Probabilistic Numerics

Probabilistic numerical computation formalises the connection between machine learning and applied mathematics. Numerical algorithms approximate intractable quantities from computable ones. They estimate integrals from evaluations of the integrand, or the path of a dynamical system described by differential equations from evaluations of the vector field. In other words, they infer a latent quantity from data. This book shows that it is thus formally possible to think of computational routines as learning machines, and to use the notion of Bayesian inference to build more flexible, efficient, or customised algorithms for computation.

The text caters for Masters' and PhD students, as well as postgraduate researchers in artificial intelligence, computer science, statistics, and applied mathematics. Extensive background material is provided along with a wealth of figures, worked examples, and exercises (with solutions) to develop intuition.

Philipp Hennig holds the Chair for the Methods of Machine Learning at the University of Tübingen, and an adjunct position at the Max Planck Institute for Intelligent Systems. He has dedicated most of his career to the development of Probabilistic Numerical Methods. Hennig's research has been supported by Emmy Noether, Max Planck and ERC fellowships. He is a co-Director of the Research Program for the Theory, Algorithms and Computations of Learning Machines at the European Laboratory for Learning and Intelligent Systems (ELLIS).

Michael A. Osborne is Professor of Machine Learning at the University of Oxford, and a co-Founder of Mind Foundry Ltd. His research has attracted £10.6M of research funding and has been cited over 15,000 times. He is very, very Bayesian.

Hans P. Kersting is a postdoctoral researcher at INRIA and École Normale Supérieure in Paris, working in machine learning with expertise in Bayesian inference, dynamical systems, and optimisation.

PHILIPP HENNIG
Eberhard–Karls–Universität Tübingen, Germany

MICHAEL A. OSBORNE
University of Oxford

HANS P. KERSTING
École Normale Supérieure, Paris

PROBABILISTIC NUMERICS

COMPUTATION AS MACHINE LEARNING

CAMBRIDGE
UNIVERSITY PRESS

CAMBRIDGE
UNIVERSITY PRESS

University Printing House, Cambridge CB2 8BS, United Kingdom

One Liberty Plaza, 20th Floor, New York, NY 10006, USA

477 Williamstown Road, Port Melbourne, VIC 3207, Australia

314–321, 3rd Floor, Plot 3, Splendor Forum, Jasola District Centre, New Delhi – 110025, India

103 Penang Road, #05-06/07, Visioncrest Commercial, Singapore 238467

Cambridge University Press is part of the University of Cambridge.

It furthers the University's mission by disseminating knowledge in the pursuit of education, learning, and research at the highest international levels of excellence.

www.cambridge.org
Information on this title:www.cambridge.org/9781107163447
DOI: 10.1017/9781316681411

© Philipp Hennig, Michael A. Osborne and Hans P. Kersting 2022

First published 2022

Printed in the United Kingdom by TJ Books Limited, Padstow Cornwall

A catalogue record for this publication is available from the British Library.

ISBN 978-1-107-16344-7 Hardback

To our families.

Measurement owes its existence to Earth
Estimation of quantity to Measurement
Calculation to Estimation of quantity
Balancing of chances to Calculation
and Victory to Balancing of chances.

Sun Tzu – *The Art of War*
§4.18: Tactical Dispositions
Translation by Lionel Giles, 1910

Contents

Acknowledgements

Many people helped in the preparation of this book. We, the authors, extend our gratitude to the following people, without whom this book would have been impossible.

We are particularly grateful to Mark Girolami for his involvement during the early stages of this book as a project. Though he could not join as an author in the end, he provided a lot of support and motivation to make this book a reality.

We would like to deeply thank the many people who offered detailed and thoughtful comments on drafts of the book: Ondrej Bajgar, Nathanael Bosch, Jon Cockayne, Michael Cohen, Paul Duckworth, Nina Effenberger, Carl Henrik Ek, Giacomo Garegnani, Roman Garnett, Alexandra Gessner, Saad Hamid, Marius Hobbhahn, Toni Karvonen, Nicholas Krämer, Emilia Magnani, Chris Oates, Jonathan Schmidt, Sebastian Schulze, Thomas Schön, Arno Solin, Tim J. Sullivan, Simo Särkkä, Filip Tronarp, Ed Wagstaff, Xingchen Wan, and Richard Wilkinson.

Philipp Hennig

I would like to thank my research group, not just for thorough proof-reading, but for an intense research effort that contributed substantially to the results presented in this book. And, above all, for wagering some of their prime years, and their career, on me, and on the idea of probabilistic numerics:

Edgar Klenske, Maren Mahsereci, Michael Schober, Simon Bartels, Lukas Balles, Alexandra Gessner, Filip de Roos, Frank Schneider, Emilia Magnani, Niklas Wahl and Hans-Peter Wieser, Felix Dangel, Frederik Künstner, Jonathan Wenger, Agustinus Kristiadi, Nicholas Krämer, Nathanael Bosch, Lukas Tatzel, Thomas Gläßle, Julia Grosse, Katharina Ott, Marius Hobbhahn, Motonobu Kanagawa, Filip Tronarp, Robin Schmidt, Jonathan Schmidt, Marvin Pförtner, Nina Effenberger, and Franziska Weiler.

I am particularly grateful to those among this group who

have contributed significantly to the development of the probnum library, which would not exist at all, not even in a minimal state, without their commitment.

Last but not least, I am grateful to my wife Maike Kaufman. And to my daughters Friederike und Iris. They both arrived while we worked on this book and drastically slowed down progress on it in the most wonderful way possible.

Michael A. Osborne

I would like to thank Isis Hjorth, for being the most valuable source of support I have in life, and our amazing children Osmund and Halfdan – I wonder what you will think of this book in a few years?

Hans P. Kersting

I would like to thank my postdoc adviser, Francis Bach, for giving me the freedom to allocate sufficient time to this book.

I am grateful to Dana Babin, my family, and my friends for their continuous love and support.

Symbols and Notation

Bold symbols (x) are used for vectors, but only where the fact that a variable is a vector is relevant. Square brackets indicate elements of a matrix or vector: if $x = [x_1, \ldots, x_N]$ is a row vector, then $[x]_i = x_i$ denotes its entries; if $A \in \mathbb{R}^{n \times m}$ is a matrix, then $[A]_{ij} = A_{ij}$ denotes its entries. Round brackets $(\cdot)$ are used in most other cases (as in the notations listed below).

Notation	Meaning
$a \propto c$	a is **proportional to** c: there is a constant k such that $a = k \cdot c$.
$A \wedge B$, $A \vee B$	The **logical conjunctions** "and" and "or"; i.e. $A \wedge B$ is true iff both A and B are true, $A \vee B$ is true iff $\neg A \wedge \neg B$ is false.
$A \otimes B$	The **Kronecker product** of matrices A, B. See Eq. (15.2).
$A \circledS B$	The **symmetric Kronecker product**. See Eq. (19.16).
$A \odot B$	The **element-wise product** (aka Hadamard product) of two matrices A and B of the same shape, i.e. $[A \odot B]_{ij} = [A]_{ij} \cdot [B]_{ij}$.
$\vec{A}, \natural\vec{A}$	$\vec{A}$ is the vector arising from stacking the elements of a matrix A row after row, and its inverse ($A = \natural\vec{A}$). See Eq. (15.1).
$\text{cov}_p(x, y)$	The **covariance** of x and y under p. That is, $\text{cov}_p(x, y) := \mathbb{E}_p(x \cdot y) - \mathbb{E}_p(x)\mathbb{E}_p(y)$.
$C^q(V, \mathbb{R}^d)$	The set of q-times **continuously differentiable functions** from V to $\mathbb{R}^d$, for some $q, d \in \mathbb{N}$.
$\delta(x - y)$	The **Dirac delta**, heuristically characterised by the property $\int f(x)\delta(x - y)\, dx = f(y)$ for functions $f : \mathbb{R} \to \mathbb{R}$.
δ_{ij}	The **Kronecker symbol**: $\delta_{ij} = 1$ if $i = j$, otherwise $\delta_{ij} = 0$.
$\det(A)$	The **determinant** of a square matrix A.
$\text{diag}(x)$	The **diagonal matrix** with entries $[\text{diag}(x)]_{ij} = \delta_{ij}[x]_i$.
$\text{d}\omega_t$	The notation for an **an Itô integral** in a **stochastic differential equation**. See Definition 5.4.
$\text{erf}(x)$	The **error function** $\text{erf}(x) := \frac{2}{\sqrt{\pi}} \int_0^x \exp(-t^2)\, \text{d}t$.
$\mathbb{E}_p(f)$	The **expectation** of f under p. That is, $\mathbb{E}_p(f) := \int f(x)\, dp(x)$.
$\mathbb{E}_{|Y}(f)$	The expectation of f under $p(f \mid Y)$.
$\Gamma(z)$	The **Gamma function** $\Gamma(z) := \int_0^\infty x^{z-1} \exp(-x)\, \text{d}x$. See Eq. (6.1).
$\mathcal{G}(\cdot; a, b)$	The **Gamma distribution** with shape $a > 0$ and rate $b > 0$, with probability density function $\mathcal{G}(z; a, b) := \frac{b^a z^{a-1}}{\Gamma(a)} e^{-bz}$.
$\mathcal{GP}(f; \mu, k)$	The **Gaussian process** measure on f with mean function μ and covariance function (kernel) k. See §4.2
$\mathbb{H}_p(x)$	The (differential) **entropy** of the distribution $p(x)$. That is, $\mathbb{H}_p(x) := -\int p(x) \log p(x)\, \text{d}x$. See Eq. (3.2).
$\mathbb{H}(x \mid y)$	The (differential) entropy of the cond. distribution $p(x \mid y)$. That is, $\mathbb{H}(x \mid y) := \mathbb{H}_{p(\cdot|y)}(x)$.
$I(x; y)$	The **mutual information** between random variables X and Y. That is, $I(x; y) := \mathbb{H}(x) - \mathbb{H}(x \mid y) = \mathbb{H}(y) - \mathbb{H}(y \mid x)$.

Notation	Meaning
I, I_N	The **identity** matrix (of dimensionality N): $[I]_{ij} = \delta_{ij}$.
$\mathbb{I}(\cdot \in A)$	The **indicator function** of a set A.
K_ν	The **modified Bessel function** for some parameter $\nu \in \mathbb{C}$. That is, $K_\nu(x) := \int_0^\infty \exp(-x \cdot \cosh(t)) \cosh(\nu t) \, dt$.
$\mathcal{L}$	The **loss** function of an optimization problem (§26.1), or the log-likelihood of an inverse problem (§41.2).
$\mathcal{M}$	The **model** $\mathcal{M}$ capturing the probabilistic relationship between the latent object and computable quantities. See §9.3.
$\mathbb{N}, \mathbb{C}, \mathbb{R}, \mathbb{R}_+$	The **natural** numbers (excluding zero), the **complex** numbers, the **real** numbers, and the **positive real** numbers, respectively.
$\mathcal{N}(x; \mu, \Sigma) = p(x)$	The vector x has the **Gaussian probability density function** with mean vector μ and covariance matrix Σ. See Eq. (3.1).
$\mathcal{N}(\mu, \Sigma) \sim X$	The random variable X is distributed according to a Gaussian distribution with mean μ and covariance Σ.
$\mathcal{O}(\cdot)$	Landau **big-Oh**: for functions f, g defined on $\mathbb{N}$, the notation $f(n) = \mathcal{O}(g(n))$ means that $f(n)/g(n)$ is bounded for $n \to \infty$.
$p(y \mid x)$	The **conditional** the probability density function for variable Y having value y conditioned on variable X having value x.
$\mathrm{rk}(A)$	The **rank** of a matrix A.
$\mathrm{span}\{x_1, \ldots, x_n\}$	The **linear span** of $\{x_1, \ldots, x_n\}$.
$\mathrm{St}(\cdot; \mu, \lambda_1, \lambda_1)$	The **Student's-t** probability density function with parameters $\mu \in \mathbb{R}$ and $\lambda_1, \lambda_2 > 0$, see Eq. (6.9).
$\mathrm{tr}(A)$	The **trace** of matrix A, That is, $\mathrm{tr}(A) = \sum_i [A]_{ii}$.
A^T	The **transpose** of matrix A: $[A^\mathsf{T}]_{ij} = [A]_{ji}$.
$\mathbb{U}_{a,b}$	The **uniform distribution** with probability density function $p(u) := \mathbb{I}(u \in (a,b))$, for $a < b$.
$\mathbb{V}_p(x)$	The **variance** of x under p. That is, $\mathbb{V}_p(x) := \mathrm{cov}_p(x, x)$.
$\mathbb{V}_{\mid Y}(f)$	The variance of f under $p(f \mid Y)$. That is, $\mathbb{H}(x \mid y) := -\int \log p(x \mid y) \, dp(x \mid y)$.
$\mathcal{W}(V, \nu)$	The **Wishart distribution** with probability density function $\mathcal{W}(x; V, \nu) \propto \lvert x \rvert^{(\nu - N - 1)/2} e^{-1/2 \, \mathrm{tr}(V^{-1} x)}$. See Eq. (19.1).
$x \perp y$	x is **orthogonal** to y, i.e. $\langle x, y \rangle = 0$.
$x := a$	The object x is **defined to be** equal to a.
$x \overset{\Delta}{=} a$	The object x is equal to a by virtue of its definition.
$x \leftarrow a$	The object x is **assigned the value** of a (used in pseudo-code).
$X \sim p$	The random variable X is **distributed according** to p.
$\mathbf{1}, \mathbf{1}_d$	A column **vector** of d **ones**, $\mathbf{1}_d := [1, \ldots, 1]^\mathsf{T} \in \mathbb{R}^d$.
$\nabla_x f(x, t)$	The **gradient** of f w.r.t. x. (We omit subscript x if redundant.)

Introduction

The Uncertain Nature of Computation

Computation is the resource that has most transformed our age. Its application has established and extracted value from globe-spanning networks, mobile communication, and big data. As its importance to humankind continues to rise, computation has come at a substantial cost. Consider machine learning, the academic discipline that has underpinned many recent technological advances. The monetary costs of modern massively parallel *graphics processing units* (GPUs), that have proved so valuable to much of machine learning, are prohibitive even to many researchers and prevent the use of advanced machine learning in embedded and other resource-limited systems. Even where there aren't hard resource constraints, there will always be an economic incentive to reduce computation use. Troublingly, there is evidence[1] that current machine learning models are also the cause of avoidable carbon emissions. Computations have to become not just faster, but more efficient.

[1] R. Schwartz et al. "Green AI" (2019); D. Patterson. "The Carbon Footprint of Machine Learning Training Will Plateau, Then Shrink" (2022).

Much of the computation consumption, particularly within machine learning, is due to problems like solving linear equations, evaluating integrals, or finding the minimum of nonlinear functions, all of which will be addressed in different chapters in this text. These so-called *numerical problems* are studied by the mathematical subfield of *numerics* (short for: *numerical analysis*). What unites these problems is that their solutions, which are numbers, have no *analytic* form. There is no known way to assign an exact numerical value to them purely by structured, rule-based thought. Methods to compute such numbers, by a computer or on paper, are of an approximate nature. Their results are not exactly right, and we do not *know* precisely how far off they are from the true solution; otherwise we could just add that known difference (or error) and be done.

That we are thus *uncertain* about the answer to a numerical problem is one of the two central insights of *probabilistic numerics* (PN). Accordingly, any numerical solver will be uncertain about the accuracy of its output – and, in some cases, also about its intermediate steps. These uncertainties are not ignored by classical numerics, but typically reduced to scalar bounds. As a remedy, PN brings statistical tools for the quantification of uncertainty to the domain of numerics.

What, precisely, are the benefits of quantifying this numerical uncertainty with probability measures?

For a start, a full probability distribution is a richer output than a sole approximation (point estimate). This is particularly useful in sequences of computations where a numerical solution is an input to the next computational task – as is the case in many applications, ranging from the elementary (matrix inversion for least squares) to the complex (solving differential equations for real-word engineering systems). In these settings, a probabilistic output distribution provides the means to propagate uncertainty to subsequent steps.

But PN's uncertainty-aware approach does not stop with quantifying the uncertainty over the final output. Rather, it offers an uncertainty-aware alternative to the design of numerical methods in two ways:

Oftentimes, numerical uncertainty already appears *within* numerical algorithms because its intermediate values are subject to approximations themselves. The resulting *intra-algorithmic* accumulation of such uncertainties calls for an appropriate amount of caution. It appears, e.g., whenever expensive function evaluations are replaced by cheaper simulations (such as when cheaper surrogate functions are used in global optimisation); or when imprecise steps are iterated (such as when ODE solvers concatenate their extrapolation steps). Probabilistic numerical methods account for these uncertainties using probability measures. This enables such methods to make smarter uncertainty-aware decisions, which becomes most salient through their formulation as probabilistic agents (as detailed below).

Moreover, probability distributions allow to more precisely encode the expected structure of the numerical problem into the solver: Numerical tasks can be solved by any number of algorithms, and it is difficult to choose among them. Not all algorithms for, say, integration, work on all integration problems. Some require the integrand to be highly regular, others only that it be continuous, or even just integrable at all. If their requirements are met, they produce a sequence of numbers that converge to the intractable solution. But they do not all converge at the same speed. In particular, algorithms that work on a restricted set of problems, when applied to a problem from that set, often converge faster than methods designed to work on a larger, less-restrictive domain. Academic research in numerics has traditionally concentrated on generic algorithms that work on large spaces of problems. Such methods are now widely available as toolboxes. These collections are valuable to practitioners because they save design time and leverage expert knowledge. But generic methods are necessarily inefficient. Generic methods are, in essence, overly cautious. The more that is known about a computation to be performed before one delves into it, the easier it will be to make progress. Some knowledge is, however, not completely certain but only expected with high probability, and thus cannot be encoded by a function space alone. A probabilistic numerical method, on the other hand, can exploit such less-than-certain expectations by distributing its *prior* probability mass to expected subsets of the function space, and away from less likely scenarios.

The mathematical toolkit of PN allows probabilistic algorithms that leverage these benefits of uncertainty quantification. Such algorithms have proven able to achieve dramatic reductions in computation.

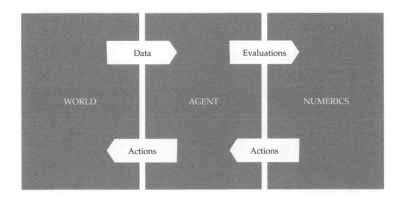

Figure 1: A computational agent interacts with the world just as its numerical algorithms interact with the agent. That is, the agent receives data from the world and selects actions to perform in the world. The numerical algorithm receives evaluations from the agent and selects computations (actions) for the agent to perform. For example, the agent might feed evaluations of an objective to an optimiser, which selects the next evaluations for the agent to make. PN recognises that a numerical algorithm is just as much an agent as one directly interacting with the world.

The second of the central insights of PN is that a numerical algorithm can be treated as an *agent*. For our purposes, an agent is an entity able to take actions so as to achieve its goals. These agents receive data from the environment, use the data to make predictions, and then use the predictions to decide how to interact with the environment. Machine learning often aims to build such agents, most explicitly within its subfield of reinforcement learning. As another example, consider an image classifier using active learning. This classifier receives labelled images, uses those to predict the labels of unlabelled images, and then uses those predictions to decide which new data should be acquired.

It is possible to treat a numerical algorithm as just such an agent, as laid out diagrammatically in Figure 1. Traditionally, a numerical method takes in data, in the form of evaluations (e.g. of an integrand), and returns predictions, or estimates (e.g. of the integral). A numerical method must also provide a rule, perhaps an adaptive one, determining which computations are actually performed (e.g. which nodes to evaluate): these are decisions. There is thus a feedback-loop: an agent that decides itself which data to collect may be inefficient by collecting redundant data, or unreliable if it neglects to probe crucially informative areas of the data-domain. Explicitly, PN treats numerical algorithms just as machine learning often treats its algorithms: as agents.

More precisely, PN is concerned with *probabilistic* agents. As above, PN uses probability distributions to quantify uncertainty. Quantified uncertainty is crucial to all agents, and numerical agents are no exception. In particular, this understanding of numerical solvers brings *probabilistic decision theory*[2] to numerics, yielding a range of advantages.

For one thing, a numerical agent must decide when to stop. Unlike in the computation of analytic expressions, there is not always an obvious end to a numerical procedure: the error in the current estimate is unknown, so it can be difficult to determine when to stop. Generic and encapsulated methods take a cautious approach, usually aiming to satisfy high demands on precision. Doing so requires many iterations, each further reducing uncertainty and improving precision, but each coming at a cost. That is, this cautious approach consumes much computation. PN provides a new solution to this problem: if uncertainty is well-quantified, we may be satisfied with (quantified) vague, and thus cheap answers. PN hence provides a principled means of stopping *early*, enabling fewer iterations, enabling a reduction in computation.

Uncertainty also guides exploration. An intelligent agent, making a decision, must weigh the uncertain consequences of its actions, occasionally gambling by taking an uncertain action, in order to explore and learn. Performing such exploration is core to effective numerics. Predictive uncertainty unlocks a fundamental means of quantifying the value of a numerical iteration, and weighing it against the real cost of the computation it

[2] M. J. Kochenderfer. *Decision Making Under Uncertainty: Theory and Application*. 2015.

will consume. There are almost always choices for the character of an iteration, such as where to evaluate an integrand or an objective function to be optimised. Not all iterations are equal, and it takes an intelligent agent to optimise the cost–benefit trade-off.

On a related note, a well-designed probabilistic numerical agent gives a reliable estimate of its own uncertainty over their result. This helps to reduce bias in subsequent computations. For instance, in ODE inverse problems, we will see how simulating the forward map with a probabilistic solver accounts for the tendency of numerical ODE solvers to systemically over- or underestimate solution curves. While this does not necessarily give a more precise ODE estimate (in the inner loop), it helps the inverse-problem solver to explore the parameter space more efficiently (in the outer loop). As these examples highlight, PN hence promises to make more effective use of computation.

The Deep Roots of Probabilistic Numerics

Probabilistic Numerics has a long history. Quite early in the history of numerical computation, people noted that its demands closely matched what was provided by the professional process of guesswork known as *statistical inference*. It seemed to those people that *probability*, central to the process of inference, might be a natural language in which to describe computation as the gathering of information. In the first chapter to his seminal nineteenth-century *Calcul des Probabilités*,[3] Henri Poincaré mused about assigning probabilities to not-yet-computed numbers:

> *Une question de probabilités ne se pose que par suite de notre ignorance: il n'y aurait place que pour la certitude si nous connaissions toutes les données du problème. D'autre part, notre ignorance ne doit pas être complète, sans quoi nous ne pourrions rien évaluer. Une classification s'opérerait donc suivant le plus ou moins de profondeur de notre ignorance.*
> *Ainsi la probabilité pour que la sixième décimale d'un nombre dans une table de logarithmes soit égale à 6 est **a priori** de 1/10; en réalité, toutes les données du problème sont bien déterminées, et, si nous voulions nous en donner la peine, nous connaîtrions exactement cette probabilité. De même, dans les interpolations, dans le calcul des intégrales définies par la méthode de Cotes ou celle de Gauss, etc.*

[3] H. Poincaré. *Calcul des Probabilités*. 1896. §I.7, pp. 30–31. Emphasis in the original.

[Roughly:] *The need for probability only arises out of uncertainty: It has no place if we are certain that we know all aspects of a problem. But our lack of knowledge also must not be complete, otherwise we would have nothing to evaluate. There is thus a spectrum of degrees of uncertainty.*
*While the probability for the sixth decimal digit of a number in a table of logarithms to equal 6 is 1/10 **a priori**, in reality, all aspects of the corresponding problem are well determined, and, if we wanted to make the effort, we could find out its exact value. The same holds for interpolation, for the integration methods of Cotes or Gauss, etc.* (Emphasis in the op. cit.)

Although Poincaré found it natural to assign probabilities to the value of determined but unknown numbers, it seems the idea of uncertainty about a fully, formally determined quantity did not sit well with a majority of mathematicians. Rather than assigning degrees of certainty about properties of a problem, it seemed more acceptable to formally state assumptions required to be *strictly* true at the onset of a theorem. When considering a particular numerical estimation rule, one can then analyse the convergence of the estimate in an asymptotic fashion, thereby formally proving that (and in which sense) the rule is admissible. This approach leaves the estimation of the rule's error after a finite number of steps as a separate and often subordinate part of the routine.

By contrast, probabilistic inference makes the formulation of probability distributions, characterising possible error, primary. These distributions will include an explicit prior on the latent quantity to be inferred, and an equally explicit likelihood function capturing the relationship of computable numbers to that latent quantity. This approach may be more or less restrictive than the asymptotic analysis described above. It might well be more cumbersome to state, subject to philosophical intricacies, and requires care to not introduce new intractable tasks along the way. Nonetheless, phrasing computation as probabilistic inference offers substantial advantages. For one thing, the approach yields a posterior probability distribution for quantities of interest that self-consistently combines estimate and uncertainty, and can approximately track their effect through several steps of the computation.

In the twentieth century, the idea of computation as inference lingered in the margins. In the 1950s and 1960s – the golden age of probability theory following the formal works of Kolmogorov – perhaps Sul'din should be mentioned as the first to return to address it in earnest.[4] He focused on the approximation of functions, a task underlying many numerical methods. In statistics, where this process is known as regression, it took on a life of its own, leading to a deep probabilistic framework studied extensively to this day, whose early probabilistic interpretations where driven by people like Sard (1963), or Kimeldorf and Wahba (1970). Parallel to Sul'din's work in Russia, the task of integration found the attention of Ajne and Dalenius (1960) in Scandinavia. The English-speaking audience perhaps first heard of these connections from Larkin (1972), who went on to write several pieces on the connection between inference and computation. Anyone who missed his works might have had

[4] Sul'din (1959); Sul'din (1960).

to wait over a decade. By then, the plot had thickened and authors in many communities became interested in Bayesian ideas for numerical analysis. Among them Kadane and Wasilkowski (1985), Diaconis (1988), and O'Hagan (1992). Skilling (1991) even ventured boldly toward solving differential equations, displaying the physicist's willingness to cast aside technicalities in the name of progress. Exciting as these insights must have been for their authors, they seem to have missed fertile ground. The development also continued within mathematics, for example in the advancement of information-based complexity[5] and average-case analysis.[6] But the wider academic community, in particular users in computer science, seem to have missed much of it. But the advancements in computer science *did* pave the way for the second of the central insights of PN: that numerics requires thinking about agents.

[5] Traub, Wasilkowski, and Woźniakowski (1983); Packel and Traub (1987); Novak (2006).
[6] Ritter (2000)

Twenty-First-Century Probabilistic Numerics

The twenty-first century brought the coming-of-age of machine learning. This new field raised new computational problems, foremost among them the presence of big data sets in the computational pipeline, and thus the necessity to sub-sample data, creating a trade-off between computational cost and precision. Numerics is inescapably important to machine learning, with popular tracks at its major conferences, and large tracts of machine learning masters' degrees, devoted to optimisation alone. But machine learning also caused a shift in perspective on modelling itself.

Modelling (or inference) used to be thought of as a passive mathematical map, from data to estimate. But machine learning often views a model as an *agent* in autonomous interaction with its environment, most explicitly in reinforcement learning. This view of algorithms as agents is, as above, central to PN.

Machine learning has been infused with the viewpoints of physicists and other scientists, who are accustomed to limits on precision and the necessity of assumptions. The Bayesian viewpoint on inference soon played a prominent (albeit certainly not the only leading) role in laying its theoretical foundations. Textbooks like those of Jaynes and Bretthorst (2003), MacKay (2003), Bishop (2006), and Rasmussen and Williams (2006) taught a generation of new students – the authors amongst them – to think in terms of generative models, priors, and posteriors. Machine learning's heavy emphasis on numerics couldn't help but lead some of those students to apply their hammer, of probabilistic inference, to the nails of the numerical problems that they encountered. These students were bound to revive questions from the history of PN. For instance, if computation is inference, should it then not be possible to build numerical algorithms that:

1. rather than taking in a logical description of their task and returning a (floating-) point estimate of its solution, instead take probability distributions as inputs and outputs?;

2. use an explicit likelihood to capture a richer, generative description of the relation between the computed numbers and the latent, intractable quantity in question?; and

3. treat the CPU or GPU as an interactive source of data?

In 2012, the authors of this text co-organised, with J. P. Cunningham, a workshop at the *Neural Information Processing Systems* conference on the shores of Lake Tahoe to discuss these questions. We were motivated by our own work on Bayesian Optimisation and Bayesian Quadrature. At the time, the wider issue seemed new and unexplored to us. By a stroke of luck, we managed to convince Persi Diaconis to make the trip up from Stanford and speak. His talk pointed us to a host of prior work.

In search of an inclusive, short title for the workshop, we had chosen to call it *Probabilistic Numerics* (PN). In the years since, this label has been increasingly used by a growing number of researchers who, like us, feel that the time has come to more clearly and extensively connect the notions of inference and computation. The 2012 workshop also marked the beginning of a fruitful collaboration between the machine learning community and statisticians like M. Girolami[7] and C. J. Oates, as well as applied mathematicians like T. J. Sullivan, I. Ipsen, H. Owhadi and others. They ensured that existing knowledge in either community was not forgotten,[8] and their research groups have since laid an increasingly broad and deep foundation to the notion of computation as *probabilistic* and also more narrowly, carefully defined *Bayesian* inference.[9] They have also undertaken a commendable effort to build a community for PN within the mathematical fields.

Although numerous interesting insights have already been reached, just as many questions are still scarcely explored. Many of them emerge from new application areas, and new associated computational problems, in the age of Big Data, GPUs, and distributed, compartmental, computation.

[7] Hennig, Osborne, and Girolami (2015)

[8] Owhadi and Scovel (2016); Oates and Sullivan (2019).

[9] Cockayne et al. (2019b)

We made a conscious decision not to use the word *Bayesian* in naming Probabilistic Numerics. We will unashamedly adopt a Bayesian view within this text, which forms a natural framework for the core ideas within PN; those ideas can also be found in many alternative approaches to machine learning and statistics. But there is also an important way in which PN can be viewed as non-Bayesian. The Bayesian norm enforces hygiene between modelling and decision-making. That is, you write down a prior capturing as much of your background knowledge as possible, and do inference to compute a posterior. Then, with that posterior, you write down a loss function and use expected loss to choose an action. The Bayesian's counterpart, the frequentist, has the loss function in mind from the outset.

However, in numerics, we are rarely afforded the luxury of using models informed by all available prior knowledge. Such models are usually more computationally expensive, in themselves, than models that are built on only weak assumptions. Sometimes, we are willing to spend a little more computation on a model to save even more computation in solving its numerical task, but other times we are not. That is, in considering an additional computation cost on a model, we must consider whether it is justified in improving performance for the given numerical task: this performance is measured by a loss function.

PN is hence, in this way, more akin to the frequentist view in muddling the loss function and the prior. That is, numerics requires us to make, in some cases, drastic simplifications to our models in order to achieve usable computational complexity. This can be conceived as letting some (vaguely specified) loss function on computation dictate which elements of the prior can be incorporated.

This Book

This book aims to give an overview of the emerging new area of Probabilistic Numerics, particularly influenced by contemporary machine learning. Even at this early point in the field, we have to concede that a complete survey is not possible: we are bound to under-represent some rapidly developing viewpoints, and apologise in advance to its authors. Our principal goals will be to study uses and roles for *uncertainty* in numerical computation, and to employ such uncertainty in making *optimal decisions* about computation.

Invariably, we will capture uncertainty in the language of *probabilities*. Any quantity that is not known to perfect (machine) precision will ideally be assigned an explicit probability distribution or measure. We will study algorithms that take and return probabilities as inputs and outputs, respectively, but also allow for uncertain, imprecise, computations to take place within the algorithm itself. These algorithms will explicitly be treated as agents, intelligently making decisions about which computations to perform. Within our probabilistic framework, these decisions will be selected as those that *minimise an expected loss.*

Along the way, we will make several foundational observations. Here is a preview of some of them, forming a quick tour through the text:

Classical methods are probabilistic   Classical methods often have clear probabilistic interpretations. Across the spectrum of numerical tasks, from integration to linear algebra, nonlinear optimisation, and solving differential equations, many of the foundational, widely used numerical algorithms can be explicitly motivated as maximum a posteriori or mean *point-estimates* arising from concrete (typically Gaussian) prior assumptions. The corresponding derivations take up a significant part of this text. These insights are crucial for two reasons.

First, finding a probabilistic interpretation for existing methods shows that the idea of a probabilistic numerical method is not some philosophical pipe dream. Probabilistic methods tangibly exist, and are as fast, and as reliable as the methods people trust and use every day – because those very methods already *are* probabilistic numerical methods, albeit they are not usually presented as such.

Second, once phrased as probabilistic inference, the classical methods provide a solid, well-studied and understood foundation for the development of *new* numerical methods and novel functionality addressing modern challenges. It may be tempting to try and invent probabilistic methods de novo; but the analytical knowledge and practical experience embodied in numerical libraries is the invaluable condensed labor of generations of skilled applied mathematicians. It would be a mistake to throw them overboard. Classical numerical methods are computationally lightweight (their cost per computational step is often constant, and small), numerically stable (they are not thrown off by small machine errors), and analytically efficient (they converge to the true solution at a "good" rate). When developing new functionality, one should strive to retain these properties as much as possible, or at least to take inspiration from the form of the classical methods. At the same time, we also have to leave a disclaimer at this point: Given the breadth and depth of numerical analysis, it is impossible to give a universal introduction in a book like this. The presentations of classical methods in these pages are designed to give a concise introduction to specific ideas, and highlight important aspects. We refer interested readers from non-numerical backgrounds to the established literature, referenced in the margins.[10]

Numerical methods are autonomous agents   We will employ the decision-theoretic, expected-loss-minimisation, framework to design numerical algorithms. Often, it is not just that the way a classical numerical method combines collected floating-point numbers into a numerical estimate can be interpreted as a posterior expectation or estimate. Additionally, the decision rule for computing those numbers in the first place also arises naturally from the underlying prior probabilistic model, through a decision-theoretic treatment. Thus, such a classical numerical algorithm can indeed be interpreted as an *autonomous agent* acting consistently with its internal probabilistic "beliefs". At first glance, this insight has primarily aesthetic value. But we will find that it directly motivates novel algorithms that act in an adaptive fashion.

Numerics should not be random   Importantly, we will *not* identify probabilistic uncertainty with *randomness*.[11] Randomness is but one possible way for uncertainty to arise. This kind is sometimes called *aleatory* or *stochastic*, in contrast to the *epistemic* uncertainty capturing a lack of *knowledge*. Probability theory makes no formal distinction between the two, they are both captured by spreading unit measure over a space of hypotheses. But there are some concepts, notably that of *bias*, which require a careful separation of these types of uncertainty. Furthermore, randomness is often used within numerics today to make (tough!) decisions, for instance, about where to make evaluations of an integrand or objective. We will argue that randomness is ill-suited to this role, as can be seen in describing a numerical algorithm as an agent (whose expected-loss-minimising action will never be returned by a random number generator). We will show (§12.3) how non-random, expected-loss-minimisation, decisions promise the reward of dramatically lowered computation consumption. This is not a fundamental rejection of the concept of Monte Carlo methods, but it reveals deep philosophical subtleties surrounding these algorithms that raise concrete

[10] The text contains a large number of notes in the margins. It is generally possible to read just the main text and ignore these offshoots. Some of them provide short reference to background knowledge for the readers' convenience. Others are entry points to related literature.

[11] §12.3 delves into this topic.

research questions.

Numerics must report calibrated uncertainty   To complete the description of classical methods as probabilistic, it does not suffice to note these methods give point estimates that arise from the most probable or expected value, the "location" of a posterior distribution. We also have to worry about the "width", captured by variance and support, of the posterior around this point estimate. We must ask whether the posterior can indeed be endowed with an interpretation as a notion of uncertainty, connected to the probable error of the numerical method. The sections that study connections to existing methods will provide some answers in this regard. We will frequently argue that certain classical methods arise from a family of *Gaussian* prior measures, parametrised by either a scalar or multivariate scale of uncertainty. All members of that family give rise to Gaussian posteriors with the same mean (which is identical to the classical method) and a posterior standard deviation that contracts at the same rate, and thus only differs by the constant scale. We will see that the contraction rate of this posterior variance is related to classical convergence rates of the point estimate (in its non-adaptive form, it is a conservative, worst-case bound on the error). We will further show that the remaining constant parameter can be inferred at runtime with minimal computational overhead, using either probabilistic, statistical, or algebraic estimation rules. Throughout, we will argue that the provision of well-calibrated quantifications of uncertainty is crucial to numerical algorithms, whether classical or new. Such reliable uncertainty underpins both the trust that can be placed in numerical algorithms and effective decision-making about computation.

Imprecise computation is to be embraced   Having adopted reliable quantifications of uncertainty, we are freed from the burden of ensuring that numerical calculations must always be highly precise. Not all numerical problems are equal: computation can be saved, in lowering precision, for the least important. From our perspective, some of the most pressing contemporary numerical problems arise in data science and machine learning, in the processing pipelines of big data sets. In these settings, data are frequently sub-sampled at runtime. This introduces stochastic disturbances to computed numbers that significantly lowers the *precision* of the computation. Yet sub-sampling also drastically reduces computational cost compared to computations on the entire data set. The trade-off between computation cost and precision results in *tuning parameters* (e.g. specifying how large a random sub-sample should be chosen) being exposed to the user, a major irk to practitioners of data science. PN here offers value in enabling optimisation of this trade-off, freeing the user of the nasty task of fiddling with parameters.

PN *consolidates numerical computation and statistical inference* Both numerical solvers and statistical-inference methods convert the information available to them into an approximation of their quantity of interest. In numerics, this information consists of evaluations of analytic expressions (or functions) – e.g. of the integrand for quadrature. In statistics, it comes as measurements (data) of observable variables. But ultimately, when viewed through the lens of information theory, these types of information are essentially the same – namely nothing but the output of a (noisy) communication channel,[12] either through an (imprecise) function or a (noisy) statistical observation. PN exploits this analogy by recasting numerical problems as statistical inference. More precisely, probabilistic numerical methods work by providing a statistical model linking the accessible function evaluations to the solution of a numerical problem, and then approximating the solution by use of statistical inference in this model. But this statistical model can be useful beyond the numerical problem at hand: should the occasion arise, it can be extended to include additional observational data containing more information. This way, the computational and observational data (information) can work together, in a *single* model, to improve the inference of the numerical solution, and of other latent variables of this joint model. Real payoffs of this probabilistic consolidation of numerics and statistics have, for example, been demonstrated for differential equations – as we will detail in §41.3.

[12] MacKay (2003), §9

Probabilistic numerical algorithms are already adding value The PN approach to global optimisation is known as Bayesian optimisation, and, in fact, Bayesian optimisation was conceived as probabilistic since its invention. Bayesian optimisation is widely used today to automatically make decisions otherwise made by human algorithm designers. Machine learning's growth has created a bewildering variety of algorithms, each with their own design decisions: the choices of an algorithm and its detailed design to be made can be framed as an "outer-loop" global optimisation problem. This problem makes careful selection of evaluations of the algorithm and its design primary, as the cost of evaluating an algorithm on a full data set is expensive enough to prevent anything approaching exhaustive search. In finding performant evaluations sooner, Bayesian optimisation saves, relative to the alternative of grid search, considerable computation on evaluations. Pre-dating the recent surge of research in wider Probabilistic Numerics, Bayesian optimisation has already blossomed into a fertile sub-community of its own, and produced significant economic impact. Chapter V is devoted to this domain, highlighting a host of new questions and ideas arising when uncertainty plays a prominent role in computation.

Pipelines of computation demand harmonisation   A probabilistic-numerics framework, encompassing all numerical algorithms, grants the ability to efficiently allocate computation, and manage uncertainty, amongst them. A newly prominent computational issue is that realistic data processing in science and industry happens not in a single computational step, but in highly engineered pipelines of compartmental computations. Each step of these chains consumes computation, and depends on and propagates errors and uncertainties. The area of uncertainty quantification[13] has developed methods to study and identify such problems, but its methods tend to add computational overhead that is not recouped in savings elsewhere. Probabilistic numerical methods, with their ability to handle uncertain inputs and produce calibrated uncertain outputs, offer a natural notion of uncertainty propagation through computational graphs. The framework of graphical models provides a scaffolding for this process. Depending on the user's needs, it is then possible to scale between simple Gaussian forms of uncertainty propagation that produce simple error bars at only minimal computational overhead, to full-fledged uncertainty propagation, with more significant computational demands. With a harmonised treatment of the uncertainty resulting from each step, and the computational costs of reducing such uncertainty, PN allows the allocation of computational resources to those steps that would benefit from it most.

Open questions   Finally, the text also highlights some areas of ongoing research, again with a focus on desirable functionality for data-centric computation.

We will *not* pay very close attention to machine precision, machine errors, and problems of numerical stability. These issues have been studied widely and deeply in numerical analysis. They play an important role, of course, and their ability to cause

[13] Sullivan (2015)

havoc should not be underestimated. But in many pressing computational problems of our time, especially those involving models defined on external data sets, the dominant sources of uncertainty lie elsewhere. Sub-sampling of big data sets to speed up a computation regularly causes computational uncertainty many orders of magnitude above the machine's computational precision. In fact, in areas like deep learning, the noise frequently dominates the signal in magnitude. This is also the reason why we spend considerable time on methods of low order: advanced methods of high order are often not applicable in the context of high computational uncertainty.

This Book and You

We wrote this book for anyone who needs to use numerical methods, from astrophysicists to deep learning hackers. We hope that it will be particularly interesting for those who are, or are aiming at, becoming a developer of numerical methods, perhaps those with machine learning or statistical training.

We invite you to join the Probabilistic Numerics community. Why should you care?

Probabilistic Numerics is beautiful   The study of PN is its own reward. It offers a unified treatment of numerical algorithms that recognises them as first-class citizens, agents in their own right.

Probabilistic Numerics is just beginning to bloom   The PN banner has been borne since Poincaré, and ours will not be the generation to let it slip. Despite these deep roots, the field's branches are only now beginning to be defined, and we can only guess at what wonderful fruit they will produce. In Chapter VII, we will describe some of the many problems open to your contributions to PN.

Probabilistic Numerics is your all-in-one toolkit for numerics   Numerics need not be considered foreign to those with statistical or machine learning expertise. PN offers a machine learning or statistics researcher the opportunity to deploy much of their existing skillset in tackling the numerical problems with which they are so commonly faced. PN allows the design of numerical algorithms that are perfectly tailored to the needs of your problem.

Probabilistic Numerics grants control of computation   PN's promise is to transform computation, sorely needed in an age of ballooning computation demands and the ever-growing evidence that its costs cannot continue to be borne.

With this, it is time to get to the substance. The next chapter provides a concise introduction to the most central arithmetic framework of probabilistic inference: Gaussian probability distributions, which provide the basic toolbox for computationally efficient reasoning with uncertainty. Readers fully familiar with this area can safely skip this chapter, and move directly to the discussion of the first and arguably the simplest class of numerical problems, univariate integration, in Chapter II.

Chapter I
Mathematical Background

Key Points

1

This chapter introduces mathematical concepts needed in the remainder. Readers with background in statistics or machine learning may find that they can skim through it. In fact, we recommend that readers skip this chapter on their first, high-level pass through this text, as the first conceptual arguments for Probabilistic Numerics will arrive in Chapter II. However, the mathematical arguments made in later chapters require the following key concepts, which must be developed here first:

§ 2 Probabilities provide the formal framework for reasoning and inference in the presence of uncertainty.

§ 3 The notion of computation as probabilistic inference is not restricted to one kind of probability distribution; but Gaussian distributions play a central role in inference on continuous-valued variables due to their convenient algebraic properties.

§ 4 *Regression* – inference on a function from observations of its values at a finite number of points is an internal operation of all numerical methods and arguably a low-level numerical algorithm in itself. But regression is also a central task in machine learning. We develop the canonical mathematical tools for probabilistic regression:

§ 4.1 Gaussian uncertainty over the weights of a set of basis functions allows inference on both linear and nonlinear functions within a finite-dimensional space of hypotheses. The choice of basis functions for this task is essentially unlimited and has wide-ranging effects on the inference process.

§ 4.2 *Gaussian processes* extend the notion of a Gaussian distribution to infinite-dimensional objects, such as functions.

§ 4.3 In the Gaussian case, the probabilistic view is very closely related to other frameworks of inference and approximation, in particular to *least-squares estimation*. This connection will be used in later chapters of this texts to connect classic and probabilistic numerical methods. In fact, readers with a background in interpolation/scattered data approximation may interpret this section as covering a first example of building a probabilistic interpretation for these numerical tasks. In contrast, from the perspective of machine learning and statistics, regression is not a computational task, but a principal form of learning. This difference in viewpoints thus highlights the fundamental similarity of computation and learning once again.

§ 4.4 Gaussian process models allow inference on *derivatives* of functions from observations of the function, and vice versa. This will be relevant in all domains of numerical computation, in particular in integration, optimisation, and the solution of differential equations.

§ 5 *Gauss–Markov processes* are a class of Gaussian process models on univariate domains whose "finite memory" allows inference at cost linear in the number of observations. The inference process is packaged into algorithms known as *filters* and *smoothers*. The dynamics of the associated stochastic process are captured by *linear stochastic differential equations*.

§ 6 Conjugate priors for the *hyperparameters* of Gaussian models allow inference on the prior mean and covariance at low computational cost.

Probabilistic Inference

Probabilities are the mathematical formalisation for the concept of *uncertainty*. Many numerical tasks involve quantities taking values x in the real vector space $\mathbb{R}^D$ for $D \in \mathbb{N}$. So consider a continuous variable $X \in \mathbb{R}$, and assume that its value x is not known precisely. Instead, it is only known that the *probability* for the value of X to fall into the set $U \subset \mathbb{R}$ is $P_X(U)$. If P_X is sufficiently regular, one can define the probability density function $p(x)$ as the Radon–Nikodym derivative of P_X with respect to the Lebesgue measure. That is, the function $p(x)$ with the property $P_X(U) = \int_U p(x)\,dx$ for all measurable sets $U \subset \mathbb{R}$. There are two basic rules for the manipulation of probabilities: If two variables $x, y \in \mathbb{R}$ are assigned the density function $p(x,y)$, then the *marginal* distribution is given by the *sum rule*

$$p(y) = \int p(x,y)\,dx,$$

and the *conditional* distribution $p(x \mid y)$ for x *given that* $Y = y$ is provided implicitly by the *product rule*

$$p(x \mid y)p(y) = p(x,y), \tag{2.1}$$

whose terms are depicted in Figure 2.1. The corollary of these two rules is *Bayes' theorem*, which describes how *prior knowledge*, combined with *data* generated according to the conditional density $p(y \mid x)$, gives rise to the *posterior* distribution on x:

$$\underbrace{p(x \mid y)}_{\text{posterior}} = \frac{\overbrace{p(y \mid x)}^{\text{likelihood}} \overbrace{p(x)}^{\text{prior}}}{\underbrace{\int p(y \mid x)p(x)\,dx}_{\text{evidence}}}.$$

When interpreted as a function of x, the conditional distribution $p(y \mid x)$ is called the *likelihood* (note it is not a probability density

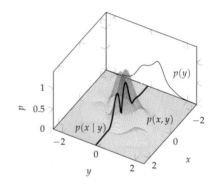

Figure 2.1: Conceptual sketch of a joint probability distribution $p(x,y)$ over two variables x, y, with marginal $p(y)$ and a conditional $p(x \mid y)$.

function of x, but of y). Computing the posterior amounts to *inference* on x from y.

Although not without competition, probability theory is widely accepted as the formal framework for reasoning with imperfect knowledge (uncertainty) in the natural sciences,[1] statistics,[2] and computer science.[3] This text accepts the general philosophical and mathematical arguments made in these texts and asks, more practically, how to use probabilistic formulations in computation.

[1] Jaynes and Bretthorst (2003)

[2] Cox (1946); Le Cam (1973); Ibragimov and Has'minskii (1981)

[3] Pearl (1988); Hutter (2010).

Gaussian Algebra

The *Gaussian* or *normal* probability distribution over $\mathbb{R}^D$ is identified by its probability density function

$$\mathcal{N}(x;\mu,\Sigma) = \frac{1}{(2\pi)^{D/2}|\Sigma|^{1/2}} \exp\left(-\frac{1}{2}(x-\mu)^\mathsf{T}\Sigma^{-1}(x-\mu)\right).$$
(3.1)

Here, a parameter vector $\mu \in \mathbb{R}^D$ specifies the *mean* of the distribution, and a *symmetric positive definite* (SPD) matrix $\Sigma \in \mathbb{R}^{D\times D}$ defines the *covariance* of the distribution[1]

$$\mu_i = \mathbb{E}_{\mathcal{N}(x;\mu,\Sigma)}(x_i), \qquad \Sigma_{ij} = \mathrm{cov}_{\mathcal{N}(x;\mu,\Sigma)}(x_i,x_j).$$

There are many ways to motivate the prevalence of the Gaussian distribution. It is sometimes presented as arising from analytic results like the central limit theorem, or the fact that the normal distribution is the unique probability distribution with mean μ and covariance Σ maximising the differential entropy functional.[2] But the primary practical reason for the ubiquity of Gaussian probability distributions is that they have convenient algebraic properties. This is analogous to the popularity of *linear* approximations in numerical computations: The main reason to construct linear approximations is that linear functions offer a rich analytic theory, and that computers are good at the basic linear operations – addition and multiplication.

In fact, the connection between linear functions and Gaussian distributions runs deeper: Gaussians are a family of probability distributions that are preserved under all linear operations. The following properties will be used extensively:

⊖ If a variable $x \in \mathbb{R}^D$ is normal distributed, then *every affine transformation* of it also has a Gaussian distribution (Fig-

[1] The matrix inverse Σ^{-1} is known as the *precision* matrix. The meaning of its elements is a bit more involved than for those of Σ, and pertains to the distribution of one or two variables *conditional* on all the others: If $p(x) = \mathcal{N}(x;\mu,\Sigma)$, then the variance of x_i conditioned on the value of $x_j, j \neq i$ is

$$\mathrm{var}_{|x_{j\neq i}}(x_i) = 1/[\Sigma^{-1}]_{ii}.$$

An interpretation for the off-diagonal elements of Σ^{-1} is that they provide the coefficients for a linear equation that determines the expectation of one element of the variable when conditioned on all the others (cf. Eq. (3.10)). Assume $\mu = 0$ for simplicity. Then, given the information $x_{j\neq i} = y$, the expectation of x_i is

$$\mathbb{E}_{|x_{j\neq i}=y}(x_i) = -\frac{1}{[\Sigma^{-1}]_{ii}}\sum_{j\neq i}[\Sigma^{-1}]_{ij}y_j.$$

More on this in a report by MacKay (2006).

[2] The entropy,

$$\mathbb{H}_p(x) := -\int p(x)\log p(x)\,dx, \quad (3.2)$$

of the Gaussian is given by

$$\mathbb{H}_{\mathcal{N}(x;\mu,\Sigma)}(x) = \frac{N}{2}(1+\log(2\pi)) + \frac{1}{2}\log|\Sigma|. \quad (3.3)$$

ure 3.1):

$$\text{if } p(\boldsymbol{x}) = \mathcal{N}(\boldsymbol{x};\boldsymbol{\mu},\Sigma),$$
$$\text{and } \boldsymbol{y} := A\boldsymbol{x} + \boldsymbol{b} \text{ for } A \in \mathbb{R}^{M\times D}, \boldsymbol{b} \in \mathbb{R}^M,$$
$$\text{then } p(\boldsymbol{y}) = \mathcal{N}(\boldsymbol{y}; A\boldsymbol{\mu} + \boldsymbol{b}, A\Sigma A^\mathsf{T}). \tag{3.4}$$

⊖ The product of two Gaussian probability density functions is another Gaussian probability distribution, scaled by a constant.[3] The value of that constant is itself given by the value of a Gaussian density function

$$\mathcal{N}(\boldsymbol{x};\boldsymbol{a},A)\mathcal{N}(\boldsymbol{x};\boldsymbol{b},B) = \mathcal{N}(\boldsymbol{x};\boldsymbol{c},C)\mathcal{N}(\boldsymbol{a};\boldsymbol{b},A+B),$$
$$\text{where } C := (A^{-1} + B^{-1})^{-1}, \tag{3.5}$$
$$\text{and } \boldsymbol{c} := C(A^{-1}\boldsymbol{a} + B^{-1}\boldsymbol{b}).$$

These two properties also provide the mechanism for *Gaussian inference*: If the variable $\boldsymbol{x} \in \mathbb{R}^D$ is assigned a Gaussian prior, and observations $\boldsymbol{y} \in \mathbb{R}^M$, given $\boldsymbol{x}$, are Gaussian distributed

$$p(\boldsymbol{x}) = \mathcal{N}(\boldsymbol{x};\boldsymbol{\mu},\Sigma) \quad \text{and} \quad p(\boldsymbol{y} \mid \boldsymbol{x}) = \mathcal{N}(\boldsymbol{y}; A\boldsymbol{x} + \boldsymbol{b}, \Lambda),$$

then both the posterior and the marginal distribution for $\boldsymbol{y}$ (the evidence) are Gaussian (Figure 3.2):

$$p(\boldsymbol{x} \mid \boldsymbol{y}) = \mathcal{N}(\boldsymbol{x};\tilde{\boldsymbol{\mu}},\tilde{\Sigma}), \quad \text{with} \tag{3.6}$$
$$\tilde{\Sigma} := (\Sigma^{-1} + A^\mathsf{T}\Lambda^{-1}A)^{-1} \tag{3.7}$$
$$= \Sigma - \Sigma A^\mathsf{T}(A\Sigma A^\mathsf{T} + \Lambda)^{-1}A\Sigma, \quad \text{and} \tag{3.8}$$
$$\tilde{\boldsymbol{\mu}} := \tilde{\Sigma}(A^\mathsf{T}\Lambda^{-1}(\boldsymbol{y} - \boldsymbol{b}) + \Sigma^{-1}\boldsymbol{\mu}) \tag{3.9}$$
$$= \boldsymbol{\mu} + \Sigma A^\mathsf{T}(A\Sigma A^\mathsf{T} + \Lambda)^{-1}(\boldsymbol{y} - (A\boldsymbol{\mu} + \boldsymbol{b})); \tag{3.10}$$

and

$$p(\boldsymbol{y}) = \mathcal{N}(\boldsymbol{y}; A\boldsymbol{\mu} + \boldsymbol{b}, A\Sigma A^\mathsf{T} + \Lambda). \tag{3.11}$$

The equivalent forms, Eqs. (3.9) & (3.10) and Eqs. (3.7) & (3.8), show two different formulations of the same posterior mean and covariance, respectively. The former pair contains a matrix inverse of size $D \times D$, the latter one of size $M \times M$. Depending on which of the two numbers is larger, it is more efficient to compute one or the other. The marginal covariance of $\boldsymbol{y}$ in Eq. (3.11) also shows up as part of Eq. (3.8). Computing this evidence term thus adds only minimal computational overhead over the computation of the posterior mean.

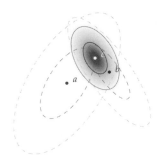

Figure 3.1: The product of two Gaussian densities is another Gaussian density, up to normalisation.

[3] This statement is about the product of two probability density functions. In contrast, the product of two Gaussian random variables is *not* a Gaussian random variable.

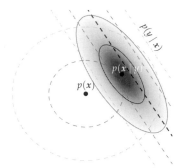

Figure 3.2: The posterior distribution $p(\boldsymbol{x} \mid \boldsymbol{y})$ arising from a Gaussian prior

$$p(\boldsymbol{x}) = \mathcal{N}(\boldsymbol{x};[1,0.5]^\mathsf{T},3^2 I)$$

and Gaussian likelihood

$$p(y = 6 \mid \boldsymbol{x}) = \mathcal{N}(6;[1,0.6]\boldsymbol{x},1.5^2)$$

is itself Gaussian. This sketch also illustrates that the likelihood function does not need to be a proper probability distribution on $\boldsymbol{x}$ (only on y). The posterior distribution can be correlated, even if the prior is uncorrelated. This phenomenon, that two a priori independent "parent" variables x_1, x_2 can become correlated by an observation $y = a_1 x_1 + a_2 x_2$ connecting the two, is known as *explaining away* (Pearl, 1988).

An important special case arises if the matrix A maps to a proper subset of x. Consider a separation of $x = [a, b]^\top$ into $a \in \mathbb{R}^d$ and $b \in \mathbb{R}^{D-d}$. The joint is[4]

$$p(x) = \mathcal{N}\left(\begin{bmatrix} a \\ b \end{bmatrix}; \begin{bmatrix} \mu_a \\ \mu_b \end{bmatrix}, \begin{bmatrix} \Sigma_{aa} & \Sigma_{ab} \\ \Sigma_{ba} & \Sigma_{bb} \end{bmatrix}\right).$$

Now consider $A = [I_d, \mathbf{0}_{D-d}]$, i.e. the "selector" map extracting a subset of size $d \leq D$. By Eq. (3.4), the *marginal* of this Gaussian distribution is another Gaussian, whose mean and covariance are simply a sub-vector and sub-matrix of the full mean and covariance, respectively (Figure 3.3)

$$p(a) = \int p(a, b)\, \mathrm{d}b = \mathcal{N}(a; \mu_a, \Sigma_{aa}). \tag{3.12}$$

Additionally using Eq. (3.6), we see that the *conditional* of a subset conditioned on its complement is also a Gaussian:

$$p(a \mid b) = \mathcal{N}(a; \mu_a + \Sigma_{ab}(\Sigma_{bb})^{-1}b, \Sigma_{aa} - \Sigma_{ab}(\Sigma_{bb})^{-1}\Sigma_{ba}). \tag{3.13}$$

Since marginalisation (sum rule) and conditioning (product rule) are the two elementary operations of probability theory, "Gaussian distributions map probability theory to linear algebra" – to matrix multiplication and inversion.

[4] In other words, if we only care about a small number d of a large set of D interdependent (co-varying) Gaussian variables, then that marginal can be computed trivially, by selecting elements from the mean vector and covariance matrix. On the one hand, this property shows that covariance only captures a limited amount of structure. On the other, this makes it possible to consider arbitrarily large sets of variables, as long as we only have to deal with finite subsets of them. This observation is at the heart of the notion of a Gaussian process, discussed below.

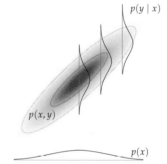

Figure 3.3: Projections and conditionals of a Gaussian are Gaussians.

Regression

▶ 4.1 Parametric Gaussian Regression

Gaussian distributions assign probability density to vectors of real numbers. In numerical applications, the objects of interest are often the output of real-valued[1] *functions* $f : \mathbb{X} \dashrightarrow \mathbb{R}$ over some input domain $\mathbb{X}$. A straightforward but powerful way to use the Gaussian inference framework on such functions is to make the assumption that f can be written as a weighted sum over a finite number F of *feature* functions $[\phi_i : \mathbb{X} \dashrightarrow \mathbb{R}]_{i=1,\ldots,F}$, as

$$f(x) = \sum_{i=1}^{F} \phi_i(x)w_i =: \Phi_x^{\mathsf{T}}w \qquad \text{with} \qquad w \in \mathbb{R}^F. \qquad (4.1)$$

The right-hand side of this equation introduces a slightly sloppy but helpful notation: Given a collection[2] $X \subset \mathbb{X}$ with elements $[X]_i = x_i \in \mathbb{X}, i = 1, \ldots, N$, we will denote by $\Phi_X \in \mathbb{R}^{F \times N}$ the matrix of feature vectors with elements $[\Phi_X]_{ij} = \phi_i(x_j)$. Similarly, we will write f_X for the vector of function values $[f(x_1), \ldots, f(x_N)]$.

The crucial algebraic property of Eq. (4.1) is that it models f as a *linear* function of the weights w. It is therefore called a *linear regression* model.[3] To perform inference on such a function within the Gaussian framework, we assign a Gaussian density over the possible values for the weight vector w, written

$$p(w) = \mathcal{N}(w; \mu, \Sigma).$$

Let us assume that it is possible to collect observations $y := [y_1, \ldots, y_N] \in \mathbb{R}^N$ of f corrupted by Gaussian noise with covariance $\Lambda \in \mathbb{R}^{N \times N}$ at the locations X (Figure 4.1). That is, according to the likelihood function[4]

[1] The formalism can be extended to complex-valued and multivariate functions, or to functions mapping virtually any input domain $\mathbb{X}$ to an output domain $\mathbb{Y}$ that can be made isomorphic to a real vector space. This generality is suppressed here to allow a more accessible presentation. The type of $\mathbb{X}$ does not matter at all since it is "encapsulated" and mapped to a real vector by the features ϕ. To capture multivariate *outputs* (or outputs that are isomorphic to the multivariate reals), the model has to return not one but several real numbers. This can be achieved by increasing the number of features and weights, i.e. by "stacking" several univariate functions. Chapter III, on linear algebra, prominently features this kind of model.

[2] We use the capital X instead of x to signify that X can really be an ordered collection of just about any type of inputs: real numbers, but also strings, graphs, etc. See e.g. §4.4 in Rasmussen and Williams (2006).

[3] This need *not* mean that f is also a linear function in x!

[4] This includes the special case $\Lambda \dashrightarrow 0$, usually written suggestively with the Dirac delta as

$$p(y \mid f) = \delta(y - f_X).$$

This corner case is important in numerical applications where function values can be computed "exactly", i.e. up to machine precision.

```
1  procedure PARAMETRIC_INFER(y, X, Λ, φ, μ, Σ)
2  │  Φ_X = φ(X)                                      // evaluate features of data
3  │  Σ̃ = (Σ^{-1} + Φ_X Λ^{-1} Φ_X^T)^{-1}              // posterior covariance
4  │                                                 // This is the most costly step, at 𝒪(F³).
5  │  μ̃ = Σ̃(Σ^{-1}μ + Φ_X Λ^{-1}y)                     // posterior mean
6  end procedure
```

Algorithm 4.1: Basic implementation of the *inference* step of parametric regression, which constructs a posterior distribution on the weights. Here, inference is performed in weight space, so the computational cost, given N observations and F features, is $\mathcal{O}(NF^2 + F^3)$. Compare with Algorithm 4.3 for the function space view, where the cost is $\mathcal{O}(N^3)$.

$$p(y \mid f) = \mathcal{N}(y; f_X, \Lambda). \tag{4.2}$$

Then the posterior over the weights w, by Eq. (3.13), is

$$
\begin{aligned}
p(w \mid y) &= \mathcal{N}(w; \tilde{\mu}, \tilde{\Sigma}), \\
\text{with} \quad \tilde{\Sigma} &:= (\Sigma^{-1} + \Phi_X \Lambda^{-1} \Phi_X^T)^{-1} \\
\text{and} \quad \tilde{\mu} &:= \tilde{\Sigma}(\Sigma^{-1}\mu + \Phi_X \Lambda^{-1}y).
\end{aligned}
$$

Using the matrix inversion lemma (Eq. (15.9)), these expressions can also be written with the inverse of a matrix in $\mathbb{R}^{N \times N}$ as

$$
\begin{aligned}
\tilde{\Sigma} &= \Sigma - \Sigma\Phi_X(\Phi_X^T\Sigma\Phi_X + \Lambda)^{-1}\Phi_X^T\Sigma, \\
\tilde{\mu} &= \mu + \Sigma\Phi_X(\Phi_X^T\Sigma\Phi_X + \Lambda)^{-1}(y - \Phi_X^T\mu).
\end{aligned}
$$

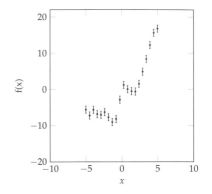

Rasmussen and Williams (2006) call this the *weight-space view* of regression. Alternatively, one can also construct a *function-space view*, a density directly over values of the unknown f: Since f is a linear map of w, Eq. (3.4) implies that the posterior over function values f_x at a finite subset $x \subset \mathbb{X}$ is

Figure 4.1: A simple nonlinear data set with i.i.d. Gaussian observation noise, i.e. $\Lambda = \sigma^2 I_N$, $\sigma \in \mathbb{R}_+$ (error-bars). Figures 4.2 and 4.3 demonstrate the effect of varying prior assumptions on the posterior induced by these observations.

$$
\begin{aligned}
p(f_x) &= \mathcal{N}(f_x; \Phi_x^T\tilde{\mu}, \Phi_x^T\tilde{\Sigma}\Phi_x) \qquad \text{with} \tag{4.3} \\
\Phi_x^T\tilde{\mu} &= \Phi_x^T\mu + \Phi_x^T\Sigma\Phi_X(\Phi_X^T\Sigma\Phi_X + \Lambda)^{-1}(y - \Phi_X\mu), \\
\Phi_x^T\tilde{\Sigma}\Phi_x &= \Phi_x^T\Sigma\Phi_x - \Phi_x^T\Sigma\Phi_X(\Phi_X^T\Sigma\Phi_X + \Lambda)^{-1}\Phi_X^T\Sigma\Phi_x.
\end{aligned}
$$

```
1  procedure PARAMETRIC_PREDICT(x, μ̃, Σ̃)           // predict at x
2  │  Φ_x = φ(x)                                     // features of x
3  │  m_x = Φ_x^T μ̃                                   // predictive mean
4  │  V_x = Φ_x^T Σ̃ Φ_x                               // predictive covariance
5  │  s_x = Φ_x^T · CHOL(Σ̃)^T · RANDNORMAL(F) + m_x   // sample
6  end procedure
```

Algorithm 4.2: Basic implementation of the *prediction* step of parametric regression in function space, using the outputs of Alg. 4.1. The cost, given D prediction locations, is $\mathcal{O}(DF)$ for the mean and element-wise variance, and $\mathcal{O}((DF)^2)$ for a full cov. Samples cost $\mathcal{O}((DF)^2)$ if the Cholesky decomposition (p. 36) of $\tilde{\Sigma}$ is available (e.g. from Alg. 4.1).

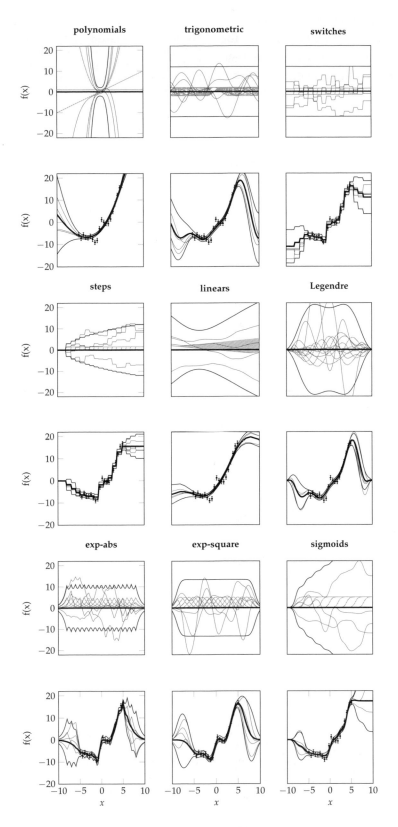

Figure 4.2: Odd-numbered rows: Priors over univariate real functions using different features. Each plot shows the underlying features Φ_x as thin grey lines, the prior mean function $\Phi_x^\mathsf{T}\mu = 0$ arising from $\mu = \mathbf{0}$, the marginal standard deviation $\operatorname{diag}(\Phi_x^\mathsf{T}\Sigma\Phi_x)^{1/2}$ for the choice $\Sigma = I$, and four samples drawn i.i.d. from the joint Gaussian over the function.

Even-numbered rows: Posteriors arising in these models from the observations shown in Figure 4.1. The feature functions giving rise to these eight different plots are the polynomials

$$\phi_i(x) = x^i, \quad i = 0, \dots, 3;$$

the trigonometric functions

$$\phi_i(x) = \sin(x/i), \quad i = 1, \dots, 8, \text{ and}$$

$$\phi_i(x) = \cos(x/i-8), \quad i = 9, \dots, 16;$$

as well as, for $i = -8, -7, \dots, 8$, the "switch" functions

$$\phi_i(x) = \operatorname{sign}(x - i);$$

the "step" functions

$$\phi_i(x) = \mathbb{I}(x - i > 0);$$

the linear functions

$$\phi_i(x) = |x - i|;$$

the first 13 Legendre polynomials (scaled to $[-10, 10]$); the absolute's exponential

$$\phi_i(x) = e^{-|x-i|};$$

the square exponential

$$\phi_i(x) = e^{-(x-i)^2};$$

and the sigmoids

$$\phi_i(x) = 1/(1 + e^{-3(x-i)}).$$

The plots highlight the broad range of behaviour accessible by varying the choice of feature functions.

Figure 4.2 shows a gallery of prior and posterior densities over function values[5] arising from the same weight-space prior $p(w) = \mathcal{N}(w; \mathbf{1}, I)$, and differing choices of feature functions ϕ. The figure also shows posterior densities arising from these priors under one particular data set of observations (shown in Figure 4.1 for reference). The figure and derivations above highlight the following aspects:

- Generalised linear regression allows inference on real-valued functions over arbitrary input domains.

- By varying the feature set Φ, broad classes of hypotheses can be created. In particular, Gaussian regression models can model nonlinear, discontinuous, even unbounded functions. There are literally *no limitations* on the choice of $\phi : \mathbb{X} \to \mathbb{R}$.

- Neither the posterior mean nor the covariance over function values (Eq. (4.3)) contain "lonely" feature vectors, but only inner products of the form $k_{ab} := \Phi_a^\mathsf{T} \Sigma \Phi_b$ and $m_a := \Phi_a \mu$. For reasons to become clear in the following section, these quantities are known as the *covariance function* $k : \mathbb{X} \times \mathbb{X} \to \mathbb{R}$ and *mean function* $m : \mathbb{X} \to \mathbb{R}$, respectively.

▶ 4.2 Gaussian Processes – Nonparametric Gaussian Inference

The basic properties of Gaussian distributions summarised in Eqs. (3.12) and (3.13) mean that computing the marginal of a high-dimensional Gaussian distribution involves only quantities of the dimensionality of the marginal. Thus one may wonder what happens if the high-dimensional distribution is in fact of *infinite* dimensionality. This limit is known as a *Gaussian process*, and extends the notion of regression to real-valued functions.

The theory and practical use of Gaussian processes are well-studied. Extended introductions can be found in the textbook by Rasmussen and Williams (2006) as well as the older book by Wahba (1990). The regularity[6] and extremal behaviour[7] of samples from a Gaussian process have been analysed in detail. As will briefly be pointed out below, Gaussian process models are also closely related to kernel methods in machine learning, in particular to kernel ridge regression. Many of the theoretical concepts in that area transfer – directly or with caveats – to the Gaussian process framework. These are discussed for example in the books by Schölkopf and Smola (2002), and Steinwart and Christmann (2008). Moreover, Berg, Christensen, and Ressel

[5] With some technical complications, Eq. (4.3) assigns a measure over an infinite-dimensional space of functions. But the plots only involve finitely many function values (albeit on a grid of high resolution), for which it suffices to consider the less tricky concept of a probability density. For more, see §4.2.2.

Exercise 4.1 (easy). *Consider the likelihood of Eq. (4.2) with the parametric form for f of Eq. (4.1). Show that the* **maximum-likelihood estimator** *for w is given by the ordinary least-squares* estimate

$$w_{ML} = (\Phi_X \Phi_X^\mathsf{T})^{-1} \Phi_X y.$$

To do so, use the explicit form of the Gaussian pdf to write out $\log p(y \mid X, w)$, take the gradient with respect to the elements $[w]_i$ of the vector w and set it to zero. If you find it difficult to do this in vector notation, it may be helpful to write out $\Phi_X^\mathsf{T} w = \sum_i w_i [\Phi_X]_{i:}$ where $[\Phi_X]_{i:}$ is the ith column of Φ_X. Calculate the derivative of $\log p(y \mid X, w)$ with respect to w_i, which is scalar.

[6] Adler (1981)
[7] Adler (1990)

(1984) provide an introduction to the theory of positive definite functions, which are a key concept in this area (see §4.2.1). With a focus on accessibility, this section provides the basic notions and algorithms required for inference in these models, as well as an intuition for the generality and limitations of Gaussian process regression.

▷ 4.2.1   Positive Definite Kernels

The main challenge in defining an "infinite-dimensional Gaussian distribution" is how to describe the infinite limit of a covariance matrix. Covariance matrices are symmetric positive definite;[8] the extension of this notion to operators is called a positive definite kernel. We approach this area from the parametric case studied in §4.1: recall from Eq. (4.3) that, for general linear regression using features ϕ, the mean vector and covariance matrix of the posterior on function values does not contain isolated, explicit forms of the features. Instead, for finite subsets $a, b \subset \mathbb{X}$ it contains only projections and inner products, of the form

[8] For more on symmetric positive definite matrices, see §15.2.

$$m_a := \Phi_a \mu \quad \text{and} \quad k_{ab} := \Phi_a^\mathsf{T} \Sigma \Phi_b = \sum_{ij=1}^{F} \phi_i(a)\phi_j(b)\Sigma_{ij}.$$

These two types of expressions are themselves functions, called

the *mean function* $m : \mathbb{X} \to \mathbb{R}$, and
the *covariance function* $k : \mathbb{X} \times \mathbb{X} \to \mathbb{R}$.

Because the features are thus "encapsulated", we may wonder whether one can construct a Gaussian regression model without explicitly stating a specific set of features. For the mean function, this is easy: since one can add an arbitrary linear shift b in the likelihood (4.2), the mean function does not actually have to be an inner product of feature functions. It can be chosen more generally, to be *any* computationally tractable function $m_a : \mathbb{X} \to \mathbb{R}$. The covariance function requires more care; but if we find an analytic short-cut for the sum of F^2 terms for a smart choice of (ϕ, μ, Σ), it is possible to use a very large, even infinite set of features. This is known as "the kernel trick".[9] It is based on one of the basic insights of calculus: Certain structured sums and series have analytic expressions that allow computing their value without actually going through their terms individually.

[9] Schölkopf (2000)

MacKay (1998) provides an intuitive example. Consider $\mathbb{X} = \mathbb{R}$, and decide to regularly distribute Gaussian feature functions with scale $\lambda \in \mathbb{R}_+$ over the domain $[c_{\min}, c_{\max}] \subset \mathbb{R}$. That is, set

$$\phi_i(x) = \exp\left(-\frac{(x-c_i)^2}{\lambda^2}\right), \qquad c_i = c_{\min} + \frac{i-1}{F}(c_{\max} - c_{\min}).$$

We also choose, for an arbitrary scale $\theta^2 \in \mathbb{R}_+$, the covariance

$$\Sigma = \frac{\sqrt{2}\theta^2(c_{\max}-c_{\min})}{\sqrt{\pi}\lambda F} I,$$

and set $\mu = 0$. It is then possible to convince oneself[10] that the limit of $F \to \infty$ and $c_{\min} \to -\infty$, $c_{\max} \to \infty$ yields

$$k(a,b) = \theta^2 \exp\left(-\frac{(a-b)^2}{2\lambda^2}\right). \tag{4.4}$$

This is called a *nonparametric* formulation of regression, since the parameters w of the model (regardless of whether their number is finite or infinite) are not explicitly represented in the computation. The function k constructed in Eq. (4.4), if used in a Gaussian regression framework, assigns a covariance of full rank to arbitrarily large data sets. Such functions are known as (positive definite) *kernels*.

Definition 4.2 (Kernel). *A positive (semi-) definite kernel is a bivariate real function $k : \mathbb{X} \times \mathbb{X} \to \mathbb{R}$ over some space $\mathbb{X}$ such that, for any set $X = [x_1, \ldots, x_N] \subset \mathbb{X}$, the matrix k_{XX} with elements*

$$[k_{XX}]_{ij} = k(x_i, x_j)$$

is positive (semi-) definite.[11] *Such functions are also known as* Mercer *kernels, positive definite functions, and, in the context of Gaussian processes, as* covariance functions.

In addition to the *Gaussian kernel* of Eq. (4.4), two further examples are the *Wiener* and *Ornstein–Uhlenbeck (exponential)* kernels over the reals (more in §5.4 and §5.5):

$$k_{\text{Wiener}}(a,b) = \min(a,b), \tag{4.5}$$
$$k_{\text{Ornstein–Uhlenbeck}}(a,b) = \exp(-|a-b|).$$

There are other limits of certain feature sets that give rise to other kernels beyond the Gaussian form of Eq. (4.4) (Exercise 4.3). These constructions are not unique – there may be other choices of ostensibly very different feature sets that, in some limit, converge to the same covariance function. Nevertheless, this explicit construction provides two insights:

[10] Proof sketch, omitting technicalities: Using Eq. (3.4), we get

$$k_{ab} = \frac{\sqrt{2}\theta^2(c_{\max}-c_{\min})}{\sqrt{\pi}\lambda F}$$
$$\cdot \sum_{i=1}^{F} e^{-\frac{(a-c_i)^2}{\lambda^2}} e^{-\frac{(b-c_i)^2}{\lambda^2}}$$
$$= \frac{\sqrt{2}\theta^2(c_{\max}-c_{\min})}{\sqrt{\pi}\lambda F} e^{-\frac{(a-b)^2}{2\lambda^2}}$$
$$\cdot \sum_{i=1}^{F} e^{-\frac{(c_i - 1/2(a+b))^2}{\lambda^2/2}}.$$

In the limit of large F, the number of features in a region of width δc converges to $F \cdot \delta c /(c_{\max}-c_{\min})$, and the sum becomes the Gaussian integral

$$k_{ab} = \frac{\sqrt{2}\theta^2}{\sqrt{\pi}\lambda} e^{-\frac{(a-b)^2}{2\lambda^2}}$$
$$\cdot \int_{c_{\min}}^{c_{\max}} e^{-\frac{(c-1/2(a+b))^2}{\lambda^2/2}} dc.$$

For $c_{\max}, c_{\min} \to \pm\infty$, that integral converges to $\sqrt{\pi}\lambda/\sqrt{2}$.

[11] It follows from the definition of positive definite matrices (§15.2) that all kernels obey $k(a,a) \geq 0$ and $k(a,b) = k(b,a)$, $\forall a,b \in \mathbb{X}$.

Exercise 4.3 (moderate). *Convince yourself that similar limits for the "switches" and "steps" feature functions in Figure 4.2 give rise to the "linear splines" and Wiener kernels listed in Figure 4.3. More examples of this form, including infinite limits of polynomial and Fourier features, can be found in a technical report by Minka (2000).*

⊖ While the covariance function (4.4) is a "sum" (an integral) over an *infinite* set of features, we had to drop the prior variance of each feature proportionally to M^{-1}, the number of features.[12] In this sense, we have spread a finite probability mass over an infinite space of features. The model may have infinitely many degrees of freedom, but not necessarily infinite modelling flexibility.

⊖ Constructing the kernel requires careful choices, like the scalar form of Σ, and feature functions with a well-defined and analytic integral limit. So the elegance of the nonparametric formulation comes at a price: while we can take *any* set of feature functions to build a parametric model, we cannot just take any bivariate function and hope that it might be a kernel.

For an intuition of how large the space of positive definite kernels is, we note that kernels form a semi-ring.

1. If k is a kernel, then αk for any $\alpha \in \mathbb{R}_+$ is a kernel.

   Proof. $v^\mathsf{T} K v > 0 \Rightarrow \alpha v^\mathsf{T} K v > 0.$ □

2. If k, h are both kernels, then $k + h$ is a kernel.

   Proof. $v^\mathsf{T}(K + H)v = v^\mathsf{T} K v + v^\mathsf{T} H v > 0.$ □

3. If k, h are both kernels, then their Hadamard product $k \odot h$, i.e. the function

   $$(k \odot h)(a, b) = k(a, b) \cdot h(a, b)$$

   is a kernel. This result is known as *Schur's product theorem* and is significantly less straightforward than the former two. A proof can be found in Bapat (1997).

4. If $\phi : \mathbb{Y} \rightarrow \mathbb{X}$ is *any* function over a space $\mathbb{Y}$, then $k(\phi(y), \phi(y'))$ is a kernel over $\mathbb{Y}$. In particular, $k(x/s, x'/s)$ is a kernel for any linear *scale* $s \in \mathbb{R}_+$.

These observations show that, although not quite as unconstrained as the choice of features for parametric regression, the space of kernels is still quite large. Among the key results of subsequent chapters is the insight that certain classic numerical algorithms can be interpreted as performing regression using

[12] Over a bounded domain $[c_{min}, c_{max}]$, the determinant of this Σ, in the limit of $M \rightarrow \infty$, converges to the finite value

$$\det \Sigma = M \cdot \frac{\sqrt{2}\theta^2}{\sqrt{\pi \lambda} M}(c_{max} - c_{min})$$

$$= \frac{\sqrt{2}\theta^2}{\sqrt{\pi \lambda}}(c_{max} - c_{min}).$$

a particular kernel. These kernels will often be associated with
rather general, unstructured priors, and it will be a natural
question whether more specific priors can be designed to better
address individual numerical problems. That is, to what degree
additional structural knowledge can help reduce the complexity
of a computation.

▷ 4.2.2   **Gaussian Process Regression**

If kernels provide an infinite-dimensional extension of positive
definite matrices, what does it mean to perform linear regression
(in the sense of Algorithms 4.1 and 4.2) with a kernel? The
probability measure implied by this use of a positive definite
kernel in a covariance model is called a Gaussian process.

Definition 4.4 (Gaussian process). *Consider a function $\mu : \mathbb{X} \to \mathbb{R}$
and a positive definite kernel $k : \mathbb{X} \times \mathbb{X} \to \mathbb{R}$. The* Gaussian process
(GP) *$p(f) = \mathcal{GP}(f; \mu, k)$ is the probability measure identified by
the property that, for any finite subset $X := [x_1, \ldots, x_N] \subset \mathbb{X}$,
the probability assigned to function values $f_X = [f(x_1), \ldots, f(x_N)]$
is given by the multivariate Gaussian probability density $p(f_X) =
\mathcal{N}(f_X; \mu_X, k_{XX})$.*[13]

The extension from parametric to nonparametric regression follows directly from Eq. (4.3). Given a Gaussian process prior
$p(f) = \mathcal{GP}(f; \mu, k)$ over an unknown function $f : \mathbb{X} \to \mathbb{R}$,
and the likelihood function from Eq. (4.2) (i.e. $p(y \mid f) =
\mathcal{N}(y; f_X, \Lambda)$), the posterior over f is a Gaussian process $p(f \mid
y) = \mathcal{GP}(f; m, \mathbb{V})$ with mean function and SPD function, $m :
\mathbb{X} \to \mathbb{R}$ and $\mathbb{V} : \mathbb{X} \times \mathbb{X} \to \mathbb{R}$, respectively, of the form

$$m_x = \mu_x + k_{xX}(k_{XX} + \Lambda)^{-1}(y - \mu_X), \qquad (4.6)$$

$$\mathbb{V}(x, x') = k_{xx'} - k_{xX}(k_{XX} + \Lambda)^{-1}k_{Xx'}. \qquad (4.7)$$

Figure 4.3 shows nine different Gaussian process priors over
$\mathbb{X} = \mathbb{R}$, alongside the posterior measures arising from the nonlinear noisy data set in Figure 4.1. The plots show the diversity
of the Gaussian process hypothesis space. GP models can be
stationary or spatially varying, and may produce smooth or
rough sample paths. The combination of basic kernels and features – using the combination rules outlined in §4.2.1 – provides
an extensive toolbox for the construction of prior models with
specific properties.

Algorithms 4.3 and 4.4 provide a compact basic implementation
for Gaussian process regression. Like Algorithms 4.1 and 4.2,

[13] It is not straightforward to show that
Definition 4.4 is well-formed, and what
restrictions have to be put on the form
of the kernel to guarantee the existence
of such a family of infinitely many Gaussian random variables. For our purposes,
it suffices to require the kernel to be
continuous on both variables to guarantee the existence of the Gaussian process. Some hints can be found on p. 1
of Wahba's book (1990) and in Adler's
(1990) in-depth treatment.

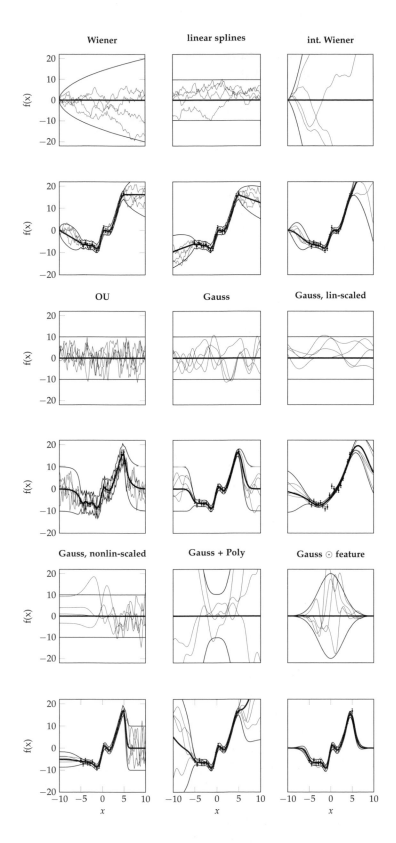

Figure 4.3: Analogous plot to Figure 4.2, for Gaussian process regression with various kernels. From top left to bottom right, the prior processes are identified by the following kernels:

the Wiener kernel (producing Brownian motion)

$$k(a,b) = \min(a,b) + c, \quad c = 10;$$

the linear spline kernel

$$k(a,b) = 1 + c - \frac{c}{10}|a-b|, \quad c = 1;$$

the integrated Wiener kernel (using $\tilde{a} := a - 10, \tilde{b} := b - 10$)

$$k(a,b) = \frac{1}{3}\min(\tilde{a}, \tilde{b})^3 + \frac{1}{2}|\tilde{a} - \tilde{b}| \min(\tilde{a}, \tilde{b})^2;$$

the exponential kernel (Ornstein–Uhlenbeck process)

$$k(a,b) = e^{-|a-b|};$$

the Gaussian (square exponential, radial basis function) kernel

$$k_{\mathrm{SE}} = e^{-(a-b)^2};$$

its linearly and nonlinearly scaling

$$k(a,b) = k_{\mathrm{SE}}(\phi(a), \phi(b))$$

for the choices

$$\phi(x) = \frac{x}{3} \text{ and } \phi(x) = \left(\frac{(x+10)}{5}\right)^3;$$

the additive combination

$$k(a,b) = k_{\mathrm{SE}}(a,b) + \sum_{i=0}^{2}(ab)^i;$$

and the point-wise product

$$k(a,b) = k_{\mathrm{SE}}(a,b) \cdot e^{-(a^2+b^2)/4}.$$

As in Figure 4.2, these examples demonstrate some of the variability among Gaussian process priors. Some processes (e.g. Wiener, spline, OU) produce sample paths that are almost surely nowhere differentiable, while others are smooth (e.g. the Gaussian kernel). Some are mean-reverting and stationary, others diverge.

```
1  procedure GP_INFER(y, X, Λ, k, m)
2      k_XX = k(X, X)                              // kernel at data
3      m_X = m(X)                                  // mean function at data
4      G = k_XX + Λ                                // data covariance
5      R = CHOL(G)               // Cholesky decomp. of data covariance
6                   // (i.e. G = R^T R). This is the most costly step, at O(N^3).
7      α = R^{-1}(R^{-1})^T(y − m_X)               // predictive weights
8  end procedure
```

Algorithm 4.3: Basic implementation of nonparametric Gaussian process *inference*. In contrast to Algorithm 4.1, inference must performed in the function space, and has cost $\mathcal{O}(N^3)$. Line 7 re-uses the upper triangular matrix R for efficiency, because linear problems with such matrices can be solved at cost $\mathcal{O}(N^2)$ by back-substitution.

they are separated into an *inference* and a *prediction step*. The computational load for inference on the GP posterior arising from N observations is dominated by the $\mathcal{O}(N^3)$ steps for a matrix square root of the so-called *Gram matrix* G – the algorithm uses the Cholesky decomposition, but other decompositions, such as eigendecompositions, could also be used in principle. The main point of such decompositions here is that they bring the matrix into a form from which linear systems can be solved in $\mathcal{O}(N^2)$ time. The cost of computing the mean function (the *mean prediction*) at a new location x_* is linear in N, computing the marginal variance at such a point is quadratic in N.

▶ **4.3   Relationship to Least-Squares and Statistical Learning**

In the case of Gaussian models, the probabilistic formalism is closely connected to other frameworks for inference, learning and approximation. This connection is helpful to connect Probabilistic Numerics with classic numerical point estimates.

A theorem due to Moore and Aronszajn[14] shows that each positive definite kernel is associated with a space of functions known as the *reproducing kernel Hilbert space* (*reproducing kernel Hilbert space* (RKHS)), defined through two abstract properties:[15]

Exercise 4.5 (easy). *Consider two functions $f : \mathbb{R}^d \to \mathbb{R}$ and $g : \mathbb{R}^d \to \mathbb{R}$, both drawn from independent Gaussian processes as $f \sim GP(\mu_f, k_f)$ and $g \sim GP(\mu_g, k_g)$. From the definition of GPs it follows that the basic Gaussian property of Eq. (3.4) carries over: If A is a (sufficiently regular) linear operator and $p(x) = \mathcal{GP}(x; m, k)$, then $p(Ax) = \mathcal{N}(Ax; Am, AkA^\mathsf{T})$. Use this property to answer the following questions.*

1. *Consider the real number $\alpha \in \mathbb{R}$. The function $\tilde{f} = \alpha \cdot f$ is also distributed according to a Gaussian process. What are its mean and covariance functions?*

2. *The sum $f + g$ is also distributed according to a Gaussian process. What is the mean function and the kernel of $f + g$?*

3. *The sum $f − g$ is also distributed according to a Gaussian process. What is the mean function and the kernel of $f − g$?*

[14] This theorem was first published by Aronszajn (1950), but he attributed it to E. H. Moore. A proof can also be found in Wahba's book (1990, Thm. 1.1.1).

[15] Schölkopf and Smola (2002), Def. 2.9.

```
1  procedure GP_PREDICT(x, α, R, m)               // predict at x ∈ X^D
2      k_xx = k(x, x)                              // prior predictive covariance
3      k_xX = k(x, X)                              // cross covariance
4      m_x = m(x) + k_xX α                         // posterior predictive mean
5      L = k_xX / R          // projection from data cov. to predictive space
6      V_x = k_xx − LL^T                           // predictive covariance
7      s_x = CHOL(V_x)^T RANDNORMAL(D) + m_x       // samples
8  end procedure
```

Algorithm 4.4: Basic implementation of nonparametric Gaussian process *prediction*. Predicting at D input locations has cost $\mathcal{O}(D^2)$ for a full covariance, and $\mathcal{O}(D)$ for a mean prediction and marginal (element-wise) variance. In the latter case, line 7 is left out, and the diagonal of V_x in line 6 can be computed cheaply using $[LL^\mathsf{T}]_{ii} = \sum_j [L_{ij}]^2$. Compare with Algorithm 4.2.

Definition 4.6. *A Hilbert space $\mathcal{H}$ of functions $f : \mathbb{X} \to \mathbb{R}$ is called an RKHS if there exists a function $k : \mathbb{X} \times \mathbb{X} \to \mathbb{R}$ such that*

1. for every $x \in \mathbb{X}$, the function $f(\tilde{x}) = k(x, \tilde{x})$ is in $\mathcal{H}$, and

2. k has the reproducing property that the values of every $f \in \mathcal{H}$ at any $x \in \mathbb{X}$ can be written as $f(x) = \langle f(\cdot), k(\cdot, x) \rangle$ (where $\langle \cdot, \cdot \rangle$ is the inner product of $\mathcal{H}$).

Using the RKHS notion the GP posterior mean estimate m_x of Eq. (4.6) can equivalently be derived as a nonparametric *least-squares* estimate, also known as the *kernel ridge regression* estimate: m_x equals the minimiser of a *regularised empirical risk* functional over the RKHS associated with k:[16]

$$m_x = k_{xX}(k_{XX} + \sigma^2 I)^{-1} y$$

$$= \arg\min_{f \in \mathcal{H}_k} \sigma^2 \|f\|_{\mathcal{H}}^2 + \frac{1}{N} \sum_{i=1}^{N} (y_i - f(x_i))^2, \qquad (4.8)$$

where $\|f\|_{\mathcal{H}}$, is the RKHS norm of f.[17] The corresponding statement for the posterior standard deviation

$$\sigma(x) := \sqrt{\mathbb{V}(x,x)} = \sqrt{k_{xx} - k_{xX}(k_{XX} + \Lambda)^{-1} k_{Xx'}} \qquad (4.9)$$

is given by the following theorem about the *worst-case approximation error* of ridge regression. For simplicity, we focus on the special case of function values observed without noise, which is most relevant for classic numerical problems.[18]

Theorem 4.8. *Let k be a positive definite kernel over $\mathbb{X}$, and $\mathcal{H}$ its associated RKHS. Consider a function $f \in \mathcal{H}$ with $\|f\|^2 \leq 1$, and a finite subset $X \in \mathbb{X}^N$. Denote $y = f_X \in \mathbb{R}^N$. Then, for any $x \in \mathbb{X}$, the approximation error between $f_x := f(x) \in \mathbb{R}$ and $m_x \in \mathbb{R}$ as defined by Eq. (4.6) is tightly bounded above by the associated GP posterior marginal variance for $\Lambda \to 0$:*

$$\sup_{f \in \mathcal{H}, \|f\| \leq 1} (m_x - f_x)^2 = k_{xx} - k_{xX} K_{XX}^{-1} k_{Xx}.$$

This statement shows that in the case of error-free evaluations of f, the posterior variance of Gaussian process regression – the Probabilists' *expected* error – equals the *worst-case* approximation error if the true function is an element of the RKHS of unit-bounded norm.[19]

Thus, if we are faced with the problem of inferring (estimating, approximating) a function $f : \mathbb{X} \to \mathbb{R}$ from observations $(x_i, y_i)_{i=1,\dots,N}$, we now have two quite different viewpoints on the very same point- and error-estimates:

[16] A proof of this theorem can be found in Kanagawa et al. (2018), a paper that also contains many other results on the connection between the GP and kernel formalisms. The proof requires an appeal to additional results, which are left out here for brevity.

[17] Note that, in this text, the meaning of the symbol k is overloaded. On the one hand, it signifies the covariance function of a *Gaussian process* (GP) and, on the other hand, the kernel of an RKHS. This double use of k is common practice due to the similarity of both cases.

[18] For the general case of $\Lambda \to 0$, see Kanagawa et al. (2018), §3.4.

Exercise 4.7 (moderate, solution on p. 359). *Prove Theorem 4.8. Hint: Use the reproducing property from Definition 4.6, and the Cauchy–Schwarz inequality*

$$|\langle f, g \rangle|^2 \leq \langle f, f \rangle \cdot \langle g, g \rangle,$$

for $f, g \in \mathcal{H}$.

[19] For clarity: The posterior standard-deviation σ_x of Eq. (4.9), in general, is not itself an element of the RKHS.

1. Assign a Gaussian process prior $p(f) = \mathcal{GP}(f; 0, k)$ over a hypothesis class of functions and use the asymptotic Gaussian likelihood $p(y \mid f) = \prod_{i=1}^{N} \delta(y_i - f(x_i))$. The resulting posterior is a Gaussian process with mean m_x and marginal variance σ_x.

2. Assume that the true function f is an element of the RKHS $\mathcal{H}_k$ associated with k, and decide to construct the regularised least-squares estimate for f within $\mathcal{H}_k$ (Eq. (4.8)), which is given by m_x. The distance between this estimate and the true $f(x)$ (if the assumption $f \in \mathcal{H}_k$ is correct!) is bounded above, up to an unknown constant (the RKHS-norm of f) by σ_x.

In many sections of this text, this equivalence between probabilistic and statistical estimation will be used to construct probabilistic re-interpretations of classic numerical methods. The juxtaposition above highlights at least one reason why it is helpful to have access to both formulations, and thus why it makes sense to study Probabilistic Numerics in addition to classic methods: in contrast to an empirical risk functional, a prior is a generative object. We can study draws from the prior to analyse and criticise the assumptions encoded in the prior. If a particular GP prior does not encode certain properties we tangibly know about our concrete problem, we may change the prior to better reflect our knowledge. It is much harder to do so based on an empirical risk. We also note that while the Gaussian inference formulation adds this additional conceptual strength, it does not take something away from the statistical one: Both in terms of intrinsic assumptions and computational demands, both are equivalent to each other.

There are, however, also subtle differences between the two formulations. In particular, draws from a Gaussian process are in general not elements of the RKHS.[20] Instead they come for a different space that, in general, is slightly "larger" and "rougher" surrounding the RKHS. This aspect will have tangible consequences for the error analysis of probabilistic numerical methods. In §II and later, we will see that probabilistic error estimates of *classic* methods are usually overly cautious on the problems that these methods are usually applied to, an indication that these methods are too generic, and can be improved upon with additional prior information.

[20] See p. 131 in Rasmussen and Williams (2006). Detailed analyses are offered by Driscoll (1973) and, more recently, Steinwart (2019). There is also a detailed discussion in §4 of Kanagawa et al. (2018).

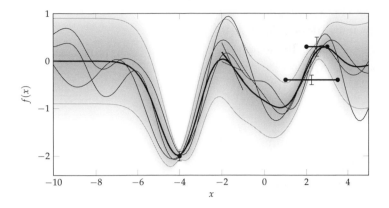

Figure 4.4: Gaussian process inference on a function f from evaluations of the function ($f(x = -4)$), its derivative ($f'(x = -1.5)$) and integrals ($\int_a^b f(x)\,dx$ for $[a, b] = [1, 3.5]$ and $[2, 3]$, plotted are the average function values, the value of the integral divided by $(b - a)$). Each observation is corrupted by Gaussian noise of varying degree (plotted error bars). These observations have a structured effect on the uncertainty assigned to function values. For example, the derivative observation constrains the derivatives of f, but contains only weak information about the absolute deviation of f from the mean function.

▶ **4.4   Inference from and on Derivatives and Integrals**

The closure of Gaussian distributions under linear projections (Eq. (3.4)) allows for an elegant extension of regression on functions from observed function values, which is of great importance for numerical uses of the Gaussian inference framework. Consider a real-valued function over a Euclidean vector space, $f : \mathbb{R}^N \dashrightarrow \mathbb{R}$, and assign the Gaussian process prior $p(f) = \mathcal{GP}(f; m, k)$. Assume that the mean function $m(x)$ and the kernel $k(x, x')$ are at least q-times continuously differentiable in all their arguments, and integrable against the measure $\nu : \mathbb{R}^N \dashrightarrow \mathbb{R}$. Then it follows[21] from Eq. (3.4) that all partial derivatives and integrals against ν are jointly Gaussian (process) distributed, with mean functions

$$\mathbb{E}\left(\frac{\partial^\ell f(x)}{\partial x_i^\ell}\right) = \frac{\partial^\ell m(x)}{\partial x_i^\ell} \quad \text{for } 0 \leq \ell \leq q,$$

$$\mathbb{E}\left(\int_a^b f(x)\,d\nu(x)\right) = \int_a^b m(x)\,d\nu(x),$$

and covariance functions of the general form

$$\text{cov}\left(\frac{\partial^\ell f(x)}{\partial x_i^\ell}, \frac{\partial^m f(x)}{\partial x_j^m}\right) = \frac{\partial^\ell \partial^m k(x, x')}{\partial x_i^\ell \partial x_j'^m},$$

$$\text{cov}\left(\int_a^b f(x)\,d\nu(x), \frac{\partial^m f(x)}{\partial x_j^m}\right) = \int \frac{\partial^m k(x, x')}{\partial x_j'^m}\,d\nu(x),$$

and analogously for mixed partial derivatives and higher-order integrals. Of course, these results can be used to perform inference on integrals from derivative observations and function values, and the other way round. This tool will be a staple of probabilistic numerical methods derived in later chapters.

[21] There are subtleties involved due to the nonparametric nature of the Gaussian process measure, so the appeal to Eq. (3.4) is simplistic, made with practicality in mind. A more precise statement is that, if L is a linear operator acting on f, then Lf is a Gaussian process with mean function Lm and covariance function LkL^*, if Lm and $Lk(\cdot, x')$ are bounded. The specific result for derivatives can be found on p. 27 in Adler (1981). For a technical treatment, see Akhiezer and Glazman (2013). Thanks to Simo Särkkä for pointing out these references. A more recent discussion is offered by Owhadi and Scovel (2015).

The kernels used in this context in later chapters include, most prominently, the Wiener process and its integrals (see §5.4). Also in wide use, mostly for algebraic convenience, is the Gaussian (aka square-exponential, radial basis function) kernel

$$k_{SE}(a,b) := \exp\left(-\frac{(a-b)^2}{2\lambda^2}\right).$$

The Gaussian kernel amounts to an extreme assumption of smoothness on f, but its extremely convenient algebraic properties nevertheless make it a versatile tool for rather regular problems, if extreme numerical precision is not the primary goal. For easy reference, we include explicit forms for the most frequent combinations of partial derivatives and integrals here, using the shorthand $\Phi(z) := \text{erf}\left(\frac{z}{\sqrt{2\lambda^2}}\right)$. If $p(f) = \mathcal{GP}(f;0,k_{SE})$, then

$$\text{cov}\left(\int_a^b f(x)dx, \int_c^d f(\tilde{x})d\tilde{x}\right) = \int_a^b \int_c^d k_{SE}(x,\tilde{x})\,dxd\tilde{x}$$

$$= \sqrt{\frac{\pi\lambda^2}{2}}\big[-(d-b)\Phi(d-b) + (d-a)\Phi(d-a)$$
$$+ (c-b)\Phi(c-b) - (c-a)\Phi(c-a)\big]$$
$$+ \lambda^2\left[-k_{SE}(d,b) + k_{SE}(d,a) + k_{SE}(c,b) - k_{SE}(c,a)\right],$$

$$\text{cov}\left(\int_a^b f(\tilde{x})d\tilde{x}, f(x)\right) = \int_a^b k_{SE}(x,\tilde{x})\,d\tilde{x} = \text{cov}\left(f(x), \int_a^b f(\tilde{x})d\tilde{x}\right)$$

$$= \sqrt{\frac{\pi\lambda^2}{2}}\left[\Phi(b-x) - \Phi(a-x)\right],$$

$$\text{cov}\left(\int_a^b f(\tilde{x})d\tilde{x}, \frac{\partial f(x)}{\partial x}\right) = \frac{\partial}{\partial x}\int_a^b k_{SE}(x,\tilde{x})\,d\tilde{x} = \text{cov}\left(\frac{\partial f(x)}{\partial x}, \int_a^b f(\tilde{x})d\tilde{x}\right)$$

$$= k_{SE}(x,b) - k_{SE}(x,a),$$

and

$$\text{cov}\left(f(x), \frac{\partial f(\tilde{x})}{\partial \tilde{x}}\right) = \frac{\partial k_{SE}(x,\tilde{x})}{\partial \tilde{x}} = -\text{cov}\left(\frac{\partial f(x)}{\partial x}, f(\tilde{x})\right)$$

$$= \frac{x - \tilde{x}}{\lambda^2}k_{SE}(x,\tilde{x}),$$

$$\text{cov}\left(\frac{\partial f(x)}{\partial x}, \frac{\partial f(\tilde{x})}{\partial \tilde{x}}\right) = \frac{\partial^2 k_{SE}(x,\tilde{x})}{\partial x \partial \tilde{x}}$$

$$= \left(\frac{1}{\lambda^2} - \frac{(x-\tilde{x})^2}{\lambda^4}\right)k_{SE}(x,\tilde{x}),$$

$$\text{cov}\left(\frac{\partial^2 f(x)}{\partial x^2}, \int_a^b f(\tilde{x})d\tilde{x}\right) = \frac{1}{\lambda^2}\left[(x-b)k_{SE}(x,b) - (x-a)k_{SE}(x,a)\right]$$

$$\text{cov}\left(\frac{\partial^2 f(x)}{\partial x^2}, f(\tilde{x})\right) = \left(\frac{(x-\tilde{x})^2}{\lambda^4} - \frac{1}{\lambda^2}\right)k_{SE}(x,\tilde{x}).$$

5

Gauss–Markov Processes
Filtering and Stochastic Differential Equations

As presented above, Gaussian process regression is a rather general formulation of inference on a function from finitely many data. However, computing the posterior's parameters associated with N real-valued data, in Eqs. (4.6) and (4.7), involves the inversion of a $N \times N$ covariance matrix; hence the computational cost of doing so in general rises faster than N (general matrix inversion has cost $\mathcal{O}(N^3)$, see also §III). This nonlinear cost is an obstacle to the application of this framework for the design of efficient numerical algorithms. Ideally, a numerical routine should be able to keep running virtually indefinitely and increase its precision over time. This requires an inference framework whose computational complexity scales at most linearly, $\mathcal{O}(N)$. Parametric regression, introduced in §4.1, has this property; but it also has a finite model capacity, thus can only compute approximations of limited quality.

Some numerical problems have a trait that offers another way to address this challenge. They construct an ordered sequence of estimates by moving along a one-dimensional path parametrised by a variable t that, for intuition, we may as well call *time*. The central examples are:

Quadrature: Univariate integration methods estimate an integral $F = \int_t f(t) \mathrm{d}t$, by evaluating f for various values $t_i \in \mathbb{R}$, stepping from one end of the integration domain to the other.

ODEs: Solvers for ordinary differential equations estimate a curve (a continuous function of univariate input) $x(t), t \in \mathbb{R}$, such that $x'(t) = f(x(t), t)$. In doing so they evaluate the multivariate function f for various values of t and x. (Often the sequence of values t_i is ordered). Of course, such solvers can be thought of as solving a univariate integration problem, where the integration path is itself an (unknown) curve

Nonlinear optimisation: Algorithms that search for local extrema $x_* = \arg\min f(x)$ of a real-valued differentiable function $f : \mathbb{R}^N \to \mathbb{R}$ usually construct a sequence of estimates $x_t \in \mathbb{R}^N$ designed to hopefully converge to the true x_*. As in the ODE setting, the estimates themselves are multivariate; but the sequence of estimates can be thought of as lying on a (discretised) curve. This notion is less precise than the two above, since it is not always clear how to account for varying step-lengths $x_t - x_{t-1}$. The locations x_t actually lie in a high-dimensional vector space with a natural Euclidean metric, so the "times" separating the points x_t are subject to some subtle scaling. Nevertheless, the notion of a time-series will turn out to be helpful anyway in §IV.

▶ 5.1   Markov Chains and Message Passing on Chain Graphs

Parametric regression models keep a finite global memory. But in the above settings, with observations on an ordered one-dimensional space, we may also try to construct models that pass a finite amount of information forward and backward along the line. This notion of a finite memory through time is formalised by the *Markov property*.[1]

[1] Markov (1906)

Definition 5.1 (Markov chain). *Consider a discrete set of latent variables (called states) $X = [x_t]_{t=0,\ldots,T}$ with joint probability density $p(X)$. Then p is a* Markov chain *if it has the* Markov property *that x_t is conditionally independent of all preceding states given the direct precursor x_{t-1}:*

$$p(x_t \mid x_0, x_1, \ldots, x_{t-1}) = p(x_t \mid x_{t-1}). \qquad (5.1)$$

In this sense, the states collected in x_t can be thought of as a kind of sufficient local memory. If we know the state at any point in time, we know all that is possible to know about the future behaviour of the system at time t. In addition, assume observations y_t that only directly relate to the local state x_t,

$$p(y_t \mid X) = p(y_t \mid x_t).$$

These two structural restrictions on a probabilistic model suffice to make inference on the latent variables linear in T. A first

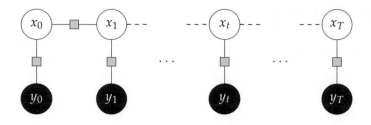

interesting observation is that it allows *recursive prediction*. Assume we have observed the *time series* $y_{0:t-1} := [y_0, \ldots, y_{t-1}]$ and want to predict the states as described by $p(x_t \mid y_{0:t-1})$. This posterior marginal distribution is given by

Figure 5.1: Graphical model (factor graph) for a Markov chain. In this bipartite notation, every white node represents a latent variable, every black node an observable, and every grey box a factor in the joint probability distribution of (X, y). Edges in the graph connect variables and observables to the factors in which they appear. The Markov property is visibly reflected in the fact that this graph is a *chain*. If all the factors are Gaussian, this is the generic form of a linear state space model. If they additionally all have the same parameters, it is a linear time-invariant model.

$$p(x_t \mid y_{0:t-1}) = \frac{\int_{j \neq t} p(X) p(y_{0:t-1} \mid X)\, dx_j}{\int p(X) p(y_{0:t-1} \mid X)\, dX}$$

$$= \frac{\int_{j \neq t} p(y_{0:t-1} \mid X_{0:t-1}) p(x_0)\, dx_0 \left(\prod_{0 < j < t} p(x_j \mid x_{j-1})\, dx_j \right) p(x_t \mid x_{t-1}) \left(\prod_{i > t} p(x_i \mid x_{i-1})\, dx_i \right)}{\int p(y_{0:t-1} \mid X_{0:t-1}) p(x_0)\, dx_0 \left(\prod_{0 < j < t} p(x_j \mid x_{j-1})\, dx_j \right) p(x_t \mid x_{t-1})\, dx_t \left(\prod_{i > t} p(x_i \mid x_{i-1})\, dx_i \right)}$$

$$= \frac{\int_{j < t} p(x_t \mid x_{t-1}) p(y_{0:t-1} \mid X_{0:t-1}) p(x_0)\, dx_0 \left(\prod_{0 < j < t} p(x_j \mid x_{j-1})\, dx_j \right)}{\int_{j < t} p(y_{0:t-1} \mid X_{0:t-1}) p(x_0)\, dx_0 \left(\prod_{0 < j < t} p(x_j \mid x_{j-1})\, dx_j \right)}$$

$$= \int p(x_t \mid x_{t-1}) p(x_{t-1} \mid y_{0:t-1})\, dx_{t-1}.$$

In other words, it is possible to iteratively compute a posterior over x_t given all previous observations, by an alternating sequence of *prediction-update* steps that only involve local quantities:

Predict: use the posterior from the previous step to compute[2]

$$p(x_t \mid y_{0:t-1}) = \int p(x_t \mid x_{t-1}) p(x_{t-1} \mid y_{0:t-1})\, dx_{t-1}. \quad (5.2)$$

If $t = 0$, start the induction with the prior $p(x_0)$.

Update: include the local observation into the posterior by Bayes' theorem:

$$p(x_t \mid y_{0:t}) = \frac{p(y_t \mid x_t) p(x_t \mid y_{0:t-1})}{\int p(y_t \mid x_t) p(x_t \mid y_{0:t-1})\, dx_t}. \quad (5.3)$$

[2] These steps are a special case of a general algorithm called *belief propagation* or the *sum-product algorithm* (Pearl, 1988; Lauritzen and Spiegelhalter, 1988). It formalises the computational cost of inference in joint probability distributions given their factorisation into local terms. There are visual formal languages capturing such factorisation properties, known as *graphical models* (e.g. Figure 5.1).

Expression (5.2) is known as the *Chapman–Kolmogorov* equation. It can be found as Eqs. (5) and (5*) in a seminal paper by Kolmogorov (1936).

The situation is only slightly more complicated if, having collected all observations $y = y_{0:T}$, one subsequently has to compute a marginal distribution $p(x_t \mid y)$ for some $0 \le t < T$. Due to the Markov property, x_t is conditionally independent of later observations given x_{t+1}:

$$p(x_t \mid x_{t+1}, y) = p(x_t \mid x_{t+1}, y_{0:t}) \qquad (5.4)$$

and of the form

$$
\begin{aligned}
&= \frac{p(x_t, x_{t+1} \mid y_{0:t})}{p(x_{t+1} \mid y_{0:t})} \\
&= \frac{p(x_{t+1} \mid x_t, y_{0:t}) p(x_t \mid y_{0:t})}{p(x_{t+1} \mid y_{0:t})} \\
&= \frac{p(x_{t+1} \mid x_t) p(x_t \mid y_{0:t})}{p(x_{t+1} \mid y_{0:t})}. \qquad (5.5)
\end{aligned}
$$

Exercise 5.2 (easy). *Show that Eq. (5.4) holds. Hint: Use Bayes' theorem and the Markov property (5.1).*

Using this, we can write the marginal posterior on x_t as follows[3]

$$
\begin{aligned}
p(x_t \mid y) &= \int p(x_t, x_{t+1} \mid y)\, dx_{t+1} \\
&= \int p(x_t \mid x_{t+1}, y) p(x_{t+1} \mid y)\, dx_{t+1} \qquad (5.6) \\
&= \int p(x_t \mid x_{t+1}, y_{0:t}) p(x_{k+1} \mid y)\, dx_{t+1}.
\end{aligned}
$$

[3] This derivation is based on the exposition in §8.1 of Särkkä (2013)

Then, we just insert Eq. (5.5) into Eq. (5.6),[4] which yields

$$p(x_t \mid y) = p(x_t \mid y_{0:t}) \int p(x_{t+1} \mid x_t) \frac{p(x_{t+1} \mid y)}{p(x_{t+1} \mid y_{0:t})}\, dx_{t+1}. \quad (5.7)$$

[4] Kitagawa (1987)

So to compute the marginal $p(x_t \mid y)$ for all $0 \le t \le T$, using the notion of time, we can think of this as first performing a *forward-pass* as described above to compute the predictions $p(x_t \mid y_{0:t-1})$ and updated beliefs $p(x_t \mid y_{0:t})$. The final update step in that pass provides $p(x_T \mid y)$, from which we can start a *backward-pass* to compute the posterior marginals $p(x_t \mid y)$ using Eq. (5.7) and all terms computed in the forward pass. This nomenclature, of *passing messages* along the Markov chain is popular in statistics and machine learning, and applies more generally to tree-structured graphs (i.e. not just chains).[5] In signal processing, where time series play a particularly central role, the forward pass is known as *filtering*, while the backward updates are known as *smoothing*. Figure 5.2 depicts the output of these methods. The next section spells out their computations in the case when the underlying state-space model is linear and Gaussian.

[5] Bishop (2006), §8.4.2

▶ 5.2 Linear Gaussian State-Space Models

The abstract form of the message passing algorithm above becomes particularly elegant if all prior and conditional distributions in the model are Gaussian, involving only linear relations.

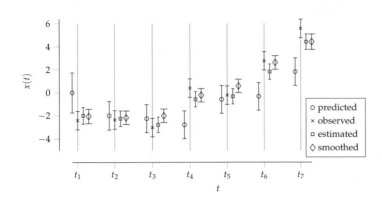

We will assume the following forms, using popular notational conventions for the linear maps involved:

$$p(x_0) = \mathcal{N}(x_0; m_0, P_0), \tag{5.8}$$

$$p(x_{t+1} \mid x_t) = \mathcal{N}(x_{t+1}; A_t x_t, Q_t),$$

$$p(y_t \mid x_t) = \mathcal{N}(y_t; H_t x_t, R_t). \tag{5.9}$$

The latter two relations are also often written, and known as, the *dynamic model* and an *measurement model*, respectively:

$$x_{t+1} = A_t x_t + \xi_t \quad \text{with} \quad \xi_t \sim \mathcal{N}(0, Q_t) \quad \text{(dynamic)},$$

$$y_t = H_t x_t + \zeta_t \quad \text{with} \quad \zeta_t \sim \mathcal{N}(0, R_t) \quad \text{(measurement)}.$$

In signal processing and control theory, the matrices A_t, H_t, Q_t, R_t are known as the *transition* and *measurement* matrices, *process noise* and *observation noise* covariances, respectively. We will sometimes use these intuitions evoking a dynamical system, but it will not always fit directly to the numerical domain. The entire setup is known as a *linear Gaussian system* in control theory. However, to avoid confusion with the regression models defined in §4.1 and §4.2 (which are also Gaussian and linear), we will use another popular convention and call this a linear Gaussian *state-space* model to stress that the inference takes place in terms of the time-varying states x_t. If the parameters are independent of time, $A_t = A, Q_t = Q, H_t = H$ and $R_t = R$, for all t, they define a *linear time-invariant (LTI) system*.

Under these assumptions, the predictive, updated and posterior marginals constructed above all retain Gaussian form. The Chapman–Kolmogorov equation (5.2) becomes

$$p(x_{t+1} \mid y_{0:t}) = \mathcal{N}(x_{t+1}; m_{t+1}^-, P_{t+1}^-), \text{ with} \tag{5.10}$$

$$m_{t+1}^- = A_t m_t \quad \text{and} \quad P_{t+1}^- = A_t P_t A_t^\mathsf{T} + Q_t. \tag{5.11}$$

```
 1  procedure FILTER(m_{t-1}, P_{t-1}, A, Q, H, R, y)
 2  |   m_t^- = A m_{t-1}                          // predictive mean
 3  |   P_t^- = A P_{t-1} A^T + Q                   // predictive covariance
 4  |   z = y - H m_t^-                             // residual
 5  |   S = H P_t^- H^T + R                         // innovation covariance
 6  |   K = P_t^- H^T S^{-1}                        // gain
 7  |   m_t = m_t^- + Kz                            // updated mean
 8  |   P_t = (I - KH) P_t^-                        // updated covariance
 9  |   return (m_t, P_t), (m_t^-, P_t^-)
10  end procedure
```

Algorithm 5.1: Single step of the Kálmán filter. Variables indexed by t are outputs, while the variables without indices are only used internally, can thus be overwritten. If the latent state is of dimensionality $x_t \in \mathbb{R}^L$ and the observations have dimensionality $y_t \in \mathbb{R}^V$, then an individual step of the filter has computational complexity $\mathcal{O}(L^3 + V^3)$ (for the inversion of S in line 6, and the matrix-matrix multiplications in the latent states in line 3, respectively).

The update, Eq. (5.3) becomes

$$p(x_t \mid y_{0:t}) = \mathcal{N}(x_t; m_t, P_t),$$

where the parameters of this distribution can be computed using the following procedure, giving explicit names to intermediate terms (capital letters denote matrices, lower case vectors):

Exercise 5.3 (easy). *Using the basic properties of Gaussians from Eqs. (3.4), (3.8) & (3.10) and the prediction-update Eqs. (5.2) & (5.3), show that Eqs. (5.10) to (5.13) hold.*

$$z_t := y_t - H_t m_t^- \qquad \text{(innovation residual)}, \qquad (5.12)$$
$$S_t := H_t P_t^- H_t^T + R_t \qquad \text{(innovation covariance)},$$
$$K_t := P_t^- H_t^T S_t^{-1} \qquad \text{(gain)},$$
$$m_t := m_t^- + K_t z_t,$$
$$P_t := (I - K_t H_t) P_t^-. \qquad (5.13)$$

Many of these terms originate from the field of control theory, where they were made popular by Rudolf Kálmán (1960). The whole prediction update scheme above is thus widely known as *the Kálmán filter*, and the quantity K_t is called the *Kálmán gain* in his honour.[6]

The "full" posterior marginals – those arising from all observations, in the past and the future – are also Gaussian,

$$p(x_t \mid y) = \mathcal{N}(x_t; m_t^s, P_t^s). \qquad (5.14)$$

Their form can be written, from Eq. (5.7), using the parameters

[6] The Kálmán gain is also known as the *optimal* gain for historical reasons (because it is the optimal sensitivity of an electrical filter designed to follow the dynamical system defined above). In our context, this name is redundant. Given the state-space model, the posterior is not just the optimal, but really the only meaningful probabilistic estimator.

```
 1  procedure SMOOTHER(m_t, P_t, A, m_{t+1}^-, P_{t+1}^-, m_{t+1}^s, P_{t+1}^s)
 2  |   G = P_t A^T (P_{t+1}^-)^{-1}                        // gain
 3  |   m_t^s = m_t + G(m_{t+1}^s - m_{t+1}^-)              // posterior mean
 4  |   P_t^s = P_t + G(P_{t+1}^s - P_{t+1}^-) G^T          // posterior covariance
 5  end procedure
```

Algorithm 5.2: Single step of the RTS smoother. Notation as in Algorithm 5.1. The smoother, since it does not actually touch the observations y_t, has complexity $\mathcal{O}(L^3)$.

```
1  procedure PREDICT(m_0, P_0, [A_t, Q_t, H_t, y_t, R_t]_{t=1,...,∞})
2  |  for t = 1,... do
3  |  |  (m_t, P_t) = FILTER(m_{t-1}, P_{t-1}, A_t, Q_t, H_t, R_t, y_t)
4  |  end for
5  end procedure
```

Algorithm 5.3: Algorithmic wrapper around Algorithm 5.1 to perform online prediction at a sequence of points t_i. PREDICT has constant memory requirements over time, and its computation cost is constant per time step. Thus inference from N observations requires N steps of Algorithm 5.1, at cost $\mathcal{O}(N(L^3 + V^3))$. See the *Bayesian ODE filter* (Algorithm 38.1); one of its special cases, the EKF0, is analogous to this Algorithm 5.3 (as discussed in §38.3.4).

of the prediction and updated beliefs, as follows:

Let $G_t := P_t A_t^\mathsf{T} (P_{t+1}^-)^{-1}$, (smoother gain)

then $m_t^s = m_t + G_t(m_{t+1}^s - m_{t+1}^-)$

and $P_t^s = P_t + G_t(P_{t+1}^s - P_{t+1}^-)G_t^\mathsf{T}$. (5.15)

These update rules are often simply called the "Kálmán smoother" or, more precisely, the (fixed interval) *Rauch–Tung–Striebel (RTS) smoother* equations.[7] The estimates computed by the Kálmán filter and smoother are depicted in Figure 5.2.

[7] Rauch, Striebel, and Tung (1965)

For reference, Algorithms 5.1 and 5.2 summarise the above results in pseudo-code, providing the individual steps for both the filter and the smoother. The wrapper algorithm PREDICT (Algorithm 5.3) solves the task of continuously predicting the subsequent state of a time series. For a finite time series running from $t = 0$ to $t = T$, the algorithm INFER (Algorithm 5.4) returns posterior marginals for every time step t. Since these marginals (that is, their means and variances) are exactly equal to those of GP regression (§4.2.2), algorithm INFER (Algorithm 5.4) is nothing but a linear-time implementation of GP regression with Markov priors.[8]

[8] Särkkä and Solin (2019), §12.4

The Kálmán filter (and smoother) are so efficient that they can be sometimes applied even if the linearity or Gaussianity of the dynamic or measurement model are violated.[9] In numerics, the case for such fast-and-Gaussian methods is even stronger

[9] Särkkä (2013), §13.1

```
1  procedure INFER(m_0, P_0, [A_t, Q_t, H_t, y_t, R_t]_{t=1,...,T})
2  |  for t = 1 : 1 : T do
3  |  |  ((m_t, P_t), (m_t^-, P_t^-)) =
4  |  |      FILTER(m_{t-1}, P_{t-1}, A_{t-1}, Q_{t-1}, H_t, R_t, y_t)
5  |  end for
6  |  for t = T - 1 : -1 : 0 do
7  |  |      (m_t^s, P_t^s) =
8  |  |      SMOOTHER(m_t, P_t, A_t, m_{t+1}^-, P_{t+1}^-, m_{t+1}^s, P_{t+1}^s)
9  |  end for
10 end procedure
```

Algorithm 5.4: Algorithmic wrapper around Algorithms 5.1 and 5.2 to perform inference for a time-series of finite length. While the runtime of this routine is also linear in T, in contrast to Algorithm 5.3, it has linearly growing memory cost, to store all the parameters of the posterior and intermediate distributions. See the *Bayesian ODE smoother* (Algorithm 38.2); one of its special cases, the EKS0, is analogous to this Algorithm 5.4 (as discussed in §38.3.4).

because (compared with conventional statistics) saved computational budget can be invested in finer discretisations. Thus, all probabilistic numerical methods in this text use Gaussian methods (such as the Kálmán filter and smoother) for probabilistic regression – with the sole exception of the probabilistic ODE solvers presented in §40.3, where a stronger case for nonparametric posteriors can be made due to highly nonlinear dynamics of ODEs. Accordingly, the standard sequential-Monte-Carlo versions of filters and smoothers, known as *particle filters and smoothers*,[10] will not appear before the ODE chapter VI. There, they will be concisely introduced in §38.4.

[10] Doucet, Freitas, and Gordon (2001)

► 5.3   Linear Stochastic Differential Equations

For a moment, let us put aside the observations y and only consider the prior defined by the dynamic model from Eq. (5.11). The predictive *means* of this sequence of Gaussian variables follow the discrete linear recurrence relation $m_{t+1} = A_t m_t$. When solving numerical tasks, the time instances t will not usually be immutable discrete locations on a regular grid, but values chosen by the numerical method itself, on a continuous spectrum. We thus require a framework creating continuous *curves* $x(t)$ for $t > t_0 \in \mathbb{R}$ that are consistent with such linear recurrence equations. For deterministic quantities, *linear differential equations* are that tool: Consider the linear (time-invariant) dynamical system for $x(t) \in \mathbb{R}^N$,

$$\frac{dx(t)}{dt} = Fx(t); \qquad \text{and assume } x(t_0) = x_0. \qquad (5.16)$$

This initial value problem is solved by the curve[11]

$$x(t) = \exp(F(t - t_0))x_0.$$

Thus, the linear ordinary differential equation (5.16), together with a set of discrete time locations $[t_0, t_1, \ldots, t_N = T]$ gives rise to the linear recurrence relation

$$x_{t_{i+1}} = A_{t_i} x_{t_i} \quad \text{with} \quad A_{t_i} = \exp(F(t_{i+1} - t_i)).$$

For clarity, the solution to a linear time-invariant ODE at discrete time locations is a linear recurrence relation. This does *not* mean that every recurrence relation can be identified with the solution of one particular linear ODE, or in fact with any ODE at all. But one way to construct recurrence relations is all we need to build interesting probabilistic inference algorithms.

[11] This uses the *matrix exponential*

$$e^X \equiv \exp(X) := \sum_i^{\infty} \frac{X^i}{i!}, \qquad (5.17)$$

where $X^i := \underbrace{X \cdots X}_{i \text{ times}}$ is the ith power of C (defining $C^0 = I$). The exponential exists for every complex-valued matrix. Among its properties are:

⊖ $e^0 = I$ (for the zero matrix);

⊖ if $Xy = YX$, then

$$e^X e^Y = e^Y e^X = e^{X+Y}.$$

Thus, every exponential is invertible:

$$\left(e^X\right)^{-1} = e^{-X};$$

⊖ if Y is invertible, then

$$e^{YXY^{-1}} = Ye^X Y^{-1},$$

thus, $\det e^X = e^{\text{tr} X}$;

⊖ if $D = \text{diag}_i(d_i)$ then $e^D = \text{diag}_i(e^{d_i})$ (using the scalar exponential). In particular, if $X = VDV^{-1}$ is the eigendecomposition of X, then

$$e^X = Ve^D V^{-1}$$

provides a practical way to compute the exponential of diagonalisable matrices. Another important way to compute matrix exponentials is if X is *nilpotent* (i.e. there exists an $m \in \mathbb{N}$ such that $X^m = 0$), in which case the exponential can be explicitly computed by Eq. (5.17).

The construction of probabilistic models for continuous time series requires a generalisation of the above construction for deterministic linear dynamic systems to stochastic processes: We need a way to build the Gaussian density around the mean prediction $m_{t_{i+1}} = A_{t_i} m_{t_i}$, such that the conditional distribution has the form of Eq. (5.10). In particular, given $x_{t_i} = m_{t_i}$, we would like a relative, or "differential" way to add a centred Gaussian disturbance $\xi_t \sim \mathcal{N}(0, Q_t)$ over the time interval $[t_i, t_{i+1}]$.

Such a generalisation is provided by *linear stochastic differential equations* (linear SDEs). Inconveniently, the stochastic paths that solve such "differential" equations are a.s. nowhere differentiable and thus have a.s. infinite total variation.[12] A rigorous definition of SDEs thus requires a new integral w.r.t. such a stochastic process (the *Itô integral*) which gives rise to a new kind of calculus. To avoid its complicated introduction, we will, however, only provide an intuitive definition of SDEs. The full-blown theory can, e.g., be found in the detailed book by Karatzas and Shreve (1991) or in the more concise one by Oksendal (2003); if slightly less rigour is acceptable to the reader, we recommend the more accessible book by Särkkä and Solin (2019).

[12] Oksendal (2003), §3.1

Above, general Gaussian processes were defined as an infinite-dimensional generalisation of finite-dimensional distributions. In similar fashion, we will define a linear SDE as the abstract object giving rise to Gaussian probabilistic recurrence relations for finite time steps.

Definition 5.4 (Linear SDE).[13] *Consider curves $x : t \in \mathbb{R} \mapsto x(t) \in \mathbb{R}^N$ for $t > t_0$. Assume matrices $F \in \mathbb{R}^{N \times N}$ and a vector $L \in \mathbb{R}^N$. For the purposes of this text, the* linear time-invariant stochastic differential equation

$$dx(t) = Fx(t)\,dt + L\,d\omega_t$$

(see below for an explanation of the notation $d\omega_t$), together with the initial value $x(t_0) = x_0$, describes the local behaviour of a unique Gaussian process, determined by the following mean and covariance function:

$$\mathbb{E}(x(t)) = e^{F(t-t_0)}x_0, \tag{5.18}$$

$$\mathrm{cov}(x(t), x(t')) = \int_{t_0}^{\min t,t'} e^{F(t-\tau)} LL^\mathsf{T} e^{F^\mathsf{T}(t'-\tau)}\,d\tau \tag{5.19}$$

$$=: k(t, t').$$

This process is known as the solution *of the SDE. In particular, this*

[13] In addition to sidestepping complications involved with general stochastic processes on the real line, the simplified definition for SDEs chosen here also attempts to avoid confusion with the definition of probabilistic algorithms for the solution of deterministic ordinary differential equations in Chapter VI. The aim in that chapter will be to cast the solution of ODEs as the construction of linear SDEs that concentrate as much probability mass as possible around the true solution. It will *not* be the aim to construct more involved stochastic processes driven by the ODE (and its unknown solution) itself.

gives rise to the discrete time stochastic recurrence relation

$$p(x_{t_{i+1}} \mid x_{t_i}) = \mathcal{N}(x_{t_{i+1}}; A_{t_i} x_{t_i}, Q_{t_i}), \qquad (5.20)$$

with

$$A_{t_i} := \exp(F(t_{i+1} - t_i)) \qquad and$$
$$Q_{t_i} := \int_0^{t_{i+1} - t_i} e^{F\tau} L L^\mathsf{T} e^{F^\mathsf{T}\tau} \, d\tau. \qquad (5.21)$$

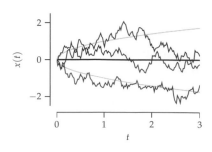

Figure 5.3: Draws from the Wiener process ω_t (here with $x_{t=0} = 0$) are paths of Brownian motion: continuous, but non-differentiable, almost everywhere. Their expected deviation from x_0 (grey lines) grows as $\sqrt{t}$.

The most basic choice $N = 1, L = 1, F = 0$ yields the SDE "$dx(t) = d\omega_t$" and thus an implicit definition of that ominous object $d\omega_t$, which is called the *increment of the Wiener process*. The solution of this SDE has (since $e^0 = 1$), the constant mean function $\mathbb{E}(x(t)) = \mu(t) = x_0$ (i.e. if we set $x_0 = 0$, vanishing mean), and the covariance function is $k(t, t') = \min(t, t') - t_0$. This solution is thus the *Wiener process*[14] with starting time t_0 (see Eq. (4.5)), which is depicted in Figure 5.3 for $t_0 = 0$. The mysterious $d\omega_t$ is, strictly speaking, nothing but a placeholder for an Itô integral; i.e. the SDE "$dx = d\omega_t$" is in essence just a shorthand for the Itô *stochastic integral equation* $x(t) = \int_0^t d\omega_s$.[15] Thus $d\omega_t / dt$ is, loosely speaking, some kind of "derivative of the Wiener process"; it is hence often thought of as Gaussian *white noise*. While this is a useful intuition, it is completely informal because a sample path from the Wiener process ω_t is almost surely not differentiable, almost everywhere. Figure 5.4 gives an intuition for state-space inference using the Wiener process itself as the prior measure.

[14] Candidates for the invention of the Wiener process include the Danish astronomer Thiele in 1880 (see a review by Lauritzen in 1981), the French mathematician Bachelier, the Austrian physicist Smoluchowski, and Albert Einstein with his *Annus Mirabilis* paper on Brownian motion (Einstein, 1906). Wiener (1923), however, was arguably the first to show the existence of the process. An impressive encyclopedic handbook on the Wiener process was provided by Borodin and Salminen (2002).

[15] See §5.2.A. in Karatzas and Shreve (1991) for more information on the stochastic-integral form of SDEs.

▶ 5.4   Polynomial Splines

An interesting class of linear SDEs arises from *integrals* of the Wiener process. This can be achieved by considering the SDE with $F \in \mathbb{R}^{(q+1) \times (q+1)}$ and $L \in \mathbb{R}^{(q+1)}$ as

$$F = \begin{bmatrix} 0 & 1 & 0 & \cdots & 0 \\ 0 & 0 & 1 & \cdots & 0 \\ \vdots & & \ddots & \ddots & \vdots \\ 0 & 0 & \cdots & 0 & 1 \\ 0 & 0 & \cdots & 0 & 0 \end{bmatrix}, \text{ and } L = \begin{bmatrix} 0 \\ 0 \\ \vdots \\ 0 \\ \theta \end{bmatrix}. \qquad (5.22)$$

This structure[16] ensures that the elements of x are derivatives of each other. So they can be interpreted as derivatives of a function $f : \mathbb{R} \to \mathbb{R}$:

$$x(t) = \begin{bmatrix} f(t) & f'(t) & f''(t) & \cdots & f^{(q)}(t) \end{bmatrix}. \qquad (5.23)$$

[16] Another common notation if the step size is fixed ($t_{i+1} - t_i = h \; \forall i$) is to scale the state space to $\tilde{x}(t) = Bx(t)$ with $B = \text{diag}(1, h, \ldots, h^q/q!)$, and a corresponding $\tilde{F} = BFB^{-1}$, $\tilde{L} = BL$ (this means $F_{i,i+1} = i/h$). In this notation, Eq. (5.23) becomes

$$\tilde{x}_i(t) = \frac{h^{i-1} f^{(i-1)}(t)}{(i-1)!}.$$

The advantage is that the resulting $\tilde{A}$ and $\tilde{Q}$ have much simpler form: $\tilde{A}$ becomes the *Pascal triangle* matrix (the upper triangular matrix containing the Pascal triangle), and the elements of Q depend on h only in a scalar fashion:

$$[\tilde{A}]_{ij} = \mathbb{I}(j \geq i) \binom{j}{i},$$

$$[\tilde{Q}]_{ij} = \frac{\theta^2 h^{2q+1}}{(2q + 3 - i - j)(q + 1 - i)!} \times \frac{1}{(q + 1 - j)!(i - 1)!(j - 1)!}.$$

This can help both with numerical stability and efficient implementations.

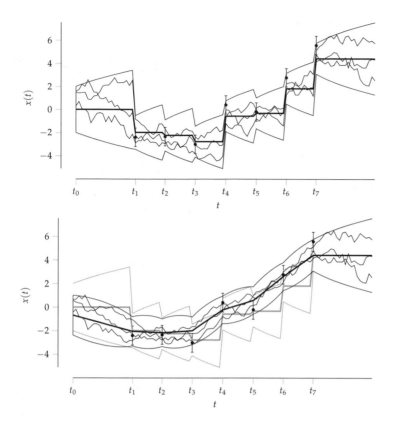

Figure 5.4: State-space inference using the most elementary Wiener process prior, i.e. the linear time invariant model with $F = 0, L = 1, H = 1$. Observations shown as black circles with error bars at two standard deviations of the Gaussian observation noise. Top: Filtering. Predictive means in solid black, two standard deviations in thin black. Three joint samples from the predictive distribution, constructed in linear time during the prediction run, are plotted in thin black, also. Bottom: Posterior distribution after smoothing (filtering distribution in grey for comparison). The posterior samples (which are indeed valid draws from the joint posterior) are produced by taking the samples from the predictive distribution and scaling/shifting them (deterministically) during the smoothing run; they do not involve additional random numbers.

The corresponding discrete-time objects A and Q contain elements that are polynomials of the time steps $h_i := t_{i+1} - t_i$. The matrix $A(h)$ is upper triangular (and Q, of course, is SPD), with elements[17] ($1 \leq i, j \leq q + 1$)

$$[A(h)]_{ij} = [\exp(Fh)]_{ij} = \mathbb{I}(j \geq i)\frac{h^{j-i}}{(j-i)!}, \qquad (5.25)$$

$$[Q(h)]_{ij} = \theta^2 \frac{h^{2q+3-i-j}}{(2q+3-i-j)(q+1-i)!(q+1-j)!}. \quad (5.26)$$

A detailed derivation of A and Q is provided in the literature.[18] The corresponding covariance functions have a tedious form, but they are also polynomials. For example, for $q = 1$ – the *integrated Wiener process* – the kernel is (for $t_0 = 0$)

$$\mathrm{cov}(f(a), f(b)) = \theta^2 \left(\frac{1}{3}\min^3(a,b) + |a - b|\frac{1}{2}\min(a,b) \right) \qquad (5.27)$$

(see also Figure 4.3). We recall that the posterior mean function of a Gaussian process is a weighted sum of kernel evaluations. Hence, under the choice (5.27) and noise-free observations of f, the posterior mean on f would be the piecewise cubic interpolant of the data (which is unique within the convex hull of the

[17] Since $\exp(X)^{-1} = \exp(-X)$, Eq. (5.25) also immediately provides

$$[A^{-1}(h)]_{ij} = \mathbb{I}(j \geq i)\frac{(-h)^{j-i}}{(j-i)!}. \quad (5.24)$$

[18] Kersting, Sullivan, and Hennig (2020), Appendix A; note that zero-based indexing is used there.

data). It is the *cubic spline*. More generally, posterior interpolants of the q-times integrated Wiener process are $2q + 1$-ic splines.

▶ 5.5   The Matérn Family

Another important base case is given by the univariate SDE (i.e. $x(t) \in \mathbb{R}$) with a negative F. For convenience further below, we will use the parametrisation $F = -1/\lambda$ and $L = 2\theta/\sqrt{\lambda}$ for $\theta, \lambda \in \mathbb{R}_+$. This setup captures the velocity of a gas particle of temperature $\theta/\sqrt{\lambda}$ in a linear (harmonic) potential well of force constant $1/\lambda$, and its solution is known as the *Ornstein–Uhlenbeck* (OU) process.[19] The SDE

[19] Uhlenbeck and Ornstein (1930)

$$\mathrm{d}x = -\frac{x}{\lambda}\,\mathrm{d}t + \frac{2\theta}{\sqrt{\lambda}}\,\mathrm{d}\omega_t$$

with $x(t_0) = x_0$ yields, with Eqs. (5.18) and (5.19),

$$\mathbb{E}(x(t)) = x_0 e^{-\frac{t-t_0}{\lambda}} \quad \text{and} \quad k(x, x') = \theta^2 \left(e^{-\frac{|t-t'|}{\lambda}} - e^{-\frac{t+t'-2t_0}{\lambda}} \right).$$

The special case of $t_0 \to -\infty$ is the stationary limit of the process. It has vanishing mean function, and covariance

[20] Matérn (1960)

$$k(t, t') = \theta^2 e^{-\frac{|t-t'|}{\lambda}}.$$

General integrals of the OU process form an important class of regression models in statistics and machine learning. The *Matérn*[20] class of covariances[21] is given, using the distance $r := |t - t'|$ by

[21] The naming of the family is due to Stein (1999). See also Rasmussen and Williams (2006), Eq. (4.16).

[22] Readers with a background in functional analysis might find it helpful to know that the RKHS arising from the Matérn kernel $k_{q+1/2}$ is norm-equivalent to the *Sobolev* space $H^{q+1}(\mathbb{R})$. See, e.g., Kanagawa, Sriperumbudur, and Fukumizu (2020).

$$k_\nu(r) = \theta^2 \frac{2^{1-\nu}}{\Gamma(\nu)} \left(\sqrt{2\nu}\frac{r}{\lambda} \right)^\nu K_\nu \left(\sqrt{2\nu}\frac{r}{\lambda} \right),$$

where K_ν is the modified Bessel function. For $\nu = q + 1/2$ with integer q, these kernels have the slightly more concrete form[22]

$$k_{q+1/2}(r) = \theta^2 \frac{\Gamma(q+1)}{\Gamma(2q+1)} \sum_{i=0}^{q} \frac{(q+i)!}{i!(q-i)!} \left(\sqrt{8\nu}\frac{r}{\lambda} \right)^{q-i} \cdot \exp\left(-\sqrt{2\nu}\frac{r}{\lambda} \right).$$

Or yet more explicitly, for the first three integer (and most popular) choices $q = 0, 1, 2$:

$$k_{1/2}(r) = \theta^2 \cdot \exp\left(-\frac{r}{\lambda} \right),$$

$$k_{3/2}(r) = \theta^2 \left(1 + \frac{\sqrt{3}r}{\lambda} \right) \cdot \exp\left(-\frac{\sqrt{3}r}{\lambda} \right),$$

$$k_{5/2}(r) = \theta^2 \left(1 + \frac{\sqrt{5}r}{\lambda} + \frac{5r^2}{3\lambda^2} \right) \cdot \exp\left(-\frac{\sqrt{5}r}{\lambda} \right).$$

The associated Gaussian processes are solutions of multivariate state-space models of the form[23]

$$dz(t) = Fz(t)\,dt + L\,d\omega_t$$

with $z \in \mathbb{R}^{q+1}$ and

$$
F = \begin{bmatrix}
0 & 1 & 0 & \cdots & 0 \\
0 & 0 & 1 & 0 & \vdots \\
\vdots & & \ddots & \ddots & 0 \\
0 & & 0 & 0 & 1 \\
-a_0 & -a_1 & \cdots & -a_{q-1} & -a_q
\end{bmatrix}
\quad \text{and} \quad
L = \begin{bmatrix} 0 \\ 0 \\ \vdots \\ 0 \\ \theta \end{bmatrix},
$$
(5.28)

where the a_i are the coefficients of the polynomial $(\xi + i\omega)^{-(q+1)}$ with $\xi := \sqrt{2\nu}/\lambda$.[24] For example, for the three values $q = 0, 1, 2$ from above, we get

$$dz(t) = -\xi z(t)\,dt + \theta\,d\omega_t,$$
(5.29)

$$dz(t) = \begin{bmatrix} 0 & 1 \\ -\xi^2 & -2\xi \end{bmatrix} z(t)\,dt + \begin{bmatrix} 0, \\ \theta \end{bmatrix} d\omega_t$$

$$dz(t) = \begin{bmatrix} 0 & 1 & 0 \\ 0 & 0 & 1 \\ -\xi^3 & -3\xi^2 & -3\xi \end{bmatrix} z(t)\,dt + \begin{bmatrix} 0 \\ 0 \\ \theta \end{bmatrix} d\omega_t.$$
(5.30)

A more general and detailed introduction to this family of stochastic processes is provided by Särkkä and Solin (2019).

▶ 5.6 Riccati Equations and Steady State

In numerical computations, we will often run a Gaussian filter for many steps through time. The question will then arise whether the algorithm will actually be able to identify an object of interest to finite uncertainty, or whether it might "lose track" over time, in the sense that the posterior predictive covariance P_i^- rises without bound. If this is not the case, does P_i^- converge to some finite value (and which one) for $i \to \infty$?

There is an elegant framework for this purpose, which is well-studied in control engineering,[25] where Kálmán filters are a foundational tool and the ability to track and control a system is of central concern. Consider a linear time-invariant system defined by the parameters A, Q, H, R. From the prediction (Eq. (5.11)) and update (Eq. (5.13)), the step from P_i^- to P_{i+1}^- is given by the *deterministic* step (since it does not involve the observation y)

[23] Hartikainen and Särkkä (2010); Särkkä, Solin, and Hartikainen (2013).

[24] This matrix F is known as the *companion matrix* of the polynomial

$$p(x) = a_0 + a_1 x^1 + \cdots + a_q x^q + x^{q+1},$$

because p is both the characteristic and the minimal polynomial of F. More in §7.4.6 of Golub and Van Loan (1996), and on pp. 405ff. of Wilkinson (1965).

Exercise 5.5 (moderate, solution on p. 360). *Find explicit forms for the matrices A_t, Q_t (Eq. (5.21)) associated with the discrete-time forms of Eqs. (5.29)–(5.30).*

[25] Bougerol (1993)

Exercise 5.6 (moderate, solution on p. 360). *Equation (5.31) demonstrates that the predictive covariances P_i^- are governed by a discrete time algebraic Riccati equation. Show that the evolution of the estimation covariances P_i and the smoothed covariances P_i^s are also described by DAREs.*

54 I Mathematical Background

$$P_{i+1}^- = AP_i^- A^\mathsf{T} - AP_i^- H^\mathsf{T}(HP_i^- H^\mathsf{T} + R)^{-1}HP_i^- A^\mathsf{T} + Q$$
$$= Q + A((P_i^-)^{-1} + H^\mathsf{T}R^{-1}H)^{-1}A^\mathsf{T}. \quad (5.31)$$

Equations of this form are known as *discrete-time algebraic Riccati equations* (DAREs).[26] Whether a DARE has a fix point, and if so, where that fix point lies, can be answered by considering the following *symplectic matrix*:[27]

$$Z = \begin{bmatrix} A^\mathsf{T} + H^\mathsf{T}R^{-1}HA^{-1}Q & -H^\mathsf{T}R^{-1}HA^{-1} \\ -A^{-1}Q & A^{-1} \end{bmatrix}.$$

If Z has no eigenvalues on the unit circle, then exactly half its eigenvalues are inside the unit circle, and the iteration (5.31) converges to a finite fix-point, known as the *steady-state* predictive covariance. To find it, consider the matrix $U \in \mathbb{C}^{2N \times 2N}$ of the eigenvectors of Z. Assume that they are sorted such that the first N columns of U correspond to the eigenvectors for eigenvalues *inside* the unit circle (and the other N columns to those *outside* the circle). Then separate U into square $N \times N$ sub-matrices as

$$U = \begin{bmatrix} U_1 & U_3 \\ U_2 & U_4 \end{bmatrix}.$$

The steady-state predictive covariance is given by

$$P_\infty^- = U_2 U_1^{-1}.$$

This solution is relatively easy to state, but it is not the numerically most efficient way to find P_∞^-. Advanced algorithms can be found in the book by Faßbender (2007). More generally, Riccati equations have been the subject of deep analysis. A classic book was written by Reid (1972). Bini, Iannazzo, and Meini (2011) provide a more recent review.

[26] The name reflects that, under some regularity assumptions, there is a continuous time limit given by the matrix differential equation

$$dP = AP + PA^\mathsf{T} - PH^\mathsf{T}R^{-1}HP + Q \quad (5.32)$$

(in the sense that the sequence of P's produced by Eq. (5.31) are solutions of Eq. (5.32)). Historically, quadratic ordinary differential equations

$$x'(t) = q(t) + a(t)x(t) + b(t)x^2(t)$$

(of which Eq. (5.32) is a matrix-valued generalisation) are named after the eighteenth-century work of Jacopo Riccati (1724).

[27] A symplectic matrix M is a matrix that satisfies $M^\mathsf{T}\Omega M = \Omega$ for some fixed nonsingular, skew-symmetric matrix Ω. In our case, e.g.,

$$\Omega = \begin{bmatrix} 0 & I \\ -I & 0 \end{bmatrix}.$$

Symplectic matrices have unit determinant. They are invertible, with $M^{-1} = \Omega^{-1}M^\mathsf{T}\Omega$, and a product of two symplectic matrices is a symplectic matrix. Hence they form a group. A *Lie* group, in fact, known as the symplectic group. Its generators are the *Hamiltonian matrices*, matrices of the form

$$X = \begin{bmatrix} A & B \\ C & -A^\mathsf{T} \end{bmatrix}$$

with symmetric matrices B, C. There is a corresponding stability analysis for the continuous-time algebraic Eq. (5.32) involving a Hamiltonian matrix.

Hierarchical Inference in Gaussian Models

As we saw in the preceding sections, the *parameters* $\Theta :=$ $\{m, k, A, b, \Lambda\}$ of a Gaussian model,

$$p(f \mid \Theta) = \mathcal{N}(f; m, k), \qquad p(y \mid f, \Theta) = \mathcal{N}(y; Af + b, \Lambda),$$

fundamentally affect the shape of the posterior on f. So what should be done if the right choice of parameters is itself unknown? The difference between a *variable* (a number of interest) and a *parameter* (a nuisance number required to specify the model, but not of central interest) is only conceptual, not formal. If the right value for a parameter is not clear a priori, the natural treatment is to assign uncertainty to it, too. For this purpose, the evidence term

$$p(y \mid \Theta) = \int p(f \mid \Theta) p(y \mid f, \Theta) \, \mathrm{d}f = \mathcal{N}(y; Am + b, k + \Lambda)$$

provides a *marginal likelihood* (also known as the *type-II likelihood*) for the parameters.[1]

Because inferring parameters involves "modelling the model", this notion is known as *hierarchical inference*. Hierarchical inference can increase the computational cost of the overall estimation, so it is not always advisable. But for some special cases of general interest, analytical forms are available. Usually, the probability distribution over the parameters itself contains numbers specifying certain parts. Those numbers are called *hyperparameters*. If one truly wanted, they too could be inferred via additional hierarchical modelling layers, *ad infinitum*, but this is not done in practice to keep computational cost finite. We will now outline such a framework for estimating the unknown mean and variance of a Gaussian model. We will employ a *conjugate prior*[2] over these hyperparamaters, i.e. a prior which

[1] More on the kind of exact marginalisation performed below, with extensions, can be found in a book by Bretthorst (1988). A more compact discussion of conjugate priors for the Gaussian is in §24.1 of MacKay (2003).

[2] An early work on conjugate priors is by Edwin Pitman (1936). An general exposition of conjugate priors for exponential families was provided by Diaconis and Ylvisaker (1979). The core idea behind conjugate priors, namely to formally treat prior knowledge like additional data, is arguably first used, albeit without much discussion, in §VI of Pierre-Simon Laplace's *Théorie analytique des probabilités* (1814, p. 364), in the famous argument about inferring probabilities from observed events, which also introduces the Gaussian approximation to the Beta integral now known as the *Laplace approximation* (1814, p. 365). There, Laplace argues that one can always use a uniform prior, since nonuniform prior knowledge can be represented by adding counts to the observations.

ensures that the posterior distribution over these hyperparameters, given data, has the same (Gaussian) form.

▶ 6.1   Inference on Scalar Parameters of Gaussians

Assume the real numbers $\boldsymbol{y} := [y_i]_{i=1,\dots,N}$ are drawn i.i.d. from a Normal distribution with unknown mean α and variance β^2,

$$p(\boldsymbol{y} \mid \alpha, \beta) = \prod_{i=1}^{N} \mathcal{N}(y_i; \alpha, \beta^2) = \mathcal{N}(\boldsymbol{y}; \alpha\mathbf{1}, \beta^2 I).$$

We would like to assign probability densities over the latent quantities α and β. Purely from an algebraic perspective (as opposed to a deeper philosophical motivation for this kind of uncertainty), it is convenient to choose a prior distribution $p(\alpha, \beta)$ of some form $p(\alpha, \beta) = \eta(\alpha, \beta; \theta)$ with hyperparameter θ, such that the posterior distribution has the same functional form η as the prior, just with updated hyperparameters $\tilde{\theta}$ instead of θ:

$$p(\alpha, \beta \mid \boldsymbol{y}) = \frac{p(\boldsymbol{y} \mid \alpha, \beta)\eta(\alpha, \beta; \theta)}{\int p(\boldsymbol{y} \mid \alpha, \beta)\eta(\alpha, \beta; \theta)\,\mathrm{d}\alpha\,\mathrm{d}\beta} = \eta(\alpha, \beta; \tilde{\theta}).$$

A prior η with this property is called *conjugate* to the likelihood $p(\boldsymbol{y} \mid \alpha, \beta)$. For the present case of a Gaussian likelihood with latent mean and variance, the standard choice of conjugate prior assigns a Gaussian distribution of mean μ_0 and variance proportional to β^2 (with scale λ_0) to α, and a Gamma distribution with parameters a_0, b_0 to the *inverse* of β. This is known as the *Gauss-Gamma*, or *Gauss-inverse-Gamma* prior, and has the hyperparameters $\theta_0 := \begin{pmatrix} \mu_0 & \lambda_0 & a_0 & b_0 \end{pmatrix}$:

$$\eta(\alpha, \beta \mid \mu_0, \lambda_0, a_0, b_0) = p(\alpha \mid \beta, \mu_0, \lambda_0)p(\beta \mid a_0, b_0)$$
$$= \mathcal{N}\left(\alpha; \mu_0, \frac{\beta^2}{\lambda_0}\right)\mathcal{G}(\beta^{-2}; a_0, b_0),$$
$$\text{where } \mathcal{G}(z; a, b) := \frac{b^a z^{a-1}}{\Gamma(a)}e^{-bz}.$$

Here, $\mathcal{G}(\cdot; a, b)$ is the Gamma distribution with shape $a > 0$ and rate $b > 0$. The normalisation constant of the Gamma distribution, and also the source of the distribution's name, is the Gamma function Γ.[3] To compute the posterior, we multiply prior and likelihood, and identify

$$p(\alpha, \beta \mid \boldsymbol{y}) \propto p(\boldsymbol{y} \mid \alpha, \beta)p(\alpha, \beta) \tag{6.2}$$
$$= \mathcal{N}(\boldsymbol{y}; \mathbf{1}\alpha, \beta^2 I)\mathcal{N}(\alpha; \mu_0, \beta^2/\lambda_0)\mathcal{G}(\beta^{-2}; a_0, b_0).$$

[3] The Gamma function is an extension of the factorial function. The Greek symbol for this function is due to Legendre who utilised two "Eulerian integrals", B, Γ (the first symbol being a capital Greek letter Beta):

$$B(m, n) = \int_0^1 x^{m-1}(1-x)^{n-1}\,\mathrm{d}x,$$
$$\Gamma(t) = \int_0^1 e^{-x}x^{t-1}\,\mathrm{d}x. \tag{6.1}$$

In the context of this text, it is a neat marginal observation that, while Legendre was interested in problems of chance, Euler's original motivation for considering those integrals, in an exchange with Goldbach, was one of *interpolation*: he was trying to find a "simple" smooth function connecting the factorial function on the reals. And indeed,

$$\Gamma(n) = (n-1)! \quad \forall n \in \mathbb{N}_{\backslash 0}.$$

Legendre is also to blame for this unsightly shift in the function's argument, since he constructed Eq. (6.1) by rearranging Euler's more direct result

$$n! = \int_0^1 (-\log x)^n\,\mathrm{d}x.$$

A great exposition on this story and the Gamma function can be found in a Chauvenet-prize-decorated article by Davis (1959). It is left as a research exercise to the reader to consider in which sense Euler's answer to this interpolation problem is natural, in particular from a probabilistic-numerics standpoint (that is, which prior assumptions give rise to the Gamma function as an interpolant of the factorials, whether there are other meaningful priors yielding other interpolations).

We first deal with the Gaussian part, using Eq. (3.5) (and some simple vector arithmetic) to re-arrange this expression as

$$\mathcal{G}(\beta^{-2}; a_0, b_0) \mathcal{N}\left(\boldsymbol{y}; \mathbf{1}\mu_0, \beta^2\left(I + \frac{\mathbf{1} \cdot \mathbf{1}^\mathsf{T}}{\lambda_0}\right)\right) \cdot \mathcal{N}\left(\alpha; \frac{\lambda_0 \mu_0 + \sum_i y_i}{\lambda_0 + N}, \frac{\beta^2}{\lambda_0 + N}\right). \qquad (6.3)$$

The second Gaussian expression is evidently a Gaussian over α, and the first one does not depend on α. To deal with the first part, we use the matrix inversion lemma, Eq. (15.9), to rewrite

$$\left(I + \frac{\mathbf{1} \cdot \mathbf{1}^\mathsf{T}}{\lambda_0}\right)^{-1} = I - \frac{\mathbf{1} \cdot \mathbf{1}^\mathsf{T}}{N + \lambda_0}.$$

This allows writing the first line of Eq. (6.3) more explicitly (leaving out normalisation constants independent of β) as

$$\mathcal{G}(\beta^{-2}; a_0, b_0) \cdot \mathcal{N}\left(\boldsymbol{y}; \mu_0, \beta^2\left(I + \frac{\mathbf{1} \cdot \mathbf{1}^\mathsf{T}}{\lambda_0}\right)\right)$$

$$\propto \left(\frac{1}{\beta^2}\right)^{a_0-1} \exp\left(-\frac{b_0}{\beta^2}\right) \cdot \left(\frac{1}{\beta^2}\right)^{N/2} \cdot \exp\left(-\frac{1}{2\beta^2}\left(\sum_{i=1}^N (y_i - \mu_0)^2 - \frac{(\sum_{i=1}^N y_i - N\mu_0)^2}{\lambda_0 + N}\right)\right). \qquad (6.4)$$

At this point, it is common practice to introduce the following substitutions, known as *sufficient statistics*:

$$\bar{\alpha} = \frac{1}{N}\sum_{i=1}^N y_i \qquad\qquad \text{sample mean,} \qquad (6.5)$$

$$\bar{\beta}^2 = \frac{1}{N}\sum_{i=1}^N (y_i - \bar{\alpha})^2 \qquad \text{sample variance,} \qquad (6.6)$$

with which the cumbersome expression in Eq. (6.4) simplifies (by shuffling sums around) to

$$\sum_{i=1}^N (y_i - \mu_0)^2 - \frac{(\sum_{i=1}^N y_i - N\mu_0)^2}{\lambda_0 + N}$$

$$= N\bar{\beta}^2 + \frac{\lambda_0 N}{\lambda_0 + N}(\bar{\alpha} - \mu_0)^2.$$

The terms in Eq. (6.4) thus have the form of a Gamma distribution over β^{-2}. All other terms suppressed by the $\propto$ sign make up the normalisation constant of the new Gauss-Gamma-posterior

$$p(\alpha, \beta \mid \boldsymbol{y}, \mu_0, \lambda_0, a_0, b_0) = \eta(\alpha, \beta \mid \mu_N, \lambda_N, a_N, b_N), \qquad (6.7)$$

with the new parameters

$$\mu_N = \frac{\lambda_0 \mu_0 + N\bar{\alpha}}{\lambda_0 + N}, \quad \lambda_N = \lambda_0 + N,$$

$$a_N = a_0 + N/2, \qquad b_N = b_0 + 1/2\left(N\bar{\beta}^2 + \frac{\lambda_0 N}{\lambda_0 + N}(\bar{\alpha} - \mu_0)^2\right). \qquad (6.8)$$

Exercise 6.1 (easy). *Assume that, instead of i.i.d. draws y_i, one observes individually scaled samples $a_i = y_i s_i$ with known scales s_i. By re-tracing the derivation, convince yourself that this situation can be addressed in the same fashion, but with new sufficient statistics*

$$\bar{\alpha} = \frac{1}{N}\sum_{i=1}^N \frac{a_i}{s_i},$$

$$\bar{\beta}^2 = \frac{1}{N}\sum_{i=1}^N \left(\frac{a_i}{s_i} - \bar{\alpha}\right)^2.$$

This will be helpful for hierarchical inference in §III.

The common interpretation for this result is that λ_N and a_N can be seen as *counters* for the number of observations collected, while μ_N and b_N are sufficient statistics for the population's mean and variance.[4] In this sense, λ_0 and $2a_0$ amount to pseudo-observations (see note 2) encoded in the prior. As N increases, μ_N (the expected value of α under the Gauss-Gamma prior) converges to the sample mean $\bar{\alpha}$, while $\mathbb{E}(\beta^2) = b_N/a_N$ converges to the sum of the sample variance and a correction term

$$\frac{\lambda_0 N}{\lambda_0 + N}(\bar{\alpha} - \mu_0)^2.$$

Intuitively, this term corrects for the fact that $\bar{\beta}^2$ is a biased estimate of the variance – the sample mean is typically closer to the samples than the actual mean is, and this bias depends on how far the initial estimate μ_0 is from the correct mean.

In applications our main interest will usually not be in the posterior distribution over the parameters (α, β), but predictions of the subsequent sample y_{N+1}. Under the hierarchical Gauss-Gamma model, this posterior distribution is the *marginal* distribution reached by integrating out the *posterior* over the hyperparameters,

$$p(y_{N+1} \mid y) = \int_{-\infty}^{\infty} \int_0^{\infty} p(y_+ \mid y, \alpha, \beta) p(\alpha, \beta \mid y) \, d\alpha \, d\beta.$$

The integral over α is easy, as it is an instance of the basic Gaussian properties above. The remaining integral over β is over the product of a Gaussian and several Gamma terms, which is given by a famous result known as[5] *Student's-t* distribution:

$$\mathrm{St}(y_{N+1}; \mu_N, {}^{a_N}/b_N, 2a_N)$$

$$:= \int_0^{\infty} \mathcal{N}(y_{N+1}; \mu_N, \beta^2) \mathcal{G}(\beta^{-2}; a_N, b_N) \, d\beta \qquad (6.9)$$

$$= \frac{\Gamma(a_N + 1/2)}{\Gamma(a_N)} \frac{b_N^{a_N}}{\sqrt{2\pi}} \left(b_N + \frac{(y_{N+1} - \mu_N)^2}{2} \right)^{-a_N - 1/2}.$$

▶ ## 6.2   Inference on Multivariate Gaussian Parameters

The derivations above can be extended to the case of *multivariate* observations $Y = \begin{bmatrix} y_1, \ldots, y_N \end{bmatrix} \in \mathbb{R}^{M \times N}$ drawn i.i.d. as

$$p(Y \mid \alpha, B) = \prod_i \mathcal{N}(y_i; \alpha, B) \qquad (6.10)$$

from a Gaussian with unknown mean vector α and unknown covariance matrix B. The corresponding conjugate prior is the

[4] The expected value of a Gamma-distributed random variable is

$$\mathbb{E}_{\mathcal{G}(z;a,b)}(z) = \frac{a}{b}.$$

[5] An alternative contender for the invention of this distribution is the German geodesist F. R. Helmert, but the endearing story of the statistician Gosset, writing under the pseudonym "Student" (1908) so as not to violate a non-disclosure agreement with the Guiness Brewery, his employer, has stuck. In fact, Helmert's 1875 letter to the *Zeitschrift für Mathematik und Physik* is an entertaining read, too. It contains a dressing-down of R. A. Mees (Professor of Physics at Göttingen) who, in an article published in the same newspaper some months prior (pp. 145 ff.), apparently misread a discussion, by Helmert, of Gauss' work on estimation of errors. The letter opens with the sentence "The point of the following is to show that Mr. Mees errs, not just in his evaluation of my work, but throughout his entire essay."

Gauss-inverse-Wishart distribution

$$p(\boldsymbol{\alpha}, B) = \mathcal{N}(\boldsymbol{\alpha}; \boldsymbol{\mu}_0, 1/\lambda_0 B) \mathcal{W}(B^{-1}; W_0, \nu_0), \qquad (6.11)$$

with the parameters $\boldsymbol{\mu}_0 \in \mathbb{R}^M$, $\lambda_0 \in \mathbb{R}_+$, a symmetric positive definite matrix W_0, and the so-called degree of freedom $\nu_0 > M - 1$. Here, $\mathcal{W}(B^{-1}; W_0, \nu_0)$ is a *Wishart distribution*,[6]

[6] Wishart (1928)

$$\mathcal{W}(B^{-1}; W_0, \nu_0) := \frac{|B^{-1}|^{(\nu_0-M-1)/2} \exp\left(-1/2\,\mathrm{tr}(W_0^{-1}B^{-1})\right)}{2^{\nu_0 M/2}|W_0|^{\nu_0/2}\Gamma_M(\nu_0/2)},$$

using what is sometimes called the *multivariate Gamma function*,

$$\Gamma_M(x) := \pi^{M(M-1)/4} \prod_{j=1}^{M} \Gamma\left(x + \frac{(1-j)}{2}\right).$$

The posterior resulting from the likelihood (6.10) and prior (6.11) emerges analogously to the derivations above. It is a Gauss-inverse-Wishart with the updated parameters

$$\boldsymbol{\mu}_N = \frac{\lambda_0 \boldsymbol{\mu}_0 + N\bar{\boldsymbol{\alpha}}}{\lambda_0 + N},$$
$$\lambda_N = \lambda_0 + N,$$
$$\nu_N = \nu_0 + N,$$
$$W_N = W_0 + N\bar{B} + \frac{\lambda_0 N}{\lambda_0 + N}(\bar{\boldsymbol{\alpha}} - \boldsymbol{\mu}_0)(\bar{\boldsymbol{\alpha}} - \boldsymbol{\mu}_0)^\mathsf{T},$$

using the multivariate forms of the sufficient statistics from Eqs. (6.5) and (6.6):

$$\bar{\boldsymbol{\alpha}} = \frac{1}{N}\sum_i \boldsymbol{y}_i,$$
$$\bar{B} = \frac{1}{N}\sum_i (\boldsymbol{y}_i - \bar{\boldsymbol{\alpha}})(\boldsymbol{y}_i - \bar{\boldsymbol{\alpha}})^\mathsf{T}.$$

[7] When comparing Eq. (6.12) to Eq. (6.9), an unexpected factor of 2 shows up here and there. This comes from differing definitions of the "counters" a_N and ν_N, which in turn are due to the standard definition of the Gamma distribution.

As above, it is also possible to marginalise over this multivariate posterior. This again yields a Student-t posterior, but a multivariate one:[7]

$$p(\boldsymbol{y}_{N+1} \mid Y, \boldsymbol{\mu}_0, \lambda_0, \nu_0, W_0) = \int p(\boldsymbol{y}_{N+1} \mid \alpha, B)p(\alpha, B \mid Y, \boldsymbol{\mu}_0, \lambda_0, \nu_0, W_0)\,d\alpha\,dB \qquad (6.12)$$

$$= \mathrm{St}_M\left(\boldsymbol{y}_{N+1}; \boldsymbol{\mu}_N, \frac{\lambda_N + 1}{\lambda_N(\nu_N - M + 1)}W_N, \nu_N - M + 1\right)$$

$$= \frac{\Gamma(\nu_N+M/2)}{\Gamma(\frac{\nu_N}{2})\nu_N^{M/2}\pi^{M/2}|W_N|^{1/2}}\left[1 + \frac{1}{\nu_N}(\boldsymbol{y}_{N+1} - \boldsymbol{\mu}_N)^\mathsf{T}W_N^{-1}(\boldsymbol{y}_{N+1} - \boldsymbol{\mu}_N)\right]^{-(\nu_N+M)/2}.$$

▶ **6.3   Conjugate Prior Hierarchical Inference for Filters**

For linear Gaussian state-space models as defined by Eqs. (5.8)–(5.9), the marginal likelihood factorises over the Markov chain:[8]

$$p(\boldsymbol{y} \mid \theta) = \prod_{i=1}^{N} p(y_i \mid \boldsymbol{y}_{1:i-1}, \theta) = \prod_{i=1}^{N} \mathcal{N}(y_i; Hm_i^-, HP_i^- H^\mathsf{T}).$$
(6.13)

In particular, for SDEs like those of the preceding §5.4 and §5.5, which can be written, with an explicit role for θ, as

$$\mathrm{d}z(t) = Fz(t)\,\mathrm{d}t + \theta \tilde{L}\,\mathrm{d}\omega_t,$$

hierarchical inference can be formulated efficiently in the filter formulation:[9] define the unit-scale predictive variance analogously to Eq. (5.21) as

$$\tilde{Q}_{t_i} := \int_0^{t_{i+1} - t_i} e^{F\tau} \tilde{L} \tilde{L}^\mathsf{T} e^{F\tau}\,\mathrm{d}\tau,$$

which extracts θ in Eq. (6.13). We get

$$p(\boldsymbol{y} \mid \theta) = \prod_{i=1}^{N} \mathcal{N}(y_i; Hm_i^-, \theta^2 H\tilde{P}_i^- H^\mathsf{T})$$

with a recursively defined $\tilde{P}^- =: A\tilde{P}A^\mathsf{T} + \tilde{Q}$, started at $\tilde{P}_0^- = P_0^-$. Given the inverse Gamma prior

$$p(\theta) = \mathcal{G}(\theta^{-2}, \alpha_0, \beta_0),$$

the posterior on θ can then be updated recursively during the filtering pass, and the analogue to Eq. (6.7) simplifies to

$$p(\theta^{-2} \mid \boldsymbol{y}_{1:N}) = \mathcal{G}\left(\theta^{-2}; \alpha_0 + \frac{N}{2}, \beta_0 + \frac{1}{2}\sum_{i=1}^{N} \frac{(y_i - Hm_i^-)^2}{H\tilde{P}_i^- H^\mathsf{T}}\right)$$
$$=: \mathcal{G}(\theta^{-2}, \alpha_N, \beta_N).$$
(6.14)

In Algorithm 5.1, this can be realised[10] by using $\tilde{Q}$ instead of Q, and adding the lines $\alpha \leftarrow \alpha + 1/2$ and $\beta \leftarrow \beta + z/2s$ after line 8 (those two variables having been initialised to $\alpha \leftarrow \alpha_0, \beta \leftarrow \beta_0$). The corresponding Student-t marginal on the state can be computed locally, if necessary, in each step.

[8] This is known as the *prediction error decomposition*, See Eq. (12.5) in Särkkä (2013).

[9] As in the preceding sections, analytic hierarchical inference on the scale θ requires noise-free observations. The same applies here. In the notation of the Kalman filter, this amounts to $R = 0$.

[10] Pseudo-code can be found in the following chapter, as Algorithm 11.2.

Summary of Part I

This chapter provided a concise introduction to Gaussian probabilistic inference. Here is a brief summary of the key results from this chapter:

- Gaussian densities provide the link between probabilistic inference and linear algebra. Though of limited expressiveness, they thus form the basis for computationally efficient inference.

- Using linear models, the Gaussian framework can be leveraged for inference on infinite-dimensional objects like functions and curves.

- Gaussian processes provide Gaussian inference on infinite-dimensional hypothesis-spaces. Even these nonparametric methods, however, embody non-trivial prior constraints. Like all consistent probabilistic models, have to spread finite probability mass over their hypothesis space.

- Gauss–Markov processes, captured by *state-space models*, allow Gaussian inference in linear time, through the algorithms known as filtering and smoothing. They are well-suited for the design of computationally lightweight inference rules, as required in numerical computation. Linear stochastic differential equations capture the continuous-time limit of these stochastic processes.

- The parameters of Gaussian models can be inferred using *hierarchical inference*. In most cases this poses a nonlinear (non-Gaussian) optimisation or inference problem. But in the special case of scale and mean of a Gaussian model, *conjugate priors* allow for analytic inference.

The following chapters will employ this toolset in concrete numerical tasks.

Chapter II
Integration

Key Points

Upon first hearing the idea of Probabilistic Numerics – that computation may be phrased as inference – the critical reader may have some fundamental questions.

- Is Probabilistic Numerics even **feasible**? Nice idea, but how might probabilistic numerical methods be built in practice?

- Are probabilistic numerical algorithms **fast**? Classic numerical methods are efficient. Bayesian inference has a reputation for high computational cost. Can probabilistic numerical methods be implemented at low complexity?

- Do probabilistic numerical algorithms **work**? In fact, what does "works" even mean here? Which analytic desiderata should probabilistic numerical methods satisfy? Classic numerical analysis, most centrally, aims to show that the point estimates of a certain method converge at a desirable *rate* towards the truth. For probabilistic numerical methods, we will likely want a similar notion. But since probabilistic methods add uncertainty as a first-class citizen, we should also be able to make analytic statements showing their uncertainty to be meaningful in some sense.

- Does probabilistic mean **stochastic**? After all, Monte Carlo methods, relying on random numbers, are a classic, well-established field of their own.

This chapter uses the elementary problem of integration to establish basic notions and give first exemplary answers to the above questions. In short, these answers are as follows:

- It is actually quite straightforward to derive **feasible** instances of probabilistic numerical algorithms. In particular, a

GP prior with a Gaussian covariance yields a first probabilistic numerical quadrature algorithm, producing good estimates for an integral given a set of evaluation nodes. Further, the placement of evaluation nodes across the integration domain, the *actions* taken by the numerical agent, can be naturally controlled by the probabilistic interpretation, by, for example, selecting information gain as a utility function. In this sense, probabilistic numerical methods really are autonomous learning agents.

⊖ We will demonstrate, in two different ways, how probabilistic numerical quadrature algorithms can be **fast**. First, many classical numerical algorithms can be directly derived as probabilistic numerical (we will repeatedly do so throughout this book to show connections). Providing an in-depth example, the trapezoidal rule is interpretable as the maximum a posteriori and mean estimator arising from a Wiener process prior on the integrand. Further, the Bayesian inference associated with the trapezoidal rule can be implemented as a Gaussian filter, at a cost identical to that of its classical equivalent. The fact that the trapezoidal rule is probabilistic numerical and the fact that the trapezoidal rule is fast prove that probabilistic numerical algorithms can be fast. We also discuss other common tractable priors for integration, and draw connections to the broader class of (classic) Gaussian quadrature rules. Such connections mean that, instead of having to "re-invent the wheel", we can use classic methods as inspiration for probabilistic ones. Second, we will show that at least one *ab-initio* probabilistic numerical quadrature algorithm, *warped sequential active Bayesian integration* (WSABI), can be *faster* than standard alternatives. This speed is not despite, but because of, the computation spent on Bayesian inference. Such computation can be seen not as overhead, but as an investment that ultimately yields dividends in returning good estimates more quickly.

⊖ Demonstrating what "**works**" means for Probabilistic Numerics, we show convergence statements for both the point estimate and the uncertainty (error estimate) of the probabilistic trapezoidal rule. The most basic uncertainty estimate is found to provide an upper, *worst-case* error bound; and we show that this error estimate can be adapted in an "empirical Bayesian" fashion, at low computational overhead, to provide better calibration, something closer to an *expected-case* estimate.

⊖ Probabilistic Numerics is not just different to **stochastic** numerics: Probabilistic Numerics is *opposed* to stochastic numerics. In the univariate setting, we show empirically that Monte Carlo integration has deficiencies over probabilistic numerical deterministic algorithms. We use this example to construct informal, generic arguments against the use of random numbers in computation.

9

Introduction

The primary tools in this chapter are Gaussian process inference (§4.3), and the state-space formulation of Gauss–Markov processes (§5), in particular in the algorithmic form of filtering and smoothing (Algorithms 5.1 and 5.2).

▶ 9.1 Motivation

Integration is a significant numerical problem in many fields of science and engineering. It is a key step in inference, where it is encountered when averaging over the many states of the world consistent with observed data. Indeed, a provocative Bayesian view is that integration is the single challenge separating us from systems that fully automate statistics. More speculatively still, such systems may even exhibit *artificial intelligence* (AI).[1]

But integration is also an operation with long history, and elementary enough to be covered at early levels of mathematical education. As such, integration provides the ideal starting point for a presentation of the intuitions driving Probabilistic Numerics and how they might be used to derive practical probabilistic numerical algorithms. This chapter will study how numerical integration – also known as *quadrature* – can be formulated as inference.

The results presented here expand and detail observations from a 1988 paper by Persi Diaconis (1988), and touch on related results by Anthony O'Hagan (1991).

As a running example, we will consider the univariate[2] function

$$f : \mathbb{R} \to \mathbb{R}^+, \qquad f(x) := \exp\left(-\left(\sin(3x)\right)^2 - x^2\right) \quad (9.1)$$

[1] M. Hutter. *Universal Artificial Intelligence*. Texts in Theoretical Computer Science. 2010.

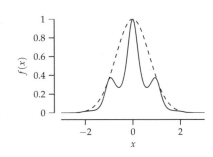

Figure 9.1: The smooth function $f(x)$ and an upper bound, the Gaussian function.

[2] We first focus on the univariate case for its pedagocial simplicity. In fact, analogously to multivariate GP regression, all below Bayesian quadrature methods extend directly to the d-dimensional case for all $d \in \mathbb{N}$. Note, however, that they – at the time of writing – are only practical up to $d \lesssim 20$ dimensions. See §10.1.2 for more details.

(Figure 9.1). The handful of symbols on paper that make up Eq. (9.1) fully specify a unique *deterministic* function. For arbitrary double precision values of $x \in \mathbb{R}$, a laptop computer can evaluate $f(x)$ to machine precision in a few nanoseconds, using only multiplication and addition, and the "atomic" functions exp and sin, which are part of elementary programming language definitions, like the GNU C library.[3] Repeated evaluations at the same value x will always return the same result. There is nothing *imprecise* about Eq. (9.1) and thus, one may argue that there is also nothing *uncertain* about the function f. However, the definite real number

$$F := \int_{-3}^{3} f(x)\,\mathrm{d}x \quad \in \mathbb{R} \tag{9.2}$$

cannot be computed straightforwardly or elementarily. Since f is clearly integrable, there is one and only one correct value of F. But this real number cannot be found in standard tables of analytic integrals.[4] And there is no atomic operation in low-level libraries providing its value to machine precision. Despite the formal clarity of Eq. (9.1), we are evidently *uncertain* about the value of F, because we cannot provide a correct value for it without further work. This is *epistemic* uncertainty, the kind arising from a lack of knowledge.

But it is easy to constrain the value of F to a finite domain: Because $f(x)$ is strictly positive, $F > 0$. A second glance at Eq. (9.1) lets us notice that f is bounded above by the Gaussian function:

$$f(x) \leq g(x) := \exp(-x^2) \quad \forall x \in \mathbb{R}.$$

Thus,

$$0 < F < \int_{-\infty}^{\infty} g(x)\,\mathrm{d}x = \sqrt{\pi}.$$

Hence it is possible to define a proper prior measure over the value of F, for example the uniform measure $p(F) = \mathbb{U}_{(0,\sqrt{\pi})}(F)$. Thus, if we can collect "data" Y that is related to F through some correctly defined and sufficiently regular likelihood function $p(Y \mid F)$, then the resulting posterior $p(F \mid Y)$ will converge towards the true value F, at an asymptotically optimal rate for this likelihood.[5] The question is thus, which prior, and which likelihood, should we choose?

▶ 9.2 Monte Carlo

Before introducing a probabilistic formulation of integration, it is helpful to briefly consider a popular *non*-probabilistic, but

[3] www.gnu.org/software/libc. There is a fuzzy boundary between what constitutes an "atomic" operation and a numerical algorithm. We will be pragmatic and define the libc as the set of atomic operations. A more abstract notion, in line with the purposes of this text, albeit also less concrete, is as follows: consider an algorithm a, a map $a(\theta) = \hat{\omega}$ taking inputs $\theta \in \Pi$ from some space Π that define a computational task with a true (potentially unknown) solution ω, and returning an estimate $\hat{\omega}$. If there are values of θ that the algorithm accepts without throwing an error, such that the resulting $\hat{\omega}$ deviates from the true ω by more than machine precision, then we might call a a *numerical* method, otherwise a low-level, atomic routine. Put succinctly, a numerical method produces an estimate that may be off, while an atomic routine just returns correct numbers. Hence, numerical methods can benefit from a non-trivial notion of uncertainty, while in atomic routines the associated uncertainty is always nil. This is not meant to be a perfectly rigorous definition of the term, and it is imperfect (for example, numerical methods also often have precision parameters and budgets to tune and spend, an aspect ignored by this definition), but a precise definition is not needed in practice anyway.

[4] Gradshteyn and Ryzhik (2007)

Exercise 9.1 (inspirational, see discussion in §9.3). *Even without appealing to the Gaussian integral, we could also bound f from above with the unit function $u(x) = 1$ on the integration domain, and would arrive at the looser bounds $0 < F < 6$. On the other hand, if we allow the use of the function* erf *(which is also in* glibc*), we could refine the upper bound to the definite integral over g, arriving at $0 < F < \sqrt{\pi}\,\mathrm{erf}(3)$. In which sense is this more "precise" prior more "correct"? Is there a* most correct, *or optimal* prior? *There is no immediate answer to these questions, but it is helpful to ponder it while reading the remainder of this chapter.*

[5] Le Cam (1973)

stochastic, way to compute integrals. That is, an approach based on the use of random numbers. Methods that compute using summary statistics of random numbers are known as *Monte Carlo (MC) methods*. They are a mainstay of computational statistics.

Assume the task is to compute $F = \int_a^b f(x)\,\mathrm{d}x$, for some generic integrable function f. Consider a probability measure $p(x)$ over the domain (a, b) that has the following properties:

1. $p(x) > 0$ wherever $f(x) \neq 0$ in (a, b); and

2. it is possible to draw random samples from p at acceptable computational cost (that is, using a source of uniform random numbers and a small number of atomic operations).

For the example integrand f with the integration limits $(a, b) = (-3, 3)$ from Eq. (9.1), the uniform measure $p(x) = \mathbb{U}_{-3,3}(x)$ fulfils these properties. Another possibility is the Gaussian measure restricted to $[-3, 3]$, that is,

$$p(x) = \begin{cases} \frac{1}{\mathrm{erf}(3)\sqrt{\pi}} \exp\left(-x^2\right) & \text{if } |x| \leq 3, \\ 0 & \text{else.} \end{cases} \tag{9.3}$$

Draws from Eq. (9.3) could, for example, be constructed relatively efficiently by *rejection sampling*.[6]

Using N i.i.d. samples $x_i \sim p(x), i = 1, \dots, N$ from any such p, we can construct the *importance sampling* estimator

$$\hat{F} := \frac{1}{N} \sum_{i=1}^{N} w(x_i), \tag{9.4}$$

using the function $w(x) := f(x)/p(x)$, which is well-defined by our above assumptions on $p(x)$. The logic of this procedure is depicted in Figure 9.2.

Note that, in contrast to F, the estimator $\hat{F}$ is a *random* number. By constructing $\hat{F}$, we have turned the problem (9.1) – inferring an uncertain but unique deterministic number – into a stochastic, statistical one. This introduction of external stochasticity introduces a different form of uncertainty, the *aleatory* kind, a lack of knowledge arising from randomness (more in §12.3). Because we have full control over the nature of the random numbers, it is possible to offer a quite precise statistical analysis of $\hat{F}$:

Lemma 9.2. *If F is integrable, the estimator $\hat{F}$ is unbiased. Its variance is*

$$\mathrm{var}(\hat{F}) = \frac{1}{N} \mathrm{var}_p(w), \tag{9.5}$$

[6] Robert and Casella (2013), §2.3

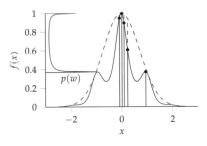

Figure 9.2: Monte Carlo integration. Samples are drawn from the Gaussian measure $p(x)$ (unnormalised measure as dashed line, samples as black dots), and the ratio $w(x) = f(x)/p(x)$ evaluated for each sample. The histogram plotted vertically on the left (arbitrary scale) shows the resulting distribution $p(w) = \int w(x)\,\mathrm{d}p(x)$. Its expected value, times the normalisation $\mathrm{erf}(3)\sqrt{\pi}$, is the true integral. Its standard deviation determines the scale for convergence of the Monte Carlo estimate.

assuming $\mathrm{var}_p(w)$ *exists. Hence, the standard deviation (the square root of the variance, which is a measure of expected error) drops as* $\mathcal{O}(N^{-1/2})$ *– the convergence rate of Monte Carlo integration.*

This is a strong statement given the simplicity of the algorithm it analyses: random numbers from almost any measure allow estimating the integral over *any integrable function*. This integrator is "good" in the sense that it is unbiased, and its error drops at a known rate.[7] The algorithm is also relatively cheap: it involves drawing N random numbers, evaluating $f(x)$ once for each sample, and summing over the results. Given all these strong properties, it is no surprise that Monte Carlo methods have become a standard tool for integration. However, there is a price for this simplicity and generality: as we will see in the next section, the $\mathcal{O}(N^{-1/2})$ convergence rate is far from the best possible rate. In fact, we will find ourselves arguing that it is the *worst* possible convergence rate amongst sensible integration algorithms.

Monte Carlo is not limited to problems where samples can be drawn exactly. Where exact sampling from a distribution is difficult, Monte Carlo is often practically realised through *Markov-Chain Monte Carlo* (MCMC). These iterative methods do not generally achieve the $\mathcal{O}(N^{-1/2})$ convergence rate, but they can still be shown to be *consistent*, meaning that their estimate of the integral asymptotically converges to its true value.

▶ 9.3   Relevance and Limitations of Prior Knowledge

The Monte Carlo method returns a "frequentist" statistical estimator: a random number whose distribution has known good properties. The strength of this approach is that the analysis of Lemma 9.2 requires only few assumptions. In particular, it involves almost no restrictive requirements on the integrand f. In practice, however, it is not necessary to be so cautious, for we invariably *do* know quite a lot about the integrand f – after all, the computer performing the computation must have access to a definition of f in a formal language: the source code encoding f. That description is bound to reveal additional information about the integrand. In our running example, we can inspect Eq. (9.1) to see that it is bounded above and below, smooth, etc.

How much performance can be gained if the algorithm is allowed *some* assumptions about the integrand – some *prior information*? This chapter introduces a probabilistic class of algorithms for integration, known as *Bayesian quadrature* (BQ).[8] We will discover that some classical integration rules, in partic-

Proof of Lemma 9.2. $\hat{F}$ is unbiased because its expected value is

$$\langle \hat{F} \rangle = \frac{1}{N} \sum_i \int_a^b w(x_i)p(x_i)\,\mathrm{d}x_i = F,$$

given that the draws x_i are i.i.d., and assuming that the $w(\cdot)$ function is known (more on this later). As $\hat{F}$ is a linear combination of i.i.d. random variables, the variance of $\hat{F}$ is immediately a linear combination of the respective variances:

$$\mathrm{var}(\hat{F}) = \frac{\sum_i \mathrm{var}_p(w_i)}{N^2} = \frac{\mathrm{var}_p(w)}{N}.$$

□

[7] The multiplicative constant $\mathrm{var}_p(w)$ can even be estimated at runtime! Albeit usually not without bias. See also Exercise 9.3 for some caveats.

Exercise 9.3 (moderate, solution on p. 361). *One of the few assumptions in Lemma 9.2 is the existence of* $\mathrm{var}_p(w)$. *Try to find an example of a simple pair of integrand* f *and measure* p *for which this assumption is violated.*

[8] See O'Hagan (1991). The term "Bayesian quadrature" is used ambiguously to mean a broad class of methods based on the idea of integration as probabilistic inference, or to refer to O'Hagan's specific algorithm, or something in between, for example any quadrature rule derived from a Gaussian process prior. We use it in the first, general sense.

ular the fundamental *trapezoidal rule*, arise naturally from this perspective.

Constructing a probabilistic quadrature method requires two ingredients. Together they form a general recipe that will also feature for all other probabilistic numerical methods:

1. A **model** describing the relationship between the *latent* object of interest and the *computable* quantities. That is, a joint probability measure $\mathcal{M} := p(F, Y)$ over the integral F and a data set $Y := [f(x_1), \ldots, f(x_N)]$ of function values. Assuming sufficient regularity of $\mathcal{M}$, the product rule (2.1) allows to write $\mathcal{M}$ as a *generative model* in terms of a prior $p(F)$ and a likelihood $p(Y \mid F)$ for F. Such a generative model will usually involve the integrand itself as a latent variable, because (as Y consists of evaluations of f) F and Y are independent when conditioned on f:

$$p(F, Y) = p(F)\, p(Y \mid F) = \int p(F \mid f)\, p(Y \mid F, f)\, \mathrm{d}p(f)$$
$$= \int p(F \mid f)\, p(Y \mid f)\, \mathrm{d}p(f).$$

Thus, the posterior on F can be computed via the posterior on f:

$$p(F \mid Y) = \int p(F \mid f)\, \mathrm{d}p(f \mid Y).$$

The model thus encodes *assumptions*, not just over the integrand, but also over its relationship to the numbers being computed to estimate it.

2. A **design rule** governing the choice of nodes $X := [x_1, \ldots, x_N]$ where f is evaluated by the computer. In general, such design rules will be a function mapping the model $\mathcal{M}$, the previous choices $\{x_j\}$ and previously collected data $Y_{<i} := \{y_j := f(x_j) \mid j < i\}$ to the decision x_i. If the rule explicitly includes previous evaluations $Y_{<i}$, it will be called *adaptive* or *closed-loop*. If X is chosen based solely on the model, the model is called *non-adaptive*, or *open-loop*. A non-adaptive design may be less sample-efficient, but can also have lower computational cost, as the design can be precomputed. We will discuss both non-adaptive and adaptive approaches in §10.2. The role of the design rule is thus to translate the information encoded in the model – and, for adaptive rules, the collected observations – into actions of the agent.

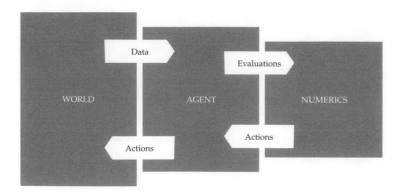

Figure 9.3: An agent, and its model of the
world, must necessarily be simpler and
smaller than the world itself. Similarly,
a numerical algorithm, and its model
of the problem, must be simpler and
smaller than the problem itself.

It is tempting to try and construct the model M by encoding
as much valid prior information as possible in a probability
measure. But this philosophical desire for a maximally informative prior must be balanced against practical constraints. We are
looking for a probability measure M that not only puts high
mass close to the truth, but also allows the *efficient computation*
of a posterior $p(F \mid Y)$, using only atomic operations.

A potential criticism of the probabilistic viewpoint on computation is that there is really only one acceptable prior – the
one that puts unit probability mass on the true solution on the
task, thus expresses zero uncertainty. But such a "perfect", or
"informed", prior would be just as analytically intractable as the
numerical task itself, and thus of no practical concern. Asking
for a probabilistic numerical method using the perfect prior
is analogous to asking for a classical method that returns the
correct answer without performing a single computation, or to
posit that a learning machine is only "well-posed" if it does not
require any training data. The goal must be to construct *tractable*
priors that have various desirable properties. For instance, these
priors should give rise to non-trivial uncertainty at intermediate points in the computation. Figure 9.3 illustrates the point:
models must be simpler than the problem modelled.

10

Bayesian Quadrature

This section will introduce Bayesian quadrature as a practical tool for numerical integration, and will give the key procedures needed to apply it to real problems.

We will tackle the generic integration problem of computing

$$F = \int_{\mathcal{X}} f(x) \, d\nu(x), \tag{10.1}$$

where $\nu(x)$ is a measure.[1] The domain of integration, $\mathcal{X}$, is, in practical applications, often a bounded interval, such as $[a, b] \subset \mathbb{R}$. The integration problem (10.1) is written as univariate, which will be the setting motivating the majority of this chapter. We will, however, also explain in §10.1.2 how Bayesian quadrature can be generalised to multivariate problems.

As we already saw in Chapter I, Gaussian process models for f are a fundamental tool for efficient formulations of inference. And indeed they allow for an analytic formulation of integration as probabilistic inference. Because Gaussian measures are closed under linear maps (see Eq. (3.4)), they are, in particular, also closed under integration. Following the exposition of §4.4, a generic Gaussian process prior $p(f) = \mathcal{GP}(f; m, k)$ over the integrand amounts to a joint Gaussian measure over both the function values collected in $Y := [f(x_1), \dots, f(x_N)]$ and the integral F:

$$p(F, Y) = \int p(F, Y \mid f) \, p(f) \, df = \int \delta\left(F - \int_{\mathcal{X}} f(x) \, d\nu(x)\right) \prod_{i=1}^{N} \delta\left(y_i - f(x_i)\right) p(f) \, df$$

$$= \mathcal{N}\left(\begin{bmatrix} Y \\ F \end{bmatrix} ; \begin{bmatrix} m_X \\ \int_{\mathcal{X}} m(x) \, d\nu(x) \end{bmatrix}, \begin{bmatrix} k_{XX} & \int_{\mathcal{X}} k_{Xx} \, d\nu(x) \\ \int_{\mathcal{X}} k_{xX} \, d\nu(x) & \iint_{\mathcal{X}} k_{xx'} \, d\nu(x) d\nu(x') \end{bmatrix} \right).$$

Here we have used the Dirac point measure δ as a likelihood term to encode *exact*, perfectly certain, observations of f at

[1] The example of Eq. (9.2) can either be seen as integrating the function $f(x) = e^{-\sin^2(3x)}$ against the Gaussian measure $\nu(x) = e^{-x^2}$, or as integrating the f from Eq. (9.1) against the Lebesgue measure.

the locations X. The conditional for F given Y, the posterior $p(F \mid Y)$, is a univariate Gaussian distribution[2] with parameters $\mathfrak{m} \in \mathbb{R}$ and $\mathfrak{v} \in \mathbb{R}_+$, given by

$$p(F \mid Y) = \mathcal{N}\left(F; \mathfrak{m}, \mathfrak{v}\right), \tag{10.2}$$

where

$$\mathfrak{m} := \int_{\mathcal{X}} m_x + k_{xX} k_{XX}^{-1}(Y - m_X)\, \mathrm{d}\nu(x) \tag{10.3}$$

$$= \mathfrak{m}_0 + \mathfrak{k}_X^\mathsf{T} k_{XX}^{-1}(Y - m_X),$$

$$\mathfrak{v} := \iint_{\mathcal{X}} k_{xx'} - k_{xX} k_{XX}^{-1} k_{Xx'}\, \mathrm{d}\nu(x)\mathrm{d}\nu(x') \tag{10.4}$$

$$= \mathfrak{K} - \mathfrak{k}_X^\mathsf{T} k_{XX}^{-1} \mathfrak{k}_X.$$

These expressions are tractable if there are analytic forms for the following three univariate and bivariate integrals:[3]

$$\mathfrak{m}_0 := \int_{\mathcal{X}} m(x)\, \mathrm{d}\nu(x) \in \mathbb{R}, \tag{10.5}$$

$$\mathfrak{k}(x_i) := \int_{\mathcal{X}} k(x, x_i)\, \mathrm{d}\nu(x) \in \mathbb{R}, \tag{10.6}$$

$$\mathfrak{K} := \iint_{\mathcal{X}} k(x, x')\, \mathrm{d}\nu(x)\mathrm{d}\nu(x') \in \mathbb{R}_+. \tag{10.7}$$

When these expressions are available, Eq. (10.2) amounts to an analytic map of the observations Y onto a probability measure over F with support on the entirety of, or a subset of, the real numbers. These integrals do not involve the integrand f, but the kernel k (and m) instead. Embedding the single integrand in a hypothesis class of many possible true functions (the support of the prior) in this way thus turns the intractable problem of exact integration into tractable, uncertain inference.

Notably, the posterior mean in Eq. (10.2) can be written as an affine function of Y:

$$\mathfrak{m} = F_0 + w^\mathsf{T} Y = F_0 + \sum_{i=1}^{N} w_i y_i, \tag{10.8}$$

with offset $\quad F_0 := \mathfrak{m}_0 - \mathfrak{k}_X^\mathsf{T} k_{XX}^{-1} m_X,$

and weights $\quad w_i := \sum_{j=1}^{N} \mathfrak{k}_{x_j} [k_{XX}^{-1}]_{ji}, \quad i = 1, \ldots, N.$

The construction so far just provides *a* probability measure over F without making any claims on its usefulness. But we would like to interpret that measure as a probabilistic *estimate*, of F, treating the posterior mean $\mathfrak{m}$ as a point estimator for F, and the posterior variance $\mathfrak{v}$ as an estimate of its square error, a notion of uncertainty. Not all Gaussian process priors will be equally

[2] Eq. (10.2) can also be reached by first forming the posterior $p(f \mid Y) =$

$$\mathcal{GP}(f; m_x + k_{xX}k_{XX}^{-1}(y - m_X),$$
$$k_{xx'} - k_{xX}k_{XX}^{-1}k_{Xx'}),$$

and using the closure of this Gaussian process under the (linear) integration operation.

[3] In practical application ν is often a probability measure. For example, in probabilistic statistics and machine learning, the typical situation is that $\nu(x)$ is a prior measure on x, while $f(x)$ is a likelihood function arising from some data. In such settings $\mathfrak{k}(x)$ equals the *kernel mean embedding of ν in the RKHS of k*, and Bayesian quadrature is related to the notion of *kernel herding* from the kernel community in machine learning. For more, see Smola et al. (2007) and Huszar and Duvenaud (2012).

"good" for a particular integration problem. To argue for one prior over another, we thus need to show that either quantity has analytic properties supporting this interpretation of point estimate and error estimate. This analysis will be provided, for a specific model choice, in §11.1.5.

▶ 10.1   Models

After the abstract introduction, we turn to describe tangible models for Bayesian quadrature. By default, we consider the real domain, $\mathcal{X} = \mathbb{R}$, although more general cases will also be presented.

Given a fixed set of nodes, integration requires two choices: that of the measure $\nu(x)$ and the model for the integrand. The measure $\nu(x)$ is often stipulated by the problem. It may also be possible to choose $\nu(x)$ to ease the resulting integration problem. For example, given a real domain, a Gaussian ν may be taken for the convenience of the resulting numerical integration problem.

We can now turn to the choice of model. Within Bayesian quadrature, the choice of GP prior for the integrand leads to two further choices: that of the prior mean $m(x)$ and the prior covariance $k(x, x')$. As above, these choices are not free, but have to be made such that the integrals in Eqs. (10.5)–(10.7) remain tractable. The mean m represents an initial guess for the integrand, while the covariance should aim to capture both the deviation of the true integrand from m and knowledge about analytic structure of the integrand beyond that represented by m e.g. periodicity or differentiability.

In practice, the prior mean function m is almost always taken as zero: $m(x) = 0$. It is rare that an integrand is known sufficiently well ahead of its evaluation to support any better-informed choice. The zero mean function has the additional practical advantage of rendering m_0 from Eq. (10.5) trivially zero, and thereby simplifying the posterior mean equation for the integral, Eq. (10.3).

As in §6, this chapter will exclusively use a *scaled* covariance family, separating a simple *scale* $\theta \in \mathbb{R}$ from a "unit" kernel $\tilde{k}(x, x')$,

$$k(x, x') := \theta^2 \, \tilde{k}(x, x'). \qquad (10.9)$$

The unit kernel $\tilde{k}$ captures more intricate structure, and will control the shape of the posterior and thus the *rate* at which the uncertainty contracts. The scale θ can then be inferred hierarchically as introduced in §6, to find the scale constant. That is because the scale θ also shows up multiplicatively in the posterior on F:

$$p(F \mid Y) = \mathcal{N}\left(F; \int_{\mathcal{X}} m_x + \tilde{k}_{xX}\tilde{k}_{XX}^{-1}(Y - m_X)\,\mathrm{d}x, \right.$$

$$\left. \theta^2 \iint_{\mathcal{X}} \tilde{k}_{xx'} - \tilde{k}_{xX}\tilde{k}_{XX}^{-1}\tilde{k}_{Xx'}\,\mathrm{d}x\mathrm{d}x' \right).$$

▷ **10.1.1   Gaussian Covariance / Squared-Exponential Kernel**

Within this family of covariances is the Gaussian covariance discussed in §4.4, which can also be written indirectly using the Gaussian density function as

$$k(x, x') = \theta^2 \mathcal{N}(x; x', \lambda^2).$$

When paired with the Gaussian measure

$$\nu(x) = \mathcal{N}(x; \mu, \sigma^2),$$

it yields tractable results (listed in §4.4) for the integrals required for Bayesian quadrature (Eqs. (10.5)–(10.7)). For convenience, we repeat that the posterior for the integral F given evaluations $Y = [f(x_1), \ldots, f(x_N)]$ is

$$p(F \mid Y) = \mathcal{N}(F; \mathfrak{m}, \mathfrak{v}),$$

where

$$\mathfrak{m} = \mathfrak{k}_X^{\mathsf{T}} k_{XX}^{-1} Y,$$
$$\mathfrak{v} = \mathfrak{K} - \mathfrak{k}_X^{\mathsf{T}} k_{XX}^{-1} \mathfrak{k}_X.$$

For the pairing of a Gaussian measure, zero prior mean and Gaussian covariance, we arrive at

$$[\mathfrak{k}]_i = \theta^2 \mathcal{N}(x_i; \mu, \lambda^2 + \sigma^2) \in \mathbb{R}, \quad \text{for } i \in \{1, \ldots, N\},$$

$$\mathfrak{K} = \frac{\theta^2}{\sqrt{2\pi(2\sigma^2 + \lambda^2)}} \in \mathbb{R}.$$

Now we have all the ingredients for a practical Bayesian quadrature procedure for univariate problems.

▷ **10.1.2   Multivariate Integrals**

Multivariate integrals are common. Fortunately, Bayesian quadrature is, in principle, readily extended to integrals over d variables (which we compile into the d-dimensional vector x). This extension requires only the choice of a Gaussian process prior over the d-dimensional space that yields tractable integrals against the measure. For instance, if the domain is $\mathbb{R}^d$, with multi-variate Gaussian measure

$$v(x) = \mathcal{N}(x; \mu, \Sigma),$$

and we take a GP with zero prior mean and multi-dimensional Gaussian covariance

$$k(x, x') = \theta^2 \mathcal{N}(x; x', \Lambda), \qquad (10.10)$$

we arrive at (where x_i is the ith node, a d-dimensional vector)

$$[\mathfrak{k}]_i = \theta^2 \mathcal{N}(x_i; \mu, \Lambda + \Sigma) \in \mathbb{R}, \quad \text{for } i \in \{1, \ldots, N\},$$
$$\mathfrak{K} = \theta^2 \left(\det 2\pi(2\Sigma + \Lambda) \right)^{-\frac{1}{2}} \in \mathbb{R}.$$

In practice, however, such a simple BQ model is unlikely to work well in high dimension. In general, multivariate integration is plagued by the "curse of dimensionality": the volume to be integrated over grows exponentially in dimension. As a consequence, if the number of evaluations does not grow similarly exponentially, a high-dimensional volume will be only sparsely explored by the evaluations. As a result, the higher the dimension, the greater the importance of the model, and the lesser the importance of evaluations of the integrand. The Gaussian covariance (10.10) is particularly poor in high dimension. The light tails of the Gaussian covariance prevent an evaluation from having influence over GP predictions at far-removed locations: exactly what is necessary in order to predict anything other than the GP prior mean in sparsely-explored spaces. At the time of writing, Bayesian quadrature is thus rarely used in dimension greater than around 20.

▷ **10.1.3   Other Tractable Models**

We conclude this section with a survey of tractable models for Bayesian quadrature. Table 10.1 reviews other pairings of prior measure $v(x)$ and Gaussian process kernel $k(x, x')$ that yield tractable results for the Bayesian quadrature equations, Eqs. (10.5)–(10.7). All assume a zero prior mean. This table is, by no means, to be considered exhaustive: a creative mind may be able to frame a given problem in additional ways to yield computable results. In doing so, it may be guided by the concrete interpretation of the model choice as a prior on functions. For example, one may consider the properties of samples from the prior to gain intuition for their fit to a particular problem. Classic quadrature methods also form a similar "zoo" of choices

$\mathcal{X}$	ν	k	Reference
$[0,1]^d$	Unif$(\mathcal{X})$	Wendland TP	Oates et al. (2019a)
$[0,1]^d$	Unif$(\mathcal{X})$	Matérn Weighted TP	Briol et al. (2019)
$[0,1]^d$	Unif$(\mathcal{X})$	Gaussian	Use of error function
$\mathbb{R}^d$	Mix. of Gaussians	Gaussian	Kennedy (1998)
$\mathbb{S}^d$	Unif$(\mathcal{X})$	Gegenbauer	Briol et al. (2019)
Arbitrary	Unif$(\mathcal{X})$ or mix. of Gauss.	Trigonometric	Integration by parts
Arbitrary	Unif$(\mathcal{X})$	Splines	Wahba (1990)
Arbitrary	Known moments	Polynomial TP	Briol et al. (2015)
Arbitrary	Known $\partial \log \nu(x)$	Gradient-based kernel	Oates, Girolami, and Chopin (2017); Oates et al. (2019a)

Table 10.1: A non-exhaustive list of distribution ν and kernel k pairs that provide a closed-form expression for both the kernel mean $\int k(\cdot, x)\,dx$ and the initial error $\mathfrak{K}$ from Eq. (10.7). Here TP refers to the tensor product of one-dimensional kernels, and $\mathbb{S}^d$ indicates the d-sphere $\{x = (x_1, \ldots, x_{d+1}) \in \mathbb{R}^{d+1} : \|x\|_2 = 1\}$. This table is adapted from Briol et al. (2019).

(see Table 11.1), but choosing between them is a less intuitive process, and adding to them is even harder, because there are only analytical, rather than constructive, means to do so without the interpretation of a prior. Interpretability is a key strength of PN.

▶ 10.2 Node Selection

The Bayesian quadrature model engenders a natural design rule. That is, thinking of the design rule as resulting from the minimisation of an expected loss, one loss function immediately suggests itself: the square error. The expected loss is then equal to the variance of $p(F \mid Y)$, $\mathfrak{v}$ (the expected square error after receiving the evaluation Y). The resulting design rule selects the locations $X = [x_1, \ldots, x_N]$ such that $\mathfrak{v}$ is minimised (note that $\mathfrak{v}$ is a function of X, a fact we will make explicit here):[4]

$$X = \arg\min_{\tilde{X} \in \mathbb{R}^N} \mathfrak{v}(\tilde{X}).$$

Designing the optimal grid for such a rule, even for regular kernels, can be challenging, because the corresponding multivariate optimisation problem can, in general, have high computational complexity.[5] However, instead of finding an *optimal* grid, one can also *sample*, at cost $\mathcal{O}(N^3)$, a draw from the *N-determinantal point process* (DPP) associated with k. Results by Bardenet and Hardy (2019) suggest that doing so causes only limited decrease in performance over the optimal deterministic grid design (which amounts to the maximum a posteriori assignment under the N-DPP). Belhadji, Bardenet, and Chainais (2019) offer further support for the use of determinantal point process sampling for integrands known to live in an RKHS.[6]

[4] Because the entropy of a Gaussian is a monotonic function of its variance (3.3), this design rule can also be phrased in an information-theoretic way as choosing the "most informative" design – that which minimises the conditional entropy of F given Y.

[5] Ko, Lee, and Queyranne (1995)

[6] The point of these papers does not disagree with our general argument, in §12.3, against the use of random sampling. Rather, these results show that allowing minor deviations from the optimal design can drastically reduce computational complexity at negligible decrease in performance. The necessary "samples" can even be drawn in a deterministic way.

Recall from Eq. (10.4) that the variance, v, of the integral does not depend on the values of the observations, Y, at all. Hence this is an open-loop, non-adaptive design criterion. This is simultaneously a good and a bad property of all Gaussian models. It means an evaluation pattern can be chosen a priori and does not need to be adapted at runtime, potentially saving computation time. However, the independence of the variance from Y also implies that the error estimate (and the evaluation locations) will be based entirely on prior assumptions, and will not depend on the collected function values themselves. These facts may feel disquieting: should we not hope that the evaluations inform both our confidence and the locations of future evaluations? To address these concerns, adaptive Bayesian quadrature schemes have been devised.

▷ 10.2.1   **Adaptive Selection**

Adaptive Bayesian quadrature schemes have, broadly, adopted non-Gaussian models, thereby shedding both the good and bad of such models. To motivate such models, note that many integration problems possess non-negative integrands. The classic case is probabilistic inference, where many integrands are a product of non-negative densities like likelihoods and priors. A particularly common case is the model evidence (or marginal likelihood),

$$\underbrace{p(\mathcal{D})}_{F} = \int \underbrace{p(\mathcal{D} \mid x)}_{f(x)} \, \underbrace{p(x) \, dx}_{d\nu(x)} .\qquad(10.11)$$

As noted in the motivation for this chapter, §9.1, solving such integrals may also be a key step towards AI. To date, all known Bayesian quadrature schemes that are adaptive (according to our definition in §9.3) consider this setting of non-negative integrands.

The first attempt at adaptive Bayesian quadrature[7] was termed *doubly-Bayesian quadrature* (BBQ) for the (Bayesian) decision-theoretic treatment of Bayesian quadrature. BBQ adopts an (approximate) means of modelling the logarithm of the integrand with a GP, thereby (approximately) enforcing the non-negativity of the integrand. The motivation for this model is the large dynamic range (variation over many orders of magnitude) of many probabilistic integrands: a GP on the logarithm allows the model to learn such a large dynamic range. To select nodes, BBQ uses the variance of the integral, (10.4), as a loss function, so that the expected loss is the expected square-error after evaluating at that node. As such, BBQ uses what is arguably both

[7] Osborne et al. (2012)

the most desirable model (a log-GP) and the most desirable loss function. However, BBQ employs a first-order approximation to the exponential function, along with the maintenance of a set of *candidate points* x_c at which to refine the approximation. Such approximation proves both highly computationally demanding and to express only weakly the prior knowledge of the large dynamic range of the integrand.

The first practical adaptive Bayesian quadrature algorithm was WSABI,[8] which adopts another means of expressing the non-negativity of a integrand: the square-root of the integrand $f(x)$ (minus a constant, $\alpha \in \mathbb{R}$) is modelled with a GP. Precisely,

[8] Gunter et al. (2014)

$$f(x) = \alpha + \frac{1}{2}\tilde{f}(x)^2,$$

where, given data $\mathcal{D}$,

$$p(\tilde{f} \mid \mathcal{D}) = \mathcal{GP}(\tilde{f}; \tilde{m}, \tilde{\mathbb{V}}),$$

where $\tilde{m}(x)$ and $\tilde{\mathbb{V}}(x,x')$ are the usual GP posterior mean (4.6) and covariance (4.7), respectively (and thus depend on $\mathcal{D}$). An integrand modelled as the square of a GP will have a smaller dynamic range than one modelled as an exponentiated GP. In this respect, WSABI is a step backwards from BBQ.

However, the BBQ approximations are significantly more costly, both in computation and quality, than those required for WSABI. That is, WSABI considers both linearisation and moment-matched approximation to implement the square-transformation: both prove more tractable than the linearised-exponential for BBQ. Linearisation gives the following (approximate) posterior for the integrand:

$$p(f \mid \mathcal{D}) \simeq \mathcal{GP}(f; m^{\mathcal{L}}, \mathbb{V}^{\mathcal{L}}),$$
$$m^{\mathcal{L}}(x) := \alpha + \frac{1}{2}\tilde{m}(x)^2,$$
$$\mathbb{V}^{\mathcal{L}}(x,x') := \tilde{m}(x)\tilde{\mathbb{V}}(x,x')\tilde{m}(x'). \tag{10.12}$$

The posterior for moment-matching is

$$p(f \mid \mathcal{D}) \simeq \mathcal{GP}(f; m^{\mathcal{M}}, \mathbb{V}^{\mathcal{M}}),$$
$$m^{\mathcal{M}}(x) := \alpha + \frac{1}{2}\left(\tilde{m}(x)^2 + \tilde{\mathbb{V}}(x,x)\right),$$
$$\mathbb{V}^{\mathcal{M}}(x,x') := \frac{1}{2}\tilde{\mathbb{V}}(x,x')^2 + \tilde{m}(x)\tilde{\mathbb{V}}(x,x')\tilde{m}(x'). \tag{10.13}$$

The expressions above demonstrate that both linearised and moment-matched are readily implemented. In either case, the posterior for the integrand is a GP, manipulable using the standard GP equations (e.g. Eq. (4.6) for the posterior mean and

Eq. (4.7) for the covariance). A closely related approach, *moment-matched log transformation* (MMLT),[9] instead proposed moment-matching for the (arguably more desirable) exponential transformation, which, again, proves less costly than BBQ.

[9] Chai and Garnett (2019)

As a loss function, both WSABI and MMLT use the (point-wise) variance in the *integrand* (rather than the variance in the *integral*, as per BBQ). This policy, of sampling a function where its variance is highest, is known generically as *uncertainty sampling*. That is, uncertainty sampling is the sequential design rule

$$x_{i+1} = \arg\max_{x} \mathbb{V}(x,x),$$

where $\mathbb{V}(x,x)$ is the posterior variance for the integrand (that is, $\mathbb{V}^{\mathcal{L}}(x,x)$, Eq. (10.12), for linearised WSABI and $\mathbb{V}^{\mathcal{M}}(x,x)$, Eq. (10.13), for moment-matched WSABI). Uncertainty sampling seems sensible: by reducing the point-wise variance in the integrand, we are presumably also reducing the variance in the integral so that, in the limit of evaluations, we should expect convergence of the estimate for the integral. However, uncertainty sampling is less clearly related to the ultimate goal of quadrature than targeting the variance (and hence squared error) of the integral.

For instance,[10] consider the integral

[10] Thanks to Roman Garnett for this example.

$$F = \int_0^{2\pi} f(x)\,\mathrm{d}x,$$

where $f(x) := \sin(x + \phi)$ is known, but the phase $\phi \in \mathbb{R}$ is unknown. As a result, the pointwise variance in the integrand, $\mathrm{var}(f(x))$, will depend on $p(\phi)$, and will generally be non-zero. If our loss function is the pointwise variance, we will be impelled to take evaluations (potentially many, if the evaluations are noisy) – however, these evaluations have no impact on our belief in F. Conversely, if our loss function is the variance in the integral, we need not make any evaluations at all. Given just prior information, we arrive at $p(F) = \delta(F)$: we can be certain that $F = 0$, so $\mathrm{var}(F) = 0$. In such, arguably corner cases, uncertainty sampling is clearly wasteful.

However, in practice, uncertainty sampling leads to algorithms that are usually substantially faster than BBQ. In fact, both MMLT and WSABI have demonstrated convergence that is significantly faster than Monte Carlo competitors – not in the number of evaluations, but in *wall-clock time*. As examples, Figures 10.1 and 10.2 demonstrate that WSABI can achieve a given estimation error in less time (measured in seconds) than even a sophisticated competitor like *annealed importance sampling*

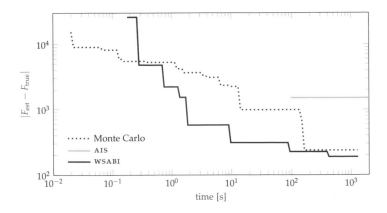

Figure 10.1:   A comparison of approaches to estimating the marginal likelihood F from Eq. (10.11) for a GP regressor fitted to real data – the yacht hydrodynamics benchmark data set (Gerritsma, Onnink, and Versluis, 1981). The required integral was eight-dimensional. This plot is adapted from Gunter et al. (2014), which contains full details.

(AIS).[11] These are remarkable results, because the algorithm for WSABI requires the maintenance of a full GP, with its costly $\mathcal{O}(N^3)$ computational scaling in N, the number of evaluations. These algorithms also require the computationally expensive management of the GP's hyperparameters. WSABI also selects evaluations at each iteration by solving a global optimisation problem, making calls to optimisation algorithms. In short, WS-ABI requires substantial computational overhead. In comparison, Monte Carlo makes use of a *(pseudo-) random number generator* (PRNG) to select evaluations, at negligible overhead cost, and a negligibly costly simple average as a model. Nonetheless, the substantial overhead incurred by WSABI, included in those measurements of wall-clock time, does not prevent WSABI from converging more quickly than Monte Carlo alternatives. Again, the overhead is perhaps better framed as an investment, whose returns more than compensate for the initial outlay. We will return to these considerations in our generic arguments against random numbers in §12.3.

Buttressing these promising empirical results, Kanagawa and

[11] Neal (2001)

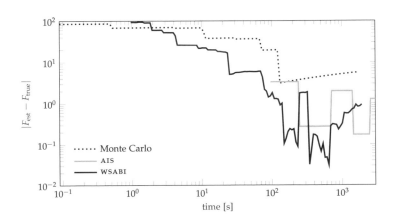

Figure 10.2:   A comparison of approaches to evaluating the marginal likelihood F from Eq. (10.11) for a GP classifier fitted to real citation network data (Garnett et al., 2012). The required integral was four-dimensional. Further details are available in the plot's original source (Gunter et al., 2014).

Hennig (2019) provide a theoretical framework for adaptive Bayesian quadrature schemes. It develops a novel property – termed *weak adaptivity* – that guarantees consistency (subject to further regularity conditions) for adaptive BQ rules with a sequential design rule given by

$$x_{i+1} = \arg\max_{x} a_i(x),$$

with

$$a_i(x) = T\big(q^2(x)\tilde{\mathbb{V}}(x,x)\big)\, b_i(x),$$

where $\tilde{\mathbb{V}}(x,x)$ is the usual GP posterior variance from Eq. (4.7), q is a positive function (e.g. the integration measure), T is the transformation (also known as warping), and $b_i(x)$ is an "adaptivity" function (in linearised WSABI, that is the square posterior mean). Weak adaptivity, loosely speaking, requires that b_i is bounded away from zero and infinity. Linearised WSABI does not technically fulfil this condition, but can be made to do so with a minor correction. Moment-matched WSABI and MMLT do satisfy the condition. Intuitively, weak adaptivity means that the method is not "too adaptive" relative to non-adaptive BQ, and so can only be "stuck for a while, but not forever". Kanagawa and Hennig (2019) also provide a worst-case bound on the convergence rate that *approaches* that of non-adaptive Bayesian quadrature. This result is weaker than that desired: empirically, we usually see adaptive schemes offer *improved* convergence over non-adaptive schemes.

Weak adaptivity plays a conceptually analogous role to the notions of *detailed balance* and *ergodicity* used to show that MCMC algorithms, likewise, can be "stuck for a while, but not forever". For MCMC the resulting insight is that, on some unknown time-scale, the mixing time of the Markov Chain, the algorithm converges like direct Monte Carlo. Similarly, weak adaptivity shows that, up to some constants, adaptive BQ works at least as well as its non-adaptive counterpart. Detailed balance and ergodicity alone don't necessarily make a good MCMC method (consistency is a very weak property, after all). However, the statistical community has used the theoretical underpinning provided by detailed balance and ergodicity as a licence to develop a diverse zoo of MCMC methods that are chiefly evaluated empirically. One may hope that the licence of weak adaptivity might enable a similar flourishing of adaptive BQ schemes.

Links to Classical Quadrature

This section returns to the univariate integration problem. In this setting, we will draw the many connections between classic and Bayesian quadrature. We will also use the setting to illustrate some deeper points about probabilistic integration, and, more broadly, about Probabilistic Numerics.

▶ **11.1 The Bayesian Trapezoidal Rule**

A particularly interesting Bayesian quadrature scheme is obtained by choosing the mean $m(x) = 0$, $\forall x$, and the covariance

$$k(x, x') = \theta^2 \left(\min(x, x') - \chi\right), \qquad (11.1)$$

with constants $\theta \in \mathbb{R}_+$ and $\chi \in \mathbb{R}, \chi < a$, to set

$$p(f) = \mathcal{GP}\left(f; 0, \theta^2 \left(\min(x, x') - \chi\right)\right). \qquad (11.2)$$

As we saw on p. 50 (see also Figure 5.3), this defines the *Wiener process* with starting time χ and intensity θ – a fundamental process, covering a particularly large hypothesis space.

So what is the integration rule arising from this prior? Assume function evaluations at an ordered set of nodes

$$X = [x_1, x_1 + \delta_1, x_1 + \delta_1 + \delta_2, \ldots, x_1 + \sum_{i=1}^{N-1} \delta_i] =: [x_1, x_2, \ldots, x_N]$$

for $\delta_i \in \mathbb{R}^+, \forall i$. To simplify the exposition, we assume $a \leq x_i \leq b \ \forall i$. The marginal prior mean m_0 of Eq. (10.5) vanishes because of the vanishing prior mean $m(x) = 0$ chosen above, and the integrals from Eqs. (10.6) and (10.7) evaluate to

$$\mathfrak{K} = \iint_a^b k(x, x') \, \mathrm{d}x \mathrm{d}x' = \theta^2 \left(\frac{1}{3}b^3 - a^2 b + \frac{2}{3}a^3 - \chi(b - a)^2\right),$$

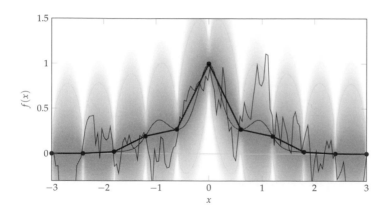

Figure 11.1: The posterior measure over f under a Wiener process prior, after 11 evaluations at equidistant points (black circles). The plot shows the piecewise linear posterior mean of this process in solid black and the probability density function as a shading. A single sample from the posterior is shown for comparison to the integrand (both thin black). The sample is clearly much less regular than the integrand.

and

$$\mathfrak{k}(x_i) = \int_a^b k(x, x_i)\, dx = \theta^2 \left(\int_a^{\min(b,x_i)} x\, dx + \int_{\min(b,x_i)}^b x_i\, dx - \chi(b-a) \right)$$

$$= \theta^2 \left(\frac{1}{2}\left(\min(b, x_i)^2 - a^2 \right) + x_i\left(b - \min(b, x_i)\right) - \chi(b-a) \right)$$

$$= \theta^2 \left(x_i b - \frac{1}{2}(a^2 + x_i^2) - \chi(b-a) \right) \text{ by the assumption } a \le x_i \le b \text{ above.}$$

These results provide one possible implementation, but as such they do not say much about the properties of this quadrature rule. As it turns out, they are a disguise for a well-known idea. A simple way to see this is to note that the posterior mean over f is not just a weighted sum of the observations Y (Eq. (10.8)), but also a weighted sum of kernel functions at the locations $\{x_i\}$:

$$\mathbb{E}_{p(f|Y)}\big(f(x)\big) = k_{xX}\underbrace{k_{XX}^{-1}Y}_{=:\boldsymbol{\alpha}} = \sum_i k(x, x_i)\alpha_i. \tag{11.3}$$

The $k(x, x_i)$ of Eq. (11.1) are piecewise linear functions, each with a sole non-differentiable locus $x = x_i$. Thus the posterior mean of Eq. (11.3) is a sum of piecewise linear functions, hence itself piecewise linear, with "kinks" – points of non-differentiability – only at the input locations X; see Figure 11.1. As this is the posterior mean conditioned on Y, that piecewise linear function with N kinks has to pass through the N nodes in Y. Assuming, for simplicity, $x_1 = a, x_N = b$, there is only one such function[1] on $[a, b]$: the *linear spline* connecting the evaluations: for $a \le x_i < x < x_{i+1} \le b$,

$$\mathbb{E}_{p(f|Y)}\big(f(x)\big) = f(x_i) + \frac{x - x_i}{\delta_i}\big(f(x_{i+1}) - f(x_i)\big).$$

The expected value of the integral is the integral of the expected value,[2] written

[1] There are some technicalities to consider if x_1 does not coincide with a, because the choice of the starting time χ affects the extrapolation behaviour on the left. One resolution is to choose the asymptotic setting $\chi \to -\infty$, which gives rise to a constant extrapolation, known as the *natural spline* (Minka, 2000) (Wahba, 1990, pp. 13–14). That same solution is also found by the filter of §11.1.1, which does not require a starting time.

[2] The two integrals can be exchanged due to Fubini's theorem, which states that this is possible whenever the (here: bivariate, over x and f) integrand is absolutely integrable, which is true for integrands fulfilling the assumptions above.

$$\mathbb{E}_{p(f|Y)}\left(\int_a^b f(x)\,\mathrm{d}x\right) = \int_a^b \mathbb{E}(f(x))\,\mathrm{d}x$$

$$= \sum_{i=1}^{N-1} \frac{\delta_i}{2}\left(f(x_{i+1}) + f(x_i)\right). \tag{11.4}$$

This is the *trapezoidal rule*.[3] It is arguably the most basic quadrature rule, second only to Riemann sums. Hence we have the following result.

[3] Davis and Rabinowitz (1984), §2.1.4

Theorem 11.1. *The trapezoidal rule is the posterior mean estimate*[4] *for the integral* $F = \int_a^b f(x)\,\mathrm{d}x$ *under any centred Wiener process prior* $p(f) = \mathcal{GP}(f;0,k)$ *with* $k(x,x') = \theta^2(\min(x,x') - \chi)$ *for arbitrary* $\theta \in \mathbb{R}_+$ *and* $\chi < a \in \mathbb{R}$.

[4] Because the mean of a Gaussian distribution coincides with the location of maximum density, the trapezoidal rule is also the maximum a posteriori estimate associated with this setup.

This is an important result: explicitly, it states that the trapezoidal rule *is* Bayesian quadrature, for a particular choice of covariance function. This foundational algorithm of classic quadrature has a clear probabilistic numerical interpretation.

It is worth noting that the trapezoidal rule's simplicity makes it rarely the best integration rule in practice. Nonetheless, we use the simplicity of the trapezoidal rule to drive intuitions applicable to all numerical methods. For stronger methods, see §10 and §11.4.

▷ **11.1.1   Alternative Derivation as a Filter**

Another way to arrive at Theorem 11.1 is to phrase the joint inference on (f,F) under the Wiener process model for the integrand as a Kalman filter (§5). Doing so provides an alternative proof of Theorem 11.1 and a convenient way to compute the posterior variance on F, which we have so far ignored in the analysis. A downside of the filtering formulation is that it does not extend to the multivariate domain: the form of Eq. (10.2) is more general. However, the filtering framework affords some generalisations, introduced below.

Further, the algorithmic implementation of the filter serves as an explicit example that a probabilistic formulation of computation need not have prohibitively high cost. In fact, the probabilistic numerical algorithm can be identical in cost to a classical form. At this point, it may be helpful to review §5.3 on *stochastic differential equations* (SDEs), from which we adopt notation.

To simplify notation, define the anti-derivative

$$F_x = \int_a^x f(\tilde{x})\,\mathrm{d}\tilde{x} \qquad \text{for } x \geq a, \tag{11.5}$$

and consider the state-space $z(x) = \begin{bmatrix} F_x, f_x \end{bmatrix}^\mathsf{T}$. This state space links the integrand and its anti-derivative, allowing the Gaussian process prior of Eq. (11.2) to equivalently be formulated as the linear SDE

$$dz(x) = Fz(x)\,dx + L\,d\omega_t \quad \text{with}$$

$$F = \begin{bmatrix} 0 & 1 \\ 0 & 0 \end{bmatrix}, \quad L = \begin{bmatrix} 0 \\ \theta \end{bmatrix}, \quad \text{and } z(\chi) = \begin{bmatrix} 0 \\ 0 \end{bmatrix}.$$

As already derived in Eqs. (5.25) and (5.26), from Eq. (5.21) we find that this SDE is associated with the discrete-time quantities (for a step of length $x_{i+1} - x_i =: \delta_i$)

$$A_i = \begin{bmatrix} 1 & \delta_i \\ 0 & 1 \end{bmatrix}, \quad Q_i = \theta^2 \begin{bmatrix} \delta_i^3/3 & \delta_i^2/2 \\ \delta_i^2/2 & \delta_i \end{bmatrix}.$$

Using $H = \begin{bmatrix} 0 & 1 \end{bmatrix}$ and setting $R = 0$ to encode the likelihood $p(y_i \mid f) = \delta(y_i = f(x_i))$, we can thus write the steps of the Kalman filter (Algorithm 5.1) explicitly,[5] and find that they simplify considerably. The mean and covariance updates in lines[6] 7 and 8 of Algorithm 5.1 are simply

$$m_i = \begin{bmatrix} [m_{i-1}]_1 + \delta_i/2(y_i + [m_{i-1}]_2) \\ y_i \end{bmatrix}, \tag{11.6}$$

$$P_i = \begin{bmatrix} [P_{i-1}]_{11} + \delta_i^3/12 & 0 \\ 0 & 0 \end{bmatrix}. \tag{11.7}$$

If we allow for an observation at $x_1 = a$, then the initial values of the SDE are irrelevant. Since we know $F_a = 0$ by definition (thus with vanishing uncertainty), the natural initialisation for the filter at $x_1 = a$ is

$$m_1 = \begin{bmatrix} 0 \\ f(a) \end{bmatrix}, \quad P_1 = \begin{bmatrix} 0 & 0 \\ 0 & 0 \end{bmatrix}.$$

The filter thus takes the straightforward form of Algorithm 11.1. This algorithm is so simple that it barely makes sense to spell it out. The significance of this result is that Bayesian inference on an integral, using a nonparametric Gaussian process with N evaluations of the integrand, can be performed in $\mathcal{O}(N)$ operations.

Put another way, the simple software implementation of the trapezoidal rule is *identical* to that of a particular Bayesian quadrature algorithm.

[5] Since the goal is to infer the definite integral F^b at the right end of the domain, there is no need to also run the smoother (Algorithm 5.2). It could be used, however, to also construct estimates for the anti-derivative F_x (Eq. (11.5)) at arbitrary locations $a \le x < b$.

[6] Note that the symbol z has a different meaning in this chapter than in Algorithm 5.1.

Exercise 11.2 (easy). *Convince yourself that Eqs. (11.6) and (11.7) indeed arise as the updates in Algorithm 5.1 from the choices or A, Q, H, R made above. Then show that the resulting mean estimate m_N at $x = b$ indeed amounts to the trapezoidal rule (e.g. by a telescoping sum). That is,*

$$\mathbb{E}(F) = \sum_{i-1}^{N-1} \frac{\delta_i}{2}(f_{i+1} + f_i),$$

$$\text{var}(F) = \frac{\theta^2}{12} \sum_{i=1}^{N-1} \delta_i^3.$$

In practice, the algorithm could thus be implemented in this simpler (and parallelisable) form. Note again, however, that this algorithm is not a good practical integration routine, only a didactic exercise. See §11.4 and in the literature cited above for more practical algorithms.

```
 1  procedure INTEGRATE(@f, a, b, N, θ)
 2      δ := (b − a)/(N − 1)                              // choose step size
 3      x ← a, y₁ = f(a), m ← 0, v ← 0,                   // initialise
 4      for i = 2, . . . , N do
 5          x ← x + δ                                     // step
 6          yᵢ ← f(x)                                     // evaluate
 7          m ← m + δ/2(yᵢ₋₁ + yᵢ)                        // update estimate
 8          v ← v + δ³/12                                 // update error estimate
 9      end for
10      return 𝔼(F) = m, var(F) = θ²v                     // probabilistic output
11  end procedure
```

Algorithm 11.1: The probabilistic trapezoidal rule formulated as a filter. The algorithm takes a handle to the integrand f, the integration limits, a, b, a budget of N evaluations, and an externally set scale θ^2 (see below for how to adapt this at runtime).

▷ **11.1.2   Uncertainty**

Formulating univariate integration as inference – as the construction of a posterior distribution over a latent quantity, under certain prior assumptions – we have "re-discovered" an old and well-trusted method for this numerical task. Though simplistic, this is an encouraging result for Probabilistic Numerics. Evidently, probabilistic numerical algorithms do not have to be abstract and involved, but can be quite simple indeed.

But the probabilistic formulation not only yielded a new way to derive the well-known trapezoidal rule, but something new: an estimator for the *error* of the trapezoidal estimate, in the form of the posterior variance v in Eq. (10.2). For the concrete choice of the Wiener process prior (11.2), we saw that this expression simply evaluates to

$$v = \text{var}_{p(f|Y,X)}(F) = \iint_a^b \mathbb{V}(x, x') \, dx dx'$$
$$= \frac{\theta^2}{12} \sum_{i=1}^{N-1} \delta_i^3. \tag{11.8}$$

We will have to ask whether this value – which, again, clearly does not depend on the collected values y_i at all – has any sensible interpretation as an error estimate. Before we address this issue, however, we find that its form can be used as a pleasingly simple way to fix the evaluation design, the step sizes $[\delta_i]_{i=1,\dots,N-1}$.

▷ **11.1.3   Regular Grids as the Maximally-Informative Design**

In many basic implementations of the trapezoidal rule, the evaluation nodes $[x_1, \dots, x_N]$ are placed on a regular grid. The above result motivates this choice probabilistically, without appealing to classical analysis. As mentioned in Eq. (10.2), a natural design rule is to require $\mathrm{var}(F)$ to be minimised. It follows from Eq. (11.8) that this is achieved precisely when the evaluation points lie on an *equidistant grid*.[7] See §11.4 for more discussion on how node-placement in classic quadrature rules relates to optimal design from the probabilistic perspective.

▷ 11.1.4   Adaptive Error Estimation

Just like the mean estimate of the trapezoidal rule (11.4), the equidistant grid as an optimal design choice for the rule is *independent* of the scale θ^2 of the prior. Hence, there is a family of models $\mathcal{M}(\theta)$, parametrised by $\theta \in \mathbb{R}_+$, so that every Gaussian process prior in that family gives rise to the same design (the same choice of evaluation nodes), and the same trapezoidal estimation rule. The associated estimate for the square error, the posterior variance, of these models is given by Eq. (11.8). If we choose the design with equidistant steps as derived above, that expression is given by

$$\mathrm{var}(F) = \frac{\theta^2}{12} \sum_{i=1}^{N-1} \left(\frac{b-a}{N-1} \right)^3 = \frac{\theta^2 (b-a)^3}{12(N-1)^2}, \qquad (11.9)$$

which means that the standard deviation $\mathrm{std}(F) = \sqrt{\mathrm{var}(F)}$, an estimate for the absolute error, contracts at a rate $\mathcal{O}(N^{-1})$, and thus more rapidly than the $\mathcal{O}(N^{-1/2})$ of the Monte Carlo estimate.

Hence the choice of the kernel k, other than the scale θ, determines the *rate* at which the error estimate $\mathrm{var}(F)$ contracts, while θ itself provides the constant *scale* of the error estimate. This situation mirrors the separation, in classical numerical analysis between *error analysis* (rate) and *error estimation* (scale). The algebraic form of the estimation rule is difficult to fundamentally change at runtime without major computational overhead, so its properties (e.g. rate) are studied by abstract analysis. The scale, on the other hand, relates to an estimate of the concrete error of the estimate, and should be estimated at runtime.

Sections 6 and 6.3 introduced the mechanism of conjugate prior hierarchical inference on θ: using a Gamma distribution to define a prior on the inverse scale θ^{-2}, the joint posterior over θ and f, F remains tractable, and can be used to address the error estimation problem. Given the prior $p(\theta^{-2}) = \mathcal{G}(\theta^{-2}; \alpha_0, \beta_0)$, the posterior on θ^{-2} can be written using the recursive terms in the Kalman filter as (reproduced for conve-

[7] To see this, first encode the assumption (made above) that the first and last node must lie on the boundaries, by setting

$$\delta_{N-1} = (b-a) - \sum_{i=1}^{N-2} \delta_i.$$

The gradient w.r.t. δ_j, $j < N-1$ is then

$$\frac{\partial \, \mathrm{var}(F)}{\partial \delta_j} = \frac{\theta^2}{4} [\delta_j^2 - \delta_{N-1}^2].$$

Setting this to zero (recall that all δ_i must be positive) gives $\delta_j = \delta_{N-1}$, $\forall j \neq N-1$. Without the formal requirement of $x_1 = a, x_N = b$, it actually turns out (Sacks & Ylvisaker, 1970 & 1985) that the best design is

$$x_i = a + (a-b)\frac{2i}{2N+1}.$$

This leaves a little bit more room on the left end of the domain than on the right, due to the time-directed nature of the Wiener process prior. E.g., for $N = 2$, the optimal nodes on $[a,b] = [0,1]$ are at $[2/5, 4/5]$.

nience from Eq. (6.14))

$$p(\theta^{-2} \mid [Y]_{1:N}) = \mathcal{G}\left(\theta^{-2}; \alpha_0 + \frac{N}{2}, \beta_0 + \frac{1}{2}\sum_{i=1}^{N}\frac{(y_i - Hm_i^-)^2}{H\tilde{P}_i^- H^\intercal}\right)$$

$$=: \mathcal{G}(\theta^{-2}, \alpha_N, \beta_N). \qquad (11.10)$$

This posterior on θ is associated with a corresponding Student-t posterior marginal on the integrand F (see Eq. (6.9)),

$$p(F \mid [Y]_{1:N}) = \int \mathcal{N}(F; \mu_{F\mid Y}, \theta\sigma_F^2)\mathcal{G}(\theta^{-2}, \alpha_N, \beta_N)\,\mathrm{d}\theta^{-2}$$

$$= \mathrm{St}\left(F; \mu_{F\mid Y}, \frac{\alpha_N}{\beta_N\sigma_F^2}, 2\alpha_N\right),$$

where $\sigma_F^2 := \mathrm{var}_{\mid Y}(F)/\theta^2$ is the standardised posterior variance for F under the "unit" kernel, and $\mu_{F\mid Y} := \mathbb{E}_{\mathcal{M}}(F \mid Y)$ is the corresponding posterior mean for F. The mean of the Student-t coincides with $\mu_{F\mid Y}$. Its variance is[8]

$$\frac{\beta_N}{\alpha_N - 1}\sigma_F^2 = \frac{\beta_0 + \frac{N}{2}\theta_{\mathrm{ML}}^2}{\alpha_0 + \frac{N}{2} - 1}\sigma_F^2. \qquad (11.11)$$

[8] E.g. Eq. (B.66) in Bishop (2006). For large values of N, the shape of the distribution approaches that of a Gaussian, with mean $\mu_{F\mid Y}$ and variance given by Eq. (11.11).

From Eq. (11.10) we see that, in contrast to Eq. (11.8), this estimated variance now actually depends on the function-values collected in Y. For the specific choice of the Wiener process prior (11.2), the values collected in β_N in Eq. (11.10) become[9]

$$\beta_N = \beta_0 + \frac{1}{2}\sum_{i=1}^{N}\frac{(y_i - Hm_i^-)^2}{H\tilde{P}_i^- H^\intercal}$$

$$= \beta_0 + \frac{1}{2}\left(\frac{f(x_1)^2}{x_1 + \chi} + \sum_{i=2}^{N}\frac{(f(x_i) - f(x_{i-1}))^2}{\delta_i}\right). \qquad (11.12)$$

[9] If necessary, the second line of Eq. (11.12) can be used to fix χ to its most likely value, given by

$$\chi_{\mathrm{ML}} :=$$

$$f(x_1)^2\left(\frac{1}{N-1}\sum_{i=2}^{N}\frac{(f(x_i) - f(x_{i-1}))^2}{\delta_i}\right)^{-1}$$

$$- x_1.$$

However, if $x_1 = a$, and the first evaluation y_1 is made without observation noise, the value of χ has no effect on the estimates.

For reference, Algorithm 11.2 on p. 97 provides pseudo-code and highlights again that this Bayesian parameter adaptation can be performed in linear cost, by collecting a running sum of the local quadratic residuals $(f(x_i) - Hm_i^-)^2$ of the filter.

What is the cost of adding uncertainty to a computation? In the case of the trapezoidal rule, Algorithm 11.2 gives the answer, which depends on how one defines computation. If we count the number of evaluations of f, then probabilistic inference can be offered at *no* computational overhead over the classic equivalent. If we count the overall number of computations, then we need to consider only the additional accumulation of the terms $f(x_i) - Hm_i^-$. Hence the overhead is a small percentage of the cost of the classic method.

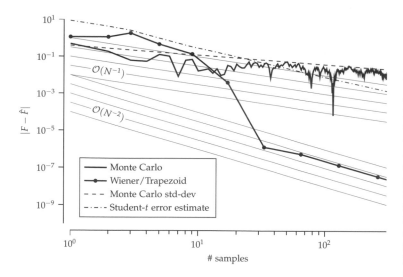

Figure 11.2: Convergence for Monte Carlo and trapezoidal rule quadrature estimates, along with different error estimates. The shown instance of Monte Carlo integration converges as $\mathcal{O}(N^{-1/2})$, as suggested by Lemma 9.2 (theoretical standard-deviation from Eq. (9.5) shown in dashed black). The trapezoidal rule overtakes the quality of the MC estimate after eight evaluations, and begins to approach its theoretical convergence rate for differentiable integrands, $\mathcal{O}(N^{-2})$ (each thin line corresponds to a different multiplicative constant). The non-adaptive GP error estimates of the form const./N (Eq. (11.9)) are under-confident. So is the adaptive Student-t error estimate (dash-dotted, as in Eq. (11.11)), reflecting the overly conservative assumption of continuity but non-differentiability in the Wiener process prior. Nevertheless, the adaptive error estimate contracts faster than the non-adaptive rate of $\mathcal{O}(N^{-1})$.

▷ **11.1.5   Convergence Rates**

How good, in practice, is the probabilistic numerical trapezoidal rule? Recall that this rule was derived by assigning, ad hoc, a Wiener process prior over the integrand f and placing evaluation nodes x_i to minimise the posterior variance on the integral F: these choices are far from canonical. Figure 11.2 compares the convergence of the estimator $\mathbb{E}_{\mathcal{M}}(F)$ with that of the Monte Carlo integration estimate. To create this plot, the true integral was evaluated to high precision using another, advanced quadrature routine.

The solid black line of the Monte Carlo estimate varies stochastically, its trend described by the standard deviation $\sqrt{\mathrm{var}_p(w)/N}$ convergence of Lemma 9.2. Compared to this stochastic rate, the trapezoidal rule estimate converges much faster: after $N = 32$ evaluations of f, the absolute error between the true integral F and the estimate $\hat{F}$ of the trapezoidal rule is roughly 1.3×10^{-6}. To reach the same fidelity with the Monte Carlo estimator, the expected number of required function evaluations is $N \sim 8.8 \times 10^{10}$, or 2.75 billion times more evaluations. So using the trapezoidal rule allows a large saving of computational cost in this situation.[10]

What is the reason for this increase in performance? The probabilistic interpretation for the trapezoidal rule offers an explanation, in form of the prior in (11.2). It defines a hypothesis space which assigns non-zero probability measure to only continuous functions f. This is a more restrictive assumption than that of Monte Carlo, which only requires the integrand to

[10] Again, the argument here is not that the trapezoidal rule is particularly efficient (it is not!), but that even the limited prior information encoded in the Wiener process allows for a drastic increase in convergence rate over the Monte Carlo rule, which can be interpreted as arising from a maximally "uninformative prior" (see §12.2).

be integrable. But of course it is a *correct* assumption, because the integrand of (9.1) is indeed continuous (even smooth).

After about $N = 64$ evaluations, the trapezoidal rule settles into a relatively homogeneous convergence at a rate of approximately $\mathcal{O}(N^{-2})$. This behaviour is predicted by classical analyses[11] of this rule for differentiable integrands like this one.[12] The probabilistically constructed non-adaptive error estimate of the trapezoidal rule (Eq. (11.8)) predicts a more conservative, slower, convergence rate $\mathcal{O}(N^{-1})$. We know from Eq. (11.9) that this is a direct consequence of the Wiener process prior assumption: draws from Wiener processes are very rough functions (almost surely continuous but not differentiable). While there is no direct classic analysis for this hypothesis class of Wiener samples itself, there is classical analysis of the Trapezoid rule for Lipschitz continuous functions that agrees with the posterior error estimate and predicts a linear error decay.[13] Even the adaptive error estimate arising from Eq. (11.11), although converging faster than the $1/N$ rate of the GP posterior standard-deviation, still yields a conservative estimate (the dash-dotted line in Figure 11.2).

The Wiener process is such a vague prior that it not only fails to capture salient analytical properties of the integrand, but also gives overly conservative estimates! This kind of insight is a strength of the probabilistic viewpoint. As we have associated the trapezoidal rule with the unnecessarily broad Wiener-process prior, that classic method, too, now seems under-constrained. Even without further analysis, we can strongly conjecture that better algorithms must be feasible for integrands like that of Eq. (9.1). And the GP prior with its defining parameters m, k provides a concrete handle guiding the search for such rules. We should seek to incorporate additional, helpful prior knowledge, to concentrate prior probability mass around the true integrand.

The space of such priors for integrands is large. It includes models that give rise to other, more advanced, classical quadrature rules (see §11.4), but also many others that are not associated with a classic method.[14] Bayesian quadrature is thus a framework for the design of customised algorithms for specific problems. The remainder of this chapter contain some examples. The following section studies one particularly straightforward way to incorporate knowledge[15] about the smoothness of the integrand.

[11] Davis and Rabinowitz (1984), p. 53

[12] The intuition for the corresponding proof is that, if the integrand is continuously differentiable, then, by the mid-point rule, the infimum and supremum of f' give an upper and lower bound on the deviation of the true integral in a segment $[x_i, x_{i+1}]$ from the integral over the linear posterior mean in that segment, and that deviation drops quadratically with the width of the segments.

[13] Davis and Rabinowitz (1984), p. 52. Note, however, that draws from the Wiener process are actually almost surely not Lipschitz. The nearest class of continuity that can be shown to contain them is that of Hölder-1/2 continuous functions; a very rough class for which the cited theorem can only guarantee $\mathcal{O}(N^{-1/2})$ convergence.

[14] Not every classical quadrature rule can be derived from a Gaussian process prior on the integrand – at least not a natural prior. An example of a method that can *not* be derived in this way is the piecewise quadratic interpolation rule

$$\int_a^b f(x)\, dx \approx \sum_{1}^{N-2} \frac{x_{i+1} - x_{i-1}}{2} \times \left(f(x_{i-1}) + 4f(x_i) + f(x_{i+1}) \right),$$

(for a regular grid $\{x_i\}_{i=1,\dots,N}$), which, depending on national allegiance, is either called *Kepler's* or *Simpson's rule*. There is actually a "contrived" probabilistic interpretation for this rule: given a fixed evaluation grid, it arises from a Gaussian prior on the weights for *piecewise* parametric polynomial features (Diaconis, 1988). But that interpretation is so far-fetched (among other problems, it requires a constant set of pre-determined evaluation nodes) as to seem useless.

[15] There is a difference between *knowledge* and *assumptions*. A prerequisite for any numerical computation is the explicit definition of the task, in a machine-readable form like (9.1) – that is, an encoding in a formal (programming) language. Thus, properties like the existence of continuous derivatives can be truly known, not just assumed.

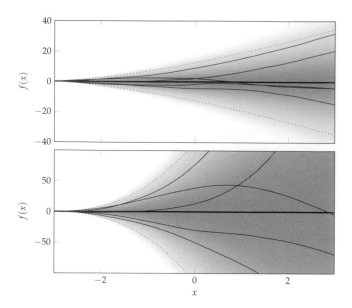

Figure 11.3: Draws from, and marginal densities of, the zero-mean integrated (top) and twice-integrated (bottom) Wiener processes. Dotted lines denote two standard deviations.

▶ 11.2   Spline Bayesian Quadrature for Smoother Integrands

If the prior behind the trapezoidal rule is too conservative, can we use the additional information, e.g. about the integrand's smoothness to build a better quadrature rule? More precisely, what if we know that the integrand is differentiable q times (but not what those derivatives are)? The Wiener process prior on f, which turned out to be the probabilistic analogue of the trapezoidal rule, is the simplest case of a more general class of quadrature rules based on polynomial spline interpolation. We can hence use the derivations provided in §5.4 to build new quadrature routines.

Let us assume that the integrand f is not just continuous, but has q continuous derivatives. We define the state

$$z(x) = \begin{bmatrix} F_a(x) \\ f(x) \\ f'(x) \\ \vdots \\ f^{(q)}(x) \end{bmatrix},$$

and again model $dz(x) = Mz(x)\,dx + L\,d\omega_t$, now with the matrices M, L as defined in Eq. (5.22). For $q = 1$, we get the *integrated Wiener process*, for $q = 2$, the *twice-integrated Wiener process* (Figure 11.3) and so on. Posterior mean functions of the integrated Wiener process are cubic splines, those of the twice-integrated Wiener process are quintic splines, etc. (Figure 11.4). Using these two, and $H = [0, 1, 0, 0, \dots]$, the standard Kalman

```
 1  procedure INTEGRATE(@f, a, b, N)
 2      x ← a                                              // initialise state
 3      m ← [0; f(a); 0_q], P̃ ← e.g. Eq. (11.13)          // define prior
 4      A, Q̃ ← e.g. Eqs. (5.25) & (5.26)
 5      α ← α_0, β ← β_0
 6      for i = 1, ..., N − 1 do
 7          x ← x + δ                                      // move
 8          m⁻ = Am                                        // predictive mean
 9          P̃⁻ = AP̃Aᵀ + Q̃                                // predictive covariance
10          z = f(x) − Hm⁻                                 // observation residual
11          s = HP̃⁻Hᵀ                                      // residual variance
12          K = 1/s P̃⁻Hᵀ                                   // gain
13          m ← m⁻ + Kz                                    // update mean
14          P̃ ← P̃⁻ − KsKᵀ                                 // update covariance
15          β ← β + z²/2s                                  // update hyperparameter
16      end for
17      E(F) ← m_1                                         // point estimate
18      var(F) ← β/(α_0 + N/2 − 1) · P̃_{11}              // error estimate
19      r ← β − β_0 − N/2                                  // model fit diagnostic (see §11.3)
20      return E(F), var(F)                                // return mean, variance of integral
21  end procedure
```

Algorithm 11.2: General probabilistic quadrature rule in Kalman filter form, including marginalisation of the intensity θ^2. Lines 3–5 define the model, the rest is a generic form of the Kalman filter with conjugate prior hierarchical inference on θ^2. The notation $@f$ is meant to imply access to the function f itself at arbitrary inputs.

filter of Algorithm 5.1 turns into a probabilistic integration method. It is reproduced with the additional lines required for hyperparameter adaptation in Algorithm 11.2. The only terms requiring some care are the initialisation. Because we do not know – at least not without further computation – the derivatives of the integrand, we should be ignorant about them at initialisation. A simplistic way to encode this is to initialise $m = [0, f(a), 0, \dots]$ and

$$P = \begin{bmatrix} 0 & 0 & \mathbf{0}_{1\times q} \\ 0 & 0 & \mathbf{0}_{1\times q} \\ \mathbf{0}_{q\times 1} & \mathbf{0}_{q\times 1} & \alpha I_q \end{bmatrix}, \tag{11.13}$$

with a "very large" value of α.

Figure 11.5 shows empirical convergence of these rules when integrating our running example of Eq. (9.1), for the choices $q = 0$ (the trapezoidal rule) through $q = 3$.

▶ **11.3 Selecting the Right Model**

We have seen how the performance of quadrature methods critically depends on how well their implicit assumptions – their model – describe the integrand. How should the model be

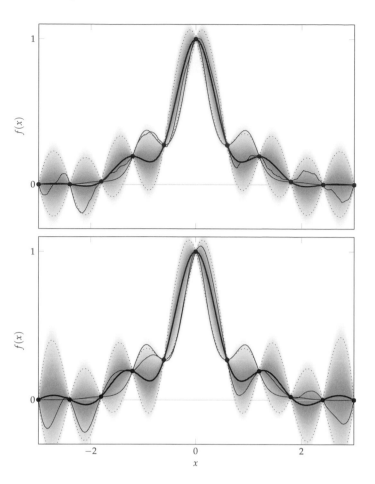

Figure **11.4**: Posteriors over the integrand f of Eq. (9.1) arising from the integrated Wiener process (top, cubic spline mean) and twice-integrated Wiener process (bottom, quintic spline mean). Compare against the priors in Figure 11.3. For further explanation, see Figure 11.1.

selected? In the unusual case that the integrand is an element of the prior hypothesis space, performance can be increased by concentrating prior mass on the integrand. In the more realistic case that the integrand is *not* in the prior space, the issue changes to how much mass the prior assigns to good approximations that are *close* to the integrand.[16] In either case, designing a good quadrature rule for one specific problem involves finding a good combination of prior mean m and covariance k so that the three integrals of Eqs. (10.5), (10.6), and (10.7) are analytically available. Recall that we introduced a diverse range of tractable possibilities for Bayesian quadrature in §10.1. Exploring this space to find the best model is daunting.

Even if we only consider Bayesian quadrature algorithms based on linear state-space models, there is a large space of potential SDEs to consider. In this setting, can the choice of model be automated? This search for the "right" prior model is itself another, potentially challenging, inference problem. In §11.1.4,

[16] Kanagawa, Sriperumbudur, and Fukumizu (2020)

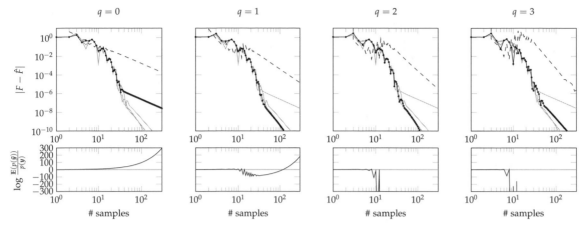

Figure 11.5: Convergence of quadrature rules from higher-order Wiener filters on the integrand of Eq. (9.1). The lower plots show the model fit statistic introduced in Eq. (11.15).

we tackled a simple version of this problem: we managed (that is, analytically marginalised, rather than selected) the model's parameter θ, the scale of uncertainty in the integral for the covariance family (10.9). For aspects of the prior other than this simple scalar term, such hierarchical inference is not always tractable. As such, its computational overhead is likely to be difficult to justify for a single integrand of modest evaluation cost.

However, inferring components of the model can still be interesting. Here we investigate doing so as a backstop mechanism, to detect if a numerical method is a poor match for the problem at hand. Consider the model class (10.9) with unit uncertainty-scale hyperparameter, $\theta = 1$. A likelihood for the model itself can be found by marginalising over the latent function f, as given in (6.13). The logarithm of this likelihood is a simple sum

$$\log p(Y \mid \mathcal{M}) = -\frac{1}{2} \sum_{i=1}^{N} \frac{(y_i - Hm_i^-)^2}{H\tilde{P}_i^- H^\mathsf{T}} - \frac{1}{2} \log |H\tilde{P}_i^- H^\mathsf{T}| + \text{const.}$$

$$(11.14)$$

To provide a reference baseline for this quantity, assume we have to *predict* this quantity before observing the values Y, but after having decided on the (regular) grid locations. Under the prior, the expected value of y_i is Hm_i^-, and the expected value of $(y_i - Hm_i^-)^2$ is just $H\tilde{P}_i^- H^\mathsf{T}$. Hence, the expected value of Eq. (11.14) for observables $\tilde{Y}$ drawn directly from the model is

$$\mathbb{E}_{\tilde{Y}\mid\mathcal{M}}\left(\log p(\tilde{Y} \mid \mathcal{M})\right) = -\frac{N}{2} - \frac{1}{2} \log |H\tilde{P}_i^- H^\mathsf{T}| + \text{const.}$$

The expected log-ratio between predicted and observed likelihood is

$$r(Y, \mathcal{M}) := \int \log \frac{p(\tilde{Y} \mid \mathcal{M})}{p(Y \mid \mathcal{M})} p(\tilde{Y} \mid \mathcal{M}) \, d\tilde{Y}$$

$$= -\frac{1}{2} \left(N - \sum_{i=1}^{N} \frac{(y_i - Hm_i^-)^2}{H\tilde{P}_i^- H^\intercal} \right) \qquad (11.15)$$

$$= \sum_{i=1}^{N} \frac{z_i^2}{2s_i^2} - \frac{N}{2} = \beta_N - \beta_0 - \frac{N}{2},$$

using the interior Kalman filter variables from Algorithm 11.2. We can see that the expected log-ratio is independent of the terms that only depend on design choices, rather than the data itself. It compares the variability of the observed data with its expectation. If $r(Y, \mathcal{M}) > 0$, then the integrand is less variable and more regular than expected under the prior, and we can expect the error estimate $\mathrm{var}_\mathcal{M}(F)$ to be conservative (i.e. the true error is likely smaller than the estimated one) – the numerical method is *under-confident*. On the other hand, if $r(Y, \mathcal{M}) < 0$, then the integrand varies more than the model would have predicted. Other, so far unexplored, areas are likely to lead to similar surprises, and thus the error estimate should not be trusted – it is *over-confident*.

Conveniently, the final line of Eq. (11.15) reveals that r is a trivial transformation of the sufficient statistic β, already collected in Algorithm 11.2! It can thus be computed at runtime without additional overhead. The bottom row of Figure 11.5 shows these values r during the integration process for the different models. We see that, although the integrand in this case is an infinitely smooth function, its derivative varies on a scale not expected by the higher-order Wiener processes. Based on the evidence, $q = 1$ appears like a good choice within this family of integrators – and indeed, the convergence rates do not rise further on increasing q.

Figure 11.7 shows another example: this time, the integrand is a true sample from an integrated ($q = 1$) Wiener process (the integrand is shown in Figure 11.6). As expected, the integrator based on the rough $q = 0$ process collects values for r that suggest its model assumptions are too rough, while the $q > 1$ integrators can detect their overconfident smoothness assumptions. For fixed values of θ, these integrators have over-confident error estimates. Posterior inference on θ adapts the error estimates so they become cautious again, but remain unreliable.

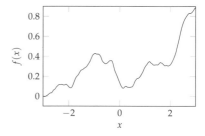

Figure 11.6: A draw from the integrated Wiener process. This particular function was used as the alternative integrand in the experiments represented in Figure 11.7.

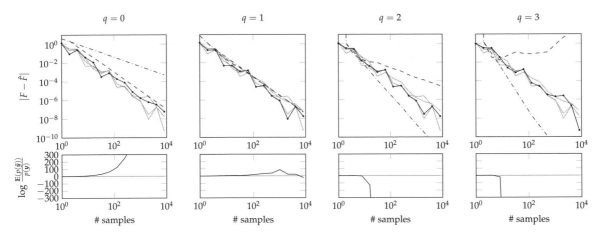

Figure 11.7: Convergence of quadrature rules when integrating a sample from a $q = 1$ times integrated Wiener process. Top row: error of the mean estimator (solid black, other values of q in grey for comparison). Dash-dotted lines are error estimates for a fixed value of θ, dashed lines are marginal variances under the Gamma prior on θ^{-2}. As in Figure 11.5, the bottom row shows the evolution of the model evidence statistic introduced in Eq. (11.15).

► 11.4   Connection to Gaussian Quadrature Rules

The detailed treatment above shows that the trapezoidal rule (both the regular grid design and the estimation rule), can be derived as a maximum a posteriori estimate arising from a Wiener process prior. The trapezoidal rule is a simple integration rule, often too simple for practical use. The most popular class of generic integration routines are known as *Gaussian quadrature rules*.[17] They are more advanced than the trapezoidal rule, and achieve significantly faster convergence on most practical problems. This section investigates the connection between Gaussian quadrature and Gaussian process regression, reviewing results by Karvonen and Särkkä (2017).

It will turn out that the probabilistic formulation of such methods is not particularly pleasing, because it yields a vanishing posterior variance on the estimate. These results nevertheless provide a reference point and intuition. The main reason to be interested in Gaussian and other classical quadrature rules, even from a probabilistic perspective, is that they are highly efficient. Figure 11.8 showcases the performance of the Gauss–Legendre on our running example, where its asymptotic convergence is very fast.

For this section, we denote the integration domain by $\Omega \subset \mathbb{R}$. Let ν be a probability measure on $\mathbb{R}$, and $f : \Omega \to \mathbb{R}$ denotes the integrand.[18] The task is to compute the integral

$$\nu(f) = \int_{\Omega} f(x)\, \mathrm{d}\nu(x).$$

A *quadrature rule* $Q = (X, \boldsymbol{w})$ is a (linear) map of f to an approx-

[17] The naming is due to a separate 1814 paper by Gauss, and unrelated to the Gaussian process prior used in Bayesian quadrature.

[18] Depending on the concrete quadrature rule in question, varying regularity requirements on Ω, ν, and f may apply. They will be assumed to hold without further comment.

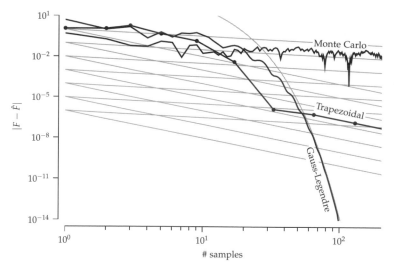

Figure 11.8: Error evolution for Gauss–Legendre quadrature on the running example of Eq. (9.1). In comparison to the Monte Carlo and Trapezoidal estimates introduced in previous sections, which each exhibit polynomial convergence rates as predicted by their corresponding error analysis, the Gaussian rule converges much faster. The curved grey line is a suggestive exponential function.

imation $Q(f)$ of $\nu(f)$ of the form

$$Q(f) := \sum_{i=1}^{N} w_i \cdot f(x_i),$$

where $X = [x_1, \ldots, x_N]$ are the *nodes* or *knots* (also sometimes called *sigma-points*) of the rule, and $w = [w_1, \ldots, w_N]$ are the *weights*.

The most popular design criterion for quadrature rules is to require the rule to be *exact* for all polynomials up to some degree.

Definition 11.3. *Let* $p_N(x) = \sum_{i=0}^{N} a_i x^i$ *be a polynomial of degree* N. *A quadrature rule* Q *is of* degree M *if it is exact with respect to* ν *for all polynomials* p_N *of degree* $N \leq M$, *i.e. if*

$$Q(p_N(x)) = \nu(p_N(x)),$$

and inexact for at least one polynomial of degree $N = M + 1$.

For any set of N pairwise different nodes $x \in \Omega^N$, there exists a quadrature rule[19] of degree at least $N - 1$. But the punchline of classical quadrature is that, if the nodes are chosen carefully, it is in fact possible to achieve degree $2N - 1$ with those N integrand evaluations. Such rules are called *Gaussian quadrature rules*:[20]

Theorem 11.4 (Gaussian quadrature). *For sufficiently regular* ν, *there exists a unique quadrature rule with* N *nodes of degree* $2N - 1$. *Its nodes are given by the roots of the* Nth ν-*orthogonal polynomial*[21] ψ_N, *and its weights* w *are all positive.*

[19] That rule is identified by the weights w satisfying the N monomial constraints $Q(x^i) = \nu(i)$ for $i = 0, \ldots, N - 1$, which amount to the Vandermonde system

$$\begin{bmatrix} x_1^0 & \cdots & x_N^0 \\ \vdots & \ddots & \vdots \\ x_1^{N-1} & \cdots & x_N^{N-1} \end{bmatrix} \begin{bmatrix} w_1 \\ \vdots \\ w_N \end{bmatrix}$$
$$= \begin{bmatrix} \nu(x^0) \\ \vdots \\ \nu(x^{N-1}) \end{bmatrix}.$$

[20] Theorem 11.4 is a simplified form of a more general result. For more see, e.g., p. 97 of Davis and Rabinowitz (1984). A proof is in Thms. 1.46–1.48 in §1.4 of Gautschi (2004).

[21] A sequence of polynomials $\{\psi_0(x), \psi_1(x), \ldots\}$ (where ψ_i is of degree i) are called *orthogonal* under the measure ν if

$$\nu(\psi_i \cdot \psi_j) = \int \psi_i(x) \cdot \psi_j(x) \, d\nu(x) = c_i \delta_{ij}.$$

For each sufficiently regular ν, this sequence exists and is uniquely identified up to the constants c_i (see §1.4 in Gautschi (2004)).

Ω	$\nu(x)$	$\{\psi_i\}$
$[-1,1]$	$1/2$	Legendre
$[-1,1]$	$1/\sqrt{1-x^2}$	Chebyshev
$[-1,1]$	$(1-x)^\alpha(1+x)^\beta$	Jacobi
$[0,\infty)$	e^{-x}	Laguerre
$(-\infty,\infty)$	e^{-x^2}	Hermite

Table 11.1: Popular cases of integration domain Ω, (unnormalised) measure ν and corresponding set of orthonormal polynomials ψ. The parameters of the measure for the Jacobi polynomials are two reals $\alpha, \beta > -1$. The special case $\alpha = \beta$ gives rise to what are termed Gegenbauer polynomials and Gauss–Gegenbauer quadrature.

A relatively small dictionary of domains, base measures and corresponding orthogonal polynomials have found wide use in practice. Some of them are listed in Table 11.1.

Karvonen and Särkkä (2017) provided the connection between these foundational rules and Bayesian quadrature. Let $[\bar{\psi}_i]_{i=0,1...}$ be a set of ortho*normal* polynomials. That is,

$$\nu(\bar{\psi}_i\bar{\psi}_j) = \int \bar{\psi}_i(x)\bar{\psi}_j(x)\,\mathrm{d}\nu(x) = \delta_{ij}.$$

Now consider the Gaussian process $p(f) = \mathcal{GP}(f;0,k)$ arising from the degenerate (i.e. finite-rank) kernel

$$k^q(x,x') = \sum_{i=0}^{q-1} c_i\bar{\psi}_i(x)\bar{\psi}_i(x'), \qquad (11.16)$$

and assume a set of positive scales $[c_i]_{i=0,1,...} \subset \mathbb{R}_+$. We might want to call this a *polynomial kernel*, but that name is already overloaded in the Gaussian process literature.

Recall from §4.1 that taking the degenerate kernel (11.16) amounts to the assumption that f can be written as $f(x) = \sum_i \bar{\psi}_i(x)v_i$ with weights $v_i \in \mathbb{R}$ drawn i.i.d. from $p(v_i) = \mathcal{N}(v_i;0,c_i)$. The following theorem shows that, for any design x, the Bayesian quadrature algorithm arising from the Gaussian process prior $p(f) = \mathcal{GP}(f;0,k^q)$ yields a quadrature rule of non-trivial degree, and the design choice that is optimal under the Bayesian perspective coincides with the Gaussian quadrature rule (i.e. the optimal one under the classic interpretation).

Theorem 11.5 (Karvonen and Särkkä, 2017). *The Bayesian quadrature rule with the kernel k^q on (Ω,ν) coincides with the classical quadrature rule Q of degree $M-1$ if, and only if, $N \le q \le M$. For such a rule, the posterior variance on the integral vanishes: $\mathfrak{v} = 0$.*

After setting $N := \frac{q}{2}$, we obtain the following statement.

Corollary 11.6 (Bayesian Gaussian Quadrature). *For each $N \in \mathbb{N}$, there is a unique N-point optimal Bayesian quadrature rule for the kernel k^{2N} on (Ω,ν), and it coincides with the Gaussian quadrature rule.*

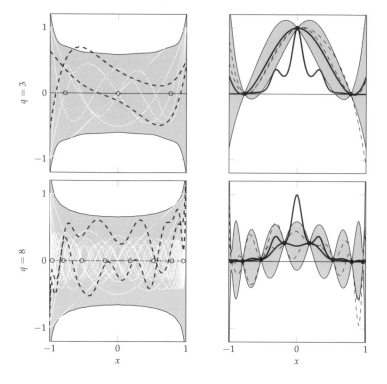

Figure 11.9: Probabilistic interpretation of Gauss–Legendre integration (that is, for $\nu(x)$ the Lebesgue measure). Priors (left) and posteriors (right) consistent with the Gauss–Legendre rules of degree $2q - 1 = 5$ (top) and 15 (bottom), respectively. The left plots show two marginal standard deviations as a shaded area, the first $2q - 1$ Legendre polynomials spanning the kernel (which are exactly integrated by the associated quadrature rule) in white, and two samples from the prior in dashed black. The right panels show the posterior after q evaluations at the nodes of the qth polynomial, again with two standard deviations as a shaded region, the posterior mean and the integrand in thick black, and two samples in dashed thin black. Even though the posterior variance on the integrand f is non-zero, the posterior variance on the integral F vanishes – the two shown samples have the same integral as the posterior mean. Changes in the scales c_i of the individual polynomials can change the means, marginal variances, and samples shown in these figures drastically, while leaving the resulting integral estimates identical.

Although this result shows certain Bayesian quadrature rules to be equivalent to Gaussian quadrature, it also highlights the *differences* between the probabilistic and the classic approach. Three key aspects are particularly worth noting:

- The equivalence class of GP priors whose associated BQ rules coincide with the Gaussian rule is large, because it includes all choices of $c \in \mathbb{R}_+^{2N}$ in the prior

$$p(v) = \mathcal{N}\big(v; 0, \mathrm{diag}(c)\big)$$

  for the weights v of $f(x) = \sum_{i=0}^{2N} v_i \bar{\psi}_i(x)$. Figure 11.9 shows priors for the particular choice $c = \mathbf{1}$, but changes to these weights can give rise to wildly different priors in the space of f. If the variances c_i decay rapidly with growing i, the prior assumes a more regular integrand, while a growing sequence of c_i amounts to the assumption of a "more variant" (though always smooth) integrand. All these choices, though, yield the same integral estimate when used in the setting of Corollary 11.6, i.e. when there are N observations at the nodes of the Nth polynomial.

- Under the posterior on f arising from the kernel k^{2N}, the variance is zero at the N nodes X of the Nth polynomial, but is generally non-zero at $x \notin X$ (see Figure 11.9). To explain this situation, note that in a set of ν-orthogonal polynomials with $c_0 > 0$, all but the constant one have vanishing expectation under ν. That is, they satisfy

$$\nu(\psi_i) = 0, \ \forall i > 0,$$

because $\psi_i(x) = \pm \psi_i(x) \psi_0(x) / \sqrt{c_0}$. In the setting of Corollary 11.6, those N evaluations exactly identify the value of the first coefficient v_0, but not necessarily those of the other coefficients. So there is flexibility left in the function values, but only in ways that do not contribute to the integral. In the posteriors shown in Figure 11.9, all sampled hypotheses, and the posterior means, share the same integral.

⊖ A related feature is that the prior of Eq. (11.16) must be parametric (of finite rank, degenerate) to yield Gaussian quadrature rules. But of course, the number N of evaluations is meant to grow as the algorithm runs. From the probabilistic perspective, this means the prior constantly becomes more general, more flexible, as N grows. Of course, its dependence on data, through N, means that this prior is not a real prior at all, at least one that an orthodox Bayesian would recognise. The price to be paid for this oddity is that it is difficult to associate a meaningful notion of uncertainty with the posterior in this simple form, because $\mathfrak{v} = 0$. It remains an open question at the time of writing, however, whether an empirical Bayesian extension is possible.

12

Probabilistic Numerical Lessons from Integration

Equipped with our survey of both current BQ approaches and their connections to classic quadrature algorithms, we will now tease out some of the intuitions that will inform the remainder of this book.

► ## 12.1 Why Be Probabilistic?

Discovering the sometimes close connections between probabilistic inference and classical quadrature methods suggests that the probabilistic approach is, at least, *no worse* than the latter, widely accepted, one. Explicitly, probabilistic numerical algorithms can be just as computationally lightweight, just as performant, and just as reliable, as classical methods – because the classical methods *are* implicitly probabilistic.

Having identified these close connections between probabilistic and classical quadrature methods, we will now emphasise their differences: in particular, the unique offerings of the probabilistic approach.

▷ ### 12.1.1 Aiding Model Customisation

Perhaps the strongest argument for the probabilistic approach is that it exposes the choice of model, as GP mean and covariance, to the user. We have seen how getting this choice right can yield methods that are substantively both more efficient and more trustworthy. If the task is to come up with an efficient quadrature rule for one specific (class of) univariate integrand, the most productive path forward is likely to be choosing a mean function m and covariance k such that samples from the associated GP match the integrand as closely as possible.[1] Of course, building a strong model entails its own design and running costs (e.g. in updating the GP with new data). For a cheap integrand, like the running example in this chapter, it is likely to be easier to simply use a standard quadrature library. That said, as we discussed for WSABI in §10.2.1, the costs of a strong model should be more properly viewed as an *investment* of computation, that, in many cases, will yield a computational return. That is, the computational overhead is more than compensated by savings in computation due to the increased efficiency of the more accurate model. Such a case is found in applications where each individual evaluation of the integrand has high evaluation cost – perhaps because it involves parsing a large data set, running a costly simulation, or even performing a physical experiment.[2] Here designing a good prior is likely to be worth the work.

[1] Analysis through the lens of the RKHS adds further analytical tools. For practical purposes, however, samples from the associated Gaussian process are arguably more explicit, and more interpretable.

[2] A recent example is in Fröhlich et al. (2021).

▶ 12.2   Monte Carlo as Probabilistic Inference

We close this chapter by returning to Monte Carlo integration for another, closer look. Now that we have realised that several classical quadrature methods can be constructed in a probabilistic fashion, it is natural to ask whether such an interpretation also exists for Monte Carlo integration. The answer is yes, as we will see in this section.

We already noted in passing that, while the trapezoidal rule amounts to the implicit assumption of a continuous integrand, Monte Carlo integration is applicable to any Borel-integrable function. This suggests that a probabilistic formulation of Monte Carlo integration will involve a very vague prior on the integrand. Thus, consider the assumption that the integrand is "white noise" with an unknown mean:

$$f(x) \sim \mathcal{GP}\big(m, k(x, x')\big),$$

where $m \in \mathbb{R}$ is an unknown constant, and $k(x, x') = \theta^2 \mathbb{I}(x = x')$ with the indicator function $\mathbb{I}(a) = 1$ if a, 0 elsewhere,[3] encoding the assumption that all function values are independent of each other, individually varying around m with variance θ^2. Following an old idea,[4] we place the Gaussian prior $p(m) = \mathcal{N}(m; 0, c^{-1})$ on the unknown constant (the precision c will be taken to the limit $c \to 0$ below). Marginalising over m, we get the prior

$$p(f \mid c) = \int p(f \mid m)p(m \mid c)\,\mathrm{d}m = \mathcal{GP}\big(f; 0, k(x, x') + c^{-1}\big)$$

[3] Readers who are justly worried that this process is not strictly well-defined can consider it as the limit case of the Gaussian process with covariance function

$$k(x, x') = \lim_{\lambda \to 0} e^{\frac{-(x-x')^2}{2\lambda^2}} \mathbb{I}_{|x-x'|<3\lambda}.$$

The restriction to a finite support is necessary for the argument below to work, it has no practically relevant effect on this probability measure. The argument here can then be performed for finite values of λ, and the result below obtained as a limit case.

[4] Blight and Ott (1975); O'Hagan and Kingman (1978).

for the integrand. Under this prior, after evaluations Y at locations $X = [x_1, \ldots, x_N]$ (assumed to be pairwise different), the posterior mean and covariance functions on f can be rearranged[5] to

$$\mathbb{E}_{|X,Y}(f(x)) = R_x^{\mathsf{T}} \bar{m} + k_{xX} k_{XX}^{-1} Y = R_x^{\mathsf{T}} \bar{m} + \sum_{i=1}^{N} \mathbb{I}(x = x_i) y_i,$$

$$\mathrm{cov}_{|X,Y}(f(x), f(x')) = k_{xx'} - k_{xX} k_{XX}^{-1} k_{Xx'} + R_x^{\mathsf{T}} (c + \mathbf{1}^{\mathsf{T}} k_{XX}^{-1} \mathbf{1})^{-1} R_{x'},$$

with

$$R_x := 1 - \mathbf{1}^{\mathsf{T}} k_{XX}^{-1} k_{Xx} = 1 - \sum_{i=1}^{N} \mathbb{I}(x = x_i), \text{ and}$$

$$\bar{m} := (c + \mathbf{1}^{\mathsf{T}} k_{XX}^{-1} \mathbf{1})^{-1} \mathbf{1}^{\mathsf{T}} k_{XX}^{-1} Y = \frac{\theta^{-2}}{c + \theta^{-2} N} \sum_{i=1}^{N} y_i.$$

[5] Rasmussen and Williams (2006), §2.7

The corresponding Gaussian posterior over the *integral* $F = \int_a^b f(x)\,dx$ has mean and variance

$$\mathbb{E}_{|X,Y}(F) = \int_a^b \mathbb{E}_{|X,Y}(f(x))\,dx = (b - a)\bar{m}, \text{ and}$$

$$\mathrm{var}_{|X,Y}(F) = \iint_a^b \mathrm{cov}_{|X,Y}(f(x), f(x'))\,dx dx' = \frac{(b-a)^2}{c + \theta^{-2} N}.$$

Evidently, for the improper limit of $c \to 0$ ("total ignorance" about the value of m), we get

$$\mathbb{E}_{|X,Y}(F) = \frac{b - a}{N} \sum_{i=1}^{N} y_i \quad \text{and} \quad \mathrm{var}_{|X,Y}(F) = \frac{\theta^2 (b-a)^2}{N}. \tag{12.1}$$

The variance θ^2 of the "white noise" around the mean m could be inferred using a Gamma prior $p(\theta) = \mathcal{G}(\theta^{-2}; \alpha_0, \beta_0)$, analogously to the procedure described in §11.1.2. For large values of N, and for the improper limit of $\alpha_0 \to 0, \beta_0 \to 0$, the resulting Gamma posterior on θ^{-2} would concentrate on its expected value[6]

$$\mathbb{E}_{\mathcal{G}(\theta^{-2}; \alpha_N, \beta_N)}(\theta^{-2}) = \frac{\alpha_N}{\beta_N} = \frac{N}{\sum_i f(x_i)^2},$$

[6] The *mode* of the Gamma distribution is at $\frac{\alpha-1}{\beta}$, which is often used as an unbiased alternative. For large N, the two estimates are asymptotically equal.

so this probabilistic method's estimate for the square error of the Monte Carlo estimate matches one that can also be constructed from Eq. (9.5) by other means. We have just found the following theorem.

Theorem 12.1. *The Monte Carlo estimate is the limit as $c \to 0$ of the maximum a posteriori estimate under the prior*

$$p(f) = \mathcal{GP}(0, \theta^2 \mathbb{I}(x = x') + c^{-1}), \tag{12.2}$$

with arbitrary $\theta \in \mathbb{R}_+$. The corresponding posterior variance estimate on the integral, $\theta^2(b-a)^2/N$, matches the convergence rate of the Monte Carlo estimator. Under this prior, any arbitrary (but non-overlapping) design $X = [x_1, \ldots, x_N]$ yields the same posterior variance on F.

A defender of Monte Carlo might argue that its most truly desirable characteristic is the fact that its convergence (see Lemma 9.2) does not depend on the dimension of the problem. Performing well even in high dimension is a laudable goal. However, the statement "if you want your convergence rate to be independent of problem dimension, do your integration with Monte Carlo" is much like the statement "If you want your nail-hammering to be independent of wall hardness, do your hammering with a banana." We should be sceptical of claims that an approach performs equally well regardless of problem difficulty. An explanation could be that the measure of difficulty is incorrect: perhaps dimensionality is not an accurate means of assessing the challenge of an integral. However, we contend that another possibility is more likely: rather than being equally good for any number of dimensions, Monte Carlo is perhaps better thought of as being equally bad.

   Recall from §10.1.2 that the curse of dimensionality results from the increased importance of the model relative to the evaluations. Theorem 12.1 makes it clear that Monte Carlo's property of dimensionality-independence is achieved by assuming the weakest possible model. With these minimalist modelling assumptions, very little information is gleaned from any given evaluation, requiring Monte Carlo to take a staggering number of evaluations to give good estimates of an integral. As a contrast, Bayesian quadrature opens the door to stronger models for integrands. The strength of a model – its inductive bias – can indeed be a deficiency if it is ill-matched to a particular integrand. However, if the model is well-chosen, it offers great gains in performance. The challenge of high dimension is in finding models suitable for the associated problems. Thus far, Probabilistic Numerics has shone light on this problem of choosing models, and has presented some tools to aid solving it. *It is now up to all of us to do the rest.* Of course, we must acknowledge that contemporary quadrature methods (both probabilistic and classical) do not work well in high-dimensional problems: indeed, they perform far worse than Monte Carlo. However, arguments like those in this chapter show that there is a lot of potential for far better integration algorithms. Such methods can work *only* in moving away from Monte Carlo, and its fundamentally limited convergence rate.

For further evidence to this point, we note that even the most general model underlying Monte Carlo integration can actually converge faster if the nodes are not placed at random. Equation (12.1) is independent of the node placement X. So if it is used for guidance of the grid design as in §11.1.3, then any arbitrary node placement yields the same error estimate (as long as no evaluation location is exactly repeated). Since the covariance k assumes that function values are entirely unrelated to each other, a function value at one location carries no information about its neighbourhood, so there is no reason to keep the function values separate from each other.

The tempting conclusion one may draw from Theorem 12.1 is that, because, under this rule, any design rule is equally good, one should just use a *random* set of evaluation nodes. This argument is correct *if* the true integrand is indeed a sample from the extremely irregular prior of Eq. (12.2). But imagine for a moment that, against our prior assumptions, the integrand f happens to be continuous after all. Now consider the choice of a regular grid,

$$X = [a, a + h, a + 2h, \ldots, b - h] \qquad \text{with} \qquad h := \frac{b - a}{N}.$$

Then, the mean estimate from Eq. (12.1) is the Riemann sum

$$\mathbb{E}_{|X,Y}(F) = h \sum_i f(x_i).$$

For functions that are even Lipschitz continuous, this sum converges to the true integral F at a *linear* rate,[7] $\mathcal{O}(N^{-1})$. That is, the poor performance of Monte Carlo is due not just to its weak model, but its use of random numbers. This insight into the advantage of regular over random node placement is at the heart of *quasi Monte Carlo* methods.[8] As we have seen above, however, it is possible to attain significantly faster convergence rates by combining non-random evaluation placements with explicit assumptions about the integrand.

Thus, from a probabilistic perspective, there is an argument for the integration rule (12.1) if there is no known regularity in the integrand (note that this is virtually never the case in practice, and other integration rules, using more informative priors, should then be preferred). But, even though this prior gives no reason itself to prefer any design X over another one,

[7] Davis and Rabinowitz (1984), §2.1.6

[8] E.g. Lemieux (2009)

it is *still* a good idea to use a regular evaluation rule, on the off chance that the true integrand is continuous after all. From these observations, we draw the contentious conclusion that it is generally a bad idea to introduce random numbers into an otherwise deterministic computation.

► **12.3   A Meditation on Randomness**

We offer a few more, provocative, thoughts on the utility of random numbers in the computation of deterministic quantities, and be it only to counter the frequent reflex to equate *probabilistic* methods with *stochastic* ones. We begin with generic arguments against the use of a (pseudo-) random number generator in computation. A PRNG:

1. does not have a coherent decision-theoretic motivation;

2. is worse at its goal of efficient exploration than a probabilistic numerical approach;

3. can be expected to be more computationally expensive in solving a numerical task; and

4. muddles subjectivity and bias.

A decision-theoretic view of randomness   What would be the probabilistic numerical view of a PRNG? In such an interpretation, the output must be the minimiser of an expected loss function. However, a PRNG is built with the intent of expressing no preference over its outputs. If we assume that the PRNG is the right approach, and try to determine the associated expected loss, the PRNG's assertion that any possible output is equally good implies that the expected loss surface is uniformly flat. Put another way, this is the assertion that the calculation demanding the PRNG is completely insensitive to its output. This is a strong assumption. An example is found in the extreme underpinnings (see Theorem 12.1) of a Monte Carlo estimate of an integral. In most real applications, there are symmetry-breaking forces at play that render some outputs (at least slightly) better than others. The best such output should always be picked. It is more common that we have a given expected loss function, with unique minimum, over a real interval. If a PRNG is used to select an action in this setting, the action will be sub-optimal, with probability one. If you accept that a random number is a decision, it is necessarily a poor one.

Exploration   But what is the right loss function for the task addressed by a PRNG? It is hard to defend a single, one-off, choice being made by a PRNG: that is, to defend the expected loss for such a choice being uniformly flat. A PRNG is perhaps more productively considered as a heuristic for making a *sequence* of decisions. The goal of this sequence (or design), $X = \{x_1, \ldots\}$, is to achieve *exploration*, which we will roughly define as providing information about the salient characteristics of some function $f(x)$. As a motivating example, consider $f(x)$ as the integrand of a quadrature problem. A PRNG provides exploration but, remarkably, requires neither knowledge or evaluations of f, nor more than minimal storage of previous choices x. These self-imposed constraints are extreme. First, in many settings, including in the quadrature case considered in this chapter, we have strong priors for f. Second, many problems (again, as in quadrature), render evaluations $f(x)$ pertinent to future choice of x: for instance, a range of x values for which $f(x)$ is observed to be flat is unlikely to require dense sampling. Third, as computational hardware has improved, memory has become increasingly cheap. Is it still reasonable to labour under computational constraints conceived in the 1940s?

The extremity of the PRNG approach is further revealed by broader consideration of the problem it aims to solve. Exploration is arguably necessary for intelligence. For instance, all branches of human creative work involve some degree of exploration. Human exploration, at its best, entails theorising, probing and mapping. This fundamental part of our intelligence is addressed by a consequentially broad and deep toolkit. Random and pseudo-random algorithms, in contrast, are painfully dumb, and are so by design.

To better achieve exploration, the Probabilistic Numerics approach is to explicitly construct a model of what you aim to explore – $f(x)$. This model will serve as a guide to optimally explorative points, avoiding the potential redundancy of randomly sampled points.

Figure 12.1, in contrast to Figure 9.3, is a cartoon indictment of the over-simplicity of a randomised approach.

▷ **12.3.1   Computation Investment**

A defender of a PRNG might argue that, in order to define an expected loss, a model and loss function must be defined and maintained. The model, and working with an expected loss, will, of course, require computation and memory: surely this will

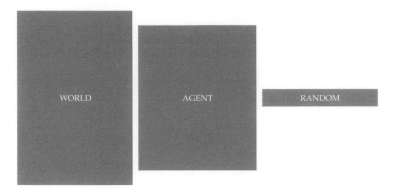

Figure 12.1: As argued in Figure 9.3, a numerical algorithm, and its model of the problem, must be simpler and smaller than the problem itself. However, a random numerical algorithm takes this to an undue extreme: its solution is too simple to be effective.

mean that the probabilistic numerical approach will be unable to provide a practical replacement for PRNG[9]. This defender of the PRNG might protest that it is most truly decision-theoretic to choose the random algorithm – that which is actually practical.

The argument here depends on an assumption: that a PRNG will lead to lower memory and computation costs than those of an explicitly probabilistic numerical algorithm. This assumption is false. As above, we would like to reframe the computation used by a probabilistic numerical algorithm not as a burden, but as an investment. That is, the computational expense incurred by a numerical algorithm must be judged at the level of the algorithm as a whole, not at the level of a single iteration. While a probabilistic numerical integrator may spend more computation than a random alternative in selecting a single node, this investment of computation may allow it to converge more quickly to a good estimate of the integral. As such, the probabilistic numerical algorithm, even if its iterations are more computationally expensive, is designed to *reduce* overall computation consumption. In this spirit, we have seen practical examples of the computational reductions possible with Probabilistic Numerics in adaptive Bayesian quadrature (§10.2).

Subjectivity and bias   Adversarial settings are often used to motivate the use of PRNGs. More concretely, if your adversary knows which specific piece of computer code (with termination rules and internal tolerances) you intend to use as a quadrature routine, that adversary can present a specific Riemann-integrable integrand that will make your code return the wrong answer. In contrast, the argument in §9.2 showed that the Monte Carlo estimator, placing its evaluation nodes randomly, does not suffer from the same problem: its estimator is guaranteed to converge.

[9] On a pedantic note, PRNGs themselves have their own – low, but non-zero – overheads. The popular Mersenne twister (Matsumoto and Nishimura, 1998) PRNG, requires 2.5 kilobytes of state and a moderate-length sequence of computational operations to generate its output.

It is unbiased on every Lebesgue-integrable function, and consistent on every square-integrable function.

Let us examine this statement more closely. At its core is the primary property of random numbers: they are *unpredictable*. This property is likely to seem intuitively clear to most readers, but is quite difficult to define precisely. Formal definitions of this property are challenging because they inevitably require a definition of all things *predictable* by a computer, a notion closely connected to computational complexity itself.[10] Thankfully, we do not actually need to understand precisely what is and is not predictable. The point of the Monte Carlo argument is that, *if* we have access to a stream of unpredictable numbers and use it to build an integration method, then no one can design an integrand that will foil our algorithm, simply because that adversary cannot predict where our method will evaluate the integrand.

The possible existence of adversarial problems motivates the construction of *unbiased* Monte Carlo estimators. Unfortunately, 'bias' is an overloaded and contested term. In the context of Monte Carlo, 'unbiased' simply means that the expected value of a random number is equal to the quantity to be estimated (Lemma 9.2). But this purely technical property draws some emotional power from the (completely unrelated!) association, in common language, of 'bias' with unfairness.[11] The technical, statistical, definition of bias, that used in defining unbiased estimators, is one term within a particular decomposition of error in predicting a data set. As argued by Jaynes,[12] this term has no fundamental significance to inference. Our goal should simply be to reduce error in the whole. ('Inductive bias',[13] meaning the set of assumptions represented within a machine learning algorithm, represents yet another distinct use of the term. In this sense, Probabilistic Numerics unashamedly *encourages* bias, through the incorporation of useful priors.)

It is important to keep in mind that the users of numerical methods are not adversaries of the methods' designers. In fact, the relationship is exactly the opposite of adversarial: users often change their problems to be better-suited to numerical methods (as, in deep learning, network architectures are chosen to suit optimisers). As a result, the majority of integrands, and optimisation objective functions, are quite regular functions. Moreover, this regularity is well-characterised and knowable by the numerical algorithm. There may be good use cases for random numbers in areas like cryptography, where a lack of information, unpredictability, is very much the point. But numerical

[10] Church (1940); Kolmogorov (1968); Loveland (1966).

[11] Pasquale (2015); O'Neil (2016).

[12] Jaynes and Bretthorst (2003), §17.2

[13] Mitchell (1980)

tasks are communicated to a numerical algorithm through the error-free, formally complete, channel of source code. In this sense, a numerical algorithm knows as much about its task as is possible. Acknowledging known regularity in a numerical task can lead to substantive performance improvements.

Formal statements of the properties of stochastic algorithms often depend on the use of "real" random numbers. The argument for random numbers in computation finally comes apart when one considers that virtually every instance of Monte Carlo methods does not actually use "real" random numbers, but only pseudo-random numbers. So the argument rests entirely on the user *not* knowing the random number generator used in the computation (and its seed). If anything, this clearly shows that computation is fundamentally conditional on prior knowledge.

We now appeal to aesthetic arguments. It seems odd that the good behaviour of, for example, your optimisation algorithm should require the hiding of information. Equally, it seems unintuitive to artificially inject additional uncertainty into a calculation that is, ultimately, designed to increase certainty.

Here are some sequences of numbers. Can you tell which one is random?

1. 6224441111111114444443333333

2. 16939937510582097494459230781 6

3. 71290426347261059020833604489 5

4. 1000111111011111111100101000001

5. 0111000001110010011011110110001 1

Here is the solution.

1. This sequence was generated by throwing a six-sided dice seven times and copying down the numbers in sequence of their occurrence, repeating the result of the *i*th throw *i* times. This sequence is "random" because it is unpredictable, but it does not pass standard tests of randomness, and a Monte Carlo integration rule using this sequence does not converge in $\mathcal{O}(N^{-1/2})$.

2. These are the 41st to 70th digits of the irrational number π. This sequence, if continued, is devoid of any structure. It is perfectly good for use in a Monte Carlo method. Unless, of course, you tell your reviewer where you got it from. Arising from one of the most widely studied numbers of mathematics, it is also anything but "random".

3. This sequence was generated by the von Neumann method,[14] a pseudo-random number generator, using the seed 908344. It is the kind of sequence used in real Monte Carlo algorithms, and – now that you know the seed – entirely deterministic. It would have been ok to use this sequence for Monte Carlo estimation up until three sentences ago, when we ripped down the veil of randomness.

[14] Von Neumann (1951)

4. These are digits taken from a CD-ROM published by George Marsaglia containing random numbers generated using a variety of physical random number generators. These digits (perhaps) were once "random". But, now that you know where we got them, they are obviously deterministic. But wait! Marsaglia's CD is actually not available online anymore. Most original copies have long been lost as retiring academics cleared out their offices. We will admit that we do not own a physical copy either. Does this revelation make those digits above random again?

5. To generate this sequence we began with a certain, secret string represented in ASCII, then dropped a coin 32 times to decide whether to flip a bit. We always started with the coin facing heads up. If it landed tails up, we flipped the bit. Here is the catch: we will not tell the height from which the coin was dropped. If we told you the drop was only five millimetres, not enough for the coin to actually turn around, then the sequence is not random. If we told you the height was two meters, then you might conclude the sequence is random. There are an awful lot of "we's" and "you's" in this argument. Evidently, randomness is very much a subjective property.

Our arguments here are not purely philosophical. A number of studies[15] have highlighted that the choice of random seed is empirically significant to the performance of popular reinforcement learning algorithms. In scientific fields, discovering that an unexpected variable affects outcomes should lead to work to uncover the mechanism. When the variable is a random seed, however, this approach is impossible: the sole purpose of a pseudo-random generator is to render the outcome an *unpredictable* function of the seed. If we are to be truly scientific, there seems no solution other than to abandon the pseudo-random generator.

[15] Henderson et al. (2018); Islam et al. (2017); Colas, Sigaud, and Oudeyer (2018); Mania, Guy, and Recht (2018).

Distinct to the seed's role within the exploration routine, the seed may also dictate the progression of a simulation of an environment. Therein, it may be a way of acknowledging environmental randomness. Environmental randomness may similarly limit our ability to improve an agent, but is due to forces outside our control. Even here, randomness is likely to be more epistemic than aleatoric, and science is possible. Indeed, simulations could be chosen to be informative for the training of the agent, rather than naïvely randomly generated.[16]

[16] Paul, Osborne, and Whiteson (2019)

Islam et al. (2017) notes that some reinforcement learning algorithms search for the best random seed, and various authors[17] advocate instead for averaging over a large number of possible seeds. Averaging, in effect, treats the seed as a random variable, an uncontrollable and unknown property of the problem that must be marginalised. However, the seed is not a feature of the problem at all. Importantly, a random seed's existence is owed to the PRNG driving the agents' exploration. In this respect, a seed is a design choice. We typically make such choices to improve the performance of our agents. When we choose to use a pseudo-random generator, we artificially bound our understanding of how to do so. Put another way, the use of a pseudo-random generator introduces a variable, the seed, that can never be improved. We have rendered our performance, in this respect, unimprovable.

[17] Mania, Guy, and Recht (2018); Colas, Sigaud, and Oudeyer (2018).

13

Summary of Part II
and Further Reading

This chapter – using a concrete univariate integral as a guide-post – built intuition about the connection between inference and computation. This led to some conceptual insights:

Classical methods can be re-framed as probabilistic. Certain elementary numerical methods can be derived precisely as maximum a posteriori estimates under equally elementary probabilistic models. More specifically, we saw that the trapezoidal quadrature rule arises as the MAP estimate under a Wiener process prior on the integrand.

Design policies arise naturally. The placement of evaluation nodes on a regular grid arose as the choice that minimises posterior variance over the integral.

Prior knowledge begets bespoke methods. We encountered the general recipe for the construction of a probabilistic numerical method. First, define a *joint generative* model (a prior and a likelihood) for the latent, intractable, quantity and the "observable" (computable) quantities. Next, construct an action rule through specifying a loss function, determining which computations to perform. For example, in integration, by aiming to reduce the variance of the posterior. By encoding knowledge in a prior measure and goals in a loss function, one can construct customised numerical methods, tailored to a specific task.

Meaningful error measures require good priors. The choice of prior determines the scale of the posterior, and hence influences how representative the posterior variance is as an error measure. Hierarchical inference allows the model class to be adapted at runtime to *calibrate* the posterior uncertainty. This calibration is epistemic – it relies on the assumption that the "unobserved" parts of the problem (here, the integrand) are subjectively similar to those already observed.

Probabilistic Numerics can be fast. Assigning a posterior probability distribution to a numerical task need not be significantly more expensive than "classic" point estimation. Even uncertainty calibration may be achieved at almost *the same cost* as the classical point estimate. Moreover, we have seen that some probabilistic numerical algorithms, like WSABI, are legitimately faster than alternatives. This leads us to frame the computation spent on probabilistic modelling as an *investment*, rather than overhead.

Imposed randomness can be harmful. While Monte Carlo estimators can be elegant from an analytic perspective, computationally, it can be counter-productive to artificially introduce randomness into an otherwise deterministic problem. Monte Carlo estimators can at best converge with stochastic rate, even on extremely regular, simple, estimation problems, like the one used in this chapter.

These observations mirror aspects of inference well known in statistics. In many ways, numerical computation and statistics share the same challenges: which model classes lead to good estimation performance, at acceptable computational cost? To which degree can the error, the deviation of the estimator from the true value, be estimated? But there is also a crucial difference between numerical tasks and statistical inference from physical data sources. In stark contrast to "real-world" statistics, e.g. in the social sciences or medicine, a numerical task is defined not through a vague concept, but in a fully descriptive formal language – the programming language encoding the task. It is thus possible, at least in principle, for the computer itself to check the validity of prior assumptions, and thus to choose among available numerical methods with differing prior measures. This prospect is the subject of contemporary research.

Software

At the time of writing, the open-source `emukit` library[1] provides a package for Bayesian quadrature with a number of different

[1] Paleyes et al. (2019), available at `emukit.github.io`

acquisition functions, including for WSABI-L. `Emukit` is an outer-loop package in the sense that it provides the active learning loop, but the surrogate model has to be coded and wrapped by the user into an emukit interface. In contrast, the `ProbNum` library[2] which focuses on the lower numerical level, additionally provides surrogate model functionality and contains a Bayesian quadrature component under active development.

[2] Code at `probnum.org`. See the corresponding publication by Wenger et al. (2021).

Further Reading

The main purpose of this chapter was to introduce core notions of probabilistic numerical computation in the simple setting of univariate integration. However, numerical integration poses a field of its own right, and remains the subject of intense study to the present day. Readers interested in deeper insights may find the following notes helpful.

Quasi-Monte Carlo

Quasi-Monte Carlo (QMC) is the name used to describe integration rules that are based on unit weights (i.e. of the algebraic form of the Monte Carlo estimator of Eq. (9.4)), but which use carefully crafted designs of low discrepancy. The error and convergence analysis of QMC methods is related to that of Bayesian quadrature, and has had some success in achieving appealing convergence rates even in the high-dimensional setting. For more on QMC and its analysis using RKHS hypothesis spaces can be found in a review by Dick et al.[3]

[3] Dick, Kuo, and Sloan (2013)

Closely Related Concepts

Related to Bayesian quadrature are topics including "kernel herding"[4] and kernel quadrature, which themselves are related to other numerical approximation methods.[5] A subtle difference between Bayesian quadrature and kernel quadrature is that the latter often allows for the kernel to change as a function of the observation nodes (in particular, to shrink as their number grows). Doing so poses conceptual problems in the Bayesian framework: it is not compatible with the philosophical notion of a prior; but more practically, this adaptation of the kernel amounts to a continuous relaxation of the associated probabilistic error estimate (which does not play such a central role in the kernel view).

[4] Chen, Welling, and Smola (2010); Huszar and Duvenaud (2012).
[5] Bach, Lacoste-Julien, and Obozinski (2012); Bach (2017).

Convergence Analysis

The theoretical treatment of convergence of Bayesian quadrature
has reached a sophistication beyond what can be presented in
this chapter. See for example, recent works by Briol et al. (2019),
and Kanagawa, Sriperumbudur, and Fukumizu (2020). In particular, both kernel quadrature and Bayesian quadrature using
translation-invariant kernels can achieve the optimal worst-case
rate for integrands constrained to lie in a Sobolev space, if certain requirements on the distribution of the design points are
fulfilled. As already mentioned above, even the more theoretically challenging case of *adaptive* Bayesian quadrature has now
been furnished[6] with results establishing asymptotic consistency (under some loose conditions).

[6] Kanagawa and Hennig (2019)

Chapter III
Linear Algebra

Key Points

In this chapter we will consider computations involving *matrices*. Here is a preview of the central results:

⊖ **Algorithmic structure** will play a prominent role. Since linear algebra methods are part of the bedrock of computation on which other methods are built, computational efficiency is particularly important. Smart book-keeping is a large part of good methods. Considerations on computational complexity will significantly constrain the choice of probabilistic models, to a class of Gaussian distributions with specific factorisation structure.

⊖ Do not be confused by the term *linear* algebra. Matrix inversion is in fact a **nonlinear** operation. This will force us to make a conscious decision when designing the probabilistic model underlying an algorithm. The model can either fit neatly with the likelihood and thus allow for more complicated observation (computation) paradigms, or fit cleanly with the latent quantity (the solution of a linear problem), and thus provide more explicit notions of posterior uncertainty. This is in contrast to integration, where the latent quantity (the integral) is linearly related to the observables (the integrand), so that both can be captured jointly in a Gaussian model.

⊖ Certain properties of a matrix (for example positive definiteness), even when known a priori, can be difficult to capture in a prior that still allows for computationally efficient inference. We may decide to *not* encode certain kinds of knowledge in favour of computational complexity. While this means that such knowledge can then not be used in the action rule of the algorithm, one may still require that resulting point estimates, and even error estimates, are consistent with it.

⊖ Putting these abstract points together, we will arrive at a concrete class of prior distributions that, when combined with certain "natural" algorithmic choices, give rise to classic iterative solvers; in particular to the seminal method of conjugate gradients. In contrast to the integration chapter, however, we will find that **calibrating uncertainty** is a much more intricate and challenging issue in linear algebra. The reason for this, put simply, is that matrices are big objects: their quadratic size means that linearly many matrix-vector projections as observations identify only a small part of the matrix.

⊖ Each chapter has a wider conceptual point that transcends the concrete numerical setting. In the case of this chapter, it is the observation that the design of a good computational prior is a trade-off between constraints set by knowledge and those set by computational considerations. Even though one may patently know some things to be true, it may be counter-productive to include this information in the prior when doing so makes the computation considerably more complex.

Required Background

In addition to the concepts of Chapter I, this chapter requires some basic linear algebra concepts, briefly reviewed in the following.

▶ **15.1 Vectorised Matrices and the Kronecker Product**

This chapter revolves around inferring matrix-valued objects. For this purpose, a matrix $A \in \mathbb{R}^{N \times M}$ will frequently be treated as a collection of NM real numbers arranged into a rectangular table, rather than an object associated with an algebraic structure. For a real matrix $A \in \mathbb{R}^{N \times M}$, the symbol $\vec{A} \in \mathbb{R}^{NM}$ will then denote the *vector* arising from stacking the elements of A row after row ("row-major" indexing[1]). It would be possible to index the elements of this vector with a single number running from 1 to NM. However, to avoid confusing translations between index sets, the elements of this vector will be indexed by the same index set $(ij) \subset \mathbb{N} \times \mathbb{N}$ as the matrix itself.

On some rare occasions it will be necessary to use the inverse operation of vectorisation – to re-shape a vectorised matrix back into rectangular form. This will be denoted by the ♮ symbol:

$$A = \natural \vec{A}. \tag{15.1}$$

The *Kronecker product* $A \otimes B$ of two matrices $A \in \mathbb{R}^{N_A \times M_A}$, $B \in \mathbb{R}^{N_B \times M_B}$ is a matrix of size $N_A N_B \times M_A M_B$ with elements

$$[A \otimes B]_{ij,k\ell} = [A]_{ik}[B]_{j\ell}. \tag{15.2}$$

This matrix maps from $\mathbb{R}^{M_A \cdot M_B}$, the space of vectorised real $M_A \times M_B$ matrices, to $\mathbb{R}^{N_A \times N_B}$, the space of vectorised $N_A \times N_B$ matrices. For $\vec{C} \in \mathbb{R}^{M_A \cdot M_B}$, and $C = \natural \vec{C}$, we have

$$[(A \otimes B)\vec{C}]_{ij} = \sum_{k\ell}[A]_{ik}[C]_{k\ell}[B]_{j\ell} = [\overrightarrow{ACB^\mathsf{T}}]_{ij}. \tag{15.3}$$

[1] This is *not* that same as stacking the matrix column-by-column ("column-major"). The latter is used in Fortran and thus also by Matlab's A(:) operator. Numpy's A.ravel() allows the user to specify the order, but defaults to row-major indexing, which is also a standard used in C. Under column-major indexing, Eq. (15.3) changes to

$$(A \otimes B)\vec{C} = \overrightarrow{(BCA^\mathsf{T})},$$

which would cause all sorts of havoc down the line.

In this sense the Kronecker product "translates" between matrix multiplication and vectorisation. The Kronecker product has a number of analytically useful properties,[2] which mostly arise from the relation

[2] van Loan (2000)

$$(A \otimes B)(C \otimes D) = AC \otimes BD. \tag{15.4}$$

Among them are

$$(A \otimes B)^{-1} = A^{-1} \otimes B^{-1},$$
$$|A \otimes B| = |A|^{\mathrm{rk}(B)} \cdot |B|^{\mathrm{rk}(A)}, \tag{15.5}$$
$$(A \otimes B) = (V_A \otimes V_B)(D_A \otimes D_B)(V_A \otimes V_B)^{-1}, \tag{15.6}$$
$$(A \otimes B)^\mathsf{T} = A^\mathsf{T} \otimes B^\mathsf{T}, \tag{15.7}$$

Exercise 15.1 (easy but instructive, solution on p. 362). *Prove Eqs. (15.4)–(15.7). Show that Eq. (15.6) is indeed the eigendecomposition of $A \otimes B$.*

where $|A|$ is the matrix determinant of A, $\mathrm{rk}(A)$ is the rank of A, and $A = V_A D_A V_A^{-1}, B = V_B D_B V_B^{-1}$ are the eigenvalue decompositions of A and B, respectively. These properties only hold assuming that these decompositions and inverses exist.

▶ **15.2   Positive Definite Matrices**

A real matrix $A \in \mathbb{R}^{N \times N}$ will be called SPD if it is symmetric ($A = A^\mathsf{T}$) and positive (semi-) definite. It is *positive (semi-) definite* if $v^\mathsf{T} A v > 0$ (if $v^\mathsf{T} A v \geq 0$) for all non-zero vectors $v \in \mathbb{R}^N$. Like all symmetric real matrices, SPD matrices have orthogonal eigenvectors. Strictly positive definite matrices have strictly positive real eigenvalues, and are thus invertible.

▶ **15.3   Frobenius Matrix Norm**

There are many norms[3] on the space of real matrices $A \in \mathbb{R}^{N \times M}$, some with certain analytical advantages over others. The *Frobenius norm* is defined by

$$\|A\|_F^2 := \mathrm{tr}(A^\mathsf{T} A) = \sum_{i=1}^N \sum_{j=1}^M A_{ij}^2 = \vec{A}^\mathsf{T} \vec{A} = \|\vec{A}\|_2^2,$$

where $\|\cdot\|_2$ is the standard Euclidean (ℓ^2) vector-norm. Of particular importance will be the generalised, *weighted Frobenius norm*, using two symmetric positive definite matrices V, W:

$$\|A\|_{F,V,W}^2 := \mathrm{tr}(A^\mathsf{T} V^{-1} A W^{-1}) = \vec{A}^\mathsf{T} (V \otimes W)^{-1} \vec{A}. \tag{15.8}$$

▶ **15.4   Singular Value Decomposition**

Every real matrix[4] $B \in \mathbb{R}^{M \times N}$ has a *singular value decomposition*

[3] A matrix norm $\|A\| \in \mathbb{R}$ has the property that
- $\|A\| \geq 0$,
- $\|A\| = 0$ iff $A = 0$,
- $\|\alpha A\| = |\alpha|\|A\|$ for all $\alpha \in \mathbb{R}$,
- $\|A + B\| \leq \|A\|\|B\|$.

Exercise 15.2 (easy, solution on p. 362). *Using Eq. (15.6), show that the Kronecker product of two symmetric positive definite matrices is itself SPD, then use this result to show that Eq. (15.8) does indeed define a matrix norm.*

[4] There is an analogous formulation for complex matrices, but the chapter only involves real matrices.

(SVD)

$$B = Q\Sigma U^\mathsf{T}$$

with orthonormal[5] matrices $Q \in \mathbb{R}^{N \times N}, U \in \mathbb{R}^{M \times M}$, whose columns are called the *left-* and *right- singular vectors*, respectively, and a rectangular diagonal matrix[6] $\Sigma \in \mathbb{R}^{N \times M}$ which contains non-negative real numbers called *singular values of B* on the diagonal. Assume, w.l.o.g., that $N \geq M$ and the diagonal elements of Σ are sorted in descending order, and Σ_{rr} with $r \leq M$ is the last non-zero singular value. Then Q can be decomposed into its first r columns, Q_+, and the (potentially empty) $N - r$ columns, Q_- as $Q = [Q_+, Q_-]$, and similarly $U = [U_+, U_-]$ for the columns of U. The SVD is a powerful tool of matrix analysis:

- r equals the *rank* of B: $\mathrm{rk}(B) = r$;

- the columns of U_- span the *null space* (the *kernel*) of B (those of U_+ the *pre-image* of B);

- the columns of Q_+ span the *range* (the *image*) of B (those of Q_- the *co-kernel* of B);

- the matrix $\tilde{B} = \arg\min_{\mathrm{rk}(\tilde{B})=k \leq r} \|B - \tilde{B}\|_F$ ("the best rank-k approximation to B in Frobenius norm") is given by $\tilde{B} = Q\tilde{\Sigma}U^\mathsf{T}$, where $\tilde{\Sigma}$ equals Σ except that $\tilde{\Sigma}_{ii} = 0$ for $i > k$;

- the matrix $V = \arg\min_{V^\mathsf{T}V=I} \|B - V\|_F$ ("the orthonormal matrix closest to B in Frobenius norm") is $V = QU^\mathsf{T}$.

[5] That is, $Q^\mathsf{T}Q = I_N$ and $U^\mathsf{T}U = I_M$.

[6] That is, $\Sigma_{ij} = 0$ if $i \neq j$.

▶ **15.5   Matrix Identities**

For matrices A, U, C, V, if all the inverses in the following equation exist, then the *matrix inversion lemma*[7] holds:

$$(A + UCV)^{-1} = A^{-1} - A^{-1}U(C^{-1} + VA^{-1}U)^{-1}VA^{-1}. \quad (15.9)$$

It is helpful if U is a "skinny" matrix (i.e. $U \in \mathbb{R}^{N \times M}, M \ll N$), and the inverse of A is known, because then the inverse of the larger $N \times N$ left-hand side of Eq. (15.9) can be found from the smaller $M \times M$ inverse on the right-hand side.

[7] The matrix inversion lemma has been ascribed to many different authors, including M. Woodbury, J. Sherman and W. Morrison, M. Bartlett, and I. Schur. It is likely that the result is even older than any of the corresponding works. Some historical background, along with interesting additional numerical analysis, can be found in a review by Hager (1989).

The inverse of the block matrix

$$A := \begin{bmatrix} P & Q \\ R & S \end{bmatrix} \quad \text{, if it exists, is} \quad A^{-1} = \begin{bmatrix} \tilde{P} & \tilde{Q} \\ \tilde{R} & M \end{bmatrix}, \quad (15.10)$$

with

$$M := (S - RP^{-1}Q)^{-1}, \quad \tilde{P} := P^{-1} + P^{-1}QMRP^{-1},$$
$$\tilde{Q} := -P^{-1}QM, \quad \tilde{R} := -MRP^{-1}.$$

This relationship is often attributed to I. Schur (1917). The term P is sometimes called the *pivot block*, the term M, and others of its general form, are widely called *Schur complements*.[8] This is due to its use in the Schur determinant formula, also simply known as the *determinant lemma*, which follows from the above:

$$|A| = |P| \cdot |S - RP^{-1}Q|.$$

[8] An introduction to Schur complements, including motivations for the terminology and a discussion of applications and related concepts, is provided by Cottle (1974).

It can also be re-phrased in the notation of the matrix inversion lemma above:

$$|A + UCV| = |A| \cdot |C| \cdot |C^{-1} + VA^{-1}U|. \qquad (15.11)$$

The related result for block matrices is[9]

[9] Lütkepohl (1996), §4.2.2, Eq. (6)

$$A \text{ non-singular} \quad \Rightarrow \quad \det \begin{bmatrix} A & B \\ C & D \end{bmatrix} = \det(A)\det(D - CA^{-1}B),$$

$$D \text{ non-singular} \quad \Rightarrow \quad \det \begin{bmatrix} A & B \\ C & D \end{bmatrix} = \det(D)\det(A - BD^{-1}C).$$

Introduction

Linear algebra operations like the solution of linear systems, inversion and decomposition of matrices are arguably the most basic kind of numerical computations. Alongside even more elemental operations like matrix-vector and matrix-matrix multiplication, they are the building blocks of virtually all heavyweight computation on contemporary computers. Consequently, this area has been studied to great depth, which has led to extremely well-crafted algorithms. A thorough introduction can be found in a tome by Golub and Van Loan (1996). A more recent – and only slightly less voluminous – treatment is provided by Björck (2015). Just seeing these books, each well over 700 pages thick,[1] sitting on a bookshelf should convince anyone that it would be foolish to attempt a probabilistic analysis of all of numerical linear algebra in this chapter. As in the other chapters, we will focus on a few key aspects.

One strong simplification we will make is to assume that computations can be performed with arbitrary precision. Doing so gives us a licence to ignore all questions of *numerical stability*. Seasoned numerical analysts may raise their eyebrows here – making algorithms stable to numerical errors is a core goal of research in numerical linear algebra. But in machine learning, machine precision is regularly by far the smallest source of uncertainty, dominated by issues arising from the lack of data and data-sub-sampling. By putting stability aside, we can concentrate on the question of epistemic uncertainty: what is the most efficient way to extract information about the solution of a linear system from a computer?

To simplify things further, we will focus on one particular problem – the solution of the symmetric, positive definite, real

[1] A less hefty introduction at undergraduate level is offered by Ipsen's (2009) concise book.

linear system (see Figure 16.1)

$$Ax = b, \quad \text{where } A \in \mathbb{R}^{N \times N} \text{ spd., and } x, b \in \mathbb{R}^N. \qquad (16.1)$$

Equation (16.1) can also be written as an optimisation problem: x is the unique vector that minimises the convex quadratic function

$$f(x) = \frac{1}{2}x^\mathsf{T} A x - x^\mathsf{T} b, \qquad (16.2)$$

and is thus known as *the least-squares problem*. $f(x)$ has gradient (see Figure 16.1)

$$r(x) := \nabla f(x) = Ax - b, \qquad (16.3)$$

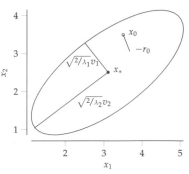

Figure 16.1: Sketch of a symmetric positive definite linear problem.

also known as the *residual* (for reasons to be introduced in §17.2). The terms residual and gradient will be used interchangeably, depending on which aspect is to be emphasised. $f(x)$ has constant Hessian matrix $\nabla \nabla^\mathsf{T} f(x) = A$. Because A is spd, it has a unique inverse, which will play such a central role that it will be afforded its own symbol:

$$A^{-1} =: H.$$

(The choice of the letter H is historic convention for inverse Hessians in optimisation.) Problem (16.1) is interesting for two reasons. First, it lies at the heart of least-squares estimation, which in turn is the basis for many basic numerical, statistical, and indeed machine learning algorithms, like Gaussian process regression (§4.2). Second, as we will see in Chapter IV, estimating spd matrices and their inverse also features in local nonlinear optimisation. In fact, some of the most core algorithms of nonlinear optimisation will arise as natural extensions of the results of this chapter.

Solving linear problems is also interesting more generally because certain other core tasks of linear algebra can be solved with algorithms that are structurally similar. In particular, there is a deep connection between iterative linear solvers and methods for computing matrix decompositions (like eigen- and singular value decompositions) through the Krylov sequence.[2] Developing a probabilistic description for (iterative) linear solvers thus holds the promise of similar advances in other linear algebra tasks.

The largest part of this chapter will be devoted to re-phrasing an existing, elementary linear algebra method – the method of conjugate gradients. The point is to build an intuition for the constraints on the model class, in particular on the choice of

[2] See §11.3 in Golub and Van Loan (1996) for an introduction. This connection is also the reason why computing the posterior uncertainty (covariance) of Gaussian process regression adds little to no overhead to just computing the associated point estimate (posterior mean). Finding the minimum of a quadratic problem requires the same considerations as characterising the geometry (Hessian) of the problem. As we have already seen in previous chapters, this has crucial implications for the complexity of Probabilistic Numerics: if we are happy to accept approximately Gaussian posteriors, then these can often be had at essentially no extra cost over the classic point estimate.

prior covariance, that are required to build a lightweight, efficient estimator for linear algebra quantities. Because they form the foundation of many computational methods, linear solvers have to work on a large class of problems at low computational cost. For the most basic methods, this also means they must not themselves require the solution of a linear problem, not even one smaller than the original one. This restriction is less important for practical applications requiring uncertainty, where one may be willing to pay a small computational overhead for probabilistic "error bars" on point estimates. In such situations, it may be convenient to use a classic (highly optimised) solver for internal computations, and construct a probabilistic estimate "around" its output, using some statistics of the solver's computations to calibrate uncertainty.

▶ 16.1   Classic Methods

The "pedestrian" solution to Problem (16.1) is *Gaussian elimination*,[3] one of the oldest algorithms known to humankind, and certainly one the best known ones, widely taught at high-school level. Gaussian elimination provides a solution for *any* simultaneously solvable set of linear equations, not just symmetric positive definite ones. It is the standard approach for small and medium-sized problems, among other reasons because it can be made numerically quite stable by ordering the operations suitably.[4] Gaussian elimination of an $N \times N$ system in general involves N intermediate steps, each involving a matrix-vector multiplication, hence the overall complexity is $\mathcal{O}(N^3)$.

However, Gaussian elimination is not an "anytime" algorithm – it only provides a correct answer after it runs to completion. In fact it can be shown[5] that if this algorithm is stopped at step $i < N$ and the computations performed until this point are used to compute an "estimate" $\hat{x}_i$ of the true solution x, then there are scenarios in which the error $\|\hat{x}_i - x\|$ can actually *grow* with every step $i < N$, and only converge suddenly on the final step $i = N$. When studying probabilistic formulations of linear algebra, we will primarily be interested in assigning uncertainty in incompletely solved problems, and thus in algorithms which improve a point estimate over the course of their run.

[3] See Gauss (1809). For a historical perspective, see Grcar (2011).

[4] In formal terms, Gaussian elimination is often captured in the so-called LU-decomposition, a notion introduced by Turing (1948). The decomposition is made numerically stable by helpful permutations of A, a process known as *pivoting*. Details can be found in §3.2–3.4 of Golub and Van Loan (1996). The LU decomposition splits the matrix A into a **Lower** and an **Upper** triangular matrix, and is a generalisation of the Cholesky decomposition (Benoit, 1924) (which only applies to SPD matrices). More can be found in Turing's very readable work.

[5] Hestenes and Stiefel (1952)

```
1  procedure CG(A(·), b, x_0)
2      r_0 = Ax_0 − b                          // initial gradient
3      d_0 = 0, β_0 = 0                         // for notational clarity
4      for i = 1, ..., N do
5          d_i = −r_{i−1} + β_{i−1}d_{i−1}      // compute direction
6          z_i = Ad_i                           // compute
7          α_i = −d_i^⊤ r_{i−1}/d_i^⊤ z_i       // optimal step-size
8          s_i = α_i d_i                        // re-scale step
9          y_i = α_i z_i                        // re-scale observation
10         x_i = x_{i−1} + s_i                  // update estimate for x
11         r_i = r_{i−1} + y_i                  // new gradient at x_i
12         β_i = r_i^⊤ r_i/r_{i−1}^⊤ r_{i−1}    // compute conjugate correction
13     end for
14 end procedure
```

Algorithm 16.1: Conjugate gradients (basic form). Adapted from Nocedal and Wright (1999). The algorithm takes as inputs the problem description (A, b) and an initial guess x_0 (often set to either **0** or b), then iteratively computes estimates x_i of typically increasing quality. The dominant computation is the matrix-vector multiplication in line 6, all other steps are of either linear or constant cost. Lines 8 and 9 could obviously be folded into the following two lines, they are kept separate here to ease the comparison to probabilistic equivalents constructed below.

Iterative solvers provide such a behaviour, and are used for large-scale problems where the cubic cost of finding the exact solution is too large to contemplate. These methods also involve individual steps of cost $\mathcal{O}(N^2)$ each. But they aim to continuously improve an initial guess $\hat{x}_0$, so that the algorithm can be stopped for $i \ll N$ and already provide a good estimate of x. The prototypical algorithm in this class is the *method of conjugate gradients* (CG),[6] an algorithm applicable to the SPD problem (16.1) above. For reference, it is displayed in Algorithm 16.1.

[6] Hestenes and Stiefel (1952)

CG consists of a single loop of iterative refinements to an estimated solution x_i of Eq. (16.1). Each iteration computes a single matrix-vector multiplication (line 6), a projection of A along a vector d_i. The other lines consist of cheaper computations that track the current estimate x_i and the current residual $r(x_i)$. The steps are determined by two "control" parameters α, β. The former, α, regulates how the observed result of the projection is used to update x_i, and latter, β, governs which projection is chosen next. Hence, this algorithmic structure fits with the separation of an active agent into an estimation (inference) and action (decision, policy) part that we already employed in the integration chapter.

The central result of this chapter on linear algebra will be the construction of a set of active probabilistic inference methods that are consistent with conjugate gradient. That is, they construct a sequence of Gaussian posterior measures associated with a mean estimate for x that equals the sequence constructed by CG. Even for readers interested in non-symmetric, non-definite problems, CG is a good starting point, as it can be generalised to larger classes of tasks. Many iterative solvers can be constructed in this way, including the *generalised minimal residual* method (GMRES)[7] and the *bi-conjugate gradient* method (BICG),[8] the *conjugate gradient squared* method (CGS),[9], and the *quasi-minimal residual* method (QMR).[10] Further, CG is closely connected to the *Lanczos processLanczos process* for approximately computing the eigenvalues of symmetric matrices,[11] and the generalisation to GMRES is analogously connected to the more general *Arnoldi process* for iterative approximation of eigenvalues.[12] A probabilistic analysis of CG thus gets us closer to a general understanding of linear algebra in terms of probabilistic inference.

There are several good textbooks available for readers interested in the classic analysis of linear algebra methods. German-speaking readers can find a great overview of all the methods mentioned above, and of their relationship to each other, in §4.3 of the book by Meister (2011). A more compact introduction to GMRES and CG in particular is also in §IV of Trefethen and Bau III (1997). The book by Parlett (1980) specifically focuses on symmetric matrices; the contents of the present chapter are related to the exposition in Chapters 12 and 13 therein.

[7] Saad and Schultz (1986)

[8] Fletcher (1975)

[9] Sonneveld (1989)

[10] Freund and Nachtigal (1991)

[11] Lanczos (1950)

[12] Arnoldi (1951)

17

Evaluation Strategies

In pursuit of a probabilistic formulation of linear algebra, it is tempting to start in the same way we started the treatment of integration in Chapter II – by writing down a family of probability measures, say, over H and x, and see if certain choices of parameters can be identified with the classic methods listed above. But due to the structured nature of linear algebra, this approach runs the risk of yielding intractable algorithms. A large part of linear algebra consists of efficient book-keeping. It is thus a better strategy to leave the probabilistic model abstract initially, and focus on algorithmic structure. Concrete implementations informed by the lessons from this section will be addressed in §19.

With this in mind, assume we want to solve the problem $Ax = b$ with a probabilistic solver that mimics the *structure* of an iterative solver like CG (Algorithm 16.1). As noted above, these methods proceed by iteratively collecting *observations* of matrix-vector multiplications $z_i = Ad_i$ of some smartly chosen vector d_i with the matrix A. The vectors d_i are termed *search directions* or *projections*. We will thus consider probabilistic methods that collect action–observation pairs $(d_i, z_i = Ad_i)_{i=0,...}$. To simplify notation, we will collect the $d_1, \ldots, d_i$ and $z_1, \ldots, z_i$ in the columns of two rectangular matrices Z_i, D_i, so that after M iterations of the method, $Z_i, D_i \in \mathbb{R}^{N \times M}$ and the *entire* set of observations can be written compactly as $Z_i = AD_i$. After each iteration, the solver constructs a posterior measure $p(A \mid D_i, Z_i)$, which can be used both to construct an estimate x_i, and to decide on the next projection d_i. For the moment, the only assumption we will make about the as-of-yet unspecified probabilistic inference scheme is that it is consistent with the observation, in the sense that it puts measure zero on all matrices

$\tilde{A}$ for which $\tilde{A}D_i \neq Z_i$. This also implies that any reasonable point estimators A_i and H_i (for $H = A^{-1}$) constructed from this probability measure should have the property

$$A_i D_i = Z_i \qquad \text{and} \qquad H_i Z_i = D_i.$$

The crucial question is, how should the solver choose the action d_{i+1} from the posterior?

▶ 17.1 Direct Methods

The most straightforward idea is to choose d_{i+1} a priori, i.e. independent of the observations Z_i. For example along a randomly chosen direction, or as $d_{i+1} = e_{i+1}$, the unit vector $e_{i+1,j} = \delta_{ij}$. One advantage of this strategy is that the directions can be chosen in a way that keeps computational cost low. To wit, sparse directions like the choice $d_i = e_i$ allow the computation of the projections $z_i = Ae_i = A_{:i}$ in linear time. This idea is at the heart of approximation methods that do not attempt to find an *optimal* solution to a linear problem, but only an ad-hoc, reasonable yet cheap projection. Such approaches can work well if outside information about the structure of the matrix is available. For instance in least-squares problems where the matrix A is constructed by the evaluation of a positive definite function, such as kernel ridge, or Gaussian process, regression. Ideas like the *Nyström* approximation[1] (the name was chosen by Baker,[2] based on the quadrature work of Nyström),[3] *inducing point* methods,[4] and *spectral* approximations,[5] and of course Gaussian eliminiation itself (i.e. LU and Cholesky decompositions), all fall in this category. M individual steps of such methods tend to have cost $\mathcal{O}(NM^2)$, linear in the size of the matrix. The downside of choosing projection directions a priori is that the solver cannot adapt to the structure of the matrix, so if the prior is badly calibrated, the solver's estimate may be bad, too. For the rest of this chapter, we turn our attention to solvers which use collected search directions to converge towards the *exact* solution of the linear problem (defined in Eq. (16.1)). Each iteration of such a method will typically have quadratic cost $\mathcal{O}(N^2)$ because it involves a generic matrix-vector multiplication, so the cost of performing M steps is $\mathcal{O}(N^2 M)$.

[1] Williams and Seeger (2000)

[2] Baker (1973), §3

[3] Nyström (1930)

[4] Snelson and Ghahramani (2005); Quiñonero-Candela and Rasmussen (2005).

[5] Rahimi and Recht (2007)

▶ 17.2 Iterative Methods

We will take an intuitive approach to constructing an algorithmic skeleton for our adaptive probabilistic solver, which will be complemented by a subtle improvement later. Our initial developments will not require symmetry of A, but we will change this later. Recall the residual (defined earlier in §16)

$$r(x) = Ax - b.$$

For *any* estimate $\tilde{x}$, wherever it may come from, the update

$$\tilde{x} \leftarrow \tilde{x} - Hr(\tilde{x})$$
$$= \tilde{x} - H(A\tilde{x} - b) = Hb = x$$

would yield the exact solution, if we had access to the exact matrix inverse H. Since the solver has access to a posterior measure $p(A \mid D_i, Z_i)$, we will assume that this measure can be used to compute some estimate H_i for H. The solver's estimate for the solution x should be consistent with H_i. This suggests the *estimation* update rule

$$x_{i+1} := x_i - H_i\, r(x_i), \qquad (17.1)$$

where the inference on H is so far left abstract.

Following our general recipe, the second part of the solver is the *action* rule, the choice for the next projection d_{i+1} of A. There are two, related but not identical, objectives for this rule: One the one hand, we would like to know the new residual $r(x_{i+1})$, if only to track process and check for convergence (remember that the problem is solved iff $r(x_{i+1}) = 0$). On the other hand, we want to efficiently collect information about A and H; i.e. explore aspects of A that will maximally improve subsequent estimates $x_{>i}$. To this end, consider the projection and accompanying observation

$$d_{i+1} := x_{i+1} - x_i = -H_i r(x_i),$$
$$z_{i+1} = Ad_{i+1}. \qquad (17.2)$$

An appealing aspect of this choice is that it allows us to compute the new residual without having to evaluate a second matrix-vector multiplication. We can simply update the residual in $\mathcal{O}(N)$ time as

$$r(x_{i+1}) = Ax_{i+1} - b = A(x_{i+1} - x_i + x_i) - b = z_{i+1} + r(x_i).$$

The downside of this action rule is that, without further analysis, there is no guarantee that it will produce particularly informative observations of A. After all, the step $x_{i+1} - x_i$ is just the *greedy* choice that moves the estimate to whatever is currently

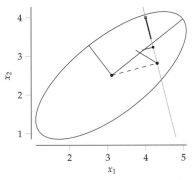

Figure 17.1: A quadratic optimisation problem: extremum as black centre, Hessian with eigen-directions represented by an ellipse with principal axes. The restriction of the quadratic to a linear sub-space is also a quadratic. The optimum in that sub-space can be found in a single division, but it is not identical to the *projection* of the global optimum onto the sub-space.

```
 1  procedure LINSOLVE_DRAFT(A(·), b, p(A))
 2  │   x_0 = H_0 b                                    // initial guess
 3  │   r_0 = A x_0 - b                                // initial gradient
 4  │   for i = 1, ..., N do
 5  │   │   d_i = -H_{i-1} r_{i-1}                      // compute optimisation direction
 6  │   │   s_i = d_i                                  // define projection
 7  │   │   y_i = A s_i                                       // observe
 8  │   │   x_i = x_{i-1} + s_i                        // update estimate for x
 9  │   │   r_i = r_{i-1} + y_i                        // new gradient at x_i
10  │   │   H_i = INFER(H | Y_i, S_i, p(A))            // estimate H
11  │   end for
12  end procedure
```

Algorithm 17.1: A draft for a probabilistic iterative linear solver. The notation $A(\cdot)$ is meant to represent a function performing multiplication with A (which does not necessarily require N^2 operations, but might). In this algorithm and others below, the line collecting the observation is marked with a bold-font comment to signify the expensive part of the iteration. Note the structural similarity to CG (Algorithm 16.1).
Line 10 is only a placeholder so far; concrete inference rules will be constructed later. In a practical implementation, lines 5 and 10 would be merged, so that no actual estimate of the quadratic matrix H has to be formed.

estimated to be the solution. However, Figure 17.1 illustrates an intuition that might inspire some hope in Eq. (17.2). Recall from (16.3) that the residual is the gradient of the quadratic objective $f(x)$. As such, if we consider the problem from an optimisation perspective, then the residual $r(x_i)$ is the direction of maximal improvement. We will just have to take care that the mapping through the estimate H_i does not destroy this beneficial aspect.

Algorithm 17.1 translates the two design choices of Eqs. (17.1) and (17.2) into more concrete pseudo-code for a first draft of our probabilistic iterative solver.[6] There is a small change to the lines in Algorithm 17.1 that amounts to a significant improvement in practice. Note that the observation in line 8 of Algorithm 17.1 is available at a point in the loop iteration before x_{i+1} is actually assigned. This offers an opportunity to already use some information from z_i within the loop, as long as it is possible to do so at low computational cost. In particular, we can re-scale the step as $d_{i+1} \leftarrow \alpha_{i+1} d_{i+1}$, using a scalar $\alpha_i \in \mathbb{R}$. Doing so introduces an ever so slight break in the consistency of the probabilistic belief: the estimate x_i in line 8 of Algorithm 17.1 will neither be equal to $H_{i-1}b$ nor to $H_i b$. But this is primarily an issue of algorithmic flow (the fact that x_i and H_i are computed in different lines of the algorithm), and the practical improvements are too big to pass on. In any case, this adaptation is also present in the classic algorithms, so we need to include it to find exact equivalences.

Indeed, under the assumption of symmetric A, the *optimal* scale α_{i+1} can be computed in linear time, using the observation in line 7. We will consider symmetric A hereafter. Consider the parametrised choice $x_i = x_{i-1} + \alpha_i d_i$. The derivative of the

[6] A minor notational complication: line 3 of Algorithm 17.1 wastes one initial matrix-vector multiplication that is not used to infer information about H. This is for generality, so that $x_0 = 0$ (and $H_0 = 0$) remains a possible choice. A related issue one may worry about: Why does the algorithm not simply set $x_i = H_i b$, which may seem like the "natural" estimate for the solution (e.g. it is the mean estimate for x if H is assigned a Gaussian measure)? Note that the update (17.1) can also be written as

$$x_{i+1} = x_i - H_i(A x_i - b)$$
$$= x_i - H_i\left(\sum_{j\leq i} A s_j + A x_0 - b\right)$$
$$= x_0 - H_i A x_0 + H_i b.$$

Hence, for $x_0 = 0$ (or $H_i A x_0 = x_0$), Eq. (17.1) is actually equal to $x_i = H_i b$. This is mostly a problem of presentation: Algorithm 17.1 is a compromise allowing both a general probabilistic interpretation while staying close to classic formulations, which typically allow arbitrary x_0.

```
1  procedure LinSolve_Project(A(·), b, p(A))
2      x_0 = H_0 b                              // initial guess
3      r_0 = Ax_0 - b                           // initial gradient
4      for i = 1, ..., N do
5          d_i = -H_{i-1} r_{i-1}               // compute optimisation direction
6          z_i = Ad_i                           // observe
7          α_i = -d_i^T r_{i-1} / d_i^T z_i     // optimal step-size
8          s_i = α_i d_i                        // re-scale step
9          y_i = α_i z_i                        // re-scale observation
10         x_i = x_{i-1} + s_i                  // update estimate for x
11         r_i = r_{i-1} + y_i                  // new gradient at x_i
12         H_i = Infer(H | Y_i, S_i, p(A))      // estimate H
13     end for
14 end procedure
```

Algorithm 17.2: Projected linear optimisation. The variables s, y are redundant with d, z, either pair could be dropped in a real implementation. Both are kept around here to provide uniform notation across algorithms. Note the structural similarity to classic iterative solvers like conjugate gradients (Algorithm 16.1). The only difference is in lines 5 and 12.

convex objective f, (16.2), in this scalar parameter is

$$\frac{\partial f(x_{i-1} + α_i d_i)}{\partial α_i} = α_i d_i^T A d_i + d_i^T (Ax_{i-1} - b)$$
$$= α_i d_i^T A d_i + d_i^T r_{i-1}.$$

This derivative is zero at

$$α_i = -\frac{d_i^T A d_i}{d_i^T r_{i-1}}.$$

Recalling that $\nabla f(x) = Ax - b$, note that this $α_i$ defines the point where ∇f is orthogonal to d_i:

$$d_i^T \nabla f(x_{i-1} + α_i d_i) = d_i^T (Ax_{i-1} + α A d_i - b) = 0.$$

Thus, line 7 of Algorithm 17.1 provides exactly the required matrix-vector multiplication $z_i = Ad_i$ to find the root of the projected gradient. Explicitly,

$$α_i = -\frac{d_i^T r_{i-1}}{d_i^T z_i}. \tag{17.3}$$

Algorithm 17.2 incorporates this insight. It involves only a few re-arrangements from Algorithm 17.1, and one new line of linear cost, to compute the optimal step size $α_i$. This algorithm will serve as the structural skeleton for the remainder of this chapter. In §19 and following, we will consider several possible choices for the inference step in line 12, and see how they relate to existing classic algorithmic families. In preparation for this step, the following sections give a brief overview over some relevant families of classic linear solvers.

18

A Review of Some Classic Solvers

Several different notions and nomenclatures are used to describe linear solvers. This section connects Algorithm 17.2, in its general form or under certain restrictions, to some popular classic concepts. This will allow us, in Corollary 18.5, to identify a requirement that probabilistic solvers have to fulfil to be equivalent to CG.

▶ 18.1 Projection Methods

Independent of the concrete inference rule in line 12, Algorithm 17.2 selects the estimate x_i as $x_i \in x_0 + \mathbb{K}_i$ with $\mathbb{K}_i = \operatorname{span}\{d_1, d_2, \ldots, d_i\}$. That is, the estimate lies in an expanding sequence of sub-spaces spanned by the search-directions. Algorithms that select the estimate as $x_i \in x_0 + \mathbb{K}_i$, for some $\mathbb{K}_i$, are known as *projection methods*.[1] Because α_i is chosen to minimise the objective f along the search direction, the resulting gradient r_{i+1} is orthogonal to d_i (but not necessarily to all d_j for $j \leq i$). More generally, there is a space $\mathbb{L}_i$ orthogonal to the gradient,

$$\nabla f(x_i) = r_i = Ax_i - b \perp \mathbb{L}_i. \qquad (18.1)$$

Methods for which $\mathbb{K} = \mathbb{L}$ are called *orthogonal* projection methods, and Eq. (18.1) is then known as the *Galerkin condition*.[2]

▶ 18.2 Conjugate Directions

A further restriction of orthogonal direction methods is formed by *conjugate directions* methods.

Definition 18.1 (Conjugate directions). *Given a symmetric matrix $A \in \mathbb{R}^{N \times N}$, two vectors $v, w \in \mathbb{R}^N$ are called A-conjugate to each other if $v^\mathsf{T} Aw = 0$. An iterative linear solver for $Ax = b$ with*

[1] Meister (2011), Def. 4.58

[2] Conversely, if $\mathbb{K} \neq \mathbb{L}$, the term *oblique-projection method* is occasionally used; Eq. (18.1) is then denoted as the *Petrov–Galerkin* condition. Galerkin's name is attached to these methods because they relate to Galerkin methods, a family of solvers for partial differential equations that solve a high- or infinite-dimensional problem by *projecting* to a lower-dimensional space.

symmetric A is called a conjugate directions method *if it chooses projections d_i that are pairwise A-conjugate to each other.*

Conjugate directions methods converge to the correct solution x in at most N steps,[3] a property called *linear consistency*. They also ensure that the gradient r_k after k steps is orthogonal to the preceding search directions,[4] i.e. $r_k^\mathsf{T} p_i = 0$ for $i < k$. So they are orthogonal projection methods.

[3] Nocedal and Wright (1999), Thm. 5.1

[4] Nocedal and Wright (1999), Thm. 5.2

The following result connects our skeletal Algorithm 17.2 to conjugate direction methods. For the sake of readability, most technical derivations have been moved to the end of the chapter.

Theorem 18.2 (proof on p. 183). *If A is symmetric, and the inference rule in line 12 of Algorithm 17.2 produces a* symmetric *estimator H_i, then Algorithm 17.2 is a conjugate directions method.*

▶ **18.3   Krylov Subspace Methods**

Another important sub-class of projection methods is formed by choosing $\mathbb{K}_i$ as the *Krylov sequence*

$$\mathbb{K}_i = \mathcal{K}^i(r_0, A) = \operatorname{span}\{r_0, Ar_0, A^2 r_0, \ldots, A^{i-1} r_0\}. \quad (18.2)$$

Such algorithms are called *Krylov subspace methods*. They include the aforementioned seminal CG and GMRES. Krylov subspace methods have been studied in great detail since the 1980s. In addition to the textbooks already mentioned above, further information can also be found in the books by Demmel (1997), Greenbaum (1997), and Saad (2003). Due to the generic form of line 12, Algorithm 17.2 is not a Krylov subspace method in general, but we will see below what we need to do to make it one.

▶ **18.4   Conjugate Gradients**

One characterisation of CG is that it is the conjugate direction method that is also a Krylov subspace method. Section 19.9 will identify a class of probabilistic models under which $\mathbb{K}_i$ is the Krylov sequence. Under this choice, Algorithm 17.2 will be shown to be equivalent to the method of conjugate gradients, based on the following technical result.

As in the preceding section, assume that the estimator H_i constructed in line 12 of Algorithm 17.2 is symmetric. Further, now assume that H_i is selected[5] such that, for all $i \geq 1$,

[5] Eq. (18.3) is obviously redundant, because the spans of S_i, Y_i, and r_i may overlap. This somewhat awkward form is deliberate, as it will later simplify the construction of concrete probability measures satisfying this restriction. Lemma 18.3 clears out the notational undergrowth, revealing that the assumption can be written much more succinctly.

$$d_i = -H_{i-1}r_{i-1} \in \text{span}\{s_1, \ldots, s_{i-1}, y_1, \ldots, y_{i-1}, r_{i-1}\}. \quad (18.3)$$

The following lemma establishes the connection to Krylov subspace methods.

Lemma 18.3 (proof on p. 184). *Assumption (18.3) is equivalent to the statement that Algorithm 17.2 is a Krylov subspace method, i.e. it is equivalent to the statement*

$$s_i \in \text{span}\{r_0, Ar_0, A^2 r_0, \ldots, A^{i-1} r_0\}. \quad (18.4)$$

We will now show the following Theorem.

Theorem 18.4 (proof on p. 184). *If A is SPD, H_i is symmetric for all $i \geq 0$, Assumption (18.3) holds, and Algorithm 17.2 does not terminate before step $k < N$, then*

$$r_i \perp r_j \quad \forall 0 \leq i \neq j \leq k,$$

and there exist $\gamma_i \in \mathbb{R}_{\backslash 0}$ for all $i < k$ so that line 12 in Algorithm 17.2 can be written as

$$d_i = -H_{i-1}r_{i-1} = \gamma_i \left(-r_{i-1} + \frac{\beta_i}{\gamma_{i-1}} d_{i-1} \right), \quad (18.5)$$

with

$$\beta_i := \frac{r_{i-1}^\mathsf{T} r_{i-1}}{r_{i-2}^\mathsf{T} r_{i-2}}.$$

Comparing Algorithm 17.2 to CG (Algorithm 16.1), we note that they are identical up to re-scaling by γ_i:

$$d_i^{\text{CG}} = \gamma_i d_i^{\text{Probabilistic}}.$$

Since the scaling $\gamma_i \in \mathbb{R}$ is cancelled by the step size α_i in line 7, the two algorithms produce the same sequence of estimates $\{x_i\}$, and we have the following result:

Corollary 18.5. *Under the assumptions of Theorem 18.4 on the estimators H_i, Algorithm 17.2 is equivalent to the method of conjugate gradients, in the sense that it produces the exact same sequence $\{x_0, x_1, \ldots, x_N\}$ of estimates as CG initialised at $x_0 = H_0 b$.*

Figure 18.1 depicts how the gradients are sampled by CG – or equivalently, if the Assumptions of Theorem 18.4 are satisfied, by Algorithm 17.2.

▶ **18.5   Preconditioning**

Krylov subspaces (Eq. (18.2)) have the following invariance properties[6] for scalars $\sigma, \tau \in \mathbb{R}_{\backslash 0}$ and orthonormal matrices U

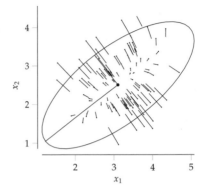

Figure 18.1: Analogous plot to Figure 17.1. The gradients at points sampled independent of the problem's structure ("needles" of point and gradient as black line, drawn from spherical Gaussian distribution around the extremum) are likely to be dominated by the eigenvectors of the largest eigenvalues. Thus, by following the gradient of the problem, one can efficiently compute a low-rank approximation of A that captures most of the dominant structure. This intuition is at the heart of the *Lanczos process* that provides the structure of conjugate gradients.

[6] Parlett (1980), §12.2.2

(i.e. $U^\mathsf{T} = U^{-1}$):

$$\text{scaling:} \qquad \mathcal{K}^m(\sigma r, \tau A) = \mathcal{K}^m(r, A),$$
$$\text{translation:} \qquad \mathcal{K}^m(r, A + \sigma I) = \mathcal{K}^m(r, A),$$
$$\text{change of basis:} \qquad \mathcal{K}^m(Ur, UAU^\mathsf{T}) = U\mathcal{K}^m(r, A). \quad (18.6)$$

A generalisation of the last Equation (18.6) is the notion of a *preconditioned* iterative solver. Take a non-singular matrix C, and consider the transformed – the *pre-conditioned* – problem

$$\tilde{A}\tilde{x} = \tilde{b} \quad \text{with} \qquad\qquad (18.7)$$
$$\tilde{A} := C^{-\mathsf{T}}AC^{-1}, \quad \tilde{x} := Cx, \quad \tilde{b} = C^{-\mathsf{T}}b.$$

If C is chosen smartly, the conjugate gradient method can converge significantly faster on the transformed system (18.7) than on the original one. As shown in Algorithm 18.1, preconditioning can be almost totally externalised from the basic solver, by adding only two additional lines, both solving a linear problem of the form $Ky = r_{k+1}$, with the matrix $K = CC^\mathsf{T}$. The ideal but impractical choice is $K = A$, which directly yields the exact solution in one step. Of course, having to compute the inverse C^{-1} of what would then be the matrix square root of A begs the question of running the solver in the first place. Good choices of pre-conditioners C are thus some form of incomplete or approximate decompositions of A that can be efficiently inverted.[7] contains a general introduction to the topic and some specific examples.

[7] For a general introduction to this topic and some specific examples, see Golub and Van Loan (1996), §11.5.

Let us return to the context of probabilistic solvers, and speak simplistically for the moment. Imagine that we find a probability measure $p_{\text{CG}}(A)$ over A consistent with the conjugate gradient method, in the sense of Theorem 18.4. Then consider a variation $p_{\text{PCG}}(A)$ of it that maps d_i to the transformed space

$$d_i \in \text{span}\{s_1, \ldots, s_{i-1}, y_1, \ldots, y_{i-1}, K^{-1}r_{i-1}\}. \qquad (18.8)$$

Then, $p_{\text{PCG}}(A)$ is consistent with a preconditioned conjugate gradient method using the pre-conditioner $K = CC^\mathsf{T}$.

Since the process of preconditioning involves using an *a priori guess* K^{-1} for the matrix inverse H to simplify the work of the solver, it will be no surprise for us to find later (Corollary 19.17) that this modification in Eq. (18.8) is associated with a change to the prior of a probabilistic solver. And, with the derivations still to follow, we can already anticipate that the ideal choice $K = A$ will be associated with a particularly "natural" prior.

```
1  procedure pCG(A(·), b, x₀)
2      r₀ = Ax₀ − b                        // initial gradient
3      g₀ = K⁻¹r₀                          // corrected gradient
4      d₀ = 0, β₀ = 0                      // for notational clarity
5      for i = 1, . . . , N do
6          dᵢ = −gᵢ₋₁ + βᵢ₋₁pᵢ₋₁          // compute direction
7          zᵢ = Adᵢ                        // compute
8          αᵢ = −dᵢᵀrᵢ₋₁/dᵢᵀzᵢ            // optimal step-size
9          sᵢ = αᵢdᵢ                       // re-scale step
10         yᵢ = αᵢzᵢ                       // re-scale observation
11         xᵢ = xᵢ₋₁ + sᵢ                  // update estimate for x
12         rᵢ = rᵢ₋₁ + yᵢ                  // new gradient at xᵢ
13         gᵢ = K⁻¹rᵢ                      // corrected gradient
14         βᵢ = rᵢᵀgᵢ/rᵢ₋₁ᵀrᵢ₋₁           // compute conjugate correction
15     end for
16 end procedure
```

Algorithm 18.1: Preconditioned conjugate gradients. Adapted from Nocedal and Wright (1999). The only difference to Algorithm 16.1 is the construction of the corrected gradient in lines 3 and 13.

► **18.6   Summary: Connecting Algorithm 17.2 to Classic Solvers**

This section cast several families of classic linear solvers in the notation of Algorithm 17.2. Doing so identified certain properties of the prior measure $p(A)$ that make Algorithm 17.2 equivalent to these classic methods: any probabilistic estimator for the matrix inverse H which is merely consistent with observations can give rise to a projection method. If the estimate is also symmetric, Algorithm 17.2 becomes a conjugate directions method. Finally, we identified certain technical properties that make the algorithm equivalent to the method of conjugate gradients, and its preconditioned generalisation.

None of these restrictions directly imply a concrete form for $p(A)$; in particular, not a Gaussian one. So the situation in linear algebra differs from that in integration, where each quadrature rule was directly associated, up to a single scalar degree of freedom, with a particular Gaussian process prior on the integrand. The underlying abstract reason is that iterative linear solvers do a comparably simple job: an $N \times N$ invertible matrix has a *finite* number N^2 of degrees of freedom. At each iteration, the solver identifies N of them perfectly, while learning nothing about the other $N(N-1)$. Because of this, the *estimation* aspect of the computation is less pronounced than in, say, integration, where a finite number of evaluations must be used to estimate an infinite sum. Linear algebra, to a significant degree, amounts to sophisticated book-keeping rather than inferring an intractable object.

This is not to say there is no use for uncertainty in linear solvers. It just so happens that classic solvers address a corner case, one less demanding of uncertainty. It is nevertheless useful to understand the connection to probabilistic inference in this domain, because uncertainty is more prominently important if:

⊖ the object of interest is an infinite-dimensional operator, rather than a finite matrix (this situation arises in the solution of partial differential equations); or

⊖ the question at hand involves the matrix inverse itself more than the estimate of the solution. For example if we want to compute Laplace approximations to large-scale models like deep neural networks,[8] which involve the *inverse* Hessian of the regularised empirical loss. Such matrices are routinely much too large to be directly inverted. But they can also have a limited number of prominent eigenvalues. If we use an iterative solver in such situations, we will be forced to stop it very early compared to the size of the matrix, and then look for a good uncertainty estimate over the "unexplored" remainder; or

⊖ the projection observations are corrupted by noise. This situation arises regularly in machine learning applications when data is sub-sampled to lower computational cost. Sometimes such situations can be re-phrased as projections of a Schur complement, which is effectively a reduction to the previous points.

[8] MacKay (1992); Daxberger et al. (2021).

A lack of restrictions is simultaneously a blessing and a curse for our search of a probabilistic interpretation of linear algebra. We may worry, if many quite different probabilistic priors can simultaneously be associated with, say, the conjugate gradient strategy, which is the *right* one? The answer we will find is: it depends. On the one hand, considerable additional prior assumptions will be required to arrive at a tractable uncertainty estimate. On the other, it will become clear that different kinds of priors may be useful to address different kinds of tasks.

Probabilistic Linear Solvers: Algorithmic Scaffold

▶ **19.1 Gaussian Distributions over Matrices**

To build a concrete solver, we need a concrete family of probability distributions over matrices. And since matrices are structured objects, constructing such a family is not entirely straightforward. There are arbitrarily many ways to define a probability measure over the elements of a real matrix. To arrive at tractable forms, though, we require a probability measure that "fits well" with observations of the form $Y = AS$.

For example, the widely known Wishart distribution[1] might at first seem like a great choice to model least-squares problems (Eq. (16.1)), since it assigns probability density to only symmetric positive definite matrices.[2] Unfortunately, the posterior arising from conditioning on the linear projections (Y, S) is not Wishart, and has no obvious compact form. However, see Exercise 19.4 and Section 15.2 for a further discussion of how the Wishart distribution can be connected, at least in approximation, to the following derivations.

Instead of the Wishart, we will once again resort to Gaussian distributions. It is straightforward to define a joint Gaussian measure over the elements of any real matrix, even a rectangular $X \in \mathbb{R}^{N \times K}$ by using the vectorisation operation (§15.1) and using the multivariate Gaussian distribution over vectors to define[3]

$$\mathcal{N}(X; X_0, \Sigma_0) := \frac{\exp\left(-\frac{1}{2}(\vec{X} - \vec{X}_0)^{\mathsf{T}}\Sigma_0^{-1}(\vec{X} - \vec{X}_0)\right)}{(2\pi)^{NK/2}|\Sigma_0|^{1/2}}, \quad (19.3)$$

where $\vec{X}_0$ is any vector in $\mathbb{R}^{NK}$, interpreted as a vectorised

[1] Wishart (1928)

[2] The Wishart distribution $\mathcal{W}(X; V, \nu)$ is the measure over symmetric matrices $X \in \mathbb{R}^{N \times N}$ with $\nu > N - 1 \in \mathbb{R}$ *degrees of freedom* and the the positive definite *scale matrix* $V \in \mathbb{R}^{N \times N}$, defined by probability density function (suppressing a complicated normalisation constant)

$$\mathcal{W}(X; V, \nu) \propto |X|^{(\nu-N-1)/2}e^{-1/2\operatorname{tr}(V^{-1}X)}. \quad (19.1)$$

It can also be characterised as the measure arising from the following generative process. Consider ν vectors $w_i \in \mathbb{R}^N$ drawn independently from $p(w_i) = \mathcal{N}(0, V)$. Then the symmetric $N \times N$ matrix

$$X = \sum_{i=1}^{\nu} w_i w_i^{\mathsf{T}} \quad (19.2)$$

has distribution $\mathcal{W}(X; V, \nu)$.

[3] We will omit the arrow over matrices in the shorthand $\mathcal{N}(\cdot; \cdot, \cdot)$. For matrices, the Gaussian distribution will always be used in this sense, so there is no risk of ambiguity.

matrix, and Σ_0 is a symmetric, positive semi-definite matrix in $\mathbb{R}^{NK \times NK}$. If Σ_0 is full rank (i.e. if it is SPD), this distribution assigns non-zero measure to *every* matrix in $\mathbb{R}^{NK}$. In particular, if X is square, this distribution assigns non-vanishing measure to symmetric and asymmetric, to positive definite and indefinite matrices, and to invertible and non-invertible ones. Sections 19.5 and 19.6 will consider what kind of restrictions to this generality can, and cannot, be readily incorporated in a Gaussian prior. For the moment, though, we consider the general form of Eq. (19.3).

▶ 19.2   A Prior over A, H, or x?

When considering probabilistic formulations of the linear problem, we have to consider what, exactly, are the uncertain aspects of the equation $Ax = b$. Is it just the vector x? Are we looking for one solution x for one particular b, or for the general inverse $H = A^{-1}$ that can solve for any b? In fact, we may even be uncertain about the elements of A themselves, because being able to perform multiplications $Ad = z$ for arbitrary $d \in \mathbb{R}^N$ (the only operation on A required for Algorithm 17.2) is not the same as having access to every element of A.[4] For the majority of this chapter, we will consider the more general problem of inferring the matrix-valued objects. Section 20.2 considers simplifications arising if one only requires one particular solution x to one particular b. This means there are principally two different ways to use a Gaussian prior in the solution of a linear system. Both have historical[5] and practical relevance.

1. One may treat the matrix A itself as the latent object, and define a joint probability distribution[6] $p(A, Y, S)$. This model class will be called *inference on A*. This approach has the advantage that the computation of the matrix-matrix product $AS = Y$ is described explicitly. This would be relevant, for example, if the main source of uncertainty is in this computation itself – if we do not actually compute exact matrix-matrix multiplications, but only approximations of it (a setting not further discussed here).

    The downside of this formulation is that it does not explicitly involve x. This is an issue because a tractable probability distribution on A may induce a complicated distribution on x. For intuition, Figure 19.1 shows distributions of the inverse of a scalar Gaussian variable of varying mean. For matrices, the situation is even more complicated, as the probability measure might put non-vanishing density on matrices that

[4] Instead, A may be an implicitly defined linear operation. For example, a convolution operation can be defined as "take the Fourier transform of x, multiply the resulting vector element-wise, then take the Fourier back-transform", and can be implemented without actually writing it out as an explicit matrix.

[5] Dennis and Moré (1977), §7.3

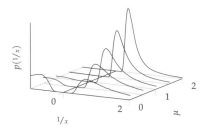

Figure 19.1: Inverses of Gaussian variables are not themselves normal distributed. The plot shows the distribution of x^{-1} if $p(x) = \mathcal{N}(x; \mu, 1)$, for five different values of μ. Since $(x + \epsilon)^{-1} \approx x^{-1} - \epsilon x^{-2}$, in the limit $|\mu| \to \infty$, the distribution approaches

$$p(x^{-1}) \approx \mathcal{N}(x^{-1}; \mu^{-1}, \mu^{-4}).$$

However, for small values of μ, the distribution becomes strongly bi-modal. It is therefore clear that we will have to resort to approximations if we want to infer both matrices and their inverse while using a Gaussian distribution to model either variable. See also Figure 19.9 for more discussion.

[6] We will generally assume that b itself is known with certainty, and thus not explicitly include it in the generative model.

do not even have an inverse to begin with.

2. The alternative is to write the solution x explicitly as

$$x = Hb$$

(recall that we assumed A to be SPD, so the inverse $H = A^{-1}$ exists), and to formulate a distribution $p(H, Y, S)$ on H. This approach will be called *inference on* H. The advantage of this formulation is that, since x is a linear function of H, simple tractable posteriors on H translate into tractable posteriors on x. The downside is that if $Y = AS$ does not hold exactly – if the computations are performed approximately – it can be difficult to capture the likelihood $p(Y, S \mid H)$.

We will focus on the special but important case that observations $Z = AD$ are made without noise. In this setting, the same set of observations can be written as linear maps of either A or H:

$$Z = AD \qquad \Longleftrightarrow \qquad D = HZ.$$

In this case, inference on A can be directly transformed into inference on H by simultaneously exchanging

$$S \leftrightarrow Y \qquad \text{and} \qquad A \leftrightarrow H.$$

Because of this connection, to avoid cluttering notation, we will consider only inference on A for the moment, and return to study inference on H later.

▶ **19.3   General Gaussian Inference**

How far can we get with a general Gaussian prior

$$p(A; A_0, \Sigma_0) = \mathcal{N}(A; A_0, \Sigma_0)$$

over the elements of A? The observations $Y = AS$ can be cast as a Dirac likelihood, the limit of a Gaussian likelihood:

$$p(S, Y \mid A) = \delta\big(\vec{Y} - (I \otimes S^{\mathsf{T}})\vec{A}\big) = \lim_{\beta \to 0} \mathcal{N}\big(Y; (I \otimes S^{\mathsf{T}})\vec{A}, \beta\Lambda\big),$$

for any constant, SPD $\Lambda \in \mathbb{R}^{NM \times NM}$ (recall that M is the number of observations: $S \in \mathbb{R}^{N \times M}$). The Kronecker product formulation shows that the observation Y is a *linear* projection of the elements of A, hence the posterior measure arising from this conditioning observation will also have Gaussian form. From Eqs. (3.10) and (3.8), it is

$$p(A \mid Y, S) = \mathcal{N}(A; A_M, \Sigma_M), \qquad (19.4)$$

with mean and covariance given by, respectively,

$$\vec{A}_M := \vec{A}_0 + \Sigma_0(I \otimes S)\underbrace{\left((I \otimes S^\mathsf{T})\Sigma_0(I \otimes S)\right)^{-1}}_{=:G_M}(\vec{Y} - (I \otimes S^\mathsf{T})\vec{A}_0), \text{ and} \qquad (19.5)$$

$$\Sigma_M := \Sigma_0 - \Sigma_0(I \otimes S)\left((I \otimes S^\mathsf{T})\Sigma_0(I \otimes S)\right)^{-1}(I \otimes S^\mathsf{T})\Sigma_0. \qquad (19.6)$$

Unfortunately, the Gram matrix G_M featuring in both mean and covariance is of size $NM \times NM$, and hence actually *larger* than the original $N \times N$ matrix. But there is little point in an inference model for the inverse of a matrix which requires computing the inverse of an even larger matrix! Thus, some structure will have to be imposed on Σ_0 to simplify the posterior's parameters, and build a practical algorithm.

We briefly reassure ourselves that, no matter the prior covariance Σ_0, the posterior of Eq. (19.4) is consistent with the observations, in the sense that it only puts non-zero mass on matrices $\tilde{A}$ obeying $\tilde{A}S = Y$. In this regard, we use the general property of Gaussian measures from Eq. (3.4) to see that the marginal distribution over the linear projection $\overrightarrow{A\tilde{S}} = (I \otimes S)^\mathsf{T}\vec{A}$ is

$$p(AS) = \mathcal{N}\left(\overrightarrow{A\tilde{S}}; (I \otimes S)^\mathsf{T}\vec{A}_M, (I \otimes S)^\mathsf{T}\Sigma_M(I \otimes S)\right) \quad (19.7)$$
$$= \mathcal{N}(\overrightarrow{A\tilde{S}}; Y, 0).$$

Hence, any sample $\tilde{A}$ from this measure is consistent with the observations. If this sample is invertible, it also has the property $\tilde{A}^{-1}Y = S$ required in Algorithm 17.2. This holds, in particular, also for the posterior mean A_M. To arrive at a practical algorithm, we will now consider two classes of covariances. Each allows efficient inference over matrix elements, and also ensures that A_M is invertible, with an analytically computable inverse. As such, they provide a good candidate for the estimators H_i used in Algorithm 17.2.

▶ **19.4   Kronecker Covariances for Efficient Computation**

The general Gaussian prior (19.3) is quite a flexible model; it allows for arbitrary covariance between any pair of matrix elements. To reduce computational cost, we can try to restrict the expressive power of Σ_0.

This situation is not unrelated to that in integration. To construct tractable integration methods in Chapter II, we had to restrict the prior to GP models with mean and covariance functions on the integrand chosen such that the posterior mean could be analytically integrated. In this chapter, we will similarly be forced to restrict the prior covariance on matrix elements to a class that allows analytic inversion of the posterior mean. While it is a somewhat ill-posed task to identify the set of all analytically integrable kernels for quadrature, we will below identify a concrete class of tractable priors for linear algebra.

A naïve choice would be to model all matrix elements as independent of each other. This corresponds to a diagonal Σ_0, and means computing G costs $\mathcal{O}(NM^2)$. However, this leads to a G whose inversion costs more than M^3 (Exercise 19.1), which is still an unacceptably high cost.

Exercise 19.1 (intermediate, and somewhat tedious. Solution on p. 362). *Consider the assumption $\Sigma_{ij,k\ell} = \delta_{ik}\delta_{j\ell}W_{ij}$, with a positive definite W. It amounts to an independent Gaussian prior, of variance W_{ij}, for every single matrix element. Show that this choice gives rise to a G in Eq. (19.5) whose inverse involves N separate positive definite matrices, each of size $M \times M$.*

A better prior would encode the fact that $\vec{A}$ is not just a long vector, but contains the elements of a square matrix. The projections terms $(I \otimes S)$, with their Kronecker product structure, already contain information about the generative process of the observations. We thus consider a Kronecker product for the prior covariance, too:[7]

$$\Sigma_0 = V_0 \otimes W_0 \qquad \text{with SPD } V_0, W_0 \in \mathbb{R}^{N \times N}. \qquad (19.8)$$

What kind of prior assumptions are we making here? If both matrices in a Kronecker product are SPD, so is their Kronecker product (see Eq. (15.6)). Hence, Eq. (19.8) yields an SPD overall covariance, and the prior assigns non-vanishing probability density to every matrix A, including non-invertible, indefinite ones, etc., despite the fact that such SPD matrices V_0, W_0 only offer

$$2 \cdot \left(1/2N(N+1)\right) = N(N+1)$$

degrees of freedom (as opposed to the $1/2N^2(N^2+1)$ degrees of freedom in a general SPD Σ_0).[8]

The prior assumptions encoded by a Kronecker product in the covariance are subtle. A few intuitive observations follow. The Kronecker covariance can be written as

$$\text{cov}(A_{ij}, A_{k\ell}) = [V_0 \otimes W_0]_{ij,k\ell} = [V_0]_{ik} \cdot [W_0]_{j\ell}. \qquad (19.9)$$

As such, it is tempting to think of V_0 as capturing covariance "among the rows" and W_0 "among the columns" (Figure 19.2). This is not entirely incorrect. Consider the following process to create a matrix $\tilde{A}$:

1. Draw N column-vectors $b_i \in \mathbb{R}^{N \times 1}, i = 1, \dots, N$ i.i.d. as

$$b_i \sim \mathcal{N}(0, V_0).$$

2. Draw N row-vectors $c_j \in \mathbb{R}^{1 \times N}, i = 1, \dots, N$ i.i.d. as

$$c_j \sim \mathcal{N}(0, W_0).$$

[7] Distributions of the form $\mathcal{N}(X; X_0, V \otimes W)$ are sometimes called a *matrix-variate normal*, due to a paper by Dawid (1981). This convention will be avoided here, since it can give the incorrect impression that this is the only possibility to assign a Gaussian distribution over the elements of a matrix, when in fact Eq. (19.3) is the most general such distribution.

[8] One helpful intuition for this situation is to convince oneself that the space of Kronecker products spans a sub-space of rank one within the space of $N^2 \times N^2$ real matrices, and that this sub-space does contain a space of SPD matrices.

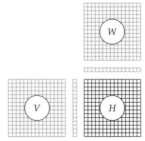

Figure 19.2: Imposing Kronecker product structure $V \otimes W$ on the prior covariance means the covariance over matrix elements is governed by two factors. V affects covariance as a function of row number, W as a function of column number. This is not quite the same as assuming the matrix itself is a product of two terms.

3. Set $\tilde{A}_{ij} = b_i c_j + A_{0,ij}$ i.e. $\tilde{A} = B \odot C + A_0$, if B and C denote the matrices resulting from arranging the vectors b_i and c_j into square matrices in the obvious way.

The matrix $\tilde{A}$ arising from this process is *not* Gaussian distributed.[9] But it indeed[10] satisfies Eq. (19.9): the covariance is Kronecker-structured.

Another helpful observation is that the marginal variance of individual matrix elements under the choice $\Sigma_0 = V_0 \otimes W_0$ is determined solely by the diagonals of the two matrices in the Kronecker product:

$$\text{var}(A_{ij}) = [V_{A0}]_{ii} \cdot [W_{A0}]_{jj}.$$

Figure 19.3 shows five samples each from two different Gaussian distributions with Kronecker product covariance.

The main takeaway is that while the Kronecker covariance does represent a helpful restriction, it is not one that limits the space of matrices that we can infer. The prior measure encompasses all matrices.

What Kronecker structure on the covariance *does* achieve is a drastic reduction of computational complexity.Choosing Σ_0 as in Eq. (19.8) shortens the posterior's mean and covariance (Eqs. (19.5) and (19.6)) to, respectively,

$$A_M = A_0 + \underbrace{(Y - A_0 S)}_{=:\Delta_M \in \mathbb{R}^{N \times M}} \underbrace{(S^\mathsf{T} W_0 S)^{-1}}_{\in \mathbb{R}^{M \times M}} \underbrace{S^\mathsf{T} W_0}_{\in \mathbb{R}^{M \times N}}, \quad \text{and} \quad (19.10)$$

$$\Sigma_M = V_0 \otimes \underbrace{\left(W_0 - W_0 S (S^\mathsf{T} W_0 S)^{-1} S^\mathsf{T} W_0 \right)}_{=:W_M}. \quad (19.11)$$

Note the absence of arrows over A_M and H_M. The posterior mean A_M is a sum of the prior mean (which can, of course, be chosen to be simple, e.g. a scalar or diagonal matrix), and an *outer product* of rank at most M. All the objects can be stored in $\mathcal{O}(NM^2)$, and they contain a single matrix inverse of only an $M \times M$ matrix. The terms in this outer product are:

Δ_M the residual between the expected value $A_0 S$ (the prediction for Y under the prior), and the actual observation,

$S^\mathsf{T} W_0 S$ the predictive covariance between the rows of the residual, and

$S^\mathsf{T} W_0$ the predictive covariance between the residual's rows and the rows of A.

[9] NB: the product of two Gaussian probability distributions is another Gaussian distribution (times a Gaussian normalisation constant). But the product of two Gaussian *random variables* is *not* itself a Gaussian random variable!

[10] This is because

$$\mathbb{E}\left(\tilde{A}_{ij}\tilde{A}_{k\ell} - \mathbb{E}(\tilde{A}_{ij})\mathbb{E}(\tilde{A}_{k\ell})\right)$$
$$= \mathbb{E}(a_i b_j a_k b_\ell) = [V_0]_{ik} \cdot [W_0]_{j\ell}.$$

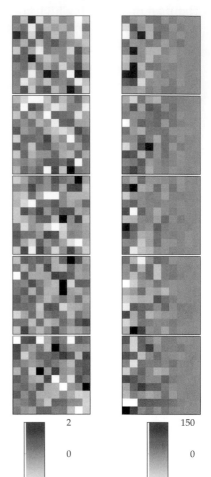

Figure 19.3: Five i.i.d. samples from the distribution $\mathcal{N}(I, V_0 \otimes W_0)$ for the choices $V_0 = W_0 = I$ (left column) and $V_0 = \text{diag}[10^4, 9^4, 8^4, \dots]$, $W_0 = I$ (right column), respectively.

Exercise 19.2 (easy). *Using Eqs. (15.2) to (15.7), prove that the choice (19.8) simplifies Eqs. (19.5) & (19.6) to (19.10) & (19.11), respectively.*

The vector Y shows up in A_M without a mapping to its left. In the simple case of $A_0 = 0$, the columns of A_M are a scaled copy of Y, with each rows transformed by W_0. This is reflected in the posterior variance: Observing linear projections of all the rows of A, given assumptions about the covariance along rows and columns, affects the "uncertainty along the rows", but not "along the columns".

The posterior mean A_M of Equation (19.10) provides an estimator for A. Algorithm 17.2 instead requires an estimator for $H = A^{-1}$. Thanks to the low-rank structure of A_M, however, it is straightforward to compute its inverse, and use it as such an estimator $H_i = A_i^{-1}$. Using the matrix inversion lemma (15.9), we find, after a few simple re-arrangements,

$$A_M^{-1} = (A_0 + \Delta_{AM}(S^\mathsf{T}W_0S)^{-1}S^\mathsf{T}W_0)^{-1} \qquad (19.12)$$
$$= A_0^{-1} + (S - A_0^{-1}Y)(S^\mathsf{T}W_0A_0^{-1}Y)^{-1}S^\mathsf{T}W_0A_0^{-1}.$$

But we remind ourselves that this inverse of the expected value of A is not the same as the expected value of the inverse! The latter is more challenging to compute. Nevertheless the following result shows that, for sensible choices of the prior parameters A_0 and W_0, the estimate A_M^{-1} exists.

Lemma 19.3. *Assume A_0 and W_0 are* SPD, *and the search directions S are chosen to be linearly independent. Then, for our assumption of* SPD A, *the inverse (19.12) exists.*

Proof. If A_0 is SPD, its inverse exists. $Y = AS$, and products of SPD matrices are SPD. Thus, $W_0A_0^{-1}A$ is SPD, hence $S^\mathsf{T}W_0A_0^{-1}AS$ invertible. $\square$

We thus have our first way to concretely realise Algorithm 17.2: Its line 12 can be implemented by assigning the Gaussian prior

$$p(A) = \mathcal{N}(A; A_0, V_0 \otimes W_0), \qquad \text{with } A_0, V_0, W_0 \text{ SPD}, \quad (19.13)$$

to A, which gives rise to the posterior mean of Eq. (19.10). If the directions S are independent, the inverse of the mean is given by Eq. (19.12) and provides the estimator H_i.[11] That is, explicitly,

$$H_i = (A_0 + \Delta_{AM}(S^\mathsf{T}W_0S)^{-1}S^\mathsf{T}W_0)^{-1}$$
$$= A_0^{-1} + (S - A_0^{-1}Y)(S^\mathsf{T}W_0A_0^{-1}Y)^{-1}S^\mathsf{T}W_0A_0^{-1}.$$

[11] If the columns of S are *not* linearly independent, this could be rectified internally in the solver by keeping track of a linearly independent sub-space. Doing so would require extra linear algebra operations (for example it could be realised using the SVD of S).

▶ **19.5   Encoding Symmetry**

We defined the problem $Ax = b$ with the assumption that A is a symmetric positive definite matrix. The priors on A or A^{-1} considered so far, however, do not encode this knowledge yet. They assign non-zero probability density to all real-valued matrices. This is not just an aesthetic shortcoming: §18.2 guarantees conjugacy of the search directions if the estimator H_M is symmetric; but the estimator of Eq. (19.12) is not symmetric in general.

We will now find that *symmetry* can be encoded in the prior, with a bit of legwork, without deviating from tractable Gaussian inference. This is because symmetry is a *linear* constraint; it can be written as the set of linear equations

$$A_{ij} - A_{ji} = 0, \qquad \forall\, 1 \le i, j \le N.$$

From Eq. (3.4), we recall that the Gaussian family is closed under such constraints. In contrast, positive definiteness is a considerably more intricate property because the positive definite cone is not a linear sub-space of $\mathbb{R}^{N^2}$. A discussion of positive definiteness follows in §19.6.

To capture symmetry, will begin by simplifying the prior covariance from Eq. (19.13) to the choice $V_0 = W_0$, i.e.

$$p(A) = \mathcal{N}(A; A_0, W_0 \otimes W_0). \qquad (19.14)$$

This step alone does not encode symmetry (samples from this distribution are still asymmetric with probability one), but it avoids technical complications in the following.

For a formal treatment, we introduce two projection operators acting on the space $\mathbb{R}^{N^2}$ of square $N \times N$ matrices:

$\Pi_\ominus : \mathbb{R}^{N^2} \twoheadrightarrow \mathbb{R}^{N^2}$, with elements

$$\Pi_{\ominus\,(ij),(k\ell)} := \tfrac{1}{2}(\delta_{ik}\delta_{j\ell} + \delta_{i\ell}\delta_{jk}),$$

is the *projection onto the space of symmetric matrices*. It has the characteristic property

$$\natural\,\Pi_\ominus \vec{X} = \tfrac{1}{2}(X + X^\mathsf{T}).$$

$\Pi_\oplus : \mathbb{R}^{N^2} \twoheadrightarrow \mathbb{R}^{N^2}$, with elements

$$\Pi_{\oplus\,(ij),(k\ell)} := \tfrac{1}{2}(\delta_{ik}\delta_{j\ell} - \delta_{i\ell}\delta_{jk}),$$

is the *projection onto the space of anti-symmetric[12] matrices*. It has the characteristic property

$$\natural\,\Pi_\oplus \vec{X} = \tfrac{1}{2}(X - X^\mathsf{T}).$$

It is easy to convince oneself that $\Pi_\ominus$ and $\Pi_\oplus$ are orthogonal projection operators that jointly span $\mathbb{R}^{N^2}$, i.e. that[13]

[12] Also known as *skew-symmetric* matrices.

[13] This also implies that every matrix $X \in \mathbb{R}^{N \times N}$ can be written as a sum of a symmetric and an antisymmetric part:

$$\vec{X} = \Pi_\ominus \vec{X} + \Pi_\oplus \vec{X},$$

which holds simply because

$$X = \tfrac{1}{2}(X + X^\mathsf{T} + X - X^\mathsf{T}).$$

$$\Pi_\ominus\Pi_\ominus = \Pi_\ominus, \qquad \Pi_\oplus\Pi_\oplus = \Pi_\oplus, \quad \text{and}$$
$$\Pi_\ominus^\mathsf{T} = \Pi_\ominus, \qquad \Pi_\oplus^\mathsf{T} = \Pi_\oplus, \quad \text{and}$$
$$\Pi_\ominus\Pi_\oplus = \Pi_\oplus\Pi_\ominus = 0_{N^2}, \qquad \Pi_\ominus + \Pi_\oplus = I_{N^2}. \qquad (19.15)$$

We also notice that, for Kronecker products of a matrix W with itself, we have (leaving out a few simple lines of algebra)

$$[\Pi_\ominus(W \otimes W)\Pi_\oplus]_{(ij),(k\ell)}$$
$$= \frac{1}{4}(W_{ik}W_{j\ell} - W_{i\ell}W_{jk} - W_{ik}W_{j\ell} + W_{i\ell}W_{jk}) = 0.$$

So a Kronecker product of this type can be written as a direct sum of a "symmetric" part and an "anti-symmetric" part:

$$W \otimes W = \underbrace{\Pi_\ominus(W \otimes W)\Pi_\ominus}_{=:W \circledS W} + \underbrace{\Pi_\oplus(W \otimes W)\Pi_\oplus}_{=:W \circledA W}.$$

These two products are known[14] as the *symmetric Kronecker product* $W \circledS W$ and the *skew-symmetric Kronecker product* $W \circledA W$, with elements

$$[C \circledS D]_{(ij),(k\ell)} = 1/2(C_{ik}D_{j\ell} + C_{i\ell}D_{jk}), \text{ and} \qquad (19.16)$$
$$[C \circledA D]_{(ij),(k\ell)} = 1/2(C_{ik}D_{j\ell} - C_{i\ell}D_{jk}).$$

They inherit some, but not all, of the great properties of the Kronecker product. In particular, when applied to symmetric matrices,[15]

$$(W \circledS W)^{-1} = W^{-1} \circledS W^{-1}.$$

However,[16] for general C and D,

$$(C \circledS D)^{-1} \neq C^{-1} \circledS D^{-1}.$$

We also have

$$(C \circledS D)\vec{X} = 1/2(CXD^\mathsf{T} + CX^\mathsf{T}D^\mathsf{T}), \text{ and}$$
$$(C \circledA D)\vec{X} = 1/2(CXD^\mathsf{T} - CX^\mathsf{T}D^\mathsf{T}). \qquad (19.17)$$

Using this framework, the *information* about A's symmetry can be explicitly written as an observation with likelihood

$$p(\ominus|\,A) = \delta(\Pi_\oplus\vec{A} - 0) = \lim_{\beta \to 0} \mathcal{N}(\vec{0}_{N^2}; \Pi_\oplus\vec{A}, \beta I_{N^2}). \qquad (19.18)$$

By Eqs. (3.8) and (3.10), the density on A resulting from conditioning the prior (19.14) with this likelihood is

$$p(A\,|\ominus) = \mathcal{N}(A; \vec{A}_0 - \Sigma_0\Pi_\oplus^\mathsf{T}(\Pi_\oplus\Sigma_0\Pi_\oplus^\mathsf{T})^{-1}(-\Pi_\oplus\vec{A}_0),$$
$$\Sigma_0 - \Sigma_0\Pi_\oplus^\mathsf{T}(\Pi_\oplus\Sigma_0\Pi_\oplus^\mathsf{T})^{-1}\Pi_\oplus\Sigma_0). \qquad (19.19)$$

[14] van Loan (2000)

Exercise 19.4 (easy). *Show that for matrices X drawn from the Wishart distribution $\mathcal{W}(X; V, v)$ (defined in Eq. (19.1)) the elements of X have the covariance*

$$\mathrm{cov}(X_{ij}, X_{k\ell}) = 2v(V \circledS V).$$

Hint: Use the generative definition of Eq. (19.2). The fourth moment of a central normal distribution is given by Isserlis' theorem (Isserlis, 1918):

$$p(a) = \mathcal{N}(a; 0, \Sigma) \Rightarrow$$
$$\mathbb{E}(a_i a_j a_k a_\ell) = \Sigma_{ij}\Sigma_{k\ell} + \Sigma_{ik}\Sigma_{j\ell} + \Sigma_{i\ell}\Sigma_{jk}.$$

[15] If $W \in \mathbb{R}^{N \times N}$ is of full rank, the matrix $W \circledS W$ has rank $1/2 N(N+1)$, the dimension of the space of all real symmetric $N \times N$ matrices. That its inverse on that space is given by $W^{-1} \circledS W^{-1}$ can be seen from Eq. (19.17). The inverse on asymmetric matrices is not defined.
[16] Alizadeh, Haeberley, and Overton (1988)

Using the Kronecker structure $\Sigma_0 = W_0 \otimes W_0$ and the identity from Eq. (19.15), the mean reduces to its symmetric part:

$$\vec{A}_0 - (\Pi_\oplus + \Pi_\ominus)\Sigma_0\Pi_\oplus^\mathsf{T}(\Pi_\oplus\Sigma_0\Pi_\oplus^\mathsf{T})^{-1}\Pi_\oplus\vec{A}_0$$
$$= (\Pi_\oplus + \Pi_\ominus)\vec{A}_0 - \Pi_\oplus\vec{A}_0 = \Pi_\ominus\vec{A}_0,$$

while the covariance simplifies to a symmetric Kronecker product:

$$\Sigma_0 - \Sigma_0\Pi_\oplus^\mathsf{T}(\Pi_\oplus\Sigma_0\Pi_\oplus^\mathsf{T})^{-1}\Pi_\oplus\Sigma_0 = \Pi_\ominus\Sigma_0\Pi_\ominus = W_0 \otimes W_0.$$

The resulting probabilistic model

$$p(A) = \mathcal{N}(A; A_0, W_0) \otimes W_0) \tag{19.20}$$

with a symmetric prior mean matrix A_0, only assigns non-zero measure to symmetric matrices; samples from Eq. (19.20) are depicted in Figure 19.4. Like for the Kronecker product covariance, this prior, too, can be conditioned to the linear observations $Y = AS$, giving a posterior

$$p(A \mid Y, S, \ominus) = \frac{\delta(Y - AS)\mathcal{N}(A; A_0, W_0 \otimes W_0)}{\int \delta(Y - AS)\mathcal{N}(A; A_0, W_0 \otimes W_0)\, \mathrm{d}A}$$
$$= \mathcal{N}(A; A_M, \Sigma_M).$$

Some algebraic footwork[17] is required to find the posterior means and covariance, the analogues to Eqs. (19.10) and (19.11). They are

$$A_M = A_0 + (Y - A_0S)(S^\mathsf{T}W_0S)^{-1}S^\mathsf{T}W_0 \tag{19.21}$$
$$+ W_0S(S^\mathsf{T}W_0S)^{-1}(Y - A_0S)^\mathsf{T}$$
$$- W_0S(S^\mathsf{T}W_0S)^{-1}S^\mathsf{T}(Y - A_0S)(S^\mathsf{T}W_0S)^{-1}S^\mathsf{T}W_0,$$

$$\Sigma_M = W_M \otimes W_M, \text{ with (as in Eq. (19.11)),} \tag{19.22}$$
$$W_M := W_0 - W_0S(S^\mathsf{T}W_0S)^{-1}S^\mathsf{T}W_0.$$

These expressions, in particular the posterior mean A_M, play a central role not just in linear solvers, but also in nonlinear optimisation. Let us take a closer look. We first note that A_M is indeed symmetric if A_0 is symmetric, because $S^\mathsf{T}Y = S^\mathsf{T}AS$ is symmetric. What is less obvious is that the expression added to A_M is of at most rank $2M$. This can be seen by defining the helpful terms

$$U := W_0S(S^\mathsf{T}W_0S)^{-1} \quad \in \mathbb{R}^{N \times M} \quad \text{and} \tag{19.23}$$
$$V := (I - 1/2US^\mathsf{T})(Y - A_0S) \quad \in \mathbb{R}^{N \times M}.$$

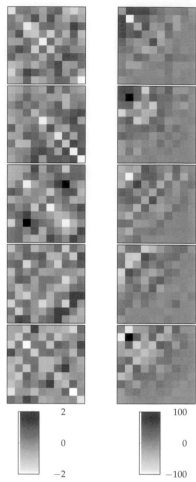

Figure 19.4: Samples from a Gaussian prior encoding symmetry. Results analogous to Figure 19.3. Five i.i.d. samples from the distribution of Eq. (19.20) for $W_0 = I$ (left column) and $W_0 = \mathrm{diag}[10^2, 9^2, 8^2, \dots]$ (right column), respectively. Note differing choice for W_0 relative to Figure 19.3, since W_0 here is in both terms of the product.

Exercise 19.5 (moderate). *Explicitly compute the evidence term*

$$\int \delta(Y - AS)\mathcal{N}(A; A_0, W_0 \otimes W_0)\, \mathrm{d}A.$$

What is its form?

[17] For a derivation, see Hennig (2015).

Exercise 19.6 (hard). *Derive the result in Eq. (19.21). In performing the derivation, try to gain an intuition for why the posterior mean (19.21) is not simply the symmetrised form $\Pi_\ominus A_M$ of the posterior mean from Eq. (19.10) (consider Eq. (19.19) for a hint).*

Using these, A_M can be written as

$$A_M = A_0 + UV^\mathsf{T} + VU^\mathsf{T} = A_0 + \begin{bmatrix} U & V \end{bmatrix} \begin{bmatrix} \mathbf{0} & I_M \\ I_M & \mathbf{0} \end{bmatrix} \begin{bmatrix} U^\mathsf{T} \\ V^\mathsf{T} \end{bmatrix}.$$

The inverse of this expression, if it exists, follows from the matrix inversion lemma:

$$A_M^{-1} = A_0^{-1} - A_0^{-1} \begin{bmatrix} U & V \end{bmatrix} \begin{bmatrix} U^\mathsf{T} A_0^{-1} U & U^\mathsf{T} A_0^{-1} V + I \\ V^\mathsf{T} A_0^{-1} U + I & V^\mathsf{T} A_0^{-1} V \end{bmatrix}^{-1} \begin{bmatrix} U^\mathsf{T} \\ V^\mathsf{T} \end{bmatrix} A_0^{-1}. \qquad (19.24)$$

There is no particularly enlightening way to simplify this expression for general model parameters A_0, W. But note that the matrix to be inverted on the right-hand side is of size $2M \times 2M$. So assuming the inverse of the prior mean A_0 is known or easy to compute, computation of this inverse estimator has complexity of *at most* $\mathcal{O}(M^3)$ (and multiplying with it has cost $\mathcal{O}(NM^2)$). Below we will find that there are special instances for which the complexity is significantly lower.

▶ **19.6   What about Positive Definiteness?**

Encoding symmetry in the prior is analytically feasible because it amounts to a linear constraint (Eq. (19.18)). Since we assume throughout this chapter that A is not just symmetric, but also positive definite, it would be desirable to also encode this information in the prior. Unfortunately, the space of positive definite matrices is a cone, a nonlinear sub-space of $\mathbb{R}^{N^2}$, the space of all (vectorised) square $N \times N$ matrices, and also a nonlinear sub-space of $\mathbb{R}^{1/2N(N+1)}$, the space of symmetric such matrices (see Figure 19.5). Information about positive definiteness can thus not be captured in a Gaussian likelihood term using only linear terms of A.

It is, however, possible to scale the parameters of the Gaussian prior post hoc to ensure that the posterior mean estimate always lies within the positive definite cone. This is helpful in so far as it means this posterior point estimate can be trusted to be admissible, and this is how this correction is used in practice. From a probabilistic perspective, however, this is not particularly satisfying since it means the model cannot make use of the known positive definiteness during inference.

The following is a minor generalisation of a derivation in a seminal review by Dennis and Moré (1977, §7.2) reproduced in some detail here because it provides valuable insights, also used in Chapter IV. Consider the symmetry-encoding prior (19.20),

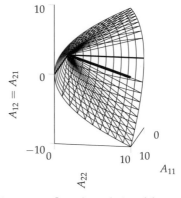

Figure 19.5: Outer boundaries of the positive definite cone within the space of symmetric 2×2 matrices (the only case that allows a plot). The thick line down the centre of the cone marks scalar matrices. The outer edge of the 2×2 positive definite cone is given by matrices A with $A_{12} = A_{21} = \pm\sqrt{A_{11}A_{22}}$.

which gives rise to the posterior mean of Eq. (19.21). Assume that the prior mean A_0 has been chosen to be symmetric positive definite. Since the posterior mean is of the same algebraic form (Gaussian, with a symmetric Kronecker product posterior covariance), the posterior can equivalently be computed iteratively, as rank-2 updates to the mean estimator. Consider the posterior belief

$$p(A \mid Y_i) = \mathcal{N}(A; A_i, W_i \otimes W_i),$$

conditioned on observations Y_i, the i matrix-vector multiplications $y_j = As_j$ for $j = 1, \dots, i$.

Using $p(A \mid Y_i)$, and given the next observation $y_{i+1} = As_{i+1}$, we can calculate a Gaussian posterior on A with the mean and covariance

$$
\begin{aligned}
A_{i+1} = A_i &+ \frac{(y_i - A_i s_i)s_i^\mathsf{T} W_i + W_i s_i (y_i - A_i s_i)^\mathsf{T}}{s_i^\mathsf{T} W_i s} \\
&- \frac{(y_i - A_i s_i)^\mathsf{T} s_i}{(s_i^\mathsf{T} W_i s_i)^2} W_i s_i s_i^\mathsf{T} W_i \\
&= A_i + uv^\mathsf{T} + vu^\mathsf{T},
\end{aligned}
\tag{19.25}
$$

for (see Eq. (19.23))

$$
\begin{aligned}
u &:= \frac{W_i s_i}{s_i^\mathsf{T} W_i s_i}, \\
v &:= (y_i - A_i s_i) - \frac{W_i s_i s_i^\mathsf{T} (y_i - A_i s_i)}{2 s_i^\mathsf{T} W_i s_i}, \\
W_{i+1} &= W_i - \frac{W_i s_i s_i^\mathsf{T} W_i}{s_i^\mathsf{T} W_i s_i}.
\end{aligned}
$$

Each posterior mean update is thus a rank-2 update. This iterative form is more manageable from an analytic perspective than the immediate form of Eq. (19.21). The idea is now to ask for a value of W_0 such that A_i can be shown by induction to be positive definite, a notion that Dennis and Moré call *hereditary positive definiteness*. For this we make use of a result from matrix perturbation theory.[18] Intuitively speaking, a rank-1 update can at most shift the eigenvalues of the original matrix up or down to the value of the nearest neighbouring eigenvalues.

Lemma 19.7. *Let $A \in \mathbb{R}^{N \times N}$ be symmetric with eigenvalues*

$$\lambda_1 \le \lambda_2 \le \dots \le \lambda_N.$$

And let $A^* = A + \alpha\, a\, a^\mathsf{T}$, with $a \in \mathbb{R}^N, \alpha \in \mathbb{R}$. If $\alpha \ge 0$, then A^* has eigenvalues λ^* such that

$$\lambda_1 \le \lambda_1^* \le \lambda_2 \le \dots \le \lambda_N \le \lambda_N^*.$$

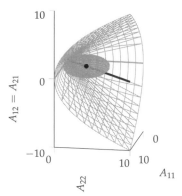

Figure 19.6: A Gaussian prior measure of mean $A_0 = 3I$ and symmetric Kronecker covariance with $W = 3I$ shown relative to the positive definite cone. The symmetric Kronecker product inherits *some* of the cone's structure in so far as the marginal variance of off-diagonal elements under this prior is half that of diagonal elements. But the distribution still assigns non-vanishing measure to the indefinite matrices outside of the cone.

[18] Wilkinson (1965), pp. 95–98

If $\alpha \leq 0$, then the eigenvalues of A^* can be arranged so that

$$\lambda_1^* \leq \lambda_1 \leq \lambda_2^* \leq \cdots \leq \lambda_N^* \leq \lambda_N.$$

Now note that the rank-2 update in Eq. (19.25) can be written as the sum of two symmetric rank-1 matrices:

$$A_{i+1} = A_i + 1/2\big((u+v)(u+v)^\mathsf{T} - (u-v)(u-v)^\mathsf{T}\big). \quad (19.26)$$

This insight can be used to arrive at the following helpful statement about rank-2 updates.

Lemma 19.8 (Dennis and Moré, Thm. 7.5). *Consider the updated estimator A_{i+1} as defined in Eq. (19.25). Assuming the A_i is positive definite, and $s_i^\mathsf{T} W_i s_i \neq 0$, the matrix A_{i+1} is positive definite if and only if $\det A_{i+1} > 0$.*

To leverage this result, we make use of the matrix determinant lemma, Eq. (15.11). Conveniently rearranged for the present context, it reads

$$\det(I + ab^\mathsf{T} + ba^\mathsf{T}) = (1 + a^\mathsf{T}b)^2 - (a^\mathsf{T}a)(b^\mathsf{T}b).$$

Thus, the determinant of the updated A_{i+1} is

$$\det A_{i+1} = \det A_i \left(\frac{(y_i^\mathsf{T} A_i^{-1} W_i s_i)^2 - (y_i^\mathsf{T} A_i^{-1} y_i)(s_i^\mathsf{T} W_i A_i^{-1} W_i s_i) + (s_i^\mathsf{T} W_i A_i^{-1} W_i s_i)(y_i^\mathsf{T} s_i)}{(s_i^\mathsf{T} W_i s_i)^2} \right).$$

Since W_i is positive semi-definite, by Lemma 19.8, A_{i+1} is thus symmetric positive definite if and only if

$$y_i^\mathsf{T} s_i > y_i^\mathsf{T} A_i^{-1} y_i - \frac{(y_i^\mathsf{T} A_i^{-1} W_i s_i)^2}{s_i^\mathsf{T} W_i A_i^{-1} W_i s_i}. \quad (19.27)$$

There are two interesting special cases for which this condition can be simplified. They are summarised in the following two statements.

Corollary 19.9. *Assume A_0 is symmetric positive definite, A_i is the posterior mean estimator of Eq. (19.21), and Algorithm 17.2 is used to construct search directions $s_i, i = 1, \ldots$ (in particular, this means the search directions are conjugate). If W_i has the property that $W_i s_i = y_i$, then all A_i are symmetric positive semi-definite. (This is the case for the unrealistic, but conceptually interesting parameter choice $W_0 = A$).*

Proof of Corollary 19.9. Under the assumptions of the Corollary, the right-hand side of Eq. (19.27) vanishes, and the condition is *always* fulfilled: by assumption A is SPD and $y_i^\mathsf{T} s_i = s_i^\mathsf{T} A s_i$. Algorithm 17.2 ensures the search directions s_i are conjugate under A, and thus

$$W_i s_i = A s_i - Y(S^\mathsf{T} Y)^{-1} Y^\mathsf{T} s_i = y_i - 0.$$

$\square$

Theorem 19.10 (proof on p. 187). *Assume $A_0 = \alpha I, W_0 = \beta I$ for $\alpha, \beta \in \mathbb{R}_+$, A_i is the posterior estimator of Eq. (19.21), and the search-directions S are conjugate to each other. Then there exists a finite $\alpha_0 > 0$, so that any choice $\alpha > \alpha_0$ ensures that all A_i are positive semi-definite.*

In general, the posterior mean is not guaranteed to be positive definite (see Figure 19.7). But Corollary 19.9 and Theorem 19.10 establish two different paths to guarantee positive definiteness of the posterior mean: Corollary 19.9 establishes that if we choose W such that $W_0 S = Y$ and set any positive definite prior mean A_0, then inference on a positive definite A will always produce positive definite posterior means (see Figure 19.8). If we consider scalar covariances instead, then Theorem 19.10 provides the weaker statement that, in that setting, it is at least possible to "drag the posterior mean into the positive definite cone" by increasing prior covariance.

Both statements, however, are dissatisfying from the probabilistic perspective for two reasons. First, they are just statements about the mean. The posterior *distribution*, being Gaussian, will always put non-zero measure on parts of the real vector-space outside of the positive definite cone. Second, these statements are of a post-hoc nature, literally: the prior still puts mass outside of the cone (see Figure 19.6). The information that A is positive definite, available *a priori*, can thus not be leveraged by the solver in its action policy. The real value of prior information is that it can change the way the algorithm acts, not just the final estimate. At the time of writing, there is no clear solution to this problem.

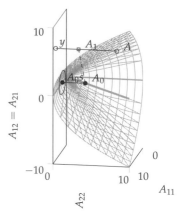

Figure 19.7: Gaussian inference under the Gaussian prior of Figure 19.6 and the projection $s = [1,0]^\mathsf{T}$, on the SPD matrix A with $A_{11} = A_{22} = 9, A_{12} = 0.7 \cdot 9$ (black circle). The plots on the "left wall" of the plot show the projections of the prior and A into the observation space $[A_{11}, A_{12}]^\mathsf{T}$. Although both the prior mean and the true matrix are symmetric positive definite, the posterior mean (black square, connected to A_0 by a dashed line) lies outside of the cone. Theorem 19.10 shows that one way to fix this is to increase the prior mean. The graphical representation of this result is that A_1 always lies on the black projection line connecting A and y (recommended instant exercise: why?). As the prior mean increases, A_1 eventually moves along that line into the cone.

▶ **19.7   Summary: Gaussian Linear Solvers**

We are interested in Gaussian inference models that can be made consistent with the evaluation strategy and the estimates constructed by iterative linear solvers for symmetric positive definite matrices. The derivations of the preceding pages show that even these comparably concrete constraints still allow for a diverse space of models. Table 19.1 summarises the four different candidates for a Gaussian framework of linear solvers. Aiming to solve $Ax = b$ for x, assuming that A is symmetric positive definite, we adopt the algorithmic paradigm of an iterative solver, as defined in Table 17.2, constructing projection-observation pairs $S = [s_1, \dots, s_M] \in \mathbb{R}^{N \times M}$ and $Y = AS = [y_1, \dots, y_M] \in \mathbb{R}^{N \times M}$.

To endow that algorithm class with a probabilistic meaning, we might directly model the matrix inverse H. Modelling H allows a joint Gaussian model over both H and the solution x. Alternatively, we might model the matrix A. Modelling A allows direct treatment of Gaussian observation noise, and still

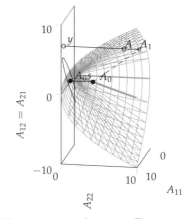

Figure 19.8: Analogous to Figure 19.7, but with the covariance choice $W = A$ considered in Corollary 19.9. Under this choice, the posterior mean always lies "to the right" of the true A along the projection line, thus in the positive definite cone.

	Asymmetric model	Symmetric model

Model for H

$$p(H) = \mathcal{N}(H_0, V_0 \otimes W_0)$$
$$p(Y, S \mid H) = \delta(S - HY)$$
$$= \lim_{\gamma \to 0} \mathcal{N}\big(\vec{S}; \overrightarrow{AY}, \gamma^2(I_N \otimes I_M)\big)$$
$$\mathbb{E}_{|Y}(H) = H_0 + (S - H_0Y)\underbrace{(Y^\mathsf{T}W_0Y)^{-1}Y^\mathsf{T}W_0}_{=:U^\mathsf{T}}$$
$$\mathbb{V}_{|Y}(H) = V_0 \otimes W_0(I - YU^\mathsf{T})$$

$$p(H) = \mathcal{N}(H_0, W_0 \otimes W_0)$$
$$p(Y, S \mid H) = \delta(S - HY)$$
$$= \lim_{\gamma \to 0} \mathcal{N}\big(\vec{S}; \overrightarrow{AY}, \gamma^2(I_N \otimes I_M)\big)$$
$$\mathbb{E}_{|Y}(H) = H_0 + \underbrace{(S - H_0Y)}_{=:\Delta}\underbrace{(Y^\mathsf{T}W_0Y)^{-1}Y^\mathsf{T}W_0}_{=:U^\mathsf{T}}$$
$$+ U\Delta^\mathsf{T} - UY^\mathsf{T}\Delta U^\mathsf{T}$$
$$\mathbb{V}_{|Y}(H) = W_0(I - YU^\mathsf{T}) \otimes W_0(I - YU^\mathsf{T})$$

Model for A

$$p(A) = \mathcal{N}(A_0, V_0 \otimes W_0)$$
$$p(Y, S \mid A) = \delta(Y - AS)$$
$$= \lim_{\gamma \to 0} \mathcal{N}\big(\vec{Y}; \overrightarrow{AS}, \gamma^2(I_N \otimes I_M)\big)$$
$$\mathbb{E}_{|Y}(A) = A_0 + (Y - A_0S)\underbrace{(S^\mathsf{T}W_0S)^{-1}S^\mathsf{T}W_0}_{=:U^\mathsf{T}}$$
$$\mathbb{V}_{|Y}(A) = V_0 \otimes W_0(I - SU^\mathsf{T})$$

$$p(A) = \mathcal{N}(A_0, W_0 \otimes W_0)$$
$$p(Y, S \mid A) = \delta(Y - AS)$$
$$= \lim_{\gamma \to 0} \mathcal{N}\big(\vec{Y}; \overrightarrow{AS}, \gamma^2(I_N \otimes I_M)\big)$$
$$\mathbb{E}_{|Y}(A) = A_0 + \underbrace{(Y - A_0S)}_{=:\Delta}\underbrace{(S^\mathsf{T}W_0S)^{-1}S^\mathsf{T}W_0}_{=:U^\mathsf{T}}$$
$$+ U\Delta^\mathsf{T} - US^\mathsf{T}\Delta U^\mathsf{T}$$
$$\mathbb{V}_{|Y}(A) = W_0(I - SU^\mathsf{T}) \otimes W_0(I - SU^\mathsf{T})$$

Table 19.1: A summary of the four difference classes of probabilistic models under consideration for the construction of linear solvers. Each cell lists the form of the prior over matrix elements, the observation likelihood, and the posterior mean and covariance over the matrix elements thus arising. See text for a discussion.

gives rise to a low-rank mean estimate for A, thus an easily computable estimate for the inverse A^{-1}. In either model class, we can also decide to explicitly model the symmetry of the matrix, or to not encode this information in the probability measure. Modelling symmetry complicates the derivations somewhat, but turns Algorithm 17.2 into a conjugate direction method.

Before making an explicit link between certain classes of classic solvers and particular choices within those four families, we point out some subtle connections and differences between these for model choices.

Although the observation likelihoods in all four cases are Dirac point masses on a projection AS or HY, these point masses arise from different limit processes: If the prior encodes symmetry, i.e. uses the symmetric Kronecker product $\otimes$, then the likelihood has to also involve a symmetric Kronecker product in the covariance – otherwise the posterior does not inherit the symmetric property, and both the posterior mean and covariances do not have the compact forms listed in Table 19.1. Without going into further details, this is the principal reason why it is not straightforward to extend this framework to the noisy setting, i.e. a situation in which matrix-vector multiplications can only be computed with (Gaussian) noise.

▶ **19.8   Consistency between beliefs on the matrix and its inverse**

As we have already noted in §19.2, there are structural differences between a Gaussian model over A and one over its inverse H. These differences reflect a larger point that one should be very careful when considering the inverse of Gaussian random variables $x \sim \mathcal{N}(\mu, \sigma^2)$ if the signal-to-noise ratio is small, $\mu/\sigma < 1$ (see Figure 19.9). But if the ratio is large, the inverse is relatively well approximated by a Gaussian itself. What does this mean for our matrix-valued Gaussian beliefs? Are there situations in which a Gaussian prior on the matrix A can be associated with a reciprocal Gaussian belief on H; and does this relationship persist as observations arrive and the posterior evolves? This section summarises some such results.[19]

Definition 19.11 (Posterior correspondence). *Consider two solvers of the form of Algorithm 17.2, one with a belief on A with prior mean A_0 and a covariance parameter W_0^A (with associated posterior mean A_M) and one maintaining a distribution on H with prior mean H_0 and covariance parameter W_0^H (with associated posterior mean H_M). We say their priors induce* posterior correspondence *if*

$$A_M^{-1} = H_M \quad \text{for } 0 \le M \le N. \tag{19.28}$$

And we speak of weak posterior correspondence *if we only have*

$$A_M^{-1} Y = H_M Y. \tag{19.29}$$

For *asymmetric* models, it is then possible to first show a general result:

Lemma 19.12. *Assume an asymmetric prior. Let $1 \le M \le N$, W_0^A, W_0^H symmetric positive definite, and assume $A_0^{-1} = H_0$. Then prior correspondence (Eq. (19.28)) holds if, and only if,*

$$0 = (AS - A_0 S)[(S^\mathsf{T} W_0^A A_0^{-1} A S)^{-1} S^\mathsf{T} W_0^A A_0^{-1} - (S^\mathsf{T} A^\mathsf{T} W_0^H A S)^{-1} S^\mathsf{T} A^\mathsf{T} W_0^H].$$

For example, a specific choice that fits this structure is $A_0 = \alpha_0 I$, $W_0^A = \beta_0 A$ paired with $H_0 = \alpha_0^{-1} I$, $W_0^H = \beta_0/\alpha_0$. A more general, and more practical form, will be developed in §21.

Symmetric models are more restricted. But we can still show weak correspondence:

Theorem 19.13. *Assume an* symmetric *prior. Let $1 \le M \le N$, W_0^A, W_0^H symmetric positive definite, and assume $A_0^{-1} = H_0$. Further*

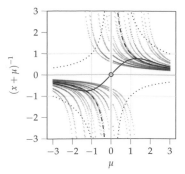

Figure 19.9: The inverse x^{-1} of a scalar Gaussian random variable $x \sim \mathcal{N}(\mu, 1)$ has a complicated distribution if $|\mu| \lesssim 1$ (see also Figure 19.1). For $\mu \neq 0$, the mean (solid line) is given, in a principal value sense, by Dawson's function (Lecomte, 2013)

$$\mathbb{E}_{\mathcal{N}(\mu,1)}(x^{-1})$$
$$= \sqrt{\frac{\pi}{2}} e^{-(x-\mu)^2/2} \operatorname{erfi}\left(\frac{x-\mu}{\sqrt{2}}\right),$$

where $\operatorname{erfi}(z) = -i\operatorname{erf}(iz)$. However, for $\mu \gg 1$, the distribution $p(x^{-1})$ is relatively well approximated by $\mathcal{N}(x^{-1}; \mu^{-1}, \mu^{-2})$ (dashed line μ^{-1}, dotted lines at $\mu \pm 2\sqrt{\mu^{-2}}$). The plot also shows 20 samples $(x+\mu)^{-1}$. For $\mu = 0$, the mean does not exist.

[19] These statements are all from Wenger and Hennig (2020), where proofs can also be found.

assume that W_0^A, A_0, W_0^H satisfy

$$W_0^A S = Y, \quad and$$
$$S^\mathsf{T}(W_0^A A_0^{-1} - A W_0^H) = 0.$$

Then weak posterior correspondence (Eq. (19.29)) holds.

▶ **19.9   Gaussian Models Consistent with Classic Solvers**

By inspecting the above in light of the theorems in §17 onward, we can now establish the following results.

Theorem 19.14 (Probabilistic projection methods). *Any Gaussian generative model on elements of A, $p(A) = \mathcal{N}(A, A_0, \Sigma_A)$ or on elements of the inverse H, $p(H) = \mathcal{N}(H, H_0, \Sigma_H)$, when used in the form of Algorithm 17.2, gives rise to a projection method.*

Proof. By Eq. (19.7), the estimator arising from these priors obeys the consistency requirement for line 12 of Algorithm 17.2 and is thus a projection method by construction.   □

Theorem 19.15 (Probabilistic conjugate direction methods). *Any Gaussian generative model with symmetric Kronecker covariance for either A or H, i.e. $p(A) = \mathcal{N}(A, A_0, W_A \otimes W_A)$ or $p(H) = \mathcal{N}(H, H_0, W_H \otimes W_H)$, with symmetric positive definite A_0, W_A or H_0, W_H, when used in Algorithm 17.2, gives rise to a conjugate direction method.*

Proof. The theorem follows immediately from Theorem 18.2, using the consistency of the Gaussian posterior (19.7), and the fact that the posterior estimates A_M^{-1} or H_M are symmetric.   □

Theorem 19.16 (Probabilistic conjugate gradients). *Consider a prior $p(H) = \mathcal{N}(H; H_0, W_H \otimes W_H)$. For all parameter choices of (H_0, W_H) with scalar $H_0 = \alpha I$ and $W_H = \beta I + \gamma H$, for $\alpha \in \mathbb{R}$ and $\beta, \gamma \in \mathbb{R}_+$, Algorithm 17.2 is equivalent to the method of conjugate gradients, in the sense that it produces the exact same sequence of estimates x_i. The same is true for the model class $p(A) = \mathcal{N}(A; A_0, W_A \otimes W_A)$ with scalar $A_0 = \alpha I$ and $W_A = \beta I + \gamma A$.*[20]

[20] Yes, W_H includes the true, inaccessible, H, and, similarly, W_A includes A. This oddity is discussed in more depth in §20.

Proof. We will make use of Theorem 18.4. First, by Theorem 19.15, the algorithm constructed here is a conjugate directions method. For Theorem 18.4 to hold, we have to show that the estimator

H_i resulting from these models and parameter choices satisfies Assumption (18.5), i.e. that the gradient r_{i-1} is mapped to $s_i = -H_{i-1}r_{i-1}$ in the span of $\{S, Y, r_{i-1}\}$. We verify that this is true by considering the image of H_i as listed in the right column of Table 19.1. For the model on H, if $S_{:i-1}$ denotes $(s_1, \ldots, s_{i-1})$ and analogously for $Y_{:i-1}$, then H_{i-1} maps any vector $v \in \mathbb{R}^N$ to the span of $\{H_0 v, S_{:i-1}, H_0 Y_{:i-1}, W_H Y_{:i-1}\}$. Hence, if H_0 is scalar and $W_H = \beta I + \gamma H$, then (since $HY = S$), r_{i-1} is mapped to the span of $\{r_{i-1}, S_{:i-1}, Y_{:i-1}\}$.

For models on A, H_{i-1} maps r_{i-1} to the span of

$$\{A_0^{-1} r_{i-1}, A_0^{-1} W_A S_{:i-1}, A_0^{-1} Y_{:i-1}, S_{:i-1}\}.$$

For a scalar A_0 and $W_A = \beta I + \gamma A$, using $AS = Y$, this is the span of $\{r_{i-1}, Y_{:i-1}, S_{:i-1}\}$. This concludes the proof. □

Corollary 19.17 (Probabilistic preconditioned conjugate gradient). *Consider a prior $p(A) = \mathcal{N}(A; \alpha K, \beta^2 K \otimes K)$ with a positive definite matrix K that can be decomposed as $K = C^\mathsf{T} C$, and scalars $\alpha, \beta \in \mathbb{R}$. Then Algorithm 17.2 is equivalent to the preconditioned method of conjugate gradients with the preconditioner K. The same is true for the model class $p(H) = \mathcal{N}(H; \tilde{\alpha} K^{-1}, \tilde{\beta}^2 (K \otimes K)^{-1})$.*

Proof. This result follows from Theorem 19.16, by noting that preconditioned CG amounts to running CG on the transformed problem $(C^{-1\mathsf{T}} A C^{-1}) C x = C^{-1\mathsf{T}} b$. If we define the transformed quantities $\tilde{A} := C^{-1\mathsf{T}} A C^{-1}$, $\tilde{x} = Cx$ and $\tilde{b} = C^{-1\mathsf{T}} b$, then by Theorem 19.16, running conjugate gradient on $\tilde{A}\tilde{x} = \tilde{b}$ is equivalent to running Algorithm 17.2 to infer $\tilde{A}$ from the prior $p(\tilde{A}) = \mathcal{N}(\tilde{A}; \alpha I, \beta^2 (I \otimes I))$. We note that this transformation of A can be written as

$$A = (C \otimes C)^\mathsf{T} \vec{\tilde{A}}.$$

Thus, by Eq. (3.4), the associated belief over A is a Gaussian of the form[21]

$$\begin{aligned} p(A) &= \mathcal{N}(A; \alpha(C \otimes C)^\mathsf{T} I, \beta^2 (C \otimes C)^\mathsf{T} (I \otimes I)(C \otimes C)) \\ &= \mathcal{N}(A; \alpha K, \beta^2 K \otimes K). \end{aligned}$$

An analogous computation for $H = (C \otimes C)^{-1} \tilde{A}^{-1}$ yields the corresponding prior for H. □

The above results, in particular Theorem 19.16, show that there is an interesting class of probabilistic interpretations for widely used iterative linear solvers. In the sense of these Theorems, we

[21] The step from the first to the second line can be shown from the definitions of the symmetric (Eq. (19.16)) and standard (Eq. (15.2)) Kronecker products.

may interpret an algorithm like CG as the policy of an agent with an internal probabilistic model for the matrix A, or its inverse H, who explicitly uses this model to iteratively estimate the solution of the linear problem $Ax = b$, and performs probabilistic inference from the observations collected in this process.

It may seem questionable that the exact A, or its inverse H, show up as possible parameter choices in Theorem 19.16. After all, these are the objects of interest in the inference scheme, and thus definitely not available at runtime. For the moment, we just note in passing that the posterior *means* H_M or A_M only contain W_H or W_A in the form $W_H Y$ and $W_A S$, respectively. Since we know $HY = S$ and $AS = Y$, respectively, we can replace $W_H Y = (\beta I + \gamma H)Y = \beta Y + \gamma S$ and, analogously $W_A S = (\beta I + \gamma A)S = \beta S + \gamma Y$. So the means, the point estimators, can be computed for these choices – they only contain aspects of the intractable W that are accessible at runtime (i.e. not A or H).

In contrast, the posterior covariances explicitly contain the matrix W. So if these error estimates are required, this "trick" cannot be used, at least not without further thought. A way to address this issue will be considered in §21. The principal idea will be that of empirical Bayesian inference: If the algorithm has already run for several iterations, and we know what structure it needs to have to be equivalent to CG, what is our best guess for a covariance matrix W that is both consistent with the algorithms' actions so far and also might preserve the equivalence in future steps? Of course, this will require some assumption of regularity about the matrix A itself.

Computational Constraints

▶ **20.1 Inference Interpretations of Algorithms vs Algorithms for Inference**

In this chapter, we have so far established that there are self-contained probabilistic inference algorithms on matrix elements whose behaviour is consistent with that of existing linear solvers. These corroborate the view that computation is inference.

On a more practical level, a corollary of these results is that we can use *existing* – efficient, stable – implementations of linear solvers, CG in particular, and treat them as a source of data, producing informative action–output pairs $(s_i, y_i = As_i)_{i=1,\ldots,M}$. Combined with the kind of structured Gaussian priors studied above, these data then give rise to posteriors on A and H, and these posteriors have convenient properties: their posterior mean is a sum of A_0 and a term of low rank, thus easy to handle both analytically and computationally. And the good convergence properties[1] of CG translate into desirable convergence properties of the Gaussian posterior.

Thus, consider the data set $S, Y \in \mathbb{R}^{N \times M}$ collected by running CG on A, b. If we adopt this practically minded approach, the desiderata for the Gaussian prior change. It no longer matters whether the prior is particularly consistent with the actions of the algorithm that collected the data. Instead, two new considerations arise:

Computational efficiency: The Gaussian posterior should have particularly low storage and evaluation cost. In particular, one would like to use the known properties of CG – orthogonal gradients, conjugate directions.

Uncertainty calibration: The posterior covariance – the main

[1] Expositions on the convergence of CG and related methods can for example be found in §5.1 (p. 112 onwards) of Nocedal and Wright (1999) and in §11.4.4. of Golub and Van Loan (1996). A frequently used result is that CG after $k + 1$ steps, assuming exact computations, finds the solution $x_{k+1} = P_k^*(A)r_0$, where P_k^* is the (matrix) polynomial of degree k that solves the following optimisation problem over all such polynomials:

$$P_k^* = \arg\min_{P_k} \|x_0 + P_k(A)r_0 - x\|_A,$$
(20.1)

where x is the true solution of $Ax = b$, and $\|v\|_A^2 := v^\mathsf{T} A v$. This result can be used to phrase the convergence in terms of the eigenvalue spectrum of A (e.g. p. 116 in Nocedal and Wright (1999)). In particular, if A has eigenvalues $\lambda_1 \leq \cdots \leq \lambda_N$, then the error of CG after $M + 1$ steps is roughly given by

$$\|x_{M+1} - x\|_A \approx (\lambda_{N-M} - \lambda_1)\|x_0 - x^*\|_A. \quad (20.2)$$

Simply put, if A has $K \ll N$ large eigenvalues and $N - K$ small ones, then CG finds a good estimate in only K steps. Since these optimisation steps are taken in the span of S_M (the Krylov sequence of Eq. (18.2)), this also means that the low-rank term in the posterior mean A_M approximately covers the dominant eigenvalues of A.

170   III Linear Algebra

"added value" of the probabilistic solver over a classic solver – should be analytically linked to the estimation error. We will find below that this intuitive desideratum is not straightforward to translate into a concrete analytical statement. Since the object of interest is matrix-valued, design criteria focussing on different aspects of the matrix lead to different choices for the prior.

Assume we want to perform inference on A with a symmetry-encoding prior $p(A) = \mathcal{N}(A; A_0, W_0 \otimes W_0)$. Both the computational and the calibration viewpoints suggest choosing

$$A_0 = 0, \text{ and}$$
$$W_0 \text{ such that } W_0 S = Y.$$

Computationally, this choice is appealing, because then the Gram matrix $S^\mathsf{T} W_0 S = S^\mathsf{T} Y = S^\mathsf{T} A S$ is diagonal (since CG produces conjugate directions), and to set $A_0 = 0$, and all terms with $S^\mathsf{T} A_0 S$ in the posterior vanish.[2] From Eq. (19.21), the posterior mean is then given simply by

$$A_M = Y(S^\mathsf{T}Y)^{-1}Y^\mathsf{T} = \sum_{m=1}^{M} \frac{y_m y_m^\mathsf{T}}{s_m^\mathsf{T} y_m} = \tilde{Y}\tilde{Y}^\mathsf{T}, \qquad (20.3)$$

and can thus be stored in form of the $N \times M$ matrix $\tilde{Y} = Y(S^\mathsf{T}Y)^{-1/2}$. Since for SPD A, $S^\mathsf{T}Y = S^\mathsf{T}AS$, is a diagonal matrix with only positive entries on the diagonal, its matrix square root can be computed simply from the real numbers $\sqrt{s_m^\mathsf{T} y_m} > 0$.

Let us again consider the hypothetical choice

$$W_0 = A.$$

We find that it is also favourable from the viewpoint of uncertainty calibration: the prior $p(A) = \mathcal{N}(A; 0, W_0 \otimes W_0)$ assigns element-wise variance

$$\mathrm{var}_{p(A)}([A]_{ij}) = \frac{1}{2}([W_0]_{ii}[W_0]_{jj} + [W_0]_{ij}^2). \qquad (20.4)$$

Thus, for elements of the diagonal, we have what might be called *perfect* calibration – the true square error equals the expected square error:

$$\frac{([A]_{ii} - \mathbb{E}_{p(A)}([A]_{ii}))^2}{\mathbb{E}_{p(A)}\left(([A]_{ii} - \mathbb{E}_{p(A)}([A]_{ii}))^2\right)} = 1. \qquad (20.5)$$

[2] A scalar $A_0 = \alpha_0 I$ is also relatively easy to handle. Because CG produces orthogonal gradients and $y_i = As_i = r_i - r_{i-1}$, the matrix $Y^\mathsf{T}Y$ is symmetric tridiagonal positive definite:

$$(Y^\mathsf{T}Y)_{ij} = y_i^\mathsf{T} y_j = (r_i - r_{i-1})^\mathsf{T}(r_j - r_{j-1})$$
$$= \delta_{ij}(r_i^\mathsf{T} r_i + r_{i-1}^\mathsf{T} r_{i-1})$$
$$+ \delta_{i,j-1} r_{i-1}^\mathsf{T} r_{i-1}$$
$$+ \delta_{i,j+1} r_i^\mathsf{T} r_i.$$

Tridiagonal problems can be efficiently solved in $\mathcal{O}(M)$ time and thus can be treated as "essentially trivial". For SPD tridiagonal systems, a concrete example is Algorithm 4.3.6 (p. 181) of Golub and Van Loan (1996). This algorithm requires $8M$ floating point operations to solve the $M \times M$ system). In LAPACK (Anderson et al., 1999), the corresponding solvers are called xPTSV (for Positive definite Tridiagonal SolVer, with x=S,D,C,Z for single, double, complex, double complex, respectively).

For off-diagonal elements, the variance is an upper error bound

$$\frac{\left([A]_{ij} - \mathbb{E}_{p(A)}([A]_{ij})\right)^2}{\mathbb{E}_{p(A)}\left(\left([A]_{ij} - \mathbb{E}_{p(A)}([A]_{ij})\right)^2\right)} = \frac{[A]_{ij}^2}{\frac{1}{2}([A]_{ii}[A]_{jj} + [A]_{ij}^2)} < 1,$$

(20.6)

because we assumed A to be SPD, and thus

$$|[A]_{ij}| \leq \sqrt{[A]_{ii}[A]_{jj}}, \qquad \forall\, 0 < i, j \leq N.$$

It would of course be preferable to achieve perfect calibration for *all* matrix elements, not just on the diagonal. But the symmetric Kronecker structure imposes restrictions on the form of the covariance, so we have to live with some trade-off. This situation is analogous to that we encountered in the chapter on integration: to infer integrals, we had to model the integrand with a GP whose covariance function (kernel) was chosen such that the posterior mean be analytically *integrated*. This cannot be achieved in general with perfect calibration, so we settled for under-confidence. In this chapter, to infer matrix inverses, we have to model the matrix with a Gaussian whose covariance is chosen such that the posterior mean can be analytically *inverted*. Again, we find that perfect calibration cannot be achieved, and settle for under-confidence.

Corollary 19.9 further supports the choice

$$W_0 = A, \qquad A_0 = 0,$$

since A_M is then always positive semi-definite. Setting $A_0 = 0$ yields a rank-deficient estimator A_M, so we cannot use the matrix inversion lemma to compute an inverse. However, the pseudoinverse[3] of A_M can be computed efficiently and has the right conceptual properties for many applications. For a factorised symmetric matrix like our $A_M = \tilde{Y}\tilde{Y}^\mathsf{T}$, the pseudoinverse is given by

$$A^+ = \tilde{Y}(\tilde{Y}^\mathsf{T}\tilde{Y})^{-2}\tilde{Y}^\mathsf{T}.$$

Since $\tilde{Y}^\mathsf{T}\tilde{Y}$ is tridiagonal symmetric positive definite, its inverse can be computed in $8M$ operations (see note 2).

Alas, we can of course not set $W_0 = A$, since A is the very matrix we are trying to infer. We could set

$$W_0 = A_M$$

in what might be called an empirical Bayesian approach. This would ensure $WS = Y$. But then the posterior variance vanishes

[3] The Moore–Penrose pseudoinverse A^+ of a matrix A is a generalisation of the inverse A^{-1} that exists for any matrix A. It is defined (for real-valued matrices) as a matrix with the properties

$$AA^+A = A,$$
$$A^+AA^+ = A^+,$$
$$(AA^+)^\mathsf{T} = AA^+,$$
$$(A^+A)^\mathsf{T} = A^+A.$$

(The concept seems to have been invented by Fredholm (1903) for operators, and discussed for matrices by Moore (1920).) The pseudoinverse yields the least-squares solution A^+b for our linear problem $Ax = b$ in the sense that

$$\|Ax - b\|_2 \geq \|AA^+b - b\|_2 \;\; \forall x \in \mathbb{R}^N.$$

For the choice $A_0 = 0$, A_M^+ can also be seen as the natural limit of the estimator A_M^{-1} arising from $A_0 = \alpha I$ for small α, because, for general A,

$$A^+ = \lim_{\alpha \to 0}(A^\mathsf{T}A + \alpha I)^{-1}A^\mathsf{T}$$
$$= \lim_{\alpha \to 0} A^\mathsf{T}(AA^\mathsf{T} + \alpha I)^{-1}.$$

(from Table 19.1):

$$W_M = W_0 - W_0 S (S^\mathsf{T} W_0 S)^{-1} S^\mathsf{T} W_0$$
$$= \tilde{Y}\tilde{Y}^\mathsf{T} - \tilde{Y}\tilde{Y}^\mathsf{T} = 0.$$

So we will have to do something more elaborate. Section 21 discusses ways to estimate a prior covariance parameter W_0 that is consistent with the choice of A_M and achieves non-zero posterior variance according to different desiderata for calibration.

▶ **20.2   Inferring the Solution x**

Across this chapter, the linear problem $Ax = b$ has been phrased in terms of finding the matrix inverse A^{-1}. This provides a way to find x for *any* $b \in \mathbb{R}^{N \times N}$. Depending on the application, however, it may be entirely enough to just solve for one specific b. In such cases the detour through the matrix inverse is not necessary, and we may wonder whether we can get away with less computational overhead. A derivation and analysis of linear solvers phrased as inference on x can be found in Cockayne et al. (2019a); the connection to matrix-based inference is further explored in Bartels et al. (2019).

This setting is where a formulation with a prior on H is more convenient than one with a prior on A. Because $x = Hb$ is a linear map of H, any Gaussian prior

$$p(H) = \mathcal{N}(H; H_0, \Sigma) \qquad \text{with } \Sigma \in \mathbb{R}^{N^2 \times N^2}$$

directly translates into a Gaussian prior on x, with

$$p(x = Hb) = \mathcal{N}(x; H_0 b, (I \otimes b)^\mathsf{T} \Sigma (I \otimes b))$$
$$=: \mathcal{N}(x; x_0, \Xi_0) \qquad \text{with } \Xi_0 \in \mathbb{R}^{N \times N}.$$

The (noise-free) observations $AS = Y$ can then be interpreted in two different ways: either as linear projections of H of the form $S = HY$, or as linear projections of $x = H^\mathsf{T} b$ of the form

$$Y^\mathsf{T} x = S^\mathsf{T} b. \tag{20.7}$$

Equation (20.7) is a statement about only the b numbers in $Y^\mathsf{T} H^\mathsf{T} b = S^\mathsf{T} b \in \mathbb{R}^M$ rather then the $N \times M$ numbers in S, highlighting that inference on x is more limited, but also less expensive, than explicit inference on H followed by a projection on b. The direct Gaussian posterior on x has the form

$$p(x \mid Y^\mathsf{T} x = S^\mathsf{T} b) = \mathcal{N}(x; x_M, \Xi_M), \tag{20.8}$$
$$\text{with} \quad x_M = x_0 + \Xi_0 Y (Y^\mathsf{T} \Xi_0 Y)^{-1} (S^\mathsf{T} b - Y^\mathsf{T} x_0),$$
$$\text{and} \quad \Xi_M = \Xi_0 - \Xi_0 Y (Y^\mathsf{T} \Xi_0 Y)^{-1} Y^\mathsf{T} \Xi_0. \tag{20.9}$$

For example, the non-symmetric prior $p(H) = \mathcal{N}(H; H_0, V \otimes W)$ induces the prior $p(x) = \mathcal{N}(x; x_0, \Xi_0)$ with $x_0 = H_0^\mathsf{T} b$ and

$$\Xi_0 = (I \otimes b)^\mathsf{T}(W_0 \otimes V_0)(I \otimes b) = (b^\mathsf{T} V_0 b) W_0.$$

On the other hand, the symmetric Kronecker-structured prior

$$p(H) = \mathcal{N}(H; H_0, W_0 \otimes W_0) \text{ induces}$$
$$p(x) = \mathcal{N}(x; x_0, \Xi_0) \text{ with } x_0 = H_0 b \text{ and}$$
$$\Xi_0 = (I \otimes b)^\mathsf{T}(W_0 \otimes W_0)(I \otimes b)$$
$$= \frac{1}{2}\left(W_0(b^\mathsf{T} W_0 b) + W_0 b b^\mathsf{T} W_0\right)$$
$$=: \frac{1}{2}\left(\beta W_0 + \tilde{b}\tilde{b}^\mathsf{T}\right) \quad \text{with } \tilde{b} := W_0 b, \beta := b^\mathsf{T} W_0 b.$$

Exercise 20.1 (medium). *The more general yet more expensive path is to condition the prior $p(H) = \mathcal{N}(H; H_0, W_0 \otimes W_0)$ on the $N \times M$ observations $S = HY$, then project onto x. The resulting posterior mean is $x_M = H_M b$, with H_M from Table 19.1. Compute this projection $H_M b$ and convince yourself that it has a more complicated form than Eq. (20.10) (e.g. it explicitly contains terms in H_0). What is the significance of these additional terms? Do they change the value of x_M? (Hint: Consider their effect on the space outside the span of $Y^\mathsf{T} W_0 b$.)*

The matrix inversion lemma yields

$$(Y^\mathsf{T} \Xi_0 Y)^{-1} = \frac{1}{2}\left(\beta(Y^\mathsf{T} W_0 Y) + Y^\mathsf{T} \tilde{b}\tilde{b}^\mathsf{T} Y\right)^{-1}$$
$$= 2\beta^{-1}(Y^\mathsf{T} W_0 Y)^{-1}\left(I - \frac{Y^\mathsf{T} \tilde{b}\tilde{b}^\mathsf{T} Y(Y^\mathsf{T} W_0 Y)^{-1}}{\beta + \tilde{b}^\mathsf{T} Y(Y^\mathsf{T} W_0 Y)^{-1} Y \tilde{b}}\right),$$

and we see from Eqs. (20.8)–(20.9) that conditioning on $S = HY$ gives rise to a posterior on x with mean

$$x_M = x_0 + (\beta W_0 Y + \tilde{b}\tilde{b}^\mathsf{T} Y)\beta^{-1}(Y^\mathsf{T} W_0 Y)^{-1}\left(I - \frac{Y^\mathsf{T} \tilde{b}\tilde{b}^\mathsf{T} Y(Y^\mathsf{T} W_0 Y)^{-1}}{\beta + \tilde{b}^\mathsf{T} Y(Y^\mathsf{T} W_0 Y)^{-1} Y \tilde{b}}\right)(S^\mathsf{T} b + Y^\mathsf{T} x_0). \quad (20.10)$$

While these terms have a tedious structure, they can be managed efficiently by keeping track of the M-dimensional vector $b^\mathsf{T} W_0 Y$ and the $M \times M$ matrix $Y^\mathsf{T} W_0 Y$. As before, this can be achieved in a particularly efficient manner if the choices W_0 and Y well-chosen relative to each other: if the observations Y are constructed by running CG and $W_0 = \omega I$, then $Y^\mathsf{T} Y$ is a tridiagonal SPD matrix.

21

Uncertainty Calibration

We know from the preceding chapters that we can use the iterations of classic CG to construct[1] a "good" (symmetric, positive definite, fast-converging, computationally efficient) mean estimate A_M. But we could have done all of this without a probabilistic formulation. The final goal of this chapter is to construct a tractable covariance that is both probabilistically consistent with A_M (i.e. both mean and covariance arise from the same generative model) and well calibrated, so that it can serve as a notion of uncertainty.

Our approach to achieve this will be to set W_0 to a matrix that acts like A on the span of S, and estimate its effect on the complement of this space using regularity assumptions about A. That is, W_0 could be chosen as the general form[2]

$$W_0 = \tilde{Y}\tilde{Y}^\mathsf{T} + \left(I - S(S^\mathsf{T}S)^{-1}S^\mathsf{T}\right)\Omega\left(I - S(S^\mathsf{T}S)^{-1}S^\mathsf{T}\right), \quad (21.1)$$

with a general SPD matrix Ω. The projection matrices surrounding Ω ensure that it only acts on the space *not* covered by $A_M = \tilde{Y}\tilde{Y}^\mathsf{T}$. For any such Ω, this choice of W_0 evidently gives rise to the posterior A_M from Eq. (20.3).

For simplicity, we will only consider the simplest form of this nature, a *scalar* matrix

$$\Omega = \omega I. \quad (21.2)$$

This is arguably a natural choice, too, because in the absence of more specific prior knowledge about A, there is no way to identify certain directions in the null-space of S over others. A scalar Ω also simplifies Eq. (21.1) because the two terms on

[1] We saw in Theorem 19.16 that $p(A) = \mathcal{N}(A; \alpha I, \beta^2 I \otimes I)$ is another prior consistent with conjugate gradient. Since it gives rise to a posterior mean that offers less of these good properties (it is more expensive, and not necessarily positive definite), it is less interesting. But its simpler structure allows a different form of uncertainty calibration, via a conjugate prior. This will not be further explored here, but interested readers can find a derivation in the appendix to this chapter, in §22.5.

[2] See Hennig (2015). Additional discussion and further experiments can be found in Wenger and Hennig (2020), which, among other things, investigates the notion of Rayleigh regression.

either side of Ω are projection matrices, thus we get

$$W_0 = \tilde{Y}\tilde{Y}^\mathsf{T} + \omega(I - S(S^\mathsf{T}S)^{-1}S^\mathsf{T}) \quad \text{and}$$

$$W_M = W_0 - W_0 S(S^\mathsf{T}W_0 S)S^\mathsf{T}W_0$$
$$= W_0 - \tilde{Y}\tilde{Y}^\mathsf{T}$$
$$= \omega(I - S(S^\mathsf{T}S)^{-1}S^\mathsf{T}).$$

The scale ω can then be interpreted as scaling the remaining uncertainty over the entire null-space of S, the space not yet explored by CG.[3] How should ω be set? We already saw in Eqs. (20.4)–(20.6) that the very (symmetric) Kronecker structure in the covariance that engenders the desirable low-rank structure of the posterior mean also restricts the calibration of uncertainty and causes a trade-off: calibrated uncertainty on the diagonal elements implies under-confidence off the diagonal, and conversely, calibrated uncertainty off the diagonal means over-confidence on the diagonal. We can thus expect to have to strike some balance between the two.

▶ **21.1   Rayleigh Regression**

Figure 21.1 shows results from an empirical example, a run of CG on a specific matrix. The SARCOS data set[4] is a popular, simple test setup for kernel regression. It was used to construct a kernel ridge regression problem $Ax = b$ with

$$A := k_{XX} + \sigma^2 I \in \mathbb{R}^{14\,828 \times 14\,828} \text{ and } b := y, \tag{21.3}$$

where k is the isotropic Gaussian kernel (Eq. (4.4)) with length-scale 2 and noise level $\sigma = 0.1$. On this problem, standard CG (Algorithm 16.1, with some adaptions for stability) was run for $M = 300$ steps. The plot shows the sequence of the *Rayleigh coefficients*, the projected values of A arising as

$$a(m) := \frac{s_m^\mathsf{T} A s_m}{s_m^\mathsf{T} s_m},$$

where s_m is the mth direction of CG. These coefficients are readily available during the run of the solver, because the term $s_m^\mathsf{T} A s_m$ (up to a linear-cost re-scaling) is computed in line 7 of Algorithm 17.2. From Eq. (21.3), there are straightforward upper and lower bounds both for elements of A and for $a(m)$. With the eigenvalues $\lambda_1 \geq \cdots \geq \lambda_N$ of A, we evidently have

$$\lambda_1 \geq a(m) \geq \lambda_N \quad \text{for all } m$$

and thus also[5]

[3] Recall, e.g. from Theorem 18.4, that for CG, the space spanned by the directions S and that of the A-projections Y are closely related. More precisely,

$$\text{span}\{r_0, r_1, \ldots, r_{m-1}\}$$
$$= \text{span}\{r_0, y_1, \ldots, y_{m-1}\}$$
$$= \text{span}\{s_1, \ldots, s_m\}$$
$$= \text{span}\{r_0, Ar_0, \ldots, A^{m-1}r_0\}.$$

For a proof, see e.g. Theorem 5.3 in Nocedal and Wright (1999).

[4] See Vijayakumar and Schaal (2000), or §2.5 in Rasmussen and Williams (2006). The data can be found, at the time of writing, at www.gaussianprocess.org/gpml/data/. It contains a time series of trajectories mapping 21-dimensional inputs $x \in \mathbb{R}^{21}$ (positions, velocities, and accelerations, respectively, of 7 joints of a robot arm) to 7 output torques. The first of these torques is typically used as the target $y(x) \in \mathbb{R}$ for regression, as was done here, too. The entire training set contains 44 484 input–output pairs. For the purposes of this experiment, to allow some comparisons to analytical values, this was thinned by a factor of $1/3$, to $N = 14\,828$ locations. The data was standardised to have vanishing mean and unit covariance.

[5] Both bounds hold because A is assumed to be SPD, thus all its eigenvalues are real and non-negative. The upper bound holds because the trace is the sum of the eigenvalues. If $k_{XX} = UDU^\mathsf{T}$ is the eigenvalue decomposition of the SPD matrix k_{XX}, then the lower bound holds because $UDU^\mathsf{T} + \sigma^2 I = U(D + \sigma^2 I)U^\mathsf{T}$. For this specific matrix, we also know from the functional form of k_{XX} (Eq. (4.4)) that $[A]_{ij} \leq 1 + \sigma^2 \delta_{ij}$, although such a bound is not immediately available for $H = A^{-1}$.

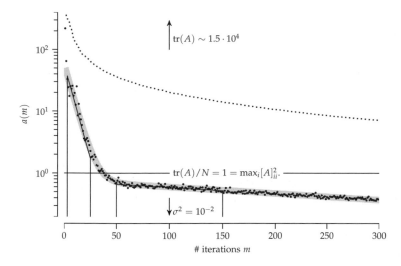

Figure 21.1: Scaled matrix projections collected by Conjugate Gradients for the SARCOS problem. The plot shows, as a function of the iteration index m, the value of the scalar projection $a(m) := (s_m^\mathsf{T} A s_m)/(s_m^\mathsf{T} s_m)$ (black circles), where s_m is the search direction of CG. These observations for $m = [3, 4, \ldots, 24, 50, 51, \ldots, 149]$ (vertical lines) are used to estimate a structured regression model for $a(m)$ (see text for details, local models as thin black lines). The regression line of that model is shown as a broad grey curve. The plot also indicates the two strict upper ($\mathrm{tr}(A)$) and lower (σ^2) bounds on the eigenvalues of A, which are clearly loose (outside the plot range). The constant value of diagonal elements, which happens to be known for this problem, is indicated by a horizontal line. For comparison, the plots also shows the values of the 300 largest eigenvalues of A (dotted line).

$$\sigma^2 \leq \frac{v^\mathsf{T} A v}{v^\mathsf{T} v} \leq \mathrm{tr}\, A \qquad \text{for any } v \in \mathbb{R}^D.$$

Since the trace is the sum of *all* N eigenvalues, this upper bound is relatively loose (as Figure 21.1 confirms). But of course we do not know the eigenvalues λ_i themselves, so constructing better uncertainty scale will require a little bit more work.

While this experimental setup is not particularly challenging for CG, Figure 21.1 shows the typical behaviour of this iterative solver. The collected projections rapidly (i.e. in $M \ll N$ steps) decay as the solver explores an expanding sub-space of relevant directions. Those directions, while not identical to the eigenvectors of A corresponding to the largest eigenvalues (shown dotted in the plot), are related to them (see Eqs. (20.1) and (20.2)). The plot shows a behaviour frequently observed in practice: A small number of initial steps (in this example, from $m = 1$ to about $m = 50$) reveal large projections a_m. Then comes a "kink" in the plot, followed by a relatively continuous decay over a longer time scale. It is tempting to think of the first phase as revealing dominant "structure" in A while the remainder is "noise". But since there are $N - 50 \gg 50$ such suppressed directions, their overall influence is still significant. We also note that, while the a_m clearly exhibit a decaying trend, they do not in fact decrease monotonically.

Since the $a(m)$ are readily available during the solver run, it is desirable to make additional use of them for uncertainty quantification – to set ω in Eq. (21.2) based on the progression of $a(m)$. One possible use for the posterior mean A_M is to construct a cheap estimator $A_M v$ for matrix-vector multiplications Av with arbitrary $v \in \mathbb{R}^N$, including for $v \in \mathbb{R}^N$ that lie outside of the span S. If this is the target application, then ω should be set to provide the right scale for such projections. Since this amounts to a statement about aspects of the matrix that have not yet been observed, it must hinge on either prior knowledge or prior assumptions about A and their implications for $a(m)$. Apart from the fact that $a(m)$ comes "for free" during the solver run, another nice aspect is that the $a(m)$ are scalar. So we can use relatively inexpensive univariate regression from the M observations of $a(m)$ to try and predict values for $a(m > M)$, and thus also the value $v^\intercal A v$. We call this process *Rayleigh regression*.[6] It is visually represented in Figure 21.1. The broad grey curve is a fit for a function of the form

[6] Wenger and Hennig (2020)

$$\hat{a}(m) = \sigma^2 + 10^{\zeta_1 + \zeta_2 m} + 10^{\zeta_3 + \zeta_4 m}, \tag{21.4}$$

with real constants $\zeta_1, \ldots, \zeta_4$. The constants were found by a least squares fit (or equivalently, but more on-message, as the posterior mean of parametric Gaussian regression) over the transformed observations $\log_{10} a(m)$ on the region $m = [3, 4, \ldots, 24]$ (for ζ_1, ζ_2) and $m = [50, 51, \ldots, 149]$ (for ζ_3, ζ_4, the contribution of the previous term can be essentially ignored in this domain, simplifying the fit). It is then possible to estimate the *average* value of a_m from any particular stopping point M to N, to get a candidate for the scale ω:

$$\omega_{\text{projections}} := \frac{1}{N - M} \int_M^N \hat{a}(m) \, dm. \tag{21.5}$$

Of course a specific parametric form like Eq. (21.4) is not always available. A more general, and more automatic model based on GP regression on the values of $\log a(m)$ can be found in Wenger and Hennig (2020).

▷ **21.1.1   Predicting General Matrix Projections**

Under the posterior $p(A) = \mathcal{N}(A; A_M, W_M \otimes W_M)$, the marginal over a matrix projection $Av = (I \otimes v)^\intercal \vec{A}$ is

$$p(Av) = \mathcal{N}\left(Av; A_M v, \underbrace{\frac{1}{2}\left(W_M v^\intercal W_M v + (W_M v)(v^\intercal W_M)\right)}_{=: \Sigma_v}\right).$$

Figure 21.2 shows results from experiments with random directions v (with elements drawn from a shifted Gaussian, uniform and binary distributions) on the SARCOS set-up described above (see figure caption). The predicted scale $\omega = 0.02$ (fitted

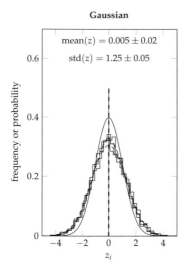
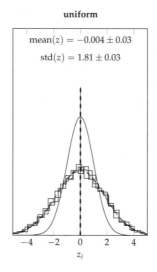
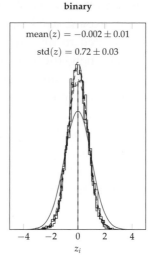

using Eq. (21.5)) is not perfect – indeed it would be surprising if it were, given the ad hoc nature of the fitted model. But it captures the scale of the vector elements quite well. The more conservative estimate $\omega = 1$, let alone the hard upper bound $\omega = \operatorname{tr} A$, would give radically larger scales. So wide in fact, that the corresponding pdf would not even be visible in the plot.

The plot also clearly shows that the sampled matrix projections are indeed modelled quite well by a Gaussian probability distribution. This is neither surprising nor particularly profound: Since the elements of v are drawn from a probability distribution $v_i \sim p_v$ independent of each other and of the elements of A, the central limit theorem applies, and the elements

$$[Av]_i = \sum_j [A]_{ij} v_j$$

are approximately Gaussian distributed with mean and variance

$$\mathbb{E}_{p_v}([Av]_i) = \mathbb{E}_{p_v}([v]_j) \sum_j [A]_{ij}, \quad \text{and}$$

$$\operatorname{var}_{p_v}([Av]_i) = \operatorname{var}_{p_v}([v]_j) \sum_j [A]_{ij}^2.$$

Hence, the fact that the elements of Av have a Gaussian distribution is not surprising. What *is* reassuring is that the Gaussian posterior on Av manages to capture the two moments of this distribution rather well, even though it does not make use of (and has no access to) p_v. That the posterior mean A_M provides a very good prediction of arbitrary matrix-vector products is a

Figure 21.2: Predicting the projection Av after $M = 300$ steps of CG on the SARCOS problem (see Figure 21.1). For this plot, the elements of a vector $v \in \mathbb{R}^{14\,828}$ were drawn i.i.d. from a unit-mean Gaussian distribution, a uniform distribution, and as binary values $[v]_i = \{-1,1\}$, respectively for each panel. To simplify computations, all steps were only performed on a subset of 4000 randomly chosen indices of Av. The plot investigates the standardised variable $z := \Sigma_v^{-1/2}(Av - \mathbb{E}_{p(A|S,Y)}(Av))$, using the matrix square root of $\Sigma_v := \operatorname{cov}_{p(A|S,Y)}(Av)$, the predictive covariance of Av under the posterior. If the probabilistic model were perfectly calibrated, the elements of this vector should be distributed like independent standard Gaussian random variables. The plot shows this standard Gaussian prediction for z_i (solid black) alongside, for three independent realisations of v, the empirical distribution of the actual elements z_i (histogram), and an empirical fit (dashed) of a Gaussian pdf to the elements of z. These means and standard deviations of such empirical distributions (estimated from 10 realisations of v, not shown) are printed in each plot. This figure uses the value for the scale ω fitted as described in §21.1.1, which gives $\omega_{\text{projections}}(M = 300) = 0.02$ (in other words, for the naïve setting $\omega = 1$, the shown solid pdf would be about 50 times wider).

testament to the ability of the *Lanczos process*Lanczos process
to quickly expand a sub-space of relevant directions, and not
in itself related to the probabilistic side. The predicted variance Σ_v is a new, fundamentally probabilistic error estimate,
emerging from the probabilistic interpretation of linear solvers.
The relatively simple and computationally cheap, hand-crafted
regression model of Eq. (21.4) on the CG step sizes manages to
find the right scale for the remaining aspects of A not captured
by the mean.

▷ **21.1.2 Predicting Individual Matrix Elements**

The above section is an example in which the prediction of an
unknown variable is apparently made *easier* by randomness. In
our kōan on randomness (§12.3), we argued that randomness removes structure. Here, the removal of structure by randomness
leaves us with a genuinely Gaussian distribution, the Gaussian
being the "least-structured" (in a maximum-entropy sense) of
all distributions of a given mean and variance over the real line.
One may argue that, in this case, the randomness is helpful
because it ensures an asymptotically perfect fit to the posterior. But the more honest statement is that this randomness
has washed out all remaining, interesting, structure. We are left
with the plain old Gaussian, that we have allowed ourselves to
model.

The estimation task becomes harder when we consider more
explicit, deterministic aspects of the latent matrix A. As a particularly glaring case, we consider the prediction of individual
matrix elements $[A]_{ij}$. The posterior marginal distribution on
these scalars under our model, conditioned on CG's observations, is (see Eq. (20.4))

$$p([A]_{ij} \mid Y, S) = \mathcal{N}\left([A]_{ij}; [A_M]_{ij}, \frac{1}{2}([W_M]_{ii}[W_M]_{jj} + [W_M]_{ij}^2)\right).$$

We already know from Eqs. (20.5)–(20.6) that there is no scalar
ω (in fact, not even a full SPD matrix W_0) such that the posterior
variance is a tight prediction for the approximation error on *all*
matrix elements. So we are forced to choose between a worst-
case, hard error bound on all matrix elements, and a reasonably
scaled error estimate that can be too small for some elements.

Figure 21.3 shows the progression of the posterior distribution for an increasing number of CG steps on the SARCOS task
introduced above (details in the caption, the Figure only shows
a small sub-set of the matrix elements for visibility). The top row

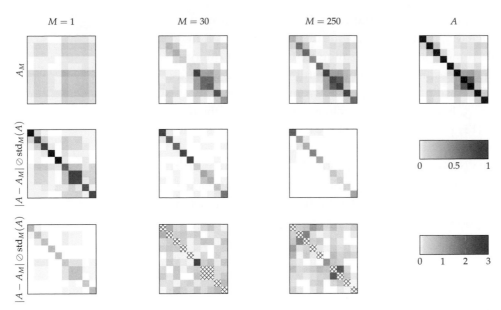

Figure 21.3: Contraction of the posterior measure on A during a CG run on the SARCOS problem (see Figure 21.1). Top row: Posterior mean A_M on a (randomly sampled) subset of 10 index pairs, after $M = 1, 30, 250$ steps of CG (the full $14\,828 \times 14,828$ matrix is too big to print). The target sub-matrix of A is shown for comparison on the right. Middle and bottom row: Absolute estimation error $|A - A_M|$, scaled element-wise by the posterior standard deviation. The middle row shows the choice for the scaling $\omega = 1$ (grey-scale from 0 to 1), the bottom row for $\omega_{\text{projection}} \approx 0.02$, the value used for Figure 21.2 (grey-scale from 0 to 3). 'Mis-scaled' entries, where the scaled error is outside of the grey-scale range, are marked with a cross-hatch pattern.

shows the posterior mean converging towards the true matrix A. The bottom row shows the element-wise posterior marginal variance,[7] for the following two different choices of the scale parameter ω:

A hard upper bound: From Eq. (20.4), we see that $\mathrm{var}_{p(A)}([A]_{ij})$ is an upper bound to the square estimation error $[A - A_M]_{ij}^2$ if

$$\frac{1}{2}([W_0]_{ii}[W_0]_{jj} + [W_0]_{ij}^2) > |A - A_M|_{ij}.$$

For symmetric positive definite matrices (which obey $|A|^2 \leq |[A_{ii}]| \cdot |[A]_{jj}|$), one way to ensure this bound holds is to set

$$\omega \geq \max_{ij}[A]_{ij}.$$

Such an element-wise bound can either be constructed explicitly by inspecting the matrix, or may be known a priori. For SPD matrices, one way to construct such a bound in $\mathcal{O}(N)$ time would be to leverage the aforementioned bound again and set $\omega = \max_i[A]_{ii}^2$. For the example of the SARCOS matrix, which is a kernel Gram matrix, this bound is known *a priori* to be 1. The resulting scaling is shown in the middle row of Figure 21.3. The Figure confirms that the variance provides an upper bound, but also shows this bound to be rather loose for off-diagonal elements (which are by far the majority of matrix elements!).

An estimated average: If instead we again use Rayleigh regression and set ω to $\omega_{\text{projections}}$ from Eq. (21.5), this will not

---

[7] Under the joint posterior, these matrix elements are correlated. So one should not try to build a mental histogram of the numbers in the plotted matrix and ask about their relative frequencies.

give an upper bound on the error. But since this bound is constructed to capture the *typical* scale of the matrix, it may provide a more aggressive scaling that, while not offering any guarantees, might be more useful in practical applications. The resulting scaling is shown in the bottom row of Figure 21.3. Note the different colour scale relative to the row above. This part of the figure shows this scaled estimate to provide a better average-case error estimate for off-diagonal elements (values of value ~ 1). On the diagonal, the error estimates can be far off, though. Some of the outliers (marked by a cross-hatch pattern) can have ratios of true to estimated error beyond 10.

22

Proofs

▶ **22.1 Proof of Theorem 18.2**

Theorem 18.2 establishes that Algorithm 17.2 amounts to a conjugate direction method if the estimator H_i is symmetric.

Proof. By induction: For the base case[1] $i = 2$, i.e. after the first iteration of the loop, we have (recall that $\alpha_1 = -d_1^\mathsf{T} r_0 / d_1^\mathsf{T} A d_1$). The symmetry of the estimator H_i is used in the third to last equality:

> [1] For this proof, it does not actually matter how the first direction d_1 is chosen.

$$d_1^\mathsf{T} A d_2 = -d_1^\mathsf{T} A(H_1 r_1) = -d_1^\mathsf{T} A(H_1(y_1 + r_0)) = -d_1^\mathsf{T} A(s_1 + H_1 r_0) = -\alpha_1 d_1^\mathsf{T} A d_1 - d_1^\mathsf{T} A H_1 r_0$$
$$= d_1^\mathsf{T} r_0 - \alpha_1^{-1} s_1^\mathsf{T} A H_1 r_0 = d_1^\mathsf{T} r_0 - \alpha_1^{-1} y_1^\mathsf{T} H_1 r_0 = d_1^\mathsf{T} r_0 - \alpha_1^{-1} s_1^\mathsf{T} r_0 = d_1^\mathsf{T} r_0 - d_1^\mathsf{T} r_0 = 0.$$

For the inductive step, assume $\{d_0, \dots, d_{i-1}\}$ are pairwise A-conjugate. For any $k < i$, using this assumption *twice* yields

$$d_k^\mathsf{T} A d_i = -d_k^\mathsf{T} A(H_i r_i)$$

$$= -d_k^\mathsf{T} A H_i \left(\sum_{j \leq i} y_j + r_0 \right)$$

$$= -d_k^\mathsf{T} A \left(\sum_{j \leq i} s_j + H_i r_0 \right)$$

$$= -d_k^\mathsf{T} A \left(\sum_{j \leq i} \alpha_j d_j + H_i r_0 \right)$$

$$= -\alpha_k d_k^\mathsf{T} A d_k - d_k^\mathsf{T} A(H_i r_0)$$
$$= d_k^\mathsf{T} r_{k-1} - d_k^\mathsf{T} r_0$$
$$= d_k^\mathsf{T} \left(\sum_{j < k} y_j + r_0 \right) - d_k^\mathsf{T} r_0 = \sum_{j < k} \alpha_j d_k^\mathsf{T} A d_j = 0.$$

□

184   III Linear Algebra

▶ 22.2   Proof of Lemma 18.3

Lemma 18.3, establishing the connection between CG and Krylov subspace methods, also helps in the proof of Theorem 18.4.

Proof of Lemma 18.3. We begin by noting that d_i and $s_i = \alpha_i d_i$ only differ by a scalar, and recall both that $y_i = As_i$ and $r_{i-1} = r_0 + \sum_{j<i} y_j$. Hence, Eq. (18.3) can immediately be shortened to

$$s_i \in \mathrm{span}\{r_0, s_1, \ldots, s_{i-1}, As_1, As_2, \ldots, As_{i-1}\}. \qquad (22.1)$$

The proof can then be completed by an almost trivial induction. For $i = 1$, the statement reads $s_i \propto r_0$. For $i > 1$, assume

$$s_{i-j} \in \mathrm{span}\{r_0, Ar_0, A^{i-2}r_0\} \qquad \forall 0 < j < i.$$

Recursive application of this assumption to Eq. (22.1) directly yields Eq. (18.4). Evidently, this derivation also implies that Eq. (18.4) can be written equivalently as

$$\begin{aligned}
d_i \in \mathrm{span}\{r_0, Ad_1, \ldots, Ad_{i-1}\} \\
= \mathrm{span}\{s_0, s_1, \ldots, s_{i-1}, r_{i-1}\} \\
= \mathrm{span}\{r_0, y_1, y_2, \ldots, y_{i-1}\} \\
= \mathrm{span}\{r_0, r_1, \ldots, r_{i-1}\}.
\end{aligned} \qquad (22.2)$$

$\square$

▶ 22.3   Proof of Theorem 18.4

Theorem 18.4 identifies a property of the probabilistic model on A that, when used in Algorithm 17.2, makes that algorithm equivalent to the method of conjugate gradients.

Proof of Theorem 18.4. Because H_i is symmetric, Theorem 18.2 holds and the algorithm is a conjugate directions method. Hence $r_i^\mathsf{T} s_{j<i} = 0$ and $s_i^\mathsf{T} As_{j<i} = s_i^\mathsf{T} y_{j<i} = 0$. Because the Theorem posits that the algorithm has not yet terminated at step i, $r_j \neq 0$ for all $j \leq i$.

The proof now again proceeds by induction. For $i = 1$, the sets S_{i-1}, Y_{i-1} are empty, so the assumption trivially amounts to $d_1 \propto r_0$. In other words, $d_1 = -\gamma_1 r_0$, for some $\gamma \neq 0$. With this choice, we get (γ_1 cancels in α_0)

$$\alpha_0 = \frac{r_0^\mathsf{T} r_0}{r_0^\mathsf{T} Ar_0}.$$

We thus have $x_1 = x_0 - \alpha_0 r_0$ and $r_1 = r_0 - \alpha_0 A r_0$. This means $r_1 \perp r_0$, so the first statement holds. Also,

$$\text{span}\{r_1, s_1, y_1\} = \text{span}\{r_0, A r_0\}, \text{ and}$$
$$d_2 = \delta_0 r_0 + \delta_1 A r_0, \text{ with } \delta_0, \delta_1 \in \mathbb{R}.$$

Because the algorithm produces conjugate directions, $d_2^{\mathsf{T}} A r_0 = d_2^{\mathsf{T}} A d_1 = 0$, thus $\delta_0 r_0^{\mathsf{T}} A r_0 + \delta_1 r_0^{\mathsf{T}} A A r_0 = 0$, i.e.

$$\delta_1 = -\frac{r_0^{\mathsf{T}} A r_0}{r_0^{\mathsf{T}} A A r_0} \delta_0, \text{ and}$$

$$d_2 = \delta_0 \left(r_0 - \frac{r_0^{\mathsf{T}} A r_0}{r_0^{\mathsf{T}} A A r_0} A r_0 \right)$$

$$= \delta_0 \left(r_0 - \alpha_0 A r_0 \frac{(r_0^{\mathsf{T}} A r_0)^2}{(r_0^{\mathsf{T}} r_0)(r_0^{\mathsf{T}} A A r_0)} \right)$$

$$= \delta_0 \underbrace{\frac{(r_0^{\mathsf{T}} A r_0)^2}{(r_0^{\mathsf{T}} r_0)(r_0^{\mathsf{T}} A A r_0)}}_{=:-\gamma_0} \left(\underbrace{r_0 - \alpha_0 A r_0}_{=r_1} + r_0 \left(\frac{(r_0^{\mathsf{T}} r_0)(r_0^{\mathsf{T}} A A r_0)}{(r_0^{\mathsf{T}} A r_0)^2} - 1 \right) \right)$$

$$= \gamma_0 \left(-r_1 + \frac{1}{\gamma_1} \left(\frac{(r_0^{\mathsf{T}} r_0)(r_0^{\mathsf{T}} A A r_0)}{(r_0^{\mathsf{T}} A r_0)^2} - 1 \right) d_1 \right).$$

We see $\gamma_0 \neq 0$, because A is SPD and $r_0 \neq 0$ by assumption (otherwise the algorithm would be converged!). To close this part, we observe that

$$r_1^{\mathsf{T}} r_1 = (r_0 - \alpha_0 A r_0)^{\mathsf{T}} (r_0 - \alpha_0 A r_0)$$

$$= r_0^{\mathsf{T}} r_0 - 2\alpha_0 r_0^{\mathsf{T}} A r_0 + \alpha_0^2 r_0^{\mathsf{T}} A A r_0$$

$$= -r_0^{\mathsf{T}} r_0 + \frac{(r_0^{\mathsf{T}} r_0)^2 r_0^{\mathsf{T}} A A r_0}{(r_0 A r_0)^2}$$

$$= r_0^{\mathsf{T}} r_0, \quad \text{and}$$

$$\left(\frac{(r_0^{\mathsf{T}} r_0) r_0^{\mathsf{T}} A A r_0}{(r_0 A r_0)^2} - 1 \right) = \frac{r_1^{\mathsf{T}} r_1}{r_0^{\mathsf{T}} r_0}.$$

Thus, we indeed have the required statement $d_2 = \gamma_0 (-r_1 + \beta_2/\gamma_1 d_1)$. For the inductive step, assume $r_k \perp r_j$ for all $k \neq j$ and $k, j < i - 1$. Further assume that

$$d_j = \gamma_j(-r_{j-1} + \beta_j d_{j-1}) \qquad \text{for all } j < i,$$

with β_j defined as in Eq. (18.5). By the Theorem's assumption (and the re-formulation of Eq. (22.2)), direction d_i can be written using scalars $\{v_j\}_{j=1,\dots,i}$ as

$$d_i = \sum_{j<i} v_j s_j + v_i r_{i-1}. \tag{22.3}$$

Because the algorithm produces conjugate directions, we have, for $\ell < i$:

$$0 = s_\ell^\mathsf{T} A d_i = v_\ell s_\ell^\mathsf{T} A s_\ell + v_i s_\ell^\mathsf{T} A r_{i-1}$$
$$= v_\ell s_\ell^\mathsf{T} A s_\ell + v_i y_\ell^\mathsf{T} r_{i-1}.$$

If $\ell < i - 1$, then the second term in this sum cancels by the first induction assumption:

$$y_\ell^\mathsf{T} r_{i-1} = (r_\ell - r_{\ell-1})^\mathsf{T} r_{i-1} \overset{\ell < i-1}{=} 0.$$

But A is positive definite and the algorithm has not converged, so $d_\ell \neq 0$, hence

$$v_\ell = 0 \qquad \text{for all } j < i - 1.$$

Equation (22.3) thus simplifies to

$$d_i = v_{i-1} s_{i-1} + v_i r_{i-1} = v_{i-1} \alpha_{i-1} d_{i-1} + v_i r_{i-1}.$$

One degree of freedom is removed because d_i must be conjugate to s_{i-1}, so

$$
\begin{aligned}
0 &= v_{i-1} \alpha_{i-1} s_{i-1}^\mathsf{T} A d_{i-1} + v_i s_{i-1}^\mathsf{T} A r_{i-1} \\
&= v_{i-1} \alpha_{i-1} s_{i-1}^\mathsf{T} A \gamma_{i-1} (-r_{i-2} + \beta_{i-1}/\gamma_{i-2} d_{i-2}) + v_i y_{i-1}^\mathsf{T} r_{i-1} \\
&= -v_{i-1} \alpha_{i-1} \gamma_{i-1} y_{i-1}^\mathsf{T} r_{i-2} + v_i (r_{i-1} - r_{i-2})^\mathsf{T} r_{i-1}, \qquad \text{and} \\
&= v_{i-1} \alpha_{i-1} \gamma_{i-1} r_{i-2}^\mathsf{T} r_{i-2} + v_i r_{i-1}^\mathsf{T} r_{i-1} \\
v_{i-1} \alpha_{i-1} &= -v_i \frac{\beta_i}{\gamma_{i-1}}.
\end{aligned}
$$

Setting $\gamma_i = -v_i \neq 0$, we thus get the required statement

$$d_i = \gamma_i \left(-r_{i-1} + \frac{\beta_i}{\gamma_{i-1}} d_{i-1} \right). \tag{22.4}$$

What remains is to show that $r_i \perp r_j \, \forall j < i$. To do so, we re-arrange the recursion property (which is now proven for all $j \leq i$), to write the preceding gradients r_j in terms of the search directions:

$$d_j = \gamma_j \left(-r_{j-1} + \frac{\beta_j}{\gamma_{j-1}} d_{j-1} \right) \quad \Leftrightarrow \quad r_{j-1} = -\frac{1}{\gamma_j} \left(d_j - \frac{\beta_j}{\gamma_{j-1}} d_{j-1} \right) \quad \text{for all } j \leq i. \tag{22.5}$$

At step i, the updated gradient is

$$r_i = A s_i + r_{i-1} = \alpha_i A d_i + r_{i-1} = -\frac{d_i^\mathsf{T} r_{i-1}}{d_i^\mathsf{T} A d_i} A d_i + r_{i-1}. \tag{22.6}$$

For $j < i - 1$, Eq. (22.5) directly shows that $r_j \perp r_i$, since r_j is then orthogonal to r_{i-1} on the one hand, and can be written as a combination of d_j and d_{j-1} on the other hand (both of which are A-conjugate to d_i). For $j = i - 1$, we use Eq. (22.6) to see

$$r_{i-1}^\mathsf{T} r_i = \frac{d_i^\mathsf{T} r_{i-1}}{\gamma_j d_i^\mathsf{T} A d_i} \left(d_i - \frac{\beta_i}{\gamma_{i-1}} d_{i-1} \right)^\mathsf{T} A d_i + r_{i-1}^\mathsf{T} r_{i-1} = \frac{1}{\gamma_i} d_i^\mathsf{T} r_{i-1} + r_{i-1}^\mathsf{T} r_{i-1},$$

and use Eq. (22.4) to get

$$r_{i-1}^\mathsf{T} r_i = -r_{i-1}^\mathsf{T} r_{i-1} + \frac{\beta_j}{\gamma_{j-1}} d_{j-1}^\mathsf{T} r_{j-1} + r_{i-1}^\mathsf{T} r_{i-1} = \frac{\beta_j}{\gamma_{j-1}} d_{j-1}^\mathsf{T} r_{j-1}.$$

But recall that $d_{j-1} \perp r_{j-1}$ by construction:

$$r_{j-1} = \alpha_{j-1} A d_{j-1} + r_{j-2} = -\frac{d_{j-1}^\mathsf{T} r_{j-2}}{d_{j-1} A d_{j-1}}.$$

Hence $r_j \perp r_i$ for all $j < i$, and the proof is completed.   □

▶ 22.4 Proof for Theorem 19.10

Theorem 19.10 states that for symmetric inference on the elements of a symmetric positive definite matrix with a scalar mean and covariance, it is possible to ensure hereditary positive definiteness of the posterior mean by shifting the scalar prior mean "far out" into the positive definite cone. Unfortunately, deriving a qualitative version of this result requires seriously tedious linear algebra derivations. So instead, Theorem 19.10 only claims that there is *some* sufficiently large value α_0 ensuring hereditary positive definiteness.

Proof of Theorem 19.10. We first note that for scalar W_0, we have $W_i = \beta(I - S(S^\mathsf{T} S)^{-1} S^\mathsf{T})$, so β cancels out of the right-hand side of Eq. (19.27), and $W_i s_i$ amounts to computing the projection of s_i onto the complement of the span of S. Now we make the inductive assumption that A_i is positive definite. If this holds, then the second term being subtracted on the right-hand side of Eq. (19.27) is strictly positive (the numerator is the square of a real number, the denominator is nonnegative because A_i is positive definite). So the right-hand side of the inequality is smaller than $y_i^\mathsf{T} A_i^{-1} y_i$. Furthermore, the left-hand side, $y_i^\mathsf{T} s_i = s_i^\mathsf{T} A s_i$ is positive, since A is assumed to be SPD. We will show that the upper bound $y_i^\mathsf{T} A_i^{-1} y_i$ can be brought arbitrarily close to zero for large values of α, so that the inequality eventually has to hold.

Consider the expression for A_i^{-1} given in Eq. (19.24). To compute $y_i^\mathsf{T} A_i^{-1} y_i$, it will be multiplied from the left and right by y_i. Since s_i is conjugate to all preceding directions by assumption $y_i^\mathsf{T} S = 0$, and thus $y_i^\mathsf{T} A_0^{-1} U = 0$, as well as $y_i^\mathsf{T} A_0^{-1} V = \frac{1}{\alpha} y_i^\mathsf{T} Y$. This insight significantly reduces the amount of work required, but still leaves some tedious derivations that prevent a quantitative result here. Inspecting Eq. (19.24), we see that we need to compute

$$y_i^\mathsf{T} A_i^{-1} y_i = \frac{1}{\alpha} y_i^\mathsf{T} y_i - \frac{1}{\alpha^2} y_i^\mathsf{T} Y M Y^\mathsf{T} y_i,$$

where M is the term in the lower right $M \times M$ block of the matrix inverse in Eq. (19.24) (and depends on α!). Its form is given by Eq. (15.10), but it requires a lengthy derivation, left out here for space, to find that its concrete form here is

$$M = (Y^\mathsf{T}(A_0^{-1} + A_0^{-1} WS(S^\mathsf{T} WA_0^{-1} WS)^{-1} S^\mathsf{T} WA_0^{-1})Y - Y^\mathsf{T} S)^{-1}$$

$$= \left(1/\alpha \left((Y^\mathsf{T} Y) - (Y^\mathsf{T} S)(S^\mathsf{T} S)^{-1}(Y^\mathsf{T} S)\right) - Y^\mathsf{T} S\right)^{-1}.$$

Hence, for $\alpha \to \infty$, $M \to -(Y^\mathsf{T} S)^{-1}$, and we have

$$y_i^\mathsf{T} A_i^{-1} y_i \xrightarrow{\alpha \to \infty} \frac{1}{\alpha} y_i^\mathsf{T} y_i + \frac{1}{\alpha^2} y_i^\mathsf{T} Y(Y^\mathsf{T} S)^{-1} Y^\mathsf{T} y_i \xrightarrow{\alpha \to \infty} 0,$$

which completes the proof. ☐

To an informal degree, this derivation also gives a rough idea of scale: since y_i is bounded above by $\lambda_{\max} \|s_i\|$, where $\lambda_{\max}$ is the largest eigenvalue of A, hereditary positive definiteness is achieved by setting α much larger than $\lambda_{\max}$.

▶ 22.5 Conjugate Prior Inference for Matrices

Section 21 introduces a method to calibrate the posterior covariance for observations collected from CG in an empirical Bayesian fashion for models with $W_A S = Y$. Such models are preferable because their associated prior mean has several good algebraic properties (see §20). But the alternative interpretation for CG from Theorem 19.16, with scalar covariance,[2]

$$p_A(A \mid \alpha_A, \beta_A) = \mathcal{N}(A; \alpha_A I, \beta_A^2 I \otimes I) \quad \text{or} \quad (22.7)$$
$$p_H(H \mid \alpha_H, \beta_H) = \mathcal{N}(H; \alpha_H I, \beta_H^2 I \otimes I),$$

allows another conceptually appealing form of uncertainty calibration, via the conjugate prior.

In principle, this is a case of applying the general framework of hyperparameter inference from conjugate priors, outlined in

[2] To avoid clutter and redundancy, the exposition below, as above, will focus on p_A, the model inferring the matrix A. Since there is little risk of confusion, the subscripts will be dropped there, so the model parameters will be denoted as α, β. The case for inference on H is entirely analogous under the exchange $A \leftrightarrow H, Y \leftrightarrow S$.

§6. Annoyingly, its application to probability measures over matrix elements raises a few tedious linear algebra complications.

To find the Gauss-Gamma posterior arising from the symmetric Gaussian prior with scalar parameters, Eq. (22.7), we use the closure of the Gaussian family under marginalisation and multiplication (Eq. (3.5)) to compute the marginal likelihood analogously to §6.2:

$$p(Y, S \mid \alpha, \beta) = \int p(Y \mid A, S) p(A \mid \alpha, \beta) \, \mathrm{d}A$$
$$= \int \delta(\vec{Y} - (I \otimes S)^\mathsf{T} \vec{A}) \mathcal{N}(\vec{A}; \alpha \vec{I}, \beta^2 (I \otimes I)) \, \mathrm{d}A$$
$$= \mathcal{N}(\vec{Y}; \alpha \vec{S}, \beta^2 (I \otimes S)^\mathsf{T} (I \otimes I)(I \otimes S)).$$

Then we multiply with the Gauss-Gamma prior to get the posterior up to normalisation

$$p(\alpha, \beta \mid Y) \propto p(Y \mid \alpha, \beta, S) p(\alpha, \beta)$$
$$= \mathcal{N}(\vec{Y}; \alpha \vec{S}, \beta^2 (I \otimes I)) \mathcal{N}(\alpha; \mu_0, \beta^2 / \lambda_0) \mathcal{G}(\beta^{-2}; a_0, b_0).$$

In the analogue to Eq. (6.2), we take care of the Gaussian part by re-arranging

$$p(\alpha, \beta \mid Y, S) \propto \mathcal{G}(\beta^{-2}; a_0, b_0) \mathcal{N}\left(\vec{Y}; \mu_0 \vec{S}, \beta^2 \left((I \otimes S)^\mathsf{T} (I \otimes I)(I \otimes S) + \vec{S} \frac{1}{\lambda_0} \vec{S}^\mathsf{T} \right) \right) \quad (22.8)$$
$$\times \mathcal{N}\left(\alpha; \Psi \left(\lambda_0 \mu_0 + \vec{S}^\mathsf{T} \left((I \otimes S)^\mathsf{T} (I \otimes I)^{-1}(I \otimes S) \right)^{-1} \vec{Y} \right), \beta^2 \Psi \right)$$

$$\text{with} \quad \Psi := \left(\lambda_0 + \vec{S}^\mathsf{T} ((I \otimes S)^\mathsf{T} (I \otimes I)(I \otimes S))^{-1} \vec{S} \right)^{-1}. \quad (22.9)$$

In contrast to its scalar analogue, this equation contains several cumbersome expressions that require further treatment before we can arrive at a manageable representation. Central among them is the marginal covariance

$$G := (I \otimes S)^\mathsf{T} (I \otimes I)(I \otimes S) \in \mathbb{R}^{NM \times NM}.$$

We can use Eq. (19.16) and the definition of the Kronecker product (15.2) to find an explicit form for this expression:[3]

$$G_{ia,jb} = \sum_{k,\ell,n,m=1}^{N} \delta_{ik} S_{\ell a} 1/2 (\delta_{kn} \delta_{\ell m} + \delta_{km} \delta_{\ell n}) \delta_{nj} S_{mb}$$
$$= 1/2 \left(\delta_{ij} (S^\mathsf{T} S)_{ab} + S_{ja} S_{ib} \right).$$

So if this matrix acts on an arbitrary $\vec{X} \in \mathbb{R}^{NM}$, the result is

$$G \vec{X} = 1/2 \overline{(X(S^\mathsf{T} S) + S X^\mathsf{T} S)}.$$

[3] It follows from the structure of the symmetric Kronecker product that the inverse of this matrix exists on the space of all matrices that can be written in the form $\vec{CS} \in \mathbb{R}^{NM}$, where $C = C^\mathsf{T} \in \mathbb{R}^{N \times N}$. Of course, in Eq. (22.8), this inverse is invariably multiplied with such matrices. If S is full rank, then this space has $NM - 1/2(M^2 - M)$ degrees of freedom, so, for $a \in \mathbb{R}_{\backslash 0}$,

$$\det(aG) = a^{NM - 1/2(M^2 - M)} \det(G).$$

To simplify Eq. (22.8), we require solutions X to problems of the type $GZ = X$, where Z is of the form $Z = CS$ with a symmetric C. This is a similar problem to the inversion of $W \otimes W$ for Eq. (19.21). Explicit constructions of such solutions can be found in the literature,[4] but one can just convince oneself by inspection that such a solution is given by

[4] Hennig (2015)

$$GX = Z$$
$$\Rightarrow \quad X = 2Z(S^\mathsf{T}S)^{-1} - S(S^\mathsf{T}S)^{-1}(Z^\mathsf{T}S)(S^\mathsf{T}S)^{-1}.$$

In this sense, we have

$$S^\mathsf{T}G^{-1}S = \mathrm{tr}\left((S^\mathsf{T}S)(S^\mathsf{T}S)^{-1}\right) = M,$$

which simplifies Ψ from Eq. (22.9) to $\Psi = (\lambda_0 + M)^{-1}$. Analogous to the scalar base case, we introduce a "sample mean" defined by[5]

$$\tilde{\alpha} := M^{-1}\,\mathrm{tr}(Y^\mathsf{T}S(S^\mathsf{T}S)^{-1}). \qquad (22.10)$$

[5] The trace in Eq. (22.10) has a particularly simple form if the directions S are A-conjugate (as is the case if they are produced by CG). In that case, $Y^\mathsf{T}S$ is a diagonal matrix, and the expression becomes

$$\mathrm{tr}(Y^\mathsf{T}S(S^\mathsf{T}S)^{-1})$$
$$= \sum_m^M (s_m^\mathsf{T}As_m)[(S^\mathsf{T}S)^{-1}]_{mm}.$$

With this the second line of Eq. (22.8), the posterior on α, becomes[6]

$$p(\alpha \mid \beta^2, Y, S) = \mathcal{N}\left(\alpha; \frac{\lambda_0\mu_0 + M\tilde{\alpha}}{\lambda_0 + M}, \frac{\beta^2}{\lambda_0 + M}\right).$$

To approach the posterior on the variance β^2, we continue to follow the guidance from Chapter I and apply the matrix inversion lemma, which yields

[6] For an intuition of this expression, note that if $S = I_{:,1:M}$ (the first M columns of the identity), then the posterior mean on α is essentially (up to regularisation) computing a running average of A's first M diagonal elements.

$$\overrightarrow{(Y - \mu_0 S)}^\mathsf{T} \overbrace{\left(G + \vec{S}\frac{1}{\lambda_0}\vec{S}^\mathsf{T}\right)^{-1}}^{=G^{-1} - \frac{(G^{-1}\vec{S})(\vec{S}^\mathsf{T}G^{-1})}{\lambda_0 + M}} \overrightarrow{(Y - \mu_0 S)}$$

$$= \overrightarrow{(Y - \mu_0 S)}^\mathsf{T}\left(2Y(S^\mathsf{T}S)^{-1} - S(S^\mathsf{T}S)^{-1}(Y^\mathsf{T}S)(S^\mathsf{T}S)^{-1} - \mu_0 S(S^\mathsf{T}S)^{-1}\right)$$
$$\quad - \frac{(M\tilde{\alpha} - M\mu_0)^2}{\lambda_0 + M}$$

$$= \mathrm{tr}(2Y^\mathsf{T}Y(S^\mathsf{T}S)^{-1} - Y^\mathsf{T}S(S^\mathsf{T}S)^{-1}Y^\mathsf{T}S(S^\mathsf{T}S)^{-1}) - 2\mu_0 M\tilde{\alpha} + \mu_0^2 M - \frac{M^2(\tilde{\alpha} - \mu_0)^2}{\lambda_0 + M}.$$

As mentioned in Note 3 above, some care must be taken when considering the number of pseudo-observations. The matrix determinant lemma (15.11) provides

$$\det \beta^2\left(G + \vec{S}\frac{1}{\lambda_0}\vec{S}^\mathsf{T}\right) = \det(\beta^2 G)\left(\frac{1}{\lambda_0} + \vec{S}^\mathsf{T}G^{-1}\vec{S}\right)$$

$$= \beta^{2(NM - 1/2(M^2 - M))}\det(G)\left(1 + \frac{M}{\lambda_0}\right).$$

So the sufficient statistics for the Gauss-Gamma posterior on α, β^2 are

$$\mu_N = \frac{\lambda_0 \mu_0 + M\tilde{\alpha}}{\lambda_0 + M},$$

$$\lambda_N = \lambda_0 + M,$$

$$a_N = a_0 + 1/2(NM - 1/2(M^2 - M)),$$

$$b_N = b_0 + 1/2\bigg(\operatorname{tr}(2Y^\mathsf{T}Y(S^\mathsf{T}S)^{-1} - Y^\mathsf{T}S(S^\mathsf{T}S)^{-1}Y^\mathsf{T}S(S^\mathsf{T}S)^{-1})$$

$$- 2\mu_0 M\tilde{\alpha} + \mu_0^2 M - \frac{M^2(\tilde{\alpha} - \mu_0)^2}{\lambda_0 + M} \bigg). \tag{22.11}$$

These expressions tell us what computations are needed to estimate the parameters α, β. But what do they mean? In contrast to the scalar case, it is not so straightforward to define this expression in terms of a sample mean and variance. To understand their structure, assume that the singular value decomposition of S is given by $S = V\Sigma U^\mathsf{T}$. Then Y can be written in the same basis as $Y = VRU^\mathsf{T}$ with a dense rectangular matrix $R \in \mathbb{R}^{N\times M}$ that – since $Y = AS$ – is given by $R = V^\mathsf{T}AV\Sigma$. Recall from the introduction (§15.4) that Σ is a "rectangular diagonal" matrix, its only non-zero elements are the singular values $\sigma_i = \Sigma_{ii}, i = 1, \ldots, M$. By Σ^{-1}, we will denote its pseudo-inverse – the rectangular diagonal matrix containing σ_i^{-1} on its diagonal. This notation drastically simplifies the expressions above. We find that[7]

$$\tilde{\alpha} = 1/M \operatorname{tr}(Y^\mathsf{T}S(S^\mathsf{T}S)^{-1}) = 1/M \operatorname{tr}(UR^\mathsf{T}\Sigma^{-1}U^\mathsf{T})$$

$$= 1/M \operatorname{tr}(R^\mathsf{T}\Sigma^{-1}) = 1/M \sum_{i=1}^{M}(V^\mathsf{T}AV)_{ii}.$$

So $\tilde{\alpha}$ is indeed an empirical average of the "diagonal" entries of A, but in the basis of the singular vectors of S. What about the unwieldy trace term in Eq. (22.11)? Transforming it into the basis of the SVD yields (note again that both sums only run to M, not N, and that $V^\mathsf{T}AV$ is symmetric by assumption)

$$\operatorname{tr}(2Y^\mathsf{T}Y(S^\mathsf{T}S)^{-1} - Y^\mathsf{T}S(S^\mathsf{T}S)^{-1}Y^\mathsf{T}S(S^\mathsf{T}S)^{-1})$$

$$= \operatorname{tr}(2UR^\mathsf{T}R\Sigma^{-2}U^\mathsf{T} - U(R^\mathsf{T}\Sigma^{-1})(R^\mathsf{T}\Sigma^{-1})U^\mathsf{T})$$

$$= \operatorname{tr}(2R^\mathsf{T}R\Sigma^{-2} - (R^\mathsf{T}\Sigma^{-1})(R^\mathsf{T}\Sigma^{-1}))$$

$$= \sum_{ij=1}^{M} 2R_{ji}R_{ji}\sigma_i^{-2} - R_{ij}R_{ji}\sigma_i^{-1}\sigma_j^{-1}$$

$$= \sum_{ij=1}^{M}(V^\mathsf{T}AV)_{ij}^2.$$

[7] Note that the surrounding orthonormal matrices V do not cancel in this trace, as the sum only runs from 1 to M, not over all elements. However, in the final state $M = N$, we indeed get $\tilde{\alpha} = 1/M \sum_{i=1}^{N} A_{ii}$.

And we see that introducing the sufficient statistic

$$\tilde{\beta}^2 := \frac{1}{M} \sum_{ij=1}^{M} \left((V^\mathsf{T} A V)_{ij}^2 - \frac{(V^\mathsf{T} A V)_{ii}(V^\mathsf{T} A V)_{jj}}{M} \right)$$

gives a result analogous to Eq. (6.8):

$$b_N = b_0 + \frac{1}{2} \left(M\tilde{\beta}^2 + \frac{\lambda_0 M}{\lambda_0 + M}(\tilde{\alpha} - \mu_0)^2 \right).$$

This is a pleasing result. The sufficient statistics compute an empirical expectation over the elements of A in the left-singular basis of S. The term $\tilde{\alpha}$ is an empirical mean over the diagonal. The more involved expression $\tilde{\beta}^2$ is an empirical sum over the squares of elements, corrected by the outer product of the means. We also note that things are particularly easy if S is an orthonormal matrix. Since then its SVD is simply given by $S = S \cdot I \cdot I$, i.e. $V = S$, we simply get $V^\mathsf{T} A V = S^\mathsf{T} A S = Y^\mathsf{T} S$. This is interesting because both direct and iterative solvers that use conjugate search directions project along a transformation of a set of orthogonal directions. For conjugate gradients, that set is the sequence of gradients (residuals) $r_i = Ax_i - b$.

23

Summary of Part III

The solution of linear systems of equations $Ax = b$ is a highly structured process that requires keeping track of just the right quantities, in the right order. Considering the process from the probabilistic perspective, we have again seen that classic iterative solvers arise as mean estimates of Gaussian models, with a highly structured surrounding posterior uncertainty. In particular, the method of conjugate gradients can be motivated in two separate ways, from Gaussian priors on either the matrix A or its inverse. The resulting posterior uncertainties (covariances) can be made to be closely related, though not identical to each other.

Conjugate gradients efficiently explores the expanding subspaces of the Krylov sequence, providing potentially rapidly converging point estimates for the solution x. Since this process perfectly identifies the solution within the sub-space, it is not surprising that a probabilistic interpretation of this process is associated with vanishing uncertainty within the subspace. In its complement, on the other hand, the solution is not identified at all. A first task for a probabilistic linear solver is thus to assign uncertainty across this part of the solution space, and adapt or calibrate this uncertainty. We saw that this can be possible under regularity assumptions on A, which allow predicting the value of upcoming projections As_m in future steps in the process of Rayleigh regression. Since this process uses observations (the Rayleigh coefficients) that are essentially already collected by CG anyway, it offers a convenient way to tune uncertainty estimates, and add predictive uncertainty to algorithms like conjugate gradients.

Along the way, we also made several structural observations that may seem marginal at first sight, but hold interesting insights, in particular:

- ⊖ Preconditioning is connected to the notion of prior information. This connection is not just intuitive, but can be made quite precise (Corollary 19.17). One way to interpret these results is that a pre-conditioner is a means to calibrate not just the initial point estimate A_0, but also the surrounding uncertainty.

- ⊖ Certain kinds of prior information, even if known with certainty, can only be imperfectly captured in the prior without sacrificing computational tractability. As a concrete example, while we can ensure that, for symmetric positive definite matrices, the posterior mean estimate is always spd, too, this cannot be captured in a Gaussian prior. In this sense, not just the probabilistic solver but CG et al. with it, are "missing out" on useful prior information about positive definiteness, in the sense that they do not directly make use of it to guide their search strategy.

- ⊖ In linear algebra, more than in other domains, performance hinges on some crucial assumptions being true, which allow for ignoring or not tracking certain quantities. In particular, the assumption that matrix-vector multiplications $As = y$ can be computed without error. If this does not hold (which is a concrete problem in machine learning wherever data-subsampling leads to stochastic imprecision), then various tacit assumptions fly out the window. We can no longer equate models on A and its inverse with each other (because $AS = Y$ is then not equivalent with $S = HY$). Even if the disturbance is Gaussian, the resulting Gaussian posterior loses its convenient algebraic structure (Eqs. (19.10) and (19.11) as well as Eqs. (19.21) and (19.22)). In general, we can thus not expect to find linear algebra methods for the "noisy" setting that come close, even in complexity, to existing iterative routines. Stochasticity has very severe effects on linear algebra.

Software

The ProbNum library[1] provides reference implementations of probabilistic linear solvers with posterior uncertainty quantification.

[1] Code at probnum.org. See the corresponding publication by Wenger et al. (2021).

Chapter IV
Local Optimisation

24

Key Points

Most of the background for this chapter is provided by Chapter I. To understand the interpretation of quasi-Newton methods, readers should first pass through Chapter III, which introduces most of the relevant concepts.

Chapter II on integration focussed on explicitly re-constructing existing numerical quadrature rules as probabilistic estimators. Chapter III on linear algebra took a similar approach, adding some new functionality to the existing methods at the end. In this chapter, we will move further away from existing methods, and develop new functionality. Classic optimisation routines will remain a reference point. But contemporary optimisation problems, in particular in the area of machine learning, pose challenges that classic methods are not particularly well-suited to address. Here, the probabilistic viewpoint offers new avenues.

We will argue in §26.1 that the key numerical challenge separating machine learning from classic numerical problems is posed by the central role of (big, external) data in the computation. When data sets are large – as they often are – data points are regularly sub-sampled for internal computations. This batching causes stochasticity, noise, of a magnitude far beyond the machine precision, and classic notions of stability are no longer applicable. It no longer makes sense to talk about a correct number that is being computed with a tiny error. A real *likelihood* function has to enter the picture. In this chapter, we will see that if this object is not properly modelled and represented in the computation, it can contribute to a number of problems that are very visible in areas like deep learning, which exhibits a rather disappointing algorithmic landscape at the time of writing this text.

Selecting algorithmic parameters: There are several "hidden" or internal quantities that control and define an optimiser. Examples addressed below include step sizes, stopping criteria, and the computational precision of observations. These hyperparameters are either absent or mere nuisances in problems where gradients can be accessed with essentially perfect certainty. But they can become real obstacles in stochastic optimisation. In fact, some parameters may even be wholly unidentified, and setting them may then require the computation of additional observables. We will find that probabilistic formulations help both in identifying and solving such problems. It is not always necessary to track a full, calibrated posterior in such cases; just using probabilistic reasoning, with likelihoods and evidences, may be enough.

Search directions: For high-dimensional stochastic optimisation problems, a frequent analytical approach is to take an optimiser designed for noise-free optimisation, then analyse its robustness to noise. This can lead to a conflation of concepts, where design choices that were originally conceived to address problems unrelated with uncertainty (e.g. underdamped dynamics of the optimisation rule) are now also used to address noise. Explicit probabilistic inference on underlying quantities of interest (like the latent gradient, which is observed with low certainty or corrupted by noise) can help separate different design aspects of an optimisation routine, and provide more nuanced ways to achieve differing desiderata.

Problem Setting

The preceding chapters on integration and linear algebra dealt with *linear* problems.[1] In this chapter, we move to more general, nonlinear tasks. This theme will then continue in the chapters on differential equations.

Nonlinear optimisation problems are another class of numerical tasks that have been studied to extreme depths. They have ubiquitous applications of massive economic relevance. As in previous chapters, the scope of this text is too limited to give a comprehensive overview, nor even to address just a significant part of the myriad different types of optimisation problems (some listed below). We will focus on the following basic set-up: consider the real-valued function $f(x) \in \mathbb{R}$ with multivariate inputs $x \in \mathbb{R}^N$. Typical values for N can vary from a handful (e.g. in control engineering) to billions (e.g. in contemporary machine learning). Throughout this chapter, we will assume that f is at least twice continuously differentiable. Slightly adapting the widely used notation, we will denote the gradient and Hessian functions of f by

$$\nabla f : \mathbb{R}^N \twoheadrightarrow \mathbb{R}^N, \qquad [\nabla f(x)]_i = \frac{\partial f(x)}{\partial x_i}, \qquad \text{and}$$

$$B : \mathbb{R}^N \twoheadrightarrow \mathbb{R}^{N \times N}, \qquad [B(x)]_{ij} = \frac{\partial^2 f(x)}{\partial x_i \partial x_j}.$$

The function f will be called *(strongly) convex* if $B(x)$ is (strictly) positive definite everywhere. We will *not* generally assume that f is convex. And we will stick to the comparably simple *unconstrained* setting. For the purposes of this chapter, we are looking for a *local minimum*[2] of f, which will be denoted by

$$x_* = \arg \min_x f(x) : \quad \Leftrightarrow \quad (\nabla f(x_*) = 0) \wedge (B(x_*) \text{ is spd}).$$

[1] Integration is a linear operation in so far as, for two functions f, g and real numbers $\alpha, \beta \in \mathbb{R}$,

$$\int \alpha f(x) + \beta g(x) \, dx$$
$$= \alpha \int f(x) \, dx + \beta \int g(x) \, dx.$$

A Gaussian (process) prior on an integrand f is thus associated with a Gaussian marginal on the integral over f. The linear algebra problems studied in Chapter III actually do not have this property, because matrix inversion is nonlinear $((A + B)^{-1} \neq A^{-1} + B^{-1})$. The principal linear property used in Chapter III is that matrix-vector multiplications $As = y$ provide a *linear* projection of the latent matrix A.

[2] One could equally well decide to look for *maxima*. The minima of f are the maxima of $-f$. Methods searching for *global* extrema are fundamentally different, and covered in Chapter V.

```
 1  procedure OPTIMISE(f, ∇f, x₀)
 2      [f₀, ∇f₀] ← [f(x₀), ∇f(x₀)]              // first evaluation
 3      [F, ∇F] ← [f₀, ∇f₀]                      // initialise storage
 4      for i = 0, 1, . . . do
 5          dᵢ ← DIRECTION(F, ∇F)                // decide search direction
 6          αᵢ ← LINESEARCH(f(xᵢ + tdᵢ), dᵢᵀ∇f(xᵢ + tdᵢ))
 7          xᵢ₊₁ ← xᵢ + αᵢdᵢ                      // move
 8          fᵢ₊₁ ← f(xᵢ₊₁)                        // observe
 9          ∇fᵢ₊₁ ← ∇f(xᵢ₊₁)                      // observe
10          if TERMINATE(∇fᵢ) then               // done?
11              return xᵢ                        // success!
12          end if
13          [F, ∇F] ← [F ∪ fᵢ₊₁, ∇F ∪ ∇fᵢ₊₁]     // update storage
14      end for
15  end procedure
```

Algorithm 25.1: Pseudo-code for a generic iterative (first-order) optimisation algorithm. For generality, this code assumes access to both the objective f and its gradient ∇f. Many practical optimisers require only the gradient. The algorithm iterates over three principal steps: decide on a search *direction* and a step *length*, then update the estimate and collect a new observation of the objective and/or its gradient. The line search subroutine deciding the step length operates on a projected, univariate sub-problem. The first part of this chapter primarily deals with the line search, the second part with the selection of directions.

(That is, we will use the notation arg min even for local minima, for simplicity). Introductions to classic nonlinear optimisation methods can be found in a number of great textbooks. Nocedal and Wright (1999) provide an accessible, practical introduction with an emphasis on unconstrained, not-necessarily-convex problems. Boyd and Vandenberghe (2004) offer a more theoretically minded introduction concentrating on convex problems. Both books also discuss constrained problems, and continuous optimisation problems that do not have a continuous gradient everywhere (so-called *non-smooth* problems). These two areas are at the centre of the book by Bertsekas (1999). Other popular types of optimisation include discrete, and mixed-integer "programs".[3] Genetic Algorithms and Stochastic Optimisation are also large communities, interested in optimising highly noisy or fundamentally rough functions (see e.g. the book by Goldberg (1989)). Such noise (i.e. uncertainty/imprecision) on function values will play a central role in this chapter – in fact, one could make the case that Probabilistic Numerics can bridge some conceptual gaps between numerical optimisation and stochastic optimisation. However, we will make the assumption that there is at least a smooth function "underneath" the noise. Stochastic and evolutionary methods are also connected to the contents of Chapter V.

[3] For historical reasons, the optimisation and operations research communities use the terms "program" and "problem", as well as "programming" and "optimisation" synonymously. A mixed integer program is a problem involving both continuous (real-valued) and discrete parameters.

Algorithms for unconstrained nonlinear optimisation often have a basic algorithmic structure (Algorithm 25.1) that mirrors that of the linear solvers discussed in Chapter III. They iteratively produce a sequence of points[4] x_i, $i = 0, \ldots, M$, that should ideally converge towards x_* in a robust and fast way. Here "robust" may mean that the sequence will converge from more or less any choice of the starting point x_0. "Fast" means that either the sequence of residuals of the estimates $\{\|x_i - x_*\|\}_{i \geq 0}$ or the sequence of function values $\{f(x_i) - f(x_*)\}_{i \geq 0}$ converge to 0 at some high rate.[5]

For many classic local optimisers, each iteration from x_i to x_{i+1} consists of the same two principal steps as for the linear solvers defined in Algorithm 17.2:

- Decide on a *search direction* $d_i \in \mathbb{R}^N$, meaning that the next iterate will have the form $x_{i+1} = x_i + \alpha_i d_i$ with $\alpha_i \in \mathbb{R}$. This step usually involves at least one call to the "black boxes" f and/or ∇f. Several options for the choice of d_i will be discussed in §28; but the naïve choice is to set $d_i = -\nabla f(x_i)$. This is known as *gradient* or *steepest descent* and is such an elementary idea that there may be no meaningful citation for its invention.[6] Exercise 25.2 shows that gradient descent actually has certain pathological properties. Nevertheless, it remains a popular algorithm.

- Fix the *step-size* α_i. This may be done by a closed-form guess about the optimal step-size. But if this step is performed by evaluating f and/or ∇f for different values of α in search of a "good" location close to the optimum along this direction, it is called a *line search*. If the line search finds the global optimum (along this univariate direction) $\alpha_* = \arg \min_\alpha f(x_i + \alpha d_i)$, it will be called *perfect*. This is an analytical device – for nonlinear problems, perfect line searches do not exist in practice, although a good line search on a convex problem can come close.

Gradient descent, both with an efficient choice of step size and a fixed step size, offers important reference points. The following two results[7] show that gradient descent with exact line searches has a linear convergence rate.

Theorem 25.1 (Convergence of noise-free, exact line search, steepest descent on quadratic functions). *Consider the strongly convex quadratic function (already studied in Chapter III)*

$$f(x) = \frac{1}{2}x^\mathsf{T}Bx - b^\mathsf{T}x, \qquad B \in \mathbb{R}^{N \times N}, b \in \mathbb{R}^N$$

with symmetric positive definite Hessian B. This function has a global minimum at $x_* = B^{-1}b$. Let $0 < \lambda_1 \leq \lambda_2 \leq \cdots \leq \lambda_N$ be the

---

[4] We will make the philosophical leap to call these iterates "estimates". That is how they are interpreted by practitioners (who can never run an optimiser to perfect convergence), and the classic convergence analysis also supports this interpretation.

[5] Several different types of rates are used in optimisation when talking about how fast a sequence $\{r_i\}_{i \in \mathbb{N}}$ converges to zero. Stephen Wright once summarised them thus:

- A **sublinear** rate, in the optimisation context, means that $r_i \to 0$, but $r_{i+1}/r_i \to 1$. An example is the decrease $r_i \leq C/i$ for some constant C.

- A **linear** or **geometric** (sometimes also **exponential**) rate means that $r_{i+1} \leq dr_i$ for a constant $0 < d < 1$. Thus $r_i \leq Cd^i$ for some constant C.

- A **super-linear** rate means $r_{i+1}/r_i \to 0$. In other words, a geometric decrease with decreasing constant $d \to 0$. We will see that this rate can only be achieved with comparably elaborate algorithms.

- A **quadratic** rate means that $r_{i+1} \leq dr_i^2$ for some constant d (which may even be larger than 1 and still allow convergence if r_0 is sufficiently small!). This is the rate of Newton's method. Achieving it generally requires access to the Hessian function B.

In a quadratic decrease, the number of leading digits in x_i that match those of x_* doubles at each iteration. The consensus is that, in high-dimensional problems, this should be fast enough for anybody.

[6] Cauchy may be a contender, in 1847. See Lemaréchal (2012).

[7] Thms. 3.3 and 3.4 in Nocedal and Wright (1999). The proof for the first one is in Luenberger (1984).

eigenvalues of B. Then the sequence of iterates of steepest descent with exact line searches[8]

$$x_{i+1} = x_i - \left(\frac{\nabla f_i^\mathsf{T} \nabla f_i}{\nabla f_i^\mathsf{T} B \nabla f_i} \right) \nabla f_i$$

satisfies

$$\|x_{i+1} - x_*\|_B^2 \leq \left(\frac{\lambda_N - \lambda_1}{\lambda_N + \lambda_1} \right)^2 \|x_k - x_*\|_B^2. \qquad (25.1)$$

Two special cases to consider: in an isometric problem (all eigenvalues equal to each other), the iteration converges in one step. On the other hand, if the *condition number* $\kappa(B) = \lambda_N/\lambda_1$ is very large, then this bound is essentially vacuous, because the constant on the right-hand side of Eq. (25.1) is almost unit. Although these are just bounds, they reflect the practical behaviour of gradient descent well. The following theorem shows that these properties translate relatively directly to the nonlinear case.

Theorem 25.3 (Convergence of steepest descent on general functions). *Consider a general, twice continuously differentiable $f : \mathbb{R}^N \to \mathbb{R}$, and assume that the iterates generated by the steepest-descent method with exact steps converge to a point x_* at which $B(x_*)$ is symmetric positive definite with eigenvalues $0 < \lambda_1 \leq \cdots \leq \lambda_N$. Let c be any number with*

$$c \in \left(\frac{\lambda_N - \lambda_1}{\lambda_N + \lambda_1}, 1 \right).$$

Then for all i sufficiently large, it holds that

$$f(x_{i+1}) - f(x_*) \leq c^2 \big(f(x_i) - f(x_*) \big).$$

[8] The optimal step length used here was derived in Eq. (17.3). We use the shorthand $\nabla f(x_i) = \nabla f_i$.

Exercise 25.2 (easy, instructive, solution on p. 363). *Theorem 25.1 characterises the convergence of gradient descent if optimal step sizes can be found. Many practitioners actually just set the step size to a fixed constant, like $\alpha_i = 0.1$. This exercise may help gain an intuition for why this is problematic, and hides some underlying assumptions.*

Two wheeled robots are standing on top of a steep hill. Their task is to drive down the hill by performing "gradient descent". At every time step i, standing at location x_i, they evaluate their potential energy density $f(x_i) = \mathbb{E}(x_i)/m = g \cdot h(x_i)$, and its gradient $\nabla f(x)$, then move a step of size $\alpha = 0.1$ to the new location $x_{i+1} = x_i - \alpha \nabla f(x_i)$. Here, $x_i \in \mathbb{R}^2$ is the robots' 2D GPS co-ordinate, g is the free-fall acceleration, and $h(x_i)$ is the height of the ground at x_i. (m is the robot's mass, we use energy density rather than energy, so that this mass cancels out of all calculations).

The first robot uses SI units. For it, the starting point is $h(x_0) = 456m$ above sea level $g = 9.81m/s^2$, and the initial gradient, at x_0, is $\nabla f(x_0) = 5J/kg \cdot m$. The other robot uses Imperial units. Hence, $h(x_0) = 1496ft$ above sea, $g = 32.19ft/s^2$, and the initial gradient is $\nabla f(x_0) = 1.03 \cdot 10^{-5}Cal/oz \cdot ft$. How far will either robot move in its first step, and (assuming $h(x)$ is locally well-described by a linear function), what is the new energy at x_1?

Step-Size Selection – a Case Study

In the linear problem, solving for x in $Ax = b$, the line search step turned out to be trivial – once the observation $z_i = Ad_i$ was computed, α_i could be computed in a single analytic step involving an inner product between two vectors. This does not work in the nonlinear setting; but line searches are still considered an easier problem than the "outer loop" deciding on the direction d_i. In fact, line search methods are often presented as essentially a solved problem,[1] while the choice of search direction is still the subject of contemporary research. But in stochastic optimisation problems (definition below), line searches are anything but straightforward. And, as Theorem 25.3 and Exercise 25.2 show, they play a crucial role in making gradient descent a practical algorithm. Thus, this chapter will begin with an extensive discussion of line searches, and only then move to the outer loop.

> [1] Nocedal and Wright (1999) discuss line searches at the start of their book, in Chapters 3.1 and 3.5. Bertsekas (1999) even relegates them to Appendix C.

The probabilistic treatment of line searches will provide a concrete example of a situation in which classic numerical routines do not meet the needs of contemporary numerical problems, and the probabilistic viewpoint provides a clean description that does not add undue overhead. We will end up building a probabilistic line search by carefully replacing all non-probabilistic aspects of a classic routine with their probabilistic equivalent, extending wherever necessary.

▶ 26.1 Numerical Uncertainty is a Feature of Data Science

We briefly digress to explain why stochastic problems are of interest in the first place. Whenever we have made connections to classic numerical algorithms so far, we ended up re-discovering them as mean or maximum a posteriori point estimates for some unknown quantity z arising from computed numbers c under a model $\mathcal{M}$ by Bayes' theorem with a Dirac likelihood and a Gaussian prior. That is, from a posterior of the form

$$
\begin{aligned}
p(z \mid c, \mathcal{M}) &= \frac{p(z \mid \mathcal{M}) p(c \mid z, \mathcal{M})}{p(c \mid \mathcal{M})} \\
&= \frac{\mathcal{N}(z; \mu_{\mathcal{M}}, \Sigma_{\mathcal{M}}) \cdot \delta(c - P_{\mathcal{M}} z)}{\mathcal{N}(c; P_{\mathcal{M}} \mu_{\mathcal{M}}, P_{\mathcal{M}} \Sigma_{\mathcal{M}} P_{\mathcal{M}}^{\mathsf{T}})},
\end{aligned} \tag{26.1}
$$

where $P_{\mathcal{M}}$ is some linear operator, and $\mu_{\mathcal{M}}, \Sigma_{\mathcal{M}}$ are some, potentially nonparametric, prior parameters. The Dirac distribution δ in this expression encodes the underlying expectation that a computer, when told to compute $c = Pz$, actually computes that number, to machine precision. That assumption is quite natural, and fundamental to classic numerical analysis. Machine precision is not infinite, and even small disturbances can be amplified by subsequent operations to cause significant overall error. Studying such errors is the point of traditional numerical stability analysis. When this approach is applicable, it amounts to allowing the numerical method to pretend that the computational error vanishes. This simplifies the construction. If only point estimates are needed, Bayes' theorem can then often be side-stepped by easier derivations.

However, some computational tasks of contemporary interest feature errors of a more drastic nature. In such cases, the Dirac distribution in Eq. (26.1) should be replaced with an explicit likelihood. Contemporary "Big Data" tasks are one area were such *noisy* function evaluations are of central importance. Optimisation problems in machine learning typically arise when fitting a set of parameters x to a data set $\Xi := [\xi_1, \ldots, \xi_K]$ by minimising a loss or risk function $f(x) = \mathcal{L}(\Xi, x)$. This is known as (regularised) *empirical risk minimisation*.[2] The data Ξ are external, empirical quantities and should not be confused with the numbers computed by the numerical method. Often, the loss can be written generally as a sum over the data-points and a *regulariser* r that does not depend on the data (the regulariser may also be nil)

$$
\mathcal{L}(\Xi, x) = r(x) + \frac{1}{K} \sum_{k=1}^{K} \ell(\xi_k, x), \tag{26.2}
$$

with loss terms $\ell(\xi_k, x)$ involving only one individual datum. Examples of this setting include most popular deep-learning models, support vector machines, basic least-squares and logistic regressors, and maximum a posteriori inference in any

[2] This loss function is itself a corrupted estimate of the actual, inaccessible target function. The population risk

$$
\begin{aligned}
\mathcal{L}_{\text{pop.}}(x) &= r(x) + \mathbb{E}_{p_{\text{pop.}}}\left(\ell(x)\right) \\
&= r(x) + \int \ell(x) \, \mathrm{d}p_{\text{pop.}}(x),
\end{aligned}
$$

where $p_{\text{pop.}}$ is the unknown distribution from which the physical quantities are drawn in the wild. This will become relevant later in §27.2.

probabilistic models in which the generative probability $p(\Xi \mid x)$ for the data is an *exchangeable* measure. If K is a large number – if we have *Big Data* – then it may be impossible or at least inconvenient to evaluate the entire sum every time the optimisation algorithm asks for its value or its gradient. Instead, one may decide to select some "representer" points from Ξ to build what is known as a *batch* $\tilde{\Xi} := [\xi_{J_1}, \ldots, \xi_{J_M}]$ for some index set J of much reduced size $M \ll K$. This can be used to compute an approximation

$$\tilde{\mathcal{L}}(x) = r(x) + \frac{1}{M} \sum_{m=1}^{M} \ell(\xi_{J_m}, x) \approx \mathcal{L}(\Xi, x). \quad (26.3)$$

A typical approach is to draw $J \subset [1, K]$ at random in an i.i.d. fashion, and to re-draw the batch every single time the optimiser asks for a function or gradient value. In that case, the smaller sum is an unbiased estimator for the larger one and, by the central limit theorem, $\tilde{\mathcal{L}}$ is approximately *Gaussian* distributed around $\mathcal{L}$:

$$p\big(\tilde{\mathcal{L}}(x) \mid \mathcal{L}(\Xi, x)\big) \approx \mathcal{N}\big(\tilde{\mathcal{L}}(x); \mathcal{L}(\Xi, x), \sigma^2\big), \quad (26.4)$$

with variance $\sigma^2 \propto 1/M$. From the point of view of the optimiser, evaluations at different x are then disturbed by independent Gaussian noise, because the batches are re-drawn every time the optimiser requests a value of $\mathcal{L}$ or its gradient. Batching thus effectively provides a knob, which the user or the algorithm may twist to trade off computational *precision* against computational *cost*.[3] Because data set sizes K tend to be large and low-level cache sizes are limited, the balance in this decision will often be dominated by cost considerations. In deep-learning problems, even signal-to-noise ratios well below one are quite common.

The Gaussian noise introduced by batching explicitly introduces a likelihood term into the computation, and thus naturally suggests a probabilistic treatment. Knowing that classic numerical methods are associated with Dirac likelihoods, it is not surprising that classic methods for optimisation, in particular the efficient ones, tend to struggle with the noisy setting.

▶ **26.2 Classic Line Searches**

In the remainder of this section, we will study how significant computational noise can invalidate a classic numerical routine, and how this problem can be addressed from the probabilistic perspective. The object of interest will be the line search, the

Exercise 26.1 (easy, highly recommended if you have never done this before. Solution on p. 364). *Consider the basic Gaussian process regression model (using the standard notation for such tasks): Data $Y := [y_1, \ldots, y_N] \subset \mathbb{R}$ is assumed to be produced by a latent function $f : \mathbb{X} \to \mathbb{R}$ at locations $X := [x_1, \ldots, x_N]$ according to the i.i.d. Gaussian likelihood*

$$p(Y \mid f) = \mathcal{N}(Y; f_X, \sigma^2 I_N),$$

with $\sigma \in \mathbb{R}_+$ and $f_X := [f(x_1), \ldots, f(x_N)]$. Assume a general Gaussian process prior $p(f) = \mathcal{GP}(f; \mu, k)$ on the function f. Show that the posterior mean $\mathbb{E}_{p(f \mid Y, X)}(f_X)$ for the function values at X is the solution to an optimisation problem involving a loss function with the form given in Eq. (26.2), and can thus be computed with the methods discussed in this chapter (to get the notation of that equation, replace $Y \leftrightarrow \Xi$, $y_i \leftrightarrow \xi_i$, and $f_X \leftrightarrow x$). What effect does the choice of prior $p(f)$ have on this structure? Which other priors would retain the structure of Eq. (26.2)? What about the likelihood $p(Y \mid f)$? Which structure does it need to have to keep the connection to Eq. (26.2)?

---

[3] Eq. (26.4) really is an entirely quantitative, identified object that can be explicitly used in a probabilistic numerical method. Assume that $K \gg M$, and, for simplicity, that J is drawn uniformly from $[1, K]$. Further assume that the data ξ_i are drawn i.i.d. from some measure p – e.g. from $p \propto \exp(\ell(\xi \mid \bar{x}))$, recalling ℓ is the loss of a single datum and where $\bar{x}$ is the "correct" value of x. Then $\sigma^2 = \mathrm{var}(\ell(x))/M$, where $\mathrm{var}(\ell(x)) = \mathbb{E}_p\big(\ell^2(\xi, x)\big) - \mathbb{E}_p\big(\ell(\xi, x)\big)^2$. Even if $\mathrm{var}(\ell(x))$ cannot be analytically computed because p is unknown, it can be estimated empirically during the batching process at low cost overhead, using the statistic

$$\sum_j \ell^2(\xi_{J_j}, x).$$

For a while, it was difficult to access these quantities in standard deep learning libraries, but following work like that of Dangel, Kunstner, and Hennig (2020), even the established libraries are beginning to make full-batch quantities available.

internal sub-routine that determines the step-sizes of optimisers.
We start with a review of the classic solution.

As Exercise 25.2 shows, the performance of optimisation methods that iterate in steps $x_{i+1} = x_i + \alpha_i d_i$ does not just depend on the choice of search direction d_i, but also crucially on the step size $\alpha_i \in \mathbb{R}_+$. This is not just true for first-order methods like gradient descent, but also for more advanced algorithms. In linear problems, the step size can be computed analytically (see Eq. (17.3)); in nonlinear problems this is not generally possible. The task of finding a "good" step size is addressed by a line search method. Line searches solve a *univariate* optimisation problem. To stress this crucial point, we adopt a simplifying, if slightly abusive, notation: we will overload the symbol f to refer both to $f(x)$ with a multivariate input $x \in \mathbb{R}^N$, and the univariate function $f(\alpha) := f(x_i + \alpha d_i)$. The derivative of the univariate function is the *projected gradient*

$$f'(\alpha) := \frac{\partial f(x_i + \alpha d_i)}{\partial \alpha} = d_i^\mathsf{T} \nabla f(x_i + \alpha d_i) \in \mathbb{R}.$$

Note that both $f(\alpha)$ and $f'(\alpha)$ are scalars. The entirety of this section will be concerned with the problem of finding good values for α. This all happens entirely within one "inner loop", with almost no propagation of state from one line search to another. So we drop the subscript i. This is a crucial point that is often missed at first. It means that line searches operate in a rather simple environment, and their computational cost is rather small. For intuition about the following results, it may be helpful to keep in mind that a typical line search performs between one and, rarely, 10 evaluations of $f(\alpha)$ and $f'(\alpha)$, respectively.[4]

Because line searches are relatively simple yet important algorithms, we can study them in detail. The following pages start by constructing a *non*-probabilistic line search that is largely based on versions found in practical software libraries and textbooks. They are followed by their probabilistic extension.

► **26.3   The Wolfe Termination Conditions**

Building a line search requires addressing two problems: Where to evaluate the objective (the *search*), and when to stop it (the *termination*). We will start with the latter. Intuitively, it is not necessary for these inner-loop methods to actually find a *true* local

[4] We here assume that it is possible to simultaneously evaluate both the function f and its gradient f'. This is usually the case in high-dimensional, truly "numerical" optimisation tasks. The theory of automatic differentiation (e.g. Griewank (2000)), guarantees that gradient evaluations can always be computed with cost comparable to that of a function evaluation. But there are some situations in which one of the two may be difficult to access, for example because it has different numerical stability. The probabilistic line search described below easily generalises to settings in which only one of the two, or in fact any set of linear projections of the objective function, can be computed.

minimum $\alpha_* = \arg\min_\alpha f(x_i + \alpha d_i)$ of the objective – doing so may be very expensive, and all it does is move the iterate x_{i+1} forward or backward by a tiny amount, a precision that may be "washed out" quickly in the optimiser's subsequent steps. Instead, the line search should look for a point that is "good enough". Several authors have proposed ways to quantify this notion of sufficient improvement.[5] The most widely quoted formulation is by Philip Wolfe (1969). The *Wolfe conditions* consider a step length α acceptable if the following two inequalities hold, using two constants $0 \leq c_1 < c_2 \leq 1$.

[5] See e.g. §8.3 in Ortega and Rheinboldt (1970). Alternatively, see Warth and Werner (1977), or Werner (1978).

$$f(\alpha) \leq f(0) + c_1 \alpha f'(0), \qquad (26.5)$$
$$f'(\alpha) \geq c_2 f'(0). \qquad (26.6)$$

Figure 26.1 gives an intuition. The first condition (26.5) is also known as the Armijo,[6] or *sufficient decrease* condition. It requires that the function lies sufficiently below the initial function value. For $c_1 = 0$, it suffices if $f(\alpha) \leq f(0)$, i.e. the objective is just below the initial value. Positive values of c_1 impose a linear decrease.

[6] Armijo (1966)

The second condition (26.6) is called the *curvature condition* because it concerns a change in the gradient, requiring that the gradient increase beyond the initial one. These conditions are also, more specifically, known as the *weak* form of the Wolfe conditions. The *strong Wolfe conditions* add an upper bound on the gradient. They are

Exercise 26.2 (check whether you follow). *Why is it necessary to set $c_2 > c_1$?*

$$f(\alpha) \leq f(0) + c_1 \alpha f'(0), \qquad (26.7)$$
$$|f'(\alpha)| \leq c_2 |f'(0)|. \qquad (26.8)$$

(Eq. (26.7) is identical to Eq. (26.5), it is just reprinted for easy reference.) For every continuously differentiable f that is bounded

Figure 26.1: The Wolfe conditions for line search termination. Optimisation utility $f(\alpha)$ and $f'(\alpha)$ as black curves (top and bottom figure, respectively). True optimal step α_* is marked by a black circle. The sufficient-decrease condition excludes the grey region in the top figure, constraining the acceptable space to $[0, \alpha_2]$. Adding the weak curvature condition additionally excludes the lower grey region in the bottom plot (thus restricting the acceptable space now to $[\alpha_1, \alpha_2]$. The strong extension also excludes the top region (restricting to $[\alpha_1, \min\{\alpha_2, \alpha_3\}]$). All points in between are considered acceptable by the Wolfe conditions. In this example, the true extremum lies within that acceptable region, but this is not guaranteed by the conditions. (For this plot, the parameters were set to $c_1 = 0.4, c_2 = 0.5$ to get an instructive plot. These are not particularly smart choices for practical problems; see the end of §26.2.)

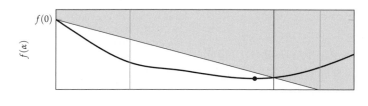

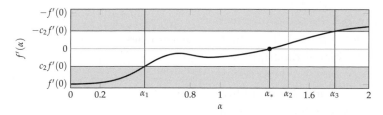

below, there exist step lengths that satisfy the conditions.[7]

As can be deduced from Figure 26.1, the Wolfe conditions do not guarantee that the true optimum lies within their bracket of acceptable step sizes (not even if the objective is convex). Nor do they strictly guarantee that the optimal step size is particularly close to the chosen one. However, they obviously prevent certain kinds of undesirable behaviour in the optimiser, like increasing function values from one step to another, or step size choices that are drastically too small. When used in combination with algorithms choosing the search directions d_i in the outer loop, the Wolfe conditions can also provide some guarantees for d_{i+1}. For example, for the BFGS method discussed in §28, the curvature condition (26.6) guarantees that d_{i+1} is a descent direction (see more in that section). Good choices for the two parameters c_1, c_2 depend a little bit on the application and the outer-loop optimisation method. But practical line searches often use lenient choices[8] with a small c_1, e.g. $c_1 = 10^{-4}$ and a large c_2, e.g. $c_2 = 0.9$. Under these settings, the conditions essentially just require a decrease in both function value and absolute gradient, no matter how small.

▶ **26.4   Search by Spline Interpolation**

The other ingredient for a classic line search is an action rule that determines where the algorithm decides to probe f and f'. For this problem, too, many different paradigms have been proposed and studied. They are guided by various motivations, such as robustness against "roughness" in the objective, speed of convergence, and others.[9] Here, we will only consider one such policy: interpolation with cubic splines. It is used in popular optimisation libraries because it is quite efficient. It is also convenient in our setting because of the close connection between cubic splines and Gaussian process regression (see §5.4).

Our interpolating line search will iteratively construct cubic local approximations of the univariate $f(\alpha)$ using collected values of f and f', at each iteration stepping to either a local minimum or an extrapolation point. Cubic spline interpolation can be phrased in various different ways, stressing different aspects.[10] In §26.5 we will re-encounter a probabilistic interpretation for them. Here is a more traditional description.[11] Figure 26.2 gives the pictorial story.

At the beginning of the line search, we only have the two numbers $f_0 := f(0)$, and $f'_0 := f'(0)$ available. So our best

[7] Nocedal and Wright (1999), Lemma 3.1

[8] Nocedal and Wright (1999), §3.1

[9] Nocedal and Wright (1999), §3.3

[10] Wahba (1990)

[11] Adapted from the presentation in Nocedal and Wright (1999), §3.5.

guess for f (see below for a more precise motivation) is a *linear* approximation

$$\hat{f}(\alpha) = f_0 + \alpha f_0'.$$

Since this linear function has no local minima, we have to decide on a first step length α_1 ad hoc. A perhaps natural choice is to set α_1 to the step length at which the *preceding* line search terminated. We compute $f_1 := f(\alpha_1)$ and $f_1' := f'(\alpha_1)$. If (f_1, f_1') satisfy the Wolfe conditions, then the line search ends.

If the Wolfe conditions are not yet satisfied, the next step depends on the gradient at α_1. If $f_1' < 0$, then the initial step was too short, and, assuming the objective is bounded below, there must be a local minimum to "the right" of α_1. This case is shown in the left panels of Figure 26.2. In this situation, we perform another extrapolation step. For example, we could set $\alpha_2 = 2\alpha_1$. On the other hand, if $f_1' > 0$, then we know that there must be a local minimum in (α_0, α_1). Because we have four numbers, f_0, f_1, f_0', f_1', available, there is a unique cubic polynomial interpolating them, given by

$$\hat{f}(\alpha) = a\alpha^3 + b\alpha^2 + \alpha f_0' + f_0, \qquad (26.9)$$

where a, b are the unique solution to the constraints $\hat{f}(\alpha_1) = f_1$ and $\hat{f}'(\alpha_1) = f_1'$. They are given by (deliberately not performing some obvious simplifications so as to show the path to the solution transparently)

$$\begin{bmatrix} a \\ b \end{bmatrix} = \frac{1}{\alpha_1^4(2-3)} \begin{bmatrix} 2\alpha_1 & -3\alpha_1^2 \\ -\alpha_1^2 & \alpha_1^3 \end{bmatrix} \begin{bmatrix} f_1 - \alpha_1 f_0' - f_0 \\ f_1' - f_0' \end{bmatrix}. \qquad (26.10)$$

The derivative $\hat{f}'$ is a quadratic function, which has a unique minimum at

$$\alpha_2 = \frac{-b + \sqrt{b^2 - 3af_0'}}{3a}.$$

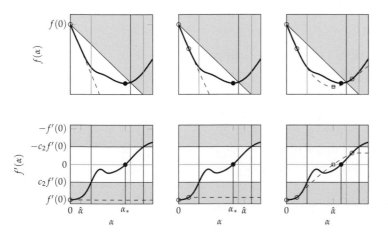

Figure 26.2: Cubic spline interpolation for searching along the line. Each (top and bottom) pair of frames shows the same plot as in Figure 26.1, showing progress of the search and interpolation steps. Left: The first evaluation only allows a linear extrapolation, which requires an initial ad hoc extrapolation step. Centre: The first extrapolation (to the second evaluation) step happened to be too small, so another extrapolation step is required. Since the "natural" cubic spline extrapolation is linear, the next step is again based on an ad hoc extension of the initial step. Right: The third evaluation finally brackets a local minimum. An interpolation step follows, using a cubic spline interpolant. The next step will be at the local minimum of the interpolant. It so happens that this point (empty square) will provide an evaluation pair that satisfies the Wolfe conditions.

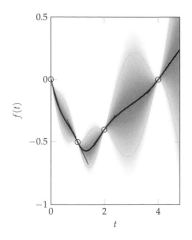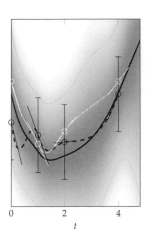

Figure 26.3: Spline interpolation can be brittle to noise. Figure adapted from Mahsereci and Hennig (2017) with permission. The left panel shows four exact evaluations of function values and derivatives, interpolated by the natural cubic spline, along with the Gaussian process posterior arising from the Wiener process prior. In this noise-free case, the GP posterior mean and the spline are identical. In the right plot, Gaussian noise was added to all four function values and gradients. The original interpolant is shown in white for reference. The noise causes oscillations in the spline interpolant (dashed black) that, in particular, cause new local minima. The GP posterior mean (solid black) reverts toward the prior mean, yielding a smoother interpolant.

This will be the next evaluation point. If $f(\alpha_2), f'(\alpha_2)$ satisfies the Wolfe conditions, the line search ends there. Otherwise, the interval is bisected: depending on the sign of $f'(\alpha_2)$ we know that the local minimum has to lie either in (α_0, α_2) or (α_2, α_1), and we can build a new cubic interpolation within that region, using the four numbers constraining it on either side.

This sequence of interval bisection by interpolation terminated by the Wolfe conditions, a popular standard in nonlinear optimisation, provides an example of the general problem, discussed above, of existing numerical methods that do not generalise well to situations with significant uncertainty or noise (see Figure 26.3). Let us assume that approximate evaluations $y'(\alpha) \approx f'(\alpha)$ of the gradient are available only with Gaussian observation likelihood

$$p(y'(\alpha) \mid f'(\alpha)) = \mathcal{N}(y'(\alpha); f'(\alpha), \sigma^2)$$

where the standard deviation σ is about as large as the starting value $f'(0)$ (this situation, a signal-to-noise ratio of 1, is not unrealistic in Big Data problems). Then, we may *observe* $y'(\alpha_1) > 0$, and decide to start the interpolation phase of the line search, even though the *true* value $f'(\alpha_1)$ is negative. Once such an erroneous bisection decision is taken, the line search is headed down a dead-end street, from which it cannot recover, at least not in its basic form. The Wolfe criteria, too, may be erroneously evaluated as satisfied even though they are not, or the other way round.

► **26.5   Probabilistic Line Searches**

This section constructs an "uncertain" extension to the line search paradigm that is more robust to evaluation noise in both the objective and its gradient. The content is based on Mahsereci and Hennig (2015).[12] The resulting *probabilistic line search* allows efficient local step-size selection in noisy settings. In doing so, it also generalises and formalises the notion of a line search as a sequence of decision problems. An implementation can be found online.[13]

A word of caution: The line search developed below provides a rigorous solution to the instability of its classic progenitor. It performs robustly on large multi-layer perceptions and logistic regression models on comparably small data sets such as MNIST or CIFAR10 and stochastic gradients of non-trivial noise Figure 26.6). On some other networks architectures, and on large data sets, it is still outperformed by standard methods and hand-tuned parameters. Some hypotheses for why this may be the case can be found in Schneider, Dangel, and Hennig (2021). In any case, as presented here, the method does provide a "textbook" example for how deterministic/nonprobabilistic numerical routines can be methodologically generalised to the stochastic/probabilistic setting:

We will identify instances of point estimation and deterministic decision making in the classic deterministic line search developed above, and explicitly replace them with probabilistic inference and uncertain decisions. In total we have to make three such changes:

⊖ the spline interpolation rule has to be extended to noisy observations;

⊖ the decision rule for where to probe the objective function has to reflect the fact that no region of inputs can be "bisected away" deterministically;

⊖ the Boolean Wolfe termination criteria have to be replaced with a *probability* of having found a suitable input point.

It will turn out that all three of these issues can be addressed jointly, by casting spline interpolation as the noise-free limit of Gaussian process regression.

[12] For a longer version with much more details, see Mahsereci and Hennig (2017).

[13] https://github.com/ProbabilisticNumerics/probabilistic_line_search

▷ **26.5.1 Cubic Spline Interpolation Replaced by Gaussian Regression**

Recall from §5.4, specifically Eq. (5.27), that the total solution of the stochastic differential equation

$$\mathrm{d} \begin{bmatrix} f(\alpha) \\ f'(\alpha) \end{bmatrix} = \begin{bmatrix} 0 & 1 \\ 0 & 0 \end{bmatrix} \begin{bmatrix} f(\alpha) \\ f'(\alpha) \end{bmatrix} \mathrm{d}\alpha + \begin{bmatrix} 0 \\ q \end{bmatrix} \mathrm{d}\omega_t, \qquad (26.11)$$

with initial value $f(0) = f'(0) = 0$ is given by the Gaussian process with kernel

$$\mathrm{cov}(f(a), f(b)) = \theta^2 \left(\frac{1}{3}\mathrm{min}^3(a,b) + |a - b|\frac{1}{2}\mathrm{min}(a,b) \right).$$

We will confirm below that, like the kernel itself, posterior means arising from this prior and a Gaussian likelihood are piecewise cubic polynomials that, in the limit of noise-free observations, revert to the cubic spline interpolant.

Thus, we can generalise the spline interpolation rule used in the non-probabilistic line search to the noisy setting, using Gaussian process regression as the framework. Since modelling Gaussian observation noise within the Gaussian process regression model adds essentially no computational overhead compared to the noise-free case, the resulting probabilistic line search will have computational cost similar to its classic counterpart.

We only have to take some care with the likelihood. The following model captures the situation described in Eq. (26.2).

Model 26.3. *Assume the Gaussian likelihood*

$$p(Y \mid f) = \mathcal{N}(Y; [f(\alpha_1), \ldots, f(\alpha_K), f'(\alpha_1), \ldots, f'(\alpha_K)]^\mathsf{T}, \Lambda), \tag{26.12}$$

for $Y \in \mathbb{R}^{2K}$ with a symmetric positive definite noise covariance matrix $\Lambda \in \mathbb{R}^{K \times K}$.[14] *Further assume that Λ has the following structure:*

$$\Lambda_{ij} = \begin{cases} \sigma_{f_i}^2 & \text{if } i = j, i \leq K \\ \sigma_{f'_i}^2 & \text{if } i = j, i > K \\ \rho_i \sigma_{f_i} \sigma_{f'_i} & \text{if } i = j + K \vee j = i + K \\ 0 & \text{else} \end{cases}.$$

This form allows the noise on function values and gradients to co-vary at one location α_i with correlation coefficient ρ_i, but the noise at two different locations is assumed to be independent. This assumption is correct in the case of Eq. (26.3) if the batches are re-drawn, independently, for each pair of evaluations. We will use the shorthand $A = [\alpha_0, \ldots, \alpha_K]$ for the set of evaluation nodes.

[14] So Y is a vector containing the noisy function values in the first half, then the derivatives stacked below. We have here assumed that we always evaluate f and f' together, so the number K of observed function values and gradients is the same. Of course this could be changed, at the cost of a slightly more involved notation.

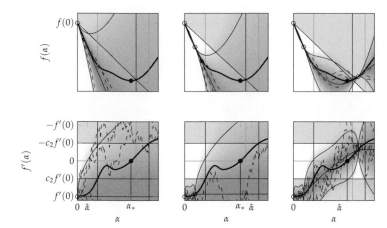

Figure 26.4: The integrated Wiener process prior yields the cubic spline interpolant as the posterior mean if the observation noise Λ vanishes. This figure shows the same data as Figure 26.2, with the Gaussian process prior (left), and posteriors after one (centre) and two (right) evaluations of the objective f and its gradient f'. Shown is the posterior mean and two marginal standard-deviations (solid lines), three samples (dashed) and the marginal density (shading). The marginal distribution on f' is a standard Wiener process (note rough, Brownian motion, samples).

For the prior, we extend the introduction from the background to deal with the nontrivial observation at the initial value $\alpha = 0$. The total solution of Eq. (26.11) conditioned on $[f(0), f'(0)]^\mathsf{T} = [f_0, f'_0]$ is a Gaussian process with mean function[15]

$$\begin{bmatrix} \mu(\alpha) \\ \mu'(\alpha) \end{bmatrix} = \begin{bmatrix} f_0 + f'_0\alpha \\ f'_0 \end{bmatrix},$$

and covariance function (kernel), using the notation $\alpha_\sqcup := \min(\alpha_a, \alpha_b)$,

$$\begin{bmatrix} k_{\alpha_a\alpha_b} & k^\partial_{\alpha_a\alpha_b} \\ \partial k_{\alpha_a\alpha_b} & \partial k^\partial_{\alpha_a\alpha_b} \end{bmatrix} := \begin{bmatrix} \mathrm{cov}(f(\alpha_a), f(\alpha_b)) & \mathrm{cov}(f(\alpha_a), f'(\alpha_b)) \\ \mathrm{cov}(f'(\alpha_a), f(\alpha_b)) & \mathrm{cov}(f'(\alpha_a), f'(\alpha_b)) \end{bmatrix}$$
$$= q^2 \begin{bmatrix} 1/3\alpha_\sqcup^3 - 1/2\alpha_\sqcup^2 + \alpha_a\alpha_b\alpha_\sqcup & -1/2\alpha_\sqcup^2 + \alpha_a\alpha_\sqcup \\ -1/2\alpha_\sqcup^2 + \alpha_b\alpha_\sqcup & \alpha_\sqcup \end{bmatrix}. \quad (26.13)$$

Then we can use the standard results from §4.2, and in particular §4.4, to compute a Gaussian process posterior measure with posterior mean function

$$\begin{bmatrix} \nu_\alpha \\ \nu'_\alpha \end{bmatrix} := \begin{bmatrix} \mu_\alpha \\ \mu'_\alpha \end{bmatrix} + \begin{bmatrix} k_{\alpha A} & k^\partial_{\alpha A} \\ \partial k_{\alpha A} & \partial k^\partial_{\alpha A} \end{bmatrix} \left(\begin{bmatrix} k_{AA} & k^\partial_{AA} \\ \partial k_{AA} & \partial k^\partial_{AA} \end{bmatrix} + \Lambda \right)^{-1} (Y - \mu^Y_A), \quad (26.14)$$

and covariance function

$$\begin{bmatrix} \kappa_{\alpha_a,\alpha_b} & \kappa^\partial_{\alpha_a,\alpha_b} \\ \partial\kappa_{\alpha_a,\alpha_b} & \partial\kappa^\partial_{\alpha_a,\alpha_b} \end{bmatrix} := \begin{bmatrix} k_{\alpha_a\alpha_b} & k^\partial_{\alpha_a\alpha_b} \\ \partial k_{\alpha_a\alpha_b} & \partial k^\partial_{\alpha_a\alpha_b} \end{bmatrix} - \begin{bmatrix} k_{\alpha_a A} & k^\partial_{\alpha_a A} \\ \partial k_{\alpha_a A} & \partial k^\partial_{\alpha_a A} \end{bmatrix} \left(\begin{bmatrix} k_{AA} & k^\partial_{AA} \\ \partial k_{AA} & \partial k^\partial_{AA} \end{bmatrix} + \Lambda \right)^{-1} \begin{bmatrix} k_{A\alpha_b} & k^\partial_{A\alpha_b} \\ \partial k_{A\alpha_b} & \partial k^\partial_{A\alpha_b} \end{bmatrix}. \quad (26.15)$$

It is relatively straightforward to see that $\nu_\alpha = \mathbb{E}_{|Y}(f(\alpha))$ is a piecewise cubic polynomial, with at most K "seams" (points of non-differentiability in f') at $\alpha_1, \ldots, \alpha_K$ (Figure 26.4). By inspection, we see that the posterior mean is a weighted sum of kernels and the prior mean. Since both the prior mean and the

[15] One way to see this is from Eqs. (5.18) and (5.19), using that F is nilpotent ($F \cdot F = 0$), thus

$$\exp(F \cdot \delta t) = \begin{bmatrix} 1 & \delta t \\ 0 & 1 \end{bmatrix}.$$

kernels $k_{\alpha A}$ and $k^\partial_{\alpha A}$ are (at most) cubic polynomials, so is the posterior mean. Analogously, the posterior mean inherits the points of non-differentiable first derivative from these kernels, at the K points $\alpha = \alpha_i$, $i = 1, \ldots, K$.

In the limit of $\Lambda \to 0$, i.e. if we assume the evaluations are available without noise, then the cubic splines of (26.9) with parameters given by Eq. (26.10) are the only feasible piecewise cubic estimate for $t \in [\alpha_0, \alpha_K]$, since then each spline is restricted by 4 conditions on either end of $[\alpha_{i-1}, \alpha_i]$, $i = 1, \ldots, K$. In this sense, the integrated Wiener process prior for f is an extension of cubic spline interpolation to non-zero values of the noise co-variance $\Lambda \in \mathbb{R}^{K \times K}$. This construction allows explicit modelling of the observation noise (Figure 26.5). The additional cost of this probabilistic line search is often negligible, even without using Kalman filtering and smoothing to speed up the computation of the GP posterior from Eqs. (26.14) and (26.15).[16]

▷ **26.5.2 Selecting Evaluation Nodes**

In the noise-free setting, our line search chose the evaluation node α_i either at an extrapolation point, following some rule for how to grow extrapolation steps, or, once an outer bound for the extrapolation has been established, as the minimum of the spline interpolant. Because it was possible to perform deterministic bisections and the interpolant is a cubic polynomial, there was always exactly one[17] such evaluation candidate. But in the noisy setting, no part of the search domain can ever be "bisected-away" with absolute certainty. Hence, the probabilistic line search will have to consider a set of candidates for the next evaluation α_i, and use some decision rule to settle on one of them. We will now first design a *finite* set of candidate points $\tau := [\tau_1, \ldots, \tau_L] \in \mathbb{R}_+$; then address the question of how to choose among them.

First, because the presence of noise makes it impossible to rule out the possibility that a local optimum lies to the right of $\alpha_{\max} := \max\{\alpha_i\}_{i=0,\ldots,K}$, our list of candidates will always include $\tau_1 = \alpha_{\max} + r_i$, where r_i is some extrapolation step. Just as in the noise-free case, the extrapolation strategy could be chosen more or less aggressive, depending on the problem setting. For high-dimensional optimisation problems in machine learning, a constant ($r_i = 1$) or linearly growing ($r_i = i$) policy may be better than the very aggressive exponential growth ($r_i = 2^i$).

To cover the domain between the previous evaluations, we will add all the local minima of the posterior mean function $\nu(\alpha)$

[16] A remark on implementation: Since Λ is block diagonal we can compute the posterior mean functions ν, ν' by filtering (§5). Then each of the K filter and smoother steps involves matrix-matrix multiplications of 2×2 matrices, as does Equation (26.10), and the computational cost of this regression procedure is only a constant multiple of that of the classic interpolation routine. However, since a typical line search performs only a very limited number ($\lesssim 10$) of function and gradient evaluations, the concrete implementation practically does not matter, and the direct form of Eq. (26.15) can be used instead. More generally, the cost overhead of this line search is often negligible when compared to the demands of computing even a single gradient if $N \gg K$.

Exercise 26.4 (advanced, discussion on p. 365). *Are there other possible choices to extend the cubic spline model to Gaussian process regression? More precisely, is there a Gaussian process prior $\mathcal{GP}(f, \mu, k)$ with mean function μ and covariance function k, such that, given observations under the likelihood (26.12), the posterior mean, for $\Lambda \to 0$, converges to the cubic spline of Eq. (26.9) with parameters (26.10) in the inner intervals $\alpha_0 < \alpha < \alpha_K$?*

[17] If the spline interpolant has no internal minimum, then the "right" end of the bisection either has negative gradient (thus we would extrapolate), or the right-most gradient is zero, and thus accepted by the Wolfe conditions.

in $[0, \alpha_{\max}] \setminus \{\alpha_i\}_{i=0,\dots,K}$, that is, excluding previous evaluation points. Because $\nu(\alpha)$ is still a cubic spline, there are still at most K such points.[18] Of course it can happen that some or all of the "cells" between evaluation points do not contain a local extremum in the posterior mean. Then these regions are not included in the list τ of candidates; and if the list only consists of the extrapolation point, then extrapolation is the only acceptable next step.

Given this now constructed list τ of L (with $L \leq K+1$) candidate points, which of these points should be chosen for the next evaluation? There are several possible ways to frame this question into a utility. Intuitively speaking, we are looking for the "most promising" candidate point τ_ℓ; where a point is promising if it is *likely* to produce a low function value and a small absolute gradient. A general way to encode this is to propose that we should choose the element $\hat{\alpha} \in \tau$ that maximises a utility

$$\hat{\alpha} = \arg\max_{\tau_\ell}\{u(\tau_\ell); \tau_\ell \in \tau\},$$

where $u(\tau) = u(p(f(\tau), f'(\tau) \mid Y))$ is a function of the marginal bivariate Gaussian posterior over the two numbers $f(\tau), f'(\tau)$. For example, it could be chosen as the *expected improvement*[19] in f over a previous best guess η, such as $\eta = \min_i\{\nu(\alpha_i)\}$, the lowest mean estimate among previous collected nodes. That is, the expected (negative) distance to η, if $f(\tau)$ is smaller than η:

$$u_{\mathrm{EI}}(\tau) = \mathbb{E}_{p(f(\tau)|Y)}(\min\{0, \eta - f(\tau)\})$$
$$= \frac{\eta - \nu(\tau)}{2}\left(1 + \mathrm{erf}\,\frac{\eta - \nu(\tau)}{\sqrt{2\kappa_{\tau\tau}}}\right) + \sqrt{\frac{\kappa_{\tau\tau}}{2\pi}}\exp\left(-\frac{(\eta - \nu(\tau))^2}{2\kappa_{\tau\tau}}\right). \tag{26.16}$$

Many other options are possible. Chapter V provides an in-depth introduction to such *Bayesian Optimisation* utilities. For example, the probability for the Wolfe conditions to hold, introduced below, can be used as another choice for u. For a practical implementation, a utility consisting of the product of u_{EI} and the Wolfe probability defined in Eq. (26.17) has been found to work well.

▷ **26.5.3   Probabilistic Wolfe Conditions**

Our classic line search would terminate if it found a point α such that the weak (or strong) Wolfe conditions (26.5) and (26.6) (or (26.8)) were satisfied. For reference, here they are again:

$$f(\alpha) \leq f(0) + c_1 t f'(\alpha) \quad \wedge \quad \begin{cases} f'(\alpha) \geq c_2 f'(0) & \text{weak} \\ |f'(\alpha)| \leq c_2 |f'(0)| & \text{strong} \end{cases}.$$

[18] These points can also still be computed in $\mathcal{O}(K)$, by evaluating the four derivatives $\nu(\alpha), \nu'(\alpha), \nu''(\alpha), \nu'''(\alpha)$ of the posterior mean, at any location t within the "cell" between two previous evaluations. These all exist, even though there is no associated posterior measure over f'' and f''', because the posterior mean is smoother than posterior samples. Together they fix the four parameters of the cubic spline (Eq. (26.9)) and thus determine the location of the internal extrema.

[19] Jones, Schonlau, and Welch (1998)

Exercise 26.5 (moderate). *As an alternative to Eq. (26.16), find the concrete value of a utility that could be called the "expected gradient improvement", given by*

$$u_{EGI} = \mathbb{E}_{p(f'(\tau)|Y)}(\min\{0, |f'(\tau)| - \eta\}),$$

where $\eta = \min_i |\nu'(\alpha_i)|$ is the lowest absolute expected gradient found so far. (The main challenge in this exercise is the computation of the first indefinite moment integral of a Gaussian distribution.)

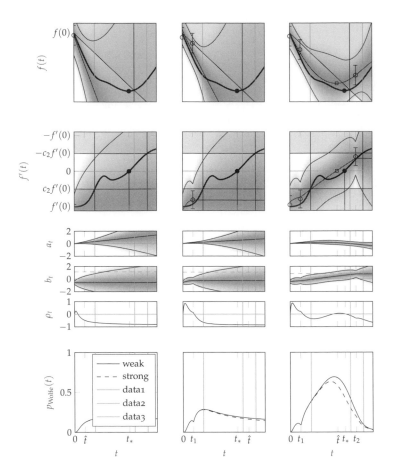

Figure 26.5: Gaussian process interpolation allows explicit modelling of observation noise. Same plot as in Figure 26.4 (samples from the belief omitted for readability) but with independent observation noise on all values of f and f'. Neither the posterior mean nor the true function now necessarily pass through the observations. But the posterior mean on f is still a differentiable piecewise cubic polynomial (and the mean on f' a continuous piecewise quadratic).

The lower half of the figure shows the belief over the two Wolfe conditions imposed by this Gaussian process posterior on (f, f'). From top to bottom: Beliefs over variables a_α (encoding the Armijo condition), b_α (encoding the curvature condition), their correlation coefficient ρ_α, and the induced probability for the weak or (approximately) strong conditions to hold. While this plot shows continuous curves for all beliefs for intuition, in an implementation, *all* these variables, even the beliefs on f and f' would only ever be computed at the finitely many evaluation nodes α_i; and a point would only be accepted if the probability for the Wolfe conditions to hold crosses a threshold *after* an evaluation has taken place there.

If the optimiser has no access to exact function values and gradients, then it is impossible to ever know *for sure* that these conditions are fulfilled at any particular point, and we can only hope to compute a probability for them to hold. This probability should arise from (and thus be consistent with) the Gaussian process model for f, f' used for the rest of the line search. In this context, it is a relief to note that the weak form of the Wolfe conditions can be written as a *linear projection* of f and f'. They amount to requiring that two scalar functions a_α and $b_\alpha \in \mathbb{R}$ are both positive at α:

$$\begin{bmatrix} a_\alpha \\ b_\alpha \end{bmatrix} := \begin{bmatrix} 1 & c_1\alpha & -1 & 0 \\ 0 & -c_2 & 0 & 1 \end{bmatrix} \begin{bmatrix} f(0) \\ f'(0) \\ f(\alpha) \\ f'(\alpha) \end{bmatrix} \geq \begin{bmatrix} 0 \\ 0 \end{bmatrix}.$$

Thanks to the closure of the Gaussian family under linear transformations (Eq. (3.4)), the Gaussian process measure on (f, f') directly implies a bivariate Gaussian measure on (a_α, b_α) for all α (see Figure 26.5). If the posterior Gaussian process measure on (f, f') is

$$p(f, f' \mid Y) = \mathcal{GP}\left(\begin{bmatrix} f \\ f' \end{bmatrix}; \begin{bmatrix} \nu \\ \nu' \end{bmatrix}, \begin{bmatrix} \kappa & \kappa^\partial \\ \partial_\kappa & \partial_\kappa^\partial \end{bmatrix} \right)$$

with the posterior mean and covariance functions ν, κ and their derivatives given by Eqs. (26.14) and (26.15), then the induced bivariate Gaussian marginal on $[a_\alpha, b_\alpha]$ is

$$p(a_\alpha, b_\alpha) = \mathcal{N}\left(\begin{bmatrix} a_\alpha \\ b_\alpha \end{bmatrix}; \begin{bmatrix} m_\alpha^a \\ m_\alpha^b \end{bmatrix}, \begin{bmatrix} C_\alpha^{aa} & C_\alpha^{ab} \\ C_\alpha^{ba} & C_\alpha^{bb} \end{bmatrix} \right),$$

with parameters (nb. $C_\alpha^{ab} = C_\alpha^{ba}$)

$$m_\alpha^a := \nu_0 - \nu_\alpha + c_1 \alpha \nu_0', \qquad m_\alpha^b := \nu'(\alpha) - c_2 \nu'(0), \text{ and}$$
$$C_\alpha^{aa} := \kappa_{00} + (c_1 \alpha)^2 \partial_\kappa_{00}^\partial + \kappa_{\alpha\alpha} + 2(c_1\alpha(\kappa_{00}^\partial - \partial_\kappa_{0\alpha}) - \kappa_{0\alpha}),$$
$$C_\alpha^{ab} := -c_2(\kappa_{00}^\partial + c_1 \alpha \partial_\kappa_{00}^\partial) + (1+c_2)\partial_\kappa_{0\alpha} + c_1 \alpha \partial_\kappa_{0\alpha}^\partial - \kappa_{\alpha\alpha}^\partial,$$
$$C_\alpha^{bb} := c_2^2 \partial_\kappa_{00}^\partial - 2c_2 \partial_\kappa_{0\alpha}^\partial + \partial_\kappa_{\alpha\alpha}^\partial.$$

And the probability for the weak Wolfe conditions to hold is given by the standardised *bivariate normal probability*[20]

$$p(a_\alpha \geq 0 \wedge b_\alpha \geq 0)$$
$$= \int_{-\frac{m_\alpha^a}{\sqrt{C_\alpha^{aa}}}}^{\infty} \int_{-\frac{m_\alpha^b}{\sqrt{C_\alpha^{bb}}}}^{\infty} \mathcal{N}\left(\begin{bmatrix} a \\ b \end{bmatrix}; \begin{bmatrix} 0 \\ 0 \end{bmatrix}, \begin{bmatrix} 1 & \rho_\alpha \\ \rho_\alpha & 1 \end{bmatrix} \right) da\,db,$$

with the correlation coefficient $-1 \leq \rho_\alpha := C_\alpha^{ab}/\sqrt{C_\alpha^{aa}C_\alpha^{bb}} \leq 1$.

The strong condition is slightly more tricky. It amounts to the still linear restriction of b_α on either side, to

$$0 \leq b_\alpha \leq -2c_2 f'(0).$$

But of course we do not have access to the exact value of $f'(0)$, just a Gaussian estimate for it. A computationally easy, albeit ad hoc, solution is to use the expectation[21] $f'(0) \approx \nu_0'$ to set an upper limit $\bar{b} := -2c_2\nu_0'$, and use it to compute an approximate probability for the strong Wolfe conditions, as

$$p(a_\alpha \geq 0 \wedge 0 \leq b_\alpha \leq \bar{b})$$
$$= \int_{-\frac{m_\alpha^a}{\sqrt{C_\alpha^{aa}}}}^{\infty} \int_{-\frac{m_\alpha^b}{\sqrt{C_\alpha^{bb}}}}^{\frac{\bar{b}-m_\alpha^b}{\sqrt{C_\alpha^{bb}}}} \mathcal{N}\left(\begin{bmatrix} a \\ b \end{bmatrix}; \begin{bmatrix} 0 \\ 0 \end{bmatrix}, \begin{bmatrix} 1 & \rho_\alpha \\ \rho_\alpha & 1 \end{bmatrix} \right) da\,db. \quad (26.17)$$

Algorithm 26.1 provides pseudo-code for the thus completed probabilistic extension of classic line searches.

[20] This is the "bivariate error function", the generalisation of the univariate Gaussian cumulative density
$$\int_{-\infty}^{x} \mathcal{N}(\tilde{x};0,1)\,d\tilde{x} = \frac{1}{2}\left(1 + \operatorname{erf}\left(\frac{x}{\sqrt{2}}\right)\right).$$
Just like the univariate case, there is no "analytic" solution, only an "atomic" one (in standard libraries, the error function is implemented as a special case of the incomplete Gamma function, computed either via a series expansion or a continued fraction, depending on the input. For more, see §6.2 of Numerical Recipes (Press et al., 1992). A highly accurate approximation of comparable cost to the error function was provided by Alan Genz (2004), whose personal website at Washington State University is a treasure trove of exquisite atomic algorithms for Gaussian integrals.

[21] Alternatively, one could also use the 95%-confidence lower and upper bounds $f'(0) \lesssim \nu_0' + 2\sqrt{\partial_\kappa_{00}^\partial}$ and $f'(0) \gtrsim \nu_0' - 2\sqrt{\partial_\kappa_{00}^\partial}$ to build more lenient or restrictive decision rules, respectively.

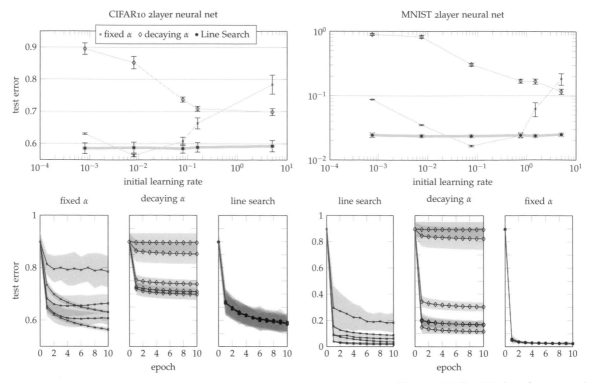

▶ 26.6   Uncertain Observations May Require Additional Observables

The likelihood defined by Eq. (26.12) contains the covariance matrix Λ, in particular its internal parameters $\sigma_{f_i}, \sigma_{f'_i}$. In a practical empirical risk minisation problem (as described by Eq. (26.3)), these variables are not necessarily known. And of course they are not present in the noise-free setting. This is a situation in which computational uncertainty introduces new complexities that have to be addressed by extra work. For example, they may require the computation of new observables that are not part of the classic paradigm. Here is one way to do this for the variances required in Λ.[22]

If the batch size M is larger than one, then $\sigma_{f_i}, \sigma_{f'_i}, \rho_i$ can be estimated empirically from the elements $\ell_m(t) := \ell(\xi_{J_m}, x(\alpha))$ of the batch objective, and its gradients $\ell'_m(\alpha) := \partial \ell_m / \partial \alpha$. In addition to the already computed empirical batch means

$$y_i = r(\alpha_i) + \frac{1}{M} \sum_{m=1}^{M} \ell_m(\alpha_i),$$

$$y'_i = d_i^\mathsf{T} \left(\nabla r(\alpha_i) + \frac{1}{M} \sum_{m=1}^{M} \nabla \ell_m(\alpha_i) \right),$$

Figure 26.6: Empirical performance of the probabilistic line search on some basic benchmarks. Figure adapted from Mahsereci and Hennig (2015). Left column: Experiments on CIFAR10 data set (Krizhevsky and Hinton, 2009). Right column: MNIST data set (http://yann.lecun.com/exdb/mnist/). The model is a 2-layer feed-forward network in either case. All plots show a comparison between stochastic gradient descent (sgd) run with *fixed* or *decaying* learning rate α, compared to an sgd optimiser initialised at the same learning rate, then controlled by the line search. Top plots: Test error after 10 training epochs vs learning rate. Bottom plots: Test error vs training epoch. Error bars show empirical standard-deviation over 20 repetitions. The uncontrolled sgd instances show strong variance in performance, while the line search quickly finds and tracks a good choice of learning rate. It does not always perform as well as the best possible learning rate, but finding that rate requires a tedious manual, or externally controlled search, while the line search requires no intervention.

[22] For simplicity, we assume independence between function values f and gradients f', setting $\rho = 0$. The extension to an empirical estimator of ρ is straightforward, but $\rho = 0$ also seems to work well in practice.

```
1  procedure PROBLINESEARCHSKETCH(f, y₀, y'₀, σ_{f₀}, σ_{f'₀})
2      T, Y, Y' ← 0, y₀, y'₀ ∈ ℝ              // initialise storage
3          t ← 1          // initial candidate equals previous step-length
4      while length(T) < 10 and no Wolfe-point found do
5          [y, y'] ← f(t)                      // evaluate objective
6          T, Y, Y' ← T ∪ t, Y ∪ y, Y' ∪ y'   // update storage
7              GP ← GPINFERENCE(t, y, y')
8          P^Wolfe ← PROBWOLFE(T, GP)          // Wolfe prob. at T
9          if any P^Wolfe > c_W then                    // done?
10             return t_* = arg max P^Wolfe            // success!
11         else                                 // keep searching!
12             T_cand ← COMPUTECANDIDATES(GP)   // candidates
13             EI ← EXPECTEDIMPROVEMENT(T_cand, GP)
14             PW ← PROBWOLFE(T_cand, GP)
15             t ← arg max(PW ⊙ EI)             // find best candidate
16         end if
17     end while
18     return error / fall-back              // no acceptable point found
19 end procedure
```

Algorithm 26.1: Pseudo-code for a probabilistic line search. Adapted from Mahsereci and Hennig (2017). The code assumes access to a function handle f that returns scaled pairs of values and gradients of the form

$$f(t) = \left[\frac{f(t) - f(0)}{f'(0)}, \frac{f'(t)}{f'(0)}\right],$$

where $t = \alpha/\alpha_{i-1}$ is the input variable scaled by the step length of the previous line search. This re-scaling allows the use of standardised scales for the GP prior, thus avoids hyperparameters. Note that all operations take place on the scalar projected gradients $\in \mathbb{R}$, not on full gradients $\in \mathbb{R}^N$. The code sets a fixed budget of 10 evaluations, after which the search aborts. In this case, a fall-back solution can be returned. For example, the point t_* that minimises the GP posterior mean. In practice, this fall-back is very rarely required.

this requires collecting the additional statistics

$$S_i = \frac{1}{M}\sum_{m=1}^{M} \ell_m^2(\alpha_i), \text{ and}$$
$$S'_i = \frac{1}{M}\sum_{m=1}^{M} (d_i^\mathsf{T}\nabla\ell_m(\alpha_i))^2, \tag{26.18}$$

then using the estimators

$$\sigma_{f_i}^2 = \frac{S_i - y_i^2}{M-1}, \qquad \sigma_{f'_i}^2 = \frac{S'_i - (y'_i)^2}{M-1}.$$

Doing so requires computing M inner products when collecting S'_i, at cost $\mathcal{O}(NM)$. However, the computation of the batch losses $\ell_m(\alpha_i)$ and gradients $\nabla\ell_m(\alpha_i)$ is usually more expensive than these inner products (in deep networks, these gradients are computed by back-propagation). And these numbers already needed to be computed for the other parts of the line search and overall optimiser anyway. Thus the empirical estimation of $\sigma_{f_i}, \sigma_{f'_i}$ only adds a minor computational overhead. Recent software packages[23] give access to these quantities at low or very low computational overhead. A more detailed discussion can be found in §5.2 of Maren Mahsereci's PhD thesis (2018), and also in the original works on the probabilistic line search.[24]

[23] E.g. Dangel, Kunstner, and Hennig (2020), software at backpack.pt

[24] Mahsereci and Hennig (2015; 2017)

Speaking more abstractly, the interesting aspect here is that
the presence of significant computational uncertainty (noise) in
an optimisation problem may not only require the design of
more general probabilistic algorithms, such as the line search
constructed here. It might also require the computation of new
quantities, for example to identify the likelihood. By giving an
explicit role to the likelihood, the probabilistic viewpoint makes
this aspect obvious. One may wonder whether non-probabilistic
formulations have in the past sometimes hidden such challenges
a bit too well.

27

Controlling Optimisation by Probabilistic Estimates

Beyond the step size, optimisation algorithms have a number of other hyperparameters that affect their performance. In the classic noise-free setting virtually all of these are either automatically set by the algorithm, or their performance is so robust to the parameter choice that a global value can be set once and for all by the designer.[1] The noisy setting complicates things both by making some decisions less straightforward, and by introducing new parameters to be tuned. In this section we will address the following two examples, one each of these cases:

⊖ Since a noisy gradient measurement will almost surely never actually return the value 'zero' – even if the optimiser should pass by the extremum of either the full-data or population loss – the issue of when to *stop* the optimiser turns from a trivial Boolean conditional in the noise-free case into an actual concern. This is a real problem in empirical risk minimisation: As it approaches the minimum of the population risk, stochastic optimisers at best begin a wasteful diffusion around the optimum that is difficult to detect. At worst, they may over-fit, i.e. "home in" to superficial features of only the empirical data set.

⊖ The batch size M is a new parameter under control of the optimiser that is not present in the classic case. Hardware characteristics often put constraints on the available choices of M. But nevertheless, a good trade-off between cost and precision can help the optimiser converge faster.

The following two sections present ways to address these issues from the probabilistic standpoint. These are just case-studies,[2] and should not be taken as the sole solutions to these issues. Quite in the contrary, both aspects have been studied by many authors in the machine learning community. The point of this section is to highlight two aspects. First, on a conceptual level, the probabilistic viewpoint offers a unifying framework in which to reason about algorithmic design. But second, practical considerations may also require us to once again ease off the Bayesian orthodoxy. Especially when it comes to nuisance parameters deep inside a low-level algorithm, not every quantity has to have a full-fledged calibrated posterior. The probabilistic framework may then still help in the derivations, but point estimates derived from the probabilistic formulation may just do the trick.

[2] The two sections are short summaries of the following two papers, respectively: Balles, Romero, and Hennig (2017) as well as Mahsereci et al. (2017). Additional information can be found in M. Mahsereci's PhD thesis (2018).

▶ **27.1   Choosing Batch Sizes**

For the moment, we consider the simple (and flawed, yet popular) case of stochastic gradient descent, i.e. the optimiser given by the update rule

$$x_{i+1} = x_i - \alpha_i \nabla \tilde{\mathcal{L}}(x_i) =: x_i - \alpha_i g_M(x_i).$$

Let us assume we have found a good value for α_i, e.g. by using the line search algorithm described above. Here we simplified the notation by introducing the shorthand $g_M(x_i)$, which explicitly exposes the batch size M in the noisy gradient $\nabla \tilde{\mathcal{L}}_M(x_i)$. By Eq. (26.3), the variance of the gradient elements scales inversely with M. If we can assume that the entire data set is very large ($K \gg M$) and that the batch elements are drawn independently of each other, then the elements of $g_M(x_i)$ are distributed according to the likelihood

$$g_M(x_i) \sim \mathcal{N}\left(\nabla \mathcal{L}(\Xi, x_i), \frac{1}{M}\Sigma(x_i)\right), \tag{27.1}$$

where $\Sigma(x)$ is the covariance between gradient elements,

$$\Sigma(x) := \frac{1}{K} \sum_{i=1}^{K} (\nabla \ell(\xi_i, x) - \nabla \mathcal{L}(\Xi, x))(\nabla \ell(\xi_i, x) - \nabla \mathcal{L}(\Xi, x))^{\mathsf{T}}.$$

We will drop the variable x from the notation below, as all subsequent considerations apply to one specific local value of x_i. The full matrix Σ is unknown, and very costly to even estimate empirically. But we already saw above (Eq. (26.18)) that the diagonal elements of Σ can be estimated relatively cheaply at runtime, by computing the additional observable

$$S = \frac{1}{M} \sum_{j=1}^{M} \nabla \ell(\xi_j, x)^{\cdot 2} - g_M(x)^{\cdot 2}, \tag{27.2}$$

where $\cdot^2$ denotes the element-wise square.

For simplicity, we will assume that the optimiser has free control over the batch size M.[3] Deciding for a concrete value of M, the optimisation algorithm now faces a trade-off: A large batch size provides a more informative (precise) estimate of the true gradient, but increases computation cost. From Eq. (27.1), the standard deviation of g_M only drops with $M^{-1/2}$, but the computation cost of course rises linearly with M. So we may conjecture that there is an optimal choice for M. It would be nice to know this optimal value; but since this is a very low-level consideration about a hyperparameter of an inner-loop algorithm, an exact answer is not as important as a cheap one. Thus, we will now make a series of convenient assumptions to arrive at a heuristic:

First, assume that the true gradient $\nabla \mathcal{L}$ is Lipschitz continuous (a realistic assumption for machine learning models) with Lipschitz-constant L. That is,

$$\|\nabla \mathcal{L}(x) - \nabla \mathcal{L}(x_i)\| \leq L\|x - x_i\| \quad \forall\, x \in \mathbb{R}^N.$$

This assumption implies a quadratic upper bound on the loss itself:[4]

$$\mathcal{L}(x_{i+1}) \leq \mathcal{L}(x_i) + \nabla \mathcal{L}(x_{i+1} - x_i) + \frac{L}{2}\|x_{i+1} - x_i\|^2.$$

Re-arranging for the stochastic gradient descent rule $x_{i+1} = x_i - \alpha_i g_i$ yields a lower bound on the *gain* in loss for the optimiser's step:

$$\mathcal{L}(x_i) - \mathcal{L}(x_{i+1}) \geq G := \alpha_i \nabla \mathcal{L}(x_i)^\mathsf{T} g_i - \frac{L\alpha_i^2}{2}\|g_i\|^2.$$

Here is where the probabilistic description becomes helpful: From Eq. (27.1), we know that $\mathbb{E}(g_i) = \nabla \mathcal{L}(x_i)$, and

$$\mathbb{E}(\|g_i\|^2) = \|\nabla \mathcal{L}(x_i)\|^2 + \frac{\mathrm{tr}\,\Sigma}{M},$$

so we can compute an *expected gain* from the next step of gradient descent, as

$$\mathbb{E}(G) = \left(\alpha_i - \frac{L\alpha_i^2}{2}\right)\|\nabla \mathcal{L}(x_i)\|^2 - \frac{L\alpha_i^2}{2M}\,\mathrm{tr}(\Sigma).$$

Since computation cost is linear in M, we consider the *expected gain per cost* $\mathbb{E}(G)/M$, which is then a rational function in M, and we can find the M that maximises this expression. It is

$$M_* = \frac{2L\alpha}{2 - L\alpha}\frac{\mathrm{tr}\,\Sigma}{\|\nabla \mathcal{L}(x_i)\|^2}. \tag{27.3}$$

[3] In practice, aspects like the cache size of the processing unit usually mean that batch sizes have to be chosen as an integer multiple of the maximal number of data points that can be simultaneously cached.

[4] See, e.g., Eq. 4.3 in Bottou, Curtis, and Nocedal (2016).

Since L is usually not known a priori and the norm of the true gradient is not accessible, we finally make a number of strongly simplifying assumptions to arrive at a concrete heuristic that does not add computational overhead. First, assume that $\nabla \mathcal{L}$ is not just Lipschitz continuous but also differentiable, and the Hessian of $\mathcal{L}$ is scalar: $B(x_i) \approx h I_N$. This means[5] that the Lipschitz constant is $L = h$ and the gradient norm can be approximated linearly as $\|\nabla \mathcal{L}(x_i)\|^2 \approx 2h(\mathcal{L}(x_i) - \mathcal{L}_*)$, where $\mathcal{L}_* = \min_{\alpha_i} \mathcal{L}(x_i + \alpha_i g_i)$ is the loss from the optimal stochastic gradient descent step size. This simplifies Eq. (27.3) to

$$M_* = \frac{\alpha}{2 - h\alpha} \frac{\operatorname{tr}\Sigma}{\mathcal{L}(x_i) - \mathcal{L}_*}.$$

Under the scalar Hessian assumption, the optimal learning rate is $\alpha = 1/h$. Since we started out assuming that the optimiser is in fact using an approximately optimal step-size, we get

$$M_* \approx \alpha \frac{\operatorname{tr}\Sigma}{\mathcal{L}(x_i) - \mathcal{L}_*}.$$

Finally, empirical risks are typically energy functions, with an optimum $\mathcal{L}_* \approx 0$. So we get an upper bound for the optimal step size as

$$M_* \leq \alpha \frac{\operatorname{tr}\Sigma}{\mathcal{L}(x_i)} \tag{27.4}$$

(recall that we have an unbiased estimate of $\mathcal{L}$ in $\tilde{\mathcal{L}}$).

This heuristic has shown good empirical performance on a number of test cases (Figure 27.1). For the purposes of this text, this result serves as another example for the use of probabilistic information in algorithm design. As in the preceding section on step-size selection, we once again face a parameter in our algorithm (the batch size M) whose optimal value is fundamentally affected by computational uncertainty. And as before, the tuning heuristic we arrive at involves the diagonal elements of the covariance matrix Σ, a quantity that would not exist in the noise-free case. We already saw in the preceding section that it can be estimated at runtime, and that doing so requires computing an additional observable (of low computational cost) that would not be part of a classic analysis.

► 27.2   **Early Stopping**

When should the optimiser stop? In the noise-free case, the answer is trivial: stop when the gradient vanishes, $\nabla f = 0$. But

[5] A detailed derivation is in the original paper by Balles, Romero, and Hennig (2017).

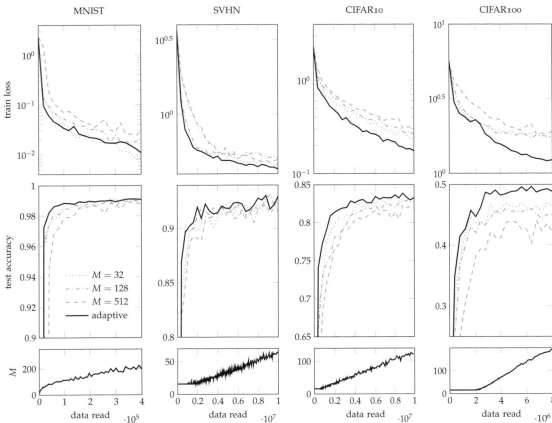

Figure 27.1: Optimisation progress of stochastic gradient descent when batch sizes are controlled by the adaptive rule of Eq. (27.4). Results reproduced from Balles, Romero, and Hennig (2017). Each column of plots shows results on a specific empirical risk minimisation problem, an image recognition task on four different standard benchmark data sets (MNIST: see Figure 26.6. Street View House Numbers: Netzer et al., 2011. CIFAR10 and 100: Krizhevsky and Hinton, 2009). Top to bottom: Training error (a measure of the optimisers' raw efficiency); test accuracy (a measure of generalisation); and the batch size M chosen by the optimiser over the course of the optimisation. Results are plotted against the number of read data-points (not the number of optimiser steps) for a fairer comparison. Especially for the moderately larger problems (CIFAR10 and CIFAR100), the adaptive schedule improves on fixed batch sizes, even though the locally chosen batch sizes generally lie within the range of the constant-M comparisons.

in the noisy case, we never know with certainty that this is the case, and the optimiser may well not actually converge to a true root of the gradient. In the empirical risk minimisation setting, this holds when significant computational noise arises from batching, but it is even a problem when the risk is computed over the *entire* data set. The real target of the optimisation problem is the population risk, which can fundamentally not be accessed because we only have access to a finite data set. This is an example where computational uncertainty and empirical uncertainty overlap.

The stopping problem has practical relevance. For contemporary machine learning models, the number N of parameters to be fitted often exceeds the number K of datapoints. In such situations, if the optimiser is not stopped, it might *over-fit* to a minimum of the empirical risk that reflects features of the data set that are only due to sampling noise, and not present in the population. The standard approach to this problem is to separate the data into a *training set* and a separate *validation set*. The optimiser only gets access to the empirical risk on the training set (possibly sub-sampled into batches). A separate monitor observes the evolution of the validation risk, and stops the optimiser when the validation risk starts rising. Apart from technicalities (reliably detecting a rise in the validation risk is itself a noisy estimation problem), the principal downside of this approach is that it "wastes" a significant part of the data on the validation set. Collecting data often has a high financial and time cost, and the data in the validation set cannot be used by the optimiser to find a more general minimum. Even if we ignore the issue of overfitting, we still need *some* way to decide when to stop the optimiser. Many practitioners just run the method "until the learning-curve is flat", which is wasteful.

This section describes a simple statistical test as an alternative, which is particularly suitable for small data sets, where constructing a (sufficiently large) validation is not feasible. It is based on work by Mahsereci et al. (2017), and makes explicit use of the observation likelihood (Eq. (27.1)). Let $p_{\text{pop.}}$ be the distribution from which data points are sampled in the wild, and f be the population risk

$$f(x) = r(x) + \int \ell(\xi, x)\, \mathrm{d}p_{\text{pop.}}(\xi).$$

Then the gradient of the empirical risk $\mathcal{L}$ is distributed as

$$p(\nabla\mathcal{L}(x) \mid f) = \mathcal{N}\left(\nabla\mathcal{L}(x); \nabla f(x), \frac{\Sigma(x)}{K}\right).$$

So the probability to observe a particular empirical loss gradient if the true population loss is actually zero is the evidence,

$$p(\nabla\mathcal{L}(x) \mid 0) = \mathcal{N}\left(\nabla\mathcal{L}(x); 0, \frac{\Sigma(x)}{K}\right).$$

Once again the quantity Σ makes an appearance. Since we already decided to estimate the diagonal of Σ empirically in the above sections, we may as well re-use the estimator S from Eq. (27.2). Making once again the simplifying assumption that the sampling noise is independent across gradient elements,[6] we get

$$p(\nabla\mathcal{L}(x) \mid 0) = \prod_{i=1}^{N}\mathcal{N}\left(\frac{\partial\mathcal{L}(x)}{\partial x_i}; 0, \frac{S_i(x)}{K}\right).$$

Analogous to the treatment in §11.3 (see Eq. (11.15)), we can now construct a log-likelihood ratio test. If the probability for the observed gradients under the assumption that the population

[6] This independence assumption is a relatively strong simplification, which may be possible to improve on with some extra work. In particular if other structural information about the data set and the model encoded in ℓ is available, a block, or low-rank structure for Σ is probably helpful.

risk vanishes is larger than the expected value of this probability, then the hypothesis that we really are close to the population optimium cannot be ruled out any more, and we may consider stopping the algorithm. This happens when

$$\log p(\nabla \mathcal{L}(x) \mid 0) - \mathbb{E}_{p(\nabla \hat{\mathcal{L}}(x)\mid 0)}(p(\nabla \hat{\mathcal{L}}(x) \mid 0)) > 0,$$

$$1 - \frac{K}{N} \sum_{i=1}^{N} \left(\frac{[\nabla \mathcal{L}(x)]_i}{S_i(x)} \right) > 0.$$

(The variable $\hat{\mathcal{L}}$ is the integration variable for the expectation.) That is, when the average gradient element is within the "error bar" estimate S.

More details can be found in Mahsereci et al. (2017). The stopping test provides another example for how probabilistic analysis of the result of computations can inform algorithm design. It also demonstrates how uncertainty arising from external and computational sources can interact with each other in practice. From the probabilistic viewpoint there is no problem with this mixing. Mathematically, uncertainties arising from different sources do not need to be distinguished formally.

28

First- and Second-Order Methods

In this section, we address the design question of iterative algorithms: in the generic update rule (see Algorithm 25.1)

$$x_{i+1} = x_i + \alpha_i d_i, \qquad \alpha_i \in \mathbb{R}, \; d_i \in \mathbb{R}^N,$$

how should the *direction* d_i be chosen? There are myriad ways to answer this question, we will discuss only a few important basic choices. Very roughly, they split into algorithms motivated by gradient descent (a first-order method), and methods motivated by the Newton–Raphson rule (a second-order method). More specifically, in §28.1 we will first discuss algorithms in which the update rule for d_i can be phrased independently for each element. That is,

$$[d_i]_n = [d_i]_n(\{f_j, \{[\nabla f_j]_n\}_{j=0,\dots,i}).$$

Section 28.3 will discuss a second type of rules that also consider interactions between gradient elements. This classification is primarily a computational consideration, not an analytic one. Some of the methods in this first class converge asymptotically faster than gradient descent; virtually all the methods in the second class converge slower than Newton's method. But element-wise rules scale more readily to very high-dimensional problems. This is one of the reasons why they are currently the popular choice in machine learning, where the number N of parameters to be optimised is frequently in the range beyond 10^6.

▶ 28.1 Element-wise Methods

Typically, the update rule is phrased in terms of some sufficient statistics kept in memory and updated locally. Here are some classic choices. In the following, all operations are element-wise.

⊖ The base case is *gradient descent*

$$x_{i+1} = x_i - \alpha_i \nabla f.$$

⊖ Gradient descent with *momentum*[1] is motivated by the Newtonian dynamics[2] of a massive particle moving, with friction, in a potential field given by f. It uses an auxiliary variable v_i, and is described by the update-rule

$$v_i = -\alpha_i(1-\beta_i)\nabla f(x_i) + \beta_i v_{i-1} \quad \text{with } \beta_i \in (0,1),$$
$$x_{i+1} = x_i + v_i.$$

$$(28.3)$$

⊖ *Nesterov's accelerated* method[3] is a variant of momentum that uses a look-ahead:

$$v_i = -\alpha_i(1-\beta_i)\nabla f(x_i + \alpha_i(1-\beta_i)v_i) + \beta_i v_{i-1},$$
$$x_{i+1} = x_i + v_i.$$

Note that this is an implicit definition, because v_i features both on the left-hand side and in the argument of ∇f. Nesterov's method will not be further discussed in this chapter, it is more readily understood in the framework of implicit ODE solvers[4]

⊖ Other recently popular algorithms include rules such as *AdaDelta*[5] and *Adam*.[6] These will not be discussed further here, but we note that these algorithms, which are specifically designed for stochastic optimisation, both retain a running average of the element-wise *square* of the gradient, similar to the statistic described in Eq. (27.2). Due to this they can in fact be interpreted as a form of "uncertainty-damping", i.e. the length of a step, in each individual dimension, is scaled by the signal-to-noise ratio. The technical details are involved, though.[7]

For the purposes of this text, it is important to note that the first three methods on this list – gradient descent, momentum, accelerated momentum – can all be motivated and analysed purely on noise-free optimisation problems. If an optimisation problem is stochastic, one can then add analysis of the noise's effect on these methods, but noise is not a principal ingredient in their construction.

We thus now turn to ask whether the presence of noise can be more explicitly encoded in these algorithms. As in previous chapters, we will thus construct generative probabilistic models

[1] Polyak (1964). Due to the derivation below, the algorithm is historically also known as the *heavy ball* method.

[2] Since this physical interpretation has an interesting connection to the probabilistic derivation below, we briefly derive it here. Assume the particle has mass m and moves in a potential given by f, with friction coefficient κ. Then its Newtonian dynamics are described by the second-order ODE

$$m\ddot{x}(t) = -\kappa\dot{x}(t) - \nabla f(x(t)). \quad (28.1)$$

A simple approximate way to solve this problem is to assume that f is locally linear (that ∇f is locally constant), which turns Eq. (28.1) into a first-order separable linear ODE in the *velocity* $v(t) := \dot{x}$. This locally constant approximation amounts to an *explicit Euler* step (see §37). Given the initial values $x(t_i) = x_i$, and $v(t_i) = v_i$, the approximate solution at time $t_{i+1} := t_i + \tau$ is then given by Eq. (28.3), with the constants given by

$$\alpha_i = 1/\kappa,$$
$$\beta_i = \exp\left(-\frac{\kappa}{m}\tau\right). \quad (28.2)$$

Note that this dynamical model reverts to that of gradient descent in the massless limit $m \to 0$ (since then $\beta \to 0$).

[3] Nesterov (1983)
[4] Nesterov's method can be derived from the Newtonian dynamics of a massive particle analogous to the derivation of the momentum method above, where the explicit Euler step is replaced with an implicit step. For further discussion of the relationship between ODE solvers and optimisation methods, see Scieur et al. (2017), and also Exercise 38.3 in Chapter VI.
[5] Zeiler (2012)
[6] Kingma and Ba (2015)
[7] Balles and Hennig (2018)

```
 1  procedure PROB_OPTIMISE(l(x), x₀)
 2      l_{x₀} ← l(x₀)                              // first evaluation
 3      L ← l_{x₀}                                  // initialise storage
 4      for i = 0, 1, … do
 5          d_i ← P_DIRECTION(L)                    // decide search direction
 6          α_i ← PLSEARCH(d_i^T l(t))              // probabilistic line search
 7          x_{i+1} ← x_i + α_i d_i                 // move
 8          l_{i+1} ← l(x_{i+1})                    // observe
 9          if TERMINATE(L) then                    // done?
10              return x_i                          // success!
11          end if
12          L ← L ∪ l_{i+1}                         // update storage
13      end for
14  end procedure
```

Algorithm 28.1: Pseudo-code for a probabilistic iterative optimisation algorithm. This is a variant of the generic classic optimiser in Algorithm 25.1. The differences to that algorithm are that the probabilistic variant assumes access to a *likelihood* $l(x) = p(y, y' \mid f(x), \nabla f(x))$ for the objective and its gradient, rather than noise-free access to those quantities. For generality, the data structure returned by the likelihood is not further specified. As a concrete example, one may think of a joint or independent Gaussian distribution over $y \in \mathbb{R}, y' \in \mathbb{R}^N$ centred on $(f, \nabla f)$, with covariance $\Lambda \in \mathbb{R}^{N+1 \times N+1}$. Observations are stored in a suitable structure L. The algorithm uses the probabilistic line search described in §26.5 to choose step-sizes. To signify that this subroutine only operates on the univariate sub-problem, line 6 uses the suggestive notation $d_i^T l(t)$ (cf. the same line in Algorithm 25.1). The search direction is computed in a decision step from the posterior on the problem arising from the data in L. Importantly, the resulting algorithm is structurally virtually identical to the classic method. The probabilistic operations are encapsulated in the subroutines. If those routines can be designed with cost comparable to the classic method, then the probabilistic optimiser need not have higher computational cost than the classics.

that revert to gradient descent and its momentum variant in the limit of a Dirac observation likelihood. Since stochastic noise is such a prevalent problem in contemporary optimisation problems, however, we will be less interested in analysing the underlying *prior* assumptions that yield these classic algorithms, and more focussed on how the presence of noise can be included explicitly in such an optimiser. The result will be a series of "add-ons" to these classic methods, rather than a probabilistic re-interpretation for them. Algorithm 28.1 shows how these can be realised within the structure of classic methods by updating specific parts of the optimisation loop. It is worth doing these extensions carefully. The probabilistic formulation allows a clear separation between the effects of observation noise and those of the geometry of the underlying smooth objective.

▶ 28.2 Probabilistic Element-wise Rules

Since the above rules are defined element-wise, we will simplify the notation for this section and use the scalar quantity $f'_n(x_i) \in \mathbb{R}$ to represent the element $[\nabla f(x_i)]_n$ of the gradient. Where the index $n \in [1, \dots, N]$ does not matter, we will also drop it. As the above methods can be motivated within the framework of noise-free gradient observations, we need to add a probabilistic estimation model for these gradients. Doing so requires a joint generative model $p(\nabla f(x))$ for the gradients – both over the N output dimensions and over the input domain $\mathbb{R}^N$. In the classic methods, this is not necessary: if one assumes the gradients to be accessible without uncertainty, there is never a need to guess what the real gradient may be. The optimiser can just check.

Once again, computational cost constraints will guide our model design just as much as knowledge about the loss function itself. To keep the element-wise structure of the above rules, we will assume that the elements of ∇f evolve independently of each other,[8] imposing the factorisation structure

$$p(\nabla f(x)) =: \prod_{n=1}^{N} p_n(f_n'(x)).$$

For the same algorithmic reasons as in previous chapters, we are again drawn to Gaussian process models as candidates for p_n. But even within that class of probabilistic models, there is now a fundamental choice to be made. The conceptually cleaner path is to define a consistent Gaussian process model over the input domain $\mathbb{R}^N$. However, this would impose the usual cubic cost in i, the number of the optimiser's iterations, a problem that would require further approximations to fix. We also know that the optimiser will only ever ask for gradients along its trajectory, which forms a univariate curve, albeit no linear sub-space of $\mathbb{R}^N$. For this reason, we make another leap of faith and treat the individual gradient observations $f_n'(x_i)$ as separate univariate time series $f_n'(t_i)$ for $t_i \in \mathbb{R}$. Inference can then be addressed with the Kalman filter (§5). This raises the question how the multivariate input x_i should be transformed into a scalar t: is the difference from one optimisation step to another unit ($t \leftarrow t + 1$) or does it have a length? For the purposes of this section, we will use the latter option, and set $t_{i+1} = t_i + \tau$ with $\tau := \|x_{i+1} - x_i\|$.

With this, we can consider two basic choices for the SDE defining the Kalman filter: The Wiener process and the Ornstein–Uhlenbeck process,

$$\mathrm{d}f_n'(t) = \qquad 0\,\mathrm{d}t + \theta_n\,\mathrm{d}\omega_t, \quad \text{and} \qquad (28.4)$$

$$\mathrm{d}f_n'(t) = -\gamma_n f'(t)\,\mathrm{d}t + \theta_n\,\mathrm{d}\omega_t, \quad \text{respectively.} \qquad (28.5)$$

Here we have allowed for separate drift (γ_n) and diffusion (θ_n) scales for each element of the gradient. They translate into the Kalman filter parameters (see Algorithm 5.1 and Eq. (5.21))

$$A_n = 1, \qquad Q = \theta_n^2 \tau \qquad \text{(Wiener)}, \quad (28.6)$$

$$A_n = e^{-\gamma_n \tau} \qquad Q = \frac{\theta_n^2}{2\gamma_n}\left(1 - e^{-2\gamma_n \tau}\right) \qquad \text{(OU)}. \qquad (28.7)$$

We recall from §5 that the Wiener process assumes the gradient elements to drift in a free random walk, while the OU process

[8] This assumption is patently incorrect, simply because ∇f is the gradient of the smooth scalar field f; thus, the gradient theorem imposes constraints on the elements of ∇f relative to each other: for any two points x_1, x_2 and any curve c from x_1 to x_2, the gradient must satisfy

$$f(x_2) - f(x_1) = \int_c \nabla f(x)\,\mathrm{d}x.$$

The discussion in §28.3 will show that including these constraints in a computationally efficient way is not straightforward. Further discussion of these issues can be found in Hennig (2013).

expects the gradients to revert to zero. As Eq. (28.7) shows, the latter model is slightly more complicated to implement, but it might provide a more realistic model of the gradients produced by an optimisation routine that actively tries to drive the gradients to zero.

Consider the behaviour of the Kalman filter (28.6) arising from the Wiener prior (28.4). Assume that, at step $i - 1$, the N independent filters for each gradient element together hold posterior (estimation) mean $m_{i-1} \in \mathbb{R}^N$ and the vector of scalar (element-wise) covariances $P_{i-1} \in \mathbb{R}^N$. To build a probabilistic version of stochastic gradient descent, we take m_{i-1} as the estimate for $\nabla f(x_i)$, so the optimiser moves to

$$x_i = x_{i-1} + \alpha_i m_{i-1}.$$

Now the optimiser collects an observation $y_i \in \mathbb{R}^N$. In the classic derivation, this is taken as a direct observation $y_i = \nabla f(x_i)$. To build a probabilistic extension, we instead use the explicit likelihood

$$p(y_i \mid \nabla f(x_i)) = \mathcal{N}(y_i; \nabla f(x_i), \operatorname{diag} R),$$

where $R \in \mathbb{R}^N$ is a vector of individual observation likelihoods – we already saw in Eqs. (26.18) and (27.2) how to build empirical estimators for this observation noise in empirical risk minimisation problems, by summing squares of gradient elements over batches. Since we can compute a noisy observation of the gradient itself, we set the observation projection in Algorithm 5.1 to $H = 1$. From Algorithm 5.1 one can then deduce (taking care to do all operations element-wise) that the updated mean and covariances at x_i will be given by the vectors (all operations element-wise!)

$$m_i = (1 - K)m_{i-1} + Ky_i \qquad \text{and}$$
$$P_i = (1 - K)P_i^- = \frac{(P_{i-1} + \theta^2 \tau)R}{P_{i-1} + \theta^2 \tau + R}, \qquad (28.8)$$

where $K = (P_{i-1} + \theta^2 \tau)/(P_{i-1} + \theta^2 \tau + R)$ is the Kalman gain. Thus the algorithm – which we might call probabilistic gradient descent – will now step to the new location

$$x_{i+1} = x_i - \alpha_i m_i = x_i - \alpha_i((1 - K)m_{i-1} + Ky_i). \qquad (28.9)$$

Despite the simplicity of these derivations, there are few interesting aspects to observe here:

Exercise 28.1 (easy, instructive). *What is the value of the Kalman gain K, and thus the update in Eq. (28.9) if the Wiener process prior (28.4) is replaced with the Ornstein–Uhlenbeck prior (28.5)? Compare the role of τ in this update with the values of Eq. (28.2) and compare the role of the friction coefficient κ in the derivation of the momentum method with that of the drift coefficient γ.*

⊖ Not surprisingly, for noise-free observations ($R = 0$), the algorithm simply reverts to gradient descent.

⊖ The diffusion scale θ introduces a new free parameter into the algorithm. Assuming that R is empirically estimated as described above, θ directly determines the gain K. So the algorithm could also be phrased in terms of K. Setting K empirically is about as hard as setting the momentum parameter β in gradient descent with momentum.

⊖ It is tempting to note the similarities between Eqs. (28.9) and (28.3) and think that we have re-constructed the momentum method in a probabilistic fashion. But the two rules are not just subtly different (note the position of the learning rate α_i inside and outside the brackets), they are also constructed from entirely different motivations. The momentum method was originally designed for noise-free problems, to address a problem with under-damped oscillations in gradient descent (hence the quite literal notion of friction). Here, we have added another feature to this method to address an entirely different challenge: the evaluation uncertainty arising from noisy gradients. In fact, it is of course possible to combine both notions with each other and build a probabilistic, smoothed, momentum method. This is perhaps important to note because the contemporary literature on stochastic optimisation, especially in the machine learning community, tends to conflate these two aspects and present the notion of momentum as a remedy for stochasticity. But noise on gradients and under-damping of gradient descent are two separate issues. If the long-term goal is to develop a clear and reliable theory for optimisation, then separate problems should be addressed by separate notions.

Research on element-wise optimisation rules motived by Kalman filtering continues, for example with the idea to use curvature information to calibrate the gain of the filter.[9]

▶ **28.3   Quasi-Newton Methods**

We now move on to optimisation rules that treat the entire gradient jointly, allowing for interactions between gradient elements. Here, too, we will focus on one sub-class of this wider area, algorithms that aim to approximate the behaviour of Newton's method and are thus known as *quasi-Newton methods*.[10] Other popular families of update rules, not discussed here, include nonlinear conjugate gradients [11] and trust-region methods.[12]

[9] Chen et al. (2020)

[10] For reasons that will become clearer below, the same class of methods has also historically been known as *secant* and *variable metric* methods.

[11] Fletcher and Reeves (1964)

[12] Winfield (1970); Powell (1975); Moré (1983).

Newton's method[13] is about the fastest optimisation method for multivariate problems anyone could wish for. A straightforward way to derive this iterative update rule is to consider the second-order Taylor expansion of the objective f around the current iterate x_i,

$$f(x_i + d) \approx f(x_i) + d^{\mathsf{T}} \nabla f(x_i) + \frac{1}{2} d^{\mathsf{T}} B(x_i) d.$$

(Recall that B is the notation for the Hessian of f.) If the Hessian is symmetric positive definite (if f is locally convex), then this quadratic approximation has a unique minimum, which defines the next Newton iterate,

$$x_{i+1} = x_i - B^{-1}(x_i) \nabla f(x_i).$$

Newton's method has some issues with convergence, in particular on non-convex problems. But when it converges, it can converge quadratically fast,[14] which is to say: very fast. The primary problem of Newton's method for medium- and large-scale problems is not its stability, but the need to compute the Hessian $B(x_i)$ and invert it (or rather, to solve the linear problem $B(x_i)z = \nabla f(x_i)$). *Quasi-Newton* methods[15] are one way to address the computational cost of Newton's method by constructing an approximation $\hat{B}(x_i)$ to $B(x_i)$. They are based on the observation that each pair of subsequent gradient observations $[\nabla f(x_i), \nabla f(x_{i-1})]$ collected by the optimiser provides information about the Hessian function, because the Hessian is the rate of change of the gradient, or more precisely:

[14] Nocedal and Wright (1999), Theorem 3.5

[15] A great contemporaneous review with extensive analysis and discussion can be found in Dennis and Moré (1977).

$$y_i := \nabla f(x_i) - \nabla f(x_{i-1}) = \bar{B}(x_{i-1} - x_i) =: \bar{B} s_i,$$

where $\bar{B}$ is the average Hessian

$$\bar{B} := \int_0^1 B(x_{i-1} + t(x_i - x_{i-1})) \, dt.$$

Thus, any matrix $\hat{B}$ that satisfies this so-called *secant-equation*

$$y_i = \hat{B} s_i \qquad (28.10)$$

is a candidate estimator for the Hessian $B(x_i)$. If we manage to invert this estimator, we have a way to estimate the Newton direction. Alternatively, if we are lucky enough to collect noise-free gradients, we could also use the inverse secant equation

$$s_i = \hat{H} y_i$$

to estimate the inverse Hessian $H = B^{-1}$.

Name	c_i	Reference
Symmetric Rank-1 (SR1)	$c_i = y_i - B_{i-1}s_i$	Davidon (1959)
Powell Symmetric Broyden	$c_i = s_i$	Powell (1970)
Greenstadt's method	$c_i = B_{i-1}s_i$	Greenstadt (1970)
DFP	$c_i = y_i$	Davidon (1959); Fletcher & Powell (1970)
BFGS	$c_i = y_i + \sqrt{\frac{y_i^\mathsf{T} s_i}{s_i^\mathsf{T} B_{i-1}s_i}} B_{i-1}s_i$	Broyden (1969); Fletcher & Powell (1970); Goldfarb (1970); Shanno (1970).

Table 28.1: The most popular members of the Dennis family, Eq. (28.11), defined by their choice of c_i (middle column); see Martinez R. (1988) for more details. Note that the names DFP and BFGS consist of the first letters of the names of their inventors (right column).

This situation sounds familiar, and indeed it is closely related to the setup discussed at length in Chapter III on linear algebra. Here as in the earlier chapter, an algorithm collects linear projections of some matrix, and has to estimate that matrix or its inverse. So we can save a lot of derivations and re-use the results from Chapter III. However, there are pitfalls in the nonlinear optimisation setting that complicate both the classic theory of quasi-Newton methods and the development of a useful probabilistic theory for them. The primary problem is that, in nonlinear optimisation, the Hessian is of course not a constant function. Since the algorithm only ever gets to collect rank-1 projections of the Hessian, it has to make assumptions not just about the aspects of the matrix it has not yet seen, but also about how previously observed aspects may have changed and become outdated over the preceding steps.

This is also the reason why there is not just one 'best' quasi-Newton method. In contrast to the linear setting, where the method of conjugate gradients is a contestant for the gold standard for spd problems, there are entire families of quasi-Newton methods. A widely studied one is the *Dennis family*[16] of update rules of the form

[16] Dennis (1971)

$$B_{i+1} = B_i + \frac{(y_i - B_i s_i)c_i^\mathsf{T} + c_i(y_i - B_i s_i)^\mathsf{T}}{c_i^\mathsf{T} s_i} - \frac{c_i s_i^\mathsf{T}(y_i - B_i s_i)c_i^\mathsf{T}}{(c_i^\mathsf{T} s_i)^2},$$
(28.11)

where $c_i \in \mathbb{R}^N$ is a parameter that determines the concrete member of the family. Quasi-Newton methods were the subject of intense study from the late 1950s to the late 1970s. The most widely used members of the Dennis family are presented in Table 28.1. Among these, the BFGS method is arguably the most popular in practice, but this should not tempt the reader to ignore the other ones. This is particularly true for problems with noisy gradients.

One can easily check that every non-zero choice of c_i yields a matrix estimate B_{i+1} that satisfies the secant equation (28.10).[17] We can also recognise in Eq. (28.11) the rank-2 update form we already know from the linear algebra chapter, for example from Eq. (19.21). Since quasi-Newton methods take a step in the direction of the estimated Newton direction,

$$x_{i+1} = x_i - \alpha_i B_{i+1}^{-1} \nabla f(x_i),$$

their algorithmic structure is very similar to that of the generic linear probabilistic solver of Algorithm 17.2. Since we used that algorithm to construct a probabilistic version of conjugate gradient, it is perhaps not surprising that quasi-Newton methods are closely related to the method of conjugate gradients. In fact, when run on the quadratic problem of Eq. (16.2), and using exact line searches, all five of the methods specifically listed above produce a sequence of estimates that is *identical* to that of the method of conjugate gradients.[18]

This connection allows us to transfer some of the results from the linear algebra chapter.[19] In particular, we can read off the following result directly from Eq. (19.21).

Corollary 28.2. *Let $W_i \in \mathbb{R}^{N \times N}$ be a spd matrix with the property $W_i s_i = c_i$. Then the Dennis family estimate (28.11) equals the posterior mean on B arising from the Gaussian prior*

$$p(B) = \mathcal{N}(B; B_i, W_i \otimes W_i)$$

and the single observation likelihood $p(y_i \mid B, s_i) = \delta(y_i - B s_i)$.

Thus, if one is interested in a direct probabilistic interpretation of quasi-Newton methods, it is possible to think about the Dennis family in terms of a Kalman filter, albeit with a somewhat disappointing choice for the underlying dynamics: Initialise the filter with $m_0 = B_0 = \epsilon I$ for some reasonable choice of ϵ, so that the first search direction s_0 of the optimiser is the negative gradient $-\nabla f(x_0)$ (this is a standard choice for such methods; alternatively, use a pre-conditioner). The algorithm performs one optimisation step, collecting the first observation pair (y_1, s_1). Now implicitly set $P_1^- = W_1^- \otimes W_1^-$ with any matrix W_1^- so that $W_1^- s_1 = c_1$, for the value of c_1 we aim to reproduce from Table 28.1. This yields a filter estimate with updated estimation mean $m_1 = \hat{B}_1$ equal to the estimate of the Dennis family member, and updated estimation covariance (from Eq. (19.11))

$$P_1 = W_1^- - W_1^- s_1 (s_1^\mathsf{T} W_1^- s_1) s_1^\mathsf{T} W_1^-.$$

[17] The DFP and BFGS methods can also be constructed as estimates of the inverse Hessian H: If, in Eq. (28.11), one replaces all instances of B with H and swaps the roles of s_i and y_i, then DFP and BFGS correspond to the respective updates in Table 28.1, where one also has to replace s_i and y_i in these equations. More details can be found in §7.3 of Dennis and Moré (1977).

[18] Dixon (1972a); Dixon (1972b).

[19] Historically, the probabilistic interpretations developed the other way round; starting with a study of quasi-Newton methods (Hennig and Kiefel, 2012), then extending towards the linear case. More about these connections, as well as proofs of some of the results quoted herein, can be found in Hennig (2015).

So far so good, but now, in the final step to complete the connection so that the next iteration still behaves like the Dennis method, we have to implicitly force the filter to add, in the prediction step, just the right terms to P_1 so that $P_2^- = A_1 P_1 A_1^\mathsf{T} + Q_1 = W_2^- \otimes W_2^-$ with an spd matrix W_2 that yields the required match $W_2 s_2 = c_2$ to the Dennis family. It turns out that such a step does not always exist, because the necessary update $W_2 - W_1$ is not always symmetric positive definite. So, beyond the special case of the linear problems discussed at length in Chapter III, we cannot hope to find a general and one-to-one interpretation of existing quasi-Newton methods as Kalman filtering models.

However, given how deep quasi-Newton methods have been studied in the past, and how long it took to develop a good theoretical grasp on them, it is perhaps not so urgent to add yet another probabilistic interpretation to them. What *is* urgently needed are efficient optimisation methods for stochastic, in particular high-dimensional stochastic optimisation problems. Here, probabilistic approaches have very recently begun to yield promising advances. For example, Wills and Schön (2017) report on stochastic quasi-Newton methods with stochastic line-search algorithms. Some ideas can also be found in Hennig (2013), and in Chapter 9 of Mahsereci (2018).

Summary

This chapter discussed uses for probabilistic reasoning in optimisation. Classic algorithms remained an important reference point. We reviewed line searches, element-wise optimisation routines, and advanced methods like quasi-Newton algorithms. But in contrast to earlier chapters, we were less interested in explicitly re-constructing these algorithms probabilistically, and instead identified some contemporary problems where these methods expose weaknesses, then addressed these problems from the probabilistic perspective:

⊖ Readers who have used classic optimisation routines, on the noise-free setups they were designed for, know such methods as well-designed black boxes. Given any reasonably well-conditioned task, they tend to converge to a good estimate without user intervention. Contemporary problems, in particular in areas like machine learning where large, subsampled data sets play a key role, introduce a significant degree of computational imprecision – uncertainty. In such settings even simple routines like gradient descent and its element-wise variants suddenly require laborious and time-consuming manual tuning by the user. From the probabilistic perspective, one cause for this problem is that classic routines implicitly assume that all numbers are computed to machine precision, a notion reflected in the Dirac likelihood we find in probabilistic interpretations of such methods. We addressed this issue in two ways. First, we introduced an explicit Gaussian likelihood. Identifying this likelihood required additional computations, of quantities that have no direct classic analogue. We found those estimators to be relatively cheap to compute, adding acceptable computational overhead. Second, we saw how internal parameter-tuning routines (the line search) of classic methods can be generalised to the probabilistic setting by taking the existing method and carefully replacing every instance of a point estimate with a probabilistic generalisation: cubic splines with integrated Wiener process regression; bisection search with a discrete Bayesian decision rule; and the Boolean Wolfe conditions with a probabilistic confidence. The resulting method once again liberates the user from frustrating parameter choices.

⊖ The core part of an iterative optimisation routine for continuous problems is formed by the decision rule that maps observed gradient values into search directions. When faced with a stochastically corrupted version of an otherwise standard optimisation problem (such as empirical risk minimisation in machine learning), it is tempting to just keep using the classic methods for high-dimensional problems and analyse their stability to the noise. The risk in this approach is that it can lead one to re-purpose algorithmic design choices originally intended to address an entirely different problem to now deal with noise. An example is the use of momentum in gradient descent (originally intended to dampen oscillations in noise-free optimisation) to stabilise against noise. Here, it can be conceptually and practically helpful to introduce an explicit probabilistic sub-routine to take care of inference, and only then combine its output with the old design tricks. Doing so can help identify some hyperparameters, or to separate challenges in an optimisation problem that arises from the objective's geometry from those originating from observation noise.

The take-away from this chapter is that Probabilistic Numerics does not always have to mean the reinvention of classic methods from an inference perspective. It can also help address new challenges, for example those arising from severe computational noise in Big Data applications. By combining the analytical and practical strengths of inference with those of classic numerical algorithms, it is possible to build new methods that address the challenges of the present, while heeding the lessons of the past. The probabilistic viewpoint here provides guardrails, a mechanism for the principled development of solutions to the issues. This is important at a time when the unsatisfactory performance of classic deterministic methods has led to a bewildering growth of new ad-hoc stochastic routines.[20] In a world where practitioners can choose among well over a hundred different optimisers, each with their own set of hyperparameters, it is less important to find one that sometimes works well, but to develop conceptual principles to guide the development of methods, that autonomously tune their parameters and work

[20] Schmidt, Schneider, and Hennig (2021)

robustly across many problems.

This chapter argued that internal hyperparameters of a numerical algorithm should not be tuned by the user, but set efficiently by the algorithm itself. Even where this approach is wholly successful, there are often also *external* parameters of a software solution that still require tuning. For example, in a machine learning system, the machine learning model itself may have to be tuned. The entire software solution then turns into a utility function to be optimised. Even a single evaluation of this global utility function then can be quite expensive, as it requires training the entire architecture to some reasonable precision. Where this is the case, *sample efficiency* (converging in fewer steps), rather than computational efficiency (cheaper steps), becomes the primary objective of algorithm design. The next chapter discusses probabilistic optimisation algorithms for such *experimental design* problems.

Chapter V
Global Optimisation

29

Key Points

This chapter presents Bayesian optimisation, the probabilistic numerical approach to global optimisation. It consists of the problem of finding the lowest point of a likely multi-modal objective function. Here, unlike in local optimisation (Chapter IV), gradients of the objective function might not exist, or might be too expensive to compute. The chapter's core messages are the following.

- ⊖ Bayesian optimisation is different from the other examples of PN in this text. First, it was conceived as an ab initio probabilistic approach, competing with a diverse range of other global optimisation algorithms. Second, at time of writing, Bayesian optimisation is already popular and successful, whether judged by citations, competition results, usage of software libraries, or economic impact.

- ⊖ A Bayesian optimiser is a probabilistic agent that acts by evaluating the objective function, receiving back data in the form of evaluations. As such, the designer of a Bayesian optimiser must make two important choices: its surrogate and its loss function.

- ⊖ The surrogate is the optimiser's model for the objective function, reflecting the designer's prior assumptions. Little is more important in practice than designing a surrogate that is well-informed about the features of the objective (particularly where the objective's input space possesses unusual features, such as graphs or strings). This surrogate must be a probabilistic model, such as a Gaussian process, as the the probabilistic treatment of uncertainty is vital to global optimisation. First, evaluations of the objective are often inexact — for instance, they may be corrupted by noise – and so the surrogate must be able to accommodate uncertain data. Second, it is always important to reason correctly about the uncertainty in unvisited regions of the objective. It is the surrogate's assessment of uncertainty that controls the challenging task of exploration.

⊖ The loss function quantifies how exploration should be balanced against exploitation, i.e. against focusing on an identified mode of the objective. The choice of loss function is non-trivial, as the task of finding the optimum can be sensibly framed in a number of distinct ways. When mapped through the surrogate, each loss function leads to a different expected loss, known as an acquisition function, each with different strengths and weaknesses.

Introduction

Chapter IV presented methods designed to find the extremum[1] of an objective function that is assumed to be convex. These methods are often used on objectives that are, instead, multimodal: in such a case, they will converge only to the mode of the objective nearest (in some sense) their starting position. We will refer to such methods as providing *local optimisation*.

Global optimisation, as its name suggests, instead tackles the problem of finding the global minimiser x_* of an, e.g., multimodal objective $f(x) \in \mathbb{R}$, where $f(x_*) := \min_x f(x)$ is the minimum of all local modes of the function[2]. This is a much more challenging problem, demanding the balancing of the *exploration-exploitation trade-off*.[3]

Exploitation corresponds to making an evaluation with a high probability of improvement. Typically, an exploitative move is an evaluation whose result is known with high confidence, usually near a known low function value, and that is expected to yield an improvement, perhaps an improvement over that known low function value, even if only an incremental one. Exploitation hence typically hones in on a local mode, as would be performed by local optimisation.

Exploration instead corresponds to evaluating the objective in a region of high uncertainty. Such an evaluation is high risk, and may be expected to supply no improvement over existing evaluations at all. Nonetheless, exploration is warranted by improbable, high-payoff, possibilities: such as finding an altogether new local mode.

Exploration is hard. To be clear, for most problems, it is not difficult to find evaluations that are high-uncertainty. The search domain is normally enormous[4] and begins as uniformly high-uncertainty. The low-uncertainty regions produced by our

[1] Without loss of generality, our discussion in this chapter will focus on minimisation. Maximisation can be achieved by minimising the negative of the objective.

[2] Note that f may have no minimum at all – $\min_x f(x)$ is, however, defined if f is continuous and the domain is compact (Garnett, 2022).

[3] This term is more common in the multi-armed bandit and reinforcement learning literatures (Sutton and Barto, 1998).

[4] For instance, if the search domain is $[0,1]^D$, evaluating just the corners of the search box will require 2^D evaluations. This number for a realistic problem, say with $D = 20$, could easily exceed the permitted budget of evaluations.

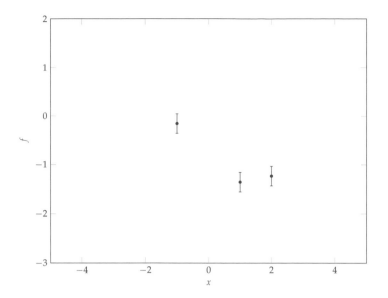

Figure 30.1: A global optimisation problem. We are given an objective function $f(x)$, which can be evaluated (possibly corrupted by observation noise) for any chosen location x. The objective may be expensive to evaluate, limiting the number of such evaluations: in the figure, only three evaluations have been gathered thus far. We must choose future evaluation locations so as to determine the objective's minimiser x_* and/or minimum $f(x_*)$.

existing evaluations are few, like stars dotted in the void. The challenge of exploration is hence in sifting through the mass of uncertainty to find the evaluation that best promises potential reward. This is a challenge common to many aspects of intelligence: think of artistic creativity, or venture capital, or simply finding your lost keys. When humans explore, we draw upon some of our most profoundly intelligent faculties: we theorise, probe and map. As such, exploration for global optimisation motivates sophisticated algorithms.

Relative to local optimisation, global optimisation typically:

⊖ is less amenable to theoretical treatment;

⊖ requires more computation for the process of optimisation itself (distinct from that required for the evaluation of the objective), and is hence used predominately for objectives whose expense, in computation, time and/or money, justifies the computational overhead; and

⊖ has a computational cost that scales more poorly in the dimension of the objective (e.g. convergence only being reliable in practice for problems of no more than around 20 independent, relevant, inputs).

An illustration of a global optimisation problem is provided in Figure 30.1.

Despite such obstacles, research into global optimisation has been spurred on by the importance and ubiquity of its applications. These encompass robotics,[5] sensor networks,[6] en-

[5] Calandra et al. (2014a)

[6] Garnett, Osborne, and Roberts (2010)

vironmental monitoring,[7] and software engineering,[8] amongst many more. The real world is very often more complex than convex. To address non-convex problems, a zoo of competing global optimisation techniques have been developed. Popular approaches include evolutionary methods, branch-and-bound methods and Monte-Carlo-based algorithms.[9]

Bayesian optimisation is a probabilistic framework for global optimisation. It is an exception to other probabilistic numerics approaches: it was directly conceived from a probabilistic viewpoint, with no direct non-probabilistic predecessor (although there is, of course, a rich literature on non-probabilistic global optimisation).[10] Although still a young area by the standards of applied mathematics,[11] compared to other areas discussed in this text, Bayesian optimisation is already a surprisingly mature, developed field, and has developed a rich set of algorithms. In this chapter, our ambition is to provide a compact take on Bayesian optimisation from a probabilistic-numerics perspective: more comprehensive overviews of Bayesian optimisation exist elsewhere.[12]

[7] Marchant and Ramos (2012)
[8] Hoos (2012)

[9] Weise (2009)

[10] cf. Horst and Tuy (2013) and Mitchell (1998)
[11] Bayesian optimisation's rich history, detailed in Garnett (2022), is perhaps best traced back to Kushner (1962).

[12] Garnett (2022)

31

Bayesian Optimisation

As for any probabilistic numerical procedure, it is important to distinguish the two components of a Bayesian optimisation algorithm: its prior and its loss function. Its prior must provide a model for the objective function, $p(f)$, and hence also for its minimum, $p(f(x_*))$[1], whereas the loss function specifies the goals of optimisation.

[1] Both densities exist under mild assumptions (Garnett, 2022).

► **31.1 Prior**

The prior for global optimisation must, first, act as a means of modelling the objective function. In the language of global optimisation, a prior for the objective can be viewed as providing a *surrogate*[2] for the objective. A surrogate is usually viewed as a function informative of, but easier to optimise than, the objective itself. Indeed, as we will discuss in §31.2, Bayesian optimisation does require optimising over a function derived from the prior. The choice of such a prior will seem familiar from our efforts in Chapter II to construct prior distributions for integrand functions. There, we concentrated on priors that reflected expectations that the integrand be smooth or otherwise structured to some degree; the objective is another function for which we are likely to have such expectations. Indeed, if there were no structure at all, optimisation could be no more effective than attempting to find a needle in a haystack. Just as in Bayesian quadrature, Bayesian optimisation predominantly uses Gaussian process priors encoding strong structure. An illustration of how a GP prior can inform optimisation is provided in Figure 31.1. Other choices include random forests[3] and neural networks.[4] As a generalisation, the attractive scaling (of the computational cost, in both the number of evaluations and

[2] A surrogate is the equivalent of the model within numerical integration.

[3] Hutter, Hoos, and Leyton-Brown (2011)

[4] Snoek et al.; Springenberg et al. (2015; 2016); Springenberg et al. (2016).

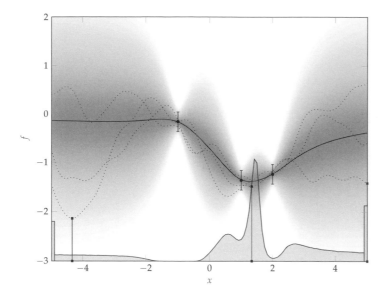

Figure 31.1: A Bayesian answer to the global optimisation problem is to assign a GP prior to the latent function. This particular GP prior arises from a zero prior mean and rational quadratic kernel with unit length scale and degree of freedom $\alpha = 0.5$. Given the three observations from Figure 30.1, we plot: the GP posterior mean as a dark line; marginal densities as shading; three sample functions as dotted lines; and the location of each sample's minimum as squares. This GP gives rise to an (intractable) *probability density function* (PDF) over the location, x_*, of the function's minimum. This is plotted along the bottom of the figure. For this univariate problem, and given sufficient computational resources, we can represent this PDF as a histogram from exhaustive sampling. Note that there is a finite probability for the minimum to lie exactly at the domain boundary (one of the samples is an example case).

the number of dimensions) of these alternative models is often offset by the poorer calibration of their credibility intervals (uncertainties).[5] Managing such uncertainty is at the heart of the exploration-exploitation trade-off faced in global optimisation.

[5] Shahriari et al. (2016)

While the most common setting for Bayesian optimisation is $x \in X \subset \mathbb{R}^d$, for compact X, this is by no means a fundamental constraint for this class of techniques. Any domain for x for which an appropriate prior $p(f(x))$ can be defined is feasible. It is not uncommon in Bayesian optimisation to consider richer input spaces, including those that are discrete, or that correspond to graph-based representations (of, for example, molecules).[6]

[6] Gómez-Bombarelli et al. (2016)

▶ 31.2   Loss Function

Effective Bayesian optimisation depends crucially on the choice of a faithful loss function. The loss function for Bayesian optimisation quantifies how the exploration-exploitation trade-off should be negotiated. When first considering a loss function for optimisation, it might be thought that the goal to be achieved is simply specified: find the minimum. However, the goal of finding the minimum may be encoded in at least several distinct but plausible ways.

1. First, our loss might be the lowest function value evaluated, such that our goal is to uncover as low a function value as possible: we will call this the *value loss* (VL).

2. Alternatively, our loss might be the entropy in the *location* of

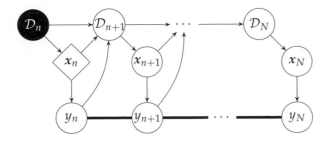

Figure 31.2: A conceptual sketch of the Bayesian optimisation decision problem. Given the current data set, $\mathcal{D}_n$, we must decide upon the decision variable (represented as a diamond node) x_n. The objective is then evaluated, returning $y_n = f(x_n)$, and (x_n, y_n) added to $\mathcal{D}_n$ to give $\mathcal{D}_{n+1}$. Given $\mathcal{D}_{n+1}$, a decision will be made about x_{n+1} — as this decision belongs to the future, and depends on uncertain y_n, x_{n+1} is uncertain. This pattern repeats until the final decision, for the input to be returned to the user, x_N, must be made and the final value, y_N, returned. Note that the diagram does define a graphical model (Bayesian network), but its joint distribution is challenging to determine. Considered a graphical model, all variables along the dark line are to be taken as dependent.

the minimum, x_*, which we will call the *location-information loss* (LIL). Figure 31.1 depicts a posterior for the minimiser x_*, whose entropy would serve as the LIL.

3. Another competing possibility is the *value-information loss* (VIL), equal to the entropy in the *value* of the minimum, $f(x_*)$.

These are not the only plausible candidate losses; we will meet alternatives below. Crucial to distinguishing these losses is a careful treatment of the end-point of the optimisation. The loss function must make precise what is to happen to the set of obtained objective evaluations once the procedure ends, and how valuable this outcome truly is. One crucial question is that of when our algorithm must terminate. Termination might be upon the exhaustion of an a priori fixed budget of evaluations, or, alternatively, when a particular criterion of performance or convergence is reached. The former assumption of a fixed budget of N evaluations is the default within Bayesian optimisation, and will be taken henceforth.

We present in Figure 31.2 the decision problem for Bayesian optimisation. We seek to illustrate the iterative nature of optimisation and its final termination. In particular, the terminating condition for optimisation will often require us to select a single point[7] in the domain to be returned: we will denote this point as x_N. At the termination of the algorithm, we will define the full set of evaluation pairs gathered as $\mathcal{D}_N := \{(x_i, y_i) \mid i = 0, \ldots, N-1\}$. Here the ith evaluation is $y_i = f(x_i)$. We will assume, for now, that evaluations are exact, hence noiseless. The returned point will often be limited to the set of evaluation locations, $x_N \in \mathcal{D}_N$, but this need not necessarily be so.[8]

The importance of the loss function can be brought out through consideration of the consequences of the terminal decision of the returned point, x_N. With our notation, the loss

[7] We will regard this final point as additional to our permitted budget of N evaluations.

[8] In the absence of noise, limiting to the set of evaluation locations enforces the constraint that the returned function value (the putative minimum) is known with complete confidence. This is not unreasonable; however, in some settings, the user may be satisfied with a more diffuse probability distribution over the returned value: such considerations, of course, motivate the broader probabilistic-numerics vision. It is worth noting that the limitation to the set of evaluation locations does not permit returning unevaluated points, even if their values are known exactly. As an example where this is important, consider knowing that a univariate objective is linear: then, any pair of evaluations would specify exactly the minimum, on one of the two edges of a bounded interval. In such a case, would we really want to require that this minimum could not be returned until it had been evaluated?

functions can be defined as follows:

$$\lambda_{\text{VL}}(x_N, y_N, \mathcal{D}_N) = y_N,$$
$$\lambda_{\text{LIL}}(x_N, y_N, \mathcal{D}_N) = \mathbb{H}(x_* \mid x_N, y_N, \mathcal{D}_N),$$
$$\lambda_{\text{VIL}}(x_N, y_N, \mathcal{D}_N) = \mathbb{H}(f(x_*) \mid x_N, y_N, \mathcal{D}_N). \quad (31.1)$$

It is not difficult to find an application demanding each of these three losses. The value loss would be appropriate if the final evaluation, y_N, provided a persistent object with worth equal to the objective value. An example might be optimising the activity of a drug molecule: after the budget of expensive trials (evaluations) has been exhausted, the best of the trialled molecules is chosen for further development. The value loss hinges entirely on the returned value y_N, subsequent to which no future evaluations (no variation) will be permitted. Recall that our definitions (31.1) assume exact observations – in §32.3, we will consider the case in which evaluations are corrupted by noise.

The location-information loss might be appropriate if, at the end-point of the optimisation process, it were possible to make evaluations with inputs in some neighbourhood of x_N (rather than exactly at x_N, as is considered by the value loss). For instance, in the drilling of an oil well, after drilling a certain number of test wells down into a plane, it might be possible to drill a small distance sideways from the best well until an even better location were found. The location-information loss might also be appropriate if the selected location for the minimum x_N was corrupted by a noise contribution ϵ before the ultimate value $y_N = f(x_N + \epsilon)$ was realised.

The value-information loss might be appropriate if the minimum were a quantity of scientific interest, as is the equilibrium state in an economic model of loss-minimising consumers. Here, it is not the minimum itself that has value, but what its determination reveals about the world around us.

As in any application of decision theory, the quantity that most directly determines our actions is not the loss, but the expected loss. In Bayesian optimisation, the term *acquisition function* (or, less commonly, *infill function* or *query selection function*) is used to describe expected loss functions.[9] We will henceforth place ourselves at the nth step in the optimisation procedure, such that the optimiser has gathered a set of evaluation pairs, $\mathcal{D}_n = \{(x_i, f(x_i)) \mid i = 0, \ldots, n-1\}$ (where $n \leq N$, the total budget of evaluations). Then, an acquisition function $\alpha(x_n)$ is considered to be a function of the next evaluation location, x_n: its optimum represents the optimal placement for this next eval-

[9] The acquisition function fills the same role as a design rule in integration.

uation.[10] It is also used to describe other functions used for selecting evaluations: we will develop some of these subtleties below. An acquisition function is also sometimes distinguished from a *recommendation strategy* used to select the final putative location for the minimum, x_N. In a decision theoretic, probabilistic numeric, framework, the acquisition function should be derived from a loss function defined on the results of the final selection: we have no need for a separate recommendation strategy.

Within an acquisition function, an expectation must be computed over the variables in Figure 31.2 that are neither already observed ($\mathcal{D}_n$) nor decided upon (x_n). That is, an expected loss for Bayesian optimisation must, in general, marginalise not just the evaluations, $y_n, \ldots, y_N$, but also the future locations $x_n, \ldots, x_N$. This marginalisation is typically impossible in closed-form.[11] Kushner (1964) asserted that the full, multiple-step, expected loss

"depends on the locations of the future observations, and it is generally so complicated that it usually is not a practical calculation with present-day computing equipment".

Computing this expected loss remains profoundly challenging to this day. We will tackle this problem in §32.4. Until then, we will adopt severe *myopic* (short-sighted) approximations that ignore the potential impact of all future evaluations other than the very next one, $f(x_n)$. Kushner (1964) motivates myopic approximations by noting that the surrogate model is often wrong, encoding assumptions that do not hold for the objective at hand. Non-myopic approaches, in forecasting the impact of many future evaluations, rely more heavily on the model than do myopic approaches. Speaking roughly, performance may be aided by reducing reliance upon a model that is wrong – when the model is wrong, a myopic approach may be helpfully conservative. As another justification for this approximation, as described by Hennig and Schuler (2012), note that, unlike general planning problems, active inference does not suffer from 'dead ends'. That is, the consistency of Bayesian inference means that an uninformative evaluation can always be overcome by future informative evaluations: it will always remain possible to learn the entire function. The myopic loss functions that we will describe will all, to some degree, promote exploration and perform reasonably in practice.

Under a myopic approximation, the expected loss (associated with loss function λ) will take the form of the acquisition

[10] More precisely, in the literature, the term acquisition function is more commonly used to describe a function that is to be *maximised* to determine the next evaluation location. Nonetheless, to maintain consistency with our expected-loss framework, we will use the term acquisition function to describe a function that is to be *minimised* rather than maximised. In some cases, this will result in us describing acquisition functions as the negation of their more common forms.

[11] One exception is that of independent, discrete-valued, evaluations y (Gittins, 1979). This is a substantially simpler setting than one which takes a prior, like a GP, that allows an evaluation for one location to be informative of others. Other, uninteresting, exceptions exist: for instance, the expected loss is closed-form for a loss function equal to a constant, ignoring the evaluations.

function

$$\alpha(x_n \mid \mathcal{D}_n) = \mathbb{E}\big(\lambda(x_n, y_n, \mathcal{D}_n)\big)$$
$$= \int \lambda(x_n, y_n, \mathcal{D}_n)\, p(y_n \mid \mathcal{D}_n)\, \mathrm{d}y_n.$$

Having evaluated at x_n, we will then use the acquisition function $\alpha(x \mid \mathcal{D}_{n+1})$ to select x_{n+1}. Note that $\alpha(x \mid \mathcal{D}_n)$ will be similar, but not identical, to $\alpha(x \mid \mathcal{D}_{n+1})$: the former's underlying probability distributions, such as $p(y_n \mid \mathcal{D}_n)$, will have been updated in light of new data, (x_n, y_n) (becoming less diffuse in the process). Some such distributions, notably $p(x_N \mid \mathcal{D}_{n+1})$, and hence $p(y_N \mid \mathcal{D}_{n+1})$, must also reflect that there are fewer future evaluations remaining. Referring back to Figure 31.2, we observe that the posterior for x_N (the returned location) at the nth step, $p(x_N \mid \mathcal{D}_n)$, will be more diffuse than that at the $(n+1)$th step, $p(x_N \mid \mathcal{D}_{n+1})$, even if the nth evaluation is entirely uninformative. With fewer remaining evaluations, there will be fewer potential surprises (such as the discovery of a new mode of the objective) in the future to consider: such surprises can lead to large changes in beliefs about the location of the minimum. With fewer such surprises in store, it is reasonable for the optimisation agent to be more confident about its actions in the future, at the final, Nth, step. Importantly, for coherent optimisation, the loss function itself should remain the same throughout the optimisation algorithm.

Most acquisition functions, aiming to balance both exploitation and exploration, will be non-convex. That is, there will be a diverse set of potentially valuable locations (some near existing modes, others far removed from them) at which to evaluate the objective. As such, practical Bayesian optimisation requires the use of a further global optimiser to optimise the acquisition function and hence select the next evaluation location.

You could be forgiven for stumbling over the previous sentence. If our stated goal is global optimisation, what have we achieved in re-framing this in such a way as to require yet another global optimisation problem? The answer is found in the realisation that the acquisition function is more amenable to optimisation than the original objective function. To begin, the acquisition function is usually substantially less expensive than the objective: for instance, it can be evaluated on a computer, where the objective might require the drilling of an oil well. Second, the acquisition function usually admits closed-form expressions for its gradient and Hessian, where the objective may not: this additional information can greatly aid optimisation. A final argument is that performance is usually relatively insensitive to the optimisation of the acquisition function: even local minima of the acquisition function will usually result in usefully informative evaluations. As such, the optimiser used for the acquisition function can be taken as something relatively cheap and dirty, without necessarily sacrificing ultimate performance.

Such considerations are common in numerics: it is common for one numerical problem to require the solution of another. There is a roughly perceived hierarchy of algorithms, with more important algorithms (like quadrature) permitted to call less important algorithms (like linear solvers). As discussed in §, one goal of Probabilistic Numerics is to formalise this hierarchy, by designing numerical algorithms that universally communicate probability distributions, and propagate uncertainty throughout a pipeline of algorithms. In such a setting, it is not impossible to imagine that design decisions hitherto underpinned only by intuition, such as the rule that the optimisation of the acquisition function is relatively unimportant for performance, might be a naturally emergent result.

Value Loss

The VL is perhaps the most intuitive of the loss functions described in §31.2, and has been developed through a number of avenues within Bayesian optimisation.

► ## 32.1 Expected Improvement

Let us begin a tour through the canonical combination of prior and loss function for Bayesian optimisation: a GP prior (see §4.2) with the *expected improvement* (EI) acquisition function.[1] The latter is best seen as an approximation to the value loss. Figure 32.1 provides an illustration of the combination of EI and a GP.

[1] Mockus, Tiesis, and Žilinskas (1978)

Let us place ourselves at the nth step in the optimisation procedure, such that the optimiser has gathered a set of evaluation pairs, $\mathcal{D}_n = \{(x_i, f(x_i)) \mid i = 0, \ldots, n-1\}$ (where $n < N$, the total budget of evaluations). We will again assume exact, noiseless, evaluations. The GP posterior for the objective, $p(f \mid \mathcal{D}_n) = \mathcal{GP}(f; m, \mathbb{V})$, has posterior mean function $m(x)$ and posterior covariance function $\mathbb{V}(x)$. We now make the approximation[2]

[2] Note that, under this approximation, the loss is not a function of x_N.

$$\lambda_{\text{VL}}(x_N, f(x_N), \mathcal{D}_N) \simeq \lambda_{\text{EI}}(\mathcal{D}_{n+1}) := \min_{i \in \{0, \ldots, n\}} f(x_i).$$

Recall that $\mathcal{D}_{n+1}$ includes x_n and $f(x_n)$. This approximation is myopic as discussed in 31.2: it disregards all future evaluations other than $f(x_n)$. The approximation also restricts the returned location x_N to the set of evaluations; consequently, the returned location is the one that corresponds to the lowest evaluation. This assumption removes the dependence of the loss on x_N. Defining the lowest function value available at the nth step as

$$\eta := \min_{i \in \{0, \ldots, n-1\}} f(x_i),$$

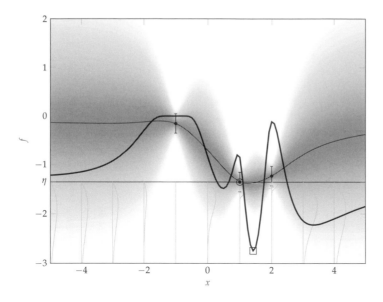

Figure 32.1: The *expected improvement* (EI) acquisition function at x is the expected amount that $f(x)$ improves upon the current lowest evaluation, η (marked by a circle). Naturally, the expected improvement cannot be worse than zero. The light grey curves at integer values of x are the integrands $(f(x) - \eta)p(f(x) \mid \mathcal{D}_{n-1})$ of Eq. (32.1), whose integral is the acquisition function, $\alpha_{\mathrm{EI}}(x)$, at those values of x. On a grid of example locations, the plot shows as a dark, thick line the resulting acquisition function $\alpha_{\mathrm{EI}}(x)$. Its maximiser, marked with a square, gives the best possible location for the next evaluation, x_n. Note that this plot considers noisy evaluations, tackled more fully in §32.3.

we can simply rewrite the loss as

$$\lambda_{\mathrm{EI}}(\mathcal{D}_{n+1}) = \min\{\eta, f(x_n)\}.$$

The expected loss is hence

$$\mathbb{E}\big(\lambda_{\mathrm{EI}}(\mathcal{D}_{n+1})\big) = \int \min\{\eta, f(x_n)\} p\big(f(x_n) \mid \mathcal{D}_n\big) \, \mathrm{d}f(x_n)$$

$$= \eta + \int \min\{0, f(x_n) - \eta\} p\big(f(x_n) \mid \mathcal{D}_n\big) \, \mathrm{d}f(x_n)$$

$$= \eta + \int_{\eta}^{\infty} 0 \times p\big(f(x_n) \mid \mathcal{D}_n\big) \, \mathrm{d}f(x_n)$$

$$+ \int_{-\infty}^{\eta} \big(f(x_n) - \eta\big) p\big(f(x_n) \mid \mathcal{D}_n\big) \, \mathrm{d}f(x_n)$$

$$= \eta + \int_{-\infty}^{\eta} \big(f(x_n) - \eta\big) p\big(f(x_n) \mid \mathcal{D}_n\big) \, \mathrm{d}f(x_n).$$

Just as promised by its name, this expected loss does indeed consider the expected improvement over the current best point, η. Note that, owing to this text's preference for minimisation over maximisation, "improvement" here is considered as being better when more negative. Given that η is "in the bag", the overall outcome cannot be worse (higher) than η. The expected loss will be determined by the probability mass that $p\big(f(x_n) \mid \mathcal{D}_n\big)$ assigns to the fortunate outcomes in which $f(x_n)$ improves upon η, and the magnitude of those improvements.

To fulfil its purpose as an acquisition function, we usually rewrite this expected loss as a function of the next evaluation location, so that

$$\mathbb{E}\big(\lambda_{\mathrm{EI}}\big) = \mathbb{E}\big(\lambda_{\mathrm{EI}}\big)(x_n).$$

For convenience, our notation no longer reflects the real dependence of λ_{EI} on $\mathcal{D}_{n+1}$. To be explicit, we will pick the next evaluation location as the minimiser of $\mathbb{E}(\lambda_{\text{EI}})(x_n)$, which is identical to the minimiser of $\alpha_{\text{EI}}(x_n) := \mathbb{E}(\lambda_{\text{EI}})(x_n) - \eta$,

$$\alpha_{\text{EI}}(x_n) = \int_{-\infty}^{\eta} (f(x_n) - \eta) p(f(x_n) \mid \mathcal{D}_n) \, \mathrm{d}f(x_n). \quad (32.1)$$

Now, given $p(f(x_n) \mid \mathcal{D}_n) = \mathcal{N}(f(x_n); m(x_n), \mathbb{V}(x_n))$, letting $\Phi(x; a, b^2)$ be the cumulative distribution function of the Gaussian distribution $\mathcal{N}(x; a, b^2)$,

$$\begin{aligned} \alpha_{\text{EI}}(x_n) = &- \mathbb{V}(x_n) \mathcal{N}(\eta; m(x_n), \mathbb{V}(x_n)) \\ &+ (m(x_n) - \eta) \, \Phi(\eta; m(x_n), \mathbb{V}(x_n)). \end{aligned} \quad (32.2)$$

Exercise 32.1. *(easy, solution on p. 366)*
Given Eq. (32.1), derive Eq. (32.2).

An example of this acquisition function is provided in Figure 32.1. Note that Eq. (32.2) will be low (indicating a desirable location for the next evaluation) where $m(x_n)$ is very low, and/or where $\mathbb{V}(x_n)$ is very large. The former desideratum encapsulates the drive towards exploitation, and the latter that towards exploration. As such, EI gives one means of balancing these two competing goals. That said, empirically, EI has been observed to be under-exploratory,[3] weighting its evaluations too heavily towards exploitation. This can be understood as a consequence of the myopic approximation underpinning EI. A model that believes it has only a single evaluation remaining is less likely to feel it can afford the luxury of exploration than one that has many evaluations at its disposal: the former model must focus on achieving immediate value through exploitation.

[3] Calandra et al. (2014b)

The EI acquisition function is relatively cheap to evaluate, but also multi-modal, and admits evaluations of gradient and Hessian (omitted here). The EI approach hence provides a clear example of why it can be productive to convert the optimisation of an objective into the optimisation of an acquisition function.

▶ 32.2   Knowledge Gradient

Knowledge gradient (KG)[4] is an acquisition function that allows the relaxation of one of the assumptions of EI. In particular, while KG is myopic, it does not restrict the returned point x_N to be amongst the set of evaluated locations. Instead, after the nth step of the optimisation procedure (that is, after the nth evaluation), x_N is chosen as the minimiser of the posterior mean m_{n+1} for the objective $f(x)$, which is conditioned on $\mathcal{D}_{n+1} := \{(x_i, f(x_i)) \mid i = 0, \ldots, n\}$, the set of evaluation pairs

[4] Frazier, Powell, and Dayanik (2009)

after the $(n+1)$th step. That is, KG considers the posterior mean *after* the upcoming next step.

This modification offers much potential value. Valuing improvement in the posterior mean rather than in the evaluations directly eliminates the need to expend a sample simply to return a low function value that may already be well-resolved by the model. For instance, if the objective is known to be a quadratic, the minimum will be known exactly after (any) three evaluations, even if it has not been explicitly evaluated. In this setting, evaluating at the minimum, as would be required by EI, is unnecessary.

KG does introduce some risk relative to EI, however. Note that the final value $f(x_N)$ may not be particularly well-resolved after the $(n+1)$th step: the posterior variance for $f(x_N)$ may be high. KG, in ignoring this uncertainty, may choose x_N such that the final value $f(x_N)$ is unreliable. That is, the final value returned, $f(x_N)$, may be very different from what the optimiser expects, $m_{N+1}(x_N)$.

The KG loss is hence the final value revealed at the minimiser of the posterior mean after the next evaluation. Let's define that minimiser as

$$\check{x}_{n+1} := \arg\min_{x'} m_{n+1}(x'),$$

where the posterior mean function,

$$m_{n+1}(x') := \mathbb{E}\big(f(x') \mid \mathcal{D}_{n+1}\big),$$

takes the convenient form of Eq. (4.6) for a GP. The KG loss can now be written as

$$\lambda_{\text{KG}}(\mathcal{D}_{n+1}) := f(\check{x}_{n+1}). \tag{32.3}$$

The expected loss, the acquisition function, is hence[5]

$$
\begin{aligned}
\alpha_{\text{KG}}(x_n) &:= \mathbb{E}\big(\lambda_{\text{KG}}(\mathcal{D}_{n+1})\big) \\
&= \int f(\check{x}_{n+1}) p\big(f(\check{x}_{n+1}) \mid f(x_n), \mathcal{D}_n\big) p\big(f(x_n) \mid \mathcal{D}_n\big) \\
&\qquad\qquad\qquad\qquad\qquad\qquad \mathrm{d}f(\check{x}_{n+1})\, \mathrm{d}f(x_n) \\
&= \int \min_{x'} m_{n+1}(x') p\big(f(x_n) \mid \mathcal{D}_n\big)\, \mathrm{d}f(x_n).
\end{aligned}
$$

Unfortunately, the KG acquisition function is not closed-form due to the required minimisation within the integral, but approximations[6] exist and have demonstrated useful empirical performance. The effect of the KG is to value *improvements in the posterior mean*, rather than simply improvements in the evaluations.

[5] Note that the KG acquisition function presented here differs from that in Frazier, Powell, and Dayanik (2009) in omitting an additive constant.

[6] Frazier, Powell, and Dayanik (2009)

The KG loss (32.3) differs in an important respect from the VL of Eq. (31.1). KG rewards improvements in the posterior mean, rather than improvements in the evaluations. The VL is influenced only by the final objective value, y_N, where KG considers the posterior mean at all locations. That is, KG values not just the next evaluation, but its impact on our beliefs about evaluations at all other locations. In this, the VL, and the resulting EI, can be seen as *local* methods, where the KG is *global*.

▶ **32.3 Noisy Expected Improvement**

It is routine in regression settings, particularly in Gaussian process regression, to manage observations y of a function f that have been corrupted by noise. Noisy observations are less common in numerics: usually, the function is evaluated using deterministic software. Nonetheless, given that Bayesian optimisation (and much of Probabilistic Numerics) is built upon a regression model, it might be expected that managing noise in optimisation might be achieved with similar confidence as that with which one manages noise in performing regression. Unfortunately, this expectation would be ill-founded. To understand why, imagine that the objective is observed only up to some i.i.d. Gaussian noise. What then should be returned as the minimum $f(x_N)$? In fact, noisy optimisation makes for an excellent case study of the importance of considering the terminating stages of optimisation.

Let us begin with EI. A simple and common approach to EI for noisy objectives would be to take the returned value as the lowest of the (noisy) evaluations. Explicitly, this approach commits to returning an evaluation that is known to have been corrupted by noise. In fact, this approach to EI for noisy evaluations introduces a version of the *winner's curse*:[7] the lowest function evaluation is probably *more noise-corrupted* than other evaluations. EI can hence be a problematic approach for objectives that are substantively corrupted by noise. For a deeper discussion of the problems of noisy EI, including proposals for overcoming these problems, see §6 and §8 of Garnett (2022).

Now let us return to KG, a more natural choice for noisy evaluations. Recall that KG rewards improvements in the posterior mean, rather than improvements in the evaluations. The surrogate model, usually a GP, will smooth over noise in the evaluations: the use of its posterior mean should ameliorate the impact of large negative noise contributions in assessing the current estimate of the minimum. As such, KG is less sensitive

[7] Thaler (1988)

Exercise 32.2. *(moderate, solution on p. 366) Take a GP prior for the objective $f(x)$, along with an i.i.d. Gaussian noise model, $y_i = f(x_i) + \varepsilon_i$, $\varepsilon_i \sim \mathcal{N}(0; \sigma^2)$. Demonstrate the effect of the winner's curse by computing the posterior for $\varepsilon_1 - \varepsilon_2$ given two observations y_1 and y_2. It may be assumed that $f(x_1)$ and $f(x_2)$ have negligible prior covariance (e.g. that x_1 and x_2 are far apart), and that their prior variances are equal. Hint: $p(\varepsilon) \neq p(\varepsilon \mid y)$.*

Figure 32.2: Imagine that we can afford two evaluations of a function on the domain indicated by the line segment. The best first evaluation location (dot), according to any ignorant prior and *myopic* acquisition function, will be the midpoint of the domain (the left plot). However, this choice means that the second and final evaluation, which will fall in one or the other halves of the domain, will leave the other half entirely unexplored (the centre plot). If a *non-myopic* strategy were used, the two evaluations could be more sensibly (and, in this case, more uniformly) distributed across the domain (the right plot).

to the winner's curse described for EI.

Another simple approach to noisy Bayesian optimisation was introduced by Osborne, Garnett, and Roberts (2009) following KG in returning the optimum of the posterior mean. The authors add one extra constraint to the KG approach: the variance in the returned value $f(x_N)$ is restricted to being no greater than a specified threshold. This additional constraint means that the approach avoids the problem of returning a putative minimum which is very uncertain. This gives another example of the importance of thinking clearly about the goals of optimisation: in this case, how important is the trustworthiness of the returned minimum?

In §33.3, we will discuss how information-theoretic approaches provide a natural solution to managing noisy function evaluations.

32.4 Overcoming Myopia – Multi-Step Look-Ahead

In §31.2, we introduced myopic approximations to the expected loss. Our motivation was the severe difficulty of computing the expected loss of an evaluation when considering the potentially many evaluations that will follow. Unfortunately, myopic approximations can introduce real performance impairments. The most important is that myopia results in a preference for exploitation over exploration. An illustration of this phenomenon is provided in Figure 32.2. A non-myopic optimiser, that knows it has the luxury of many evaluations remaining, is more likely to indulge in risky exploration over exploitation. Note also that, ideally, an optimiser should slowly shift its behaviour from explorative to exploitative over the course of optimisation. That is, early on, with a large budget of evaluations in hand, exploration is more attractive than later on. However, a myopic optimisation strategy cannot be influenced by the true number of evaluations remaining: it is static, where we would prefer dynamism.

What would it take to abandon the myopia of EI and KG and move towards a better approximation of the value loss? The challenge to be overcome is captured by Figure 31.2. Our goal is to compute the expected loss of evaluating next at x_0, $\mathbb{E}(\lambda_{\mathrm{VL}})$. If N evaluations remain, we must marginalise $N + 1$ values, $y_0, \ldots, y_N$, (recall that we're assuming that the final returned value is "free", additional to our budget) and N locations, $x_1, \ldots, x_N$. The latter random variables emerge from a decision process: x_i will be the optimiser of the ith acquisition function – we assume that all future decisions will be made optimally. That is,

$$p(x_i \mid \mathcal{D}_i) = \delta\left(x_i - \arg\min_x \mathbb{E}\left(\lambda_{\text{VL}}(x) \mid \mathcal{D}_i\right)\right). \qquad (32.4)$$

This means that the thorny problem to be solved is an interleaved sequence of numerically integrating over y_i variables and numerically optimising over x_i variables. This is a sequential decision-making problem, related to the Bellman equation and solvable, in principle, by dynamic programming.[8] Our problem shares with others of this class a cost that is exponential in the horizon, $N - n$.

The difficulty of this problem has meant that progress has been largely limited to various specialisations or relations of the generic Bayesian optimisation problem. As examples, non-myopic results have been presented for independent, discrete-valued, evaluations,[9] finding a level-set of a one-dimensional and Markov objective,[10] and active search.[11] Those approaches[12] that introduce approximations to tackle the full multi-step problem have managed to consider no more than around 20 future steps. To give a flavour of how such approaches proceed, González, Osborne, and Lawrence (2016) and Jiang et al. (2020) propose schemes in which the strong knowledge of the sequential selection of observations, as in Eq. (32.4), is set aside in favour of a model which assumes that all locations are chosen at once, as in a batch (batch Bayesian optimisation will be described in §34.1). This approximate model is depicted in Figure 32.3. This coupling of locations and removal of nesting provides a substantially simpler numerics problem, one solvable using batch Bayesian optimisation techniques for the optimisation of locations. González, Osborne, and Lawrence (2016) additionally use expectation propagation[13] for the marginalisation of their values.

[8] Jiang et al. (2019)

[9] Gittins (1979)

[10] Cashore, Kumarga, and Frazier (2015)

[11] Jiang et al. (2017)

[12] Streltsov and Vakili (1999); Osborne, Garnett, and Roberts (2009); Marchant, Ramos, and Sanner (2014); González, Osborne, and Lawrence (2016); Jiang et al. (2020).

[13] Cunningham, Hennig, and Lacoste-Julien (2011)

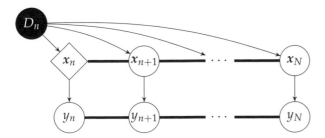

Figure 32.3: Approximate graphical model (Bayesian network) for the Bayesian optimisation decision problem. Given the current data set, $\mathcal{D}_n$, we must decide upon the decision variable (diamond node) x_n: unlike in the true problem (Figure 31.2), however, the sequential nature of the problem is ignored. All variables along the dark line are dependent.

33

Other Acquisition Functions

Acquisition functions (beyond those derived from the VL) remain an active area of research within Bayesian optimisation, and the field has produced a diverse range of proposals. In this section, we will review a few of the most prominent, and discuss their probabilistic numerical interpretation. All acquisition functions proposed in this section are myopic.

▶ **33.1 Probability of Improvement**

One of the earliest acquisition functions to be proposed[1] is PI (also known as *maximum probability of improvement* (MPI)). It is myopic, and, as with EI, defines the lowest function value available at the nth step as

$$\eta_n := \min_{i \in \{0, \ldots, n-1\}} f(x_i).$$

We will also introduce new hyperparameters, $\epsilon_n \geq 0$. Now let us define a loss function specific to the nth step:

$$\lambda_{n,\mathrm{PI}}(\mathcal{D}_{n+1}) := \mathbb{I}\big(f(x_n) \geq \eta_n - \epsilon_n\big). \tag{33.1}$$

Here $\mathbb{I}$ is the indicator function, so that the loss is 0 when $f(x_n) < \eta_n - \epsilon_n$ and 1 otherwise (expressing that the former is the preferred outcome). With that, the PI expected loss, and hence acquisition function, has the simple form

$$\alpha_{n,\mathrm{PI}}(x_n) := \mathbb{E}\big(\lambda_{n,\mathrm{PI}}(\mathcal{D}_{n+1})\big) = P\big(f(x_n) \geq \eta_n - \epsilon_n \mid \mathcal{D}_n\big).$$

The hyperparameter ϵ_n controls the degree of exploration (at the nth step), with smaller ϵ_n resulting in more exploitative behaviour. Kushner (1964) suggested setting ϵ_n to a large value for small n (so as to be more exploratory early in optimisation)

[1] Kushner (1964)

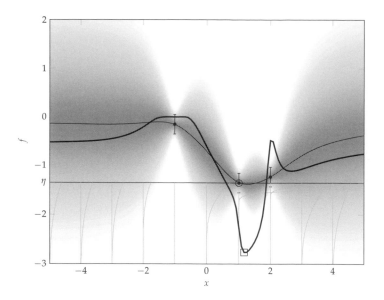

Figure 33.1: The *probability of improvement* (PI) acquisition function at x is the probability that $f(x)$ improves upon the current lowest evaluation, η (marked by a circle). The light grey curves at integer values of x describe $p\big(f(x) \mid \mathcal{D}_n\big)$ for $f(x) < \eta$. On a grid of example locations, the plot shows as a dark, thick, line the resulting negative acquisition function $-\alpha_{\mathrm{PI}}(x)$ (the integral of the grey curves), affinely rescaled for visualisation. Its maximiser, marked with a square, gives the best possible location for the next evaluation, x_n. The plot is analagous to that for EI in Figure 32.1. Note the subtle differences between the two acquisition functions: in particular, PI is the more exploitative of the two.

and to a small value for large n (so as to be more exploitative late in optimisation). Jones (2001) recommended using several values of ϵ_n, and identifying clusters of resulting x values. The hyperparameter is commonly taken as $\epsilon_n = 0$, which results in aggressively exploitative behaviour.[2] The PI acquisition function for $\epsilon_n = 0$ is depicted in Figure 33.1.

In fact, with $\epsilon_n = 0$, PI is sometimes used to (retrospectively) score the exploitativeness of evaluations that have been made by any acquisition function. Its utility here is promoted by its fixed range, $\alpha_{n,\mathrm{PI}}(x_n) \in [0,1] \subset \mathbb{R}$, with 1 deemed completely exploitative and 0 completely explorative, easing (visual) comparisons across different iterations of optimisation. Doing so is helpful in interrogating a completed Bayesian optimisation run, whatever the acquisition function. Quick inspection might reveal, for instance, that exploitation was never performed, or if the objective was inadequately explored.

Notably, this acquisition function does not distinguish between improvements of different magnitudes: any improvement (above the threshold), however small, is equally valued. This caps the potential rewards from gambling on exploration.

We could view the nth step loss function (33.1) as emerging from an approximation to a single loss function applicable across all steps,

$$\lambda_{\mathrm{PI}}(\mathcal{D}_N) = \mathbb{I}\big(f(x_n) \geq \eta_n - \epsilon_n;\quad n = 1, \ldots, N\big). \qquad (33.2)$$

From the decision-theoretic perspective, this reveals another deficiency of PI: Eq. (33.2) stipulates an odd goal for optimisation:

[2] Jones (2001)

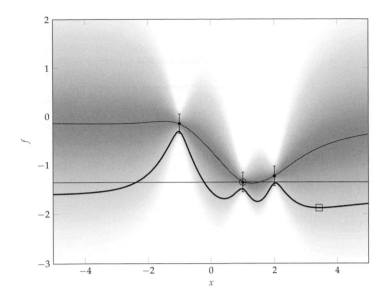

Figure 33.2: The *upper confidence bound* (UCB) acquisition function at x is a linear combination of the mean and *standard deviation* (SD) of the GP posterior. For the purposes of this plot, $\beta = 1.5$. On a grid of example locations, the plot shows as a dark, thick, line the resulting acquisition function $\alpha_{\mathrm{UCB}}(x)$ affinely rescaled for visualisation. Its maximiser, marked with a square, gives the best possible location for the next evaluation, x_n. The plot is analogous to that for EI in Figure 32.1 and PI in Figure 33.1. Note the subtle differences between the three acquisition functions: in particular, UCB (for $\beta = 1.5$) is the most explorative of the three.

incremental improvement at each step. Why should an optimiser weight each step in the optimisation process equally? The loss functions described in §31.2 instead put their emphasis on uncovering a single, exceptional, function value. A probabilistic-numerics view would argue that these goals are more coherent, and hence more suitable for optimisation.

▶ **33.2 Upper Confidence Bound**

A popular acquisition function finds its roots in the multi-armed bandit literature:[3] the UCB. Again, this acquisition function is myopic in considering no further ahead than the next function value. Rather than marginalising over that function value, y_n, this criterion adopts an optimistic approach: it assumes that y_n will take the value that is better than its expectation according to some fixed probability. Srinivas et al. (2010) framed the UCB, given a GP surrogate posterior (with mean $m(x_n)$ and variance $\mathbb{V}(x_n)$) at the proposed x_n, as

[3] Lai and Robbins (1985)

$$\alpha_{\mathrm{UCB}}(x_n) := m(x_n) - \beta_n \mathbb{V}(x_n)^{\frac{1}{2}}. \qquad (33.3)$$

Note that, owing to this text's preference for minimisation over maximisation, Eq. (33.3) describes a lower confidence bound rather than an upper confidence bound – we use the term UCB out of tradition. The first term in Eq. (33.3), the posterior mean, $m(x_n)$, rewards exploitation, by encouraging evaluation near to existing low evaluations. The second term, proportional to the posterior standard deviation, $\mathbb{V}(x_n)^{\frac{1}{2}}$, promotes exploration.

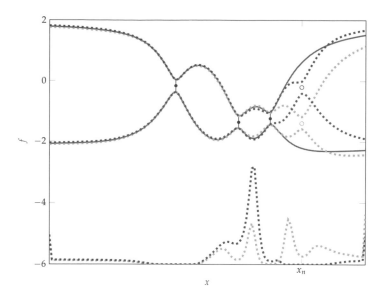

Figure 33.3: The information-theoretic rationale for Bayesian optimisation: when considering a proposed next evaluation location x_n, one should *marginalise* over potential observations y_n to be collected at this point. The plot shows two equally-probable potential scenarios for two different potential values of y_n. Each of the two potential observations would lead to a change in the GP posterior (represented using dashed lines), which in turn would give rise to a *global* change of the distribution over the minimiser (each corresponding $p(x_*)$ shown using matching dashed lines at the bottom of the plot, at arbitrary scale).

The parameter $\beta_n \in \mathbb{R}^+$ explicitly specifies the exploration-exploitation trade-off. For an appropriately large choice of β_n, UCB can be made more explorative than EI; as you will recall from Eq. (32.2), the myopia of EI can lead to insufficient exploration. As such, the greater explorative nature of UCB has been observed to yield superior performance to that of EI and PI.[4] Figure 33.2 illustrates this UCB acquisition function.

The severely optimistic assumption underlying UCB is motivated through the resulting simplicity of the acquisition function. This lends itself to theoretical treatment, yielding, for instance, regret bounds.[5] This theory also provides schedules for the adaptation of β_n as a function of n. Nonetheless, it is difficult to reconcile UCB with a defensible loss function (see Exercise 33.1). As such, this class of approaches has no known (sensible) probabilistic numerical interpretation[6].

▶ **33.3   Information-Theoretic Approaches**

Let us now return to the two alternatives to the *value loss* (VL) developed in detail above: the *location-information loss* (LIL) and *value-information loss* (VIL), which we collectively describe as *information-theoretic*. The LIL and VIL select observations that best yield information about the minimiser and minimum, respectively. Note, first, that the meanings of exploration and exploitation are not completely clear for an information-theoretic approach. In an information-theoretic approach, the worth of an evaluation is not contained within its value, as would be true for

[4] Calandra et al. (2014b)

[5] Srinivas et al. (2010); Freitas, Smola, and Zoghi (2012).

Exercise 33.1. *(hard, solution on p. 367)* *Derive a loss function for which the UCB acquisition function (33.3) is the myopic expected loss, given that the posterior for y_n is that from a GP:* $\mathcal{N}(y_n; m(x_n), \mathbb{V}(x_n))$.

[6] That said, an interesting re-interpretation of the UCB criterion is provided by Jones (2001)).

an exploitative evaluation with the VL, but instead is contained in the information it yields. As such, all evaluations selected by an information-theoretic method are in some sense exploratory: the sole goal of these methods is to gather information.

For reasons similar to those discussed in §31.2, implementing information-theoretic loss functions exactly is computationally infeasible. To improve tractability, existing information-theoretic approaches adopt (like the other approaches above) myopia. Nonetheless, information-theoretic approaches do possess some advantages over their equally-myopic alternatives. Recall that, as mentioned in §32.2, EI is local: it values improvements only at the location of the next evaluation. PI and UCB are equally local. On the other hand, even if treated myopically, the LIL and VIL are truly global: they value information about the entire domain. This can be of value in improving exploration, which, in turn, can improve performance. As discussed above, the myopia underpinning alternative acquisition functions leads to under-exploratory behaviour.

Several myopic acquisition functions based on the LIL have been proposed, differing only in implementation details. An illustration of such approaches is given by Figure 33.3. Recall that the LIL demands minimisation of the entropy of x_*. More precisely, under the myopic approximation, which considers only the impact of the next, $(n+1)$th, step, we must consider the loss function

$$\lambda_{\text{LIL}}(\mathcal{D}_{n+1}) = \mathbb{H}(x_* \mid \mathcal{D}_{n+1}).$$

This loss, of course, depends on the y_n, unobserved at the current (nth) step.

Typically, x_* is continuous, an element of $\mathbb{R}^d$. But determining the distribution for this minimiser, $p(x_*)$, on a continuous domain is intractable. For one thing, note from Figure 33.3 that $p(x_*)$ may give a finite probability (mass) to the minimiser x_* being exactly at a boundary. As a result of these difficulties, all implementations of the LIL to date discretise x_*: this then requires only the maintenance of a (discrete) probability distribution. The approximation of x_* as discrete also enables its entropy to be more easily computed,

$$\mathbb{H}(x_* \mid \mathcal{D}_{n+1}) = -\sum_i P(x_{*,i} \mid \mathcal{D}_{n+1}) \log P(x_{*,i} \mid \mathcal{D}_{n+1}).$$

If x_* is (correctly) treated as continuous, we might think to use a differential entropy, which suffers from two significant drawbacks: it is not invariant to changes of variables; and it is difficult to compute. These pathologies can be addressed through approaches described in §8.8 of Garnett (2022).

The first acquisition functions built on the LIL are named *informational approach to global optimisation* (IAGO)[7] and *entropy search* (ES).[8] They differ in implementation details: while these differences are of practical significance, they will not concern us here. Both consider an acquisition function that is the myopic expected loss

$$\alpha_{\text{IAGO}}(x_n) = \alpha_{\text{ES}}(x_n)$$
$$= \mathbb{E}\big(\lambda_{\text{LIL}}(\mathcal{D}_{n+1})\big)$$
$$= \int \mathbb{H}(x_* \mid \mathcal{D}_{n+1}) p(y_n \mid x_n, \mathcal{D}_n) \, dy_n$$
$$=: \mathbb{E}_{y_n}\big(\mathbb{H}(x_* \mid y_n, x_n, \mathcal{D}_n)\big).$$

$\mathbb{E}_{y_n}\big(\mathbb{H}(x_* \mid y_n, x_n, \mathcal{D}_n)\big)$ is a *conditional entropy*, the expected entropy in x_* after an observation y_n whose value is currently unknown.

Predictive entropy search (PES)[9] is an alternative acquisition function derived from the LIL. It first notes that

$$\arg\min_{x_n} \mathbb{E}_{y_n}\big(\mathbb{H}(x_* \mid y_n, x_n, \mathcal{D}_n)\big)$$
$$= \arg\max_{x_n} \mathbb{H}(x_* \mid \mathcal{D}_n) - \mathbb{E}_{y_n}\big(\mathbb{H}(x_* \mid y_n, x_n, \mathcal{D}_n)\big),$$

as the prior entropy of the minimiser is independent of the next measurement. PES then makes use of the identity

$$I(x_* ; y_n) = \mathbb{H}(x_* \mid \mathcal{D}_n) - \mathbb{E}_{y_n}\big(\mathbb{H}(x_* \mid y_n, x_n, \mathcal{D}_n)\big)$$
$$= \mathbb{H}(y_n \mid x_n, \mathcal{D}_n) - \mathbb{E}_{x_*}\big(\mathbb{H}(y_n \mid x_*, x_n, \mathcal{D}_n)\big), \tag{33.4}$$

where $I(\cdot\,;\cdot)$ is the mutual information between two random variables, and $\mathbb{E}_{x_*}(\mathbb{H}(y_n \mid x_*, x_n, \mathcal{D}_n))$ is the conditional entropy of y_n given the random variable x_*. Eq. (33.4) yields the acquisition function

$$\alpha_{\text{PES}} = -\mathbb{H}(y_n \mid x_n, \mathcal{D}_n) + \mathbb{E}_{x_*}\big(\mathbb{H}(y_n \mid x_*, x_n, \mathcal{D}_n)\big).$$

This acquisition function will select identical evaluations to those of ES and IAGO. Nonetheless, the rearrangement is well-motivated, following the arguments of the *Bayesian active learning by disagreement* (BALD) algorithm,[10] which itself relies on old insights about the mutual information. First, $\mathbb{H}(y_n \mid x_n, \mathcal{D}_n)$ is straightforward to calculate: it is the entropy of a univariate Gaussian. The second term requires the computation of another univariate Gaussian's entropy: $\mathbb{H}(y_n \mid x_*, x_n, \mathcal{D}_n)$. This

[7] Villemonteix, Vazquez, and Walter (2009)
[8] Hennig and Schuler (2012)

[9] Hernández-Lobato et al. (2015)

[10] Houlsby et al. (2011)

is complicated by having to condition on x_* being a minimiser, achieved readily in practice through heuristics like ensuring that the objective at x_* has zero gradient and positive curvature. The term must also be marginalised over the posterior over the minimiser, $P(x_* \mid \mathcal{D}_n)$; a task whose central difficulty is constructing that posterior. In comparison, ES/IAGO require $P(x_* \mid y_n, x_n, \mathcal{D}_n)$ (so as to compute its entropy). The principal difference between ES/IAGO and PES is that $P(x_* \mid y_n, x_n, \mathcal{D}_n)$ must be constructed afresh for each proposed sampling location, x_n, whereas $P(x_* \mid \mathcal{D}_n)$ need only be constructed once per step n.

The VIL was first proposed by Hoffman and Ghahramani (2015) giving an acquisition function known as *output-space entropy search* (OPES). Follow-on work[11] produced an acquisition function known as *max-value entropy search* (MES) that provided some improvements in implementation. These acquisition functions both modify PES only in replacing the minimiser, x_*, with the minimum, y_*,

[11] Wang and Jegelka (2017)

$$
\begin{aligned}
\alpha_{\mathrm{OPES}} &= \alpha_{\mathrm{MES}} \\
&= -\mathbb{H}(y_n \mid x_n, \mathcal{D}_n) + \mathbb{E}_{y_*}\big(\mathbb{H}(y_n \mid y_*, x_n, \mathcal{D}_n)\big).
\end{aligned}
$$

As discussed in §31.2, the VIL may be preferred to the LIL for some applications. Moreover, OPES and MES have advantages in implementation over PES. For instance, the posterior for the minimum, $p(y_* \mid \mathcal{D}_n)$, is univariate, whereas the posterior for the minimiser, $P(x_* \mid \mathcal{D}_n)$, has dimension equal to that of the search domain.

Returning to the discussion in §32.3, all the information-theoretic acquisition functions described above are relatively robust to noise in the objective function. Information-theoretic acquisition functions reward the information yielded by an observation, rather than measuring characteristics of the observation itself, as do EI, UCB, and PI. In particular, all information-theoretic acquisition functions are influenced by prospective observations only through their impact on entropy terms. So long as posteriors given the noisy observations can be obtained, such entropy terms will naturally accommodate the noise.

Figure 33.4 depicts a comparison of the information-theoretic acquisition functions from this section against those of previous sections.

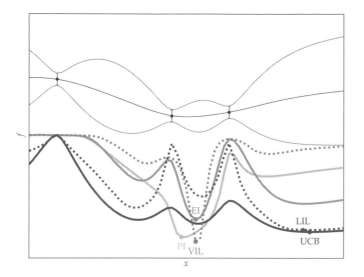

Figure 33.4: A direct comparison of many of the acquisition functions in this chapter. Since each has its own units of measure and given that only the location of the extremum matters (indicated by a dot), each acquisition function is plotted on a different (arbitrary) scale. Recall that IAGO, ES and PES are differing implementations of the same underlying loss function, LIL, with OPES and MES likewise representing different implementations of VIL. We caution that the exact locations of the acquisition function optima, indicated by labelled vertical bars, are not particularly general, and can be changed significantly through seemingly innocuous variations in the data and the GP model.

▶ **33.4   Portfolios of Acquisition Functions**

The acquisition functions described in this chapter each possess various limitations. One answer to such limitations is to propose the use of a *portfolio* of multiple acquisition functions[12] – the hope is that an average over different acquisition functions will be less vulnerable to the failure modes of any individual one of those averaged acquisition functions. This approach requires, first, finding the best candidate evaluation location according to each acquisition function in the portfolio, forming a set of candidates. The actual location chosen is then the element of that set that maximises an independent *meta-criterion*.

Of course, any decision-theoretic problem requires a single loss function to be chosen. Considering multiple acquisition functions (which correspond to distinct expected loss functions) is inconsistent with this view. However, the portfolio Bayesian optimisation approaches do, in fact, operate according to a single loss function: that inherent in the meta-criterion. The acquisition functions within the portfolio are typically computationally cheap, such as EI, PI and UCB. The meta-criterion, on the other hand, is expensive but powerful: for instance, Shahriari et al. (2014) choose the LIL loss function of §33.3. Portfolio approaches, then, are useful in providing a cheap heuristic for the optimisation of an expensive meta-criterion.

[12] Hoffman, Brochu, and Freitas (2011); Shahriari et al. (2016).

34

Further Topics

▶ **34.1 Batch Evaluation**

It is not uncommon in optimisation to be permitted many simultaneous evaluations of the objective: this is known as *batch* optimisation. For instance:

- ⊖ several time-consuming drug trials might be run in parallel, with the goal of determining the most effective drug molecule;

- ⊖ in optimising machine learning model architectures, many such architectures might be simultaneously evaluated to exploit parallel computing resources; and

- ⊖ in searching for optimal policy parameters, one (or many) agent-based simulations of an economic system may be able to be run simultaneous with a real-world trial.

Batch optimisation requires proposing a set of evaluation locations, x_B, before knowing the values $f(x_B)$ at (any) of the locations. Here the Probabilistic Numerics framing of Bayesian optimisation offers an explicit joint probability distribution over the values $f(x_B)$, acknowledging the probabilistic relationships amongst the batch. These relationships are crucial to selecting a good batch, where desiderata include the exclusion of redundant measurements (that are likely to return the same information) and the balancing of exploration against exploitation.

The technical challenges of batch Bayesian optimisation are bespoke to the different priors and acquisition functions. Batch approaches exist for EI[1] (sometimes called *multi-point* EI), UCB[2], KG[3], PES[4], and for a flexible family of acquisition functions[5] (particularly, EI).

[1] Ginsbourger, Le Riche, and Carraro (2008, 2010); Chevalier and Ginsbourger (2013); Marmin, Chevalier, and Ginsbourger (2015); Marmin, Chevalier, and Ginsbourger (2016); Wang et al. (2016); Rontsis, Osborne, and Goulart (2020).

[2] Desautels, Krause, and Burdick (2012); Daxberger and Low (2017).

[3] Wu and Frazier (2016); Wu et al. (2017).

[4] Shah and Ghahramani (2015)

[5] Azimi, Fern, and Fern (2010); Azimi, Jalali, and Fern (2012); González et al. (2016).

▶ 34.2   Reinforcement Learning

Bayesian optimisation has connections to, but distinctions from reinforcement learning.[6] Both reinforcement learning and Bayesian optimisation address a (partially-observed) Markov decision process. As a first point of distinction, however, reinforcement learning and Bayesian optimisation tackle slightly different problems. Reinforcement learning cares about the returned evaluation at every iteration of the procedure (typically by considering some discounted sum of evaluations as the objective), where optimisation should properly care only about the final returned value. In Bayesian optimisation, it is comparatively more acceptable to make an exploratory evaluation that has low expected value. In reinforcement learning, it is also much more common for the evaluation to change the state of the function: the agent actually modifies the objective function in its choice of evaluations. This is usually not the case for optimisation (for which there is no state).

> [6] Sutton and Barto (1998)

Second, the methods used in reinforcement learning and Bayesian optimisation are distinct. Reinforcement learning usually attempts to learn a policy to govern the agent's behaviour, whereas Bayesian optimisation is more explicitly concerned with a decision-theoretic approach.

Third, there's a cultural difference. Reinforcement learning is often used as the primary, outer system; Bayesian optimisation is usually used internally within larger machine learning systems (for instance, to tune their hyperparameters: see §34.3). Interestingly, Bayesian optimisation has been used within reinforcement learning: **paul_alternating_2016 (paul_alternating_2016)** use a scheme that alternates between Bayesian quadrature to marginalise environmental variables and Bayesian optimisation for policy search.

▶ 34.3   Application: Automated Machine Learning

One of the most prominent current uses of Bayesian optimisation is to tune the configuration (particularly hyperparameters) of (other) machine learning algorithms.[7] This broad field is known as Automated Machine Learning, or AutoML. Bayesian optimisation has many arguments in its favour for this application. The objective function is typically computationally expensive: it might be the validation loss or negative-log-likelihood of a model that takes hours to train. Indeed, the objective itself might include some acknowledgement of that computational

> [7] Bergstra et al. (2011); Hutter, Hoos, and Leyton-Brown (2011); Snoek, Larochelle, and Adams (2012).

cost, e.g. the error achieved per second.[8] The arguments of the objective, such as hyperparameters, might include regularisation penalties (parameters of the prior), architecture choices, and the parameters of internal numerics procedures (such as learning rates). Conveniently, there are often not more than 10 or 20 such hyperparameters that are known to be important: the dimensionality of such problems is compatible with Bayesian optimisation. In real-world cases, these hyperparameters have been historically selected manually by practitioners: it is not difficult to make the case for the automated alternative provided by Bayesian optimisation. As such, Bayesian optimisation is a core tool in the quest for automated machine learning.[9] As one example, Bayesian optimisation was used to tune the hyperparameters of AlphaGo for its high-profile match against Lee Sodol[10].

Perhaps most interestingly, from a Probabilistic Numerics perspective, there are many characteristics of the objective that can be used to inform the choice of prior and loss function. First, note that the relevance of some hyperparameters to an objective function for hyperparameter tuning is often conditional on the values of other hyperparameters. This includes examples in which the objective has a variable number of hyperparameters: we may wish to search over neural network architectures with a variable number of layers. In that case, whether the number of hidden units in the third layer will influence the objective will be conditional on the value of the hyperparameter that specifies the number of layers. The covariance function of a GP surrogate can be chosen to capture this structure, leading to improved Bayesian optimisation performance.[11]

Another common feature of hyperparameter tuning problems is that the objective can return partial information even before its computation is complete. Concretely, such computation is used in training a machine learning model, typically through the use of a local optimiser (see Chapter IV). Even before that local optimisation has converged, its early stages can be predictive of the ultimate value of the objective. This is observable through the familiar decaying-exponential shape of so-called *training curves* or *learning curves*, giving training loss as a function of the number of iterations of local optimisation. If the early parts of a training curve do not promise a competitive value after more computation is spent (a value strongly correlated with or equal to the associated objective function value), it might make sense to abort the computation prematurely. This intuition was incorporated into a Bayesian optimisation model

[8] Snoek, Larochelle, and Adams (2012)

[9] See, e.g., www.ml4aad.org/automl and autodl.chalearn.org.

[10] Chen et al. (2018)

[11] Swersky et al. (2013)

with some success by Swersky, Snoek, and Adams (2014). Their approach built a joint model over training curves (internal to each objective function evaluation) and the objective function itself: an excellent example of Bayesian optimisation's ability to incorporate structure.

Relatedly, hyperparameter tuning problems often allow evaluations of variable fidelity. An observation of higher fidelity is usually associated with higher computational cost. The canonical example is the choice of training set size. A larger training set requires more computation to evaluate the loss on that training set, but the result will be more informative about how effective the associated model would be for the full data set. In this case, the *size* of the training set can itself be taken as a variable for optimisation. Given this variable, a bespoke Bayesian optimisation model (comprising both a novel surrogate model and loss function capturing the variable cost) can be produced.[12] Resulting algorithms can offer orders-of-magnitude acceleration in finding effective hyperparameter settings.

[12] Nickson et al. (2014); Klein et al. (2017); McLeod, Osborne, and Roberts (2015).

▷ **34.3.1   Software**

At the time of writing, dozens of open-source Bayesian optimisation libraries exist. Many implement all of the acquisition functions introduced in this chapter. There are further open-source Bayesian optimisation packages specialised to particular applications, notably hyperparameter tuning. We recommend the open-source emukit package,[13], which provides a full-featured sublibrary for Bayesian optimisation, if only because emukit additionally supports other PN methods.

[13] Paleyes et al. (2019), available at emukit.github.io

Chapter VI
Solving Ordinary
Differential Equations

Key Points

The solution $x(t)$, $t \in [0, T]$, of an *ordinary differential equation (ODE)* is defined as the integral of a vector field f along its own path $\{x(s); \ 0 \le s \le t\}$ up to time t; see Eq. (37.2). Accordingly, solving ODEs is often described as the "nonlinear" extension of univariate integration, since the subset of ODEs whose vector field is independent of x are quadrature problems over t. These linear instances can, therefore, be solved by all integration methods from Chapter II. Probabilistic solvers for ODEs, however, also require an iterative learning of $x(t)$ (using its own previous estimates) and a tracking of its accumulated uncertainty over time. Nonetheless, those that model x by a GP should reduce to Bayesian quadrature (as they do!).

There is, however, another (perhaps less obvious) connection with the above-presented material: on the one hand, ODEs are the mechanistic model for a dynamical system without observations of x. On the other hand, time series (or temporal signals) are, vice versa, the statistical description of a dynamical system *with* available observations of x, but *without* a mechanistic model – which can be estimated by filtering and smoothing, as explained in §5.3. The probabilistic framework will naturally unify these two complementary viewpoints by applying the latter to the former, that is filters and smoothers to ODEs – leading to a wide class of ODE solvers called *ODE filters and smoothers*.

The topic of ODEs has been extensively studied by numerical analysts. Likewise, probabilistic ODE solvers are, compared to algorithms for other domains, relatively well-understood and begin to match parts of the deep classic theory. On the proving ground of inverse problems, they can already improve upon classic methods. The principal take-aways of this chapter are:

⊖ Approximating the solution of an ODE, $x : [0, T] \to \mathbb{R}^d$ with

initial value $x(0) = x_0 \in \mathbb{R}^d$, can be regarded as curve fitting
of a time series using information about $x'(t)$, $0 = t_0 < t_1 <
\cdots < t_N = T$, from evaluations of f. To this end, we can (a
priori) jointly model $[x, x']$ with a GP and treat its approximation as a GP regression problem, with the usual cubic
cost of $\mathcal{O}(N^3)$ in the number of time steps $\{t_1, \ldots, t_N\}$. If we
restrict our choice of GP priors to Gauss–Markov processes,
then the GP posterior can be computed by Bayesian filters
(and smoothers) in linear time $\mathcal{O}(N)$. This view engenders a
broad family of ODE solvers, now known as *ODE filters and
smoothers*, which, like in signal processing, span the entire
spectrum of fast-and-Gaussian (extended) Kalman filters to
expressive-but-slower particle filters.

⊖ If there is an additional final condition on $x(T)$ (i.e. if the
ODE is a boundary value problem), similar fast-and-Gaussian
solvers can be constructed.

⊖ All modelling assumptions of such an ODE filter or smoother
can be concisely captured by a probabilistic (Bayesian) *state
space model* (SSM), consisting of a dynamic model (a prior) and
a measurement model (a likelihood). Given such a SSM, an
ODE filter or smoother computes the posterior distribution
which for some SSMs requires approximations. The choice
of SSM and approximate inference schemes, therefore, completely defines an ODE filter or smoother, whose parameters
(most importantly: the step size) can be adapted in a probabilistic manner. Notably, the integrated-Wiener-process (IWP)
prior is the most suitable dynamic model for generic ODEs
because it extrapolates with Taylor polynomials; if more is
known, other ("biased") priors can, however, be more precise.

⊖ Like in previous chapters, specific models yield ODE filters
(of the fast-and-Gaussian type) that coincide with classic
methods. Other choices lead to completely new solvers that
encode new kinds of prior knowledge and output more detailed representations of the (potentially multimodal) set of
plausible trajectories.

⊖ The main analytical desiderata for ODE solvers are high
polynomial convergence rates and numerical stability – as
well as (additionally for probabilistic methods) a calibrated
posterior uncertainty. For extended Kalman ODE filters with
an IWP prior (and, locally, with other priors), global convergence rates on par with standard methods hold, namely of
the same order as the number of derivatives contained in

the SSM. In this setting, the expected numerical error (the posterior standard deviation) is well-calibrated in the sense that it asymptotically matches these convergence rates. For the MAP estimate, such rates even hold in more SSMs. Recent practical implementations have drastically improved the numerical stability of these methods.

⊖ Unlike in previous chapters, there is an important line of probabilistic numerical methods for ODEs that fundamentally deviates from the philosophy of this book, i.e. from applying GP regression to numerics. These *perturbative solvers* do not compute a posterior distribution $p(x \mid \{f(\hat{x}(t_i))\}_{i=1}^{N})$, but instead design a stochastic simulator by perturbing some classic numerical method – such that the size of these stochastic perturbations are proportional to the numerical error. Its randomised simulations are then, in a similar vein to particle ODE filters, considered to be samples from the distribution over the set of numerically possible trajectories (given a numerical integrator and a discretisation). These nonparametric methods are more expressive, but need to simulate the ODE multiple times. Unlike Gaussian solvers, they can represent bifurcations and chaos.

⊖ If their output distribution is used as a likelihood, both ODE filters (or smoothers) and perturbative solvers can prevent overconfidence in (otherwise likelihood-free) ODE inverse-problems. If an extended Kalman ODE filter or smoother is employed, then this likelihood is even twice differentiable, and its gradients (and Hessians) can greatly increase the sample efficiency and, thereby, the overall speed of existing inverse-problem solvers. To date, the usefulness of probabilistic ODE solvers has also been demonstrated in a few additional settings.

⊖ Efficient implementations of ODE filters and smoothers are available as part of the ProbNum Python-package.[1]

[1] Code at probnum.org. See the corresponding publication by Wenger et al. (2021).

36

Introduction

Since their invention by Isaac Newton and Gottfried Wilhelm Leibniz in the seventeenth century, differential equations have become the standard mathematical description of any (continuous) dynamical systems with explicitly known mechanics. Broadly defined as any equation that relates one (or more) functions and their derivatives, there are two main categories: *ordinary differential equations* (ODEs) and *partial differential equations* (PDEs).[1] While ODEs contain derivatives in only one independent variable (e.g. time), PDEs contain partial derivatives in multiple independent variables (e.g. three-dimensional space). In this text, we restrict our attention to ODEs and only give some pointers to probabilistic solvers for PDEs in §41.4.

Over the centuries, mathematical analysts have provided a deep and beautiful theory for ODEs which has been compiled into many comprehensive books – such as the ones by Arnold (1992) and Teschl (2012). Nonetheless, closed-form solutions are only known for very few ODEs and numerical approximations are needed in all other cases. The numerics of ODEs has therefore become an equally well-explored analytical topic. The accumulated classical numerical theory is, for example, presented in the excellent textbooks by Hairer, Nørsett, and Wanner (1993), Hairer and Wanner (1996), Deuflhard and Bornemann (2002), and Butcher (2016). The following setup will allow us to be undistracted by some analytical corner cases and focus on the introduction of (probabilistic) numerical methods.

Definition 36.1. *We say that an* ordinary differential equation *(ODE) is a relation of the form*

$$x'(t) = f(x(t)) \qquad \text{for all } t \in [0, T], \qquad (36.1)$$

between a curve $x : [0, T] \to \mathbb{R}^d$ *on a interval* $[0, T] \subset \mathbb{R}$ *and a*

[1] *Stochastic* differential equations (SDEs), which relate a *stochastic process* with its derivatives, are not included in this definition; see §5.3.

vector field (aka dynamics) $f : V \to \mathbb{R}^d$ on some non-empty open set $V \subseteq \mathbb{R}^d$.

By this definition, we restrict our attention to first-order autonomous ODEs – but this comes without loss of generality, as higher-order ODEs can be reformulated as first-order[2] and as we only exclude the (mathematically analogous) non-autonomous case $f(x(t),t)$ to declutter our notation.[3]

Definition 36.2. *We say that $x : [0, T] \to \mathbb{R}^d$ is a* solution *of the* initial value problem *(IVP)*

$$x'(t) = f(x(t)), \quad \text{for all } t \in [0, T],$$
$$\text{with initial value} \quad x(0) = x_0 \in \mathbb{R}^d. \tag{36.2}$$

If there is an additional final condition $x(T) = x_T \in \mathbb{R}^d$, *then Eq. (36.2) turns into a* boundary value problem *(BVP).[4]*

Note that, under this definition, IVPs can be ill-posed; in particular, some ODEs do not have a well-defined solution, either when Eq. (36.2) is satisfied for multiple[5] choices of x or when a local solution x on $[0, t]$, $0 < t < T$, cannot be extended[6] to the entire interval $[0, T]$. BVPs, of course, only admit a solution if x_T equals the final value $x(T)$ of a solution of the underlying IVP. Consequently, the solutions of many IVPs (and even more BVPs) are not well-defined. Since there is nothing to approximate in these cases, the whole concept of a numerical error loses its meaning. Fortunately, the next two theorems will enable us to exclude such cases by requiring the following assumptions.

Assumption 36.3. *The set $V \subseteq \mathbb{R}^d$ is open and $x_0 \in V$. The vector field $f : V \to \mathbb{R}^d$ is locally Lipschitz continuous, i.e. for each open subset $U \subseteq V$ there exists a constant $L_U > 0$ such that*

$$\|f(x) - f(y)\| \leq L_U \|x - y\|, \quad \text{for all } x, y \in U.$$

While more general preconditions for uniqueness and existence exist in the literature,[7] the following version of the Picard–Lindelöf theorem[8] is adapted to Definition 36.1 and will suffice for our purposes.

Theorem 36.4 (Picard–Lindelöf theorem). *Under Assumption 36.3, let us choose a $\delta > 0$ such that $\overline{B_\delta(x_0)} := \{x \in \mathbb{R}^d : \|x - x_0\| \leq \delta\} \subset V$ and set $M := \sup_{x \in \overline{B_\delta(x_0)}} \|f(x)\|$. Then there exists a unique* local *solution $x : [0, T] \to \mathbb{R}^d$ of the IVP (36.2) for all $T \in [0, \delta/M]$. More specifically, if $V = \mathbb{R}^d$ and $M < \infty$, then there exists a unique* global *solution $x : [0, \infty) \to \mathbb{R}^d$, i.e. for $T = \infty$.*

[2] Most classical methods can only solve first-order ODEs, which is no restriction to their applicability: any ODE of nth order,
$$x^{(n)}(t) = f\left(x^{(n-1)}(t), \ldots, x'(t), x(t)\right),$$
can be transformed into an ODE of first-order by defining the new object
$$\tilde{x}(t) := [x(t) \quad x'(t) \quad \cdots \quad x^{(n)}(t),]^\mathsf{T}$$
which implies a first-order ODE with the modified vector field
$$\tilde{f}(\tilde{x}(t)) = \left[x'(t), \ldots, x^{(n-1)}(t), f\left(\tilde{x}^{(1:n-1)}(t)\right)\right]^\mathsf{T}.$$
This, however, hides the derivative-relation of the components of $\tilde{x}(t)$. In Probabilistic Numerics, this structure can be explicitly modelled in a state-space model; see Exercise 38.2 and Bosch, Tronarp, and Hennig (2022) who considered second-order ODEs directly.

[3] Note, however, that we ignore, as most textbooks, the more general case of implicit ODEs
$$0 = F\left(x^{(n)}(t), \ldots, x(t)\right)$$
because only little is known about them; see Eich-Soellner and Führer (1998).

[4] Strictly speaking, this is only a special case of a BVP; the boundary condition can more generally be $g(y(a), y(b)) = 0$ for an arbitrary function g.

[5] **Example:** Consider the ODE $x'(t) = 2\,\text{sign}(\sqrt{|x(t)|})$ which admits a unique solution for all $x_0 \neq 0$. However, if $x_0 = 0$, then the curves
$$x(t) = \begin{cases} 0, & \text{for } t \in [0, t_0] \\ \pm(t - t_0)^2, & \text{for } t \in (t_0, T] \end{cases}$$
are solutions for all $t_0 \in [0, T]$.

[6] **Example:** Consider the ODE $x'(t) = x(t)^2$. Its solution
$$x(t) = \frac{x_0}{1 - x_0 t}$$
only exists on $[0, 1/x_0]$ and cannot be extended beyond its singularity at $t = 1/x_0$.

[7] For the most general existence and uniqueness results we are aware of, see §2.3. in Teschl (2012).

[8] Our Theorem 36.4 is a modified version of Theorem 2.2 from Teschl (2012), where a proof is provided.

To ensure sufficient regularity of such an x, we need an additional assumption.

Assumption 36.5. *The vector field f is $(q-1)$-times continuously differentiable, i.e. $f \in C^{q-1}(V, \mathbb{R}^d)$, for some $q \in \mathbb{N}$.*

Theorem 36.6 (Regularity of IVP solutions). *Under Assumptions 36.3 and 36.5, the unique solution x is one order more regular than f, i.e. $x \in C^q([0,T], \mathbb{R}^d)$.*[9]

[9] Cf. Lemma 2.3. in Teschl (2012).

Proof. By induction over $q \in \mathbb{N}$. Theorem 36.4 implies that x is well-defined; the base step ($q = 1$) then follows directly from the ODE (36.2) with continuous f by use of the fundamental theorem of calculus. The inductive step ($q \to q+1$) is obtained by differentiating the ODE for the $(q+1)$th time.   □

In the sequel, we will restrict our attention to IVPs with a well-defined solution $x \in C^q([0,T], \mathbb{R}^d)$ for some $q \in \mathbb{N}$ and some $T > 0$ – such as, amongst others, those satisfying Assumptions 36.3 and 36.5.[10] Moreover, to simplify the notation, we will, w.l.o.g., set $V = \mathbb{R}^d$.

With these preparations in place, we will from here on focus on numerics. A numerical IVP solver (aka ODE solver) is any algorithm that receives an IVP $(f, x_0, [0,T])$ as inputs, and computes a (discrete or continuous-time) approximation of $x : [0,T] \to \mathbb{R}^d$ as an output.[11] A *probabilistic IVP solver* (or *probabilistic ODE solver*) outputs a probability distribution over x instead – either by iteratively updating a prior on x (§38) or by sampling from the set of numerically possible approximations of x (§40). But, first, we will give an intuitive introduction to classical ODE solvers.

[10] This will allow probabilistic numerical solvers to model q derivatives in a state-space model; see §38.1. Note that this is no restriction of their applicability since, for $q = 1$, Assumption 36.5 is implied by Assumption 36.3, which is the standard assumption of classical numerical analysis. Thus, the probabilistic solvers (which we will introduce in §38 and §40) are as generically applicable as classical methods.

[11] We will exclusively focus on IVPs for the most parts, and only briefly treat the topic of BVPs in §41.1.

Classical ODE Solvers
as Regression Methods

From a physics viewpoint, the solution $x \in C^q([0, T], \mathbb{R}^d)$ of an IVP can be thought of as the flow of a massless particle in the force field $f \in C^{q-1}(\mathbb{R}^d, \mathbb{R}^d)$ starting at x_0. Hence, any estimate $\hat{x}(t)$ of $x(t)$ always comes with a derivative estimate y_t, written

$$y_t := f(\hat{x}(t)) \overset{\hat{x}(t) \approx x(t)}{\approx} f(x(t)) \overset{(\text{ODE})}{=} x'(t), \qquad (37.1)$$

which can be used to construct a local linearisation $\hat{x}(t+h) = \hat{x}(t) + hy_t$ to extrapolate forwards. This is the underlying principle of all ODE solvers. Euler's method represents this principle in its purest form as it simply iterates this linear extrapolation along time; see Figure 37.1 for a graphical depiction.

Figure 37.1 also highlights the important fact that, after the first step, a numerical solver essentially follows another IVP – with the same f, but initial value $x(t) = \hat{x}(t)$. This is why one often considers the *flow* of the ODE

$$\Phi_t(a) := a + \int_0^t f(x(s)) \, ds, \qquad (37.2)$$

where $x(t) = \Phi_t(a)$ is the solution of the IVP (36.2) with initial value $x(0) = a$.

Given any numerical estimate $\hat{x}(t)$, standard ODE solvers now extrapolate from t to $t + h$ by approximating this flow $\Phi_h(\hat{x}(t))$ as precisely and cheaply as possible. In fact, Euler's method can simply be interpreted as using a first-order Taylor expansion, $\hat{x}(t+h) = \hat{x}(t) + hy_t$, to approximate $\Phi_h(\hat{x}(t))$. Hence, it is only natural that Euler's method produces (by Taylor's theorem) a local error of $\mathcal{O}(h^2)$, and (after $N = T/h \in \mathcal{O}(1/h)$ steps) a global error of $\mathcal{O}(h)$.

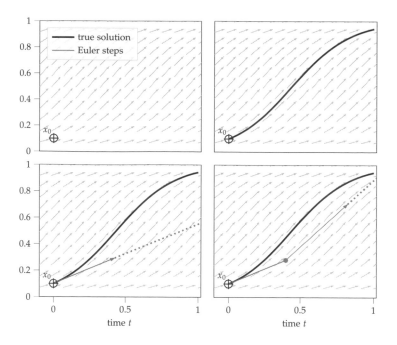

time t time t

Figure 37.1: The underlying principle: An ODE solvers receives an IVP, i.e. an initial value x_0 and a rule f to get the derivatives at every point which are depicted by the grey arrows (upper left). The true IVP solution is a trajectory of a massless particle along these derivatives (upper right). In the beginning we can extrapolate with the true derivative; Euler's method simply linearises with it (lower left). This procedure is iterated, but at a numerical estimate (solid circle) and with an imprecise derivative for extrapolation (lower right); see Eq. (37.1).

To achieve higher polynomial rates than Euler, one just has to extrapolate with better approximations of $\Phi_h(\hat{x}(t))$. In most of classical numerics, this is achieved by either of two families of methods: single-step and multi-step methods. They both construct higher-order Taylor expansions of $\Phi_h(\hat{x}(t))$ – either by collecting additional information from Eq. (37.1) at multiple sub-steps of one step $[t, t+h]$ (single-step) or by exploiting the already-collected information $\{y_{t-h} = f(\hat{x}(t-h), y_{t-2h} = f(\hat{x}(t-2h), \dots\}$ from multiple previous steps (multi-step). In both cases, the underlying principle of Eq. (37.1) remains unchanged; but the thus-created information is then used to construct a better regression (in the form of a better polynomial extrapolation)[1] of the flow Φ at every step. In the worst case, the convergence rate will then, of course, depend on how many summands of the Taylor series of $\Phi_h(\hat{x}(t))$ are matched in each step. Fortunately, this Taylor series is known[2] to be

$$\Phi_h\left(\hat{x}(t)\right) = \sum_{i=0}^{\infty} \frac{h^i}{i!} f^{\langle i \rangle}\left(\hat{x}(t)\right), \qquad (37.3)$$

where the $\{f^{\langle i \rangle}\}_{i=0}^{\infty}$ are recursively defined by $f^{\langle 0 \rangle}(a) := a$, $f^{\langle 1 \rangle}(a) := f(a)$, and

$$f^{\langle i \rangle}(a) := [\nabla_x f^{\langle i-1 \rangle} \odot f](a), \qquad (37.4)$$

where $\odot$ denotes the elementwise product. Any solver that matches the first $p \in \mathbb{N}$ summands of Eq. (37.3) will accordingly

[1] In fact, Nordsieck (1962) already observed that "...all methods of numerical integration are equivalent to finding an approximating polynomial...".

[2] Eq. (37.3) follows from $\frac{\partial^i}{\partial t^i} \Phi_h(\hat{x}(t)) = f^{\langle i \rangle}(\hat{x}(t))$, which is proved in Appendix E of Kersting, Sullivan, and Hennig (2020) by iterative application of the chain rule. This formula can also be obtained as a consequence of Faà di Bruno's formula, as given by Lemma 2.8 in Hairer, Nørsett, and Wanner (1993).

have local convergence rates of $\mathcal{O}(h^{p+1})$, and global rates of $\mathcal{O}(h^p)$. Such solvers are called pth-order methods.

A numerical solver thus decomposes the numerical problem of solving ODEs – i.e. of fitting the curve $x(t) = \Phi_t(x_0)$ – into a series of local regressions of $\Phi_h(\hat{x}(t))$. Moreover, a pth-order single-step solver (such as a pth-order Runge–Kutta) matches the first p derivatives $\{f^{\langle i\rangle}(\hat{x}(t)); i = 1,\ldots,p\}$ of $\Phi_h(\hat{x}(t))$ at $h = 0$ in every step. This is to say that, at every step $t \to t + h$, it *locally* performs Hermite interpolation[3] of $\Phi_h(\hat{x}(t))$ with data

[3] Spitzbart (1960)

$$\left\{\Phi_0(\hat{x}(t)) \stackrel{!}{=} \hat{x}(t), \ \frac{\partial^i}{\partial t^i}\Phi_t(\hat{x}(t))\Big|_{t=0} \stackrel{!}{=} f^{\langle i\rangle}(\hat{x}(t)); \quad i = 1,\ldots,p\right\}.$$
(37.5)

However, since $\hat{x}(t) \approx x(t)$ and thus $\Phi_t(\hat{x}(t)) \approx \Phi_t(x(t))$, it is unclear how these local regressions should be combined globally. Classical solvers simply pretend that estimates on the right-hand side of the data assignments ($\stackrel{!}{=}$) in Eq. (37.5) relate to the true IVP solution, instead to the flow map started at $\hat{x}(t)$. This would mean that, given a discretisation $0 = t_0 < t_1 < \cdots < t_N = T$, the solver uses iterated Hermite interpolation of $x(t + h)$ from the data

$$\left\{x(t) \stackrel{!}{=} \hat{x}(t), \ x^{(i)}(t) \stackrel{!}{=} f^{\langle i\rangle}(\hat{x}(t)); \quad i = 1,\ldots,p\right\}. \quad (37.6)$$

This removal of the flow map Φ from Eq. (37.5) to Eq. (37.6) means that the solver, after every completed step, falsely assumes that its current estimate $\hat{x}(t)$ is the true $x(t)$ – a property of classical numerics, referred to as *uncertainty-unawareness*.[4] To satisfy this overly-optimistic internal assumption of the solver, one would have to replace $\hat{x}(t)$ by the exact $x(t)$ in the entire data set, Eq. (37.6). Iterated local Hermite interpolation on this more informative (but, to the solver, inaccessible) data set indeed yields a more accurate regression of x – which is numerically demonstrated in Figure 37.2 for the popular fourth-order Runge–Kutta method (RK4).

[4] For more details on uncertainty-(un)awareness in numerics see §1 in Kersting (2020).

As a remedy, we can build more "uncertainty-aware" numerical solvers by modelling the ignored uncertainty with probability distributions, that is by adding appropriate noise to the Hermite extrapolation performed by classical ODE solvers (as in the generic GP regression from §4.2.2).

But our probabilistic, regression-based view of numerics will lead us further than that, beyond the conventional categories of single-step and multi-step methods. To see how, let us first recall that classical solvers iterate local Hermite interpolations on $t \to t + h$ using the data set from Eq. (37.6) for each respective

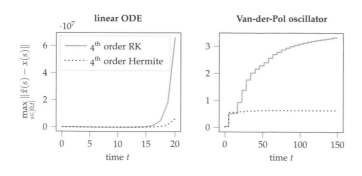

Figure 37.2: Comparison of the maximal error on fourth-order Runge–Kutta (RK) and iterated fourth-order Hermite interpolation with exact data (i.e. $x(t)$ instead of $\hat{x}(t)$ in Eq. (37.6)) on the linear and the Van-der-Pol ODE. The linear system is given by $x'(t) = x(t)$, $x(0) = 1.0$ and the Van-der-Pol system by $(x_1(t), x_2(t)) = (\mu(x_1(t) - \frac{1}{3}x_1(t)^3 - x_2(t)), \frac{x_1(t)}{\mu})$, $x(0) = (2, -5)$, $\mu = 5$. The graphs show the maximal error up to time t. As expected, Hermite interpolation produces a lower error.

time t. But, as long as we have a $\hat{x}(t)$ when needed, nothing prevents us from using the union of these data sets for all times t visited by the solver. Second, we recall from above that even our first (direct and unaltered) interpretation of ODE solvers as iterated local regression with higher derivatives, from Eq. (37.5), is constructed from the sole principle of Eq. (37.1). Hence – if we trust our regression methods to aggregate the information about x' from Eq. (37.1) at least as skillfully as the classical ODE solvers – we can treat any evaluation $f(\hat{x}(t))$ at a numerical estimate $\hat{x}(t)$ of $x(t)$ as what it is: data on $x'(t)$.

Via these two considerations, we thus regard both the local clustering of all derivative information from a finite number of steps (or sub-steps) and the ensuing local derivation of higher-derivative information as artificial constructs. After discarding them, we arrive at the insight that, given a discretisation $0 = t_0 < t_1 < \cdots < t_N = T$, approximating the ODE solution $x : [0, T] \to \mathbb{R}^d$ is nothing but a regression on the data set

$$\left\{ x(0) \stackrel{!}{=} x_0, \ x'(t_n) \stackrel{!}{=} f(\hat{x}(t_n)); \quad n = 0, \ldots, N \right\}, \quad (37.7)$$

where $\hat{x}(t_n)$ is a numerical estimate of $x(t_n)$. This regression problem might appear to be defined in a circular way, since computing $\hat{x}(t_n)$ is the very goal of the problem. But this will be no problem because ODE solvers – just like the Gauss–Markov regression tools from §5 that we will employ – go through time sequentially. Hence, at every t_n, there is a $\hat{x}(t_n)$ readily available (e.g. the predictive mean conditioned on the preceding steps). In other words, the global regression problem of Eq. (37.7) is revealed to the ODE solver one step at a time (i.e. as a time series).

Below, we will show how this regression formulation is rigorously realised in a *state-space model* (ssm), without the circular appearance of $\hat{x}$ in the problem formulation. While it will (for full generality) employ a different kind of information z_n (see Eq. (38.13)), the connection to y_t from Eq. (37.1) will become ev-

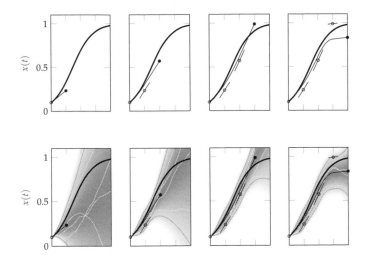

Figure 37.3: Sketch contrasting classic and probabilistic ODE solvers. Four steps of size h, true solution in black. Top row: Classical solvers construct an extrapolation $\hat{x}(t_i)$ (solid black circle) which, in this example, is also used as the probing point $\tilde{x}(t_i)$ to construct an observation $y_i = f(\tilde{x}(t_i), t_i)$. Bottom row: Probabilistic solvers do the same, but return a probability measure $p(x(t))$ (grey delineated shading, with lightly coloured samples), rather than the point estimate $\hat{x}(t)$ (although for example the mean of p could be used as such an estimate). For a well-calibrated classic solver, the estimate $\hat{x}$ should lie close to the true solution. The same applies for the mean (or mode) estimate of a Gaussian probabilistic solver; but additionally, the width (standard deviation) of the posterior measure should also be meaningfully related to the true error. In the case of the (nonparametric) perturbative solvers the resulting samples should accurately capture the entire distribution of numerically possible trajectories; e.g. by covering both sides of a bifurcation (Figure 38.2).

ident via an intuitive (but less general) SSM in §38.3.4. Bayesian regression of $x(t)$ in such a SSM is then performed by methods known as *ODE filters and smoothers*. The difference between a classical and a probabilistic solver is visualised in Figure 37.3.

▶ 37.1   A Brief History of Probabilistic ODE Solvers

John Skilling (1991) was the first to recognise that ODEs can, and perhaps should, be treated as a Bayesian (GP) process regression problem. But two decades passed by before, in parallel development, Hennig and Hauberg (2014) and Chkrebtii et al. (2016) set out to elaborate on his vision. While both papers used GP regression as a foundation, the data generation differed. Hennig and Hauberg (2014) generated data by evaluating f at the posterior predictive mean, and Chkrebtii et al. (2016) by evaluating f at samples from the posterior predictive distribution, i.e. at Gaussian perturbations of the posterior predictive mean. This difference stemmed from separate motivations: Hennig and Hauberg had the initial aim to deterministically reproduce classical ODE solvers in a Bayesian model, as had been previously achieved in e.g. Bayesian quadrature. Chkrebtii et al., on the other hand, intended to sample from the distribution of solution trajectories that are numerically possible given a Bayesian model and a discretisation. Thus, these two papers founded two distinct lines of works which we call *ODE filters and smoothers* and *perturbative solvers*;[5] see §38 and §40 respectively.

The former approach, after an early success of reproducing Runge–Kutta methods (Schober, Duvenaud, and Hennig, 2014),

[5] This is not the only categorisation of probabilistic ODE solvers. Another possible distinction would be nonparametric vs Gaussian or deterministic vs randomised which would both group the particle ODE filter/smoother with the perturbative solvers.

Note that the perturbative solvers have been called "sampling-based" solvers in several past publications.

294 VI Solving Ordinary Differential Equations

acquired its name from the recognition that Kalman filtering is a much faster form for probabilistic ODE solvers, than conventional GP regression (Schober, Särkkä, and Hennig, 2019). This first filtering formulation was conceptually somewhat vague, which was rectified when Tronarp et al. (2019) introduced a rigorous state-space model that unlocks all Bayesian filters and smoothers for ODEs (§38). Since then, several publications have further developed the theory and practice of these *ODE filters and smoothers*.

The perturbative approach, on the other hand, was next, in a seminal paper by Conrad et al. (2017), divorced from its initial Bayesian formulation. Instead of imposing a prior, Conrad et al. (2017) proposed to model the local numerical errors as suitably-scaled random variables which are added after every step of a classical solver. In contrast to Chkrebtii et al. (2016), the resulting samples are therefore drawn from the distribution of solution trajectories that are numerically possible *given a classical solver* and a discretisation. This non-Bayesian viewpoint became the predominant approach in this line of work. Since then, several publications have introduced and analysed multiple perturbative solvers – not necessarily with additive perturbations (Abdulle and Garegnani, 2020) – that output samples in this framework.

Due to the selection of authors, this text focuses on ODE filters and smoothers in great detail – while only providing a careful presentation of some of the most important perturbative methods and theorems, as well as a comprehensive referencing of the literature.

38

ODE Filters and Smoothers

As explained in the last section, an ODE solver makes use of evaluations of f as information about the derivative $x'(t_i)$ at discrete time points $0 = t_0 < t_1 < \cdots < t_N = T$ along the time interval $[0, T]$ to infer the continuous-time signal $x : [0, T] \dashrightarrow \mathbb{R}^d$ that solves the IVP (36.2). This lead us to regard IVPs as regression problems with data on $[x, x']$ according to Eq. (37.7). While in principle all (time-series) regression methods are now applicable to ODEs by this reformulation, we will once again take a Bayesian view and use linear-time Gauss–Markov regression by Bayesian filtering and smoothing (as introduced in §5). To this end, we first (as always in Bayesian inference) need to provide a statistical model consisting of a prior $p(x)$ and a likelihood for $p(f(\hat{x}) \mid x)$ – or (counter-intuitively, but more generally) a likelihood depending on $f(\hat{x})$ to condition directly on the ODE $x'(t) = f(x(t))$. The latter will take the form of the general SSM of §38.1.2, and the former will emerge as a linear-Gaussian alternative model for one of the algorithms (the EKF0) in §38.3.4. These SSMs will then in §38.3 allow us to solve ODEs with Bayesian (Kalman) filters and smoothers. This chapter thus consists of a description of models for ODEs (§38.1 and §38.2) and a presentation of methods to do inference in these models (from §38.3 on).

▶ 38.1 State Space Models (SSMs) for ODEs

Before we can define algorithms, we need a model. But only some models admit fast algorithms, and – as we are only able to match the linear-in-time-steps cost, $\mathcal{O}(N = T/h)$, of classical solvers in the Markovian *state-space models (SSMs)* of §5 – we restrict ourselves to such SSMs. To this effect, we model the prior on $x : [0, T] \to \mathbb{R}^d$ by a Gauss–Markov process – which we refer to as the (continuous-time) *dynamic model* because it models the evolution of x along $[0, T]$. Our Bayesian model is completed by adding a likelihood, aka a (continuous-time)[1] *measurement model.*

▷ **38.1.1   ODEs as Continuous-Time Filtering Problems**

We use a stochastic process $X(t)$ (referred to as *the system* in the filtering-theory literature) to jointly model $x(t)$ and $x'(t)$ such that

$$x(t) \sim X^{(0)}(t) := H_0 X(t), \text{ for some matrix } H_0 \in \mathbb{R}^{d \times D}, \quad (38.1)$$

$$x'(t) \sim X^{(1)}(t) := H X(t), \text{ for some matrix } H \in \mathbb{R}^{d \times D}. \quad (38.2)$$

The entire vector-valued function modelled by $X(t)$ will be denoted by the *state vector* $\vec{x} : [0, T] \to \mathbb{R}^D$, i.e. $\vec{x}(t) \sim X(t)$. It contains x and x' via

$$x(t) = H_0 \vec{x}(t), \quad \text{and} \quad x'(t) = H \vec{x}(t). \quad (38.3)$$

Hence, a prior $p(\vec{x})$ on $\vec{x}$ immediately implies a joint prior $p(x, x')$ whose marginal $p(x)$ is the prior on the ODE solution x. Due to $\vec{x}(t) \sim X(t)$, this prior distribution $p(\vec{x})$ is nothing but the law of $X(t)$ which (as in Definition 5.4) we define by a linear time-invariant SDE, written

$$dX(t) = F X(t) \, dt + L \, d\omega_t, \quad (38.4)$$

with Gaussian initial condition

$$X(0) \sim \mathcal{N}(m_0, P_0), \quad (38.5)$$

where ω_t denotes a standard Wiener process. In the standard case where $x_0 \in \mathbb{R}^d$ is known without uncertainty (i.e. $P_0 = 0$), the initial distribution is Dirac, namely $p(x(0)) = \delta(x(0) - x_0)$. From Eqs. (5.20) and (5.21), we already know that this yields

$$p(\vec{x}(t)) = \mathcal{N}(\vec{x}(t); A(t)m_0, A(t)P_0 A(t)^\mathsf{T} + Q(t)), \quad (38.6)$$

for all $t \in [0, T]$, with matrices

$$A(t) := \exp(tF), \quad \text{and} \quad Q(t) := \int_0^t e^{F\tau} L L^\mathsf{T} e^{F^\mathsf{T} \tau} \, d\tau,$$

as in Eq. (5.21). Now, with the aid of the nonlinear transformation

$$g : \mathbb{R}^D \to \mathbb{R}^d, \quad \xi \mapsto H\xi - f(H_0 \xi), \quad (38.7)$$

we can define the *state misalignment*[2] $z(t) := g(\vec{x}(t))$ which is equal to 0 for all $t \in [0,T]$, since $\vec{x}(t)$ solves the ODE (36.1) due to (38.3). Again, we model this feature by a (this time, non-Gaussian) Markov process

$$z(t) \sim Z(t) := g(X(t)) = HX(t) - f(H_0X(t)), \quad (38.8)$$

called the *observation process*.[3]

By this construction, the law of $Z(t)$ is equal to the push-forward measure $g_*(p(\vec{x}(t)))$. Observing that $z(t) = 0$ for all $t \in [0,T]$ under the likelihood[4]

$$p(z(t) \mid \vec{x}(t)) = \delta(g(\vec{x}(t))) \quad (38.9)$$

now amounts to conditioning on all information contained in the IVP, (36.2). Thus, the Picard–Lindelöf theorem (Theorem 36.4) ensures that the solution to this continuous-time filtering problem is indeed the true $x : [0,T] \to \mathbb{R}^d$ – or, in other words, that there is no posterior uncertainty: $p(x \mid z \equiv 0) = \delta(x - x(t))$. While this continuous-data limit case already hints at the favourable convergence properties of this approach (see §39.1), we will first have to discretise the processes $(X(t), Z(t))$ – which will lead to a discrete-time SSM and actual numerical algorithms.

▷ 38.1.2   A Discrete-Time SSM for ODEs

In practice, we have only a finite computational budget. Hence, the above continuous-time formulation of the ODE filtering problem is intractable. We thus consider a discretisation $0 = t_0 < \cdots < t_N = T$ with step sizes $h_n := t_n - t_{n-1}$. By restricting the continuous-time processes $X(t)$ and $Z(t)$ to these time points $\{t_n\}_{n=0}^N$, we obtain discretised versions of the prior (Eq. (38.6)) and the likelihood (Eq. (38.9)). From these we can now, after denoting $\vec{x}(t_n)$ and $z(t_n)$ by x_n and z_n, assemble the following *discrete-time* SSM:

$$p(x_0) = \mathcal{N}(x_0; m_0, P_0), \quad (38.10)$$
$$p(x_{n+1} \mid x_n) = \mathcal{N}(x_{n+1}; A(h_{n+1})x_n, Q(h_{n+1})), \quad (38.11)$$
$$p(z_n \mid x_n) = \delta(z_n - g(x_n)), \quad (38.12)$$
$$\text{with data } z_n = 0. \quad (38.13)$$

It resembles the linear-Gaussian SSM from Eqs. (5.8)–(5.9) – with the only difference that now $H_n x_n = g(x_n)$ and $R_n = 0$ in Eq. (38.12), which makes it nonlinear.[5] As this is a complete and rigorous SSM, all of Bayesian filters and smoothers can now, in principle, be applied to ODEs right away.

[2] For more intuition on this state misalignment, see §4 in Kersting, Sullivan, and Hennig (2020).
[3] The pair of system $X(t)$ and observations $Z(t)$ define a (continuous-time) stochastic filtering problem which consists of computing the distribution of $X(t)$, given $\{Z(s); 0 \le s \le t\}$. Its general solution is the stochastic process $\mathbb{E}(X_t \mid \mathcal{G}_t)$, where $\mathcal{G}_t$ is the σ-algebra generated by $\{Z(s); 0 \le s \le t\}$; see Thm. 6.1.2 in Oksendal (2003).

Exercise 38.1. *In the filtering-theory literature, the observation process $Z(t)$ is often defined by an SDE as well. Derive this SDE from Eqs. (38.8) and (38.4) by use of Itô's lemma. For which ODEs is this SDE a Gaussian process?*

[4] Recall that $z(t) \overset{\Delta}{=} g(\vec{x}(t))$.

[5] It might, however, be advantageous to add a positive variance $R > 0$ to Eq. (38.12), e.g. to facilitate particle filtering or to account for an inexact vector field f. This leads to a likelihood of the form

$$p(z_n \mid x_n) = \mathcal{N}(z_n; g(x_n), R).$$

Note, however, that this ssm is only known since its introduction by Tronarp et al. (2019); all preceding publications employed a less-general linear-Gaussian ssm which we will also define below in Eqs. (38.31)–(38.33). The new nonlinear ssm (38.10)–(38.13), instead, leaves the task of finding approximations to the inference algorithm and, in this way, engenders both Gaussian (§38.3) and non-Gaussian inference methods (§38.4).

This difference between the SSMs in the literature is at the heart of a common source of confusion over the new ssm (38.10)–(38.13): To some readers, it might appear that the constant data $z_n = 0$ contains no information whatsoever. But this is mistaken because the use of information does not only depend on the data but also on the likelihood. While in the regression-formulation of classical solvers (§37) the data was an evaluation of f, this dependence on f is now hidden in the likelihood via the definition of g, Eq. (38.7). Since $g(x_n)$ is by construction equal to 0 for the true $x_n = \vec{x}(t_n)$, the observation of the constant data $z_n = 0$ amounts by the form of the likelihood, Eq. (38.12), to "conditioning on the ODE" by imposing that $x'(t_n) \stackrel{!}{=} f(x(t_n))$ – which is similar to Eq. (37.7). In §38.3.4, we will explain how the alternative linear-Gaussian ssm echoes the logic of classical solvers.

Exercise 38.2 (SSMs for higher-order ODEs). *Many ODEs are originally formulated as a higher-order ODE; see note 3 of §36. Most classical solvers reduce such a higher-order ODE to a system of first-order ODEs, and solve it instead. One advantage of ODE filters is that they can solve a higher-order ODE directly, by using a different ssm. How does the ssm (38.10)–(38.13) have to be changed in order to model the following nth-order ODE?*

$$x^{(n)}(t) = f\left(x^{(n-1)}(t), \dots, x'(t), x(t)\right).$$

How many derivatives (at a minimum) have to be included in this modified ssm? (See Bosch, Tronarp, and Hennig (2022) for a solution in the case of second-order ODEs.)

▶ **38.2   Choice of Prior**

Before we get to the algorithms, we conclude our exposition of SSMs for ODEs with a discussion of the dynamic model $p(x_{n+1} \mid x_n)$ of Eq. (38.11) and its underlying continuous-time prior $p(\vec{x}(t))$ of Eq. (38.6). This exposition of the prior is completed by a description of the initialisation of $p(x_0)$ in §38.2.1. As the likelihood (measurement model) of Eq. (38.12) is (prior to approximations of it) fully determined by f, this prior is our only available modelling choice in the SSM of Eqs. (38.10)–(38.13).

Let us recall that this prior is nothing but the law of the solution $X(t)$ of the linear time-invariant SDE (38.4) – which spans all standard Gauss–Markov priors, such as the ones from §5.4 and §5.5. While we can freely choose from this class of priors, some are more suitable for ODEs than others. One prior stands out in particular: the q-times integrated Wiener process (IWP),[6] where $q \in \mathbb{N}$ is the number of modelled derivatives. To simplify the notation, we will from now on w.l.o.g.[7] assume that $d = 1$.

It is natural to consider the subset of priors which model x and the derivatives of x as its coordinates.[8] To this effect, we construct $X \overset{\Delta}{=} [X^{(0)}, \dots, X^{(q)}]^{\mathsf{T}}$ such that its coordinates are the derivatives, i.e. $x^{(i)} \sim X^{(i)}$ for all $i = 0, \dots, q$.[9] As this imposes that $dX^{(i-1)}(t) = X^{(i)}(t)dt$ for $i = 1, \dots, q$, this construction restricts the first q rows of the SDE (38.4) such that its drift and diffusion matrices read

$$F = \begin{bmatrix} 0 & 1 & 0 & \dots & 0 \\ 0 & 0 & 1 & 0 & \vdots \\ \vdots & & \ddots & \ddots & 0 \\ 0 & & 0 & & 1 \\ -a_0 & -a_1 & \cdots & -a_{q-1} & -a_q \end{bmatrix} \quad \text{and} \quad L = \begin{bmatrix} 0 \\ 0 \\ \vdots \\ 0 \\ \sigma \end{bmatrix}.$$

The last row can still be set flexibly by choosing the scale $\sigma > 0$ of the Wiener process and the non-negative drift coefficients $(a_0, \dots, a_q) \geq 0$ – which parametrise the Matérn covariance family with $\nu = q + 1/2$, as we saw in §5.5.

Although Matérn priors are popular for GP regression, they have (in their general form) not yet been explored for ODE filtering. Only the special case of $(a_0, \dots, a_{q-1}) = \mathbf{0}$ has been studied, where the only free parameter is $a_q \geq 0$. In this case, $X(t)$ is the q-times integrated Ornstein–Uhlenbeck process with (mean-reverting) drift coefficient a_q. While this prior can be advantageous for some exponentially decreasing curves (such as radioactive decay),[10] it is, to date, not known if these advantages extend to more ODEs.

Meanwhile, the q-times IWP, which sets $(a_0, \dots, a_q) = \mathbf{0}$, has become the standard prior for ODEs because the q-times IWP extrapolates (as we saw in §5.4) by use of polynomial splines of degree q. And this polynomial extrapolation also takes place for the derivatives: under the q-times IWP prior, the ith mean of the dynamic model (38.11) is, by Eq. (5.24), for all $i = 1, \dots, q+1$

[6] The IWP is also referred to as the integrated Brownian motion in the literature.

[7] See Appendix B of Kersting, Sullivan, and Hennig (2020) for why this comes with no loss of generality.

[8] In fact, the only exception to this choice is the below-discussed Fourier SSM from Kersting and Mahsereci (2020) which models the Fourier coefficients instead.

[9] Note that this implies that $H_0 = [1, 0, \dots, 0]$ and $H = [0, 1, 0, \dots, 0] \in \mathbb{R}^{1 \times (q+1)}$ in Eqs. (38.1) and (38.2).

[10] Magnani et al. (2017)

given by

$$[A(h_{n+1})x_n]_i = \sum_{k=i}^{q+1} \frac{h_{n+1}^{k-i}}{(k-i)!} [x_n]_k, \qquad (38.14)$$

i.e. by a $(q + 1 - i)$th-order Taylor-polynomial extrapolation. In particular, the solution state ($i = 1$) is predicted forward by a qth-order Taylor expansion, which is by Taylor's theorem (absent additional information about x) the best local model.[11] Note that this is in keeping with classical solvers which – in light of Eq. (37.3) – extrapolate forward along Taylor polynomials of the flow of the ODE.[12]

Therefore, it is only natural that the IWP is the standard prior for ODEs, and that any deviation from it requires specific prior knowledge on the solution $x : [0, T] \to \mathbb{R}^d$. Hence, the utility of adapting prior-selection strategies from GP regression depends on how much knowledge on x can be extracted from f. With this in mind – to draw from the full inventory of GP priors – one can even go beyond the Matérn class and use state-space approximations of non-Markov covariance functions.[13] The frequent case of periodic ODEs (oscillators) can, following earlier work on GP regression,[14] be modelled by such a state-space approximation of the periodic covariance functions.[15] Remarkably, this model extrapolates with a Fourier (instead of a Taylor) expansion – which is indeed how a periodic signal x is usually approximated. Unfortunately, Fourier series are (unlike Taylor series) global models, and therefore the utility of this periodic model is (so far) limited to fast-and-rough extrapolations with large step sizes after an initial learning period. It remains to be seen whether this (or another) radical deviation from the Taylor-expansion logic of classical numerics can give solvers that can compete with probabilistic solvers that use the IWP prior.

> #### 38.2.1 Initialisation

To fully determine the prior, we now consider the Gaussian initial distribution $p(x_0) = \mathcal{N}(x_0; m_0, P_0)$ of Eq. (38.10), which corresponds to $X(0)$ from Eq. (38.5) in continuous time. Here, we restrict our attention to the standard case of SSMs that model the first q derivatives of x.[16] If x_0 is known (that is $[m_0]_1 = x_0$), then all q derivatives are determined by

$$x^{(i)}(0) = f^{\langle i \rangle}(x_0), \qquad (38.15)$$

[11] This insight will be the basis of the convergence-rates analysis of §39.1.1.

[12] Accordingly, all known equivalences with classical models hold for the IWP prior; see Schober, Särkkä, and Hennig (2019).

[13] For a comprehensive overview of such approximations, see §12.3 in Särkkä and Solin (2019).
[14] Solin and Särkkä (2014)
[15] Kersting and Mahsereci (2020)

[16] That is, we exclude the Fourier model, see note 8.

with the recursively defined $f^{\langle i \rangle}$ from Eq. (37.4). Hence, the ideal initialisation is

$$m_0 = \left[x_0, f(x_0), f^{\langle 2 \rangle}(x_0), \ldots, f^{\langle q \rangle}(x_0) \right]^\mathsf{T} \in \mathbb{R}^{q+1},$$

$$P_0 = \mathbf{0} \in \mathbb{R}^{(q+1) \times (q+1)}.$$

Krämer and Hennig (2020, §3.1) recognised that this can be efficiently achieved by Taylor-mode automatic differentiation (AD).[17] This way, the computational complexity grows at most quadratically in the order of the approximation – instead of exponentially for standard AD. In this case, P_0 is set to zero.

[17] Bettencourt, Johnson, and Duvenaud (2019)

▶ 38.3 Gaussian ODE Filters and Smoothers

In the last section, a generally-applicable discrete-time SSM for ODEs was introduced in Eqs. (38.10)–(38.13). By virtue of this model, the numerical solution $x : [0, T] \to \mathbb{R}^d$ can now be solved by Bayesian filtering and smoothing on this SSM. Recall that we already encountered the most prototypical Bayesian filters and smoothers – the Kalman filter and Rauch–Tung–Striebel smoother (aka Kalman smoother) – in Algorithms 5.3 and 5.4. For ODEs we will, however, not limit ourselves to these elementary methods, but include all applicable filters and smoothers (including non-Gaussian ones).[18] This leads to *Bayesian ODE filtering* and *Bayesian ODE smoothing* which are defined in Algorithms 38.1 and 38.2. To include all filters and smoothers, the algorithmic descriptions here are more general in that they only contain the high-level procedural steps, and not the precise algebraic computations (which will differ from method to method). Note that the model adaptation and step-size selection in lines 4 and 5 of Algorithm 38.1 are optional (but recommended). We therefore postpone their description to §38.5.

[18] The most important filters and smoothers can, e.g., be found in Särkkä (2013).

To define an ODE filter, we thus have to determine the prediction and the update step, in lines 6 and 8 of Algorithm 38.1. For an ODE smoother, only line 5 of Algorithm 38.2 has to be defined additionally. An ODE filter or smoother is named by adding "ODE" to its classical name; e.g. the "particle filter" becomes the "particle ODE filter". The term "Gaussian ODE filters and smoothers" refers to any ODE filter or smoother that outputs Gaussian approximations of the posterior. Since any smoother is an extension of a filter, we sometimes use the word "filters" instead of "filters and smoothers".

Below, we will spell out these computations for the filters and smoothers that we consider most useful for ODEs – ordered

```
1  procedure ODE FILTER(f, x(0), p(x_{n+1} | x_n))
2     initialise p(x_0)                    // with available information about x(0)
3     for n = 0 : 1 : N − 1 do
4        optional: adapt dynamic model p(x_{n+1} | x_n)
5        optional: choose step size h_n > 0
6        predict p(x_{n+1} | z_{1:n}), from p(x_n | z_{1:n})        // by (38.11)
7        observe the ODE: z_{n+1} = 0                  // according to (38.13)
8        update p(x_{n+1} | z_{1:n+1}), from p(x_{n+1} | z_{1:n})   // by (38.12)
9     end for
10    return {p(x_n | z_{1:n}); n = 0, . . . , n}
11 end procedure
```

Algorithm 38.1: *Bayesian ODE filtering* iteratively computes a sequence of predictive and filtering distributions. Recall from the graphical model of filtering (Figure 5.1) (with z instead of y) that the sequential form of this inference procedure (i.e. the for-loop) is legitimate. The form of the computations in lines 6–8 depend on the choice of filter. The initialisation (line 2) is explained in §38.2.1. The optional (but recommended) lines 4 and 5 are detailed in §38.5.

by statistical complexity from Gaussian to Monte-Carlo approximations, i.e. from extended Kalman ODE filters via iterated extended Kalman ODE filters to particle ODE filters.[19] But, to prevent confusion, we will first explain why Gaussian ODE filters are statistically admissible for nonlinear ODEs whose true posterior is non-Gaussian.

[19] As well as the corresponding smoother (in all cases). Note that this is not a complete list of ODE filters discussed in the literature, as it e.g. leaves out the unscented Kalman ODE filter; see §2 in Tronarp et al. (2019). These, as well as completely new ODE filters, can be obtained by inserting the corresponding computations into Algorithm 38.1, or (for smoothers) into Algorithm 38.2.

▷ **38.3.1   The Cost-Accuracy Trade-off: Why Use Gaussian Solvers for Nonlinear ODEs?**

The SSM from Eqs. (38.10)–(38.13) is nonlinear, and thus yields non-Gaussian posteriors. It does so for good reasons: while the rest of the book mostly uses Gaussians for their faster computational speed, ODE solutions are almost always highly nonlinear (and often even chaotic). Hence, the arguments for non-Gaussian posteriors are more compelling than they were for the other numerical problems in this book. To satisfy this need, we will later present solvers (the particle ODE filter and the perturbative solvers) which output a Monte-Carlo representation of the non-Gaussian posterior.[20]

[20] Or, in case of most perturbative solvers, of a set of numerically possible trajectories.

Nonetheless, the inevitable trade-off between computational speed and statistical accuracy (which is central to numerics) is equally real for ODEs. In this regard, it is instructive to remember that even in signal processing with real data – where the need for fast algorithms can sometimes be less critical, since the

```
1  procedure ODE SMOOTHER(f, x(0), p(x_{n+1} | x_n))
2     {p(x_n | z_{1:n}), p(x_n | z_{1:n−1})}_{n=0,...,N} =
3              ODE FILTER(f, x(0), p(x_{n+1} | x_n))
4     for n = N − 1 : −1 : 0 do
5        compute p(x_n | z_{1:N}), from p(x_{n+1} | z_{1:N})     // by (38.26)
6     end for
7  end procedure
```

Algorithm 38.2: *Bayesian ODE smoothing* extends Alg. 38.1 by iteratively updating its output, the filtering distributions $p(x_n | z_{1:n})$, to the full posterior $p(x_n | z_{1:N})$. Note that, in line 3, the filter additionally returns the posterior predictive distributions $p(x_n | z_{1:n−1})$ which it, for all n, computes as an intermediate step anyway; see line 6 of Alg. 38.1.

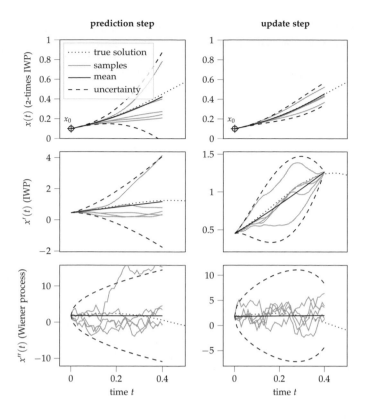

Figure 38.1: Depiction of the first step of the EKF0 with 2-times IWP prior initialised at x_0 and the implied derivatives as in (38.15). In the prediction step (left column), the predictive distribution $p(x_1)$ is computed by extrapolating forward in time along the dynamic model. The samples can be thought of as different possibilities for the trajectory of $x(t)$, $x'(t)$ and $x''(t)$ (from the top to the bottom row). Then, in the update step (right column), the predictive distribution is conditioned on $x'(t_1) = f(m_1^-)$ (recall that the intuitive SSM can be used in the Gaussian case). This yields the filtering distribution $p(x_1 \mid z_1)$ whose samples are now restricted to those with a first derivative of $f(m_1^-)$ at t_1. The uncertainty (dashed line) is drawn at two standard deviations in both directions of the mean, thus capturing a 95% credible interval. Note the reduction of uncertainty after conditioning on z_1.

The same procedure is then repeated for $t_1 \to t_2$, that is all possible trajectories (samples) are predicted forward in time, and then restricted to $x'(t_2) = f(m_2^-)$ in the subsequent update step. (Second step not depicted.)

frequency of data cannot be increased by shortening the step size as in numerics – Gaussian methods are often used first.[21] Thus, it is only natural that we will recommend Gaussian ODE filters (and smoothers) as a standard choice – unless nonparametric uncertainty quantification is especially relevant.[22]

[21] Särkkä (2013), §13.1

[22] See §38.6 for more details.

▷ ### 38.3.2   The Extended Kalman Filters and Smoothers

To define an ODE filter in the framework of Algorithm 38.1, we (as explained above) only have to specify the prediction and update step. Since our dynamic model Eq. (38.11) is linear-Gaussian, all Gaussian ODE filters can, given a Gaussian

$$p(x_n \mid z_{1:n}) = \mathcal{N}(x_n; m_n, P_n), \qquad (38.16)$$

compute an *exact predictive step*, written

$$p(x_{n+1}) = \mathcal{N}(x_{n+1}; m_{n+1}^-, P_{n+1}^-), \qquad \text{with} \qquad (38.17)$$
$$m_{n+1}^- = A(h_{n+1})m_n, \quad P_{n+1}^- = A(h_{n+1})P_n A(h_{n+1})^{\mathsf{T}} + Q(h_{n+1}).$$

The update step is, however, more complicated as it involves the nonlinear mapping f (via g). To stay in the Gaussian family, we thus have to approximate f by a simpler function. As is common use,[23] we use Taylor approximations around the predictive mean m_{n+1}^- which makes the update tractable. We will restrict our attention to the most important cases of a zeroth and first-order Taylor approximation. The resulting methods are known as the (zeroth and first-order) *extended Kalman ODE filter* – or *EKF0* and *EKF1* abbreviated.[24]

[23] Särkkä (2013), §5.1

[24] Tronarp et al. (2019), §2.4

In terms of specific computations, the EKF0 and EKF1 thus perform the following *approximate update step* using the data $z_{n+1} = 0$, where the difference between the EKF0 and EKF1 lies in the choice of $\tilde{H}$:

$$\hat{z}_{n+1} := f(H_0 m_{n+1}^-) - H m_{n+1}^-, \quad \text{(innovation residual)} \quad (38.18)$$

$$S_{n+1} := \tilde{H} P_{n+1}^- \tilde{H}^\mathsf{T} + R_{n+1}, \quad \text{(innovation cov.)} \quad (38.19)$$

$$K_{n+1} := P_{n+1}^- \tilde{H}^\mathsf{T} S_{n+1}^{-1}, \quad \text{(gain)} \quad (38.20)$$

$$m_{n+1} := m_{n+1}^- + K_{n+1} \hat{z}_{n+1}, \quad (38.21)$$

$$P_{n+1} := (I_D - K_{n+1} \tilde{H}) P_{n+1}^-. \quad (38.22)$$

The resulting (posterior) filtering distribution of this step is – just like at the end of the previous step, Eq. (38.16) – a Gaussian $p(x_{n+1} \mid z_{1:n+1}) = \mathcal{N}(x_{n+1}; m_{n+1}, P_{n+1})$. Thus, these filters never leave the Gaussian exponential family, which is why they are instances of *Gaussian ODE filters*.

If $\tilde{H} = H$, this is the EKF0,[25] which is depicted in Figure 38.1. This case can be thought of as an exact update after replacing f by the constant function $\xi \mapsto f(H_0 m_{n+1}^-)$.[26] If instead $\tilde{H} = H - J_f(H_0 m_{n+1}^-) H_0$, where J_f denotes the Jacobian matrix of f, this is the EKF1; it can be interpreted as an exact update after replacing f by its linearisation $\xi \mapsto f(H_0 m_{n+1}^-) + J_f(H_0 m_{n+1}^-)[\xi - H_0 m_{n+1}^-]$.

[25] Cf. Eqs. (5.12)–(5.13) to see the similarity of the EKF0 with the standard Kalman filter.
[26] Tronarp et al. (2019), Proposition 2

Note that the variance $R \geq 0$ can – despite its absence from the likelihood Eq. (38.12) – be chosen positive because the approximations of f cause the likelihood-data pair to be inaccurate.[27] We, however, recommend to use $R = 0$ as the default choice.

[27] In the same way, the impact of an only-approximately known ODE can also be captured by an increase in $R \geq 0$; see Kersting, Sullivan, and Hennig (2020, §2.3).

The so-computed filtering distributions $p(x_n \mid z_{1:n}) = \mathcal{N}(x_n; m_n, P_n)$ of the EKF0 and EKF1 can then be extended to the full-posterior (smoothing) distributions $p(x_n \mid z_{1:N}) = \mathcal{N}(x_n; m_n^S, P_n^S)$ by the following computations:

$$G_n := P_n A(h_{n+1})^\mathsf{T} (P_{n+1}^-)^{-1}, \quad \text{(gain)} \quad (38.23)$$

$$m_n^s := m_n + G_n \left(m_{n+1}^s - m_{n+1}^- \right), \quad (38.24)$$

$$P_n^s := P_n + G_n \left(P_{n+1}^s - P_{n+1}^- \right) G_n^\mathsf{T}. \quad (38.25)$$

These backward-recursion equations are, simply, an exact Gaussian execution of the well-known smoothing equation:[28]

[28] We already provided this equation in Eq. (5.7).

$$p(x_n \mid z_{1:N}) = p(x_n \mid z_{1:n}) \int \left[\frac{p(x_{n+1} \mid x_n) p(x_{n+1} \mid z_{1:N})}{p(x_{n+1} \mid z_{1:n})} \right] \mathrm{d}x_{n+1}, \qquad (38.26)$$

which (in our SSM) does not differ between the EKF0 and EKF1 because their dynamic model $p(x_{n+1} \mid x_n)$ is the same.

With this in mind, we define the (zeroth and first-order) *extended Kalman ODE smoothers*, EKS0 and EKS1,[29] as the instances of Algorithm 5 that employ the EKF0 or EKF1 in line 3 and then compute line 5 by Eqs. (38.23)–(38.25). The resulting smoothing-posterior distributions $p(x_n \mid z_{1:N}) = \mathcal{N}(x_n; m_n^s, P_n^s)$ can be extended beyond the time grid $\{t_n\}_{n=0}^N$ by interpolation along the dynamic model, Eq. (38.11), and therefore contain the same information as the full GP posterior of Eqs. (4.7) and (4.6).[30]

[29] In some recent publications, the EKS0 and EKS1 are referred to as EK0 and EK1 – because smoothing has become the default (see §38.6).

[30] This was also discussed above for generic Gaussian smoothers in §5.2.

Remark (Relation to Bayesian quadrature). *Before introducing more ODE filters, let us briefly clarify the relation to Bayesian quadrature (BQ) – namely that the EKF0/EKS0 is a generalisation of BQ in the following sense: if the ODE is really just an integral (i.e. $x'(t) = g(t)$), then its solution is given by*

$$x(t) = x_0 + \int_0^t g(s) \, \mathrm{d}s. \qquad (38.27)$$

Thus, computing $x(t)$ by approximating the integral in Eq. (38.27) with the Kalman-filter version of BQ (Algorithm 11.2 from §11.2) is equivalent to solving the ODE

$$x'(s) = g(s), \ s \in [0, t], \qquad \text{with initial value } x(0) = x_0,$$

by the EKF0 or EKS0.[31]

[31] See Proposition 1 in Tronarp et al. (2019) for the details of this equivalence.

Exercise 38.3 (Recognise the shared principle). *Recall gradient filtering for optimisation from Eq. (28.8). Prove that this gradient filtering coincides with the EKF0, when applied to the gradient-flow ODE $x'(t) = \nabla f(t)$, by showing that the filtering means m_n and covariance matrices P_n are the same for all $n = 0, \dots, N$.*

▷ **38.3.3   Iterated Smoothers for MAP Inference**

In the last section, we presented the extended Kalman ODE filters and smoothers (EKF0/1 and EKS0/1) as the standard method for approximate Gaussian inference of ODE solutions. But almost nothing can be said about the true non-Gaussian posterior that these Gaussians approximate, and therefore we will (in the next section) introduce the particle ODE filter which outputs a Monte-Carlo representation to the true posterior. Since particle filtering comes at significantly higher cost than Gaussian filtering, we present in this section how (as a compromise) one can approximate the maximum a posteriori (MAP) estimate by another Gaussian ODE smoother. This is a compromise because the MAP estimate is the most likely value under the true posterior, i.e. the most likely sample trajectory computed by the particle ODE filter. Unlike the previous filtering and smoothing mean, it is defined as the solution of the so-called *global MAP problem*, a non-convex optimisation problem which consists of maximising the posterior $p(\vec{x}(t) \mid z_{1:N} = 0)$.[32] Let us denote this MAP estimate by

$$\vec{x}^*(t) := \underset{\vec{x}(t)}{\arg\min} \left[-\log\left(p\left(\vec{x}(t_{0:N}) \mid z_{1:N} = 0\right)\right) \right]. \quad (38.28)$$

[32] See §2.3 in Tronarp, Särkkä, and Hennig (2021). Also note that, according to Proposition 3 in the same paper, Eq. (38.29) is equivalent to optimisation in an RKHS.

Since our prior (38.6) is Markovian, its value at the discretisation $\{t_i\}_{i=0}^N$ can be written as

$$\vec{x}^*(t_{0:N}) = \underset{\vec{x}(t_{0:N})}{\arg\min} \left[\|\vec{x}(0) - m_0\|_{P_0}^2 + \sum_{n=1}^N \|\vec{x}(t_n) - A(h_n)\vec{x}(t_{n-1})\|_{Q(h_n)}^2 \right], \quad (38.29)$$

subject to $z_{1:N} = 0$. Here, for a fixed positive definite matrix P, $\|x\|_P := x^\mathsf{T} P^{-1} x$ is the Mahalanobis norm associated with P. By use of Eq. (38.1), we can extract a global MAP estimate

$$x^*(t) := H_0 \vec{x}^*(t), \quad (38.30)$$

which includes the discrete-time MAP estimate $x^*(t_{0:N}) := H_0 \vec{x}^*(t_{0:N})$. While $x^*(t_{0:N})$ is not directly related to the EKS0 or EKS1, it can be approximated by more involved Gaussian filters and smoothers: namely by the iterated extended Kalman smoother (IEKS).[33] The corresponding filter is the iterated extended Kalman filter (IEKF).[34] These methods iterate the EKS1 and EKF1, respectively, as we will see next.[35]

[33] Bell (1994)

[34] Bell and Cathey (1993)

[35] In fact, we could also call them IEKF1 and IEKS1, but it is not necessary to distinguish them from other iterated methods here.

Recall from Eq. (38.21) how the EKF1 computes the filtering mean m_{n+1} from the predictive mean m_{n+1}^-, and recall from Eq. (38.24) how the EKS1 computes the smoothing mean m_n^S from m_n. The IEKF and IEKS now simply iterate these computations, but with a re-linearisation around the new estimate. That is, they linearise f around m_{n+1} and m_n^S and then repeat the computations of Eqs. (38.21) and (38.24) with this new linearisation. This procedure is then iterated until convergence to a fixed point. The hope is that these fixed points will be related to the MAP estimate: the IEKF, indeed, computes the local MAP estimate (i.e. for one isolated step in time). The IEKS, on the other hand, will (under some additional conditions) converge to a local minimum of the non-convex global MAP problem. Although this local minimum is not always a global minimum, the IEKS is often considered to be a suitable estimator of the global MAP estimate. It, therefore, is the probabilistic ODE solvers that approximates the true posterior best, while maintaining fast Gaussian computations without sampling. More details on the IEKF/IEKS and the MAP problem can be found in the literature.[36]

We will return to this link between the IEKS and the global MAP estimate in §39.1.1 which contains convergence rates for the MAP estimate (and thus for the IEKS, *if* its fixed point is the global MAP).

[36] Tronarp, Särkkä, and Hennig (2021), §3.2

▷ ### 38.3.4   A Linear-Gaussian SSM for the EKF0

The above ssm (38.10)–(38.13) is a general and rigorous Bayesian model for ODEs – and it is sufficient to understand it, hence this section is optional reading. But the general ssm is only known since its introduction by Tronarp et al. (2019), the EKF0 (and by extension also: the EKS0) have been introduced before in a different ssm – under the name "Kalman ODE filter"[37] and "Gaussian ODE filter".[38] This older ssm dealt with the necessary approximations due to nonlinearity from f in a fundamentally different way: instead of considering them as a part of the inference method, the approximations were included in the ssm itself – which is thus linear-Gaussian so that exact inference is possible.

[37] Schober, Särkkä, and Hennig (2019); Kersting and Hennig (2016).

[38] Kersting, Sullivan, and Hennig (2020)

This is conceptually somewhat vague because approximations are (strictly speaking) part of the method, and not the model. Nonetheless, it matches the common statistical practice of modelling nonlinear or non-Gaussian systems with linear-Gaussian ones, to enable faster methods. Moreover – as we will explain next – it resembles the classical logic where ODE solvers treat evaluations $f(\hat{x}(t))$ as data on $x'(t)$; see Eq. (37.1).

For the EKF0, this linear-Gaussian ssm is given by

$$p(x_0) = \mathcal{N}(x_0; m_0, P_0), \tag{38.31}$$

$$p(x_{n+1} \mid x_n) = \mathcal{N}(x_{n+1}; A(h_{n+1})x_n, Q(h_{n+1})),$$

$$p(y_n \mid x_n) = \mathcal{N}(y_n; Hm_n^-, R_n), \tag{38.32}$$

$$\text{with data} \quad y_n = f(H_0 m_n^-), \tag{38.33}$$

where m_n^- is the mean of the predictive distribution $p(x_n \mid y_{1:n-1})$. Since $H_0 m_n^-$ is the most likely estimate for $x(t_n)$ given $y_{1:n}$, the analogy between this y_n and the data $f(\hat{x}(t_n))$ of classical solvers from Eq. (37.7) should be evident. The likelihood (38.32) resembles a probabilistic version of the (implicitly-used) classical Dirac likelihood $p(f(\hat{x}(t_n)) \mid x(t_n)) = \delta(x'(t_n) - f(\hat{x}(t_n)))$, where y_n and Hm_n^- play the roles of $f(\hat{x}(t_n))$ and $x'(t_n)$ respectively.

Next, we will give an intuitive derivation of Eqs. (38.32) and (38.33) for some given $n \in \{0, \ldots, N\}$. In a recursive manner, we assume that the filtering distribution $p(x_{n-1} \mid y_{1:n-1})$ is a Gaussian $\mathcal{N}(x_{n-1}; m_{n-1}, P_{n-1})$ with mean m_{n-1} and covariance P_{n-1}. Then, integration over x_{n-1} yields

$$p(x_n \mid y_{1:n-1}) = \int p(x_n \mid x_{n-1}) p(x_{n-1} \mid y_{1:n-1}) \, dx_{n-1}$$
$$\overset{(38.32)}{=} \mathcal{N}(x_n; m_n^-, P_n^-),$$

with predictive mean $m_n^- = A(h_n) m_{n-1}$ and covariance $P_n^- = A(h_n) P_{n-1} A(h_n)^\mathsf{T} + Q(h_n)$. Recall that, by Eq. (38.3), the predictive normal distributions over $x(t_n)$ and $\dot{x}(t_n)$ are now given by

$$p(x(t_n) \mid y_{1:n-1}) = \mathcal{N}(x(t_n); H_0 m_n^-, H_0 P_n^- H_0^\mathsf{T}), \quad \text{and}$$
$$p(\dot{x}(t_n) \mid y_{1:n-1}) = \mathcal{N}(\dot{x}(t_n); Hm_n^-, HP_n^- H^\mathsf{T})). \tag{38.34}$$

To generate data, we observe that – as for the classical solvers – our estimate of $x(t_n)$ given the information $y_{1:n-1}$ can be extracted by mapping it through f. This results in the non-Gaussian pushforward measure $f_*(p(x(t_n) \mid y_{1:n-1}))$. To ensure closed-form Gaussian computations, we approximate it by moment-matching which yields

$$f_*(p(x(t_n) \mid y_{1:n-1})) \approx \mathcal{N}(y_n; \mu_n, V_n), \quad \text{with moments}$$
$$\mu_n := \int f(\xi) \, d\mathcal{N}(\xi; H_0 m_n^-, H_0 P_n^- H_0^\mathsf{T}), \quad \text{and} \tag{38.35}$$
$$V_n := \int [f(\xi) - \mu][f(\xi) - \mu]^\mathsf{T} \, d\mathcal{N}(\xi; H_0 m_n^-, H_0 P_n^- H_0^\mathsf{T}). \tag{38.36}$$

Unfortunately, these integrals have to be numerically approximated by quadrature, i.e. by a weighted sum of evaluations as in Eq. (10.8). To match the speed of standard classical solvers which evaluate f only once for every t_n, we use only a single evaluation for these intervals, namely the most-informative one at the mean m_n^-. This gives us the data $y_n = f(H_0 m_n^-)$. For the likelihood, we simply insert the mean Hm_n^- of (38.34) (i.e. the expected derivative) as the expectation, and $R_n \geq 0$ as the variance which is supposed to capture the missing uncertainties – from not computing the integrals in (38.35) and (38.36), as well as from the predictive covariance $HP_n^- H^\mathsf{T}$ on $\dot{x}(t_n)$. Note, however, that the standard choice is $R_n = 0$, which ignores these uncertainties. It is standard because it reproduces classical methods, as Schober, Särkkä, and Hennig (2019) demonstrated.[39] In view of the uncertainty-unawareness of classical solvers (discussed in §37) this is unsurprising.[40]

As the above construction shows, the linear-Gaussian SSM (38.31)–(38.33) can be thought of as an application of GP regression with data on the derivative[41] to ODEs. It is related to the EKF0 on the general nonlinear SSM (38.10)–(38.13) in that it already includes the zeroth-order Taylor expansion of f in its model. More precisely, Kalman filtering on the linear-Gaussian SSM (38.31)–(38.33) with $R_n = 0$ is the same algorithm as EKF0 – as can easily be seen by comparing the Kalman-filtering update step with Eqs. (38.18)–(38.22) in the EKF0 case ($\tilde{H} = H$).

Nevertheless, this alternative SSM is not a rigorous model since the data y_n – as in classical numerics; see Eq. (37.1) – depends via m_n^- on all previous computations (and thereby on the prior, the likelihood, and previous data $y_{1:n-1}$).[42] While it is useful for intuition, the nonlinear SSM (38.10)–(38.13) has become the standard and is used in the rest of this text.

Remark (Terminology). *As noted above, the existing literature using the Gaussian SSM (38.31)–(38.33) has different names for the EKF0 and EKF1. There, the terms "Kalman ODE filter" and "extended Kalman ODE filter" refer to the EKF0 and EKF1 respectively.*

▶ 38.4 Particle ODE Filters and Smoothers

As mentioned above, the update step (i.e. the conditioning on the nonlinear ODE) renders all Gaussian posteriors inexact. Fortunately, the general SSM (38.10)–(38.13) can accommodate all filters and smoothers, whether Gaussian or not, in the form of Algorithms 38.1 and 38.2. As the true posterior is nonparametric for almost all ODEs, it can only be captured by a step-wise sequence of Monte Carlo approximations at the discrete time points $\{t_i\}_{i=1}^N$, i.e. by use of so-called sequential Monte Carlo (SMC) methods or *particle filters* (and *smoothers*). As they are only used here in this – otherwise Gaussian – book, we will now, to give intuition, introduce them in a very dense way, tailored for the context of this chapter.[43]

To this end, we first recall from Algorithm 38.1 that there are (parameter and model adaptation aside) only two computational steps in ODE filtering: computing $p(x_{n+1} \mid z_{1:n})$ from $p(x_n \mid z_{1:n})$ ("predict"), and computing $p(x_{n+1} \mid z_{1:n+1})$

[39] See §39.3 for these connections with classical methods.

[40] To make the SSM (38.31)–(38.33) more uncertainty-unaware, Kersting and Hennig (2016) proposed to capture the uncertainty from the quadrature approximation of (38.35) and (38.36) by Bayesian quadrature and add it to R_n in (38.32).

[41] Solak et al. (2002)

[42] In fact, Wang, Cockayne, and Oates (2018) showed that, at the point of their writing, no rigorous Bayesian ODE solver existed in that they do not satisfy the criteria specified by Cockayne et al. (2019b). This was, however, before the introduction of the rigorous SSM (38.10)–(38.13), which has not been examined in this regard.

[43] See e.g. Doucet, Freitas, and Gordon (2001) for a general introduction. A detailed collection of popular particle filters (and smoothers) is provided by Chapters 7–11 of Särkkä (2013). For ODEs, the original presentation is to be found in §2.7 of Tronarp et al. (2019).

("update") from $p(x_{n+1} \mid z_{1:n})$. The predictive distribution $p(x_{n+1} \mid z_{1:n})$ linking both steps is thus only a means to obtain the filtering distribution $p(x_{n+1} \mid z_{1:n+1})$. In the Gaussian case, this intermediate $p(x_{n+1} \mid z_{1:n})$ was Gaussian, which ensured that the updated $p(x_{n+1} \mid z_{1:n+1})$ was Gaussian as well. In the non-Gaussian case, however, all three of these distributions are nonparametric and have to be represented by sets of (weighted) samples. While $p(x_{n+1} \mid z_{1:n})$ cannot be used to compute $p(x_{n+1} \mid z_{1:n+1})$ in closed form, it is still necessary to provide a distribution that serves as a bridge from $p(x_n \mid z_{1:n})$ to $p(x_{n+1} \mid z_{1:n+1})$.

In other words, a *proposal distribution* (aka *importance distribution*) $\pi(x_{n+1} \mid x_n, z_{1:n+1})$ is called for that is informed by $p(x_{n+1} \mid z_{1:n})$ and serves as a "best guess" for $p(x_{n+1} \mid z_{1:n+1})$, given a value (sample) of x_n. In a way, the predictive distribution $p(x_{n+1} \mid z_{1:n})$ is nothing but a computationally convenient proposal distribution that allows for computing closed-form Gaussian updates without sampling. An even more general description of the ODE filter than the one in Algorithm 38.1 would therefore replace $p(x_{n+1} \mid z_{1:n})$ with a generic proposal $\pi(x_{n+1} \mid x_n, z_{1:n+1})$ in lines 6 and 8. Then, the prediction step can be thought of as the construction of the proposal distribution, with the help of Eq. (38.11), and the update step as importance sampling with this proposal. We will now detail how such an update by importance sampling works.

Given a sampling representation of the preceding filtering distribution, written

$$p(x_n \mid z_{1:n}) \approx \sum_{i=1}^{M} w_n^{(i)} \delta\left(x_n - x_n^{(i)}\right), \tag{38.37}$$

we can, for any proposal distribution π, construct a sampling representation for the new time point, written

$$p(x_{n+1} \mid z_{1:n+1}) \approx \sum_{i=1}^{M} w_{n+1}^{(i)} \delta\left(x_{n+1} - x_{n+1}^{(i)}\right), \tag{38.38}$$

as follows. First, we observe by Bayes' theorem that

$$p\left(x_{n+1} \mid x_n^{(i)}, z_{1:n+1}\right) = p\left(x_{n+1} \mid z_{n+1}, x_n^{(i)}, z_{1:n}\right)$$
$$\propto p\left(z_{n+1} \mid x_{n+1}, x_n^{(i)}, z_{1:n}\right) p\left(x_{n+1} \mid x_n^{(i)}, z_{1:n}\right) \tag{38.39}$$
$$= \frac{p\left(z_{n+1} \mid x_{n+1}\right) p(x_{n+1} \mid x_n^{(i)})}{\pi(x_{n+1} \mid x_n^{(i)}, z_{1:n+1})} \pi\left(x_{n+1} \mid x_n^{(i)}, z_{1:n+1}\right),$$

where we used the Markov properties of the SSM (see Figure 5.1) in the last step. Now, the importance-sampling step follows. We draw a set of samples from the proposal distribution

$$x_{n+1}^{(i)} \sim \pi\left(x_{n+1} \mid x_n^{(i)}, z_{1:n+1}\right), \quad \text{for all } i = 1, \dots, M,$$

whose respective (normalised) weights are, by virtue of Eq. (38.39), recursively given by[44]

$$w_{n+1}^{(i)} \propto w_n^{(i)} \frac{p(z_{n+1} \mid x_{n+1}^{(i)}) p(x_{n+1}^{(i)} \mid x_n^{(i)})}{\pi(x_{n+1}^{(i)} \mid x_n^{(i)}, z_{1:n+1})}. \quad (38.40)$$

The desired Monte-Carlo approximation (38.38) is thereby completely specified. This process of sequentially moving from Eq. (38.37) to Eq. (38.38) on its own forms – when combined with an initialisation $x_0^{(i)} \sim p(x_0)$, $w_0^{(i)} = 1/M$ – a well-defined filter known as *sequential importance sampling* (SIS). To avoid the weights to "degenerate" to (nearly) zero, it is necessary to regularly resample the particles from the sampling distribution (38.38), which resets the weights to $1/M$.[45] The addition of this resampling to SIS completes the definition of the *particle filter*.[46] When applied to ODEs, such a *particle ODE filter* indeed (as we hoped) approximates the true nonparametric posterior $p(x_n \mid z_{1:n})$ with the standard Monte-Carlo error-rate of $\mathcal{O}(M^{-1/2})$.[47] Figure 38.2 depicts how a particle ODE filter with 30 particles accurately captures a bifurcation.[48]

Whether applied to ODEs or not, the performance of particle filter depends – along with the modelling and approximation choices already present in Gaussian filters – on the design of the resampling and, most importantly, of the proposal distribution π. For instance, simply setting π equal to the dynamic model $p(x_{n+1} \mid x_n)$ yields the *bootstrap filter*. When more computational overhead is admissible, one can also compute closer approximations of the optimal proposal, i.e. of $p(x_n \mid x_{n-1}, z_n)$, by use of the posterior of any Gaussian filter.[49] As in the Gaussian case, there are canonical ways to extend any particle ODE filter to a particle ODE smoother.[50]

▶ **38.5 Uncertainty Calibration and Step-Size Adaptation**

We have now concluded the high-level introduction of ODE filters and smoothers (Algorithms 38.1 and 38.2), and turn our attention to the remaining details, namely the uncertainty calibration and step-size adaptation in lines 4 and 5 of Algorithm 38.1. As we will see, the step-selection will naturally follow from the calibration of σ^2 via local error estimates. Like all previous publications on this topic, we only consider the EKF0 and EKF1.[51]

[44] Note that the recursion (38.40) is only valid under the modest additional assumption that

$$\pi(x_{0:n+1} \mid z_{1:n+1})$$
$$= \pi(x_{n+1} \mid x_{0:n}, z_{1:n+1}) \pi(x_{0:n} \mid z_{1:n});$$

see Eq. (7.19) in Särkkä (2013).

[45] Särkkä (2013), §7.4

[46] Särkkä (2013), §7.5

[47] Tronarp et al. (2019), Thm. 1

[48] Due to the resampling step, the particles tend to form clusters. Hence, the amount of particles appears to decrease in time t, although it actually remains constant. A close look reveals that these clusters also branch out sometimes.

[49] See Eqs. (24) and (25) in Tronarp et al. (2019).

[50] Särkkä (2013), §11

[51] Since smoothers inherit the uncertainty calibration and step sizes from their underlying filters, they do not require an additional treatment. All statements on filters in this section also hold for the corresponding smoothers.

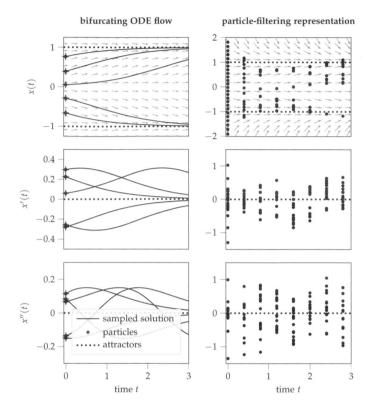

Figure 38.2: Bifurcation detection by use of particle ODE filtering. We consider the Bernoulli ODE

$$x'(t) = rx(t)(1 - |x(t)|),$$

with rate $r = 1.25$. Its flow bifurcates at 0, and then asymptotically concentrates at the attractors at ± 1. We assume that we don't know which side of this bifurcation we are on at $t = 0$; more precisely, we set $p(x_0) = \mathcal{N}(x_0; 0.05, 0.25^2)$. This incomplete knowledge can stem either from an unknown initial value or from numerical inaccuracy from previous computations for $t < 0$. Accordingly, in the notation of Eq. (37.2), the true distribution for each $t \geq 0$ is the push-forward measure $[\Phi_t]_*(p(x_0))$, which we simulate in the left column. For a growing t, this is an increasingly bimodal distribution at ± 1 with vanishing derivative $x'(t)$. This non-Gaussian distribution is nicely captured by the particle ODE filter (right column). Here, we employed a bootstrap ODE filter with 30 particles, a 2-times IWP prior and step size $h = 0.4$. Note that a Gaussian (Kalman) ODE filter (just like any classical ODE solver) would only capture the middle sample solution of the left column and thus miss the bifurcation completely; cf. Figure 38.1.

▷ **38.5.1   Global Uncertainty Calibration**

The validity of the posterior distributions does not only depend on the convergence rates of the mean (see §39.1.1 and §39.1.2), but also on the width of the (co-)variance. This posterior variance scales (in the Gaussian case: linearly) with the prior variance σ^2 – as can be seen from Eq. (4.7) for general GP regression.

The standard estimator for σ^2 is (absent prior knowledge) the maximum-likelihood (ML) estimator, which maximises the likelihood

$$p(z_{1:N} \mid \sigma^2) = p(z_1 \mid \sigma^2) \prod_{n=2}^{N} p(z_n \mid z_{1:n-1}, \sigma^2).$$

Computing the factors $p(z_n \mid z_{1:n-1}, \sigma^2)$ exactly is, however, as expensive as solving the ODE. Approximations, such as the ones from Chapter 12 in Särkkä (2013), are therefore necessary.

Fortunately, Tronarp et al. (2019) provided an elegant quasi-ML estimator for the EKF0 and EKF1, written

$$\widehat{\sigma^2} = \frac{1}{N} \sum_{n=1}^{N} \hat{z}_n^\mathsf{T} \breve{S}_n^{-1} \hat{z}_n, \tag{38.41}$$

where $\check{S}_n$ is the innovation covariance S_n of Eq. (38.19) if we set $\sigma := 1$.[52] Since $\widehat{\sigma^2}$ is based on the EKF0/EKF1 likelihood approximations, it is strictly speaking only a *quasi*-ML estimate.[53] But, for the same reason, it comes at almost no additional cost, and can be efficiently used to calibrate the width of the posterior. We refer to Bosch, Hennig, and Tronarp (2021) for more details.

For particle filters, the adaptation of σ^2 is more difficult and no simple estimator has been proposed. There is, however, vast literature on this topic that is summarised in §4.4 of Tronarp et al. (2019).

[52] A multidimensional generalisation for $d \geq 2$ was added by Bosch, Hennig, and Tronarp (2021), in the case of the EKF0.

[53] Lindström, Madsen, and Nielsen (2015), §5.4.2

▷ **38.5.2   Local Uncertainty Calibration**

A local version of the global Eq. (38.41), i.e. a quasi-ML estimate for a single step of the EKF0, was already proposed earlier:[54]

[54] Schober, Särkkä, and Hennig (2019)

$$\widehat{\sigma_n^2} = \hat{z}_n^{\mathsf{T}} \left[H\check{Q}(h_n)H^{\mathsf{T}} \right]^{-1} \hat{z}_n, \qquad (38.42)$$

where $\check{Q}(h_n)$ is the matrix $Q(h_n)$ if we set $\sigma^2 = 1$. A multivariate extension is also available.[55] For any $n \in \{1, \ldots, N\}$, this local estimate $\widehat{\sigma_n^2}$ is designed to capture the *added* numerical uncertainty in the step $t_{n-1} \dashrightarrow t_n$ of size h_n. While it ignores the accumulated uncertainty from previous steps, it lends itself perfectly to local error estimation.

[55] Bosch, Hennig, and Tronarp (2021)

▷ **38.5.3   Local Error Estimation**

In classical numerics, the difference between the extrapolations of a solver and a less-accurate one are commonly used as a local error estimate. For example, the canonical Dormand–Prince method[56] (aka *ode45* in Matlab) is a fifth-order Runge–Kutta method whose error estimates are obtained by comparison with a fourth-order RK method.

[56] Dormand and Prince (1980)

While the EKF0/EKF1 does not provide such a comparison, its probabilistic nature instead provides expected local errors in the form of the standard deviations of the predictive distribution $p(x_n \mid z_{1:n-1})$. More formally, in every step $(t_{n-1} \dashrightarrow t_n)$ of size h_n, the covariance matrix of the expected additional error is, by Eq. (38.11), $Q(h_n)$ with the calibrated σ from Eq. (38.42). From the entries of this $Q(h_n)$, one can now construct local error estimates. At first glance, it might seem most natural to use $\sqrt{H_0 Q(h_n) H_0^{\mathsf{T}}}$, the expected additional error on $x(t_n)$, as such an error estimate. While this is indeed a valid choice, the relevant publications[57] recommend

[57] Schober, Särkkä, and Hennig (2019); Bosch, Hennig, and Tronarp (2021).

$$D(h_n) := \sqrt{\tilde{H} Q(h_n) \tilde{H}^{\mathsf{T}}}$$

instead, with $\tilde{H}$ as in Eq. (38.19). Indeed, this $D(h_n)$ is arguably better-calibrated because it is the covariance of the additional residual $\hat{z}_n$ in step $(t_{n-1} \dashrightarrow t_n)$, i.e. of the very quantity used to calibrate σ^2 in Eq. (38.42). But regardless of the specifics of its construction, this cheap *probabilistic error estimate $D(h_n)$* can now be used in place of a classical error estimate in existing step-size control methods.

▷ **38.5.4   Step-Size Selection**

Step-size selection in ODE solvers aims to find step sizes that are as large as possible (to limit the computational cost), and as small as necessary (to limit the numerical error). To this end, one usually sets a local error tolerance $\bar{\varepsilon} > 0$ as an upper bound. If indeed $D(h_n) \leq \bar{\varepsilon}$, the step h_n is accepted. If not, the step size is decreased in a pre-specified way, and the decreased step is tested in the same way – until a sufficiently small step is found.

This step-size selection scheme can be executed in differ-ent ways. The most canonical way is the *proportional control algorithm*,[58] which employs the new reduced step size

$$h_n^{\text{new}} = h_n \rho \left[\frac{\bar{\varepsilon}}{D(h_n)} \right]^{\frac{1}{q+1}},$$

where $q + 1 \in \mathbb{N}$ is the local convergence rate (see Theorem 39.2) and $\rho \in (0, 1]$ is a safety factor. Other reduction methods (as well as more details) are mentioned in the relevant publications.[59] To date, step-size control has only been introduced for the EKF0 and EKF1.

Another approach to local error estimation and step-size adaptation in SSMs for probabilistic differential equation was derived from Bayesian statistical design[60] for the perturbative method by Chkrebtii et al. (2016).

▶ **38.6   Which ODE Filter/Smoother Should I Choose?**

We conclude our exposition of ODE filters and smoothers with a brief recommendation on how to choose from them. We are here concerned with the choice of *method* once a ssm has been decided on.[61] It is instructive to compare this section with §13.1 in Särkkä (2013) where the same question is considered for filtering/smoothing with regular data.

Which ODE filter/smoother should I choose? *Short answer: We recommend the EKS1.* The reasons for this recommendation are the following: First of all, the Gaussian filters and smoothers

[58] Hairer, Nørsett, and Wanner (1993), §II.4

[59] Schober, Särkkä, and Hennig (2019); Bosch, Hennig, and Tronarp (2021).

[60] Chkrebtii and Campbell (2019)

[61] The choice of prior was discussed in §38.2.

are much faster and more stable than the non-Gaussian ones (particle filtering). Among the Gaussian ones, the first-order versions (EKF1 and EKS1) make use of the Jacobian of f (available by automatic differentiation).[62] This tends to produce a more precise mean with better-calibrated uncertainty. Moreover, smoothing returns (unlike filtering) the full GP posterior distribution which exploits the whole data set $z_{1:N}$ along the entire time axis $[0, T]$ – while maintaining the $\mathcal{O}(N)$ complexity of filtering, both in the number of steps and of function evaluations. Therefore the EKS1 is, altogether, our default recommendation.

But a *longer answer* would also involve other methods. As a first alternative to the EKS1, both the EKF1 and the EKS0 recommend themselves. The EKF1 omits the smoothing pass (38.23)–(38.25) backwards through time. It is therefore a bit cheaper, i.e. its cost $\mathcal{O}(N)$ has a smaller constant. This can, e.g., be advantageous when only the distribution at the final time T (where the filtering and smoothing distributions coincide) is of interest.

The EKS0, on the other hand, does not require the Jacobian. Compared with the EKS1, this again reduces the constant in the $\mathcal{O}(N)$ cost. The Jacobian is beneficial to solve stiff ODEs and to calibrate the posterior uncertainty accurately. But when rough uncertainty estimates suffice, the EKS0 is an attractive cheaper alternative for non-stiff ODEs.

Lastly, the EKF0 combines both of the modifications of the EKF1 and EKS0, with respect to the EKS1. It is thus appropriate for the intersection of cases where the EKF1 and EKS0 are suitable.

The other above-mentioned ODE filters and smoothers are more expensive and trickier to implement efficiently. Hence, we recommend to only consider them in very specific cases. For instance, if the MAP estimate is desired, the IEKS is best suited to compute it. The particle ODE filter should only be used when capturing non-Gaussian structures is crucial. It is thus not really an alternative to Gaussian ODE filters and smoothers, but rather to the perturbative solvers of §40.

Efficient implementations of our recommended choice (the EKS1), and its next best alternatives (EKF1, EKS0, EKF0) are readily available in the ProbNum package.

▶ 38.7   Implementation in the ProbNum Package

The ProbNum package[63] contains efficient implementations of ODE filters and smoothers in Python. New algorithmic im-

[62] Griewank and Walther (2008), §13

[63] Code at probnum.org. See the corresponding publication by Wenger et al. (2021).

provements are continuously added. At the time of writing, it contains the EKF0, the EKF1 and the unscented Kalman ODE filter – as well as the corresponding smoothers: EKS0, EKS1, and unscented Kalman ODE smoother. The efficiency of the `ProbNum` implementation is ensured by the recent improvements in numerical stability (§39.2) and step-size control (§38.5.4) which were published alongside experimental demonstrations of their practical utility.[64]

[64] Krämer and Hennig (2020); Bosch, Hennig, and Tronarp (2021).

39

Theory of ODE Filters and Smoothers

We will now focus on the theoretical properties of ODE filters and smoothers. In classical numerics, there are two main analytical desiderata: *convergence rates* and *numerical stability*.

The *convergence rates* describe how quickly the numerical error $\|\hat{x} - x\|$ converges to zero when the step size h goes to zero, i.e. when the invested computational budget goes to infinity. As we explained in §37, these rates are usually polynomial since the (polynomial) Taylor expansion is, absent very specific restrictions, the optimal extrapolation. Accordingly, the convergence rates of ODE filters and smoothers known today are also polynomial; they are presented in §39.1.1 and §39.1.2. Notably, in two specific settings, equivalence with classical methods gives even higher polynomial convergence rates; see §39.3. Like all probabilistic solvers, ODE filters raise the additional question of their uncertainty (variance) calibration; §39.1.1 contains a result relating thereto.

While the convergence rates capture the behaviour of an ODE solver for "sufficiently small" step sizes h, it might exhibit inconvenient behaviour for practical step sizes $h > 0$. In particular, the numerical solution $\hat{x}$ can exhibit rapid variations although the analytical solution x does not – a phenomenon known as *numerical instability*. This usually happens in so-called *stiff ODEs*,[1] which are hard to define rigorously, but usually contain some term in f that can cause rapid variations in $\hat{x}$. In §39.2, we will present a first A-stability result (for the EKF1) as well as recent algorithmic improvements that increase the stability of the necessary numerical linear algebra (for the EKF0 and EKF1). Note that we here employ a wider definition of *numerical stability* (that includes its meaning in linear algebra) than normally used for classical ODE solvers, which do not rely

[1] Hairer and Wanner (1996)

on numerical linear algebra to the same extent.

Finally we will detail in §39.3 some links between ODE filters and classical methods, namely how the EKF0 is connected to the trapezoidal rule and Nordsieck methods. Throughout §39, we will simplify the notation by assuming w.l.o.g. that the step size $h > 0$ is constant.

▶ 39.1   Convergence Rates

ODE filters and smoothers apply techniques from signal processing (or scattered-data approximation) to numerical analysis. Accordingly, their convergence rates can be analysed with either the tools of classical numerical analysis[2] (i.e. by Grönwall's inequalities) or of scattered-data approximation[3] (i.e. by optimisation in an RKHS) – which we explore in §39.1.1 and §39.1.2 respectively. Both approaches yield similar, but distinct result: namely global convergence rates of h^q if q derivatives are modelled, but under different assumptions and restrictions.

[2] Kersting, Sullivan, and Hennig (2020)

[3] Tronarp, Särkkä, and Hennig (2021)

▷ 39.1.1   Classical Convergence Analysis

In this section, we follow Kersting, Sullivan, and Hennig (2020) in executing a classical convergence analysis of order $q \in \mathbb{N}$. To this end it is, just like for Runge–Kutta methods,[4] necessary to ensure that q derivatives exist and the remainder of the qth-order Taylor expansions of x are sufficiently small. This is secured by the following assumption.

[4] Hairer, Nørsett, and Wanner (1993), §II.2

Assumption 39.1. *Let $f \in C^q(\mathbb{R}^d, \mathbb{R}^d)$ for some $q \in \mathbb{N}$. Furthermore, let f be globally Lipschitz and let all its derivatives of order up to q be uniformly bounded and globally Lipschitz. In other words, we assume that there exists some $L > 0$ such that $\|D^\alpha f\|_\infty \leq L$ for all multi-indices $\alpha \in \mathbb{N}_0^d$ with $1 \leq \sum_i \alpha_i \leq q$, and $\|D^\alpha f(a) - D^\alpha f(b)\| \leq L\|a - b\|$ for all multi-indices $\alpha \in \mathbb{N}_0^d$ with $0 \leq \sum_i \alpha_i \leq q$.*

Under these conditions, the (by Taylor's theorem: optimal) local convergence rate of $\mathcal{O}(h^{q+1})$ are obtained in the following theorem.

Theorem 39.2. *Let the prior be a q-times integrated Wiener process or q-times integrated Ornstein–Uhlenbeck process[5] for some $q \in \mathbb{N}$, let $R > 0$ and let $m(h)$ be the filtering mean computed by one step of the EKF0. Then, under Assumption 39.1, there exists a constant $C > 0$ such that for all sufficiently small $h > 0$*

[5] See §38.2 for the definition of these priors.

$$\|m_0(h) - x(h)\| \leq Ch^{q+1}.$$

Proof. By bounding all relevant quantities and applying Taylor's theorem. See the proof of Theorem 8 in Kersting, Sullivan, and Hennig (2020) for details. □

As in classical numerics, the implied[6] global convergence rates are $\mathcal{O}(h^q)$, which are satisfied under some additional restrictions.

Theorem 39.3. *Under the same assumptions as in Theorem 39.2, let us add the restrictions that $q = 1$, that the prior is a q-times integrated Wiener process and that $R \in \mathcal{O}(h^q)$ is constant for all times t_n, $n = 1, \ldots, N$. Then, there exists a constant $C(T) > 0$, depending on final time $T > 0$, such that for all sufficiently small $h > 0$*

$$\|m(T) - x(T)\| \le C(T)h^q,$$

where $m(T) := H_0 m_N$ denotes by Eq. (38.3) the posterior mean estimate of $x(T)$ computed by the EKF0. The same bound holds for the EKS0.

Proof. By a combination of fixed-point arguments and a specific version of the discrete Grönwall's inequality; see the proof of Theorem 14 in Kersting, Sullivan, and Hennig (2020) in case of the EKF0. The extension to the EKS0 follows because, at the final time T, the filtering and smoothing distribution are equal.[7] □

In the same setting, the posterior standard deviation is *asymptotically well-calibrated* in the sense that it globally converges to zero with the same rate.

Theorem 39.4. *Under the same assumptions and restrictions of Theorem 39.3, there exists a constant $C(T) > 0$ such that the final posterior standard deviation $\sqrt{P(T)} := \sqrt{H_0 P_N H_0^\intercal}$ is bounded by*

$$\sqrt{P(T)} \le C(T)h^q,$$

for both the EKF0 and EKS0.[8]

Proof. See Theorem 15 in Kersting, Sullivan, and Hennig (2020). □

The main shortcoming of the global convergence results from Theorems 39.3 and 39.4 is their restriction to $q = 1$. Fortunately, they were published alongside experiments that demonstrated their validity for $q \in \{2, 3\}$.[9] In the meantime, experimental evidence for choices up to $q = 11$ was added.[10] Hence, it is widely believed that Theorem 39.3 can be extended to a general $q \in \mathbb{N}$.

[6] Strictly speaking, one can obtain even faster convergence rates because filters exchange information between adjacent steps via the derivatives – like multi-step methods do. §39.3 presents two settings (for $q = 1$ and $q = 2$), where the EKF0 indeed has global convergence rates of order h^{q+1}.

[7] This extension to smoothing was not contained in the original work by Kersting, Sullivan, and Hennig (2020), but was later pointed out by Krämer and Hennig (2020).

[8] Recall, from Eq. (38.22), the notation P_N for the posterior variance.

[9] See §9 in Kersting, Sullivan, and Hennig (2020).

[10] See §4 in Krämer and Hennig (2020).

▷ **39.1.2   Convergence Analysis by Scattered-Data Interpolation**

While the above classical analysis is based directly on the recursion equations of the EKF0, an alternative analysis obtains convergence rates directly from the state-space formulation of Eqs. (38.10)–(38.13). This analysis is due to Tronarp, Särkkä, and Hennig (2021); we follow their construction in this section.

First, recall from Eq. (38.28) that the global MAP estimate $\vec{x}^*(t)$ maximises the posterior $p(\vec{x}(t) \mid z_{1:N} = 0)$ – i.e. it maximises the prior under the restriction that the *information operator*[11] $\mathcal{Z}$ (which extracts the data z_n from the ODE) is zero for all $\{t_n\}_{n=0}^N$. More formally, by Eq. (38.18), this (nonlinear) operator is

$$\mathcal{Z}[\bullet] := \frac{\mathrm{d}}{\mathrm{d}t}[\bullet] - f[\bullet], \tag{39.1}$$

and ODE filters and smoothers infer x by conditioning on

$$\mathcal{Z}[\boldsymbol{X}](t_i) = 0.$$

By use of $\mathcal{Z}$, Tronarp, Särkkä, and Hennig (2021) describe the approximation of the MAP estimate $\vec{x}^*(t)$ as scattered-data interpolation in Sobolev spaces.[12] In this framework, compared to Assumption 39.1, no Lipschitz and boundedness conditions but one additional derivative are required.

Assumption 39.5. *Let $f \in C^{q+1}(\mathbb{R}^d, \mathbb{R}^d)$ for some $q \in \mathbb{N}$.*

The following theorem is a simplified version of Theorem 3 from Tronarp, Särkkä, and Hennig (2021).

Theorem 39.6. *Under Assumption 39.5 and for any prior $\boldsymbol{X}(t)$ of smoothness q,[13] there exists a constant $C(T) > 0$ such that*

$$\sup_{t \in [0,T]} \left\| \int_0^t \mathcal{Z}[x^*(s)] \, \mathrm{d}s \right\| \leq C(T) h^q, \tag{39.2}$$

where $x^*(t) = H_0 \vec{x}^*(t)$ is the MAP estimate of $x(t)$ given a discretisation $0 = t_0 < t_1 < \cdots < t_N = T$.[14]

Proof. The proof idea is to first analyse (with the help of tools from nonlinear analysis) which regularities the information operator $\mathcal{Z}$ inherits from f under Assumption 39.5, and then to apply results from scattered-data interpolation in the Sobolev space associated with the prior $\boldsymbol{X}(t)$. Details in Tronarp, Särkkä, and Hennig (2021), Theorem 3.   □

As F. Tronarp pointed out to us in personal communication, the convergence rates of the MAP then follow as a corollary.

[11] For a rigorous definition of information operators, see Cockayne et al. (2019b, §2.2).

[12] Wendland and Rieger (2005); Arcangéli, López de Silanes, and Torrens (2007).

[13] That is, for any process with a.s. q-times differentiable sample paths. In particular, this includes the Matérn family with $\nu = q + 1/2$ (§38.2) and its special cases: the q-times integrated Wiener process and Ornstein–Uhlenbeck process. See §2.1 in Tronarp, Särkkä, and Hennig (2021) for an alternative definition of such priors by use of Green's functions.

[14] Recall Eq. (38.30).

Corollary 39.7. *If Assumption 39.5 holds and f is globally L-Lipschitz continuous for some constant $L > 0$, then, for any prior $X(t)$ of smoothness q,[13] there exists a constant $C(T) > 0$ such that*

$$\sup_{t\in[0,T]} \|x^*(t) - x(t)\| \leq C(T)h^q,$$

where $x^*(t) = H_0 \vec{x}^*(t)$ is the MAP estimate of $x(t)$ given a discretisation $0 = t_0 < t_1 < \cdots < t_N = T$.[14] (NB: In particular, this uniform bound also holds for the discrete MAP estimate $x^*(t_{0:N})$ which the IEKS aims to estimate; see §38.3.3.)

Proof. By the fundamental theorem of calculus (with $x^*(0) = x(0) = x_0$), the triangle inequality, and Eq. (39.1), we have

$$\|x^*(t) - x(t)\| = \left\| \int_0^t \frac{d}{dt} x^*(s) - f(x(s))\, ds \right\|$$

$$\leq \underbrace{\left\| \int_0^t \mathcal{Z}[x^*(s)]\, ds \right\|}_{\leq\, C(T)h^q,\ \text{by (39.2)}} + \underbrace{\left\| \int_0^t f(x^*(s)) - f(x(s))\, ds \right\|}_{\leq\, \int_0^t L\,\|x^*(s) - x(s)\|\, ds}.$$

Now, application of the integral form of Grönwall's inequality (see e.g. Lemma 2.7 in Teschl (2012)) concludes the proof.   □

▷ **39.1.3   Discussion of Convergence-Rate Results**

Like Theorem 39.3, Corollary 39.7 also proves global convergence rates of $\mathcal{O}(h^q)$ of an estimate to the true solution $x(t)$. But apart from that, these two theorems are separated by multiple major differences – in addition to the aforementioned difference between Assumptions 39.1 and 39.5. To begin with, Corollary 39.7 is applicable to any prior with q derivative, while Theorem 39.3 is restricted to an EKF0 with q-times IWP prior and $q = 1$. The main restriction of Corollary 39.7 is, instead, that it only provides convergence rates for the MAP estimate $x^*(t)$ which the standard (extended) Kalman filters and smoothers do not approximate for a nonlinear f. Fortunately, as we discussed in §38.3.3, the iterated extended Kalman smoother (IEKS) does converge to a local minimum of the non-convex discrete-time MAP problem from Eq. (38.29), but it is unclear when this local minimum coincides with the global minimum $\vec{x}^*(t_{0:N})$. Thus, Corollary 39.7 (strictly speaking) does not contain convergence rates for any particular algorithm.

Nonetheless, it is another indicator that (extended) Kalman ODE filters and smoothers – which, after all, compute MAP estimates given local approximations to f – estimate x with a global numerical error $\mathcal{O}(h^q)$ if the first q derivatives of x exist and are appropriately modelled in the state space. In fact, the corresponding experiments[15] report that not only the IEKS (but also the EKS0 and EKS1!) exhibit these qth-order convergence rates of the MAP estimate $x^*(t)$. Moreover, the difference between the EKS1 and IEKS appears to be small in these experiments.

It will be up to future research to find the exact conditions on f and on the prior $X(t)$ under which these convergence rates hold for each filter and smoother. To this end, both generalising Theorem 39.3 to $q \in \{2, 3, \dots\}$ and replacing $x^*(t)$ with an output of an actual algorithm in Corollary 39.7 seem like promising ways forward.

Compared to classical methods, the h^q global convergence rates are optimal and on-par with Runge–Kutta methods, if we ignore the possibility of information sharing between steps – i.e. if we regard it as a single-step method. This is because the rate of an iterated Taylor expansion with q derivatives is also h^q. But, since an ODE filter that models q derivatives has information from the previous steps stored in these derivatives,[16] it is in a way more like a multi-step method which can achieve even higher rates in some settings – as we will see in §39.3.

▶ **39.2 Numerical Stability**

The excellent polynomial convergence rates of ODE filters and smoothers will, however, only be obtained when their computations are numerically stable. This is of particular importance for stiff ODEs.[17] To characterise the ability of an ODE solver to solve stiff equations, multiple notions of *stability* of an ODE solver exist. The most common of these notions (A-stability) has been proved for the EKF1,[18] but does not hold for the EKF0; see §39.2.1. But there are additional stability concerns for Gaussian ODE filters (and smoothers) as they heavily rely on numerical linear algebra.[19] The resulting rounding errors can – in particular if many derivatives are included in the ssm – make ODE filters unstable, even for non-stiff ODEs. Fortunately, these linear-algebra instabilities were decisively rectified by a recent publication[20] that we summarise in §39.2.2. As in the existing literature, we only consider the q-times integrated Wiener process (IWP) prior in this section.[21]

[15] Tronarp, Särkkä, and Hennig (2021), §7

[16] See Exercises 39.14 and 39.15.

[17] Hairer and Wanner (1996)

[18] Tronarp et al. (2019), §3

[19] Recall Eqs. (38.17)–(38.25). In particular, Eqs. (38.20) and (38.24) involve matrix inversions.

[20] Krämer and Hennig (2020)

[21] Recall from §38.2 why the IWP is the standard prior.

▷ **39.2.1   A-Stability**

A-stability is the most common criterion for the numerical stability of an ODE solver. It is defined by the solver's asymptotic performance on the so-called *Dahlquist test equation*, written

$$x'(t) = \Lambda x(t), \qquad x(0) = x_0 \neq 0, \qquad (39.3)$$

for some real[22] matrix Λ whose eigenvalues lie in the unit circle around zero, i.e. for which $\lim_{t \to \infty} x(t) = 0$. An ODE solver is said to be *A-stable*, if and only if its numerical estimate $\hat{x}(t)$ also converges to zero (for a fixed step size $h > 0$) as $t \to \infty$.[23] Accordingly, a Gaussian ODE filter is A-stable if and only if its mean estimate $H_0 m_n$ goes (for a fixed step size $h > 0$) to zero, as $n \to \infty$.

The following recursion holds by Eqs. (38.17)–(38.21) for the predictive mean m_n^- of both the EKF0 and EKF1 (but with different K_n):

$$m_{n+1}^- = [A(h) - A(h)K_n B]\, m_n^-, \qquad (39.4)$$

where $B = H - H_0 \Lambda$. In particular, we have $B = [-\Lambda, I, 0, \dots, 0]$ in case of the q-times IWP prior. If $K_\infty = \lim_{n \to \infty} K_n$ exists[24] and if $[A(h) - A(h)K_\infty B]$ has eigenvalues in the unit circle, then Eq. (39.4) implies that this ODE filter is A-stable.

Theorem 39.8 (Tronarp et al., 2019). *The EKF1 and EKS1 with a q-times IWP prior are A-stable.*

Proof. Theorem 2 in Tronarp et al. (2019) shows (using filtering theory)[25] that indeed, for the EKF1, K_∞ exists and $[A(h) - A(h)K_\infty B]$ has eigenvalues in the unit circle. As explained above, the A-stability of the EKF1 follows. For the corresponding smoother (EKS1), the claim follows from the fact that, at the final time (and thus also for $t \to \infty$), the smoothing mean coincides with the filtering mean.   □

Note that Tronarp et al. (2019) use a different terminology in their Theorem 2. The term "Kalman filter" there is the optimal estimator in the SSM (38.10)–(38.13) which here is linear-Gaussian due to $f(x) = \Lambda x$. In other words, "Kalman filter" there signifies the method we call EKF1. In Tronarp et al. (2019), this equivalence is exploited in Corollary 1 which is essentially our Theorem 39.8. Importantly, the EKF0 is not A-stable (see Exercise 39.9).

The A-stability of the EKS1 was recently demonstrated on a very stiff version of the Van-der-Pol ODE.[26] There are other

---

[22] In the classical literature $\Lambda \in \mathbb{R}^{d \times d}$ is a complex matrix, but ODE filters are only designed for real-valued ODEs. Hence, we here use the real-valued analogue (39.3) instead; cf. Eq. (31) in Tronarp et al. (2019).

[23] Dahlquist (1963)

[24] The limit Kalman gain K_∞ indeed exists in some important cases; see §3.1 in Schober, Särkkä, and Hennig (2019) and Proposition 10 in Kersting, Sullivan, and Hennig (2020).

[25] Anderson and Moore (1979), p. 77

Exercise 39.9. *Show that the EKF0 is not A-stable. To this end, consider the one-dimensional ODE (39.3) with $\Lambda = -\alpha < 0$, and show that (for any given step size $h > 0$) the filtering mean $H_0 m_n$ does not converge to 0 as $n \to \infty$, if α is large enough. How large does α have to be for this?*

[26] Bosch, Hennig, and Tronarp (2021), §6.1

less-common notions of stability which have (at the time of writing) not been discussed in the context of ODE filtering.

▷ **39.2.2   Stability of Linear-Algebra Operations**

As detailed in §3, Gaussian inference requires nothing but (numerical) linear algebra, i.e. nothing but matrix-vector and matrix-matrix operations. These are all (up to rounding errors) exact – with the exception of matrix inversions (in particular, if the state-space dimension D is large). The same is true for Gaussian ODE filters and smoothers since they are in essence an iterative application of Gaussian inference.[27] The required inversion of the (covariance) matrices can be facilitated by the Cholesky decomposition – or by the QR decomposition if the matrix is only positive-semidefinite.[28]

But this does not solve an even more fundamental problem: the accumulation of rounding errors, which can be insignificant in other cases, but play a decisive role here. To see why, consider the diffusion matrix $Q(h)$ for step size $h > 0$ from Eq. (38.11). For the q-times IWP prior, its entries are[29]

$$[Q(h)]_{ij} = \sigma^2 \frac{h^{2q+3-i-j}}{(2q+3-i-j)(q+1-i)!(q+1-j)!},$$

for $i, j = 1, \ldots, q+1$. Thus, $Q(h)$ has entries that span $2q$ orders of magnitude, from $\mathcal{O}(h^{2q+1})$ to $\mathcal{O}(h)$, which leads to ill-conditioned matrix computations for large q.[30] To alleviate this problem, a recent publication[31] suggested to use the **re-scaled variable** $T^{-1}x$ instead of x, with transformation matrix

$$T := \sqrt{h} \operatorname{diag}\left(\frac{h^q}{q!}, \frac{h^{q-1}}{(q-1)!}, \ldots, h, 1\right). \qquad (39.5)$$

In the underlying continuous-time model, this variable transformation $\tilde{X} = T^{-1}X$ amounts to using

$$\mathrm{d}\tilde{X}(t) = T^{-1}FT\tilde{X}(t)\,\mathrm{d}t + T^{-1}L\,\mathrm{d}\omega_t, \qquad (39.6)$$

instead of the original SDE (38.4).[32] In the discrete-time SSM, this leads to an analogously-transformed initial distribution and predictive distribution, written

$$p(x_0) = \mathcal{N}(x_0; T^{-1}m_0, T^{-1}P_0T^{-\mathsf{T}}), \qquad (39.7)$$
$$p(x_{n+1} \mid x_n) = \mathcal{N}(x_{n+1}; T^{-1}A(h)Tx_n, T^{-1}Q(h)T^{-\mathsf{T}}),$$

instead of Eqs. (38.10) and (38.11).[33] In other words, we replaced the original predictive matrices (A, Q) from Eq. (38.13) with the new ones $(\bar{A} := T^{-1}A(h)T,\ \bar{Q} := T^{-1}Q(h)T^{-\mathsf{T}})$ to

[27] Recall Eqs. (38.17)–(38.25).

[28] Krämer and Hennig (2020), §3.4

[29] This was already stated in Eq. (5.26). A detailed derivation (with zero-based indexing!) can be found in Appendix A of Kersting, Sullivan, and Hennig (2020).

[30] In fact, this ill-conditioning has prevented earlier work to test the expected $\mathcal{O}(h^q)$ convergence rates beyond $q = 4$. But Krämer and Hennig (2020) could, by virtue of their stabilising implementation, test these rates up to $q = 11$; see their Figure 3.

[31] Krämer and Hennig (2020), §3.2

[32] Cf. the alternative Nordsieck transformation of Eq. (39.14).

[33] Note that, for notational simplicity, we here assumed a constant step size h. See Krämer and Hennig (2020) for a generalisation to variable step sizes $\{h_n\}_{n=0}^N$ (in zero-based indexing!).

obtain Eq. (39.7). As desired, these new matrices are now scale-invariant:

$$[\bar{A}]_{ij} = \mathbb{I}(j \geq i)\binom{q+1-i}{q+1-j}, \qquad [\bar{Q}]_{ij} = \frac{\sigma^2}{2q+3-i-j}, \qquad (39.8)$$

for all $i, j \in \{1, \ldots, q+1\}$, where the entries of $\bar{A}$ are binomial coefficients. The new projection matrices from Eq. (38.3) are accordingly given by

$$\bar{H}_0 := H_0 T, \qquad \bar{H} := HT. \qquad (39.9)$$

After this transformation, the Gaussian ODE filter/smoother works in the re-scaled variables $(\frac{q!}{h^q}x(t), \ldots, x^{(q)}(t))$ instead of the original $(x(t), \ldots, x^q(t))$. This stabilises the computations in two ways: first, the entries (and thus the condition number) become independent of h.[34] Second, $(\bar{A}, \bar{Q})$ can be pre-computed for varying step sizes, which is not possible for the step-size dependent matrices (A, Q).

[34] Krämer and Hennig (2020), Table 1

We conclude this section by summarising the other major contribution[35] by Krämer and Hennig (2020) to the numerical stability of the linear algebra in Gaussian ODE filters (and smoothers): the **square-root implementation** of Kalman filters which, instead of the full covariance matrices, tracks their matrix square-roots. The resulting *square-root filters* (of which multiple variants exist)[36] have roughly the same computational complexity, but better numerical stability.

[35] Note that we already covered their third contribution (initialisation by automatic differentiation) in §38.2.1.

[36] Grewal and Andrews (2001), §6.5

There exist multiple definitions of the matrix square-root $\sqrt{A}$ of a matrix A. Here, it signifies any matrix such that $A = \sqrt{A}\sqrt{A}^\mathsf{T}$. This matrix $\sqrt{A}$ is not always unique. For instance, the (lower-triangular) Cholesky factors of the (symmetric positive-definite) predictive covariance matrices $\{P_n^-\}_{n=1}^N$ are their matrix square-roots under our definition.

With this in mind, we follow Krämer and Hennig (2020) to propose the following square-root implementation for the EKF0 and EKF1. First, we observe, in view of Eq. (38.17), that the predictive covariance matrix was constructed via the factorisation

$$P_{n+1}^- = \begin{bmatrix} A_n L_P & L_Q \end{bmatrix} \begin{bmatrix} L_P^\mathsf{T} A^\mathsf{T} \\ L_Q^\mathsf{T} \end{bmatrix}, \qquad (39.10)$$

where L_P and L_Q are the respective Cholesky factors of P_n and $Q(h_{n+1})$. This means that $[A_n L_P, L_Q] \in \mathbb{R}^{(q+1)\times 2(q+1)}$ is already a matrix-square root of P_{n+1}^-. But, as a symmetric positive-definite matrix, P_{n+1}^- admits a lower-dimensional square-root, namely the upper-triangular R from its Cholesky decomposition:[37]

[37] Note that this R has nothing to do with the R_{n+1} in Eq. (38.19).

$$P_{n+1}^- = R^\mathsf{T} R. \qquad (39.11)$$

Fortunately, this R can be obtained without assembling P_{n+1}^- from its square-root factors as in Eq. (39.10), since it (as Exercise 39.10 reveals) is equal to the upper-triangular factor of the QR decomposition of $[A_n L_P, L_Q]^\mathsf{T}$. Hence, we may replace the original prediction step (39.10) by the lower-dimensional matrix multiplication (39.11) in which the Cholesky factor R is efficiently obtained by a QR decomposition of $[A_n L_P, L_Q]^\mathsf{T}$ (i.e. without ever computing P_{n+1}^-).

Thereby, the filter can summarise the predictive distribution of Eq. (38.17) by (m_{n+1}^-, R) instead of (m_{n+1}^-, P_{n+1}^-). In the subsequent update step, the innovation-covariance matrix S of Eq. (38.19) can again be captured by its Cholesky factor which is (via analogous reasoning) again available (without assembling S) in the form of the upper-triangular QR-factor of $(HR)^\mathsf{T}$. The conditioning on z_{n+1} from Eqs. (38.20)–(38.22) can then be executed solely by use of this Cholesky factor of S.[38] Finally, the resulting filtering distribution $\mathcal{N}(m_{n+1}, P_{n+1})$ is obtained directly from the previously computed Cholesky factors. Again, the computation of P_{n+1} is replaced by computing its Cholesky factor instead.

Altogether, this square-root implementation represents all required covariance matrices (including the hidden, intermediate ones) by their Cholesky matrix square-root. Since the Cholesky factors of the matrices P_{n+1}^-, S and P_{n+1} can be obtained by QR decompositions of already-available matrix square-roots, they never have to be assembled – which further reduces the computational cost.

We refer the reader to Appendix A[39] in Krämer and Hennig (2020) for a complete description of this square-root implementation, and to the book by Grewal and Andrews (2001) for more implementation ideas which might help address the remaining practical challenges.[40] All of the above-described tricks are included in the ProbNum Python-package.[41]

▶ **39.3   Connection with Classical Solvers**

The probabilistic reproduction of classical numerical methods has, especially in its early days, been a central strategy of PN to invent practical probabilistic solvers. For ODE filtering, this changed when Tronarp et al. (2019) introduced the rigorous SSM of Eqs. (38.10)–(38.13) because, from then on, new research could also draw from the accumulated wisdom of signal processing (instead of numerical analysis). Since then, most ODE

Exercise 39.10. *Prove the claim in the text, i.e. show that the upper-triangular matrix in the QR decomposition of $[A_n L_P, L_Q]^\mathsf{T}$ is the transpose of the lower-triangular Cholesky factor of P_{n+1}^-. (For a solution, see §3.3 in Krämer and Hennig (2020).)*

[38] For details, see Appendix A.3 in Krämer and Hennig (2020).

[39] In particular, the square-root versions of the EKS0 and EKS1 are detailed in their Appendix A.4.

[40] These are mainly the efficient integration of high-dimensional and very stiff ODEs; see §5 in Krämer and Hennig (2020). In this regard, Krämer et al. (2021) recently published a further advance demonstrating that ODE filters can efficiently solve ODEs in very high dimensions.

[41] Code at probnum.org. See the corresponding publication by Wenger et al. (2021).

filters and smoothers were designed directly from the first principles of Bayesian estimation in SSMs, without attempting to imitate classical numerical solvers. While some loose connections have been observed,[42] it has not been studied in detail how the whole range of ODE filters and smoothers relates to classical methods. Nonetheless, earlier research[43] has established one important connection – in the form of an equivalence between the EKF0 with IWP prior[44] (more precisely, its filtering mean) and *Nordsieck methods*,[45] which we will discuss in §39.3.2. But, first, we will present another, more elementary, special case.[46]

▷ 39.3.1 Equivalence with the Explicit Trapezoidal Rule

In the case of the 1-times IWP prior and $R = 0$, the Kalman gains $\{K_n\}_{n=1}^N$ are the same for all n. In other words, it is always in its steady state $K_\infty = \lim_{n \to \infty} K_n$. Therefore, the recursion for the Kalman-filtering means $\{m_n\}_{n=0}^N$ is independent of n which leads to the following equivalence.

Proposition 39.11 (Schober, Särkkä and Hennig, 2018). *The EKF0 with 1-times IWP prior and $R = 0$ is equivalent to the explicit trapezoidal rule (aka Heun's method). More precisely, its filtering mean estimates $\hat{x}_n := H_0 m_n$ of $x(t_n)$ follow the explicit trapezoidal rule, written*

$$\hat{x}_{n+1} = \hat{x}_n + \frac{h}{2} \left(f(\hat{x}_n) + f(\tilde{x}_{n+1}) \right), \qquad (39.12)$$

with $\tilde{x}_{n+1} := \hat{x}_n + h f(\hat{x}_n)$.

Proof. See Proposition 1 in Schober, Särkkä, and Hennig (2019), where the explicit trapezoidal rule is referred to as "the P(EC)^1 implementation of the trapezoidal rule". $\square$

▷ 39.3.2 Equivalence with Nordsieck Methods

Classical introductions to Nordsieck methods can be found in most textbooks.[47] To comprehend Nordsieck methods in our context, let us first recall from Eqs. (38.1)–(38.3) that ODE filters do not only model the ODE solution $x(t)$, but a larger state vector $\vec{x}(t)$, which contains at least $x(t)$ and $x'(t)$. For the most important priors, $\vec{x}(t)$ is simply the concatenation of the first q derivatives, written

$$\vec{x}(t) = \left[x(t), x'(t), \ldots, x^{(q)}(t) \right]. \qquad (39.13)$$

In this section we again restrict our attention to the standard prior, the q-times IWP.[48] Now, recall that the dynamics of $\vec{x}(t)$

[42] For instance, it has been repeatedly pointed out that both the EKF1 and the classical *Rosenbrock methods* make use of the Jacobian matrix of f.

[43] Schober, Särkkä, and Hennig (2019)

[44] It is unsurprising that the equivalences are only known for the IWP prior as it is the only one with Taylor predictions; see Eq. (38.14).

[45] Nordsieck (1962)

[46] Note that, even earlier, the pioneering work by Schober, Duvenaud, and Hennig (2014) showed an equivalence between a *single Runge–Kutta step* and GP regression with an IWP prior. However, as it relies on imitating the sub-step structure of Runge–Kutta methods, this equivalence cannot be naturally reproduced with ODE filters. Therefore, we do not further discuss this result here.

[47] We especially recommend §III.6 in Hairer, Nørsett, and Wanner (1993).

[48] See §38.2.

is modelled by the solution $X(t)$ of the SDE (38.4) which can be transformed as in Eq. (39.6). Previously in Eq. (39.5), we chose the transformation matrix T such that the computations became less step-size dependent and more stable. As an alternative we now use a different transformation matrix, written

$$T_{\text{Nord}} := \text{diag}\left(1, \frac{1!}{h}, \frac{2!}{h^2}, \ldots, \frac{(q-1)!}{h^{q-1}}, \frac{q!}{h^q}\right). \quad (39.14)$$

This choice is motivated by the insight (see §37) that standard ODE solvers construct an approximating polynomial for $x(t)$ that (in every step) captures as many summands of its Taylor series (37.3) as possible. Indeed, the so-transformed system $X_{\text{Nord}}(t) := T_{\text{Nord}}^{-1} X(t)$ now models the re-scaled state-space vector

$$\vec{x}_{\text{Nord}}(t) = \left[x(t), hx'(t), \frac{h^2}{2}x''(t) \ldots, \frac{h^q}{q!}x^{(q)}(t)\right], \quad (39.15)$$

instead of the original $\vec{x}(t)$ of Eq. (39.13). In the classical literature, $\vec{x}_{\text{Nord}}(t)$ is called the *Nordsieck vector* whose entries are the first q Taylor summands of $x(t+h) = \Phi_h(x(t))$; see Exercise 39.12.

Analogously to Eq. (39.8), we can now derive the Nordsieck form of the prediction matrices; in particular, for A we obtain the Pascal upper-triangle matrix $\bar{A} \overset{\Delta}{=} \bar{A}_{\text{Nord}}$ with entries

$$[\bar{A}]_{ij} = \mathbb{I}(j \geq i)\binom{j-1}{i-1}.$$

For H, we now have $\bar{H} := [0, h^{-1}, 0, \ldots, 0]$ due to Eq. (39.9); $H_0 = [1, 0, \ldots, 0]$ remains unchanged.[49] The recursion of the means $\{m_n\}_{n=0}^N$ (computed by the EKF0) is after combining prediction (38.17) and update (38.21) given by

$$m_{n+1} = [I - K_{n+1}\bar{H}]\bar{A}(h)m_n + K_{n+1}f(H_0\bar{A}m_n), \quad (39.16)$$

where m_n and K_n are also re-scaled into Nordsieck form. Formulated without a statistical frame, a Nordsieck method $\widehat{\vec{x}}(t) \overset{\Delta}{=} \widehat{\vec{x}}_{\text{Nord}}(t)$ executes the prediction and update step in a single step:[50]

$$\widehat{\vec{x}}(t+h) = [I - l\bar{H}]\bar{A}\widehat{\vec{x}}(t) + hlf(H_0\bar{A}\widehat{\vec{x}}(t)), \quad (39.17)$$

where the weight vector l can be freely chosen to define the method. The structural resemblance of the recursions for filtering (39.16) and Nordsieck methods (39.17) should be evident – with the main difference that the Kalman gain K_{n+1} plays the role of l, but can unlike l depend on n.[51] And, in fact, these two

Exercise 39.12. *In Eq. (37.3) a Taylor series of the ODE flow, started at a numerical estimate $\hat{x}(t)$, was given as an extrapolation model. In contrast, the definition of the Nordsieck vector $\vec{x}_{\text{Nord}}(t)$ is not dependent on a numerical estimate. This difference stems from the "uncertainty-unawareness" of classical methods, discussed in §37. To understand this phenomenon, show that*

$$f^{\langle i\rangle}(x(t)) = x^{(i)}(t),$$

where $f^{\langle i\rangle}$ is defined as in Eq. (37.4). (Hint: use induction over $i \in \mathbb{N}$.) Then, show that it follows immediately that the qth-order Taylor expansion of $\Phi_h(x(t))$ is equal to the sum of the entries of $\vec{x}_{\text{Nord}}(t)$.

[49] Remember that, for the IWP prior, we have $H_0 = [1, 0, \ldots, 0]$ and $H = [0, 1, 0, \ldots, 0] \in \mathbb{R}^{1\times(q+1)}$.

[50] Cf. Eq. (28) in Schober, Särkkä, and Hennig (2019).

[51] The h in front of the l in Eq. (39.17) comes from the re-scaled observation matrix $\bar{H}$. Since the gain is re-scaled in the same way, it is hidden in K_{n+1} in Eq. (39.16).

recursions are the same in the steady state of the filter, i.e. after K_{n+1} has reached its limit $K_\infty := \lim_{n\to\infty} K_n$.[52] Note, however, that K_∞ depends on the SSM on which the EKF0 performs inference. While more equivalences with different Nordsieck methods should hold, the following result is so far the only one known.

[52] For the details, see §3.1 in Schober, Särkkä, and Hennig (2019).

Theorem 39.13 (Schober, Särkkä, and Hennig, 2018). *The EKF0 with 2-times IWP prior and $R = 0$ is a Nordsieck method of third order, after its Kalman gain has reached its steady state $K_\infty = \lim_{n\to\infty} K_n$. In particular, if initialised in this steady state, we have*

$$\|m(T) - x(T)\| \le C(T)h^3.$$

Proof. First, derive the steady-state Kalman gain: $K^\infty = [\frac{3+\sqrt{3}}{12}, 1, \frac{3-\sqrt{3}}{2}]^\top$. Then, insert K^∞ as the Nordsieck weight-vector l into Theorem 4.2 from Skeel (1979), which yields global convergence rates of order h^3. For the details, see Theorem 1 in Schober, Särkkä, and Hennig (2019). $\square$

Remark. *For the q-times IWP prior with $q = 2$, this theorem gives h^{q+1} instead of the h^q convergence rates suggested by Theorem 39.3 and Corollary 39.7, but only in the steady state. These rates indeed hold in practice.[53]*

[53] Schober, Särkkä, and Hennig (2019), Figure 4

In the same way, one could interpret any instance of the EKF0 (in its steady state) as a Nordsieck method. But there is no guarantee that the corresponding Nordsieck method is practically useful for at least two reasons: First, the numerical stability could be insufficient if more than two derivatives are included (see §39.2.2); second, the order of such a method will depend on the entries of K^∞ according to Theorem 4.2. from Skeel (1979).

Exercise 39.14 (Information sharing between adjacent steps). *The equivalence with the trapezoidal rule (39.12) shows how the EKF0 uses both y_{n-1} and y_n in the step from t_{n-1} to t_n. It is therefore smarter than Euler's method $\hat{x}_n = \hat{x}_{n-1} + hy_{n-1}$ which only uses y_{n-1}. Which part of the recursion, the prediction (38.17) or the update (38.21), are responsible to go from Euler's method to the trapezoidal rule? In other words, how do you have to alter Eq. (38.17) or Eq. (38.21) to fit only Euler's method instead of the trapezoidal rule?*

Exercise 39.15 (ODE filters in steady state as multi-step methods). *Recall from Eq. (39.15) that the Nordsieck vector for the q-times*

IWP prior models $x(t)$ and its first q derivatives. At any given discrete time point t_n $(n = 0, \ldots, N)$, the filtering mean estimate for $x(t_n)$, computed by the EKF0, will of course depend on all previous function evaluations $\{y_i = f(H_0 m_i^-)\}_{i=1}^n$. But, in the steady state, the mean estimates for the q modelled derivatives $[x'(t_n) \ldots, x^{(q)}(t_n))]$ will depend only on a finite number $j \in \mathbb{N}$ of these function evaluations, namely on $\{y_i = f(H_0 m_i^-)\}_{i=n-j+1}^n$. What is j for a given $q \in \mathbb{N}$?

40

Perturbative Solvers

So far in this chapter on ODEs, all methods (with the sole exception of the particle ODE filter) were probabilistic, *but not stochastic*. By this, we mean that they use probability distributions to approximate $x(t)$, but are not randomised (i.e. they return the same output when run multiple times). This design choice stems from a conviction held by some in the PN community[1] that it is never optimal to inject stochasticity into any deterministic approximation problem – except in an adversarial setting where it can be provably optimal. This view is, however, not shared by others who make the following arguments in favour of randomisation in ODE solvers.

Consider any classical single-step method, e.g. Runge–Kutta, whose local numerical error is in $\mathcal{O}(h^{q+1})$ for some $q \geq 1$ and whose global numerical error is consequently in $\mathcal{O}(h^q)$. After computing an estimate $\hat{x}(h)$ in the first step $(0 \rightarrow h)$, it goes on to compute the second step starting at $\hat{x}(h)$. In other words, the second step is equal to the first step for a *different* IVP, namely for the same ODE with the new initial value $x_0 = \hat{x}(h)$ (assuming that the ODE is autonomous). This means in the notation of Eq. (37.2) that, after computing $\hat{x}(h)$, the ODE solver tries to follow the flow map $\Phi_{t-h}(\hat{x}(h))$, in order to approximate $x(t)$. But, strictly speaking, the only thing that we know after the first step is that there is a constant $C > 0$ such that $x(h) \in B_{Ch^{q+1}}(\hat{x}(h))$. In view of this, we might as well try to follow any one of the possible flow maps $\{\Phi_{t-h}(a) : a \in B_{Ch^{q+1}}(\hat{x}(h))\}$, in order to compute $x(t)$.[2] For any later time $s > h$, the impact of the numerical error at time h on our knowledge of $x(s)$ will thus depend on the spread of $\{\Phi_{s-h}(a) : a \in B_{Ch^{q+1}}(\hat{x}(h))\}$, in addition to all subsequent numerical errors. Hence, the uncertainty

[1] See the corresponding discussion in §12.3.

[2] Recall that, for this reason, we called classical solvers "uncertainty-unaware" in §37.

over later estimates will be larger if $\Phi_t(a)$ is highly sensitive on a – that is, if $x(t)$ is highly sensitive on the initial value x_0.

Fortunately, this *sensitivity on initial values* has been extensively studied.[3] Since Edward Lorenz's seminal work on weather models,[4] it is known that even simple ODEs, such as the Lorenz equations,[5] can be so sensitive to initial values that the system's long-term behaviour is impossible to predict – a phenomenon known as *chaos*. Clearly, such chaotic long-term behaviour cannot be captured by Gaussians (or any other parametric family).[6] But even in most non-chaotic ODEs, the long-term effect of the numerical errors is non-Gaussian.

▶ 40.1 Randomisation by Locally Adding Noise

But how can we capture such a non-Gaussian distribution of possible trajectories, given a classical solver with local error in $\mathcal{O}(h^{q+1})$? The first answer was provided by Conrad et al. (2017) who proposed to imitate the numerical error by *adding* a calibrated Gaussian random variable after every step.[7] More formally, let $\Psi_h : \mathbb{R}^d \to \mathbb{R}^d$ be our classical deterministic solver of local order $q+1$ on a time mesh $\{t_n\}_{n=0}^N$, i.e. $\hat{x}(t_n) = \Psi_{h_n}(\hat{x}(t_{n-1}))$ with nth step size $h_n := t_n - t_{n-1}$.

Assumption 40.1. *The numerical method $\Psi_h : \mathbb{R}^d \to \mathbb{R}^d$ has uniform local numerical error of order $q+1$, i.e. there exists some constant $C > 0$ such that for any step size $h > 0$:*

$$\sup_{u \in \mathbb{R}^d} \|\Psi_h(u) - \Phi_h(u)\| \leq Ch^{q+1}.$$

Under this assumption, the local error in the nth step, $\varepsilon_n(h_n) := \Psi_{h_n}(\hat{x}(t_{n-1})) - \Phi_{h_n}(\hat{x}(t_{n-1}))$, is in $\mathcal{O}(h_n^{q+1})$, for all $n \in \{1, \dots, N\}$. This unknown error $\varepsilon_n(h_n)$ is now modelled by a random variable $\xi_n(h_n)$:

$$\varepsilon_n(h_n) \sim \xi_n(h_n) := \int_0^{h_n} \chi_n(s)\,\mathrm{d}s, \qquad (40.2)$$

where χ_n is a stochastic process on $[0, h_n]$ that models the off-mesh error accumulation between t_{n-1} and t_n.[8]

Assumption 40.2. *Let the error processes $\{\chi_n\}_{n=1}^N$ be independent. For each n, let χ_n be a zero-mean GP defined on $[0, h_n]$ such that, for all $t \in [0, h_n]$,*

$$\mathbb{E}\left(\|\xi_n(t)\xi_n(t)^\mathsf{T}\|_F^2\right) \leq Ct^{2p+1},$$

where $\|\cdot\|_F$ is the Frobenius norm and $C > 0$ is a constant independent of the step sizes $\{h_n\}_{n=1}^N$.[9]

[3] See, e.g., §2.4. in Teschl (2012).

[4] Lorenz (1963)

[5] The Lorenz equations with constants (σ, ρ, β) are:

$$\begin{aligned} x_1' &= \sigma(x_2 - x_1), \\ x_2' &= x_1(\rho - x_3) - x_2, \qquad (40.1) \\ z' &= x_1 x_2 - \beta x_3. \end{aligned}$$

[6] Recall that, in Figure 38.2, we already observed an elementary instance of chaos in the form of a bifurcation at $x = 0$.

[7] An even earlier perturbative solver was introduced by Chkrebtii et al. (2016). This method performs a GP regression on stochastically generated data; i.e. it shares the Bayesian GP-regression view with Gaussian ODE filters, while stochastically generating its "data" by evaluating f at a sample, i.e. of a perturbation of the predictive mean used in Eq. (38.33)); see §2.3 in Schober, Särkkä, and Hennig (2019) for a detailed discussion of this difference. While an important early advance, this method uses the same vague formulation of GP regression as the early ODE filters in the linear-Gaussian SSM (38.31)–(38.33), and only converges with linear rate ($q = 1$) to the true $x(t)$. Therefore, we here focus on later solvers without these shortcomings.

[8] Note the fundamental difference with ODE filters: while ODE filters put their model (the prior) on $x(t)$ as in Eq. (38.4), Conrad et al. instead put their probabilistic model (40.2) over the numerical error.

[9] This assumption can be relaxed; cf. Assumption 3.3 in Lie, Stuart, and Sullivan (2019).

Given the error model (40.2) and the numerical solver Ψ_h on a mesh $\{t_n\}_{n=0}^N$, the algorithm by Conrad et al. now outputs a sequence of random variables $\{\hat{X}_n\}_{n=0}^N$ according to the recursion

$$\hat{X}_n = \Psi_{h_n}(\hat{X}_{n-1}) + \xi_n(h_n), \quad \hat{X}_0 = x_0. \qquad (40.3)$$

In this method, the assumed numerical error $\xi_n(h_n)$ is added to every iteration of the solver Ψ_{h_n} and each random sample of $\{\hat{X}_n\}_{n=0}^N$ is considered a possible numerical approximation.[10]

Perturbing a carefully-designed classical method Ψ_h as in Eq. (40.3) might lead to a higher numerical error for any fixed step size $h > 0$. But if the variance of $\xi_n(h_n)$ is small enough, it might not lower the convergence rate – as the following theorem shows where $h := \max_{n=1,\dots,N} h_n$ denotes the largest step size. But first, we need to assume some regularity on f.

Assumption 40.4. *The vector field f admits a $t^* \in (0,1]$ and $C \geq 1$ such that, for $0 < t^* < t$, the flow map Φ_t is globally Lipschitz with Lipschitz constant $\mathrm{Lip}(\Phi_t) \leq 1 + Ct$.[11] (This assumption is satisfied if f is globally Lipschitz.)*

Theorem 40.5 (Lie, Stuart, and Sullivan, 2019, generalised from Conrad et al., 2017).[12,13,14] *Suppose Assumptions 40.1, 40.2 and 40.4 hold and fix $x_0 \in \mathbb{R}^d$. Furthermore, for all $t \subset [0,T]$, assume that $\Psi_t(Y) \in L^2$ for all random variables $Y \in L^2$. Then, there exists a constant $C > 0$ (independent of h) such that the randomised probabilistic solver (40.3) converges in mean-square. That is,*

$$\mathbb{E}\left(\max_{n=0,\dots,N} \|\hat{X}_n - x(t_n)\|^2\right) \leq Ch^{2\min(p,q)}.$$

In particular, the expected global error is of rate $\min(p,q)$:

$$\mathbb{E}\left(\max_{n=0,\dots,N} \|\hat{X}_n - x(t_n)\|\right) \leq Ch^{\min(p,q)}. \qquad (40.4)$$

Proof. See Theorem 3.4. in Lie, Stuart, and Sullivan (2019). $\square$

This is an important result for the following reason. Recall from Assumptions 40.1 and 40.2 that the randomised solver (40.3) tries to mimic the local numerical error of order $\mathcal{O}(h^{q+1})$ by adding Gaussian[15] noise with standard deviation in $\mathcal{O}(h^{p+1/2})$. Now, Eq. (40.4) ensures that the expected global error converges with the lower rate of p and q. This means that, if the added noise is sufficiently small (i.e. $p \geq q$), the random output $\hat{X}_{0:N}$ from Eq. (40.3) is (in expectation) "not worse" than the deterministic estimate $\hat{x}(t_{0:N})$ computed by the classical method Ψ_h – in

Exercise 40.3. *Choose Ψ_h as a fourth-order Runge–Kutta method and implement the perturbative solver (40.3) with a small fixed step size $h > 0$ and a Gaussian error model $\xi_n(h)$ with an appropriate variance. Then, apply it to the Lorenz system (40.1) and draw some samples of $\{\hat{X}_n\}_{n=0}^N$. What does the distribution of sampled trajectories look like, as $n \to \infty$?*

[10] For a pictorial representation of this randomised method, see Figure 2 in Conrad et al. (2017).

[11] The flow map Φ_t is defined in Eq. (37.2).

[12] Theorem 40.5 is a simplified version of the most general result, Theorem 3.4 in Lie, Stuart, and Sullivan (2019).

[13] The first version of this result, Theorem 2.2 in Conrad et al. (2017), was more restrictive in that the maximum was outside the expectation and f was assumed to be globally Lipschitz.

[14] Note that Lie, Stahn, and Sullivan (2022) provided an extension of this theorem to operator differential equations in Banach spaces.

[15] Note that we only assume Gaussianity of perturbations for simplicity. In fact, Theorem 3.4 by Lie, Stuart, and Sullivan (2019) also holds for a class of non-Gaussian perturbations; see their Assumption 3.3.

the sense that both the expected global error of the former and the fixed global error of the latter are in $\mathcal{O}(h^q)$. However, if the added noise is larger than that (i.e. $p < q$), then the expected global error is only in $\mathcal{O}(h^p)$, i.e. larger than without randomisation.

This is intuitive. Loosely speaking, it means that one can at most perturb the local error (in $\mathcal{O}(h^{q+1})$) by a slightly larger[16] additive noise (in $\mathcal{O}(h^{q+1/2})$) without reducing the global convergence rate. Accordingly, Conrad et al. (2017) recommend choosing $p := q$, i.e. to add the maximum admissible stochasticity that still preserves the accuracy of the underlying deterministic method Ψ_h.

[16] Due to the independence of random variables $\zeta_n(h_n)$, $n = 1, \ldots, N$, an order of $h^{q+1/2}$ in the local noise is already sufficiently small to have an expected global error of h^q; see Remark 8 in Abdulle and Garegnani (2020).

▶ **40.2   Randomised Step Sizes for Geometric Integrators**

The algorithm (40.3), however, has two shortcomings. First, even if the convergence rate is maintained (i.e. if $p \geq q$), the additive noise will usually increase the global error for any fixed $h > 0$. Second, if the underlying integrator Ψ_h is geometric[17] – i.e. it preserves geometric properties such as mass conservation, symplecticity, or conservation of first integrals – then these are not maintained after adding noise. As a remedy, Abdulle and Garegnani (2020) proposed to randomise the step sizes $\{h_n\}_{n=1}^N$ instead of adding noise. Formally, this amounts to replacing each h_n with a random variable H_n. The resulting method then follows the recursion

[17] Hairer, Lubich, and Wanner (2006)

$$\hat{X}_n = \Psi_{H_n}(\hat{X}_{n-1}), \quad \hat{X}_0 = x_0, \tag{40.5}$$

i.e. the stochasticity was, compared to Conrad et al.'s method (40.3), transferred from the random additive noise $\zeta_n(h_n)$ to the random step size H_n.[18] Here, $\hat{X}_n$ is treated as a stochastic simulation of $x(t_n)$, at time $t_n = \sum_{i=1}^n h_i$. And, indeed, this alternative perturbative method comes with the same convergence guarantees as in the additive case (Theorem 40.5). The following assumption on $\{H_n\}_{n=1}^N$ takes the place of Assumption 40.2.

[18] For a pictorial representation of Eq. (40.5), see Figure 2 in Abdulle and Garegnani (2020).

Assumption 40.6. *The random variables $\{H_n\}_{n=1}^N$ satisfy the following properties, for all $n \in \{1, \ldots, N\}$:*

(i) $H_n > 0$ *a.s.*,

(ii) *there exists $h > 0$ such that $\mathbb{E}(H_n) = h$,*

(iii) *there exists $p \geq 1/2$ and $C > 0$ independent of n such that*

$$\mathbb{E}\left(|H_n - h|^2\right) \leq Ch^{2p+1},$$

(iv) (if the integrator Ψ_t is implicit) H_n is a.s. small enough for Ψ_t to be well-posed.

Theorem 40.7 (Abdulle and Garegnani, 2020). *Suppose Assumptions 40.1 and 40.6 hold. Furthermore, let f be globally Lipschitz and $t_n = nh$ for $n = 1, 2, \ldots, N$, where $Nh = T$. Then, there exists a constant $C > 0$ (independent of h) such that the randomised probabilistic solver (40.5) converges in mean-square. That is*

$$\max_{n=0,\ldots,N} \mathbb{E}\left(\left\| \hat{X}_n - x(t_n) \right\|^2 \right) \leq Ch^{2\min(p,q)}.$$

In particular, the global maximum of expected errors is of rate $\min(p,q)$:

$$\max_{n=0,\ldots,N} \mathbb{E}\left(\left\| \hat{X}_n - x(t_n) \right\| \right) \leq Ch^{\min(p,q)}.$$

Proof. See Theorem 2 in Abdulle and Garegnani (2020). □

Just like Theorem 40.5, Theorem 40.6 shows that the local error rate of $q+1$ and the local standard deviation of $p+1/2$ combine to a convergence rate of $\min(p,q)$. For the same reasons as above, it is again recommended to choose $p = q$. Note that, like in a weaker earlier version of Theorem 40.5 by Conrad et al., the maximum is outside of the expectation here and f is assumed to be globally Lipschitz. For Theorem 40.5 these restrictions were later lifted by Lie, Stuart, and Sullivan (2019); maybe this is also possible for Theorem 40.6. Since the desired properties of geometric integrators hold for all $h > 0$, they a.s. carry over to a sample of $\{\hat{X}_n\}$ from Eq. (40.5).[19]

Notably, both of these methods can be thought of as frequentist as they sample i.i.d. approximations of $x(t)$. The particle ODE filter (from §38.4), on the other hand, is Bayesian as it computes a dependent set of samples that approximate the true posterior distribution. While there are first experimental comparisons (Tronarp et al., 2019, §5.4), more research is needed to understand the differences between all of these nonparametric solvers. There are further important methods – such as the aforementioned one by Chkrebtii et al. (2016) as well as stochastic versions of linear multistep methods[20] and of implicit solvers.[21] Finally, note that Abdulle and Garegnani (2021) recently published an extension of their ODE solver (40.5) to PDEs by randomising the meshes in finite-element methods.

[19] Abdulle and Garegnani (2020), Thm. 4

[20] Teymur, Zygalakis, and Calderhead (2016)

[21] Teymur et al. (2018)

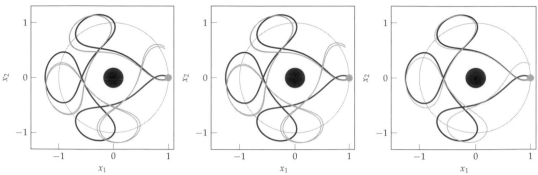

Figure 40.1: Estimating an Arenstorf orbit. Each figure shows two large point masses (black and grey circle, representing earth and moon) orbiting around each other, along with the true (black curve) and estimated orbits (grey curves) of a spacecraft following the IVP (40.6)–(40.7). The estimated orbits are computed by different probabilistic-numerical methods: the additive-noise perturbative method (40.3) (left plot), the randomised-step perturbative method (40.5) and EKF0 with 1-times IWP prior and $R = 0$ (§38.3.2). Both perturbative methods use Heun's method (i.e. $q = 2$ in Assumption 40.1) as the underlying integrator Ψ such that they are comparable with the filter due to Proposition 39.11. All solvers receive the same budget of 50 000 equidistant steps; the perturbative methods compute two samples, each with 25 000 equidistant steps. Already for the amount of two samples, we can see that the filtering mean (because it takes twice as many steps) is a much more accurate estimate than any of the samples. This difference will be even larger when the budget is split over more samples. Details in text.

▶ **40.3   Perturbative vs Gaussian Methods**

Ultimately, all of these nonparametric solvers offer non-Gaussian uncertainty quantification at a higher computational cost than Gaussian ODE filters and smoothers – in the number of evaluations of f, not necessarily in wall-clock time, as further discussed below. Unfortunately, at the time of writing, there are no strong analytical tools available yet to explain or study the value of this structured uncertainty. Generally speaking, we expect perturbations to be practical in the same settings as particle ODE filtering; see the discussion in §38.6. But the utility of nonparametric (vs Gaussian) methods remain a hotly debated topic because of the inevitable trade-off between computational speed and statistical rigour.

While other opinions exist, proponents of fast-but-approximate methods (such as the authors of this text) have phrased this trade-off as follows. Assume that a perturbative solver would need S samples to capture the numerical distribution of trajectories "sufficiently well", for a step size $h > 0$. Then, the budget of these samples could (absent parallelisation) equally well be spent on one sample with step size h/S. This single estimate will be more precise, and in some (but not all)[22] settings, one precise sample might be preferable to a set of S less precise samples. But, this sample will offer no uncertainty quantification whatsoever: it is just a perturbed classical method and has no advantage over its unperturbed version. Extended Kalman ODE filters, on the other hand, are designed to compute a good estimate together with a calibrated standard variation as an uncertainty estimate – which of course also causes overhead, but not in the amount of evaluations of f.

For a depiction of this intuition, consider Figure 40.1. It reproduces a classic three-body problem from astronomy: the search for a periodic "Arenstorf orbit" of a spacecraft between

[22] See Figure 38.2 for an example where multiple samples may be preferable.

two astronomical objects.[23] This concrete example setup is taken from Hairer, Nørsett, and Wanner (1993, p. 129). Figure 40.1 shows two bodies (representing earth and moon) of mass $1 - \mu$ and μ, respectively, rotating in a plane around their common centre of mass, with a third body of negligible mass orbiting them in the same plane. The equations of motion are given by the ODE system

$$x_1'' = x_1 + 2x_2' - \mu' \frac{x_1 + \mu}{D_1} - \mu \frac{x_1 - \mu'}{D_2}, \qquad (40.6)$$

$$x_2'' = x_2 - 2x_1' - \mu' \frac{x_2}{D_1} - \mu \frac{x_2}{D_2},$$

$$D_1 = ((x_1 + \mu)^2 + x_2^2)^{3/2},$$

$$D_2 = ((x_1 - \mu')^2 + x_2^2)^{3/2},$$

$$\mu = 0.012277471 \quad \text{and} \quad \mu' = 1 - \mu.$$

[23] Hairer, Nørsett, and Wanner (1993), p. 129

It is known that there are initial values that give closed, periodic orbits. One example is

$$x_1(0) = 0.994, \qquad x_1'(0) = 0, \qquad x_2(0) = 0,$$

$$x_2'(0) = -2.00158510637908252240537862224,$$

$$T = 17.0652165601579625588917206249. \qquad (40.7)$$

Each plot shows the true solution (found by a Runge–Kutta solver with tiny step size) as a black curve which is approximated by a different probabilistic ODE solvers (grey curves) in each plot. The first plot depicts two samples from the additive-noise perturbative solver (40.3), the second two samples from the randomised-step perturbative solver (40.5), and the third the posterior mean of a EKF0 with 1-times IWP prior (all based on Heun's method). In the first plot, the employed additive noise model is $\xi_n(h) \sim \mathcal{N}(0, [10^4 \cdot h^{2q+1}]I_2)$ for each step n; see Assumption 40.2. In the second plot, the randomised step H_n is drawn from a uniform distribution, $H_n \sim \mathcal{U}(h - 10^4 \cdot h^{2q+1}, h + 10^4 \cdot h^{2q+1})$ for each step n; see Assumption 40.6. For both perturbative solvers, the width of the distribution was scaled such that the samples are visibly different while maintaining the quality of the original integrator Ψ.

These plots visualise the trade-off between statistical flexibility and computational speed: Given a fixed budget, since the perturbative methods can take fewer steps per sample, the precision of the samples is greatly reduced – compared to a single estimator with more steps (from ODE filtering or otherwise). This effect is already pronounced for two samples, and will only increase for a larger number of samples. Since a numerical error acts like a statistical bias, the empirical mean of samples cannot be expected to rise as the number of (independent) samples goes up – to increase the quality, one has to increase the number of steps per solve, not the number of solves.

While the ODE filter appears more useful in this experiment, it should be noted that ODE filters also cause an overhead to compute their posterior uncertainty. While it stays inside the linear $\mathcal{O}(N)$ cost in the number of steps N, the constant is increased by a margin depending on the implementation. A comparison in wall-clock time could therefore be different, but is difficult to study in a principled way as it will depend on the ODE (e.g. on the cost to evaluate f). Nonetheless, we emphasise that the wall-clock overhead of ODE filters can instead be spent on a limited number of samples – even in the fast implementation of ODE filters in the ProbNum package (§38.7).

Moreover, perturbative methods *do* pick up more structure than Gaussian solvers. While it is difficult to generally assess *which* additional structure, this can be recognised more clearly in specific situations. For example, Chkrebtii et al. (2016) and Conrad et al. (2017) demonstrated that their solvers pick up the strange attractor of the Lorenz equations (40.1). And in computational neuroscience, Oesterle et al. (2021) recognised that the numerical uncertainty from solving the ODEs of neuronal models, such as the Hodgkin–Huxley model, critically affects how accurately they are simulated. This effect can be sufficiently strong to change the behaviour of the simulation *qualitatively*, even adding or removing individual spikes from the simulation. Notably, they were able to capture this structure by the perturbative solvers of Conrad et al. (2017), Eq. (40.3), and of Abdulle and Garegnani (2020), Eq. (40.5). It seems difficult to achieve this with Gaussian methods.

Which type of probabilistic solver should be used, then, depends on the application and the role of uncertainty quantification over point estimation in it. If the error estimate is more of a diagnostic for the quality of the point estimate, ODE filters may make better use of computational resources. If a structured uncertainty estimate is sought, then independent paths may be a more useful tool – in particular for chaotic or bifurcating ODEs like Figure 40.1. However, we stress again that, at the point of writing, the meaning of the structure of the independent samples is poorly understood from an analytical perspective. Future research will hopefully uncover a clearer picture.

41

Further Topics

The preceding sections of this chapter on ODEs were mainly concerned with forward solutions of IVPs. While we aspired to provide a comprehensive treatment of these algorithms and their theory above, there is more related research that we did not cover. In this section, we touch upon some of these topics briefly and provide additional pointers to related publications.

▶ **41.1 Boundary Value Problems**

In Definition 36.1, we defined a boundary value problem (BVP) as an IVP with an additional final value:[1,2]

$$x'(t) = f(x(t), t) \quad \text{for all } t \in [0, T],$$
$$\text{with } \textit{boundary values} \quad x(0) = x_0 \text{ and } x(T) = x_T.$$

In the same way as for IVPs (§38.2), we can model the BVP solution $x(t)$ and its derivative $x'(t)$ by a GP prior $p(\vec{x}(t_{0:N}))$, such that $x(t) = H_0 \vec{x}(t_{0:N})$ and $x'(t) = H\vec{x}(t_{0:N})$ are contained in $\vec{x}(t)$. The BVP posterior distribution is now written

$$p(\vec{x}(t_{0:N}) \mid z_{1:N} = 0, x(T) = x_T), \quad (41.1)$$

i.e. it is (compared with IVPs) additionally conditioned on $x(T) = x_T$. If f is linear, i.e. if $f(x,t) = M(t)x + s(t)$, the likelihood is linear and the BVP posterior (41.1) for any Gaussian prior $p(\vec{x}(t))$ can be computed in closed form by standard GP regression (§4.2). The resulting probabilistic BVP solver was proposed by John et al.,[3] based on previous work on probabilistic solvers for linear PDEs.[4] Furthermore, John et al. generalised this idea to a nonlinear f by use of quasi-linearisation, an application of Newton's method that partitions the BVP into a series of linear BVPs to which the linear solver is then applied.

[1] We here inserted the argument t into f because it is relevant to explain the work by John, Heuveline, and Schober (2019); everywhere else, we could w.l.o.g. omit it.

[2] Note that in general, as mentioned in Definition 36.1, there is a more general boundary condition $g(x(0), x(T)) = 0$. Accordingly, the referenced probabilistic BVP solvers are not limited to our restrictive definition which only serves to declutter the notation.

[3] John, Heuveline, and Schober (2019), §3

[4] Cockayne et al. (2017a), §3

Note, however, that these methods do not restrict the prior to Markov processes, and therefore do not exploit the linear-time state-space formulation of GPs that made ODE filtering and smoothing possible for IVPs.

Fortunately, this gap was closed by constructing a SSM for BVPs.[5] To see how, recall that our SSM (38.10)–(38.13) was designed for IVPs and thus does not include the final condition $x(T) = x_T$. But it can be extended to BVPs by adding the Dirac likelihood

$$p(x_T \mid x_N) = \delta(x_T - H_0 x_N),$$

to incorporate x_T as data on $x(T) = H_0 x_N$ (recall that $T = N/h$). Inference in this augmented SSM is now the same as in the original SSM – with the sole difference that, in the final step, the solver does not only condition on $z_N = 0$ but also on $H_0 x_N = x_T$.[6] Consequently, as for IVPs, we can either use the EKS0 or EKS1,[7] after linearising f, or employ an iterated extended Kalman smoother (IEKS) to compute the MAP estimate $x^*(t_{0:N})$ from Eq. (38.30).[8] In fact, Krämer and Hennig (2021) demonstrated that the latter solver (IEKS) converges quickly on test problems. It yields (due to its linear-time complexity) a significant speed-up over John, Heuveline, and Schober (2019), includes step-size selection as well as hyperparameter-calibration schemes, and is therefore the state-of-the-art in PN for BVPs.

Such probabilistic BVP solvers have (in previous forms without the linear-time formulation) been applied to numerically approximate shortest paths and distances on Riemannian manifolds. This approach has concrete applications in fields such as Riemannian statistics and brain imaging where quantifying the numerical uncertainty plays an important role for the final objective. This was first recognised by Hennig and Hauberg (2014) and further exploited by Schober et al. (2014). The current state of the art was provided by Arvanitidis et al. (2019). However, note that, in principle, all above (newer) probabilistic BVP solvers are applicable to this task as well.

▶ **41.2   Inverse Problems**

One main purpose of PN is to consistently pass numerical uncertainty along computational chains. This should enable an efficient distribution of computational budget, in order to minimise the negative effect of all sources of uncertainty on the final objective.[9] A particularly well-studied chain involving ODEs is the *ODE inverse problem*. Inverse problems, in general, consist

----

[5] Krämer and Hennig (2021)

[6] A graphical model for this augmented SSM with two likelihoods is presented in Figure 2 of Krämer and Hennig (2021). Note, however, that they also include the initial value x_0 with a likelihood – instead of regarding it as part of the prior, as we did in §38.2.1. Despite this, both approaches are equivalent in that they yield the same algorithms. In fact, Krämer and Hennig also take up our prior view by introducing the concept of a *bridge prior*, i.e. a prior that incorporates both the initial and final value.

[7] For BVPs, both boundary values contain equal information. Hence, filtering is less natural as it moves only in one direction through time.

[8] See §38.3.2 and §38.3.3 for these two approaches, respectively.

[9] See paragraph *"Pipelines of computation demand harmonisation"* in Section "This Book" in the Introduction of this text.

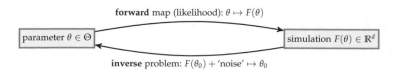

forward map (likelihood): $\theta \mapsto F(\theta)$

| parameter $\theta \in \Theta$ | | simulation $F(\theta) \in \mathbb{R}^d$ |

inverse problem: $F(\theta_0) + \text{`noise'} \mapsto \theta_0$

Figure 41.1: Depiction of a generic inverse problem. An ODE inverse problem is the special case where the output $F(\theta)$ is the solution $x : [0, T] \to \mathbb{R}^d$ of the parametrised IVP, Eq. (41.2).

of inferring the parameter for which some *forward map* outputs some given data. More formally, assume that some forward map $F : \mathbb{R}^n \to \mathbb{R}^d$ is given and that we can simulate its output $F(\theta) \in \mathbb{R}^d$ for any given parameter $\theta \in \Theta \subset \mathbb{R}^n$. Given such a (potentially noisy) simulation $F(\theta_0)$, the inverse problems now conversely consists of recovering the unknown parameter θ_0 that gave rise to this data $F(\theta_0)$; see Figure 41.1. This estimation is complicated by the fact that many inverse problems are ill-posed, e.g. when there are two parameters $\tilde{\theta}_0 \neq \theta_0$ such that $F(\theta_0) = F(\tilde{\theta}_0)$.

Standard inverse problem solvers simply try out several parameters ("samples") $\{\theta_i\}_{i=0}^S$ and compare their simulations $\{F(\theta_i)\}_{i=0}^S$ with $F(\theta_0)$. Roughly speaking, the smaller $\|F(\theta_i) - F(\theta_0)\|$, the more likely it is considered for θ_i to be close to θ_0. This process is usually guided by statistical principles such as MCMC. In fact, random-walk Metropolis methods remain the go-to solution for most applications.[10] While this is valid in the limit of infinitely many simulations, the number of samples S required to infer θ_0 satisfactorily can be very large. Thus, entire research fields such as approximate Bayesian computation (ABC), simulation-based inference, and likelihood-free inference have taken aim at reducing this high computational cost.[11]

An *ODE inverse problem* is now simply an inverse problem whose forward map is the solution of an IVP (36.2) with added parameter $\theta \in \Theta \subset \mathbb{R}^n$,[12] i.e. of the IVP

$$x'(t) = f(x(t), \theta) \quad \text{for all } t \in [0, T],$$
$$\text{with } \textit{initial value} \quad x(0) = x_0 \in \mathbb{R}^d. \tag{41.2}$$

Simulating the forward map F thus amounts to approximating the solution of the IVP (41.2), i.e. $F(\theta) = x_\theta \overset{\Delta}{=} x$ for any chosen θ. The data, which we denote by z, is thus equal to $x_{\theta_0} = F(\theta_0)$ (under additive, zero-mean Gaussian noise) at M discrete time points $0 < t_1 < \cdots < t_M \leq T$, i.e.

$$z(t_i) := x(t_i) + \xi_i \in \mathbb{R}^d, \quad \xi_i \sim \mathcal{N}(0, \sigma^2 I_d),$$

which we stack to form a data vector z written

$$z := \begin{bmatrix} z_1(t_1), \ldots, z_1(t_M), \ldots, z_d(t_1), \ldots, z_d(t_M) \end{bmatrix}^\mathsf{T} \in \mathbb{R}^{dM}.$$

[10] Tarantola (2005), §2.4

[11] A recent survey of these closely related fields was provided by Cranmer, Brehmer, and Louppe (2020).

[12] The initial value x_0 can also be added to the parameter vector θ.

Again, we will w.l.o.g. assume $d = 1$. Analogously, we combine the values of the true solution x_{θ_0} at $\{t_i\}_{i=1}^{M}$ to form the stacked vector x_{θ_0} such that the probability of observing z reads

$$p(z \mid x_{\theta_0}) = \mathcal{N}\left(z; x_{\theta_0}, \sigma^2 I_M\right). \tag{41.3}$$

To obtain the likelihood of the forward problem, we now (given some θ) have to integrate over $p(x_\theta \mid \theta)$. In classical methods (i.e. without uncertainty quantification), $p(x_\theta \mid \theta)$ is assumed to be a.s. equal to the employed numerical estimate $\hat{x}_\theta$, i.e. $p(x_\theta \mid \theta) := \delta(x_\theta - \hat{x}_\theta)$. This yields the *uncertainty-unaware likelihood*, written

$$p(z \mid \theta) = \int p(z \mid x_\theta) p(x_\theta \mid \theta) \, dx_\theta \tag{41.4}$$

$$\overset{(41.3)}{=} \mathcal{N}\left(z; \hat{x}_\theta, \sigma^2 I_M\right), \tag{41.5}$$

which is then tacitly taken for the "true" likelihood.

Fortunately, the output of any probabilistic ODE solver, when applied to the parametrised IVP (41.2) with fixed θ, is (by its very nature) a carefully designed version of $p(x_\theta \mid \theta)$.[13] It is thus natural to, after choosing a probabilistic ODE solver, insert its output distribution for $p(x_\theta \mid \theta)$ in Eq. (41.4). This yields a different $p(z \mid \theta)$ than the conventional *uncertainty-unaware likelihood* (41.5). For large step sizes $h > 0$ (i.e. for large numerical uncertainty relative to the statistical noise σ^2), the resulting *uncertainty-aware likelihood* indeed corrects for the overconfidence of the unaware likelihood, as is demonstrated in Figure 41.2 for the EKF0.

In this new statistical model, one can now do statistical inference of θ_0 as needed. Depending on the precise shape of $p(z \mid \theta)$ (stemming from the probabilistic solver), different inference schemes recommend themselves and have been explored in the literature – both for perturbative solvers[14] and Gaussian ODE filters.[15]

In the case of *perturbative solvers*, most publications have followed the Bayesian approach to inverse problems,[16] wherein a prior $p(\theta)$ over the parameter space Θ is added to the model. Solving the corresponding Bayesian inverse problem now consists of computing the posterior distribution

$$p(\theta \mid z) \propto p(\theta) \left[\int p(z \mid x_\theta) p_h(x_\theta \mid \theta) \, dx_\theta \right], \tag{41.6}$$

where we inserted Eq. (41.4) for the likelihood, with superscript h added to $p(x_\theta \mid \theta)$ to highlight the dependence on the step

[13] Remember that, due to multiple trade-offs (fast vs accurate, Gaussian vs non-parametric, choice of prior, etc.), there is no uniquely correct way to construct $p(x_\theta \mid \theta)$ – just like there is no single true regression for any data. Nonetheless, the distinction between ignoring and accounting for the uncertainty is pivotal.

[14] The list of perturbative inverse-problem solvers includes the papers by Chkrebtii et al. (2016), Conrad et al. (2017), Teymur et al. (2018), Lie, Sullivan, and Teckentrup (2018), and Abdulle and Garegnani (2020).

[15] Kersting et al. (2020)

[16] Dashti and Stuart (2017)

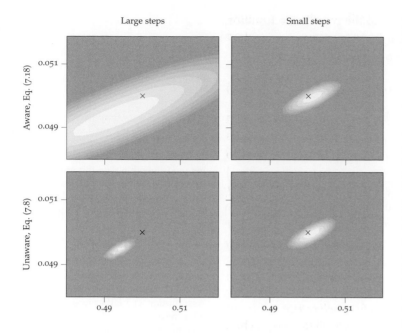

Large steps   Small steps

Figure 41.2: Uncertainty-(un)aware likelihoods w.r.t. (θ_1, θ_2) of the Lotka–Volterra ODE

$$x_1' = \theta_1 x_1 - \theta_2 x_1 x_2,$$
$$x_2' = -\theta_3 x_2 + \theta_4 x_1 x_2,$$

with fixed $(\theta_3, \theta_4) = (0.05, 0.5)$ and $x_0 = (20, 20)$. An EKF0 with 1-times IWP prior was used to construct $p(x_\theta \mid \theta)$, leading to the uncertainty-aware likelihood (41.12) in the top row. The black cross marks the true parameter. The unaware likelihood (bottom row) is overconfident for the large step size ($h = 0.2$), i.e. for large P, while the aware likelihood is well-calibrated such that the true parameter has non-zero likelihood. For the small step size ($h = 0.025$) this effect is less pronounced since P is small. This figure is adapted from Figure 2 in Kersting et al. (2020). This removal of overconfidence has also been demonstrated for perturbative solvers, see e.g. Figures 5 and 6 in Conrad et al. (2017), or Figures 3 and 11 in Abdulle and Garegnani (2020).

size h. The posterior, Eq. (41.6), is (in general) not available in closed form and has to be approximated by a suitable sampling scheme. The aforementioned reduction of overconfidence (see Figure 41.2) in this uncertainty-aware posterior has been demonstrated in multiple experiments.[17] Due to the stochasticity of the forward map $p_h(x_\theta \mid \theta)$, a pseudo-marginal MCMC approach is particularly suited to approximate the posterior.[18] Convergence guarantees of such inference schemes to the numerical-error-less posterior (i.e. when indeed $\hat{x}_\theta = x_\theta$ for all θ), as $h \to 0$, were proved by Lie, Sullivan, and Teckentrup (2018).

[17] See e.g. Figures 5 and 6 in Conrad et al. (2017), or Figures 3 and 11 in Abdulle and Garegnani (2020).

[18] Abdulle and Garegnani (2020), §8

In the case of *ODE filters and smoothers*, the (to date) only publication is Kersting et al. (2020). Like the perturbative approaches, it managed to reduce the overconfidence in the likelihood by inserting an EKF0 in lieu of a classical ODE solver, as Figure 41.2 demonstrates. But, on top of that, it exploited the resulting, more structured Gaussian form of the likelihood to estimate its gradients and Hessian matrices in the following way.

First, let us assume w.l.o.g. that $h > 0$ is fixed, and recall, from Eqs. (38.1) and (38.2), that the functions x and x' are a priori jointly modelled by a Gauss–Markov process, written

$$p\left(\begin{bmatrix} x \\ x' \end{bmatrix}\right) = \mathcal{GP}\left(\begin{bmatrix} x \\ x' \end{bmatrix}; \begin{bmatrix} x_0 \\ f(x_0) \end{bmatrix}, \begin{bmatrix} k & k^\partial \\ \partial k & \partial k^\partial \end{bmatrix}\right),$$

where the functions $k^\partial = \partial k(t, t')/\partial t'$, $\partial k = \partial k(t, t')/\partial t$ and

$\partial k^\partial = \partial^2 k(t,t')/\partial t \partial t'$ are derivatives of the covariance function k. The EKS0[19] thus computes (for a fixed $\theta \in \Theta$) a posterior GP whose marginals at the data time points $\{t_i\}_{i=1}^M$ reads

$$p(x_\theta \mid \theta) = \mathcal{N}(x_\theta; m_\theta, P), \qquad (41.7)$$

where the posterior mean is given by[20]

$$m_\theta \overset{(4.6)}{=} x_0 \mathbf{1}_M + k^\partial{}_{\mathbb{T}_M \mathbb{T}_N} \left[\partial K^\partial{}_{\mathbb{T}_N \mathbb{T}_N} \right]^{-1} [y_{1:N} - f(x_0, \theta)\mathbf{1}_N] \quad (41.8)$$

with $\mathbb{T}_N = \{jh\}_{j=1}^N$, $y_{1:N} = [f(m_\theta^-(h), \theta), \ldots, f(m_\theta^-(Nh), \theta)]^\mathsf{T}$, and $\mathbf{1}_M = [1, \ldots, 1]^\mathsf{T} \in \mathbb{R}^M$. While the dependence of m_θ^- on θ is at least as involved as the dependence $f(x, \theta)$ on θ, the following simplifying assumption fortunately holds for many ODEs.[21]

Assumption 41.1. *The dependence of f on θ is linear. More precisely, we assume that $f(x, \theta) = \sum_{i=1}^n \theta_i f_i(x)$, for some continuously differentiable $f_i : \mathbb{R}^d \to \mathbb{R}^d$, for all $i = 1, \ldots, n$. (Note that no linearity assumption is placed on the f_i.)*

Under this assumption, Eq. (41.8) becomes[22]

$$m_\theta = \begin{bmatrix} \mathbf{1}_M & J \end{bmatrix} \begin{bmatrix} x_0 \\ \theta \end{bmatrix} = x_0 \mathbf{1}_M + J\theta, \qquad (41.9)$$

where the Jacobian-matrix estimator $J = KY$ is the product of the *kernel pre-factor*[23]

$$K = k^\partial{}_{\mathbb{T}_M \mathbb{T}_N} \left[\partial K^\partial{}_{\mathbb{T}_N \mathbb{T}_N} \right]^{-1} \in \mathbb{R}^{M \times N} \qquad (41.10)$$

and the *data matrix* $Y \in \mathbb{R}^{N \times n}$ with entries

$$[Y]_{ij} = f_j(m_\theta^-(ih)) - f_j(x_0), \qquad (41.11)$$

where f_j is as in Assumption 41.1. It is important to note that our notation omits that $[Y]_{ij}$ actually depends on θ via the predictive mean $m_\theta^-(ih)$. For any $i \in \{1, \ldots, N\}$, this $m_\theta^-(ih)$ changes with θ through the import of θ on the previous steps up to time $t = ih$ – which is a nonlinear and potentially highly sensitive dependence. Nonetheless, all local ("first-order") effects are captured by the linearisation, Eq. (41.9). Therefore, it is not unreasonable to hope that J will be a useful estimator of the true Jacobian of the map $\theta \mapsto m_\theta$, despite ignoring the global ("higher-order") dependence of the true Jacobian on θ via Y.[24] In any case, Kersting et al. (2020) proceeded to demonstrate the usefulness of this heuristic estimator J for the inference of θ, as we will see next.

[19] While Kersting et al. (2020) considered the EKF0, we here present the analogous construction for the EKS0 because it is easier to comprehend.

[20] We here, for its simplicity, use the notation of the linear-Gaussian SSM (38.31)–(38.33) to work with the EKF0 and EKS0. This is admissible because Kalman filtering (and smoothing) on this SSM is equal to the EKF0 and EKS0 on the general SSM (38.10)–(38.13) which yields Eq. (41.8); see §38.3.4. For notational simplicity we set $R = 0$, but a non-zero $R > 0$ can simply be added to $\partial k^\partial{}_{\mathbb{T}_N \mathbb{T}_N}$ if needed.

[21] In fact, most ODEs collected in Hull et al. (1972, Appendix I), a standard set of ODE benchmarking problems, satisfy Assumption 41.1 either immediately or after re-parametrisation. In particular, Assumption 41.1 does not restrict the numerical difficulty of the ODE since f inherits all inconveniences from the $\{f_i\}_{i=1}^n$ for which nothing (but the usual continuous differentiability) is assumed.

[22] Note that Eq. (41.9) reveals how easily x_0, if unknown, can be treated as an additional parameter.

[23] K is called a *pre*-factor because it is (absent any adaptation of the SSM to θ) independent of θ and can thus be pre-computed for all forward solutions at once.

[24] The precise Jacobian matrix can be computed at an additional cost by sensitivity analysis (Rackauckas et al., 2018). The Jacobian estimator J, on the other hand, comes as an almost-free byproduct of the forward solution with EKF0 or EKS0: it is simply the product of the pre-computable K (41.10) and the previously collected function evaluations (41.11). Exact sensitivity analysis, in contrast, requires more expensive global computations along the entire time axis $[0, T]$.

To this end, we observe that, again, insertion of the probabilistic numerical likelihood (41.7) for $p(x_\theta \mid \theta)$ in Eq. (41.4) yields an *uncertainty-aware likelihood*

$$p(z \mid \theta) = \mathcal{N}(z; m_\theta, P + \sigma^2 I_M),\qquad (41.12)$$

which is depicted in Figure 41.2. By plugging (41.9) into (41.12), we now obtain the estimators

$$\hat{\nabla}_\theta \mathcal{L}(z) := -J^\top \left[P + \sigma^2 I_M \right]^{-1} [z - m_\theta],\quad \text{and}\quad (41.13)$$

$$\hat{\nabla}_\theta^2 \mathcal{L}(z) := J^\top \left[P + \sigma^2 I_M \right]^{-1} J \qquad (41.14)$$

for the gradient and Hessian of the corresponding log-likelihood $\mathcal{L}(z) := \log p(z \mid \theta)$.[25] Both of these estimators can then be inserted into any existing gradient-based sampling or optimisation method to infer θ_0. Classically, such gradient and Hessian estimators are not accessible without an additional sensitivity analysis (Rackauckas et al., 2018).

To summarise, we have seen how the EKF0 gives rise to an uncertainty-aware[26] likelihood (41.12) with freely available estimators for its gradient (41.13) and Hessian (41.14). Our exposition followed Kersting et al. (2020) who, however, executed this strategy for the EKF0 (and not the EKS0). The filtering case is more complicated (because the equivalence with GP regression only holds locally), but essentially analogous. For the filtering case, the experiments in Kersting et al. (2020) demonstrate that, indeed, the resulting gradient-based inference schemes are significantly more efficient (i.e. they need fewer forward ODE solutions) than their gradient-free counterparts – both for MCMC sampling and for optimisation. Recently, Tronarp, Bosch, and Hennig (2022) introduced another method to solve ODE inverse problems by insertion of ODE filtering/smoothing into the likelihood.

Future research should try to link these two uncertainty-aware approaches, MCMC (by perturbations) and Gaussian approximations (by filtering). Notably, the particle ODE filter or smoother (§38.4) could alternatively be used to compute $p_h(x_\theta \mid \theta)$ in the perturbative scheme of Eq. (41.6).

Finally, we want to point out that the numerical error in inverse problems can also be modelled without explicitly employing a probabilistic ODE solver – by instead modelling the discretisation error as random variables and estimate their variance jointly with the ODE parameter (Matsuda and Miyatake, 2021).

[25] Note that the size of these gradient and Hessians scale, as desired, inversely with the combined uncertainty of the numerical error P and statistical noise $\sigma^2 I_M$. This means that they inherited the uncertainty-awareness of the probabilistic likelihood (41.12).

[26] See Figure 41.2.

▶ **41.3   Probabilistic Synthesis of Numerical Simulations and Observational Data**

Recall that one ensuing benefit of a well-designed probabilistic numerical method is the possibility to extend its probabilistic model to include observational data.[27] Classical methods, in contrast, do not treat numerical information probabilistically and are thus not able to jointly exploit numerical and statistical information. PN envisions to leverage this larger set of information for better, faster inference.

For ODE filters and smoothers, this hope was recently put into practice.[28] More precisely, they extended the SSM (38.10)–(38.13) to include additional linear observations $y_{1:M}^{\text{obs}} = [y_1^{\text{obs}}, \ldots, y_M^{\text{obs}}]$ of the ODE solution x at specific time points through another likelihood

[28] Schmidt, Krämer, and Hennig (2021)

$$p(y_n^{\text{obs}} \mid H^{\text{obs}} x_n) = \mathcal{N}(y_n^{\text{obs}}; H^{\text{obs}} x_n, R^{\text{obs}}), \qquad (41.15)$$

with $H^{\text{obs}} \in \mathbb{R}^{k \times D}$ and $0 \leq R^{\text{obs}} \in \mathbb{R}^{k \times k}$, for some $M \in \mathbb{N}$ and $k \in \{1, \ldots, D\}$. By this construction, this statistical data y^{obs} is incorporated in the same way as the numerical data $z = [z_1, \ldots, z_N]$ – in the sense that the observation likelihood (41.15) has the same form as the numerical likelihood (38.12). Hence, the resulting *extended* SSM is nothing but the previous SSM whose likelihood now also includes (41.15). This model is particularly advantageous because it is still a probabilistic SSM.[29]

For the application of inferring the latent force model of an ODE from observational data, Schmidt, Krämer, and Hennig (2021) go on to detail how to add a dynamic model for the latent force to the extended SSM, and how to then use the EKF1/EKS1 to infer this latent force model from data – in a *single* filtering/smoothing loop, i.e. jointly with the ODE solution and in linear time. This effectively removes an entire outer for-loop that is usually wrapped around classical solvers, leading to drastic performance increases (in real, wall-clock time, even accounting for the computational overhead of the EKF1/EKS1 over classic packaged solvers).

As a concrete example they use data from the *Covid-19 pandemic*, which provides an intuitive idea for the kind of data and mechanistic knowledge typical for real-world problems. We know that infection numbers are driven by a dynamic process that can be described approximately by an ODE (the widely used SIRD family of models), but that this model contains various unknown quantities – in their example, the time-varying contact rate among the population, modelled by a latent Gaussian process. But these infection numbers are also counted empirically. Both the mechanistic knowledge about infection dynamics and the empirical information provided by the case counts provide information that the EKF1/EKS1 can directly incorporate via an observation model as in Eq. (41.15). This allows inference on the latent contact rate in a single forward pass (rather than a laborious outer loop to fit the ODE solution), directly followed by forward simulation.

This insight is crucial from the point of view of machine learning. It is quite typical for real-world inference problems involving dynamical systems to feature both some knowledge about the underlying dynamics (up to some unknown parameters or latent forces, for example) and to observe some physical quantities. For such dynamical systems described by *PDEs*, Girolami et al. (2021) presented a similar way to fuse numerical and observational information by use of a probabilistic numerical PDE solver.

▶ **41.4   Partial Differential Equations (PDEs)**

PDEs are an equally well-established field of Probabilistic Numerics, but are beyond the scope of this text. We here only point to the relevant literature and link it to the above material on ODEs.

For linear PDEs, it is possible to construct *exact* probabilistic meshless methods by conditioning a (Gaussian) prior over the PDE solution on evaluations of the right-hand side. The corresponding Bayesian PDE solver was introduced by Cockayne et al. (2017a).[30] These methods were then applied to PDE-constrained inverse problems by Cockayne et al. (2017b) and to a real-world engineering problem by Oates et al. (2019b). However, as in the case of ODEs, exact inference is not possible for nonlinear PDEs, and approximations are necessary. To this end, Wang et al. (2021) introduced a first extension of the linear solvers to nonlinear PDEs. This line of work is philosophically similar to ODE filters and smoothers (§38). Importantly, Krämer, Schmidt, and Hennig (2022) showed how ODE filters – in combination with discretising space by a Gaussian process interpretation of finite difference methods – can be used to solve time-dependent PDEs.

There are also other probabilistic PDE solvers which follow the paradigm of perturbative solvers (§40). Chkrebtii et al. (2016) applied their ODE solver, without modifications, to

[30] This approach is particularly related to this chapter because, on linear ODEs, they coincide with the EKS0.

a parabolic PDE. Echoing their ODE solver (40.3), Conrad et al. (2017) provided a distinct solver for linear elliptic PDEs by perturbing a standard finite element method (FEM) with an additive random field. By a similar extension of their ODE solver (40.5), Abdulle and Garegnani (2021) introduced a FEM with randomised meshes. Another probabilistic modification of FEMs, which synthesises finite element models with data from external measurements, was proposed by Girolami et al. (2021); see §41.3.

There are further related approaches. For instance, Raissi, Perdikaris, and Karniadakis (2017) solve PDEs by use of probabilistic machine learning. Owhadi (2017) and Owhadi and Zhang (2017) employ gamblets to solve PDEs with rough coefficients.

Chapter VII
The Frontier

42

So What?

You've read the book: what should you do now? As you've learned, the future of Probabilistic Numerics (PN) is wide open, and your contributions to its shaping would be welcome. Many fundamental mathematical, engineering, and philosophical issues within the field remain to be addressed. In this section, we will highlight some open questions that are likely to influence the academic discussion on PN for at least the coming decade.

▶ **42.1   Where Will Probabilistic Numerics Find Application?**

The Probabilistic Numerical offerings of superior computation usage and uncertainty quantification are broadly applicable. However, to date, as detailed in Chapter V, PN has had substantive impact within only one application: global optimisation, particularly for hyperparameter tuning. Where will the next breakthrough success for PN be found? Relatedly, what software would best support the usage of PN?

▶ **42.2   Can Randomness be Banished from Computation?**

In §12.3, we argued against the use of randomness in computation. However, the non-random alternatives to most existing stochastic numerical algorithms are not practical. Can the Probabilistic Numerical view help to construct such alternatives that are both effective and lightweight?

▶ **42.3   Can we Scale Probabilistic Numerics?**

In some domains, notably Bayesian optimisation and Bayesian quadrature, PN remains limited by its practical restriction to

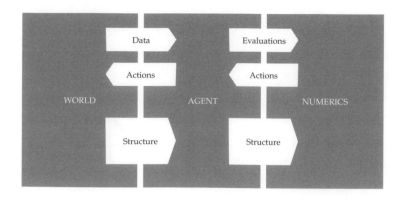

Figure 42.1: An adaption of Figure 1. A priori known structure is important to computational agents interacting with the world. Hard-coding knowledge, whether through architectural symmetries or priors, is superior to having to learn it from data. Identically, such structure is important to Probabilistic Numerical agents.

comparably low-dimensional problems. Can PN truly be made to scale to higher-dimensional problems in these settings? Solutions are likely to entail both better prior models and smart engineering. Note that this challenge has arguably already been overcome in the domains of differential equations and linear algebra, at least in the sense that, there, PN scales just as well as competing classic methods, and achieves very comparable runtimes. But for integration in particular, MCMC methods continue to provide a formidable competitor.

▶ **42.4   How Can Numerics be Tailored?**

This book has argued that structure is central to the performance of numerical algorithms (as per Figure 42.1). Numerical algorithms that are tailored to the needs of a problem will perform much better than generic algorithms. Examples were particularly rich in Chapter II (integration). Of course, Chapter III (linear algebra) also underlined that there are constraints on incorporating structure into algorithms that must be exceedingly lightweight. A core open question remains: how is such structure to be designed?

One approach is to leave the tailoring of a numerical algorithm to a human designer. We have argued that a user familiar with probabilistic modelling are well-equipped for such tailoring. If such a user has additionally acquired experience with a particular problem, there is likely to be no-one better placed to build a performant numerical algorithm. This user's time at the coalface of the problem, their hard-won intuitions, can be distilled into priors. These priors, the embodiment of human work, will save much computation work.

However, humans cannot be expected to design a unique

numerical algorithm for each required instance. Many numerical problems, hidden within nested layers of an intelligent system, remain inscrutable to the system's human overseer. Even if the overseer were omniscient, no human would have the capacity to design each and every numerical algorithm within a large system. For these reasons, automation is essential to numerical tailoring.

How should such automation be introduced? As we have mentioned, there is an obvious source of prior information about most numerical problems: its source code. Parsing this code to infer the structure of a partner numerical algorithm seems very useful. Of course, constraints on computation mean that not all features of the source can be incorporated. How should the decision of which structure to incorporate be automatically made?

The domain of ODEs provides an interesting pointer outside of the box. Here PN methods have recently shown drastic improvements in runtime over classic methods in situations where the numerical problem (here, the ODE) provides mechanistic structure to an otherwise empirical inference problem.[1] This provides a hint that prior information in computation may take a different form to the traditional notion in statistics. Perhaps it is not so much that human users provide priors explicitly. But that, by interacting more directly with each other through the probabilistic framework, computational steps can *inform* each other in a way that removes the need for some computations.

[1] Schmidt, Krämer, and Hennig (2021)

► 42.5   Can Probabilistic Numerical Models Be Identified at Runtime?

Section 42.4 posed questions about how to construct Probabilistic Numerical models. In addressing such questions, we might draw from existing analysis of statistical models, for instance, within statistical learning theory. Such analysis usually focusses on the information content of samples with respect to the model. Simply put, learning theorists ask whether a certain statistical model can principally be identified from a certain data source, and at which rate this identification is possible. When statistical concepts are applied to numerical computations, the cost of performing the computation enters the theoretical analysis as a new quantity of interest. Given a particular numerical task, one may try to find a solution by using computational resources in many different ways. An elaborate prior distribution, perhaps constructed from an automated analysis of the source code defining the numerical task, followed by a small number of well-chosen "observations" of a function involved in the numerical task? Or perhaps a very simple, lightweight prior, combined with a large number of "observations"? The practical requirement that numerical computations themselves have to be fundamentally tractable on a binary computer imposes a structural constrained on the model space that is currently not understood.

▶ **42.6   What Can We Say about Numerical Error given Finite Computation?**

Section 42.5 asked what kind of computational tasks can be solved in principle. The natural extension is to ask to which degree the error of a computation (the correct amount of uncertainty over it) can be identified at runtime, and at what computational cost. Evidently, as in all statistical settings, the precise error (here of a computation) cannot be found live, at runtime – if this were possible, one could simply subtract this error from the current estimate, and would arrive at a precise, tractable answer to the supposedly intractable numerical task. Nonetheless, we have seen throughout this book that the statistical toolbox *does* provide a useful variety of means of assessing the error. In fact, the scale, and some structure of the error can often be estimated at runtime with minimal or negligible computational overhead! As elsewhere in statistics, meaningful inference has to rely on assumptions of regularity and structure. But more work is needed to understand the precise limits of such statistical uncertaintly calibration.

▶ **42.7   What Does Uncertainty Mean within Probabilistic Numerics?**

Some questions within PN cannot be separated from philosophy. For example, there is an ongoing, deep, discussion about the meaning of uncertainty in the result of a deterministic computation.[2] In many ways, this discussion mirrors general charges levelled against probabilistic inference in the statistics and machine learning communities. By removing the ability to appeal to "randomness of nature", the numerical setting highlights the philosophical challenges of the probabilistic framework. But there are also some aspects that are genuinely unique to the numerical setting. Not all complicate the argument: some even simplify things. For example, prior assumptions can be argued for or against with much more precision in the numerical setting,

[2] Fillion and Corless (2014)

because a numerical task is defined in a formal (programming) language. Still, many members of the involved academic communities remain skeptical of the notion of uncertainty over the result of a computation. These central philosophical questions find new evidence and urgency within PN.

▶ 42.8 Can Computational Pipelines Be Harmonised?

As argued in the Introduction, PN offers a framework for managing pipelines of numerical algorithms. Constructing such a framework promises both rigorous quantification of uncertainty and computational savings. However, to date, little work on Probabilistic Numerical pipelines has been completed. Promising foundations for such work are to be found in the study of graphical models, particularly of message passing (featured in §5.1). Graphical models are an exceedingly powerful concept for the design of probabilistic models, and the automated construction of efficient inference algorithms.[3]

[3] Basic introductions can be found in the textbooks by Bishop (2006) and Barber (2012); an impressive, encyclopedic, treatment is provided by Koller and Friedman (2009).

▶ 42.9 Are There Limits to the Probabilistic Synthesis of Numerical and Statistical Information?

The statistical model – used by a probabilistic numerical methods to link numerical information to its quantity of interest – can sometimes be augmented to include observational data.[4] This information fusion between statistics and numerics has been shown to yield significant performance increases.[5]

From a pure information- or decision-theoretic viewpoint, there should be no limits to this approach. No matter if truly noisy or just approximate, all (uncertain) information can be expressed by probability distributions and exploited by use of probabilistic inference, that is by PN.

Future research will determine how far this equivalence can be taken, and whether a firm distinction between *statistical inference* and *numerical computation* should really be maintained.

[4] See paragraph "PN *consolidates numerical computation and statistical inference*" in the Introduction for the details of this argument.

[5] See §41.3 for a concrete example application.

Chapter VIII
Solutions to Exercises

Solutions to Exercises

Selected Exercises from Chapter I "Mathematical Background"

Solution to Exercise 4.7. Define the short-hand $w_i(x) = [K_{XX}^{-1} k_{Xx}]_i$ for the regression weights. To show the theorem, we insert the definition of m_x from Eq. (4.6) and use the reproducing property of k to write all instances of $f(x)$, $f(x_i)$ as an inner product:

$$s(x) := \sup_{f \in \mathcal{H}, \|f\| \leq 1} (m_x - f_x)^2 = \sup_{f \in \mathcal{H}, \|f\| \leq 1} \left(\sum_{i=1}^{N} f(x_i) w_i(x) - f_x \right)^2$$

$$= \sup_{f \in \mathcal{H}, \|f\| \leq 1} \left\langle \sum_i w_i(x) k(\cdot, x_i) - k(\cdot, x), f(\cdot) \right\rangle_{\mathcal{H}}^2.$$

Consider the function

$$\bar{f}_x(\cdot) := \frac{\sum_i w_i(x) k(\cdot, x_i) - k(\cdot, x)}{\| \sum_i w_i(x) k(\cdot, x_i) - k(\cdot, x) \|}.$$

By Definition 4.6, $\bar{f}_x$ is in $\mathcal{H}$, and it clearly has unit norm. We thus have

$$\left\langle \sum_i w_i(x) k(\cdot, x_i) - k(\cdot, x), \bar{f}_x(\cdot) \right\rangle_{\mathcal{H}}^2 \leq s(x),$$

because $s(x)$ is a supremum over such RKHS functions. But we also have, from the Cauchy–Schwarz inequality,

$$s(x) \leq \| \sum_i w_i(x) k(\cdot, x_i) - k(\cdot, x) \|^2 \cdot 1$$

$$= \left\langle \sum_i w_i(x) k(\cdot, x_i) - k(\cdot, x), \bar{f}_x(\cdot) \right\rangle_{\mathcal{H}}^2.$$

Thus, $s(x)$ is bounded above and below by that expression, so has to be equal to it. Using the reproducing property once again, we can rewrite:

$$
\begin{aligned}
s(x) &= \left\langle \sum_i w_i(x)k(\cdot, x_i) - k(\cdot, x), \bar{f}_x(\cdot) \right\rangle_{\mathcal{H}}^2 \\
&= \left\| \sum_i w_i(x)k(\cdot, x_i) - k(\cdot, x) \right\|_{\mathcal{H}}^2 \\
&= \sum_{ij} w_i(x)w_j(x)k(x_i, x_j) - 2\sum_i w_i(x)k(x, x_i) + k(x, x) \\
&= k_{xx} - k_{xX}K^{-1}k_{Xx},
\end{aligned}
$$

which completes the proof. $\qquad\qquad\qquad\qquad\qquad\qquad\qquad$ □

Solution to Exercise 5.5.   The main challenge in this exercise is to compute the matrix exponential of $F\delta t$ in $dz(t) = Fz(t)dt + Ld\omega$. The way to do this is to see that, by construction (from Eq. (5.28)), the three F matrices in Eqs. (5.29)–(5.30) (of size $N \times N$ for $N = 1, 2, 3$) have only the one degenerate eigenvalue $\lambda = -\xi$, and the corresponding eigenvector is given by $u \in \mathbb{R}^N$ with

$$
[u]_i = (-1)^{N-1-i}\xi^{-(N-1-i)}, \qquad i = 1, \dots, N.
$$

Thus, the eigenvalue of $A = \exp(Fh)$ is $e^{-\xi h}$, and one can find the three forms:

$$
\begin{aligned}
A_0 &= \exp(-\xi h), \\
A_1 &= \exp\left(h \begin{bmatrix} 0 & 1 \\ -\xi^2 & -2\xi \end{bmatrix} \right) = e^{-\xi h} \begin{bmatrix} \xi h + 1 & h \\ -\xi^2 h & (1 - \xi h) \end{bmatrix}, \\
A_2 &= \exp\left(h \begin{bmatrix} 0 & 1 & 0 \\ 0 & 0 & 1 \\ -\xi^3 & -3\xi^2 & -3\xi \end{bmatrix} \right) \\
&= e^{-\xi h} \begin{bmatrix} {}^1\!/_2(\xi^2 h^2 + 2\xi h + 2) & h(\xi h + 1) & {}^1\!/_2 h^2 \\ -{}^1\!/_2\xi^3 h^2 & -(\xi^2 h^2 - \xi h - 1) & -{}^1\!/_2 h(\xi h - 2) \\ {}^1\!/_2\xi^3 h(\xi h - 2) & \xi^2 h(\xi h - 3) & {}^1\!/_2(\xi^2 h^2 - 4\xi h + 2) \end{bmatrix}.
\end{aligned}
$$

The form for Q then just requires a comparably straightforward element-wise integral over polynomials in h.

Solution to Exercise 5.6.   For the estimation covariances P_i, the DARE corresponding to Eq. (5.31) is

$$
P_{i+1} = \tilde{Q} + \tilde{A}((P_i)^{-1} + \tilde{H}^{\mathsf{T}}\tilde{R}^{-1}\tilde{H})^{-1}\tilde{A}^{\mathsf{T}}. \qquad (42.1)
$$

Its parameters are transformations of those of the discrete-time system:

$$\tilde{H} := HA, \qquad \tilde{Q} := (Q^{-1} + H^{\mathsf{T}}R^{-1}H)^{-1}, \quad (42.2)$$
$$\tilde{R} := R + HQH^{\mathsf{T}}, \qquad \tilde{A} := \tilde{Q}Q^{-1}A. \qquad (42.3)$$

For the smoothed covariances P_i^s, let us write the corresponding DARE as

$$P_{i+1}^s = \hat{Q} + \hat{A}((P_i^s)^{-1} + \hat{H}^{\mathsf{T}}\hat{R}^{-1}\hat{H})^{-1}\hat{A}^{\mathsf{T}}.$$

Finding its parameters is more tricky if one tries to derive them from scratch, but becomes simpler once one has found the above DARE for P. Phrased in terms of the variables from Eqs. (42.2) and (42.3), they are

$$\hat{H} := \tilde{H}\tilde{A}, \qquad \hat{Q} := (\tilde{Q}^{-1} + \tilde{H}^{\mathsf{T}}\tilde{R}^{-1}\tilde{H})^{-1},$$
$$\hat{R} := \tilde{R} + \tilde{H}\tilde{Q}\tilde{H}^{\mathsf{T}}, \qquad \hat{A} := \hat{Q}\tilde{Q}^{-1}A.$$

A hint in case you are confused how to even reach a recursive statement for P^s: Start by re-arranging the smoother update Eq. (5.15) so that it only contains terms in P and P^s (i.e. not in P^-):

$$P_t^s = P_t + P_t A^{\mathsf{T}}((AP_tA^{\mathsf{T}} + Q)^{-1}P_{t+1}^s - I)(AP_tA^{\mathsf{T}} + Q)^{-1}AP_t.$$

Now write down the same equation for $t+1$, and replace all occurrences of P_{t+1} using (42.1). Then use the matrix inversion lemma, Eq. (15.9) to simplify the expression.

Selected Exercises from Chapter II "Integration"

Solution to Exercise 9.3. As an example of a pair f, p leading to pathological variance, consider the case if both the intregrand f and the proposal p are centred Gaussian measures

$$f(x) = \mathcal{N}(x; 0, s^2) = \frac{1}{\sqrt{2\pi s^2}} \exp\left(-\frac{x^2}{2s^2}\right), \quad \text{and}$$
$$p(x) = \mathcal{N}(x; 0, \sigma^2)$$

and set $s^2 > \sigma^2$. This question is a variation on Exercise 29.13 from MacKay (2003). MacKay also suggests the following interesting extension: implement MC integration for this situation, and examine the *empirical* mean and variance of this estimator as the number of drawn samples increases.

Selected Exercises from Chapter III "Linear Algebra"

Solution to Exercise 15.1.   Equations (15.4)–(15.7) follow directly from the definition in Eq. (15.2). For example, for Eq. (15.3):

$$[(A \otimes B)\vec{C}]_{ij} = \sum_{k\ell} A_{ik} B_{j\ell} C_{k\ell} = \sum_{k} A_{ik} \overrightarrow{CB^\intercal}_{kj} = \overrightarrow{ACB}_{ij}.$$

It is advantageous to prove Eq. (15.6) next. It follows directly from Eq. (15.4) using the eigendecomposition $A = V_A D_A V_A^{-1}$ (remember that D_A and D_B are diagonal matrices, containing eigenvalues $\lambda_{A,i}$ and $\lambda_{B,j}$ on their diagonals). To see that it is indeed the eigendecomposition of $A \otimes B$, we simply use Eq. (15.4) and the definition (15.2) again to see that the matrix $V_A \otimes V_N$ has the property

$$\begin{aligned}[(A \otimes B)(V_A \otimes V_B)]_{ij,k\ell} &= [(V_A \otimes V_B)(D_A \otimes D_B)]_{ij,k\ell} \\ &= \sum_{ab} V_{A,ia} V_{B,jb} \delta_{ak} \delta_{b\ell} \lambda_{A,a} \lambda_{B,b} \\ &= \lambda_{A,a} \lambda_{B,b} (V_A \otimes V_B)_{ia,jb}.\end{aligned}$$

Hence, this matrix contains the eigenvectors of $A \otimes B$ in its columns, and the eigenvalues are $\lambda_{A\otimes B,ab} = \lambda_{A,a} \lambda_{B,b}$. Using the previous result, we can now show Eq. (15.5), using properties of the determinant ($|AB| = |A||B|$) and the eigendecomposition (the determinant is the product of the eigenvectors)

$$|A \otimes B| = |V_A \otimes V_B||D_A \otimes D_B||V_A \otimes V_B| = |D_A \otimes D_B|.$$

Note again that $(D_A \otimes D_B)$ is a diagonal matrix with diagonal entries $(D_A \otimes D_B)_{ij,ij} = \lambda_{A,i} \lambda_{B,j}$. So its determinant is

$$|A \otimes B| = \prod_{ij} \lambda_{A,i} \lambda_{A,j} = \left(\prod_i \lambda_{A,i}^{\mathrm{rk}\,B} \right) \left(\prod_j \lambda_{B,j}^{\mathrm{rk}\,A} \right).$$

Solution to Exercise 15.2.   The fact that the Kronecker product of two SPD matrices is SPD follows directly from the results to Exercise 15.1. To see that Eq. (15.8) defines a matrix norm, simply note that it is a Euclidean vector-norm on $\vec{A}$, and thus inherits all the properties defined in note 3, on p. 128.

Solution to Exercise 19.1.   This is primarily an exercise in performing nested sums. Choosing $\Sigma_{ij,k\ell} = \delta_{ik} \delta_{j\ell} W_{ij}$ gives

$$((I \otimes S^\intercal)\Sigma)_{nm,k\ell} = \sum_{ij}^{N} \delta_{ni} S_{jm} \delta_{ik} \delta_{j\ell} W_{ij} = \delta_{nk} W_{k\ell} S_{\ell m},$$

and thus the Gram matrix G has elements

$$((I \otimes S^\mathsf{T})\Sigma(I \otimes S))_{nm,ab} = \sum_{k\ell}^{N} \delta_{nk} W_{k\ell} S_{\ell m} \delta_{ka} S_{\ell b}$$

$$= \delta_{na} \sum_{\ell}^{N} W_{n\ell} S_{\ell m} S_{\ell b}.$$

The remaining sum, with its non-trivial structure, can be written as computing the elements of a tensor $C_{nmb} \in \mathbb{R}^{N \times M \times M}$, whose computation requires $\mathcal{O}(N^2 M^2)$ operations (note that it is "symmetric" under exchange of m and b). The Kronecker symbol in front of the sum indicates that G can be written in block diagonal form, with N *different* blocks of $M \times M$ matrices, collected in C. So the inversion of G costs $\mathcal{O}(NM^3)$ (even though this is less than the cost of computing the elements of G themselves). One tempting way out is to assume that W is a rank-one object. This is of course not really acceptable since it restricts the model class severely, but leads to a pleasing insight. For choosing $W_{n\ell} = w_n w_\ell$ gives

$$G_{nmm,ab} = \delta_{na} w_n \left(S^\mathsf{T}(\operatorname{diag} w)S\right)_{mb}$$

$$= \left(\operatorname{diag} w \otimes \left(S^\mathsf{T}(\operatorname{diag} w)S\right)\right)_{nm,ab},$$

which is not a surprise, since this choice amounts to setting $\Sigma = \operatorname{diag} w \otimes \operatorname{diag} w$.

Selected Exercises from Chapter IV "Local Optimisation"

Solution to Exercise 25.2.   The first robot moves a distance of $\|x_1 - x_0\| = 0.1 \times \nabla f(x_0)[\mathrm{m}] = 0.5\,\mathrm{m}$, where the potential energy density is approximately

$$f(x_1) \approx f(x_1) - \|x_1 - x_0\| \nabla f(x_0)$$

$$= 4\,473\,\frac{\mathrm{J}}{\mathrm{kg}} - 0.5\,\mathrm{m} \times 5\frac{\mathrm{J}}{\mathrm{kg} \cdot \mathrm{m}} = 4\,448\,\frac{\mathrm{J}}{\mathrm{kg}}.$$

The second robot makes the literally microscopic step $0.1 \times \nabla f(x_0)[\mathrm{ft}] = 1.03 \times 10^{-6}\,[\mathrm{ft}] \approx 0.3\,\mathrm{\mu m}$, to where the potential energy density is

$$f(x_1) = 3.031 \times 10^{-2}\,\frac{\mathrm{Cal}}{\mathrm{oz}} - 1.03 \times 10^{-6}\,\mathrm{ft} \times 1.03 \times 10^{-5}\,\frac{\mathrm{Cal}}{\mathrm{oz} \cdot \mathrm{ft}}$$

$$= 3.031 \times 10^{-2}\,\frac{\mathrm{Cal}}{\mathrm{oz}} = 4\,473\,\frac{\mathrm{J}}{\mathrm{kg}}$$

(i.e., the energy density is unchanged, up to four significant digits). The point of this exercise is to show that gradient descent with a fixed step-size, although it may initially seem like the intuitive approach to optimisation, is not a well-defined algorithm. If the units of measure of f are $[f]$ and the units of x are $[x]$, then the units of ∇f are $[f]/[x]$, so adding a constant multiple of ∇f to x makes no sense. To get a meaningful algorithm, the step size α has to have units itself, and they must be $[x]^2/[f]$. This is the case, for example, for Newton's method.

The reason gradient descent with fixed step size has long been popular for some problem classes (like deep learning) is an implicit assumption that f has been smartly designed such that the Hessian's eigenvalues are all approximately unit, i.e. that the problem is well-conditioned. In this example, this holds for SI units: Moving about half a meter (similar to the length of human step) in between re-alignments is a plausible paradigm. The necessary pre-conditioning is sometimes concious, sometimes unconscious. For example, the deep learning community has found many "tricks of the trade"[6] to facilitate learning with neural networks (e.g. weight initialisation, data standardisation, etc.), many with the conscious or unconscious aim to condition the optimisation problem.

[6] Hinton (2012); Goodfellow, Bengio, and Courville (2016).

Solution to Exercise 26.1. We consider the finite set of function values $f_X \in \mathbb{R}^N$. The exercise stipulates a Gaussian prior $p(f_X)$ and likelihood $p(Y \mid f_X)$. For Gaussians, the location of the mean and maximum of the pdf coincide. Thus, the posterior mean $m_X = \mathbb{E}_{p(f_X|Y)}(f_X)$ is equal to the *maximum* of the product of prior and likelihood

$$m_X = \arg\max p(f_X)p(Y \mid f_X).$$

(The evidence is not a function of f_X, thus does not affect the location of the maximum and can be ignored.) The location of maxima is not affected by any monotonic re-scaling. So we can take the logarithm (a monotonic transformation) of the posterior. The logarithm of a Gaussian (again ignore all constant scaling factors) is a quadratic form. Because we are interested in minimisation instead of maximisation, we also multiply by (-1), to get

$$
\begin{aligned}
m_X &= \arg\min - \log p(f_X) - \log p(Y \mid f_X) \\
&= \underbrace{\frac{1}{2}(f_X - \mu_X)^\mathsf{T} k_{XX}^{-1}(f_X - \mu_X)}_{=\frac{1}{2}\|f_X-\mu_X\|_{k_{XX}}^2 =: r(x)} + \frac{1}{2}\|Y - f_X\|^2 \\
&= r(x) + \frac{1}{2}\sum_{i=1}^{N}(Y_i - f(x_i))^2.
\end{aligned}
$$

Which is clearly of the form of Eq. (26.2). MAP inference on the latent quantity w in probabilistic models (here, $w = f_X$) can generally be identified with regularised empirical risk minimisation if the data are conditionally independent given w. That is, if

$$p(Y \mid w) = \prod_{i=1}^{N} p(y_i \mid w).$$

A well-known theorem by de Finetti[7] states that this is the case if the likelihood is *exchangeable* (invariant under permutations of the data). However, the opposite direction does not always work: not all regularisers $r(w)$ and not all loss functions $\ell(y_i; w)$ can be interpreted as the negative logarithm of a prior and likelihood, respectively, since their exponential may not have finite integral, and thus can not be normalised to become a probability measure. For example, the *hinge loss* used in support vector machines is not the logarithm of a likelihood.[8]

Discussion of Exercise 26.4.   Some formal discussion of this problem can be found in §6.3 of Rasmussen and Williams (2006). The following argument gives an intuition: assume we do not want to encode the evaluation nodes t_i in the model a priori (i.e., we want the model to produce cubic spline mean functions in the noise-free, $\Lambda \to 0$, limit of *any* choice of t_i). Recall again that this posterior mean is a weighted sum of the covariance function $k(t_a, t_b)$ of our Gaussian process model. Hence, that kernel k has to be a piecewise cubic polynomial in t_a and t_b, with discontinuities in the second derivative only for $t_a = t_b$, at the evaluation nodes. That is, assuming our case of $t_a, t_b > 0$, it must be possible to write k as a polynomial in $|t_a - t_b|$, plus polynomial terms in t_a and t_b.[9] Hence, the posterior marginal variance $\mathrm{var}(f(t))$, which is also a weighted sum, of terms $k_{t,t_a} k_{t,t_b}$, is always at most a polynomial containing terms $|t_a - t_b|^\ell$ with $0 \leq \ell \leq 6$. Thus, it is certainly possible to construct priors which, given Y with likelihood (26.12), assign a different absolute uncertainty to each input location t but still revert to the cubic spline mean in the limit $\Lambda \to 0$. But their qualitative behaviour is equivalent in the sense that the marginal standard deviation (the "sausage of uncertainty" around the posterior mean) is locally cubic in t. This is again an instance of the deeper insight that, since a Gaussian process posterior mean and (co-)variance both involve the same kernel, a classic numerical estimate that is a particular least-squares MAP estimator is consistent with only a restricted set of probabilistic posterior error estimates in the sense of posterior standard-deviations.

[7] Diaconis and Freedman (1980)

[8] For further discussion, see pp. 144–145 in Rasmussen and Williams (2006).

[9] This is not contradicted by the form of Eq. (26.13), since

$$\min(t_a, t_b) = 1/2(|t_a + t_b| - |t_a - t_b|).$$

Selected Exercises from Chapter V "Global Optimisation"

Solution to Exercise 32.1.   We compute:

$$
\alpha_{\mathrm{EI}}(\boldsymbol{x}_n) = \int_{-\infty}^{\eta} f(\boldsymbol{x}_n)\, \mathcal{N}\big(f(\boldsymbol{x}_n); m(\boldsymbol{x}_n), \mathbb{V}(\boldsymbol{x}_n)\big)\, \mathrm{d}f(\boldsymbol{x}_n)
$$

$$
- \eta \int_{-\infty}^{\eta} \mathcal{N}\big(f(\boldsymbol{x}_n); m(\boldsymbol{x}_n), \mathbb{V}(\boldsymbol{x}_n)\big)\, \mathrm{d}f(\boldsymbol{x}_n)
$$

$$
= \int_{-\infty}^{\eta} f(\boldsymbol{x}_n)\, \frac{1}{\sqrt{2\pi\mathbb{V}(\boldsymbol{x}_n)}} \exp -\frac{1}{2}\frac{\big(f(\boldsymbol{x}_n) - m(\boldsymbol{x}_n)\big)^2}{\mathbb{V}(\boldsymbol{x}_n)}\, \mathrm{d}f(\boldsymbol{x}_n)
$$

$$
- \eta\, \Phi\big(\eta; m(\boldsymbol{x}_n), \mathbb{V}(\boldsymbol{x}_n)\big)
$$

$$
= \int_{-\infty}^{\eta - m(\boldsymbol{x}_n)} \frac{z + m(\boldsymbol{x}_n)}{\sqrt{2\pi\mathbb{V}(\boldsymbol{x}_n)}} \exp -\frac{1}{2}\frac{z^2}{\mathbb{V}(\boldsymbol{x}_n)}\, \mathrm{d}z
$$

$$
- \eta\, \Phi\big(\eta; m(\boldsymbol{x}_n), \mathbb{V}(\boldsymbol{x}_n)\big)
$$

$$
= -\sqrt{\frac{\mathbb{V}(\boldsymbol{x}_n)}{2\pi}} \int_{-\infty}^{\eta - m(\boldsymbol{x}_n)} \frac{-z}{\mathbb{V}(\boldsymbol{x}_n)} \exp -\frac{1}{2}\frac{z^2}{\mathbb{V}(\boldsymbol{x}_n)}\, \mathrm{d}z
$$

$$
+ m(\boldsymbol{x}_n)\, \Phi\big(-m(\boldsymbol{x}_n); 0, \mathbb{V}(\boldsymbol{x}_n)\big)
$$

$$
- \eta\, \Phi\big(\eta; m(\boldsymbol{x}_n), \mathbb{V}(\boldsymbol{x}_n)\big)
$$

$$
= -\sqrt{\frac{\mathbb{V}(\boldsymbol{x}_n)}{2\pi}} \left(\exp -\frac{1}{2}\frac{z^2}{\mathbb{V}(\boldsymbol{x}_n)}\right)_{-\infty}^{\eta - m(\boldsymbol{x}_n)}
$$

$$
+ \big(m(\boldsymbol{x}_n) - \eta\big)\, \Phi\big(\eta; m(\boldsymbol{x}_n), \mathbb{V}(\boldsymbol{x}_n)\big)
$$

$$
= -\mathbb{V}(\boldsymbol{x}_n)\mathcal{N}\big(\eta; m(\boldsymbol{x}_n), \mathbb{V}(\boldsymbol{x}_n)\big)
$$

$$
+ \big(m(\boldsymbol{x}_n) - \eta\big)\, \Phi\big(\eta; m(\boldsymbol{x}_n), \mathbb{V}(\boldsymbol{x}_n)\big). \qquad \square
$$

Solution to Exercise 32.2.   With a GP prior for the objective $f(x)$, we have the multi-variate Gaussian prior for the two function values $f_1 := f(x_1)$ and $f_2 := f(x_1)$ (assuming zero covariance between $f(x_1)$ and $f(x_2)$),

$$
p\left(\begin{bmatrix} f_1 \\ f_2 \end{bmatrix}\right) = \mathcal{N}\left(\begin{bmatrix} f_1 \\ f_2 \end{bmatrix}; \begin{bmatrix} m_1 \\ m_2 \end{bmatrix}, \underbrace{\begin{bmatrix} C_1 & 0 \\ 0 & C_2 \end{bmatrix}}_{=:C}\right).
$$

If we take an i.i.d. Gaussian noise model, $y_i = f_i + \varepsilon_i$, $\varepsilon_i \sim \mathcal{N}(0; \sigma^2)$, and using standard Gaussian identities (see §3), we can compute in closed-form the joint distribution,

$$
p\left(\begin{bmatrix} \varepsilon_1 \\ \varepsilon_2 \\ y_1 \\ y_2 \end{bmatrix}\right) = \mathcal{N}\left(\begin{bmatrix} \varepsilon_1 \\ \varepsilon_2 \\ y_1 \\ y_2 \end{bmatrix}; \begin{bmatrix} 0 \\ 0 \\ m_1 \\ m_2 \end{bmatrix}, \begin{bmatrix} \sigma^2 & 0 & \sigma^2 & 0 \\ 0 & \sigma^2 & 0 & \sigma^2 \\ \sigma^2 & 0 & C_1 + \sigma^2 & 0 \\ 0 & \sigma^2 & 0 & C_2 + \sigma^2 \end{bmatrix}\right).
$$

We can now calculate the posterior for the noise contributions:

$$p\left(\begin{bmatrix}\varepsilon_1\\\varepsilon_2\end{bmatrix}\middle|\begin{bmatrix}y_1\\y_2\end{bmatrix}\right)$$

$$=\mathcal{N}\left(\begin{bmatrix}\varepsilon_1\\\varepsilon_2\end{bmatrix};\sigma^2(C+\sigma^2I)^{-1}\begin{bmatrix}y_1-m_1\\y_2-m_2\end{bmatrix},\sigma^2I-\sigma^4(C+\sigma^2I)^{-1}\right)$$

$$=\mathcal{N}\left(\begin{bmatrix}\varepsilon_1\\\varepsilon_2\end{bmatrix};\sigma^2\begin{bmatrix}(C_1+\sigma^2)^{-1}(y_1-m_1)\\(C_2+\sigma^2)^{-1}(y_2-m_2)\end{bmatrix},\text{diag}\begin{bmatrix}\sigma^2-\sigma^4(C_1+\sigma^2)^{-1}\\\sigma^2-\sigma^4(C_2+\sigma^2)^{-1}\end{bmatrix}\right).$$

Note that if an observation y_i is lower than its prior mean m_i, the expected value for the noise contribution is negative. We will now assume that $C_1=C_2=\Sigma$, and, finally, calculate the posterior for the difference between noise contributions:

$$p\left(\varepsilon_1-\varepsilon_2\middle|\begin{bmatrix}y_1\\y_2\end{bmatrix}\right)=\mathcal{N}\left(\varepsilon_1-\varepsilon_2;\sigma^2(\Sigma+\sigma^2I)^{-1}(y_1-y_2-(m_1-m_2)),2\sigma^2-2\sigma^4(C_2+\sigma^2)^{-1}\right).$$

For clarity, we will now additionally assume that $m_1=m_2$. It can hence be seen that the expected value of the difference between noise contributions is proportional (with positive constant of proportionality $\sigma^2(\Sigma+\sigma^2I)^{-1}$) to the difference between observations. As such, and exploiting the linearity of expectation: if y_1 is smaller than y_2, the expected value for ε_1 is also smaller than ε_2. When combined with our note above, we conclude that if y_1 and y_2 are both lower than their prior means (as is typical for putative minima), the lower of the two is likely to have the noise contribution of larger magnitude.

Solution to Exercise 33.1. Our goal is to find a $\lambda(x_n,\mathcal{D}_n)$ such that the myopic expected loss is equal to the UCB criterion. That is, we require a loss function λ_{UCB} such that

$$\int\lambda_{\text{UCB}}(x_n,\mathcal{D}_n)p(y_n\mid\mathcal{D}_{n-1})\,dy_n=-m(x_n)-\beta_n\mathbb{V}(x_n)^{\frac12}.$$

There are many such solutions: the most trivial is

$$\lambda_{\text{UCB}}(x_n,\mathcal{D}_n)=-m(x_n)-\beta_n\mathbb{V}(x_n)^{\frac12},\qquad(42.4)$$

which expresses no dependence on the function value y_n at all. This is incompatible with the stated goal of optimisation to find low function values.

Another solution is the contrived loss function

$$\lambda_{\text{UCB}}(x_n,\mathcal{D}_n)=y_n\,\delta\left(y_n-\left(-m(x_n)-\beta_n\mathbb{V}(x_n)^{\frac12}\right)\right).\qquad(42.5)$$

The expectation of this loss against $p(y_n \mid \mathcal{D}_{n-1})$ will trivially produce an expected loss equal to the UCB acquisition function, (33.3).

Further solutions can be found by writing

$$\int \lambda_{\text{UCB}}(x_n, \mathcal{D}_n) p(y_n \mid \mathcal{D}_{n-1}) \, dy_n$$
$$= -\int y_n p(y_n \mid \mathcal{D}_{n-1}) \, dy_n - \beta_n \left(\int (y_n - m(x_n))^2 p(y_n \mid \mathcal{D}_{n-1}) \, dy_n \right)^{\frac{1}{2}},$$

$$\int (\lambda_{\text{UCB}}(x_n, \mathcal{D}_n) + y_n) p(y_n \mid \mathcal{D}_{n-1}) \, dy_n = -\beta_n \left(\int (y_n - m(x_n))^2 p(y_n \mid \mathcal{D}_{n-1}) \, dy_n \right)^{\frac{1}{2}}$$

and, multiplying both sides by $\beta_n \mathbb{V}(x_n)^{\frac{1}{2}}$,

$$\beta_n \mathbb{V}(x_n)^{\frac{1}{2}} \int (\lambda_{\text{UCB}}(x_n, \mathcal{D}_n) + y_n) p(y_n \mid \mathcal{D}_{n-1}) \, dy_n$$
$$= -\beta_n^2 \int (y_n - m(x_n))^2 p(y_n \mid \mathcal{D}_{n-1}) \, dy_n.$$

One possible solution has the integrand of the left-hand side equal to that of the right, so that

$$\beta_n \mathbb{V}(x_n)^{\frac{1}{2}} (\lambda_{\text{UCB}}(x_n, \mathcal{D}_n) + y_n) = -\beta_n^2 (y_n - m(x_n))^2.$$

We can hence finally arrive at

$$\lambda_{\text{UCB}}(x_n, \mathcal{D}_n) = -\beta_n (y_n - m(x_n))^2 \mathbb{V}(x_n)^{-\frac{1}{2}} - y_n. \quad (42.6)$$

Note that, as $\beta_n > 0$ and $\mathbb{V}(x_n) > 0$, this loss function is a concave quadratic in y_n. This is inappropriate for optimisation: it neglects the fact that the loss should lead to an unambiguous preference for y_n to be as low (e.g. large and negative) as possible. Speaking informally, a user would not be delighted if y_n was returned as positive infinity, whereas Eq. (42.6) would award such an outcome infinitely negative loss.

Note that all loss functions (Eqs. (42.4), (42.5), and (42.6)) implictly depend on the prior mean and covariance functions of the underlying GP, so as to be able to compute the GP posterior mean $m(x_n)$ and variance $\mathbb{V}(x_n)$ given $\mathcal{D}_n$. It is odd that the loss function should depend on the prior in this way; it implies that, even for identical outcomes, the loss will be different for different priors. In the case of Eq. (42.5), it is indefensible that the loss depends on y_n in no other way: that is, it is only if $y_n = m(x_n) + \beta_n \mathbb{V}(x_n)^{\frac{1}{2}}$ that Eq. (42.5) is non-zero.

More on this topic can be found in §6.1 of Garnett (2022).

References

Abdulle, A. and G. Garegnani. "Random time step probabilistic methods for uncertainty quantification in chaotic and geometric numerical integration". *Statistics and Computing* 30.4 (2020), pp. 907–932.

– "A probabilistic finite element method based on random meshes: A posteriori error estimators and Bayesian inverse problems". *Computer Methods in Applied Mechanics and Engineering* 384 (2021), p. 113961.

Adler, R. *The Geometry of Random Fields*. Wiley, 1981.

– *An introduction to continuity, extrema, and related topics for general Gaussian processes*. Vol. 12. Lecture Notes-Monograph Series. Institute of Mathematical Statistics, 1990.

Ajne, B. and T. Dalenius. "Några Tillämpningar av statistika idéer på numerisk integration". *Nordisk Mathematisk Tidskrift* 8.4 (1960), pp. 145–152.

Akhiezer, N. I. and I. M. Glazman. *Theory of linear operators in Hilbert space*. Vol. I& II. Courier Corporation, 2013.

Alizadeh, F., J.-P. A. Haeberley, and M. L. Overton. "Primal-Dual interior-point methods for semidefinite programming: Convergence rates, stability and numerical results". *SIAM Journal on Optimization* (1988), pp. 746–768.

Anderson, B. and J. Moore. *Optimal Filtering*. Prentice-Hall, 1979.

Anderson, E. et al. *LAPACK Users' Guide*. 3rd edition. Society for Industrial and Applied Mathematics (SIAM), 1999.

Arcangéli, R., M. C. López de Silanes, and J. J. Torrens. "An extension of a bound for functions in Sobolev spaces, with applications to (m, s)-spline interpolation and smoothing". *Numerische Mathematik* 107.2 (2007), pp. 181–211.

Armijo, L. "Minimization of functions having Lipschitz continuous first partial derivatives". *Pacific Journal of Mathematics* (1966), pp. 1–3.

Arnold, V. I. *Ordinary Differential Equations*. Universitext. Springer, 1992.

Arnoldi, W. "The principle of minimized iterations in the solution of the matrix eigenvalue problem". *Quarterly of Applied Mathematics* 9.1 (1951), pp. 17–29.

Aronszajn, N. "Theory of reproducing kernels". *Transactions of the AMS* (1950), pp. 337–404.

Arvanitidis, G. et al. "Fast and Robust Shortest Paths on Manifolds Learned from Data". *The 22nd International Conference on Artificial Intelligence and Statistics, AISTATS*. Vol. 89. Proceedings of Machine Learning Research. PMLR, 2019, pp. 1506–1515.

Azimi, J., A. Fern, and X. Z. Fern. "Batch Bayesian Optimization via Simulation Matching". *Advances in Neural Information Processing Systems, NeurIPS*. Curran Associates, Inc., 2010, pp. 109–117.

Azimi, J., A. Jalali, and X. Z. Fern. "Hybrid Batch Bayesian Optimization". *Proceedings of the 29th International Conference on Machine Learning, ICML*. icml.cc / Omnipress, 2012.

Bach, F. "On the equivalence between kernel quadrature rules and random feature expansions". *Journal of Machine Learning Research (JMLR)* 18.21 (2017), pp. 1–38.

Bach, F., S. Lacoste-Julien, and G. Obozinski. "On the Equivalence between Herding and Conditional Gradient Algorithms". *Proceedings of the 29th International Conference on Machine Learning, ICML*. icml.cc / Omnipress, 2012.

Baker, C. *The numerical treatment of integral equations*. Oxford: Clarendon Press, 1973.

Balles, L. and P. Hennig. "Dissecting Adam: The Sign, Magnitude and Variance of Stochastic Gradients". *Proceedings of the 35th International Conference on Machine Learning, ICML*. Vol. 80. Proceedings of Machine Learning Research. PMLR, 2018, pp. 413–422.

Balles, L., J. Romero, and P. Hennig. "Coupling Adaptive Batch Sizes with Learning Rates". *Proceedings of the Thirty-Third Conference on Uncertainty in Artificial Intelligence, UAI*. AUAI Press, 2017.

Bapat, R. *Nonnegative Matrices and Applications*. Cambridge University Press, 1997.

Barber, D. *Bayesian reasoning and machine learning*. Cambridge University Press, 2012.

Bardenet, R. and A. Hardy. "Monte Carlo with Determinantal Point Processes". *Annals of Applied Probability* (2019).

Bartels, S. et al. "Probabilistic linear solvers: a unifying view". *Statistics and Computing* 29.6 (2019), pp. 1249–1263.

Belhadji, A., R. Bardenet, and P. Chainais. "Kernel quadrature with DPPs". *Advances in Neural Information Processing Systems, NeurIPS*. 2019, pp. 12907–12917.

Bell, B. M. "The Iterated Kalman Smoother as a Gauss—Newton Method". *SIAM Journal on Optimization* 4.3 (1994), pp. 626–636.

Bell, B. M. and F. W. Cathey. "The iterated Kalman filter update as a Gauss– Newton method". *IEEE Transaction on Automatic Control* 38.2 (1993), pp. 294–297.

Benoit. "Note sûre une méthode de résolution des équations normales provenant de l'application de la méthode des moindres carrés a un système d'équations linéaires en nombre inférieure a celui des inconnues. Application de la méthode a la résolution d'un système défini d'équations linéaires. (Procédé du Commandant Cholesky)". *Bulletin Geodesique* (1924), pp. 67–77.

Berg, C., J. Christensen, and P. Ressel. *Harmonic Analysis on Semigroups — Theory of Positive Definite and Related Functions*. Springer, 1984.

Bergstra, J. et al. "Algorithms for Hyper-Parameter Optimization". *Advances in Neural Information Processing Systems, NeurIPS*. 2011, pp. 2546–2554.

Bertsekas, D. *Nonlinear programming*. Athena Scientific, 1999.

Bettencourt, J., M. Johnson, and D. Duvenaud. "Taylor-mode automatic differentiation for higher-order derivatives". *NeurIPS 2019 Workshop Program Transformations*. 2019.

Bini, D., B. Iannazzo, and B. Meini. *Numerical solution of algebraic Riccati equations*. SIAM, 2011.

Bishop, C. *Pattern Recognition and Machine Learning*. Springer, 2006.

Björck, Å. *Numerical Methods in Matrix Computations*. Springer, 2015.

Blight, B. J. N. and L. Ott. "A Bayesian Approach to Model Inadequacy for Polynomial Regression". *Biometrika* 62.1 (1975), pp. 79–88.

Borodin, A. N. and P. Salminen. *Handbook of Brownian Motion - Facts and Formulae*. 2nd edition. Probability and Its Applications. Birkhäuser Basel, 2002.

Bosch, N., P. Hennig, and F. Tronarp. "Calibrated adaptive probabilistic ODE solvers". *Artificial Intelligence and Statistics (AISTATS)*. 2021, pp. 3466–3474.

Bosch, N., F. Tronarp, and P. Hennig. "Pick-and-Mix Information Operators for Probabilistic ODE Solvers". *Artificial Intelligence and Statistics (AISTATS)*. 2022.

Bottou, L., F. E. Curtis, and J. Nocedal. "Optimization Methods for Large-Scale Machine Learning". *arXiv:1606.04838 [stat.ML]* (2016).

Bougerol, P. "Kalman filtering with random coefficients and contractions". *SIAM Journal on Control and Optimization* 31.4 (1993), pp. 942–959.

Boyd, S. and L. Vandenberghe. *Convex Optimization*. Cambridge University Press, 2004.

Bretthorst, G. *Bayesian Spectrum Analysis and Parameter Estimation*. Vol. 48. Lecture Notes in Statistics. Springer, 1988.

Briol, F. et al. "Frank-Wolfe Bayesian Quadrature: Probabilistic Integration with Theoretical Guarantees". *Advances in Neural Information Processing Systems, NeurIPS*. 2015, pp. 1162–1170.

Briol, F.-X. et al. "Probabilistic Integration: A Role in Statistical Computation?" *Statistical Science* 34.1 (2019), pp. 1–22.

Broyden, C. "A new double-rank minimization algorithm". *Notices of the AMS* 16 (1969), p. 670.

Butcher, J. C. *Numerical Methods for Ordinary Differential Equations*. 3rd edition. John Wiley & Sons, 2016.

Calandra, R. et al. "Bayesian Gait Optimization for Bipedal Locomotion". *Learning and Intelligent OptimizatioN (LION8)*. 2014a, pp. 274–290.

Calandra, R. et al. "An experimental comparison of Bayesian optimization for bipedal locomotion". *Proceedings of the International Conference on Robotics and Automation (ICRA)*. 2014b.

Cashore, J. M., L. Kumarga, and P. I. Frazier. "Multi-Step Bayesian Optimization for One-Dimensional Feasibility Determination" (2015).

Chai, H. R. and R. Garnett. "Improving Quadrature for Constrained Integrands". *The 22nd International Conference on Artificial Intelligence and Statistics, AISTATS*. Vol. 89. Proceedings of Machine Learning Research. PMLR, 2019, pp. 2751–2759.

Chen, R. T. Q. et al. "Self-Tuning Stochastic Optimization with Curvature-Aware Gradient Filtering". *Proceedings on "I Can't Believe It's Not Better!" at NeurIPS Workshops*. Vol. 137. Proceedings of Machine Learning Research. PMLR, 2020, pp. 60–69.

Chen, Y., M. Welling, and A. J. Smola. "Super-Samples from Kernel Herding". *Proceedings of the Twenty-Sixth Conference on Uncertainty in Artificial Intelligence, UAI*. AUAI Press, 2010, pp. 109–116.

Chen, Y. et al. "Bayesian optimization in AlphaGo". *arXiv:1812.06855 [cs.LG]* (2018).

Chevalier, C. and D. Ginsbourger. "Fast Computation of the Multi-Points Expected Improvement with Applications in Batch Selection". *Learning and Intelligent Optimization*. Lecture Notes in Computer Science. Springer Berlin Heidelberg, 2013, pp. 59–69.

Chkrebtii, O. A. and D. Campbell. "Adaptive step-size selection for state-space probabilistic differential equation solvers". *Statistics and Computing* 29 (2019), pp. 1285–1295.

Chkrebtii, O. A. et al. "Bayesian solution uncertainty quantification for differential equations". *Bayesian Anal.* 11.4 (2016), pp. 1239–1267.

Church, A. "On the concept of a random sequence". *Bulletin of the AMS* 46.2 (1940), pp. 130–135.

Cockayne, J. et al. "Probabilistic Numerical Methods for Partial Differential Equations and Bayesian Inverse Problems". *arXiv:1605.07811v3 [stat.ME]* (2017a).

Cockayne, J. et al. "A Bayesian conjugate gradient method (with discussion)". *Bayesian Analysis* 14.3 (2019a), pp. 937–1012.

Cockayne, J. et al. "Bayesian Probabilistic Numerical Methods". *SIAM Review* 61.4 (2019b), pp. 756–789.

Cockayne, J. et al. "Probabilistic numerical methods for PDE-constrained Bayesian inverse problems". *AIP Conference Proceedings* 1853.1 (2017b), p. 060001.

Colas, C., O. Sigaud, and P.-Y. Oudeyer. "How Many Random Seeds? Statistical Power Analysis in Deep Reinforcement Learning Experiments". *arXiv:1806.08295 [cs.LG]* (2018).

Conrad, P. R. et al. "Statistical analysis of differential equations: introducing probability measures on numerical solutions". *Statistics and Computing* 27.4 (2017), pp. 1065–1082.

Cottle, R. "Manifestations of the Schur complement". *Linear Algebra Applications* 8 (1974), pp. 189–211.

Cox, R. "Probability, frequency and reasonable expectation". *American Journal of Physics* 14.1 (1946), pp. 1–13.

Cranmer, K., J. Brehmer, and G. Louppe. "The frontier of simulation-based inference". *Proceedings of the National Academy of Sciences* (2020).

Cunningham, J., P. Hennig, and S. Lacoste-Julien. "Gaussian Probabilities and Expectation Propagation". *arXiv:1111.6832 [stat.ML]* (2011).

Dahlquist, G. G. "A special stability problem for linear multistep methods". *BIT Numerical Mathematics* 3 (1963), pp. 27–43.

Dangel, F., F. Kunstner, and P. Hennig. "BackPACK: Packing more into Backprop". *8th International Conference on Learning Representations, ICLR*. 2020.

Dashti, M. and A. M. Stuart. "The Bayesian Approach to Inverse Problems". *Handbook of Uncertainty Quantification*. Springer International Publishing, 2017, pp. 311–428.

Davidon, W. *Variable metric method for minimization*. Tech. rep. Argonne National Laboratories, Ill., 1959.

Davis, P. "Leonhard Euler's Integral: A Historical Profile of the Gamma Function." *American Mathematical Monthly* 66.10 (1959), pp. 849–869.

Davis, P. and P. Rabinowitz. *Methods of Numerical Integration*. 2nd edition. Academic Press, 1984.

Dawid, A. "Some matrix-variate distribution theory: Notational considerations and a Bayesian application". *Biometrika* 68.1 (1981), pp. 265–274.

Daxberger, E. and B. Low. "Distributed Batch Gaussian Process Optimization". *PMLR*. 2017, pp. 951–960.

Daxberger, E. et al. "Laplace Redux-Effortless Bayesian Deep Learning". *Advances in Neural Information Processing Systems, NeurIPS*. Vol. 34. 2021.

Demmel, J. W. *Applied Numerical Linear Algebra*. SIAM, 1997.

Dennis, J. "On some methods based on Broyden's secant approximations". *Numerical Methods for Non-Linear Optimization*. 1971.

Dennis, J. E. and J. J. Moré. "Quasi-Newton methods, motivation and theory". *SIAM Review* 19.1 (1977), pp. 46–89.

Desautels, T., A. Krause, and J. W. Burdick. "Parallelizing Exploration-Exploitation Tradeoffs with Gaussian Process Bandit Optimization". *Proceedings of the 29th International Conference on Machine Learning, ICML*. icml.cc / Omnipress, 2012.

Deuflhard, P. and F. Bornemann. *Scientific Computing with Ordinary Differential Equations*. Vol. 42. Springer Texts in Applied Mathematics. Springer, 2002.

Diaconis, P. "Bayesian numerical analysis". *Statistical decision theory and related topics* IV (1988), pp. 163–175.

Diaconis, P. and D. Freedman. "Finite exchangeable sequences". *The Annals of Probability* (1980), pp. 745–764.

Diaconis, P. and D. Ylvisaker. "Conjugate priors for exponential families". *The Annals of Statistics* 7.2 (1979), pp. 269–281.

Dick, J., F. Y. Kuo, and I. H. Sloan. "High-dimensional integration: the quasi-Monte Carlo way". *Acta Numerica* 22 (2013), pp. 133–288.

Dixon, L. "Quasi-Newton algorithms generate identical points". *Mathematical Programming* 2.1 (1972a), pp. 383–387.

– "Quasi Newton techniques generate identical points II: The proofs of four new theorems". *Mathematical Programming* 3.1 (1972b), pp. 345–358.

Dormand, J. and P. Prince. "A family of embedded Runge-Kutta formulae". *Journal of computational and applied mathematics* (1980), pp. 19–26.

Doucet, A., N. de Freitas, and N. Gordon. "An Introduction to Sequential Monte Carlo Methods". *Sequential Monte Carlo Methods in Practice*. Statistics for Engineering and Information Science. Springer, New York, NY, 2001, pp. 3–14.

Driscoll, M. "The reproducing kernel Hilbert space structure of the sample paths of a Gaussian process". *Probability Theory and Related Fields* 26.4 (1973), pp. 309–316.

Eich-Soellner, E. and C. Führer. "Implicit Ordinary Differential Equations". *Numerical Methods in Multibody Dynamics*. Vieweg+Teubner Verlag, 1998, pp. 139–192.

Einstein, A. "Zur Theorie der Brownschen Bewegung". *Annalen der Physik* (1906), pp. 371–381.

Faßbender, H. *Symplectic methods for the symplectic eigenproblem*. Springer Science & Business Media, 2007.

Fillion, N. and R. M. Corless. "On the epistemological analysis of modeling and computational error in the mathematical sciences". *Synthese* 191.7 (2014), pp. 1451–1467.

Fletcher, R. "A new approach to variable metric algorithms". *The Computer Journal* 13.3 (1970), p. 317.

– "Conjugate Gradients Methods for Indefinite Systems". *Dundee Biennial Conference on Numerical Analysis*. 1975, pp. 73–89.

Fletcher, R. and C. Reeves. "Function minimization by conjugate gradients". *The Computer Journal* (1964), pp. 149–154.

Fowler, D. and E. Robson. "Square root approximations in Old Babylonian mathematics: YBC 7289 in context". *Historia Mathematica* 25.4 (1998), pp. 366–378.

Frazier, P., W. Powell, and S. Dayanik. "The Knowledge-Gradient Policy for Correlated Normal Beliefs". *INFORMS Journal on Computing* 21.4 (2009), pp. 599–613.

Fredholm, E. I. "Sur une classe d'équations fonctionnelles". *Acta Mathematica* 27 (1903), pp. 365–390.

Freitas, N. de, A. J. Smola, and M. Zoghi. "Exponential Regret Bounds for Gaussian Process Bandits with Deterministic Observations". *Proceedings of the 29th International Conference on Machine Learning, ICML*. icml.cc / Omnipress, 2012.

Freund, R. W. and N. M. Nachtigal. "QMR: a Quasi-Minimal Residual Method for non-Hermitian Linear Systems". *Numerische mathematik* 60.1 (1991), pp. 315–339.

Fröhlich, C. et al. "Bayesian Quadrature on Riemannian Data Manifolds". *Proceedings of the 38th International Conference on Machine Learning, ICML*. Vol. 139. Proceedings of Machine Learning Research. PMLR, 2021, pp. 3459–3468.

Garnett, R. *Bayesian Optimization*. Cambridge University Press, 2022.

Garnett, R., M. A. Osborne, and S. J. Roberts. "Bayesian optimization for sensor set selection". *ACM/IEEE International Conference on Information Processing in Sensor Networks*. ACM. 2010, pp. 209–219.

Garnett, R. et al. "Bayesian Optimal Active Search and Surveying". *Proceedings of the 29th International Conference on Machine Learning, ICML*. icml.cc / Omnipress, 2012.

Gauss, C. F. *Theoria motus corporum coelestium in sectionibus conicis solem ambientium*. Perthes, F. and Besser, I.H., 1809.

– "Methodus nova integralium valores per approximationem inveniendi". *Proceedings of the Royal Scientific Society of Göttingen*. Heinrich Dieterich, 1814.

Gautschi, W. *Orthogonal Polynomials—Computation and Approximation*. Oxford University Press, 2004.

Genz, A. "Numerical computation of rectangular bivariate and trivariate normal and *t* probabilities". *Statistics and Computing* 14.3 (2004), pp. 251–260.

Gerritsma, J., R. Onnink, and A. Versluis. "Geometry, resistance and stability of the delft systematic yacht hull series". *International shipbuilding progress* 28.328 (1981).

Ginsbourger, D., R. Le Riche, and L. Carraro. "A multi-points criterion for deterministic parallel global optimization based on Gaussian processes" (2008).

– "Kriging is well-suited to parallelize optimization". *Computational Intelligence in Expensive Optimization Problems* 2 (2010), pp. 131–162.

Girolami, M. et al. "The statistical finite element method (statFEM) for coherent synthesis of observation data and model predictions". *Computer Methods in Applied Mechanics and Engineering* 375 (2021), p. 113533.

Gittins, J. C. "Bandit processes and dynamic allocation indices". *Journal of the Royal Statistical Society. Series B (Methodological)* (1979), pp. 148–177.

Goldberg, D. *Genetic Algorithms in Search, Optimization, and Machine Learning*. Addison-Wesley, 1989.

Goldfarb, D. "A family of variable metric updates derived by variational means". *Mathematics of Computation* 24.109 (1970), pp. 23–26.

Golub, G. and C. Van Loan. *Matrix computations*. Johns Hopkins University Press, 1996.

Gómez-Bombarelli, R. et al. "Automatic chemical design using a data-driven continuous representation of molecules". *arXiv:1610.02415 [cs.LG]* (2016).

González, J., M. A. Osborne, and N. D. Lawrence. "GLASSES: Relieving The Myopia Of Bayesian Optimisation". *Proceedings of the 19th International Conference on Artificial Intelligence and Statistics, AISTATS*. Vol. 51. JMLR Workshop and Conference Proceedings. JMLR.org, 2016, pp. 790–799.

González, J. et al. "Batch Bayesian Optimization via Local Penalization". *Proceedings of the 19th International Conference on Artificial Intelligence and Statistics, AISTATS*. Vol. 51. JMLR Workshop and Conference Proceedings. JMLR.org, 2016, pp. 648–657.

Goodfellow, I. J., Y. Bengio, and A. Courville. *Deep Learning*. MIT Press, 2016.

Gradshteyn, I. and I. Ryzhik. *Table of Integrals, Series, and Products*. 7th edition. Academic Press, 2007.

Grcar, J. "Mathematicians of Gaussian elimination". *Notices of the AMS* 58.6 (2011), pp. 782–792.

Greenbaum, A. *Iterative Methods for Solving Linear Systems*. Vol. 17. SIAM, 1997.

Greenstadt, J. "Variations on variable-metric methods". *Mathematics of Computation* 24 (1970), pp. 1–22.

Grewal, M. S. and A. P. Andrews. *Kalman Filtering: Theory and Practice Using MATLAB*. John Wiley & Sons, Inc., 2001.

Griewank, A. *Evaluating Derivatives: Principles and Techniques of Algorithmic Differentiation*. Frontiers in Applied Mathematics. SIAM, 2000.

Griewank, A. and A. Walther. *Evaluating Derivatives*. Cambridge University Press, 2008.

Gunter, T. et al. "Sampling for Inference in Probabilistic Models with Fast Bayesian Quadrature". *Advances in Neural Information Processing Systems, NeurIPS*. 2014, pp. 2789–2797.

Hager, W. "Updating the Inverse of a Matrix". *SIAM Review* 31.2 (1989), pp. 221–239.

Hairer, E., C. Lubich, and G. Wanner. *Geometric numerical integration: structure-preserving algorithms for ordinary differential equations*. Vol. 31. Springer Science & Business Media, 2006.

Hairer, E., S. Nørsett, and G. Wanner. *Solving Ordinary Differential Equations I – Nonstiff Problems*. 2nd edition. Vol. 8. Springer Series in Computational Mathematics. Springer, 1993.

Hairer, E. and G. Wanner. *Solving Ordinary Differential Equations II – Stiff and Differential-Algebraic Problems*. 2nd edition. Vol. 14. Springer, 1996.

Hartikainen, J. and S. Särkkä. "Kalman filtering and smoothing solutions to temporal Gaussian process regression models". *IEEE International Workshop on Machine Learning for Signal Processing (MLSP), 2010*. 2010, pp. 379–384.

Helmert, F. "Über die Berechnung des wahrscheinlichen Fehlers aus einer endlichen Anzahl wahrer Beobachtungsfehler". *Zeitschrift für Mathematik und Physik* 20 (1875), pp. 300–303.

Henderson, P. et al. "Deep Reinforcement Learning That Matters". *Proceedings of the Thirty-Second AAAI Conference on Artificial Intelligence*. AAAI Press, 2018, pp. 3207–3214.

Hennig, P. "Fast Probabilistic Optimization from Noisy Gradients". *Proceedings of the 30th International Conference on Machine Learning, ICML*. Vol. 28. JMLR Workshop and Conference Proceedings. JMLR.org, 2013, pp. 62–70.

– "Probabilistic Interpretation of Linear Solvers". *SIAM Journal on Optimization* (2015), pp. 210–233.

Hennig, P. and S. Hauberg. "Probabilistic Solutions to Differential Equations and their Application to Riemannian Statistics". *Proceedings of the Seventeenth International Conference on Artificial Intelligence and Statistics, AISTATS*. Vol. 33. JMLR Workshop and Conference Proceedings. JMLR.org, 2014, pp. 347–355.

Hennig, P. and M. Kiefel. "Quasi-Newton methods: A new direction". *International Conference on Machine Learning, ICML*. 2012.

Hennig, P., M. Osborne, and M. Girolami. "Probabilistic numerics and uncertainty in computations". *Proceedings of the Royal Society of London A: Mathematical, Physical and Engineering Sciences* 471.2179 (2015).

Hennig, P. and C. Schuler. "Entropy search for information-efficient global optimization". *Journal of Machine Learning Research* 13.Jun (2012), pp. 1809–1837.

Hernández-Lobato, J. M. et al. "Predictive Entropy Search for Bayesian Optimization with Unknown Constraints". *Proceedings of the 32nd International Conference on Machine Learning, ICML*. Vol. 37. JMLR Workshop and Conference Proceedings. JMLR.org, 2015, pp. 1699–1707.

Hestenes, M. and E. Stiefel. "Methods of conjugate gradients for solving linear systems". *Journal of Research of the National Bureau of Standards* 49.6 (1952), pp. 409–436.

Hinton, G. "A practical guide to training restricted Boltzmann machines". *Neural Networks: Tricks of the Trade*. Springer, 2012, pp. 599–619.

Hoffman, M., E. Brochu, and N. de Freitas. "Portfolio Allocation for Bayesian Optimization". *UAI 2011, Proceedings of the Twenty-Seventh Conference on Uncertainty in Artificial Intelligence*. AUAI Press, 2011, pp. 327–336.

Hoffman, M. and Z. Ghahramani. "Output-Space Predictive Entropy Search for Flexible Global Optimization". *NIPS workshop on Bayesian optimization*. 2015.

Hoos, H. H. "Programming by optimization". *Communications of the ACM* 55.2 (2012), pp. 70–80.

Horst, R. and H. Tuy. *Global optimization: Deterministic approaches*. Springer Science & Business Media, 2013.

Houlsby, N. et al. "Bayesian Active Learning for Classification and Preference Learning". *arXiv:1112.5745 [stat.ML]* (2011).

Hull, T. et al. "Comparing numerical methods for ordinary differential equations". *SIAM Journal on Numerical Analysis* 9.4 (1972), pp. 603–637.

Huszar, F. and D. Duvenaud. "Optimally-Weighted Herding is Bayesian Quadrature". *Proceedings of the Twenty-Eighth Conference on Uncertainty in Artificial Intelligence, UAI*. AUAI Press, 2012, pp. 377–386.

Hutter, F., H. Hoos, and K. Leyton-Brown. "Sequential Model-Based Optimization for General Algorithm Configuration". *Proceedings of LION-5*. 2011, pp. 507–523.

Hutter, M. *Universal Artificial Intelligence*. Texts in Theoretical Computer Science. Springer, 2010.

Ibragimov, I. and R. Has'minskii. *Statistical Estimation: Asymptotic Theory*. Springer, New York, 1981.

Ipsen, I. *Numerical matrix analysis: Linear systems and least squares*. SIAM, 2009.

Islam, R. et al. "Reproducibility of Benchmarked Deep Reinforcement Learning Tasks for Continuous Control". *arXiv:1708.04133 [cs.LG]* (2017).

Isserlis, L. "On a formula for the product-moment coefficient of any order of a normal frequency distribution in any number of variables". *Biometrika* 12.1/2 (1918), pp. 134–139.

Jaynes, E. and G. Bretthorst. *Probability Theory: the Logic of Science*. Cambridge University Press, 2003.

Jiang, S. et al. "Efficient Nonmyopic Active Search". *Proceedings of the 34th International Conference on Machine Learning, ICML*. Vol. 70. Proceedings of Machine Learning Research. PMLR, 2017, pp. 1714–1723.

Jiang, S. et al. "Efficient nonmyopic Bayesian optimization and quadrature". *arXiv:1909.04568 [cs.LG]* (2019).

– "BINOCULARS for efficient, nonmyopic sequential experimental design". *Proceedings of the 37th International Conference on Machine Learning, ICML*. Vol. 119. Proceedings of Machine Learning Research. PMLR, 2020, pp. 4794–4803.

John, D., V. Heuveline, and M. Schober. "GOODE: A Gaussian Off-The-Shelf Ordinary Differential Equation Solver". *Proceedings of the 36th International Conference on Machine Learning, ICML*. Vol. 97. Proceedings of Machine Learning Research. PMLR, 2019, pp. 3152–3162.

Jones, D. "A taxonomy of global optimization methods based on response surfaces". *Journal of Global Optimization* 21.4 (2001), pp. 345–383.

Jones, D., M. Schonlau, and W. Welch. "Efficient global optimization of expensive black-box functions". *Journal of Global Optimization* 13.4 (1998), pp. 455–492.

Kadane, J. B. and G. W. Wasilkowski. "Average case epsilon-complexity in computer science: A Bayesian view". *Bayesian Statistics 2, Proceedings of the Second Valencia International Meeting*. 1985, pp. 361–374.

Kálmán, R. "A New Approach to Linear Filtering and Prediction Problems". *Journal of Fluids Engineering* 82.1 (1960), pp. 35–45.

Kanagawa, M. and H. Hennig. "Convergence Guarantees for Adaptive Bayesian Quadrature Methods". *Advances in Neural Information Processing Systems, NeurIPS*. 2019, pp. 6234–6245.

Kanagawa, M., B. K. Sriperumbudur, and K. Fukumizu. "Convergence Analysis of Deterministic Kernel-Based Quadrature Rules in Misspecified Settings". *Foundations of Computational Mathematics* 20.1 (2020), pp. 155–194.

Kanagawa, M. et al. "Gaussian Processes and Kernel Methods: A Review on Connections and Equivalences". *arXiv:1807.02582 [stat.ML]* (2018).

Karatzas, I. and S. E. Shreve. *Brownian Motion and Stochastic Calculus*. Springer, 1991.

Karvonen, T. and S. Särkkä. "Classical quadrature rules via Gaussian processes". *IEEE International Workshop on Machine Learning for Signal Processing (MLSP)*. Vol. 27. 2017.

Kennedy, M. "Bayesian quadrature with non-normal approximating functions". *Statistics and Computing* 8.4 (1998), pp. 365–375.

Kersting, H. "Uncertainty-Aware Numerical Solutions of ODEs by Bayesian Filtering". PhD thesis. Eberhard Karls Universität Tübingen, 2020.

Kersting, H. and P. Hennig. "Active Uncertainty Calibration in Bayesian ODE Solvers". *Proceedings of the Thirty-Second Conference on Uncertainty in Artificial Intelligence, UAI.* AUAI Press, 2016.

Kersting, H. and M. Mahsereci. "A Fourier State Space Model for Bayesian ODE Filters". *Workshop on Invertible Neural Networks, Normalizing Flows, and Explicit Likelihood Models, ICML.* 2020.

Kersting, H., T. J. Sullivan, and P. Hennig. "Convergence Rates of Gaussian ODE Filters". *Statistics and Computing* 30.6 (2020), pp. 1791–1816.

Kersting, H. et al. "Differentiable Likelihoods for Fast Inversion of 'Likelihood-Free' Dynamical Systems". *Proceedings of the 37th International Conference on Machine Learning, ICML.* Vol. 119. Proceedings of Machine Learning Research. PMLR, 2020, pp. 5198–5208.

Kimeldorf, G. S. and G. Wahba. "A correspondence between Bayesian estimation on stochastic processes and smoothing by splines". *The Annals of Mathematical Statistics* 41.2 (1970), pp. 495–502.

Kingma, D. P. and J. Ba. "Adam: A Method for Stochastic Optimization". *3rd International Conference on Learning Representations, ICLR.* 2015.

Kitagawa, G. "Non-Gaussian State—Space Modeling of Nonstationary Time Series". *Journal of the American Statistical Association* 82.400 (1987), pp. 1032–1041.

Klein, A. et al. "Fast Bayesian Optimization of Machine Learning Hyperparameters on Large Datasets". *Proceedings of the 20th International Conference on Artificial Intelligence and Statistics, AISTATS.* Vol. 54. Proceedings of Machine Learning Research. PMLR, 2017, pp. 528–536.

Ko, C.-W., J. Lee, and M. Queyranne. "An exact algorithm for maximum entropy sampling". *Operations Research* 43.4 (1995), pp. 684–691.

Kochenderfer, M. J. *Decision Making Under Uncertainty: Theory and Application.* The MIT Press, 2015.

Koller, D. and N. Friedman. *Probabilistic Graphical Models: Principles and Techniques.* MIT Press, 2009.

Kolmogorov, A. "Zur Theorie der Markoffschen Ketten". *Mathematische Annalen* 112 (1 1936), pp. 155–160.

Kolmogorov, A. "Three approaches to the quantitative definition of information". *International Journal of Computer Mathematics* 2.1-4 (1968), pp. 157–168.

Krämer, N. and P. Hennig. "Stable Implementation of Probabilistic ODE Solvers". *arXiv:2012.10106 [stat.ML]* (2020).

Krämer, N. and P. Hennig. "Linear-Time Probabilistic Solutions of Boundary Value Problems". *Advances in Neural Information Processing Systems, NeurIPS*. 2021.

Krämer, N., J. Schmidt, and P. Hennig. "Probabilistic Numerical Method of Lines for Time-Dependent Partial Differential Equations". *Artificial Intelligence and Statistics (AISTATS)*. 2022.

Krämer, N. et al. "Probabilistic ODE Solutions in Millions of Dimensions". *arXiv:2110.11812 [stat.ML]* (2021).

Krizhevsky, A. and G. Hinton. *Learning multiple layers of features from tiny images*. Tech. rep. 2009.

Kushner, H. J. "A New Method of Locating the Maximum Point of an Arbitrary Multipeak Curve in the Presence of Noise". *Journal of Basic Engineering* 86.1 (1964), pp. 97–106.

Kushner, H. J. "A versatile stochastic model of a function of unknown and time varying form". *Journal of Mathematical Analysis and Applications* 5.1 (1962), pp. 150–167.

Lai, T. L. and H. Robbins. "Asymptotically efficient adaptive allocation rules". *Advances in Applied Mathematics* 6.1 (1985), pp. 4–22.

Lanczos, C. "An iteration method for the solution of the eigenvalue problem of linear differential and integral operators". *Journal of Research of the National Bureau of Standards* 45 (1950), pp. 255–282.

Laplace, P. *Théorie Analytique des Probabilités*. 2nd edition. V. Courcier, Paris, 1814.

Larkin, F. "Gaussian measure in Hilbert space and applications in numerical analysis". *Journal of Mathematics* 2.3 (1972).

Lauritzen, S. "Time series analysis in 1880: A discussion of contributions made by TN Thiele". *International Statistical Review/Revue Internationale de Statistique* (1981), pp. 319–331.

Lauritzen, S. and D. Spiegelhalter. "Local computations with probabilities on graphical structures and their application to expert systems". *Journal of the Royal Statistical Society. Series B (Methodological)* 50 (1988), pp. 157–224.

Le Cam, L. "Convergence of estimates under dimensionality restrictions". *Annals of Statistics* 1 (1973), pp. 38–53.

Lecomte, C. "Exact statistics of systems with uncertainties: An analytical theory of rank-one stochastic dynamic systems". *Journal of Sound and Vibration* 332.11 (2013), pp. 2750–2776.

Lemaréchal, C. "Cauchy and the Gradient Method". *Documenta Mathematica* Extra Volume: Optimization Stories (2012), pp. 251–254.

Lemieux, C. *Monte Carlo and quasi-Monte Carlo sampling*. Springer Science & Business Media, 2009.

Lie, H. C., M. Stahn, and T. J. Sullivan. "Randomised one-step time integration methods for deterministic operator differential equations". *Calcolo* 59.1 (2022), p. 13.

Lie, H. C., A. M. Stuart, and T. J. Sullivan. "Strong convergence rates of probabilistic integrators for ordinary differential equations". *Statistics and Computing* 29.6 (2019), pp. 1265–1283.

Lie, H. C., T. J. Sullivan, and A. L. Teckentrup. "Random Forward Models and Log-Likelihoods in Bayesian Inverse Problems". *SIAM/ASA Journal on Uncertainty Quantification* 6.4 (2018), pp. 1600–1629.

Lindström, E., H. Madsen, and J. N. Nielsen. *Statistics for Finance*. Texts in Statistical Science. Chapman and Hall/CRC, 2015.

Lorenz, E. N. "Deterministic Nonperiodic Flow". *Journal of Atmospheric Sciences* 20 (2 1963), pp. 130–141.

Loveland, D. "A new interpretation of the von Mises' concept of random sequence". *Mathematical Logic Quarterly* 12.1 (1966), pp. 279–294.

Luenberger, D. *Introduction to Linear and Nonlinear Programming*. 2nd edition. Addison Wesley, 1984.

Lütkepohl, H. *Handbook of Matrices*. Wiley, 1996.

MacKay, D. "The evidence framework applied to classification networks". *Neural computation* 4.5 (1992), pp. 720–736.

– "Introduction to Gaussian processes". *NATO ASI Series F Computer and Systems Sciences* 168 (1998), pp. 133–166.

– *Information Theory, Inference, and Learning Algorithms*. Cambridge University Press, 2003.

– *The Humble Gaussian Distribution*. Tech. rep. Cavendish Laboratory, Cambridge University, 2006.

Magnani, E. et al. "Bayesian Filtering for ODEs with Bounded Derivatives". *arXiv:1709.08471 [cs.NA]* (2017).

Mahsereci, M. "Probabilistic Approaches to Stochastic Optimization". PhD thesis. Eberhard Karl University of Tübingen, 2018.

Mahsereci, M. and P. Hennig. "Probabilistic Line Searches for Stochastic Optimization". *Advances in Neural Information Processing Systems, NeurIPS*. 2015, pp. 181–189.

– "Probabilistic Line Searches for Stochastic Optimization". *Journal of Machine Learning Research* 18.119 (2017), pp. 1–59.

Mahsereci, M. et al. "Early Stopping without a Validation Set". *arXiv:1703.09580 [cs.LG]* (2017).

Mania, H., A. Guy, and B. Recht. "Simple random search provides a competitive approach to reinforcement learning". *arXiv:1803.07055 [cs.LG]* (2018).

Marchant, R. and F. Ramos. "Bayesian Optimisation for Intelligent Environmental Monitoring". *NIPS workshop on Bayesian Optimization and Decision Making*. 2012.

Marchant, R., F. Ramos, and S. Sanner. "Sequential Bayesian Optimisation for Spatial-Temporal Monitoring". *Proceedings of the Thirtieth Conference on Uncertainty in Artificial Intelligence, UAI*. AUAI Press, 2014, pp. 553–562.

Markov, A. "Rasprostranenie zakona bol'shih chisel na velichiny, zavisyaschie drug ot druga (A generalization of the law of large numbers to variables that depend on each other)". *Izvestiya Fiziko-matematicheskogo obschestva pri Kazanskom universitete (Proceedings of the Society for Physics and Mathematics at Kazan University)* 15.135-156 (1906), p. 18.

Marmin, S., C. Chevalier, and D. Ginsbourger. "Differentiating the multipoint Expected Improvement for optimal batch design". *arXiv:1503.05509 [stat.ML]* (2015).

– "Efficient batch-sequential Bayesian optimization with moments of truncated Gaussian vectors". *arXiv:1609.02700 [stat.ML]* (2016).

Martinez R., H. J. "Local and Superlinear Convergence of Structured Secant Methods from the Convex Class". PhD thesis. Rice University, 1988.

Matérn, B. "Spatial variation". *Meddelanden fran Statens Skogsforskningsinstitut* 49.5 (1960).

Matsuda, T. and Y. Miyatake. "Estimation of Ordinary Differential Equation Models with Discretization Error Quantification". *SIAM/ASA Journal on Uncertainty Quantification* 9.1 (2021), pp. 302–331.

Matsumoto, M. and T. Nishimura. "Mersenne twister: a 623-dimensionally equidistributed uniform pseudo-random number generator". *ACM Transactions on Modeling and Computer Simulation (TOMACS)* 8.1 (1998), pp. 3–30.

McLeod, M., M. A. Osborne, and S. J. Roberts. "Practical Bayesian Optimization for Variable Cost Objectives". *arXiv:1703.04335 [stat.ML]* (2015).

Meister, A. *Numerik Linearer Gleichungssysteme*. Springer, 2011.

Minka, T. *Deriving quadrature rules from Gaussian processes*. Tech. rep. Statistics Department, Carnegie Mellon University, 2000.

Mitchell, M. *An introduction to genetic algorithms*. MIT press, 1998.

Mitchell, T. M. *The Need for Biases in Learning Generalizations*. Tech. rep. CBM-TR 5-110. Rutgers University, 1980.

Mockus, J., V. Tiesis, and A. Žilinskas. "The Application of Bayesian Methods for Seeking the Extremum". *Toward Global Optimization*. Vol. 2. Elsevier, 1978.

Moore, E. "On the reciprocal of the general algebraic matrix, abstract". *Bulletin of American Mathematical Society* 26 (1920), pp. 394–395.

Moré, J. J. "Recent developments in algorithms and software for trust region methods". *Mathematical Programming: The state of the art*. 1983, pp. 258–287.

Neal, R. "Annealed importance sampling". *Statistics and Computing* 11.2 (2001), pp. 125–139.

Nesterov, Y. "A method of solving a convex programming problem with convergence rate $\mathcal{O}(1/k^2)$". *Soviet Mathematics Doklady*. Vol. 27. 2. 1983, pp. 372–376.

Netzer, Y. et al. "Reading digits in natural images with unsupervised feature learning". *NIPS workshop on deep learning and unsupervised feature learning*. 2. 2011, p. 5.

Nickson, T. et al. "Automated Machine Learning on Big Data using Stochastic Algorithm Tuning". *arXiv:1407.7969 [stat.ML]* (2014).

Nocedal, J. and S. Wright. *Numerical Optimization*. Springer Verlag, 1999.

Nordsieck, A. "On numerical integration of ordinary differential equations". *Mathematics of Computation* 16.77 (1962), pp. 22–49.

Novak, E. *Deterministic and stochastic error bounds in numerical analysis*. Vol. 1349. Springer, 2006.

Nyström, E. "Über die praktische Auflösung von Integralgleichungen mit Anwendungen auf Randwertaufgaben". *Acta Mathematica* 54.1 (1930), pp. 185–204.

O'Hagan, A. "Bayes–Hermite quadrature". *Journal of Statistical Planning and Inference* (1991), pp. 245–260.

– "Some Bayesian Numerical Analysis". *Bayesian Statistics* (1992), pp. 345–363.

O'Hagan, A. and J. F. C. Kingman. "Curve Fitting and Optimal Design for Prediction". *Journal of the Royal Statistical Society. Series B* 40.1 (1978), pp. 1–42.

O'Neil, C. *Weapons of math destruction: How big data increases inequality and threatens democracy*. Crown, 2016.

Oates, C. J. and T. J. Sullivan. "A Modern Retrospective on Probabilistic Numerics". *Statistics and Computing* 29.6 (2019), pp. 1335–1351.

Oates, C. J., M. Girolami, and N. Chopin. "Control functionals for Monte Carlo integration". *Journal of the Royal Statistical Society: Series B (Statistical Methodology)* 79.3 (2017), pp. 695–718.

Oates, C. J. et al. "Convergence rates for a class of estimators based on Stein's method". *Bernoulli* 25.2 (2019a), pp. 1141–1159.

Oates, C. J. et al. "Bayesian Probabilistic Numerical Methods in Time-Dependent State Estimation for Industrial Hydrocyclone Equipment". *Journal of the American Statistical Association* 114.528 (2019b), pp. 1518–1531.

Oesterle, J. et al. "Numerical uncertainty can critically affect simulations of mechanistic models in neuroscience". *bioRxiv* (2021).

Oksendal, B. *Stochastic Differential Equations: An Introduction with Applications*. 6th edition. Springer, 2003.

Ortega, J. and W. Rheinboldt. *Iterative solution of nonlinear equations in several variables*. Vol. 30. Classics in Applied Mathematics. SIAM, 1970.

Osborne, M., R. Garnett, and S. Roberts. "Gaussian processes for global optimization". *3rd International Conference on Learning and Intelligent Optimization (LION3)*. 2009.

Osborne, M. A. et al. "Active Learning of Model Evidence Using Bayesian Quadrature". *Advances in Neural Information Processing Systems, NeurIPS*. 2012, pp. 46–54.

Owhadi, H. "Multigrid with Rough Coefficients and Multiresolution Operator Decomposition from Hierarchical Information Games". *SIAM Review* 59.1 (2017), pp. 99–149.

Owhadi, H. and C. Scovel. "Conditioning Gaussian measure on Hilbert space". *arXiv:1506.04208 [math.PR]* (2015).

– "Toward Machine Wald". *Springer Handbook of Uncertainty Quantification*. Springer, 2016, pp. 1–35.

Owhadi, H. and L. Zhang. "Gamblets for opening the complexity-bottleneck of implicit schemes for hyperbolic and parabolic ODEs/PDEs with rough coefficients". *Journal of Computational Physics* 347 (2017), pp. 99–128.

Packel, E. and J. Traub. "Information-based complexity". *Nature* 328.6125 (1987), pp. 29–33.

Paleyes, A. et al. "Emulation of physical processes with Emukit". *Second Workshop on Machine Learning and the Physical Sciences, NeurIPS*. 2019.

Parlett, B. *The Symmetric Eigenvalue Problem*. Prentice-Hall, 1980.

Pasquale, F. *The black box society: The secret algorithms that control money and information*. Harvard University Press, 2015.

Patterson, D. "The Carbon Footprint of Machine Learning Training Will Plateau, Then Shrink" (2022).

Paul, S., M. A. Osborne, and S. Whiteson. "Fingerprint Policy Optimisation for Robust Reinforcement Learning". *Proceed-*

ings of the 36th International Conference on Machine Learning, ICML. Vol. 97. Proceedings of Machine Learning Research. PMLR, 2019, pp. 5082–5091.

Pearl, J. *Probabilistic Reasoning in Intelligent Systems.* Morgan Kaufmann, 1988.

Pitman, E. "Sufficient statistics and intrinsic accuracy". *Mathematical Proceedings of the Cambridge Philosophical society.* Vol. 32. 04. 1936, pp. 567–579.

Poincaré, H. *Calcul des Probabilités.* Gauthier-Villars, 1896.

Polyak, B. T. "Some methods of speeding up the convergence of iteration methods". *USSR Computational Mathematics and Mathematical Physics* 4.5 (1964), pp. 1–17.

Powell, M. J. D. "A new algorithm for unconstrained optimization". *Nonlinear Programming.* AP, 1970.

– "Convergence properties of a class of minimization algorithms". *Nonlinear programming* 2. 1975, pp. 1–27.

Press, W. et al. *Numerical Recipes in Fortran 77: The Art of Scientific Computing.* Cambridge University Press, 1992.

Quiñonero-Candela, J. and C. Rasmussen. "A unifying view of sparse approximate Gaussian process regression". *Journal of Machine Learning Research* 6 (2005), pp. 1939–1959.

Rackauckas, C. et al. "A Comparison of Automatic Differentiation and Continuous Sensitivity Analysis for Derivatives of Differential Equation Solutions". *arXiv:1812.01892 [math.NA]* (2018).

Rahimi, A. and B. Recht. "Random Features for Large-Scale Kernel Machines". *Advances in Neural Information Processing Systems, NeurIPS.* Curran Associates, Inc., 2007, pp. 1177–1184.

Raissi, M., P. Perdikaris, and G. E. Karniadakis. "Machine learning of linear differential equations using Gaussian processes". *Journal of Computational Physics* 348 (2017), pp. 683–693.

Rasmussen, C. and C. Williams. *Gaussian Processes for Machine Learning.* MIT, 2006.

Rauch, H., C. Striebel, and F. Tung. "Maximum likelihood estimates of linear dynamic systems". *Journal of the American Institute of Aeronautics and Astronautics (AAIA)* 3.8 (1965), pp. 1445–1450.

Reid, W. *Riccati differential equations.* Elsevier, 1972.

Riccati, J. "Animadversiones in aequationes differentiales secundi gradus". *Actorum Eruditorum Supplementa* 8 (1724), pp. 66–73.

Ritter, K. *Average-case analysis of numerical problems.* Lecture Notes in Mathematics 1733. Springer, 2000.

Robert, C. and G. Casella. *Monte Carlo Statistical Methods*. Springer Science & Business Media, 2013.

Rontsis, N., M. A. Osborne, and P. J. Goulart. "Distributionally Robust Optimization Techniques in Batch Bayesian Optimization". *Journal of Machine Learning Research* 21.149 (2020), pp. 1–26.

Saad, Y. *Iterative Methods for Sparse Linear Systems*. SIAM, 2003.

Saad, Y. and M. Schultz. "GMRES: A generalized minimal residual algorithm for solving nonsymmetric linear systems". *SIAM Journal on scientific and statistical computing* 7.3 (1986), pp. 856–869.

Sacks, J. and D. Ylvisaker. "Statistical designs and integral approximation". *Proc. 12th Bienn. Semin. Can. Math. Congr.* 1970, pp. 115–136.

– "Model robust design in regression: Bayes theory". *Proceedings of the Berkeley Conference in Honor of Jerzy Neyman and Jack Kiefer*. Vol. 2. 1985, pp. 667–679.

Sard, A. *Linear approximation*. American Mathematical Society, 1963.

Särkkä, S. *Bayesian filtering and smoothing*. Cambridge University Press, 2013.

Särkkä, S. and A. Solin. *Applied Stochastic Differential Equations*. Cambridge University Press, 2019.

Särkkä, S., A. Solin, and J. Hartikainen. "Spatiotemporal learning via infinite-dimensional Bayesian filtering and smoothing: A look at Gaussian process regression through Kalman filtering". *IEEE Signal Processing Magazine* 30.4 (2013), pp. 51–61.

Schmidt, J., N. Krämer, and P. Hennig. "A Probabilistic State Space Model for Joint Inference from Differential Equations and Data". *Advances in Neural Information Processing Systems, NeurIPS*. 2021.

Schmidt, R. M., F. Schneider, and P. Hennig. "Descending through a Crowded Valley - Benchmarking Deep Learning Optimizers". *Proceedings of the 38th International Conference on Machine Learning*. Vol. 139. Proceedings of Machine Learning Research. PMLR, 2021, pp. 9367–9376.

Schneider, F., F. Dangel, and P. Hennig. "Cockpit: A Practical Debugging Tool for the Training of Deep Neural Networks". *Advances in Neural Information Processing Systems, NeurIPS*. 2021.

Schober, M., D. Duvenaud, and P. Hennig. "Probabilistic ODE Solvers with Runge-Kutta Means". *Advances in Neural Information Processing Systems, NeurIPS*. 2014, pp. 739–747.

Schober, M., S. Särkkä, and P. Hennig. "A probabilistic model for the numerical solution of initial value problems". *Statistics and Computing* 29.1 (2019), pp. 99–122.

Schober, M. et al. "Probabilistic shortest path tractography in DTI using Gaussian Process ODE solvers". *Medical Image Computing and Computer-Assisted Intervention–MICCAI 2014*. Springer, 2014.

Schölkopf, B. "The Kernel Trick for Distances". *Advances in Neural Information Processing Systems, NeurIPS*. MIT Press, 2000, pp. 301–307.

Schölkopf, B. and A. Smola. *Learning with Kernels*. MIT Press, 2002.

Schur, I. "Über Potenzreihen, die im Innern des Einheitskreises beschränkt sind." *Journal für die reine und angewandte Mathematik* 147 (1917), pp. 205–232.

Schwartz, R. et al. "Green AI". *arXiv:1907.10597 [cs.CY]* (2019).

Scieur, D. et al. "Integration Methods and Optimization Algorithms". *Advances in Neural Information Processing Systems, NeurIPS*. 2017, pp. 1109–1118.

Shah, A. and Z. Ghahramani. "Parallel Predictive Entropy Search for Batch Global Optimization of Expensive Objective Functions". *Advances in Neural Information Processing Systems, NeurIPS*. 2015, pp. 3330–3338.

Shahriari, B. et al. "An Entropy Search Portfolio for Bayesian Optimization". *arXiv:1406.4625 [stat.ML]* (2014).

Shahriari, B. et al. "Taking the human out of the loop: A review of Bayesian optimization". *Proceedings of the IEEE* 104.1 (2016), pp. 148–175.

Shanno, D. "Conditioning of quasi-Newton methods for function minimization". *Mathematics of Computation* 24.111 (1970), pp. 647–656.

Skeel, R. "Equivalent Forms of Multistep Formulas". *Mathematics of Computation* 33 (1979).

Skilling, J. "Bayesian solution of ordinary differential equations". *Maximum Entropy and Bayesian Methods* (1991).

Smola, A. et al. "A Hilbert space embedding for distributions". *International Conference on Algorithmic Learning Theory*. 2007, pp. 13–31.

Snelson, E. and Z. Ghahramani. "Sparse Gaussian Processes using Pseudo-inputs". *Advances in Neural Information Processing Systems, NeurIPS*. 2005, pp. 1257–1264.

Snoek, J., H. Larochelle, and R. P. Adams. "Practical Bayesian Optimization of Machine Learning Algorithms". *Advances in*

Neural Information Processing Systems, NeurIPS. 2012, pp. 2960–2968.

Snoek, J. et al. "Scalable Bayesian Optimization Using Deep Neural Networks". *Proceedings of the 32nd International Conference on Machine Learning, ICML.* Vol. 37. JMLR Workshop and Conference Proceedings. JMLR.org, 2015, pp. 2171–2180.

Solak, E. et al. "Derivative Observations in Gaussian Process Models of Dynamic Systems". *Advances in Neural Information Processing Systems, NeurIPS.* MIT Press, 2002, pp. 1033–1040.

Solin, A. and S. Särkkä. "Explicit Link Between Periodic Covariance Functions and State Space Models". *Proceedings of the Seventeenth International Conference on Artificial Intelligence and Statistics, AISTATS.* Vol. 33. JMLR Workshop and Conference Proceedings. JMLR.org, 2014, pp. 904–912.

Sonneveld, P. "CGS, a fast Lanczos-type solver for nonsymmetric linear systems". *SIAM Journal on Scientific and Statistical Computing* 10.1 (1989), pp. 36–52.

Spitzbart, A. "A generalization of Hermite's Interpolation Formula". *The American Mathematical Monthly* 67.1 (1960), pp. 42–46.

Springenberg, J. T. et al. "Bayesian Optimization with Robust Bayesian Neural Networks". *Advances in Neural Information Processing Systems, NeurIPS.* 2016, pp. 4134–4142.

Srinivas, N. et al. "Gaussian Process Optimization in the Bandit Setting: No Regret and Experimental Design". *Proceedings of the 27th International Conference on Machine Learning, ICML.* Omnipress, 2010, pp. 1015–1022.

Stein, M. *Interpolation of spatial data: some theory for Kriging.* Springer Verlag, 1999.

Steinwart, I. "Convergence Types and Rates in Generic Karhunen-Loève Expansions with Applications to Sample Path Properties". *Potential Analysis* 51.3 (2019), pp. 361–395.

Steinwart, I. and A. Christmann. *Support Vector Machines.* Springer Science & Business Media, 2008.

Streltsov, S. and P. Vakili. "A Non-myopic Utility Function for Statistical Global Optimization Algorithms". *Journal of Global Optimization* 14.3 (1999), pp. 283–298.

Student. "The probable error of a mean". *Biometrika* 6 (1 1908), pp. 1–25.

Sul'din, A. V. "Wiener measure and its applications to approximation methods. I". *Izvestiya Vysshikh Uchebnykh Zavedenii. Matematika* 6 (1959), pp. 145–158.

– "Wiener measure and its applications to approximation methods. II". *Izvestiya Vysshikh Uchebnykh Zavedenii. Matematika* 5 (1960), pp. 165–179.

Sullivan, T. *Introduction to uncertainty quantification*. Vol. 63. Texts in Applied Mathematics. Springer, 2015.

Sutton, R. and A. Barto. *Reinforcement Learning*. MIT Press, 1998.

Swersky, K., J. Snoek, and R. P. Adams. "Freeze-Thaw Bayesian Optimization". *arXiv:1406.3896 [stat.ML]* (2014).

Swersky, K. et al. "Raiders of the lost architecture: Kernels for Bayesian optimization in conditional parameter spaces". *NIPS workshop on Bayesian Optimization in theory and practice (BayesOpt'13)*. 2013.

Tarantola, A. *Inverse Problem Theory and Methods for Model Parameter Estimation*. SIAM, 2005.

Teschl, G. *Ordinary Differential Equations and Dynamical Systems*. Vol. 140. Graduate Studies in Mathematics. American Mathematical Society, 2012.

Teymur, O., K. Zygalakis, and B. Calderhead. "Probabilistic Linear Multistep Methods". *Advances in Neural Information Processing Systems, NeurIPS*. 2016, pp. 4314–4321.

Teymur, O. et al. "Implicit Probabilistic Integrators for ODEs". *Advances in Neural Information Processing Systems, NeurIPS*. 2018, pp. 7255–7264.

Thaler, R. H. "Anomalies: The Winner's Curse". *Journal of Economic Perspectives* 2.1 (1988), pp. 191–202.

Thiele, T. "Om Anvendelse af mindste Kvadraters Methode i nogle Tilfælde, hvor en Komplikation af visse Slags uensartede tilfældige Fejlkilder giver Fejlene en 'systematisk' Karakter". *Det Kongelige Danske Videnskabernes Selskabs Skrifter-Naturvidenskabelig og Mathematisk Afdeling* (1880), pp. 381–408.

Traub, J., G. Wasilkowski, and H. Woźniakowski. *Information, Uncertainty, Complexity*. Addison-Wesley Publishing Company, 1983.

Trefethen, L. and D. Bau III. *Numerical Linear Algebra*. SIAM, 1997.

Tronarp, F., N. Bosch, and P. Hennig. "Fenrir: Physics-Enhanced Regression for Initial Value Problems". *arXiv:2202.01287 [cs.LG]* (2022).

Tronarp, F., S. Särkkä, and P. Hennig. "Bayesian ODE solvers: The maximum a posteriori estimate". *Statistics and Computing* 31.3 (2021), pp. 1–18.

Tronarp, F. et al. "Probabilistic solutions to ordinary differential equations as nonlinear Bayesian filtering: a new perspective". *Statistics and Computing* 29.6 (2019), pp. 1297–1315.

Turing, A. "Rounding-off errors in matrix processes". *Quarterly Journal of Mechanics and Applied Mathematics* 1.1 (1948), pp. 287–308.

Uhlenbeck, G. and L. Ornstein. "On the theory of the Brownian motion". *Physical Review* 36.5 (1930), p. 823.

van Loan, C. "The ubiquitous Kronecker product". *Journal of Computational and Applied Mathematics* 123 (2000), pp. 85–100.

Vijayakumar, S. and S. Schaal. "Locally Weighted Projection Regression: Incremental Real Time Learning in High Dimensional Space". *Proceedings of the Seventeenth International Conference on Machine Learning, ICML*. Morgan Kaufmann, 2000, pp. 1079–1086.

Villemonteix, J., E. Vazquez, and E. Walter. "An informational approach to the global optimization of expensive-to-evaluate functions". *Journal of Global Optimization* 44.4 (2009), pp. 509–534.

Von Neumann, J. "Various techniques used in connection with random digits". *Monte Carlo Method*. Vol. 12. National Bureau of Standards Applied Mathematics Series. 1951, pp. 36–38.

Wahba, G. *Spline models for observational data*. CBMS-NSF Regional Conferences series in applied mathematics. SIAM, 1990.

Wang, J., J. Cockayne, and C. Oates. "On the Bayesian Solution of Differential Equations". *Proceedings of the 38th International Workshop on Bayesian Inference and Maximum Entropy Methods in Science and Engineering* (2018).

Wang, J. et al. "Parallel Bayesian Global Optimization of Expensive Functions". *arXiv:1602.05149 [stat.ML]* (2016).

Wang, J. et al. "Bayesian numerical methods for nonlinear partial differential equations". *Statistics and Computing* 31.55 (2021).

Wang, Z. and S. Jegelka. "Max-value Entropy Search for Efficient Bayesian Optimization". *Proceedings of the 34th International Conference on Machine Learning, ICML*. Vol. 70. Proceedings of Machine Learning Research. PMLR, 2017, pp. 3627–3635.

Warth, W. and J. Werner. "Effiziente Schrittweitenfunktionen bei unrestringierten Optimierungsaufgaben". *Computing* 19.1 (1977), pp. 59–72.

Weise, T. "Global optimization algorithms-theory and application". *Self-Published,* (2009), pp. 25–26.

Wendland, H. and C. Rieger. "Approximate Interpolation with Applications to Selecting Smoothing Parameters". *Numerische Mathematik* 101.4 (2005), pp. 729–748.

Wenger, J. and P. Hennig. "Probabilistic Linear Solvers for Machine Learning". *Advances in Neural Information Processing Systems, NeurIPS* (2020).

Wenger, J. et al. "ProbNum: Probabilistic Numerics in Python". 2021.

Werner, J. "Über die globale Konvergenz von Variable-Metrik-Verfahren mit nicht-exakter Schrittweitenbestimmung". *Numerische Mathematik* 31.3 (1978), pp. 321–334.

Wiener, N. "Differential space". *Journal of Mathematical Physics* 2 (1923), pp. 131–174.

Wilkinson, J. *The Algebraic Eigenvalue Problem*. Oxford University Press, 1965.

Williams, C. K. I. and M. W. Seeger. "Using the Nyström Method to Speed Up Kernel Machines". *Advances in Neural Information Processing Systems, NeurIPS*. MIT Press, 2000, pp. 682–688.

Wills, A. G. and T. B. Schön. "On the construction of probabilistic Newton-type algorithms". *IEEE Conference on Decision and Control (CDC)*. Vol. 56. 2017.

Winfield, D. H. "Function and functional optimization by interpolation in data tables". PhD thesis. Harvard University, 1970.

Wishart, J. "The generalised product moment distribution in samples from a normal multivariate population". *Biometrika* (1928), pp. 32–52.

Wolfe, P. "Convergence conditions for ascent methods". *SIAM review* (1969), pp. 226–235.

Wu, J. and P. I. Frazier. "The Parallel Knowledge Gradient Method for Batch Bayesian Optimization". *Advances in Neural Information Processing Systems, NeurIPS*. 2016, pp. 3126–3134.

Wu, J. et al. "Bayesian Optimization with Gradients". *Advances in Neural Information Processing Systems, NeurIPS*. 2017, pp. 5267–5278.

Zeiler, M. D. "ADADELTA: An Adaptive Learning Rate Method". *arXiv:1212.5701 [cs.LG]* (2012).

Index